ULTIMATE COMICS
SPIDER-MAN

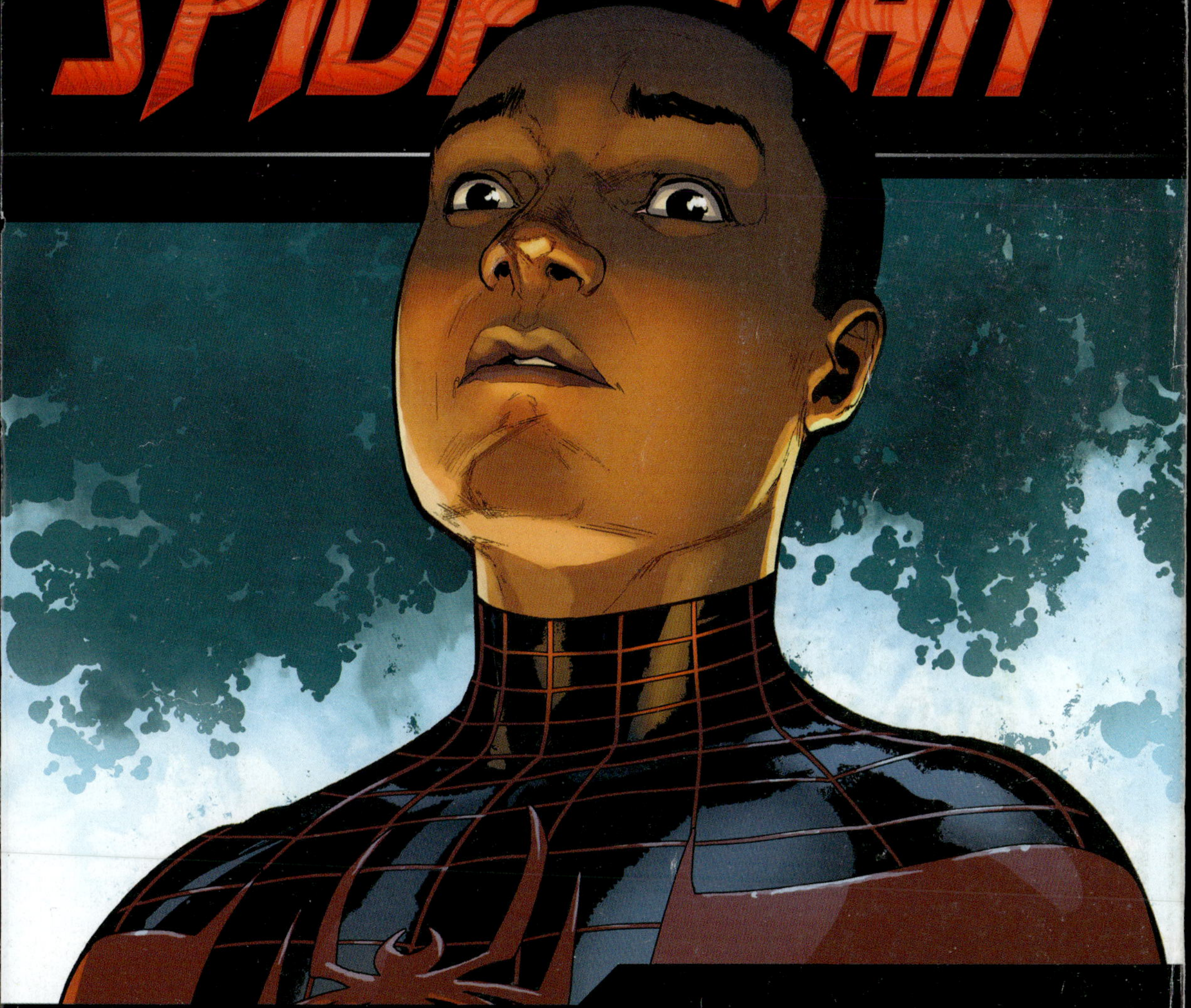

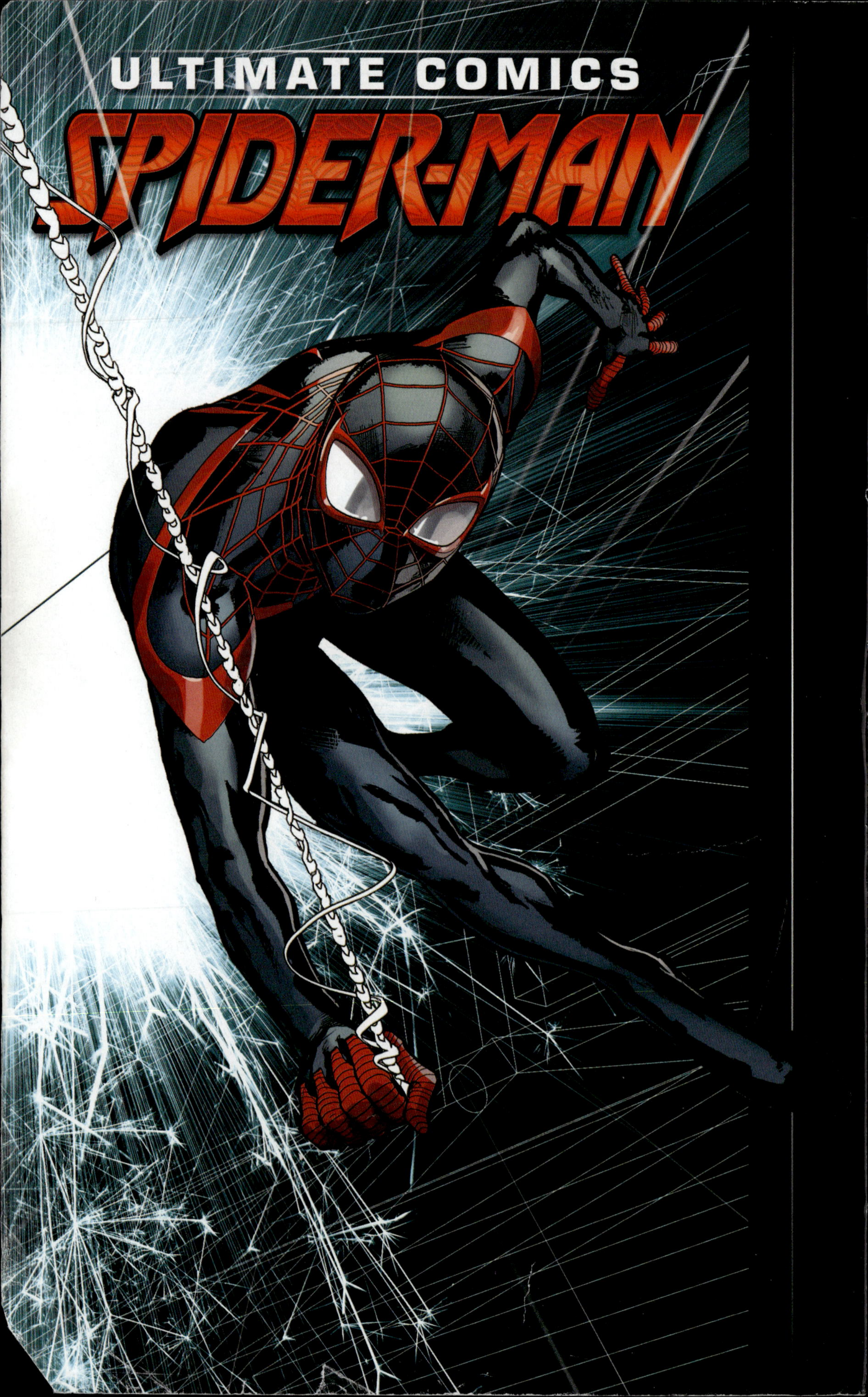
ULTIMATE COMICS
SPIDER-MAN

WRITER: **BRIAN MICHAEL BENDIS**

CATACLYSM: ULTIMATE SPIDER-MAN #1-3

ARTIST: **DAVID MARQUEZ**

COLORISTS: **JUSTIN PONSOR** WITH PAUL MOUNTS (#1)

COVER ART: **DAVID MARQUEZ** & **RAIN BEREDO**

ULTIMATE SPIDER-MAN #200

ARTIST: **DAVID MARQUEZ**

ARTISTS, MJ AND MAY PARKER SEQUENCES: **MARK BAGLEY** & **ANDREW HENNESSY**

ARTIST, GWEN STACY SEQUENCE: **MARK BROOKS**

ARTIST, MILES MORALES SEQUENCE: **SARA PICHELLI**

ARTIST, KITTY PRYDE SEQUENCE: **DAVID LAFUENTE**

COLORIST: **JUSTIN PONSOR**

COVER ART: **DAVID MARQUEZ** & **JUSTIN PONSOR**

MILES MORALES: ULTIMATE SPIDER-MAN #1-12

ARTIST: **DAVID MARQUEZ**

COLORISTS: **JUSTIN PONSOR** WITH JASON KEITH (#6)

COVER ART: **DAVID MARQUEZ** & **JUSTIN PONSOR**

LETTERER: **VC's CORY PETIT**

ASSISTANT EDITORS: **EMILY SHAW** & **CHRIS ROBINSON**

SENIOR EDITOR: **MARK PANICCIA**

SPIDER-MAN CREATED BY **STAN LEE** & **STEVE DITKO**

COLLECTION EDITOR: **JENNIFER GRÜNWALD**
ASSISTANT EDITOR: **SARAH BRUNSTAD**
ASSOCIATE MANAGING EDITOR: **ALEX STARBUCK**
EDITOR, SPECIAL PROJECTS: **MARK D. BEAZLEY**
SENIOR EDITOR, SPECIAL PROJECTS: **JEFF YOUNGQUIST**
SVP PRINT, SALES & MARKETING: **DAVID GABRIEL**
BOOK DESIGNER: **ADAM DEL RE**

EDITOR IN CHIEF: **AXEL ALONSO**
CHIEF CREATIVE OFFICER: **JOE QUESADA**
PUBLISHER: **DAN BUCKLEY**
EXECUTIVE PRODUCER: **ALAN FINE**

MILES MORALES: ULTIMATE SPIDER-MAN ULTIMATE COLLECTION BOOK 3. Contains material originally published in magazine form as CATACLYSM: ULTIMATE COMICS SPIDER-MAN #1-3, ULTIMATE SPIDER-MAN #200 and MILES MORALES: THE ULTIMATE SPIDER-MAN #1-12. First printing 2015. ISBN# 978-0-7851-9780-5. Published by MARVEL WORLDWIDE, INC., a subsidiary of MARVEL ENTERTAINMENT, LLC. OFFICE OF PUBLICATION: 135 West 50th Street, New York, NY 10020. Copyright © 2015 MARVEL No similarity between any of the names, characters, persons, and/or institutions in this magazine with those of any living or dead person or institution is intended, and any such similarity which may exist is purely coincidental. **Printed in the U.S.A.** ALAN FINE, President, Marvel Entertainment; DAN BUCKLEY, President, TV, Publishing and Brand Management; JOE QUESADA, Chief Creative Officer; TOM BREVOORT, SVP of Publishing; DAVID BOGART, SVP of Operations & Procurement, Publishing; C.B. CEBULSKI, VP of International Development & Brand Management; DAVID GABRIEL, SVP Print, Sales & Marketing; JIM O'KEEFE, VP of Operations & Logistics; DAN CARR, Executive Director of Publishing Technology; SUSAN CRESPI, Editorial Operations Manager; ALEX MORALES, Publishing Operations Manager; STAN LEE, Chairman Emeritus. For information regarding advertising in Marvel Comics or on Marvel.com, please contact Jonathan Rheingold, VP of Custom Solutions & Ad Sales, at jrheingold@marvel.com. For Marvel subscription inquiries, please call 800-217-9158. **Manufactured between 10/2/2015 and 11/9/2015 by R.R. DONNELLEY, INC., SALEM, VA, USA.**
10 9 8 7 6 5 4 3 2 1

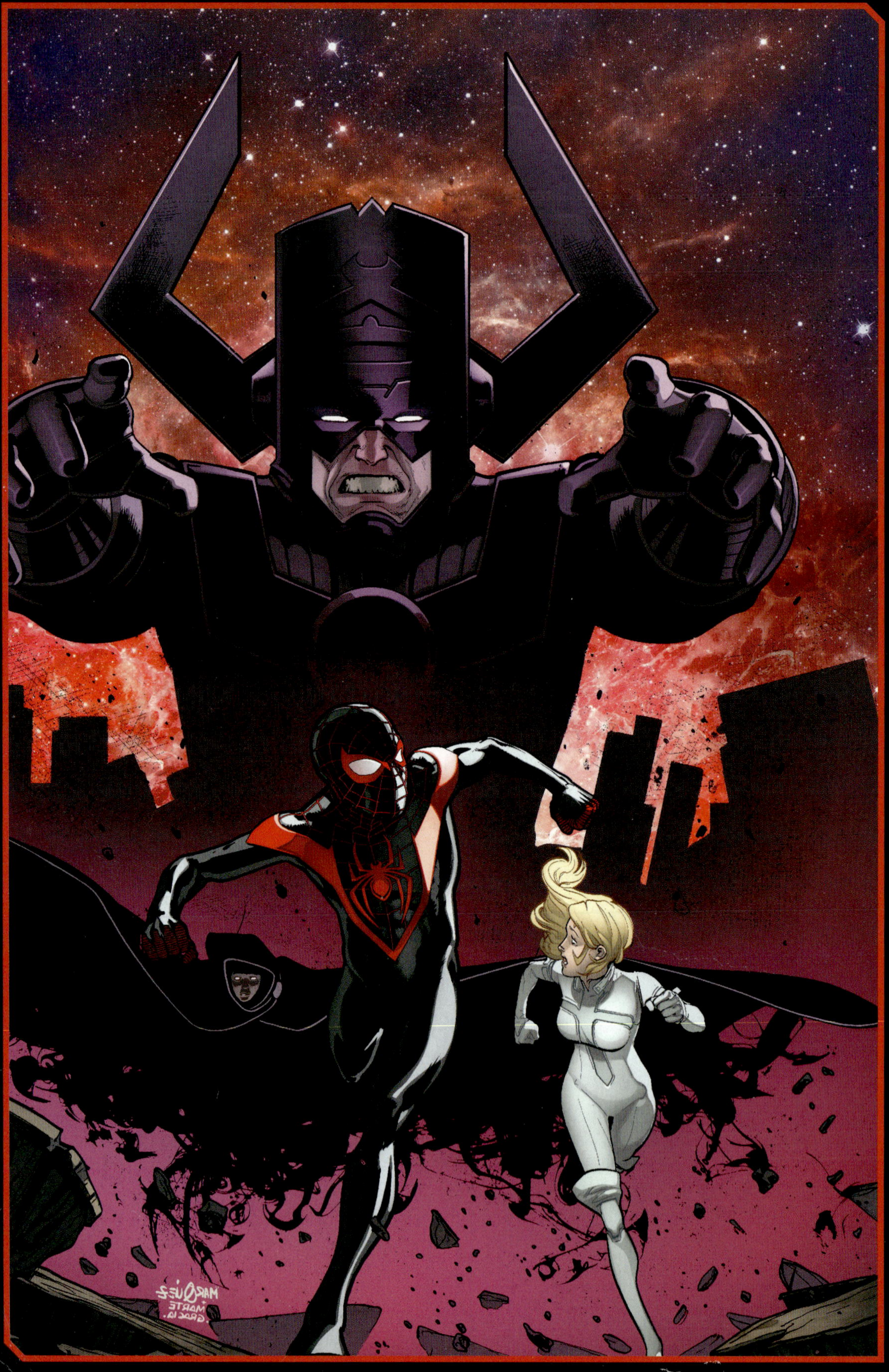

CATACLYSM: ULTIMATE SPIDER-MAN #1

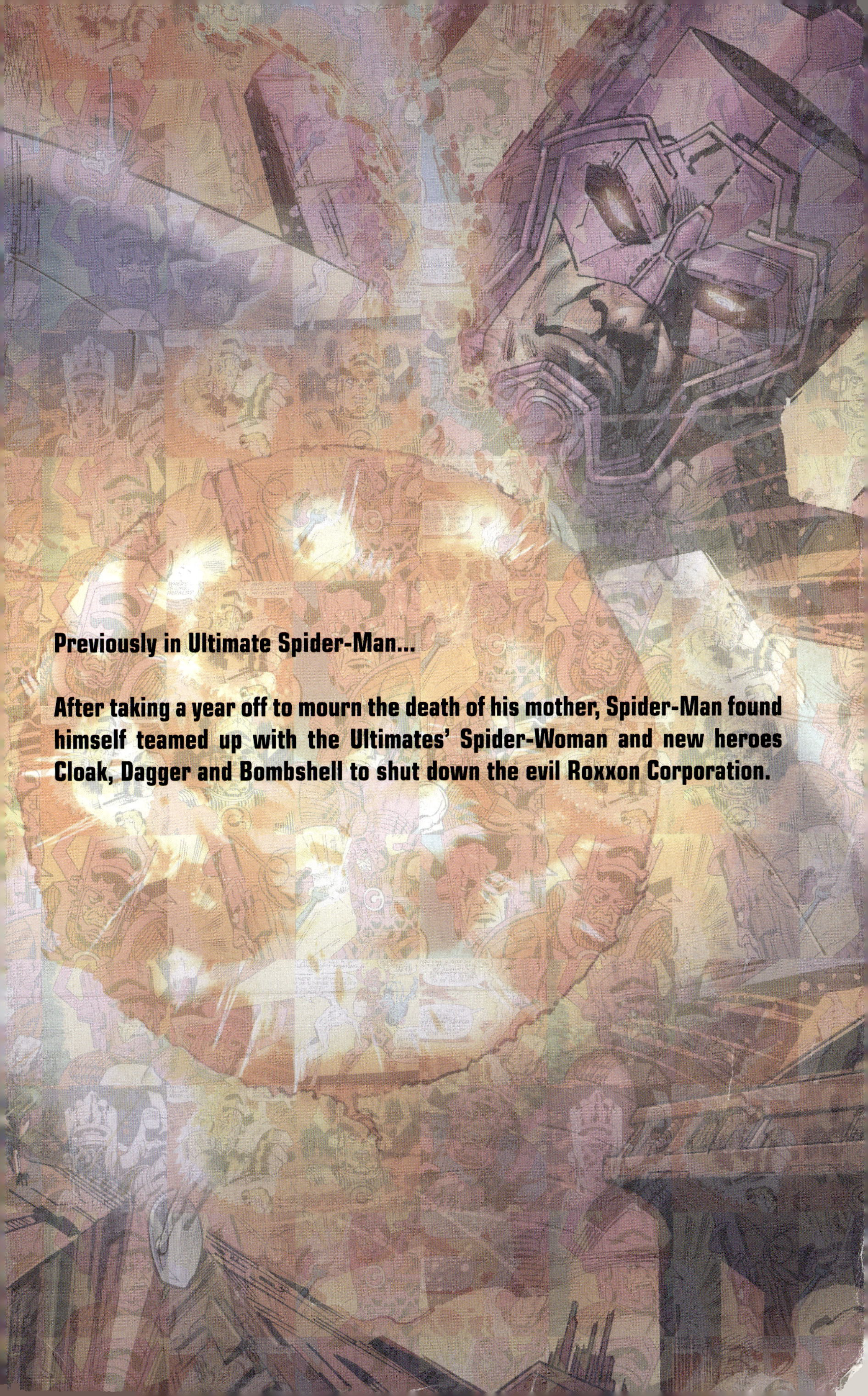

Previously in Ultimate Spider-Man...

After taking a year off to mourn the death of his mother, Spider-Man found himself teamed up with the Ultimates' Spider-Woman and new heroes Cloak, Dagger and Bombshell to shut down the evil Roxxon Corporation.

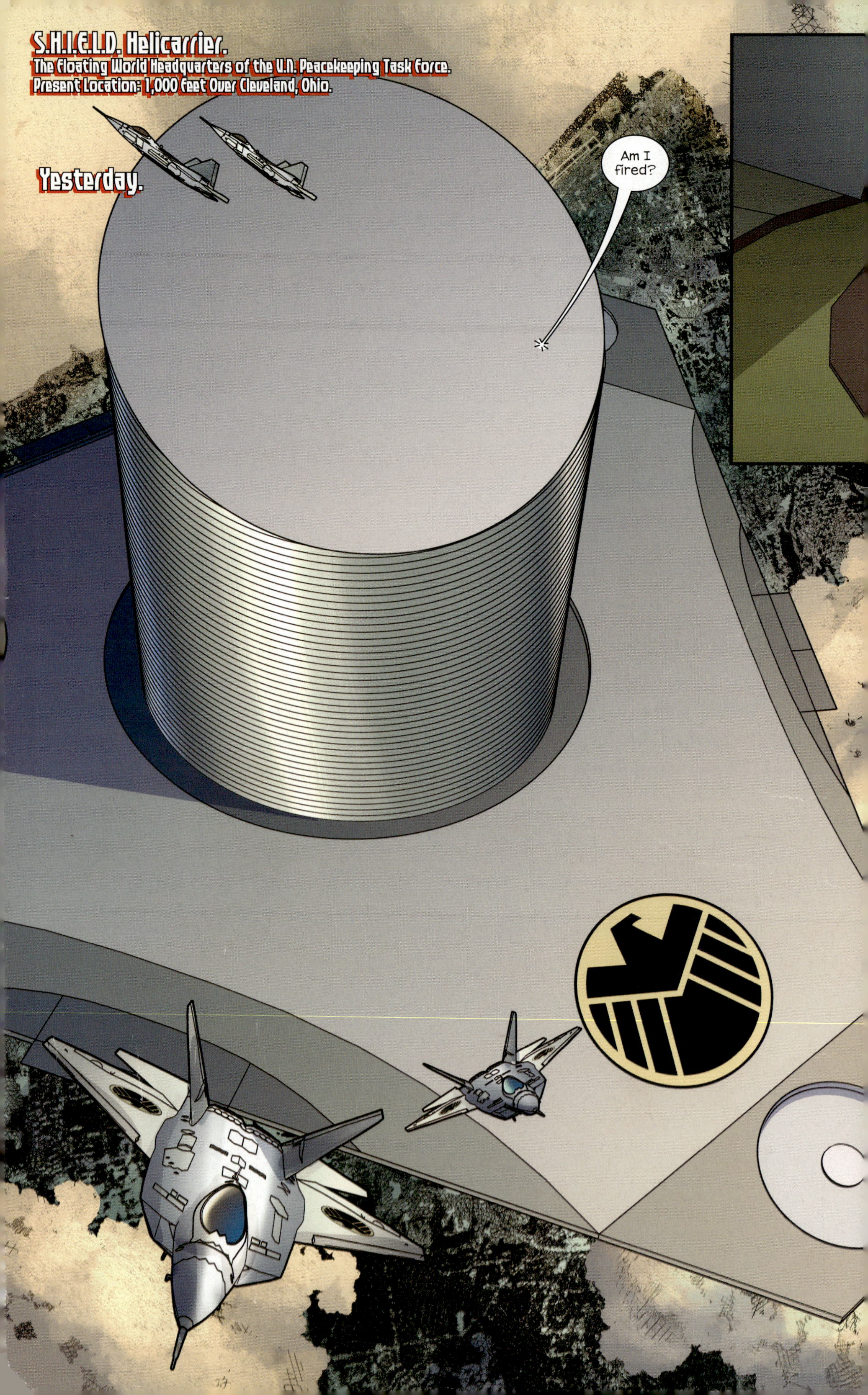
S.H.I.E.L.D. Helicarrier.
The Floating World Headquarters of the U.N. Peacekeeping Task Force.
Present Location: 1,000 Feet Over Cleveland, Ohio.
Yesterday.
Am I fired?

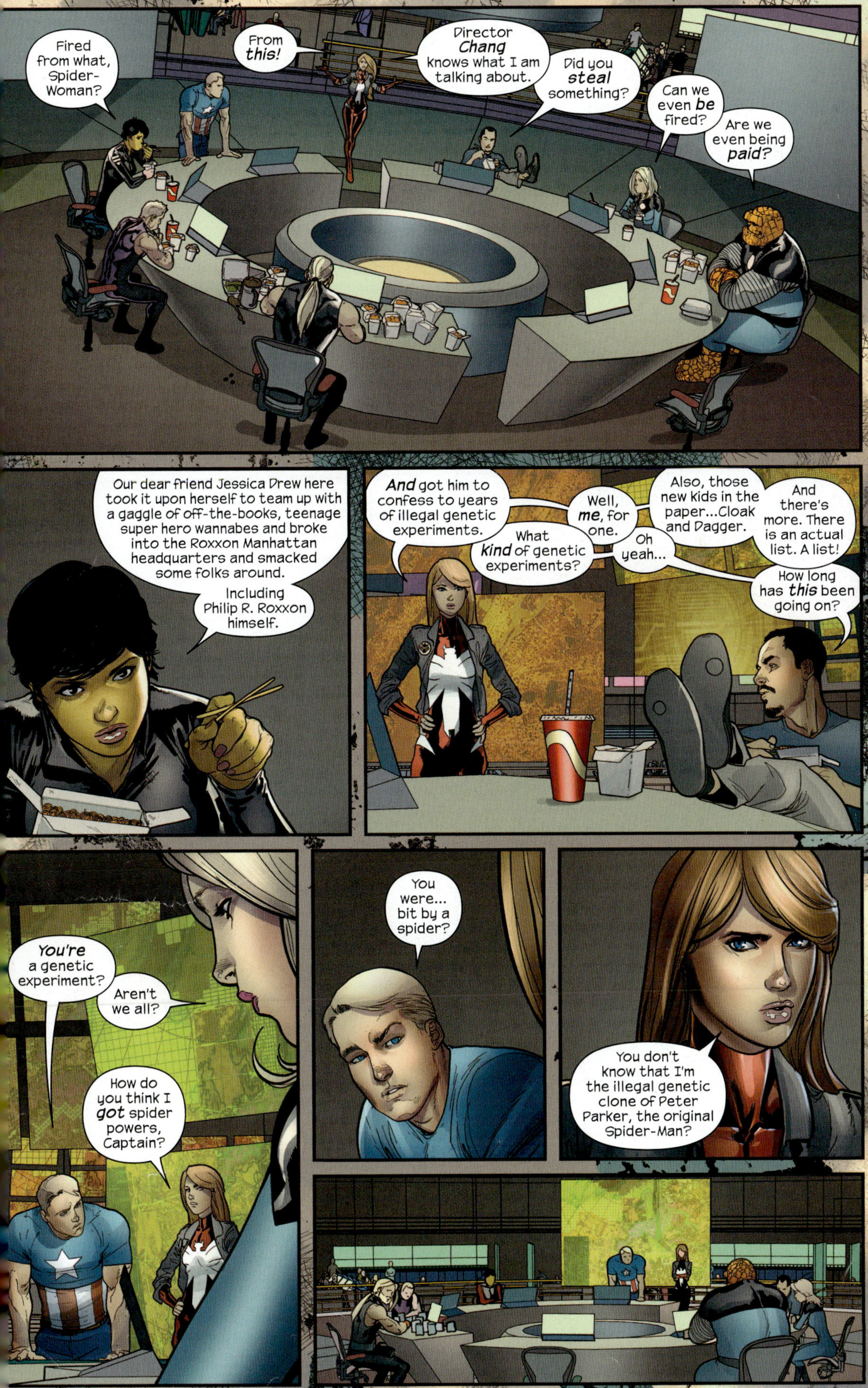

Fired from what, Spider-Woman?
From *this!*
Director *Chang* knows what I am talking about.
Did you *steal* something?
Can we even *be* fired?
Are we even being *paid?*
Our dear friend Jessica Drew here took it upon herself to team up with a gaggle of off-the-books, teenage super hero wannabes and broke into the Roxxon Manhattan headquarters and smacked some folks around.
Including Philip R. Roxxon himself.
And got him to confess to years of illegal genetic experiments.
Well, *me*, for one.
Also, those new kids in the paper...Cloak and Dagger.
And there's more. There is an actual list. A list!
What *kind* of genetic experiments?
Oh yeah...
How long has *this* been going on?
You're a genetic experiment?
Aren't we all?
How do you think I *got* spider powers, Captain?
You were... bit by a spider?
You don't know that I'm the illegal genetic clone of Peter Parker, the original Spider-Man?

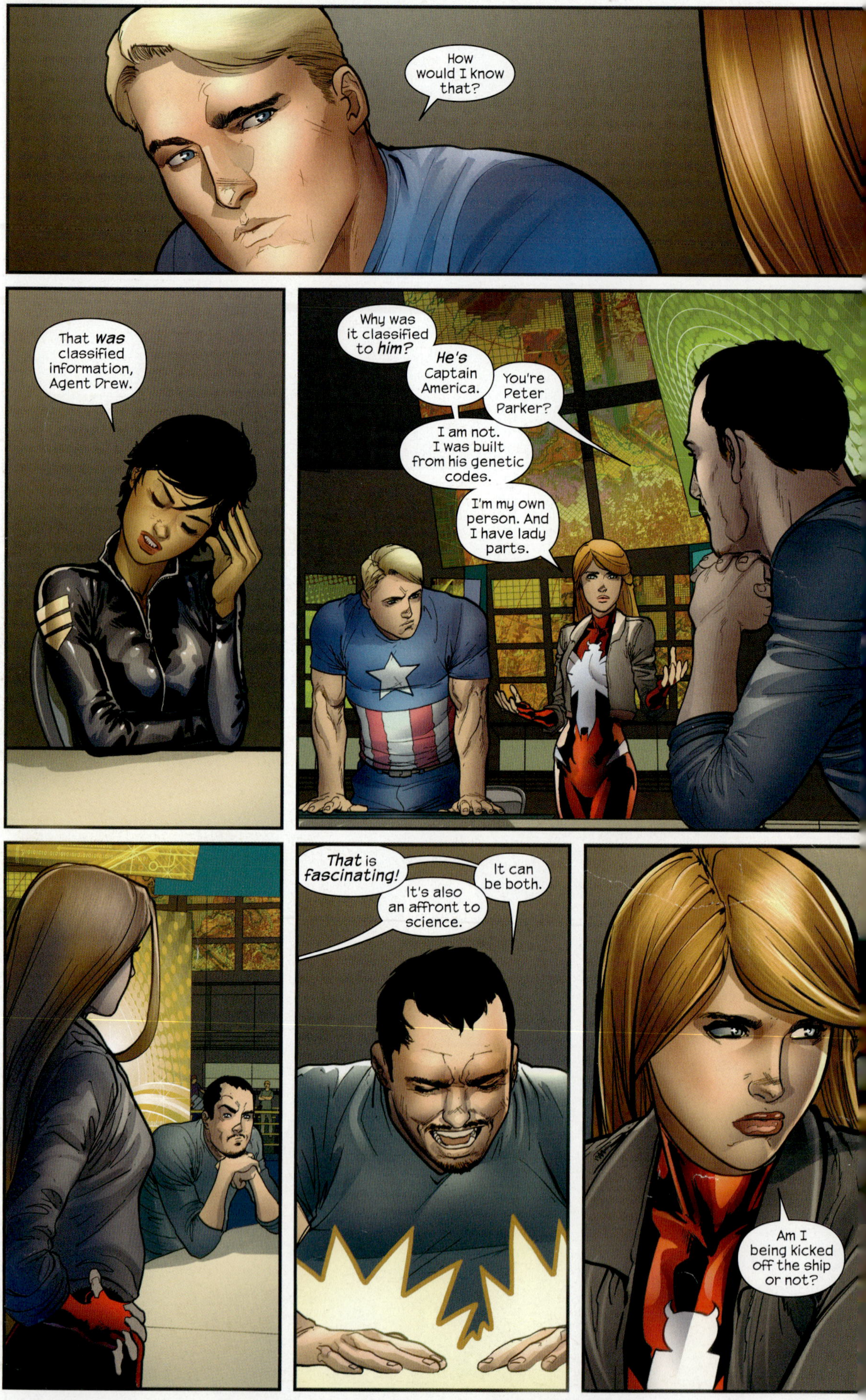
How would I know that?
That *was* classified information, Agent Drew.
Why was it classified to *him?*
He's Captain America.
You're Peter Parker?
I am not. I was built from his genetic codes.
I'm my own person. And I have lady parts.
That is *fascinating!*
It's also an affront to science.
It can be both.
Am I being kicked off the ship or not?

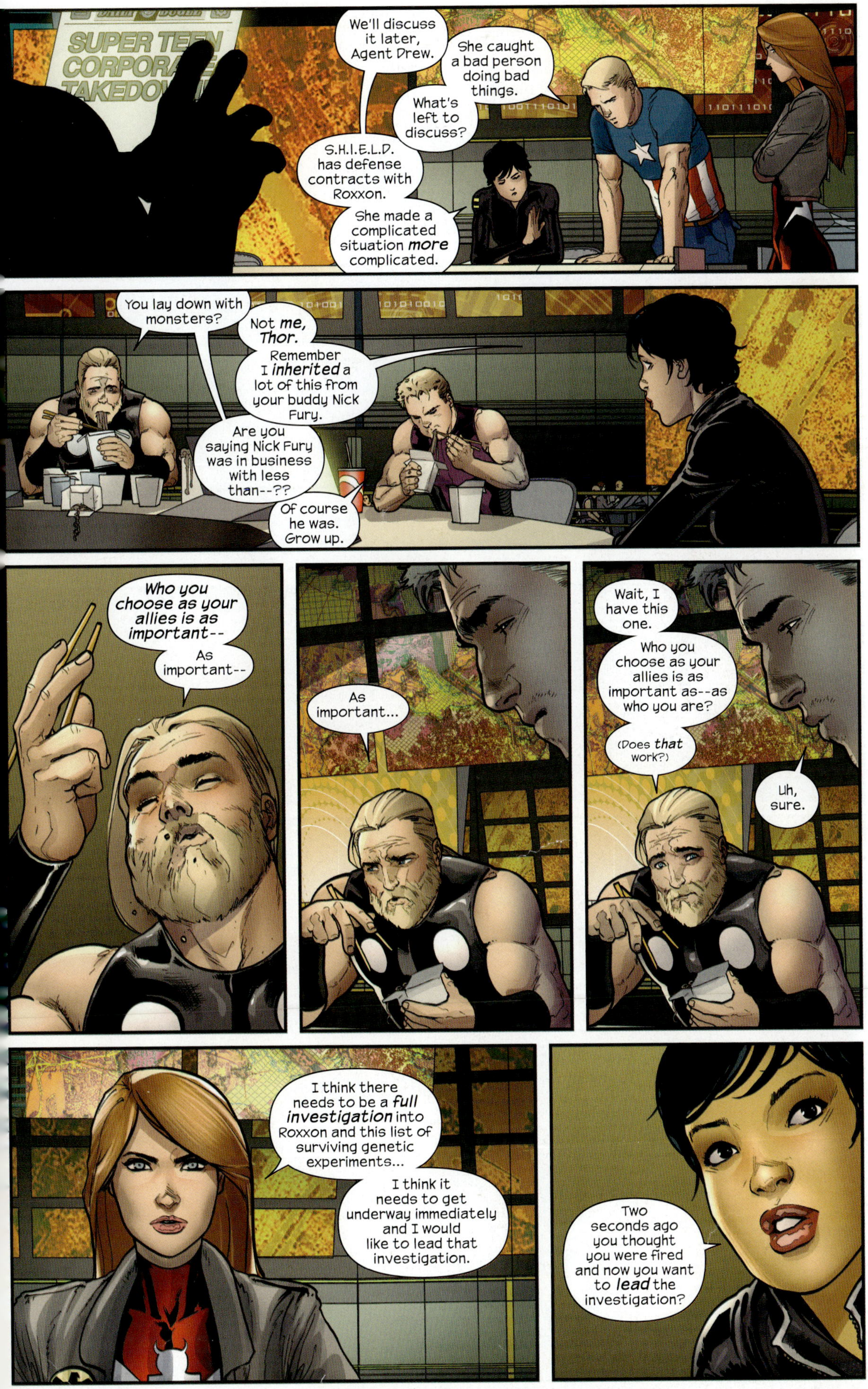
SUPER TEEN CORPORATE TAKEDOWN
We'll discuss it later, Agent Drew.
She caught a bad person doing bad things.
What's left to discuss?
S.H.I.E.L.D. has defense contracts with Roxxon.
She made a complicated situation *more* complicated.
You lay down with monsters?
Not *me, Thor.* Remember I *inherited* a lot of this from your buddy Nick Fury.
Are you saying Nick Fury was in business with less than--??
Of course he was. Grow up.
Who you choose as your allies is as important--
As important--
As important...
Wait, I have this one.
Who you choose as your allies is as important as--as who you are?
(Does *that* work?)
Uh, sure.
I think there needs to be a *full investigation* into Roxxon and this list of surviving genetic experiments...
I think it needs to get underway immediately and I would like to lead that investigation.
Two seconds ago you thought you were fired and now you want to *lead* the investigation?

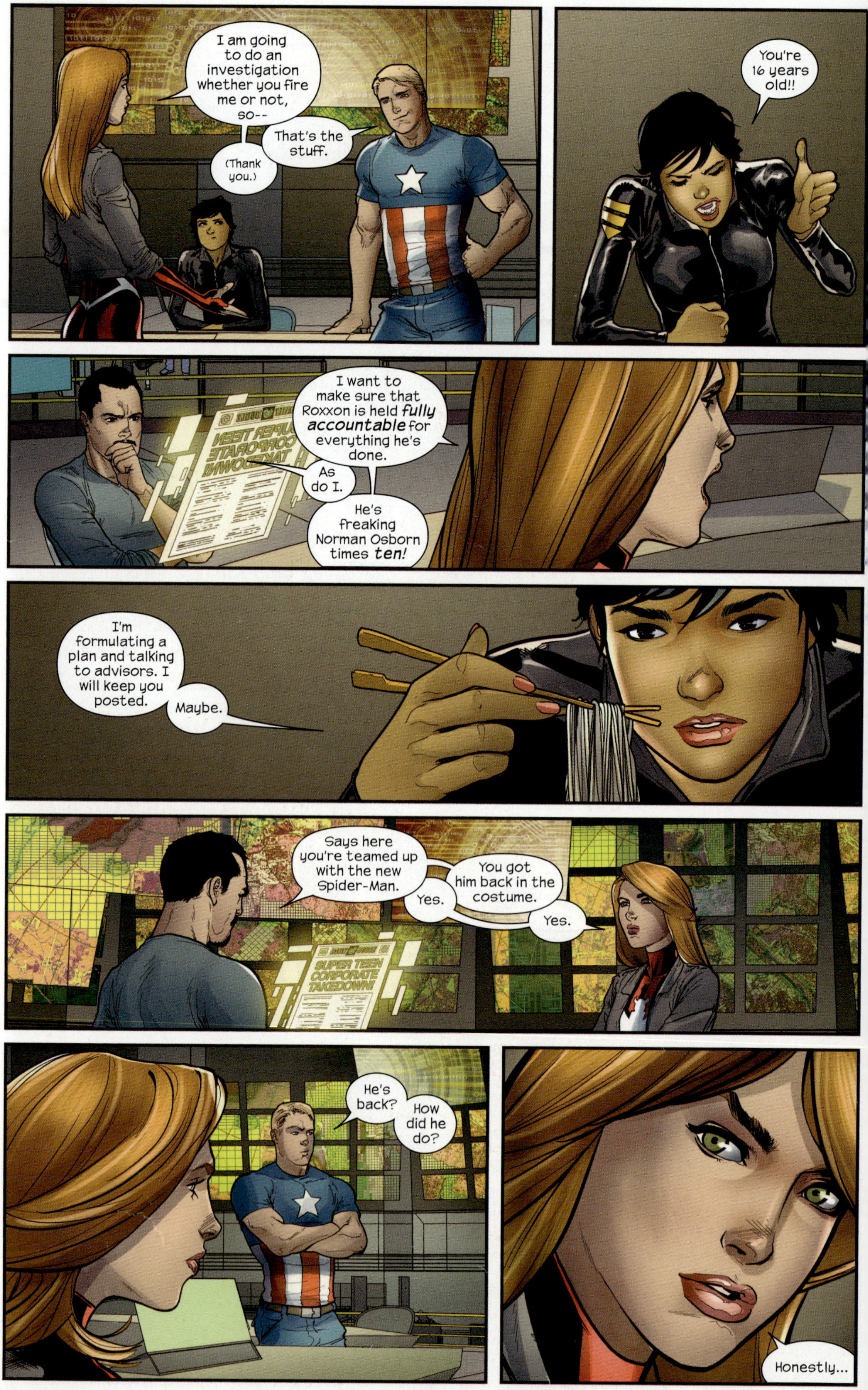
I am going to do an investigation whether you fire me or not, so--
(Thank you.)
That's the stuff.
You're 16 years old!!
I want to make sure that Roxxon is held *fully accountable* for everything he's done.
As do I.
He's freaking Norman Osborn times *ten!*
SUPER TEEN CORPORATE TAKEDOWN!
I'm formulating a plan and talking to advisors. I will keep you posted.
Maybe.
Says here you're teamed up with the new Spider-Man.
Yes.
You got him back in the costume.
Yes.
SUPER TEEN CORPORATE TAKEDOWN!
He's back?
How did he do?
Honestly...

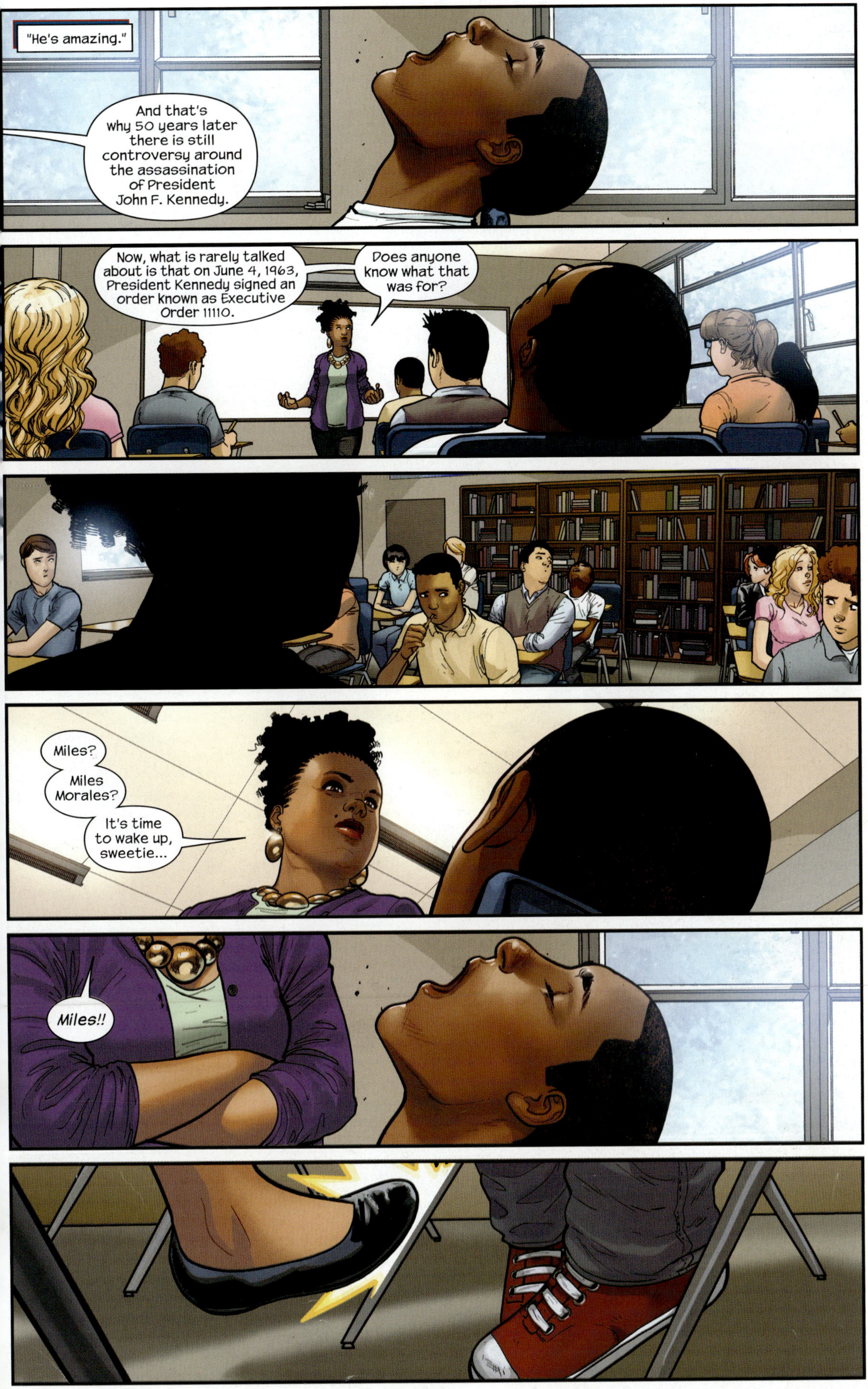

"He's amazing."
And that's why 50 years later there is still controversy around the assassination of President John F. Kennedy.
Now, what is rarely talked about is that on June 4, 1963, President Kennedy signed an order known as Executive Order 11110.
Does anyone know what that was for?
Miles?
Miles Morales?
It's time to wake up, sweetie...
Miles!!

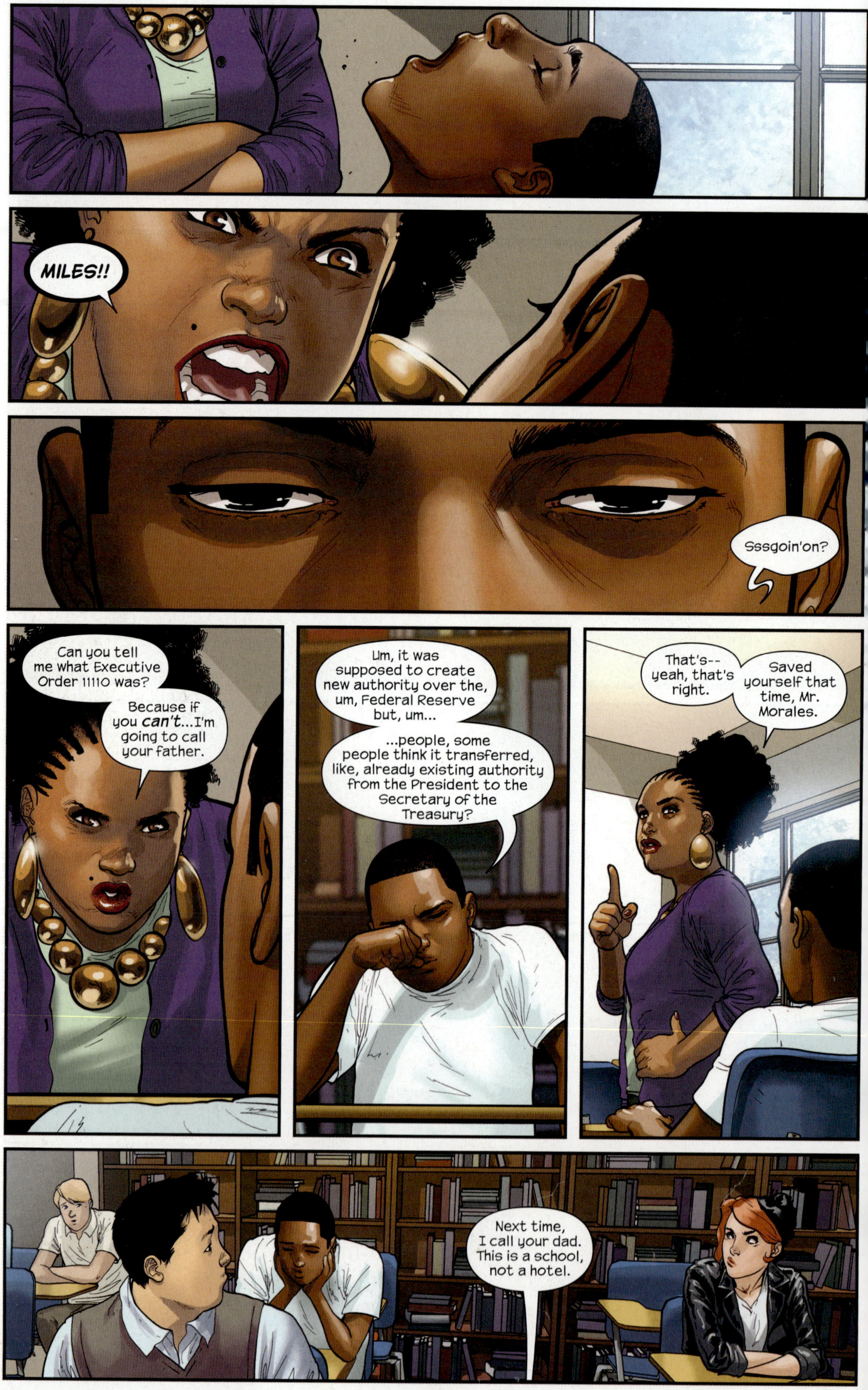
MILES!!
Sssgoin'on?
Can you tell me what Executive Order 11110 was?
Because if you *can't*...I'm going to call your father.
Um, it was supposed to create new authority over the, um, Federal Reserve but, um...
...people, some people think it transferred, like, already existing authority from the President to the Secretary of the Treasury?
That's-- yeah, that's right.
Saved yourself that time, Mr. Morales.
Next time, I call your dad. This is a school, not a hotel.

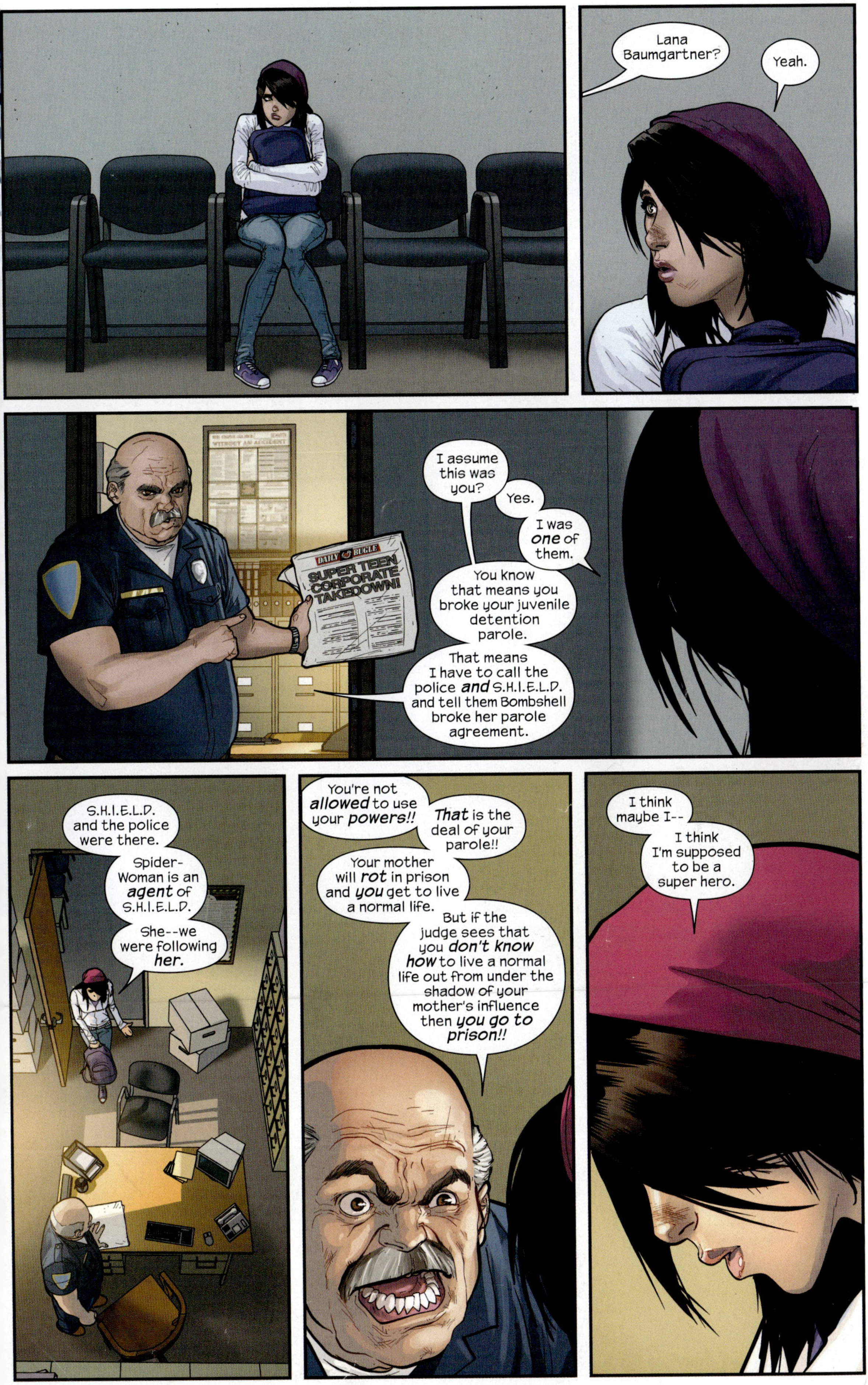
Lana Baumgartner?
Yeah.
I assume this was you?
Yes.
I was *one* of them.
You know that means you broke your juvenile detention parole.
That means I have to call the police *and* S.H.I.E.L.D. and tell them Bombshell broke her parole agreement.
DAILY BUGLE
SUPER TEEN CORPORATE TAKEDOWN!
S.H.I.E.L.D. and the police were there.
Spider-Woman is an *agent* of S.H.I.E.L.D.
She--we were following *her*.
You're not *allowed* to use your *powers!!*
That is the deal of your parole!!
Your mother will *rot* in prison and *you* get to live a normal life.
But if the judge sees that you *don't know how* to live a normal life out from under the shadow of your mother's influence then *you go to prison!!*
I think maybe I--
I think I'm supposed to be a super hero.

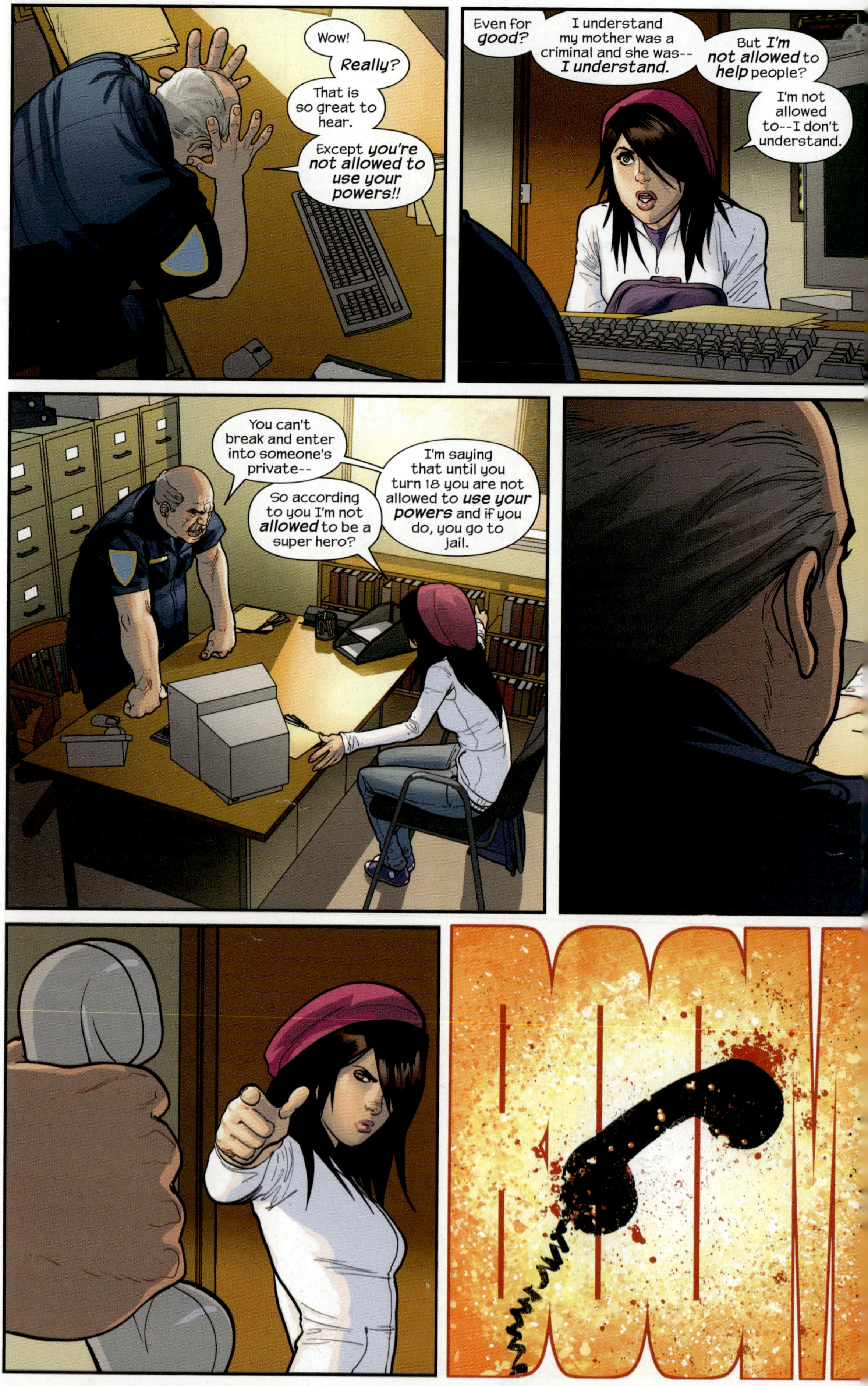

Wow!
Really?
That is so great to hear.
Except *you're not allowed to use your powers!!*
Even for *good?*
I understand my mother was a criminal and she was-- *I understand.*
But *I'm not allowed* to *help* people?
I'm not allowed to--I don't understand.
You can't break and enter into someone's private--
So according to you I'm not *allowed* to be a super hero?
I'm saying that until you turn 18 you are not allowed to *use your powers* and if you do, you go to jail.
DOOM

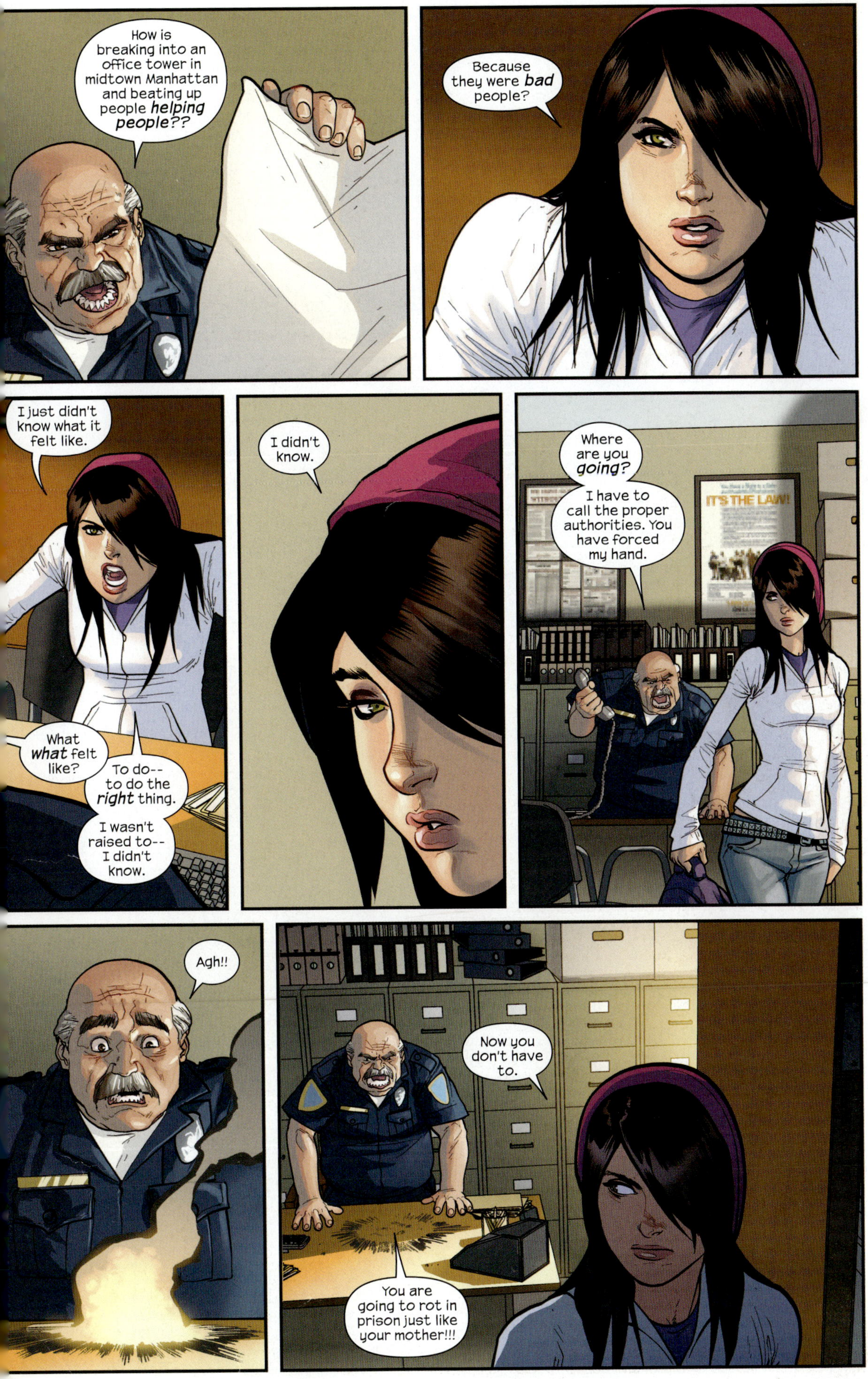
How is breaking into an office tower in midtown Manhattan and beating up people *helping people??*
Because they were *bad* people?
I just didn't know what it felt like.
What *what* felt like?
To do-- to do the *right* thing.
I wasn't raised to-- I didn't know.
I didn't know.
Where are you *going?*
I have to call the proper authorities. You have forced my hand.
IT'S THE LAW!
Agh!!
Now you don't have to.
You are going to rot in prison just like your mother!!!

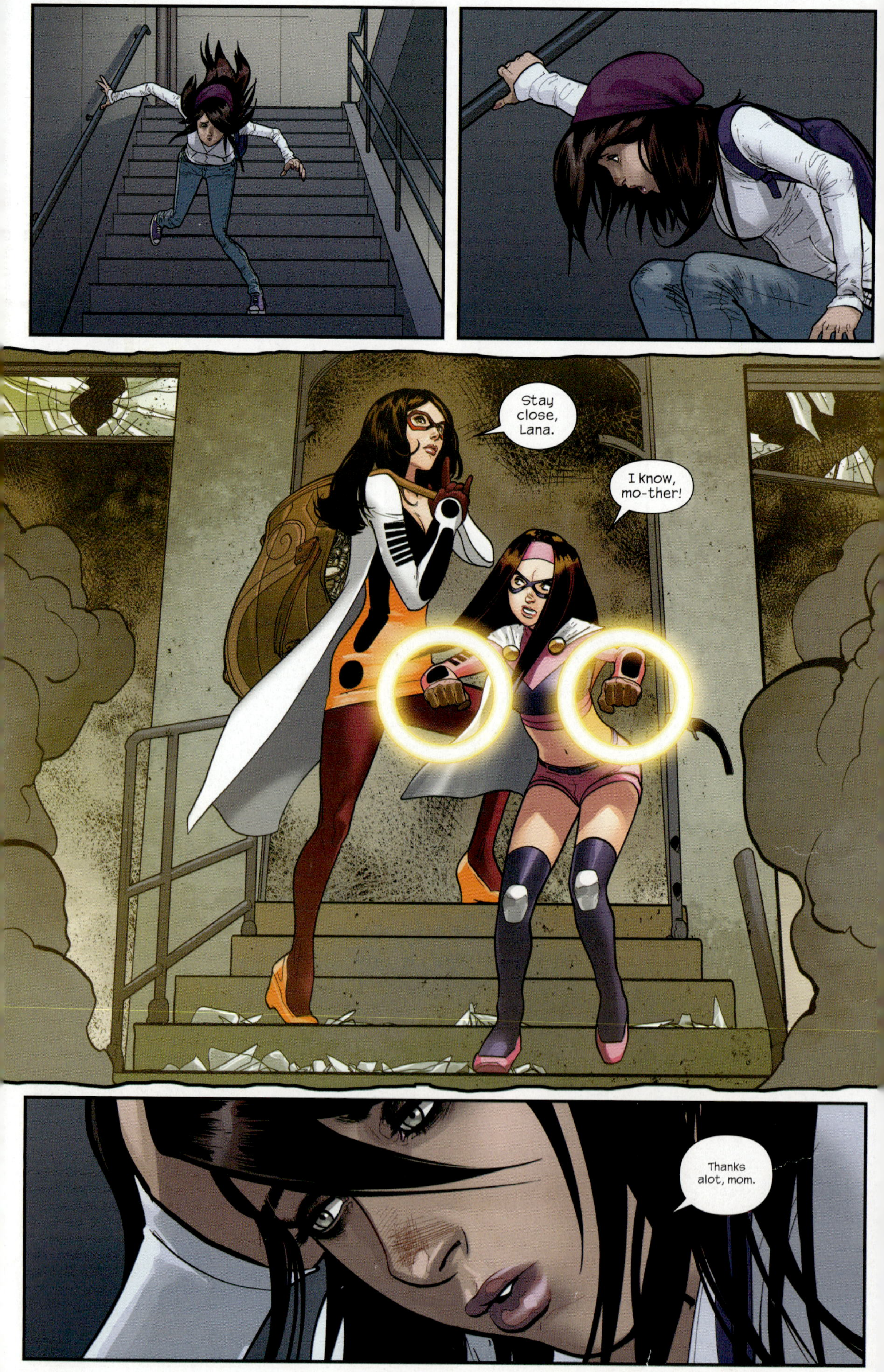
Stay close, Lana.
I know, mo-ther!
Thanks alot, mom.

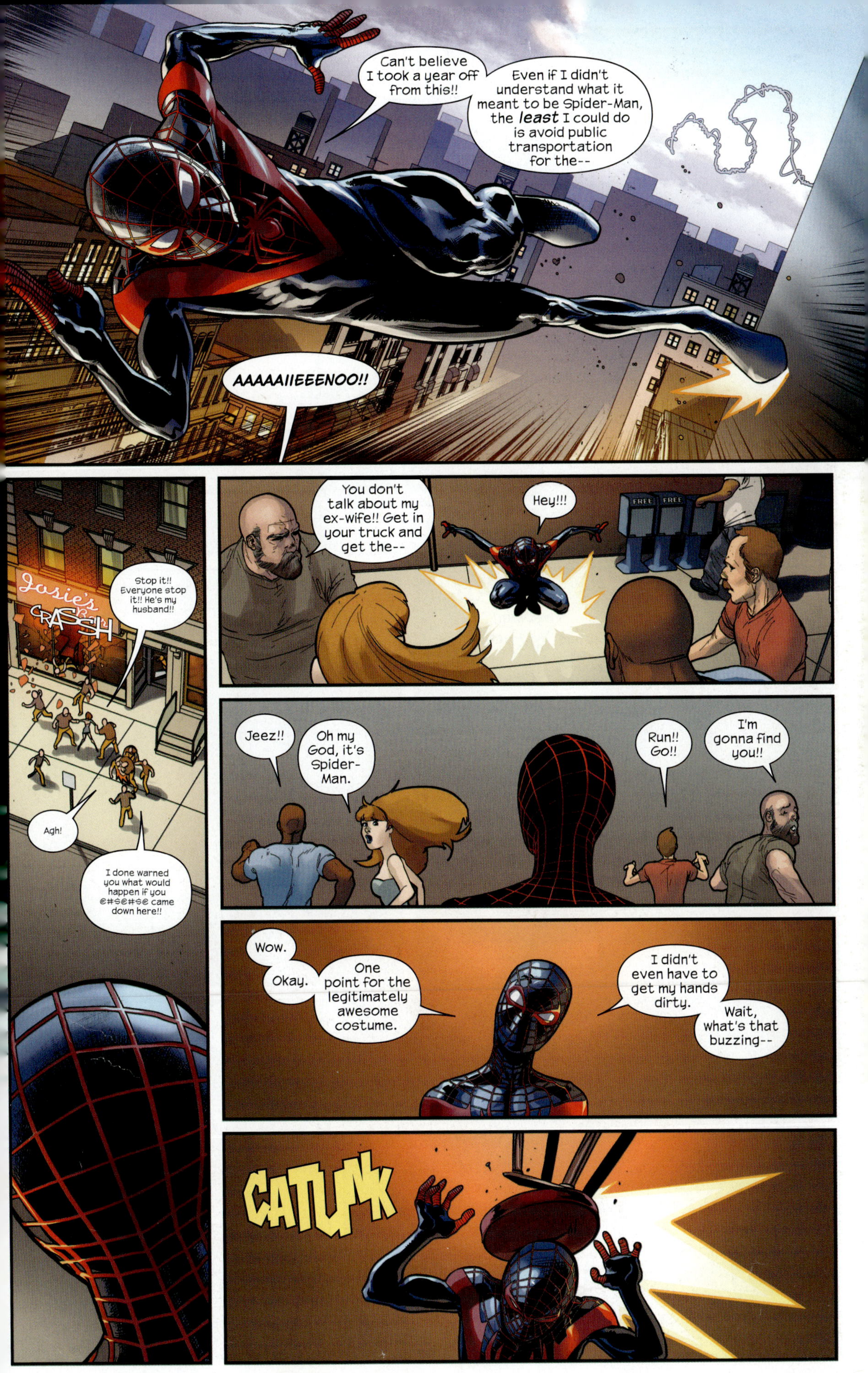
Can't believe I took a year off from this!!
Even if I didn't understand what it meant to be Spider-Man, the **least** I could do is avoid public transportation for the--
AAAAAIIEEENOO!!
Josie's Bar
CRASSH
Stop it!! Everyone stop it!! He's my husband!!
Agh!
I done warned you what would happen if you @#$@#$@ came down here!!
You don't talk about my ex-wife!! Get in your truck and get the--
Hey!!!
FREE
FREE
Jeez!!
Oh my God, it's Spider-Man.
Run!! Go!!
I'm gonna find you!!
Wow.
Okay.
One point for the legitimately awesome costume.
I didn't even have to get my hands dirty.
Wait, what's that buzzing--
CATUNK

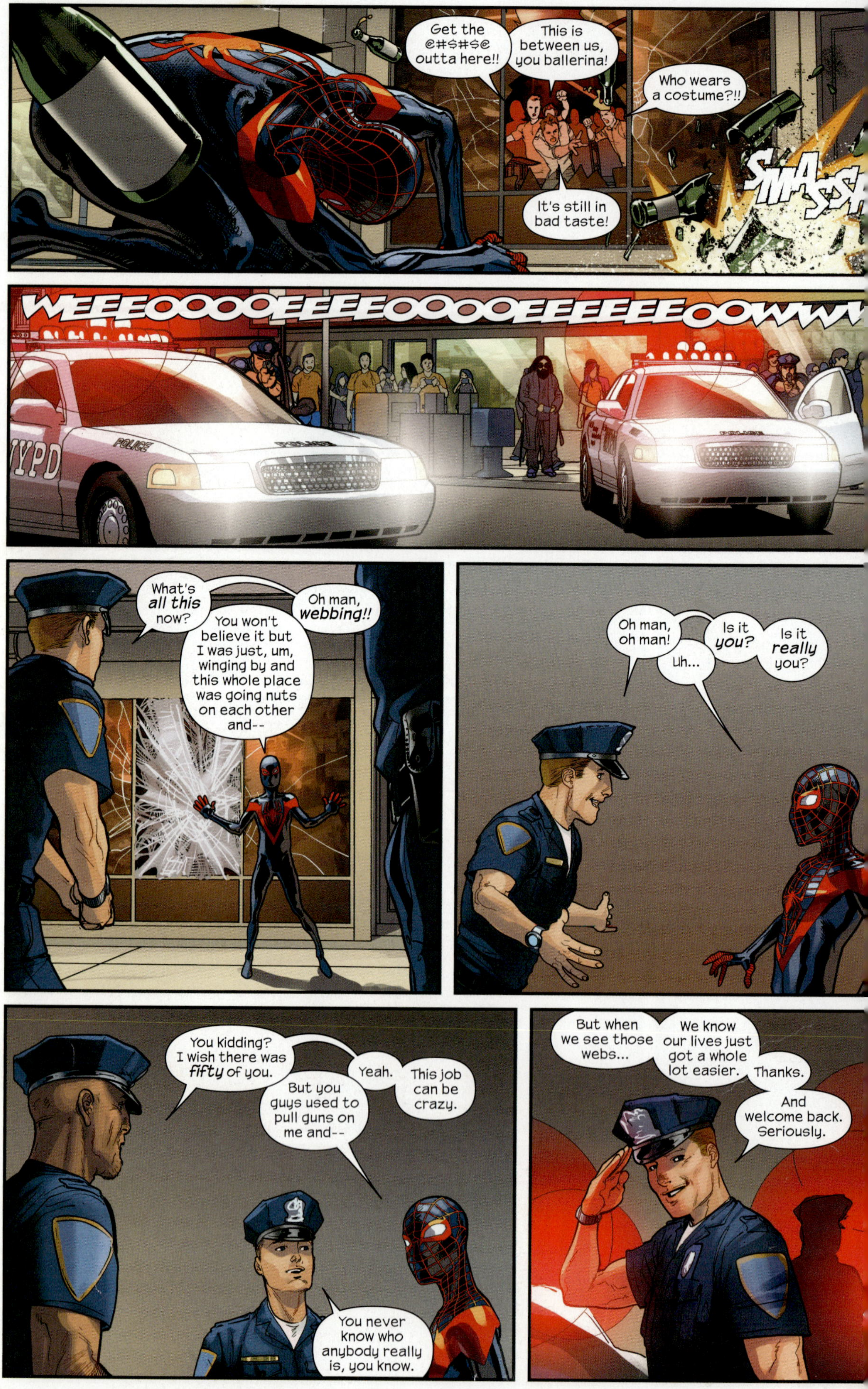
Get the @#$#$@ outta here!!
This is between us, you ballerina!
Who wears a costume?!!
It's still in bad taste!
SMASH
WEEEOOOOEEEEOOOOOEEEEEEOOWWW
NYPD
POLICE
What's all this now?
Oh man, webbing!!
You won't believe it but I was just, um, winging by and this whole place was going nuts on each other and--
Oh man, oh man!
Is it you?
Is it really you?
Uh...
You kidding? I wish there was fifty of you.
Yeah.
This job can be crazy.
But you guys used to pull guns on me and--
You never know who anybody really is, you know.
But when we see those webs...
We know our lives just got a whole lot easier.
Thanks.
And welcome back. Seriously.

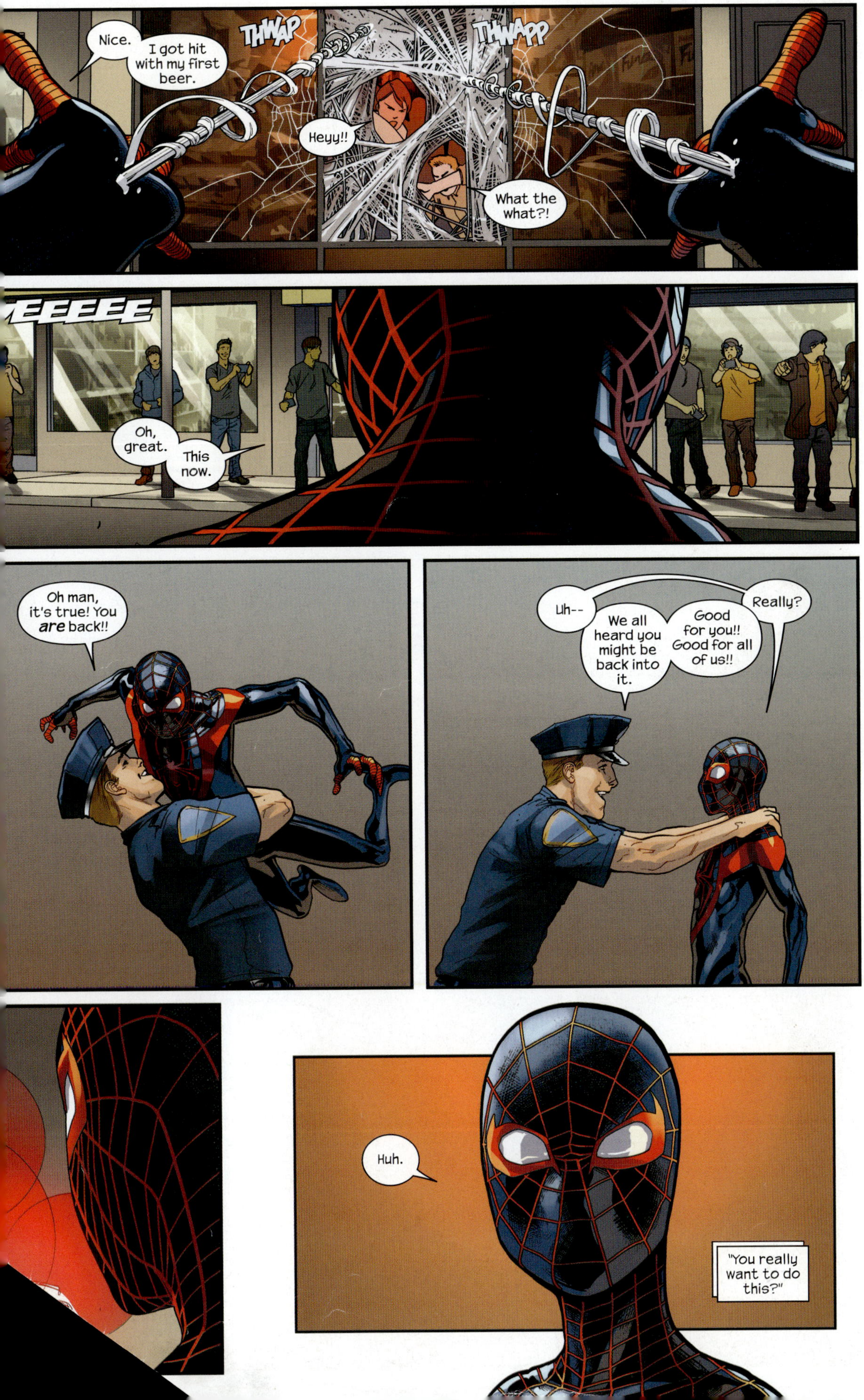
Nice.
I got hit with my first beer.
THWAP
THWAPP
Heyy!!
What the what?!
EEEEEE
Oh, great.
This now.
Oh man, it's true! You *are* back!!
Uh--
We all heard you might be back into it.
Good for you!! Good for all of us!!
Really?
Huh.
"You really want to do this?"

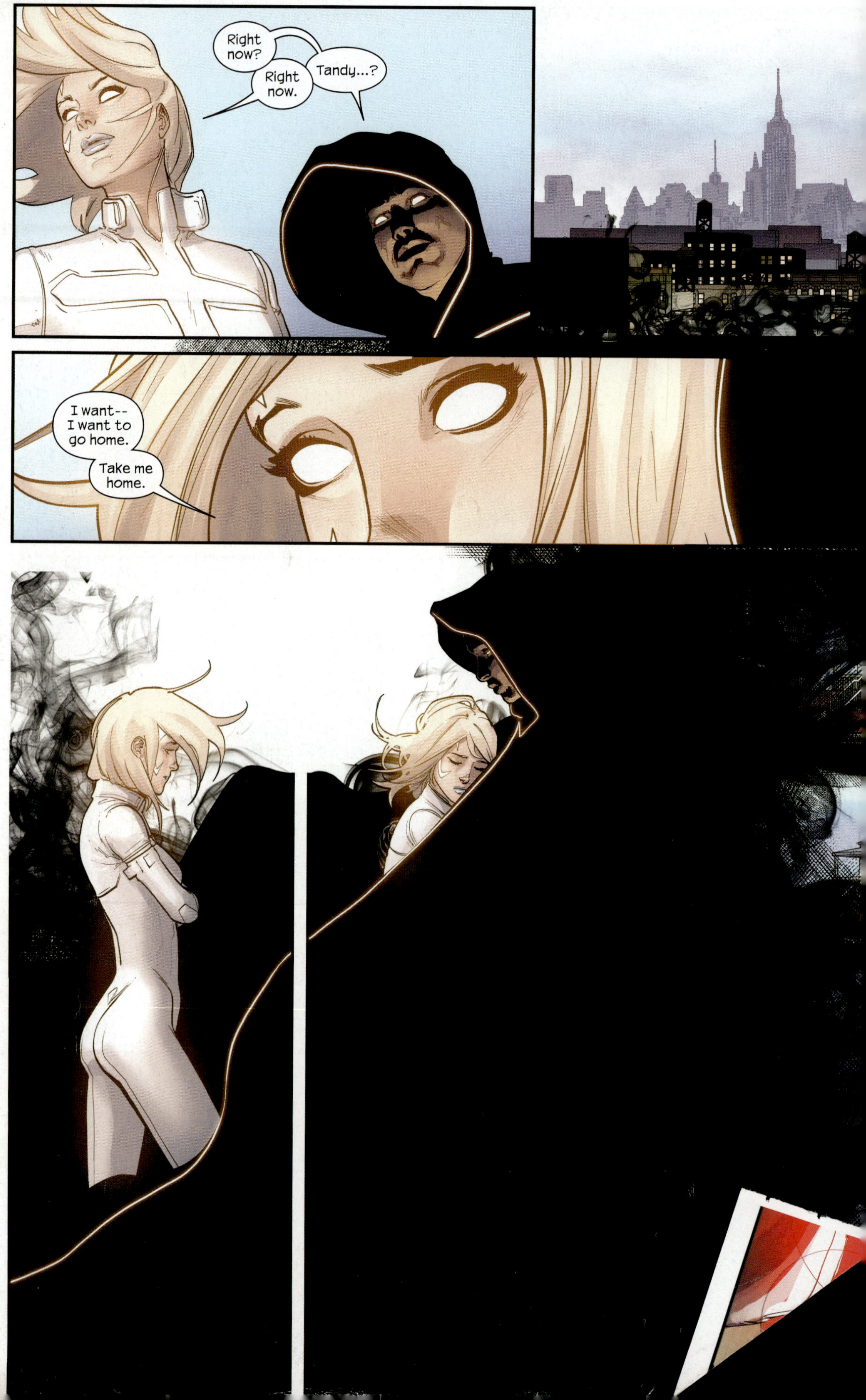
Right now?
Tandy...?
Right now.
I want--
I want to go home.
Take me home.

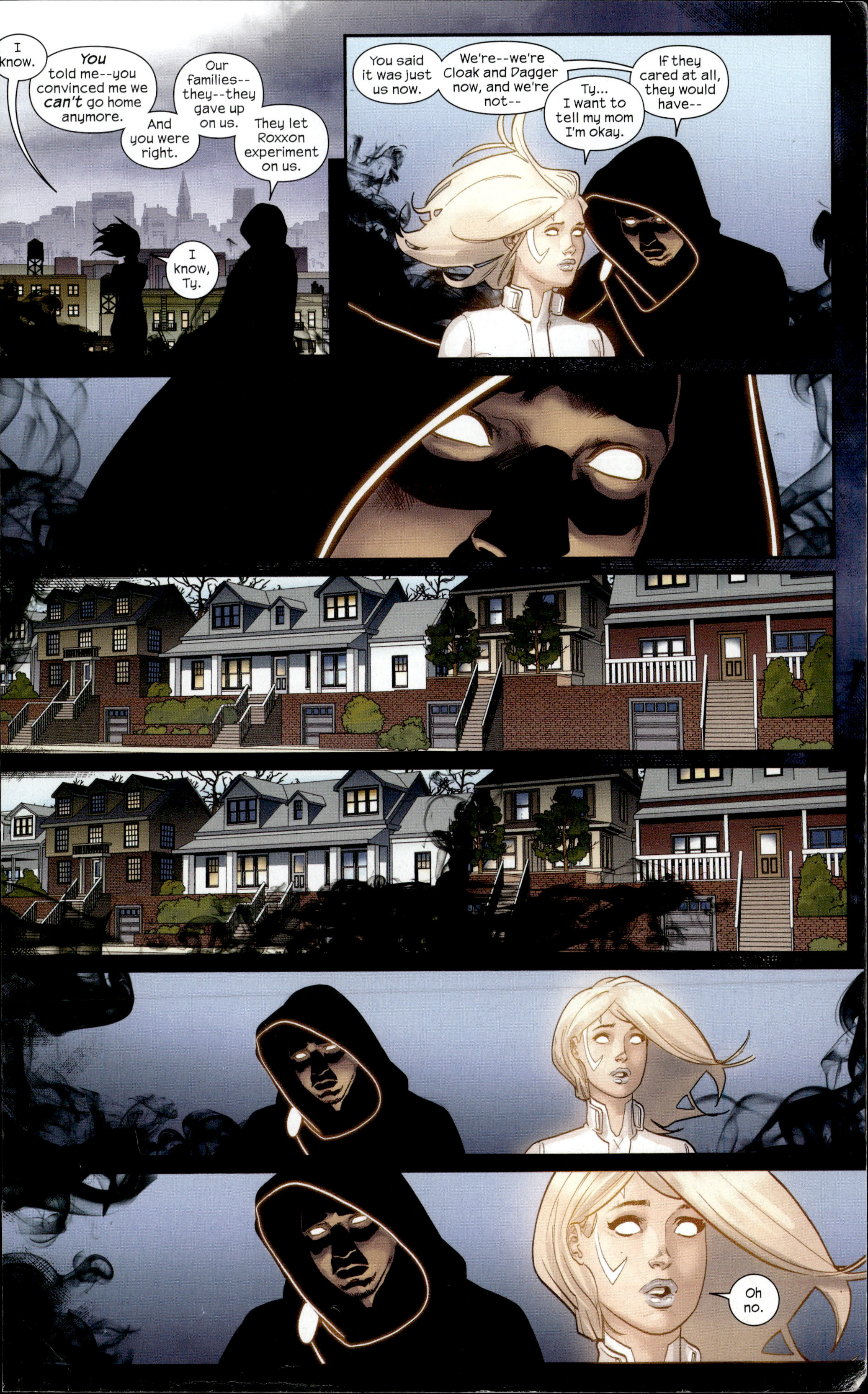
I know.
You told me--you convinced me we can't go home anymore.
And you were right.
Our families--they--they gave up on us.
They let Roxxon experiment on us.
I know, Ty.
You said it was just us now.
We're--we're Cloak and Dagger now, and we're not--
If they cared at all, they would have--
Ty... I want to tell my mom I'm okay.
Oh no.

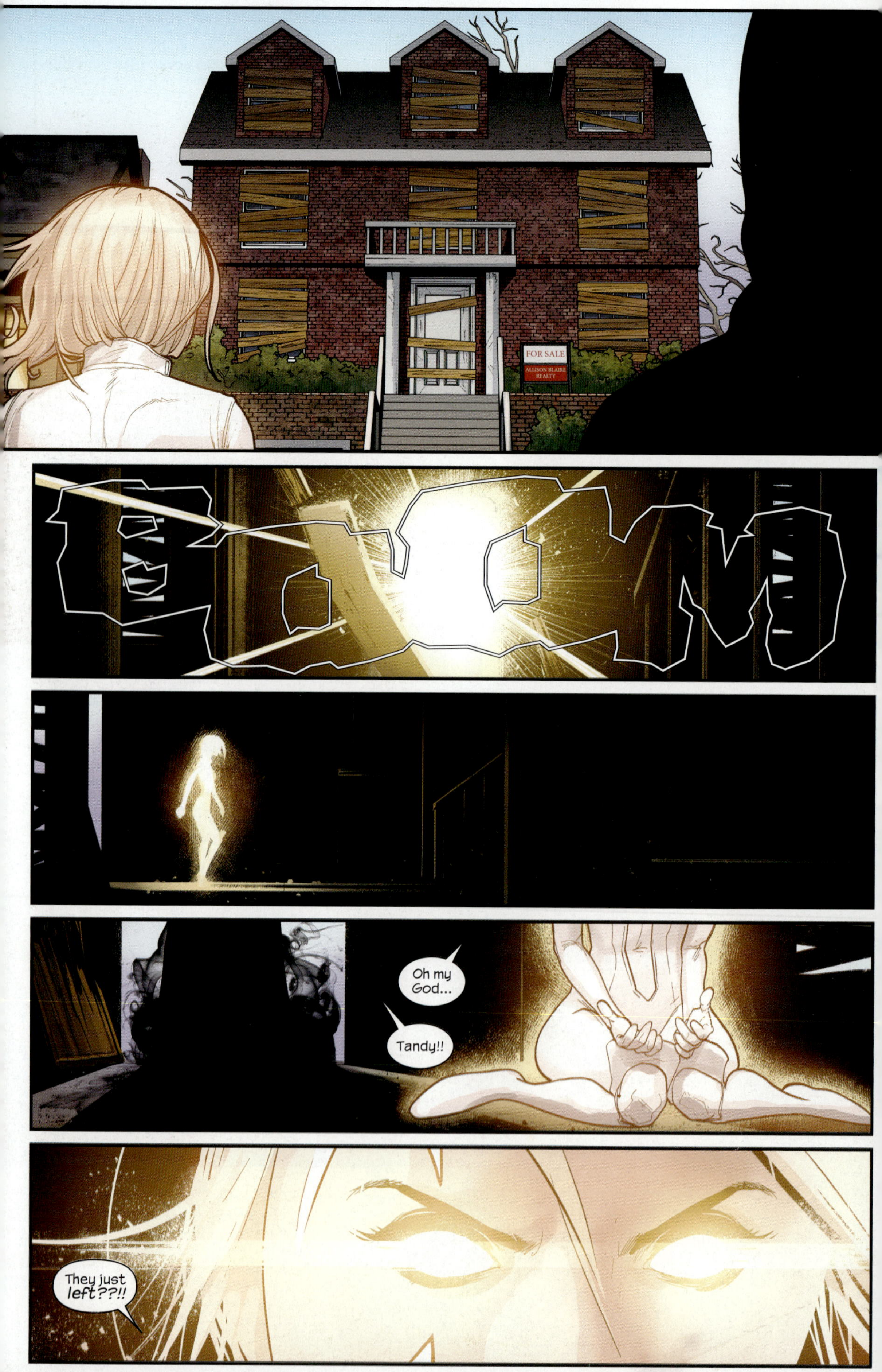
FOR SALE
ALLISON BLAIRE REALTY
BOOM
Oh my God...
Tandy!!
They just left??!!

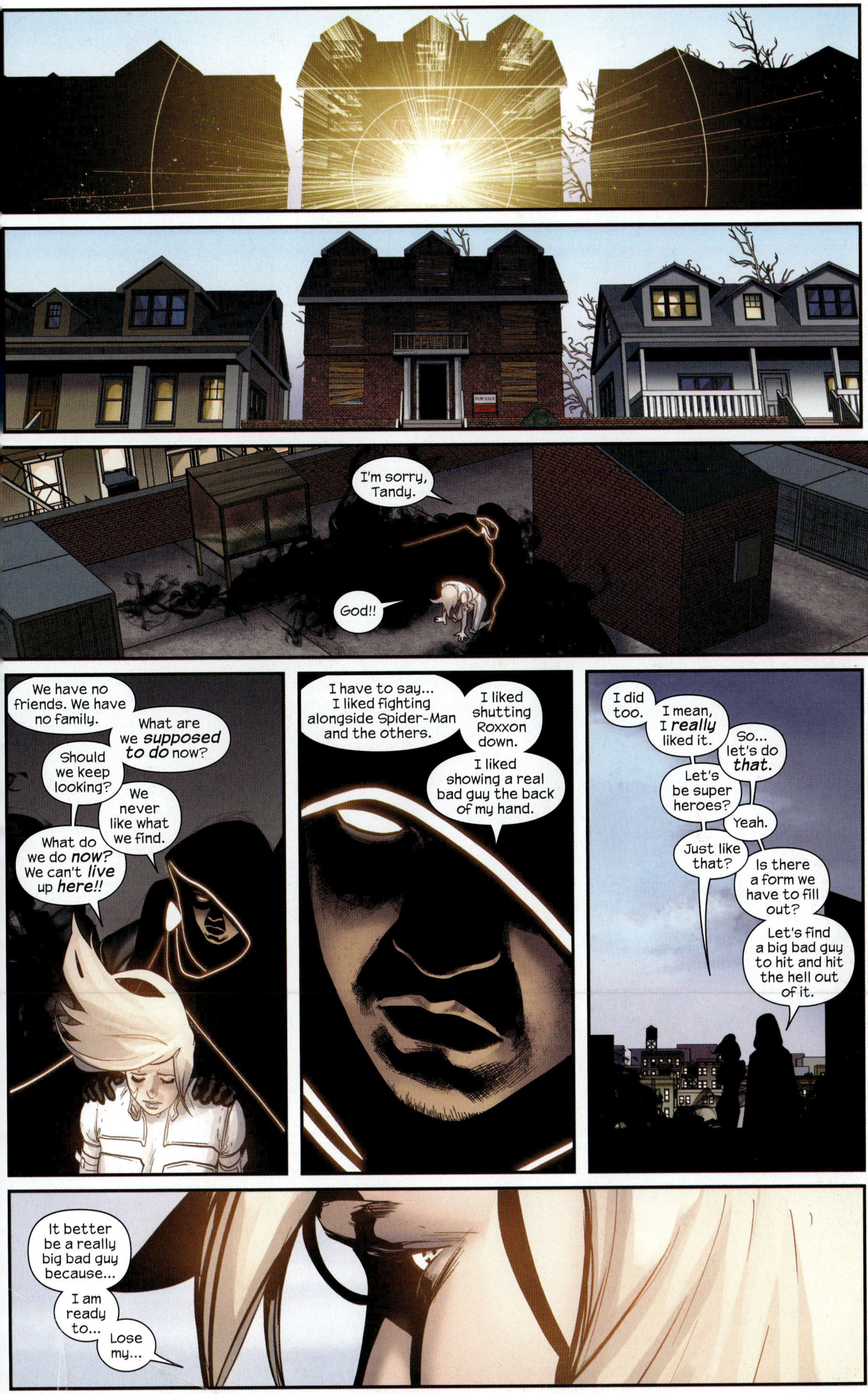

I'm sorry, Tandy.
God!!
We have no friends. We have no family.
What are we *supposed to do* now?
Should we keep looking?
We never like what we find.
What do we do *now?* We can't *live* up *here!!*
I have to say... I liked fighting alongside Spider-Man and the others.
I liked shutting Roxxon down.
I liked showing a real bad guy the back of my hand.
I did too.
I mean, I *really* liked it.
So... let's do *that.*
Let's be super heroes?
Yeah.
Just like that?
Is there a form we have to fill out?
Let's find a big bad guy to hit and hit the hell out of it.
It better be a really big bad guy because...
I am ready to... Lose my...

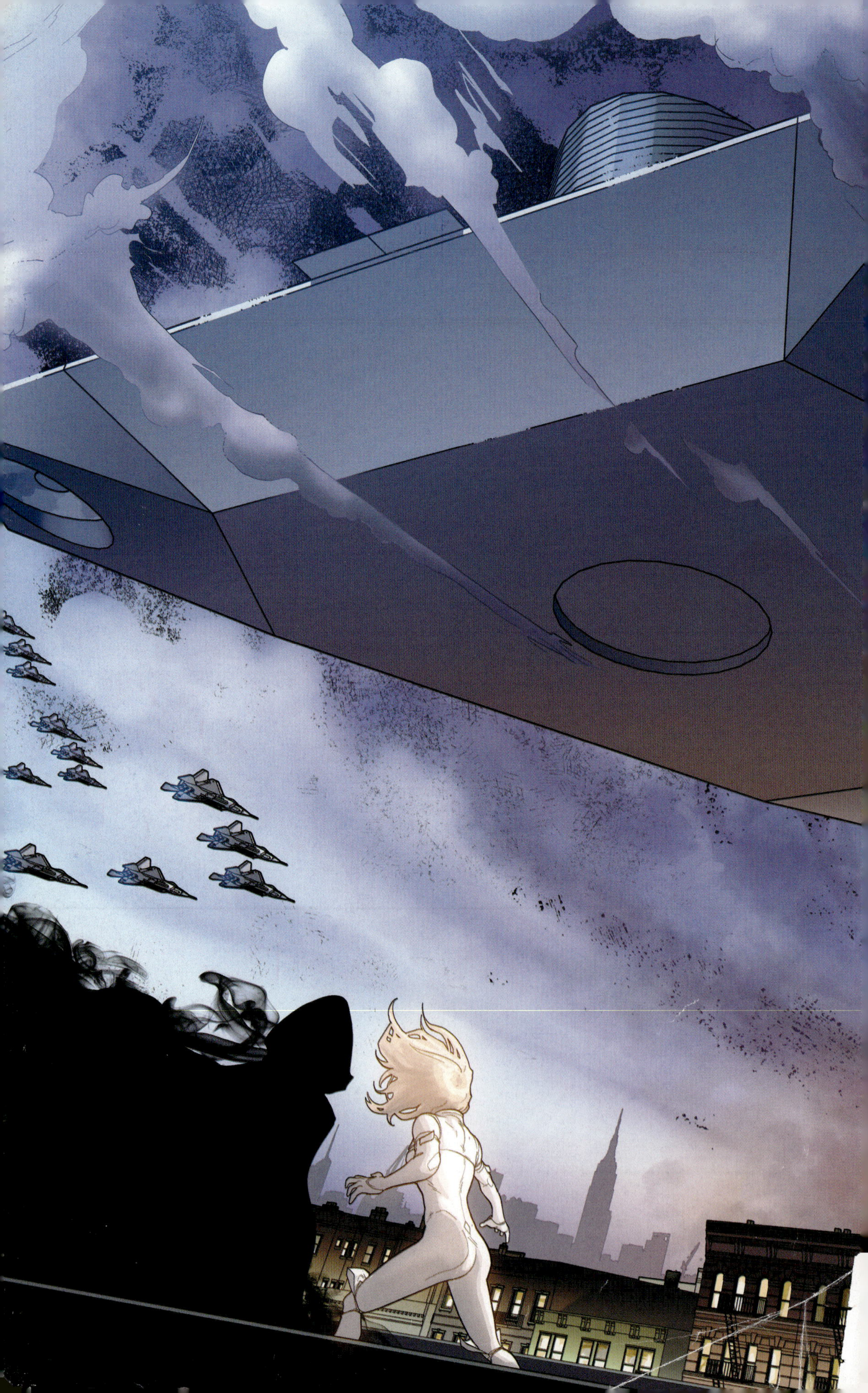

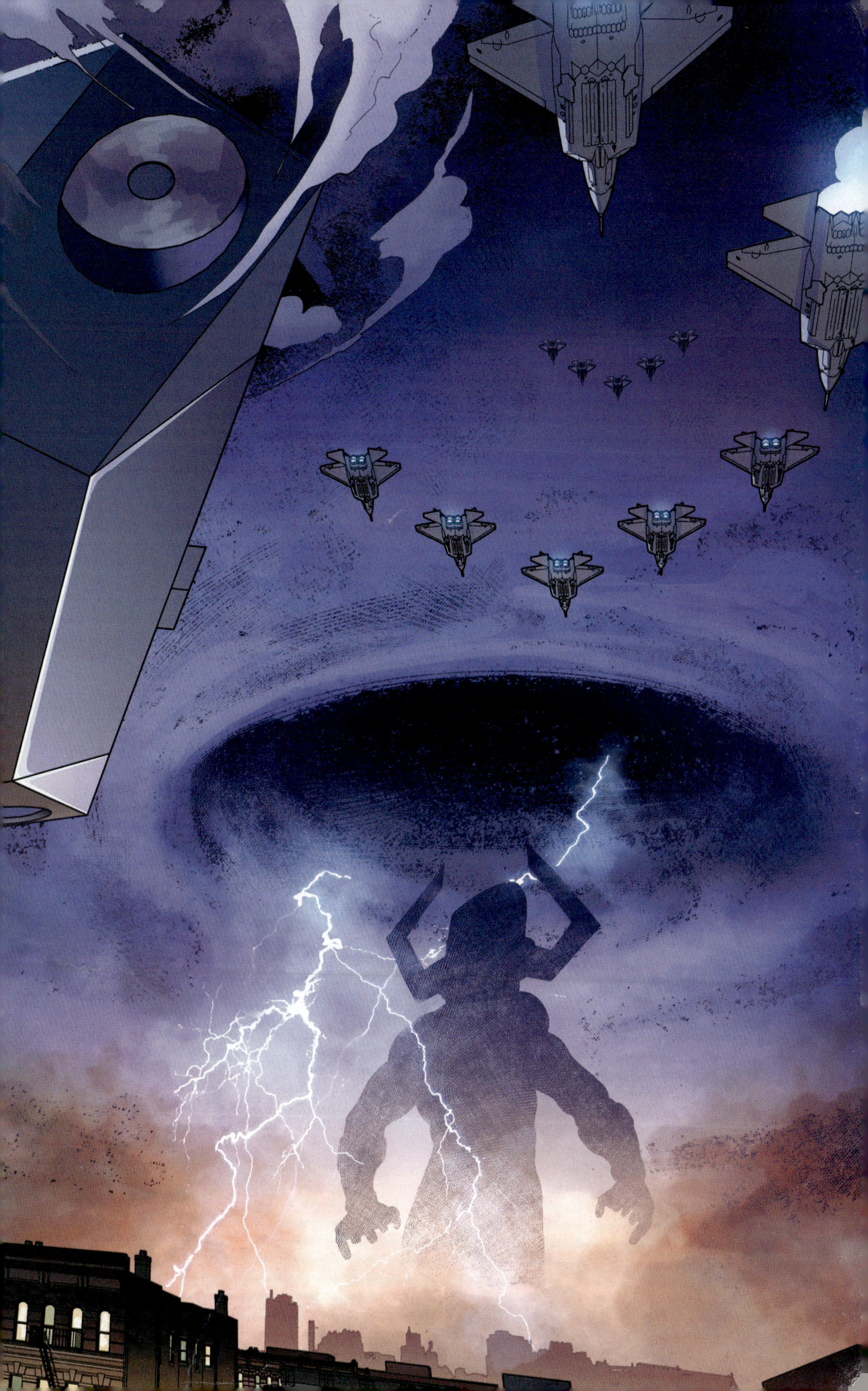

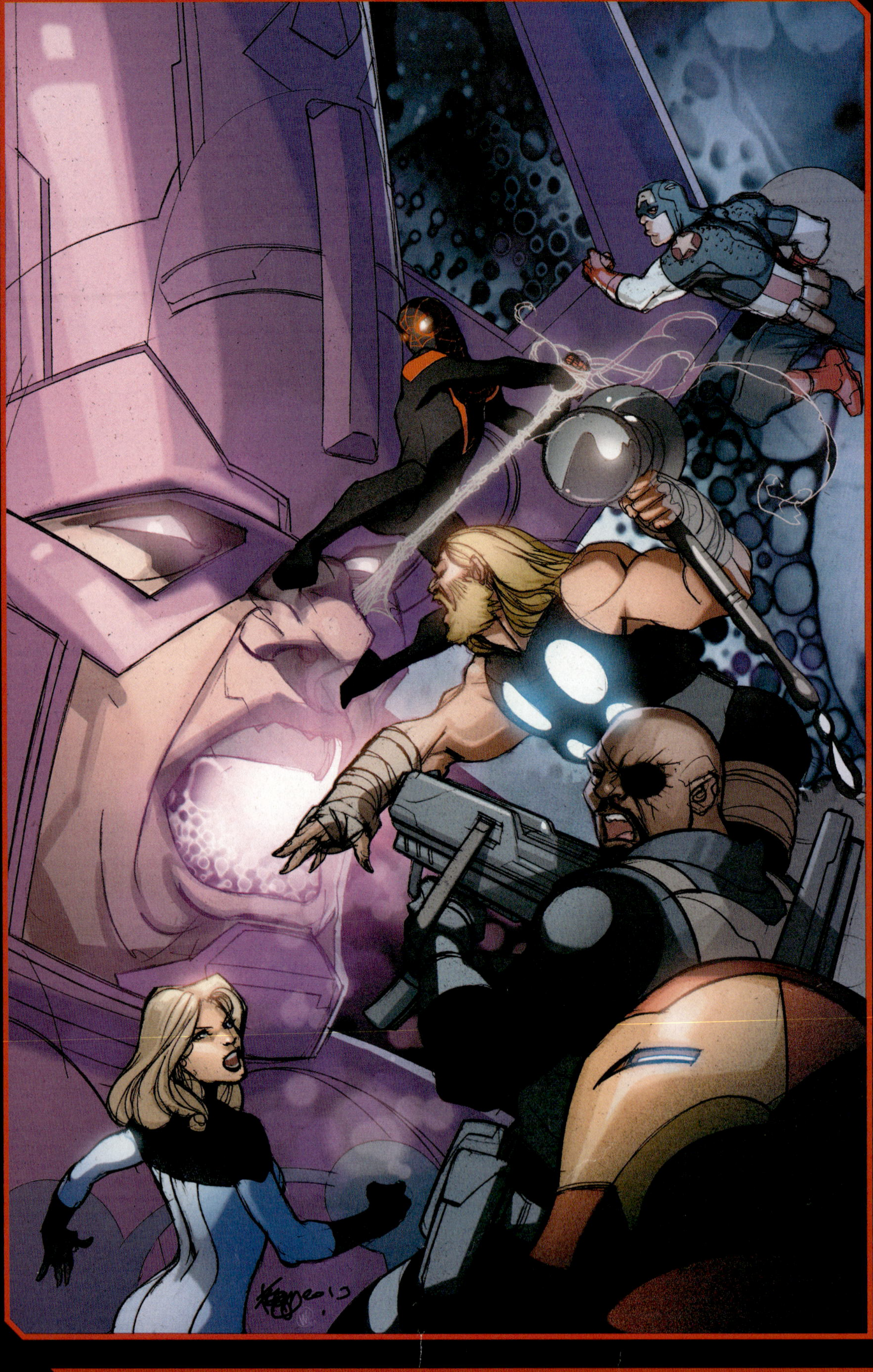

CATACLYSM: THE ULTIMATES' LAST STAND #2 VARIANT BY PASQUAL FERRY & WIL QUINTANA

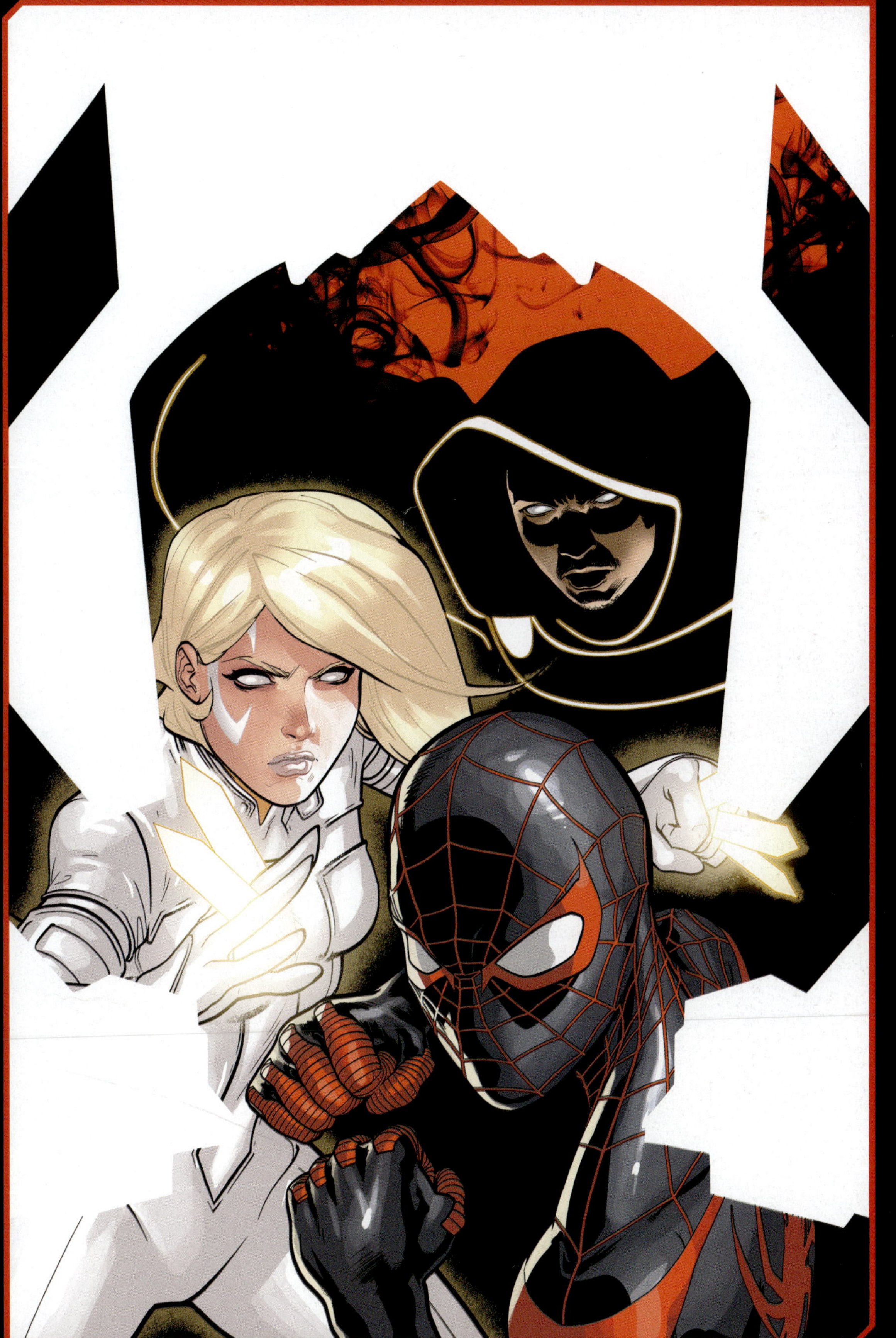

CATACLYSM: ULTIMATE SPIDER-MAN #2

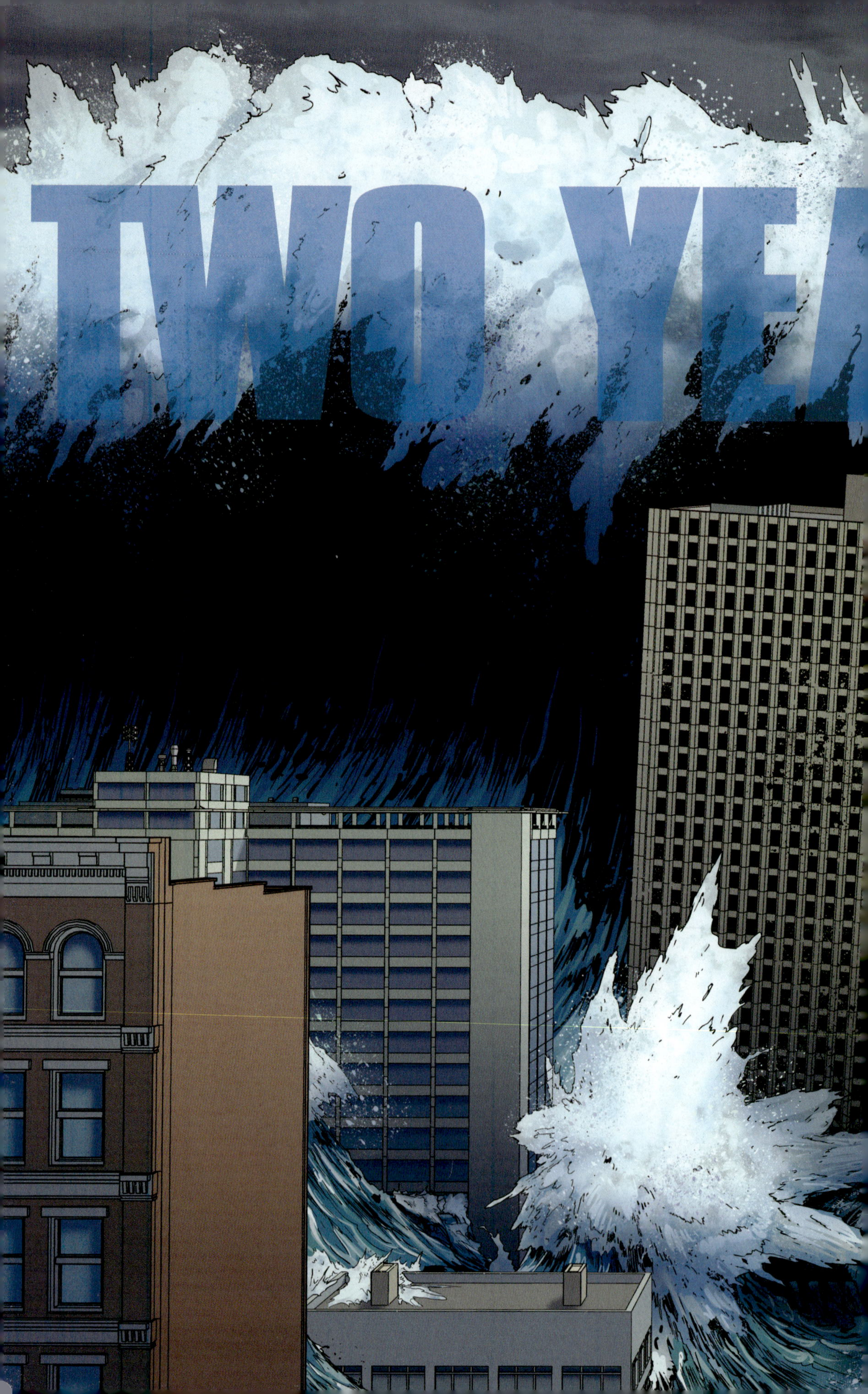
TWO YE

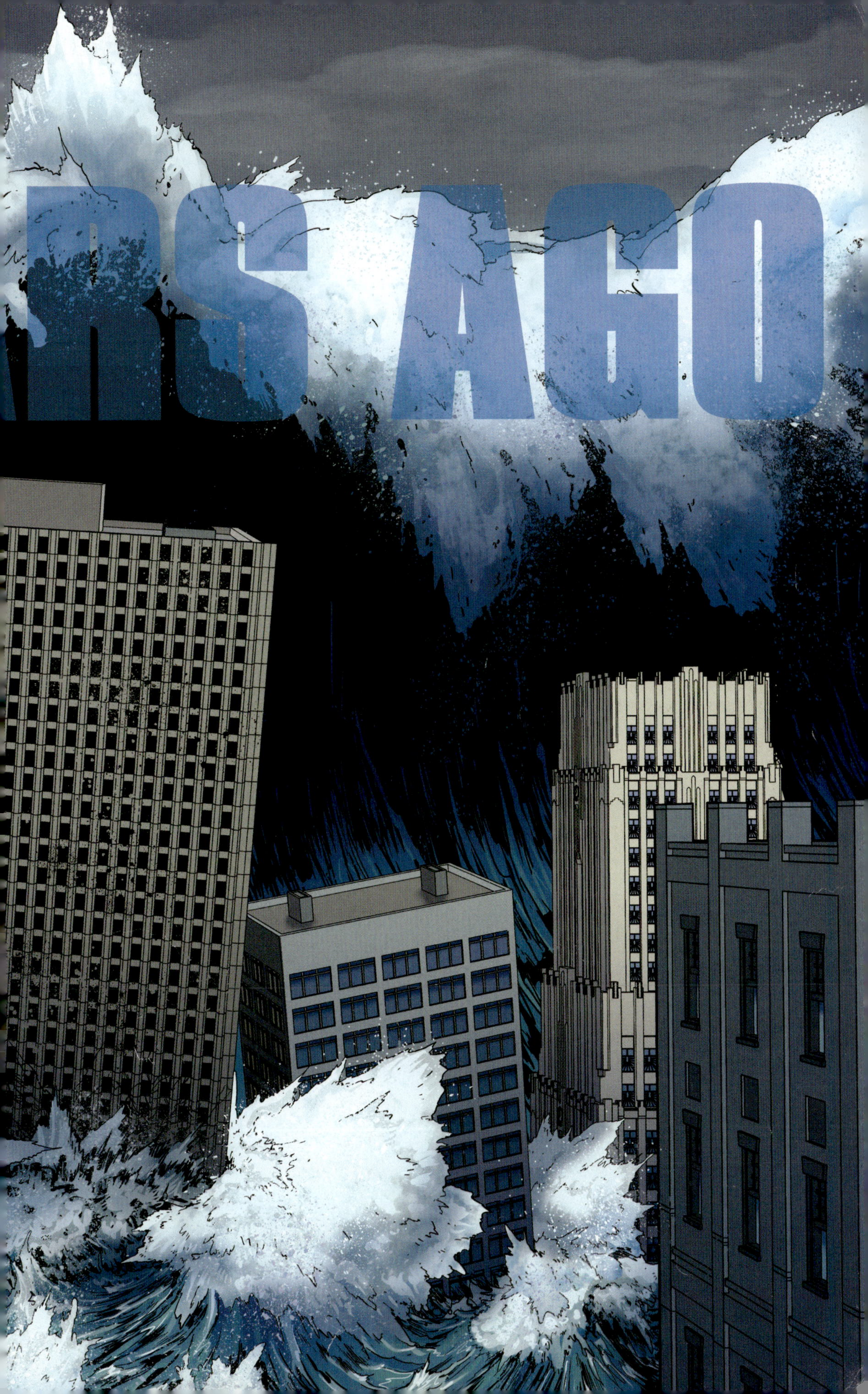
RS AGO

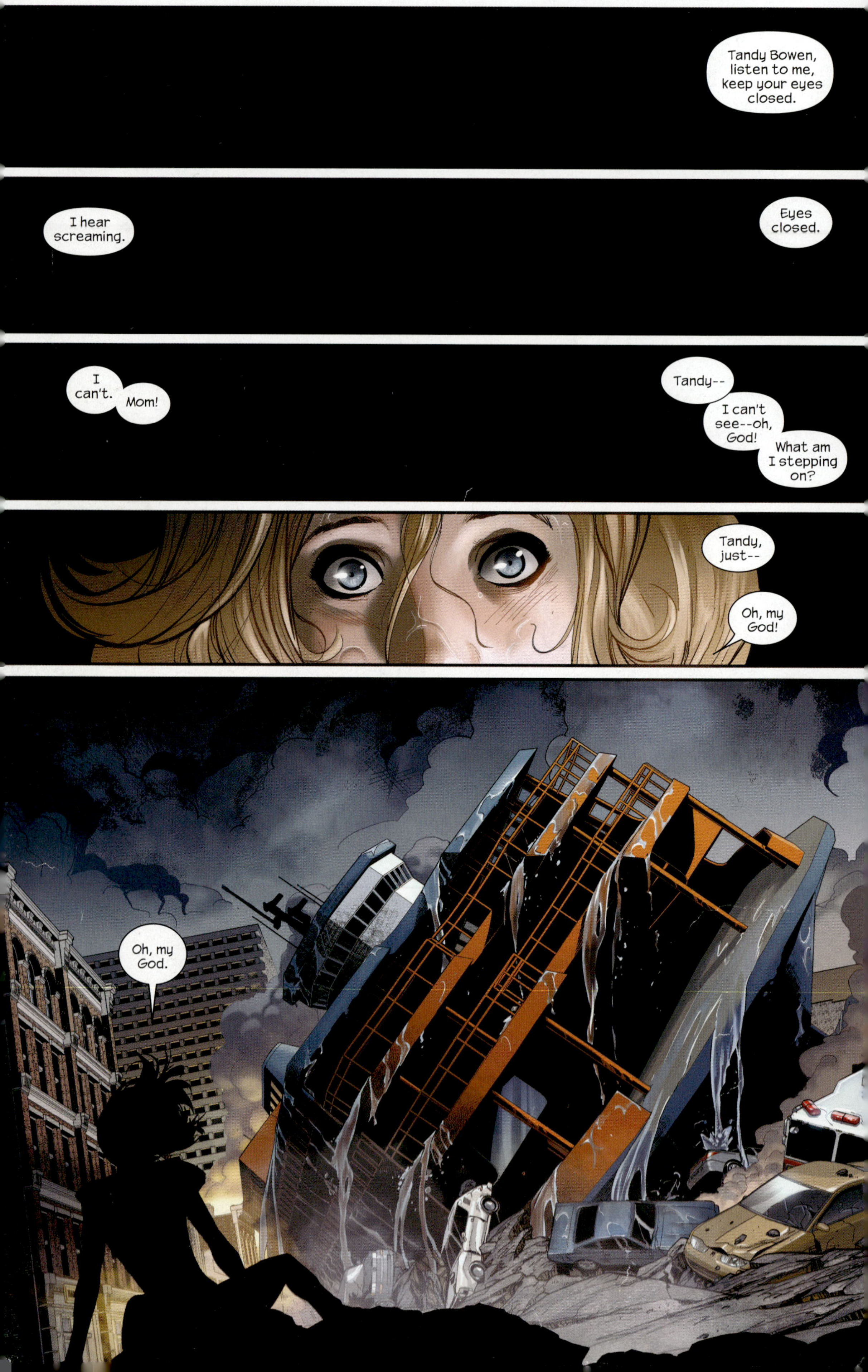
Tandy Bowen, listen to me, keep your eyes closed.
I hear screaming.
Eyes closed.
I can't.
Mom!
Tandy--
I can't see--oh, God!
What am I stepping on?
Tandy, just--
Oh, my God!
Oh, my God.

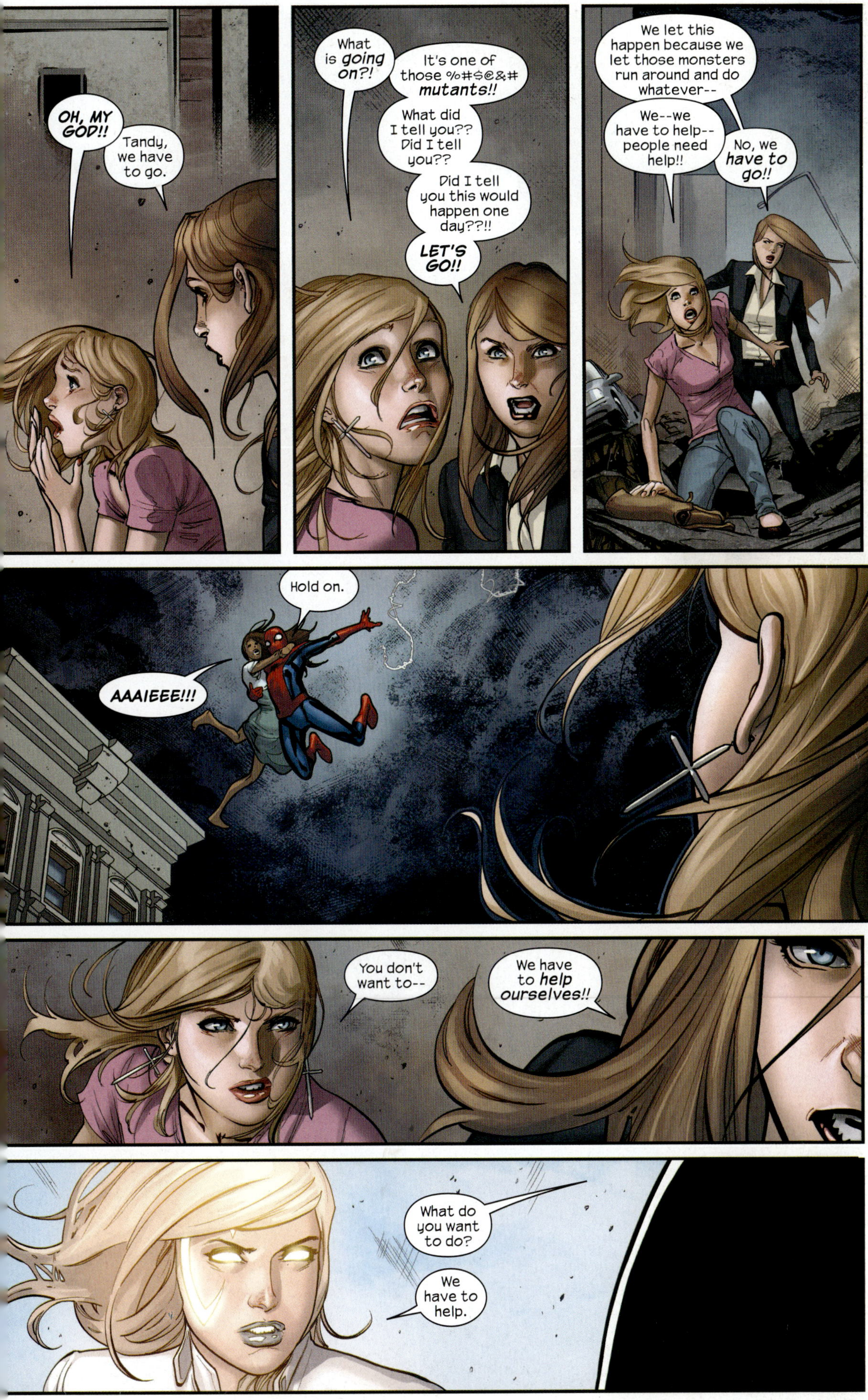
OH, MY GOD!!
Tandy, we have to go.
What is going on?!
It's one of those %#$@&# mutants!!
What did I tell you?? Did I tell you??
Did I tell you this would happen one day??!!
LET'S GO!!
We let this happen because we let those monsters run around and do whatever--
We--we have to help-- people need help!!
No, we have to go!!
Hold on.
AAAIEEE!!!
You don't want to--
We have to help ourselves!!
What do you want to do?
We have to help.

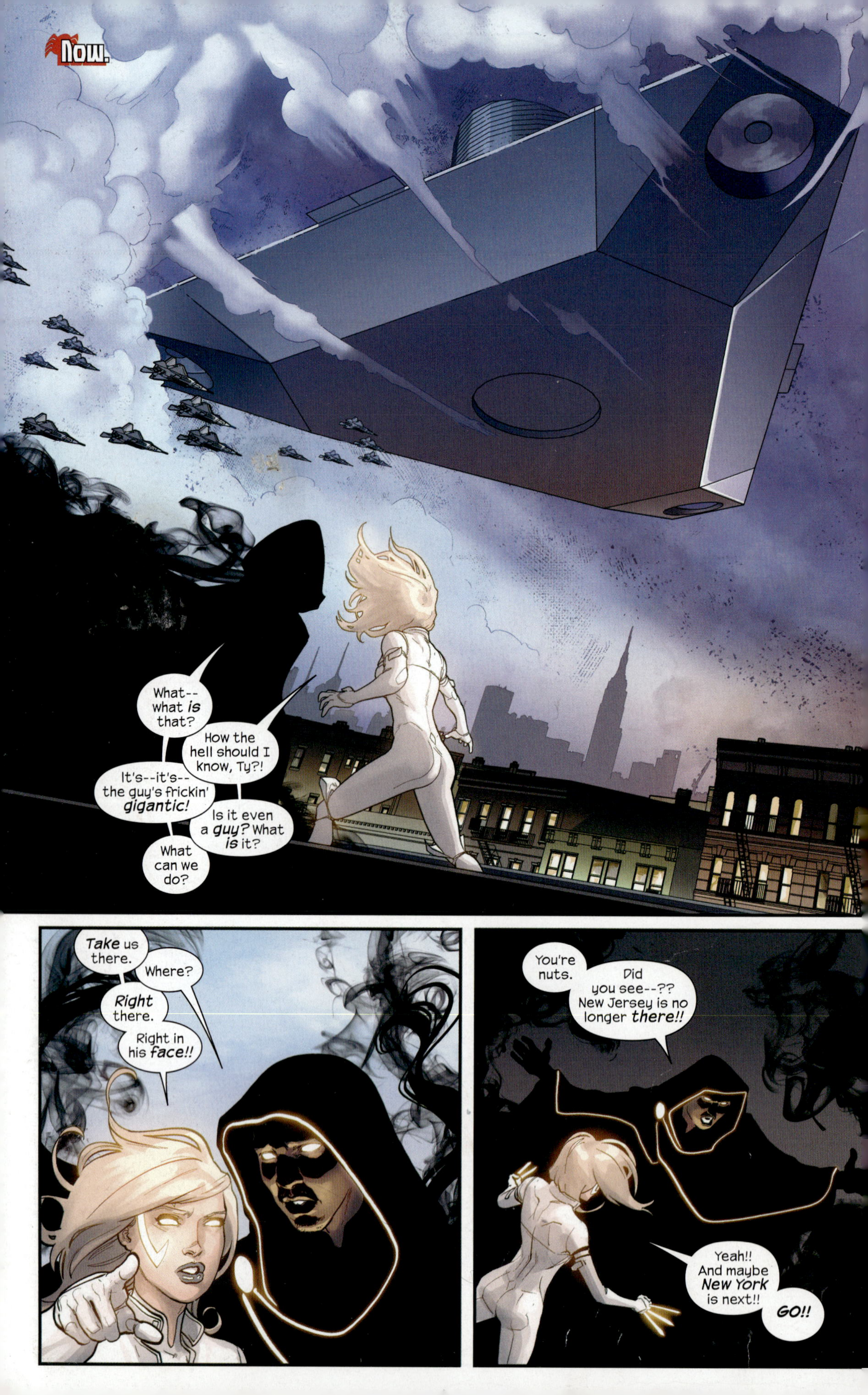
Now.
What--
what is
that?
How the
hell should I
know, Ty?!
It's--it's--
the guy's frickin'
gigantic!
Is it even
a guy? What
is it?
What
can we
do?
Take us
there.
Where?
Right
there.
Right in
his face!!
You're
nuts.
Did
you see--??
New Jersey is no
longer there!!
Yeah!!
And maybe
New York
is next!!
GO!!

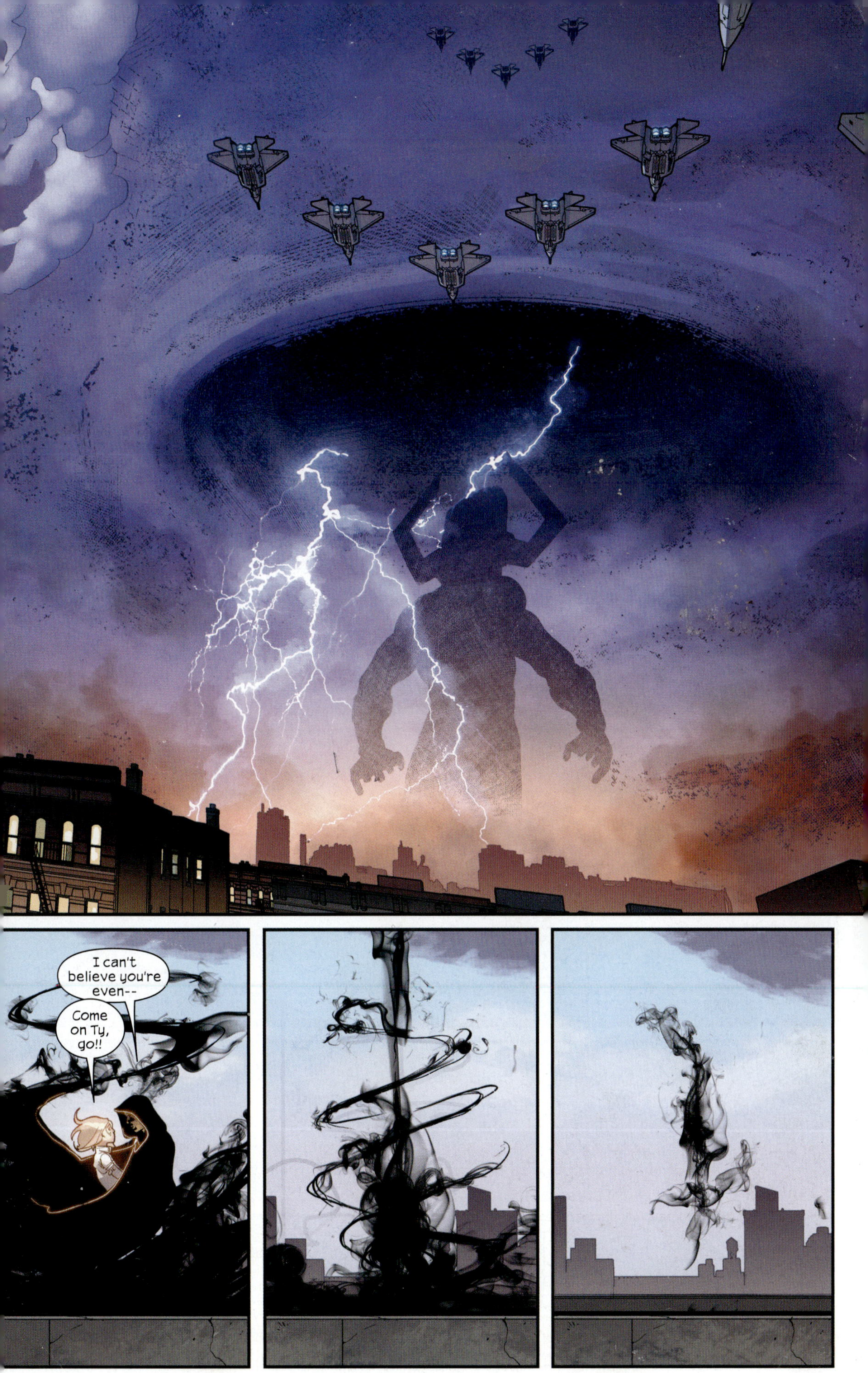
I can't believe you're even--
Come on Ty, go!!

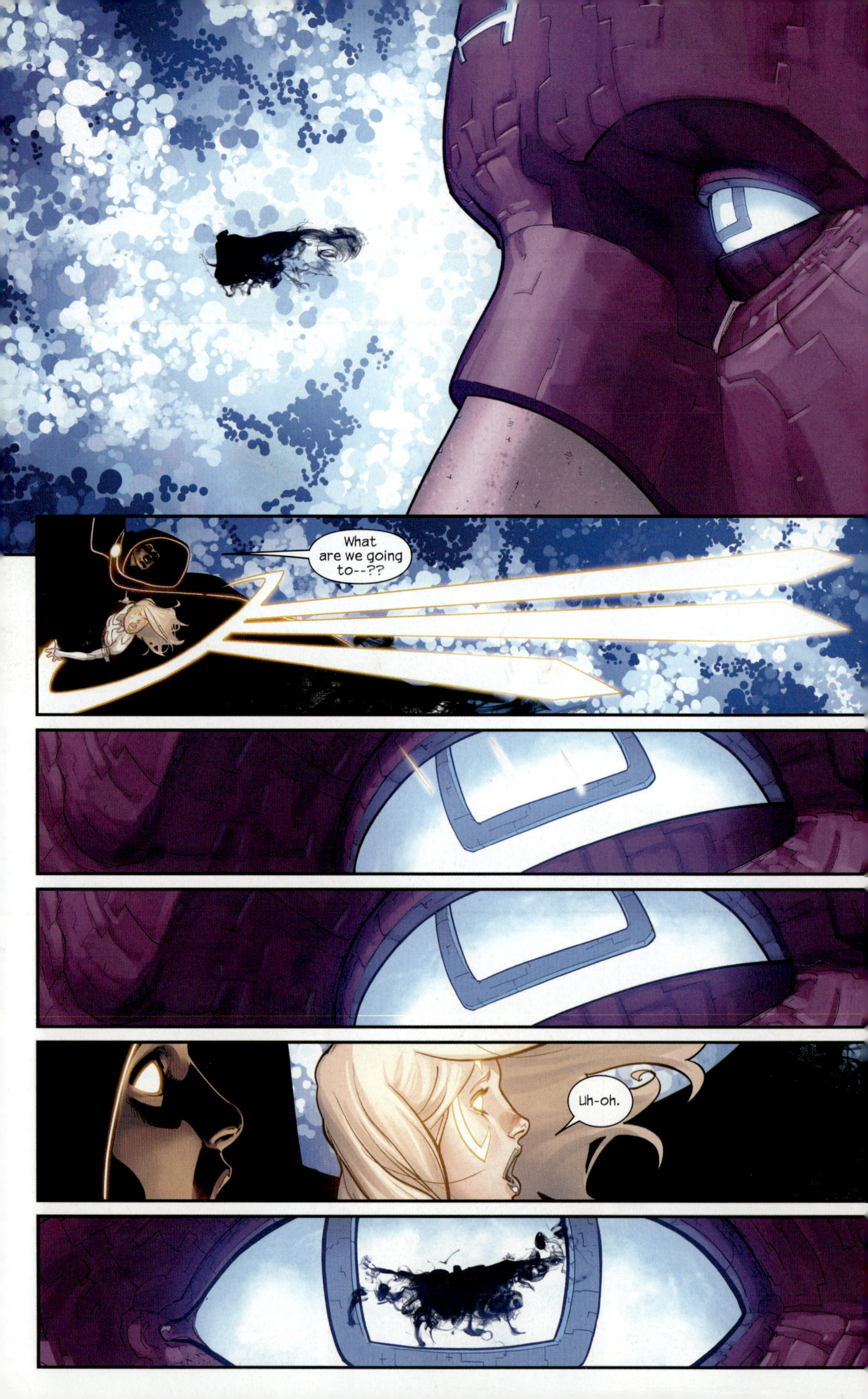
What are we going to--??
Uh-oh.

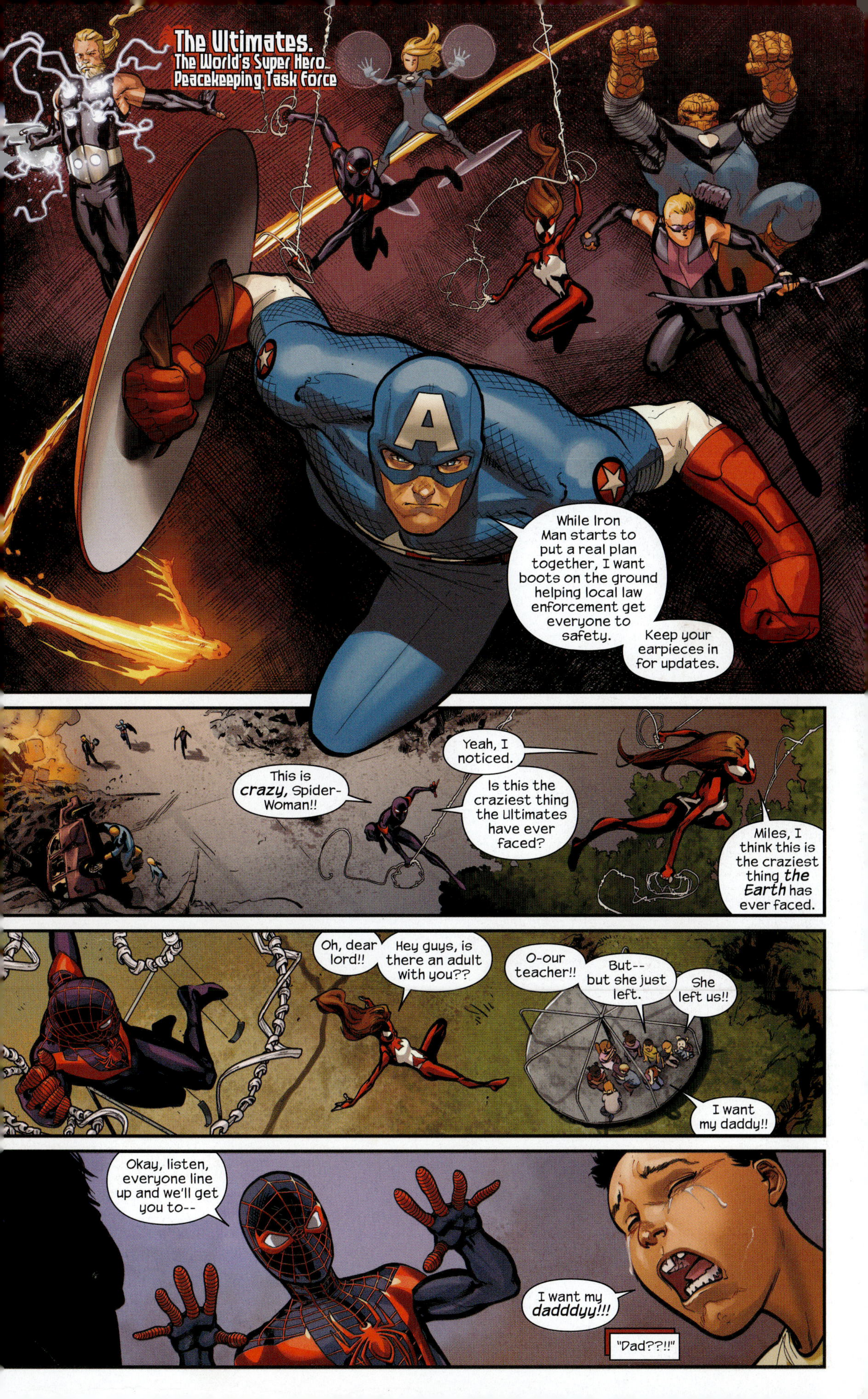
The Ultimates.
The World's Super Hero Peacekeeping Task Force
While Iron Man starts to put a real plan together, I want boots on the ground helping local law enforcement get everyone to safety.
Keep your earpieces in for updates.
This is crazy, Spider-Woman!!
Yeah, I noticed.
Is this the craziest thing the Ultimates have ever faced?
Miles, I think this is the craziest thing the Earth has ever faced.
Oh, dear lord!!
Hey guys, is there an adult with you??
O-our teacher!!
But-- but she just left.
She left us!!
I want my daddy!!
Okay, listen, everyone line up and we'll get you to--
I want my dadddyy!!!
"Dad??!!"

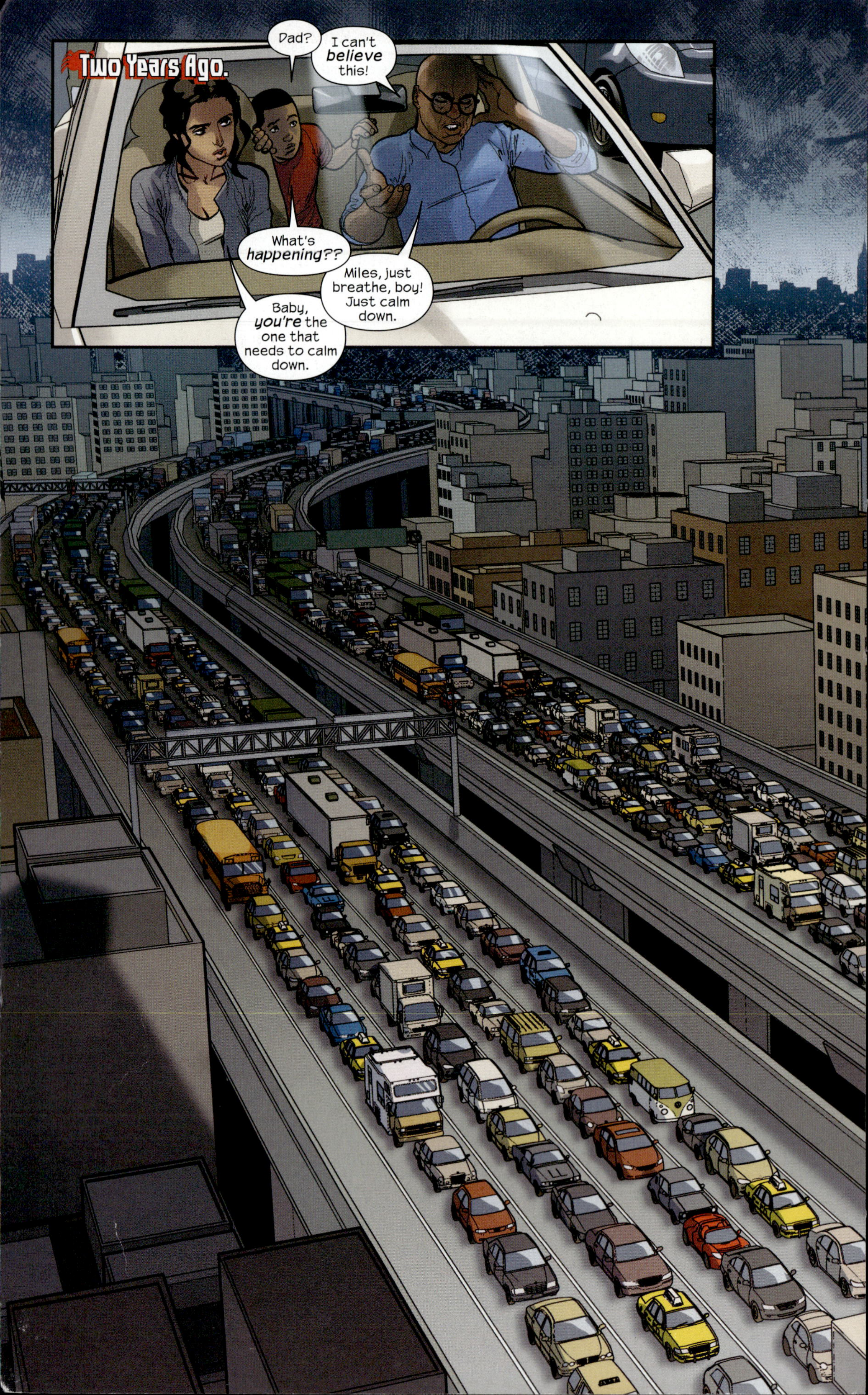
Two Years Ago.
Dad?
I can't believe this!
What's happening??
Miles, just breathe, boy! Just calm down.
Baby, you're the one that needs to calm down.

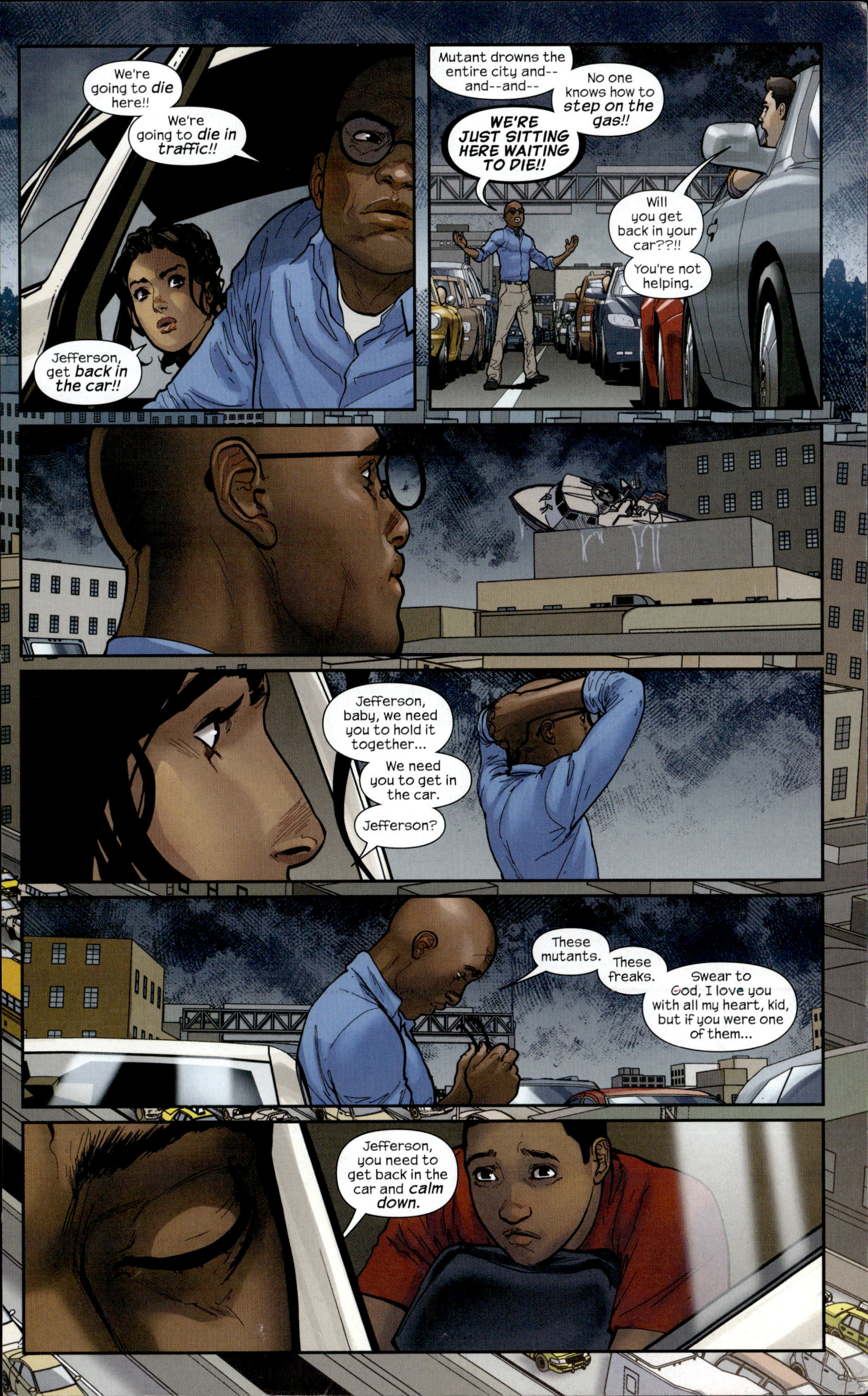
We're going to die here!!
We're going to die in traffic!!
Jefferson, get back in the car!!
Mutant drowns the entire city and-- and--and--
No one knows how to step on the gas!!
WE'RE JUST SITTING HERE WAITING TO DIE!!
Will you get back in your car??!!
You're not helping.
Jefferson, baby, we need you to hold it together...
We need you to get in the car.
Jefferson?
These mutants.
These freaks.
Swear to God, I love you with all my heart, kid, but if you were one of them...
Jefferson, you need to get back in the car and calm down.

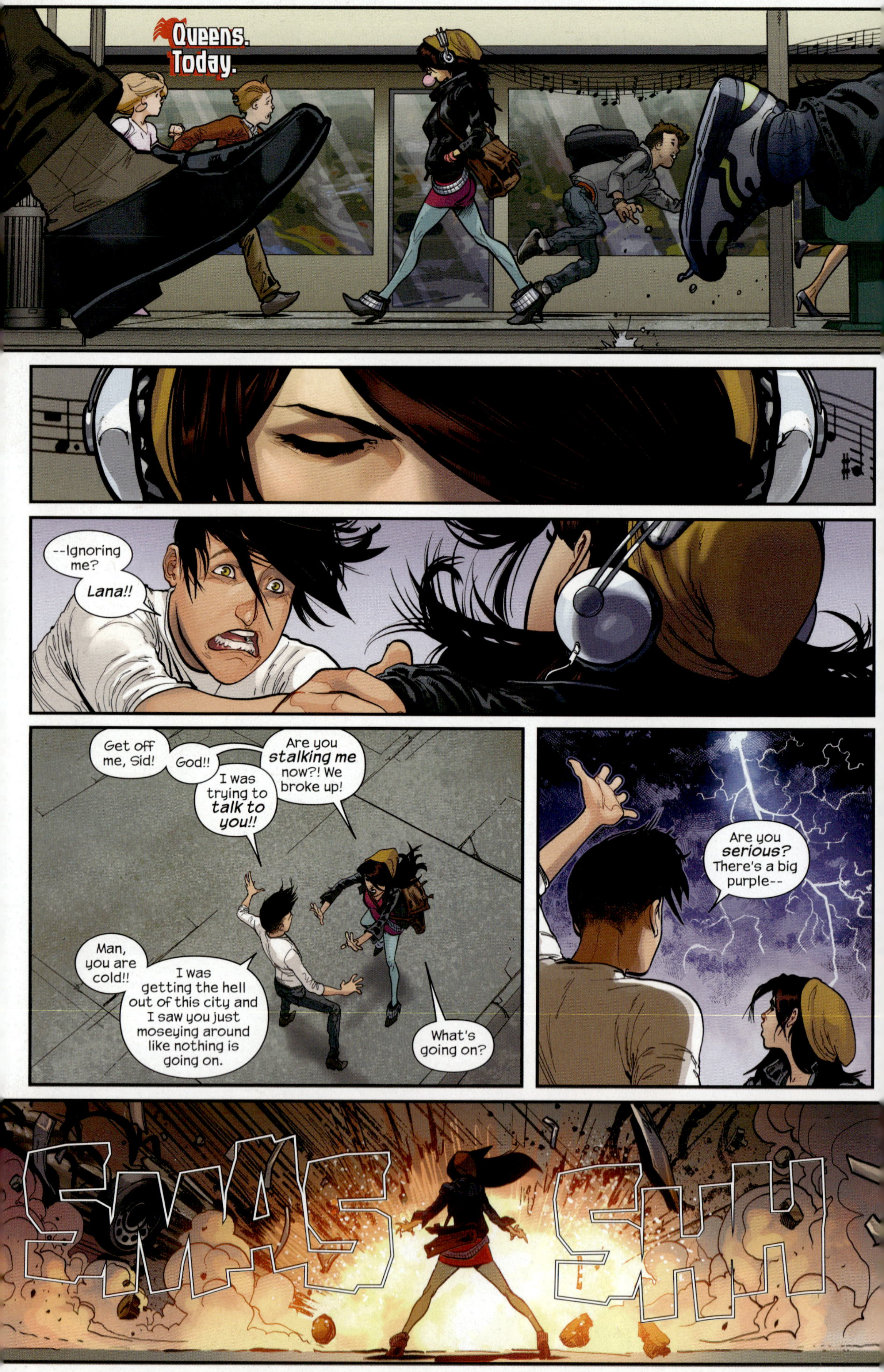
Queens. Today.
--Ignoring me?
Lana!!
Get off me, Sid!
God!!
Are you stalking me now?! We broke up!
I was trying to talk to you!!
Man, you are cold!!
I was getting the hell out of this city and I saw you just moseying around like nothing is going on.
What's going on?
Are you serious? There's a big purple--

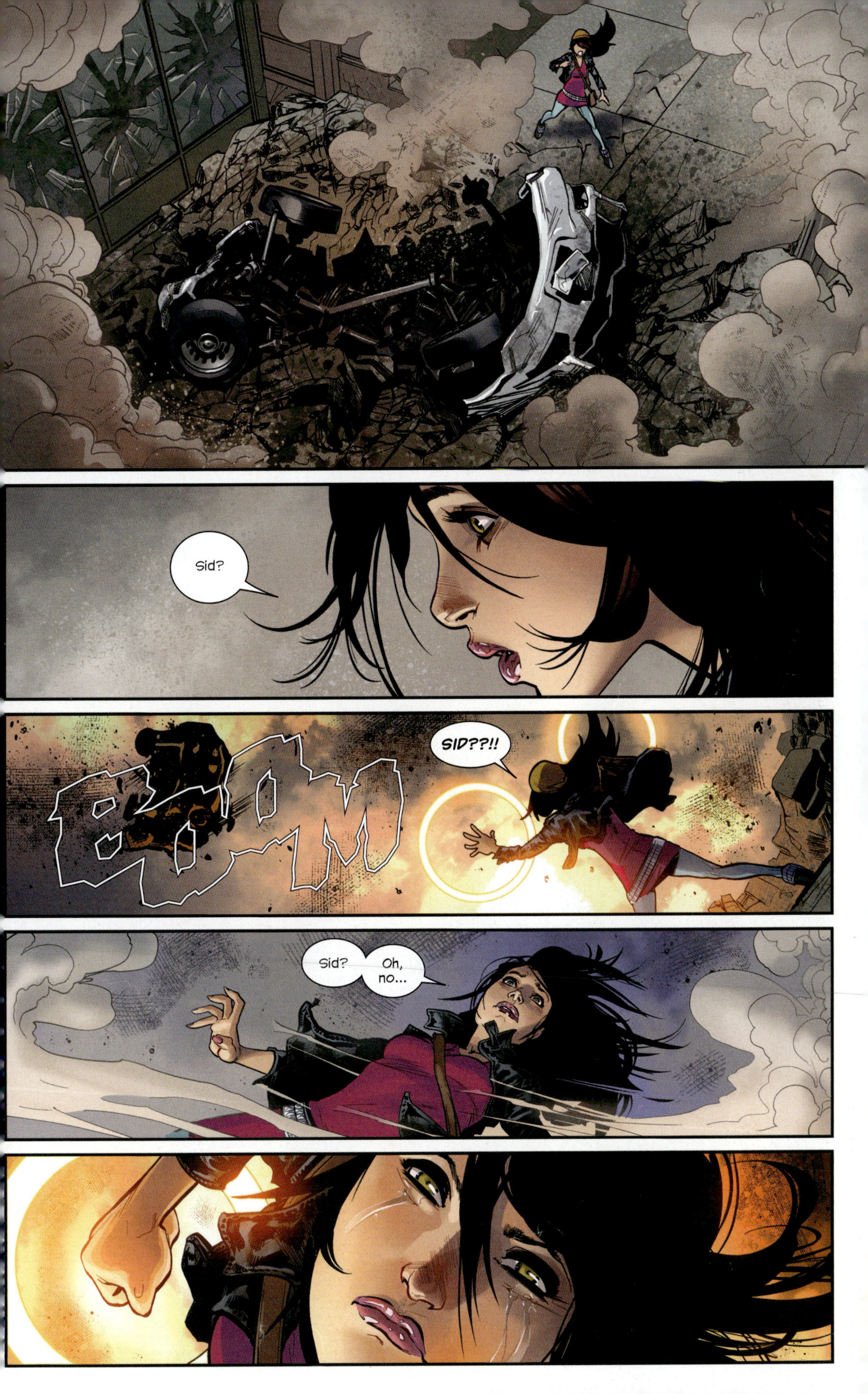
Sid?
BOOM
SID??!!
Sid?
Oh, no...

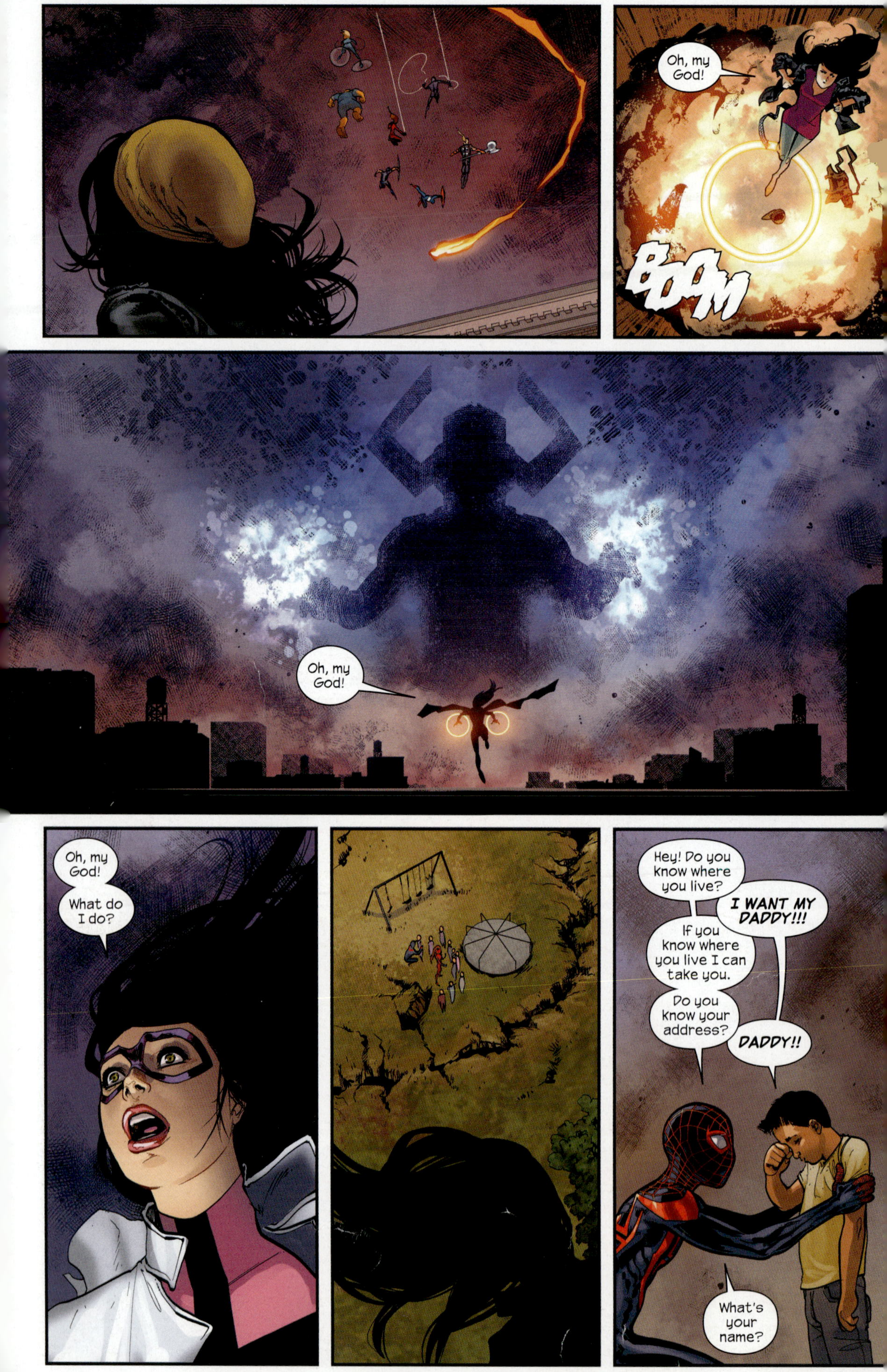
Oh, my God!
BOOM
Oh, my God!
Oh, my God!
What do I do?
Hey! Do you know where you live?
I WANT MY DADDY!!!
If you know where you live I can take you.
Do you know your address?
DADDY!!
What's your name?

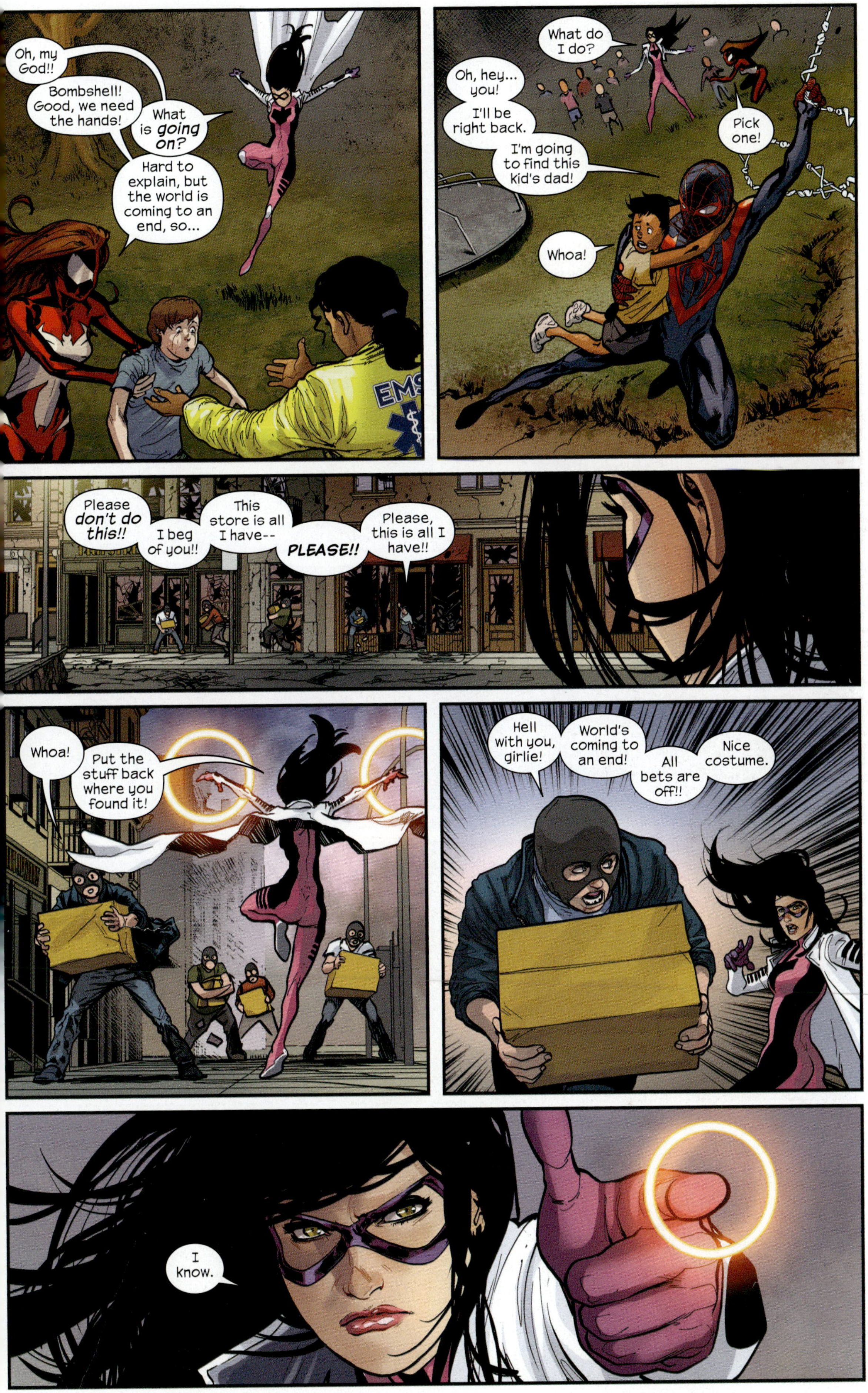

Oh, my God!!
Bombshell! Good, we need the hands!
What is *going on?*
Hard to explain, but the world is coming to an end, so...
EMS
What do I do?
Oh, hey... you!
I'll be right back.
I'm going to find this kid's dad!
Pick one!
Whoa!
Please *don't do this!!*
I beg of you!!
This store is all I have--
PLEASE!!
Please, this is all I have!!
Whoa!
Put the stuff back where you found it!
Hell with you, girlie!
World's coming to an end!
All bets are off!!
Nice costume.
I know.

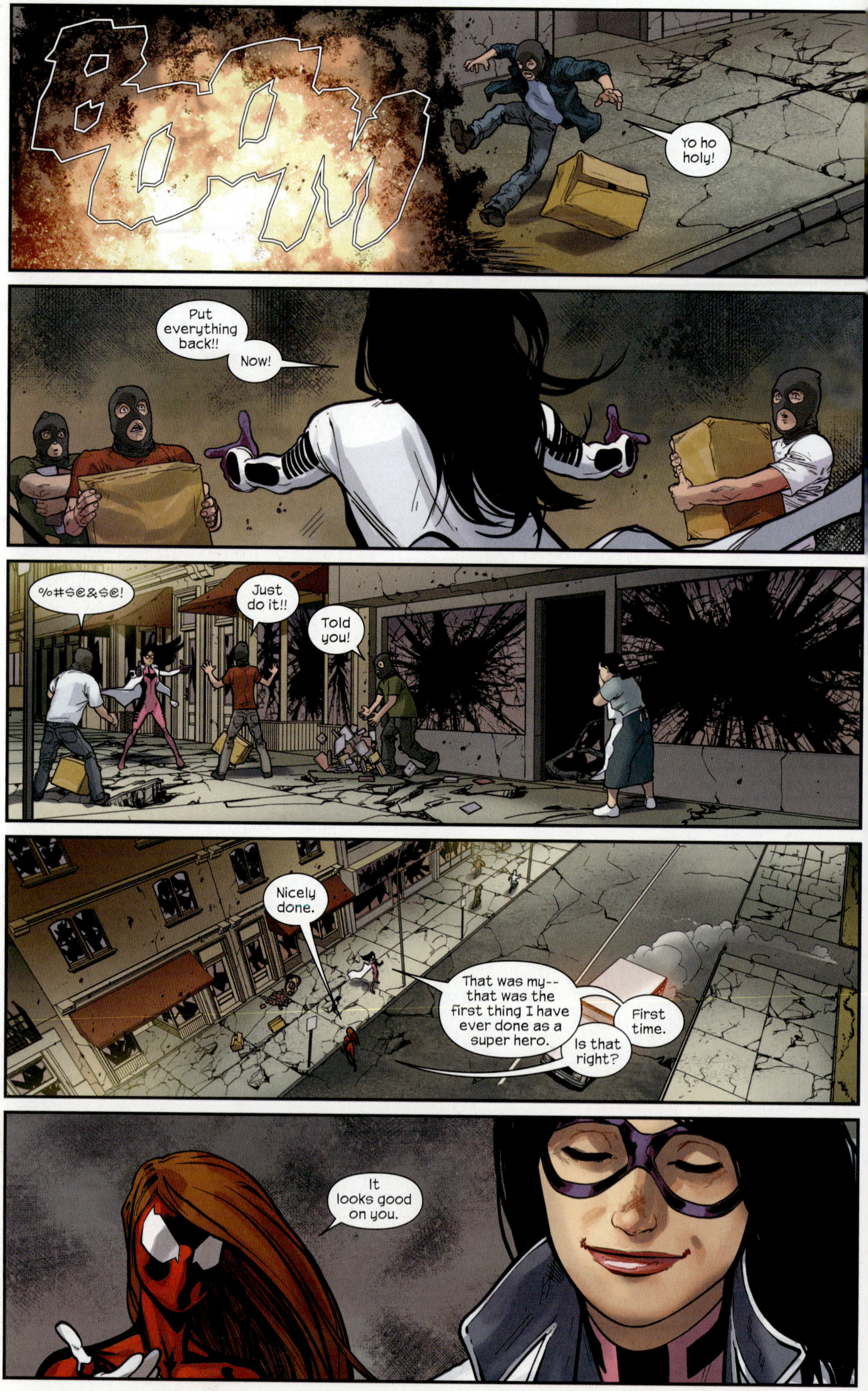
BOOM
Yo ho holy!
Put everything back!!
Now!
%#$@&$@!
Just do it!!
Told you!
Nicely done.
That was my-- that was the first thing I have ever done as a super hero.
First time.
Is that right?
It looks good on you.

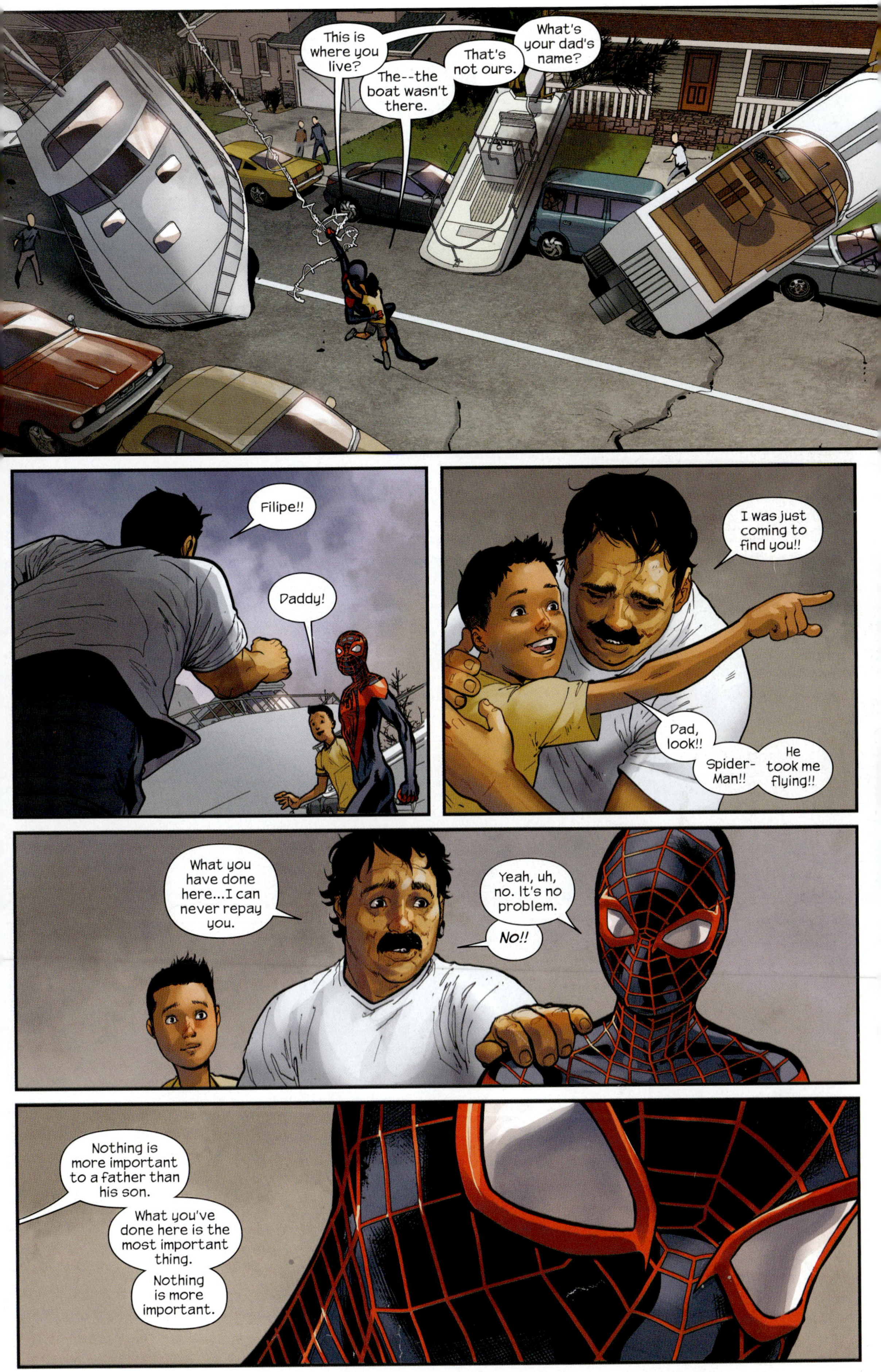
This is where you live?
The--the boat wasn't there.
That's not ours.
What's your dad's name?
Filipe!!
Daddy!
I was just coming to find you!!
Dad, look!!
Spider-Man!!
He took me flying!!
What you have done here...I can never repay you.
Yeah, uh, no. It's no problem.
No!!
Nothing is more important to a father than his son.
What you've done here is the most important thing.
Nothing is more important.

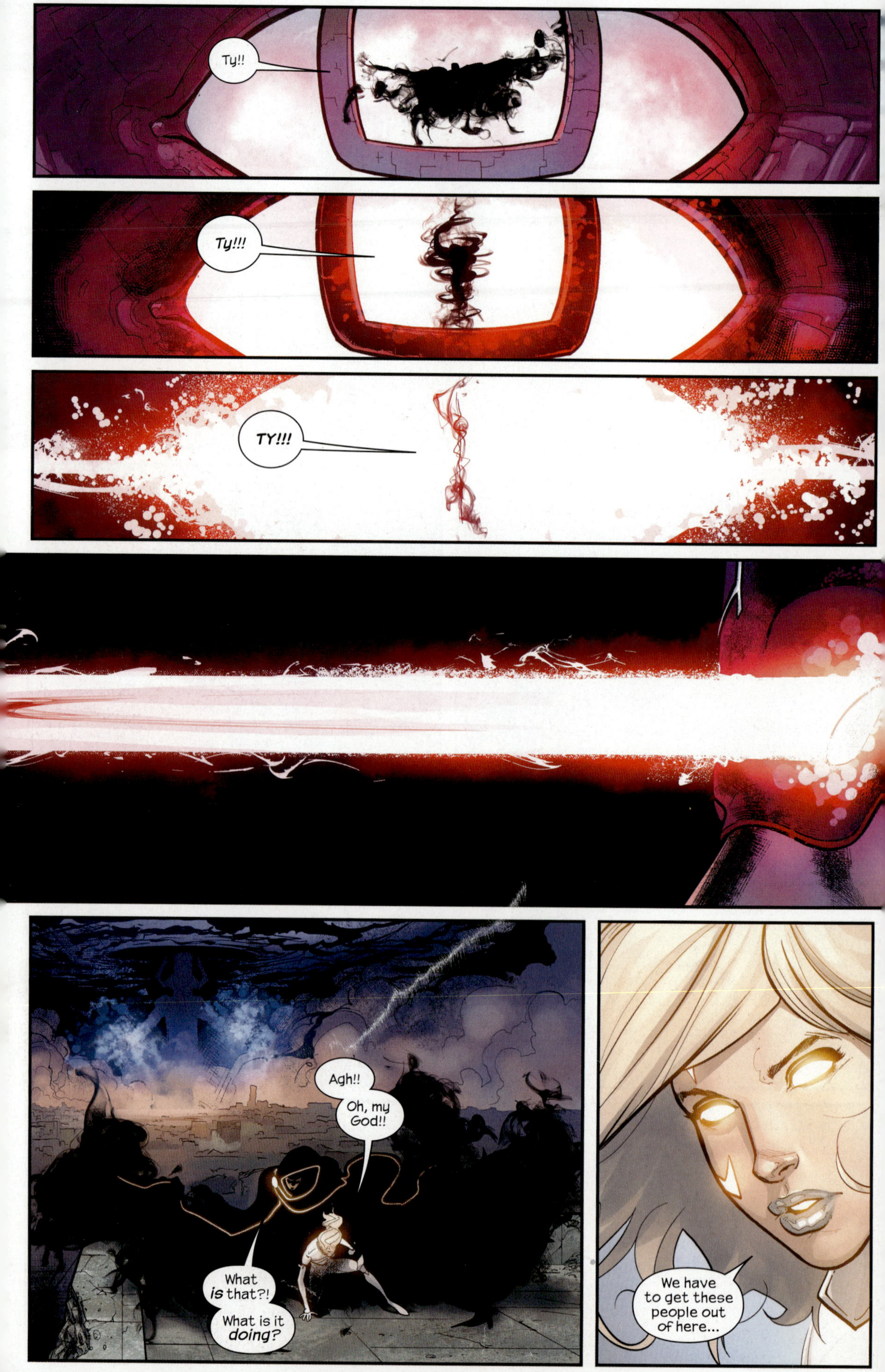
Ty!!
Ty!!!
TY!!!
Agh!!
Oh, my God!!
What *is* that?!
What is it *doing*?
We have to get these people out of here...

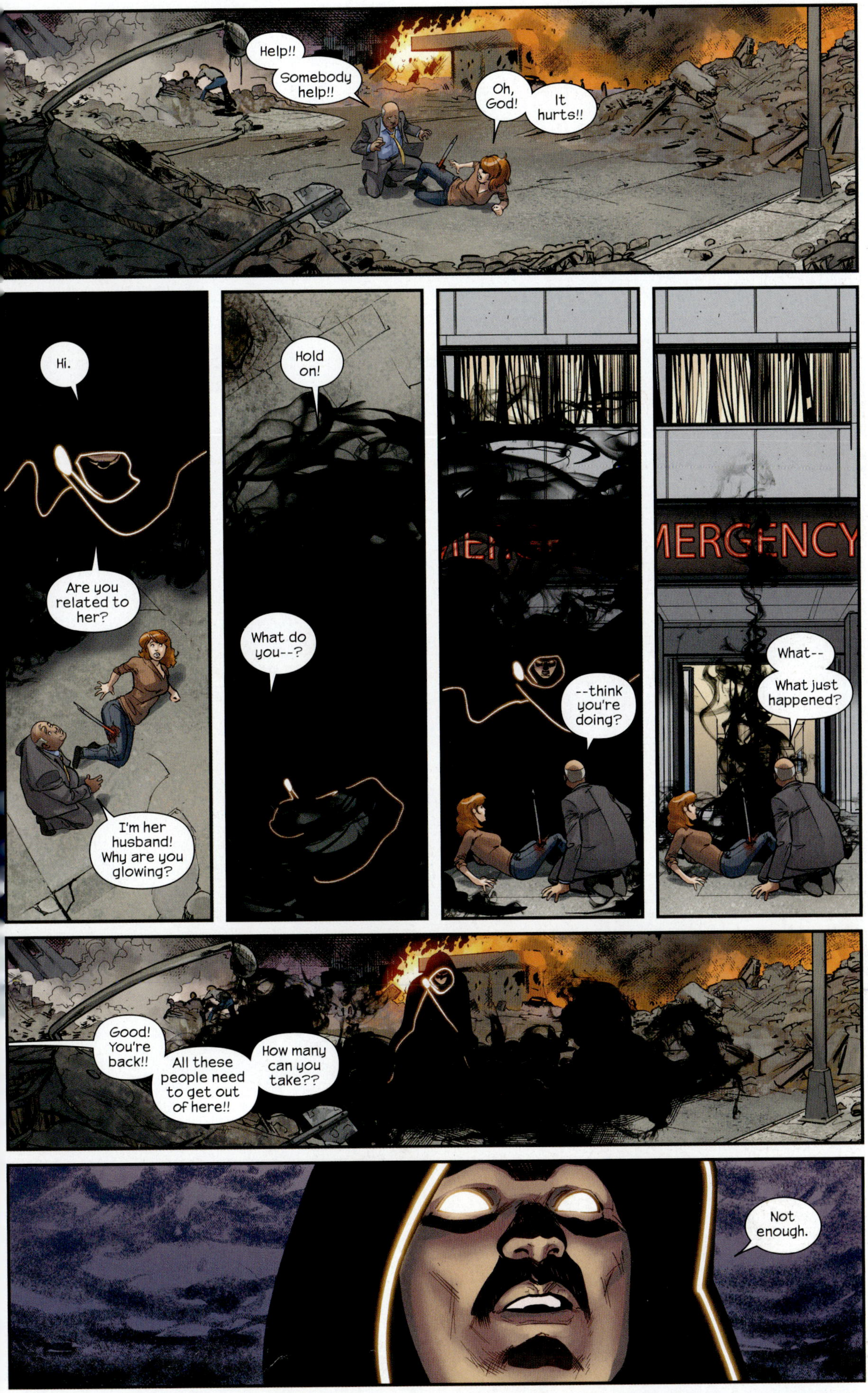
Help!!
Somebody help!!
Oh, God!
It hurts!!
Hi.
Are you related to her?
I'm her husband! Why are you glowing?
Hold on!
What do you--?
--think you're doing?
MERGENCY
What--
What just happened?
Good! You're back!!
All these people need to get out of here!!
How many can you take??
Not enough.

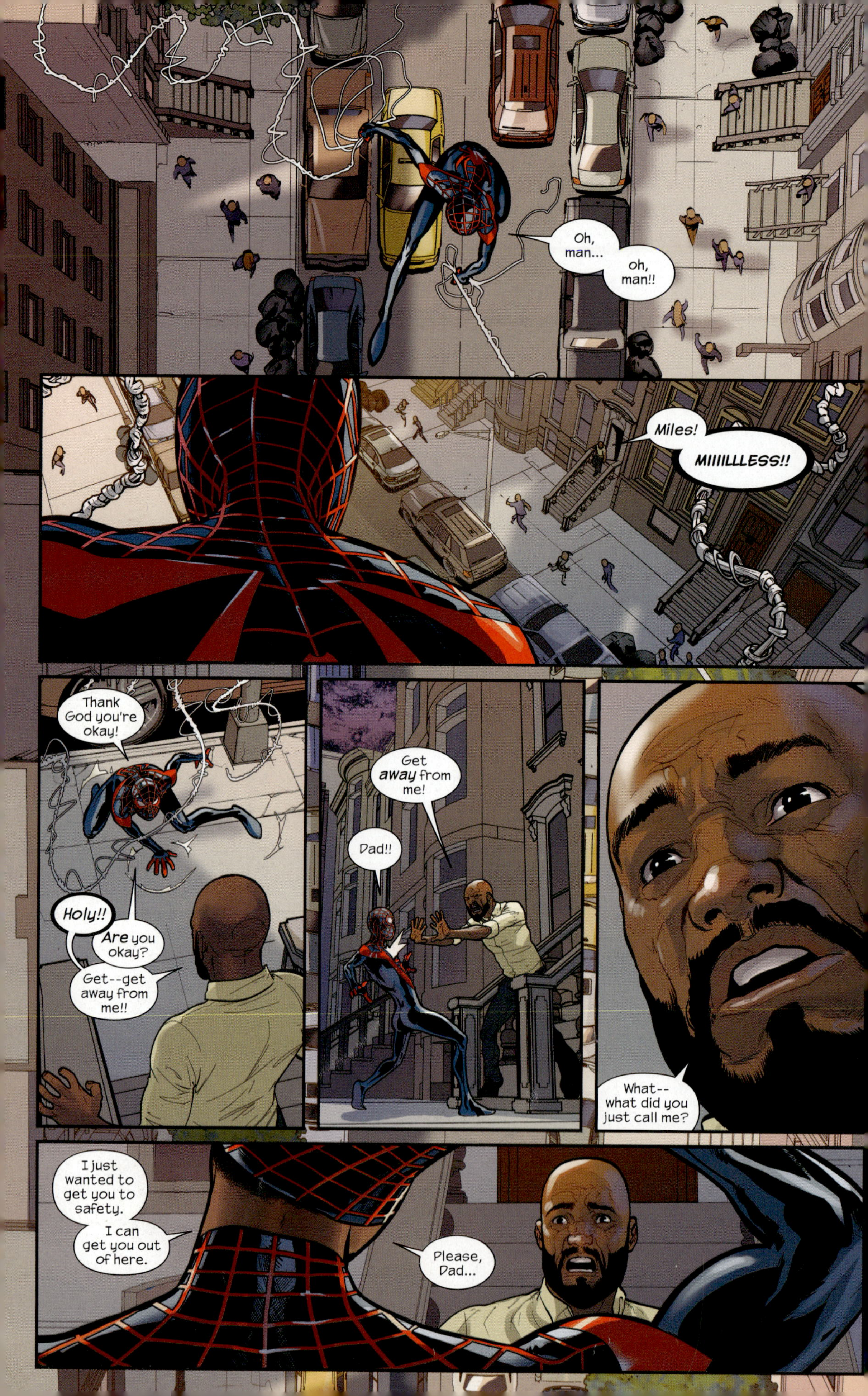
Oh, man...
oh, man!!
Miles!
MIIIILLLESS!!
Thank God you're okay!
Holy!!
Are you okay?
Get--get away from me!!
Dad!!
Get away from me!
What-- what did you just call me?
I just wanted to get you to safety.
I can get you out of here.
Please, Dad...

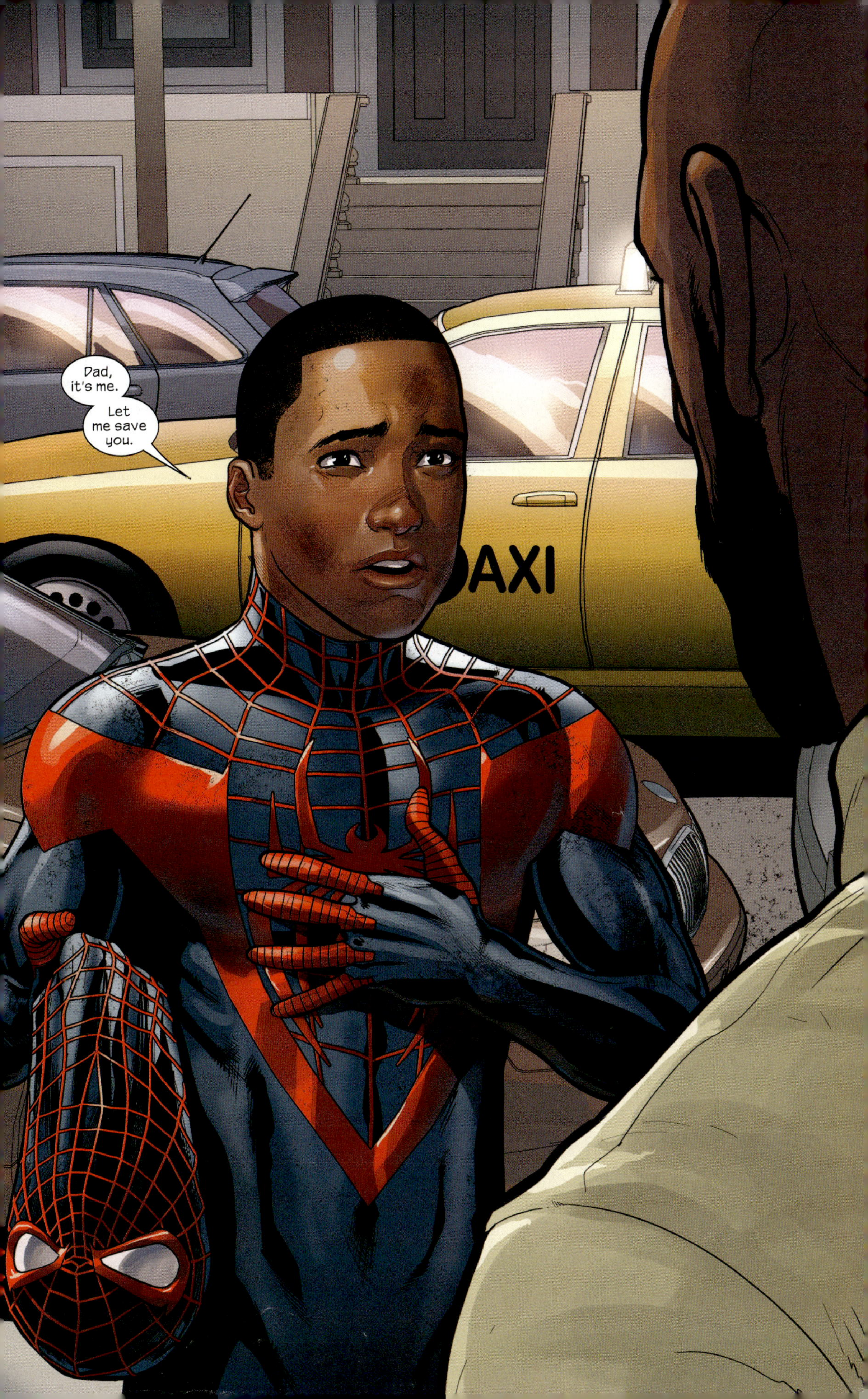
Dad, it's me.
Let me save you.
AXI

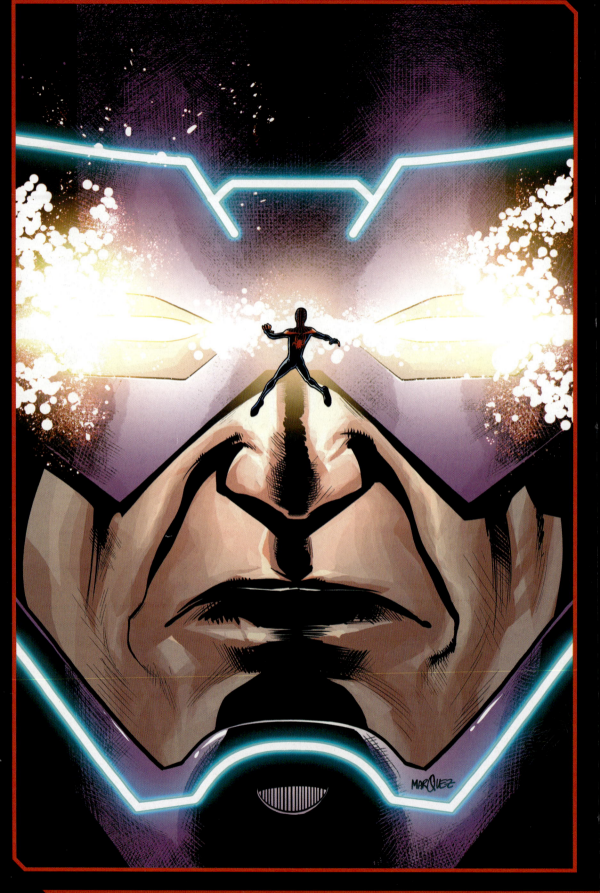

CATACLYSM: ULTIMATE SPIDER-MAN #3

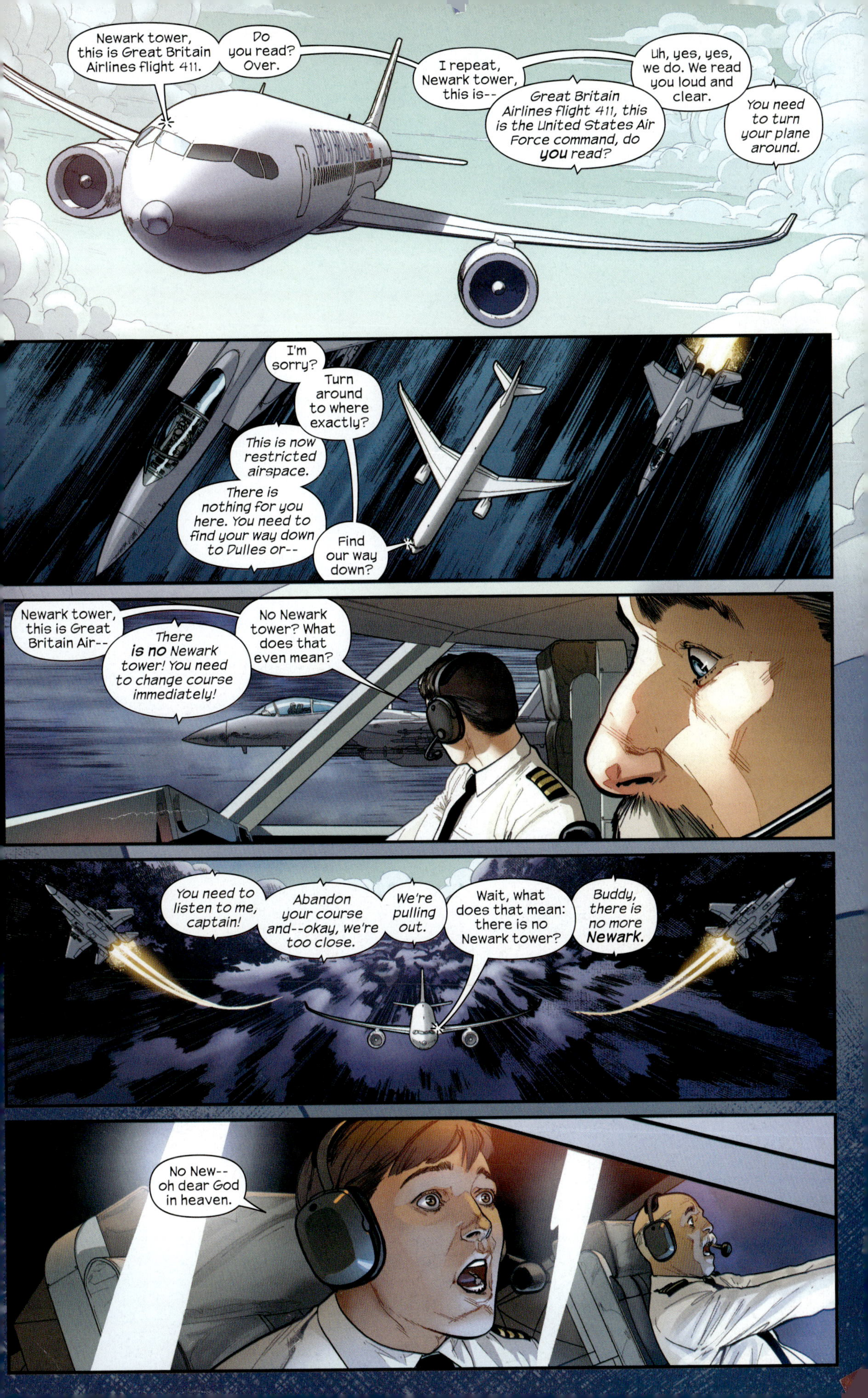
Newark tower, this is Great Britain Airlines flight 411.
Do you read? Over.
I repeat, Newark tower, this is--
Uh, yes, yes, we do. We read you loud and clear.
Great Britain Airlines flight 411, this is the United States Air Force command, do **you** read?
You need to turn your plane around.
I'm sorry?
Turn around to where exactly?
This is now restricted airspace.
There is nothing for you here. You need to find your way down to Dulles or--
Find our way down?
Newark tower, this is Great Britain Air--
There **is no** Newark tower! You need to change course immediately!
No Newark tower? What does that even mean?
You need to listen to me, captain!
Abandon your course and--okay, we're too close.
We're pulling out.
Wait, what does that mean: there is no Newark tower?
Buddy, there is no more **Newark.**
No New-- oh dear God in heaven.

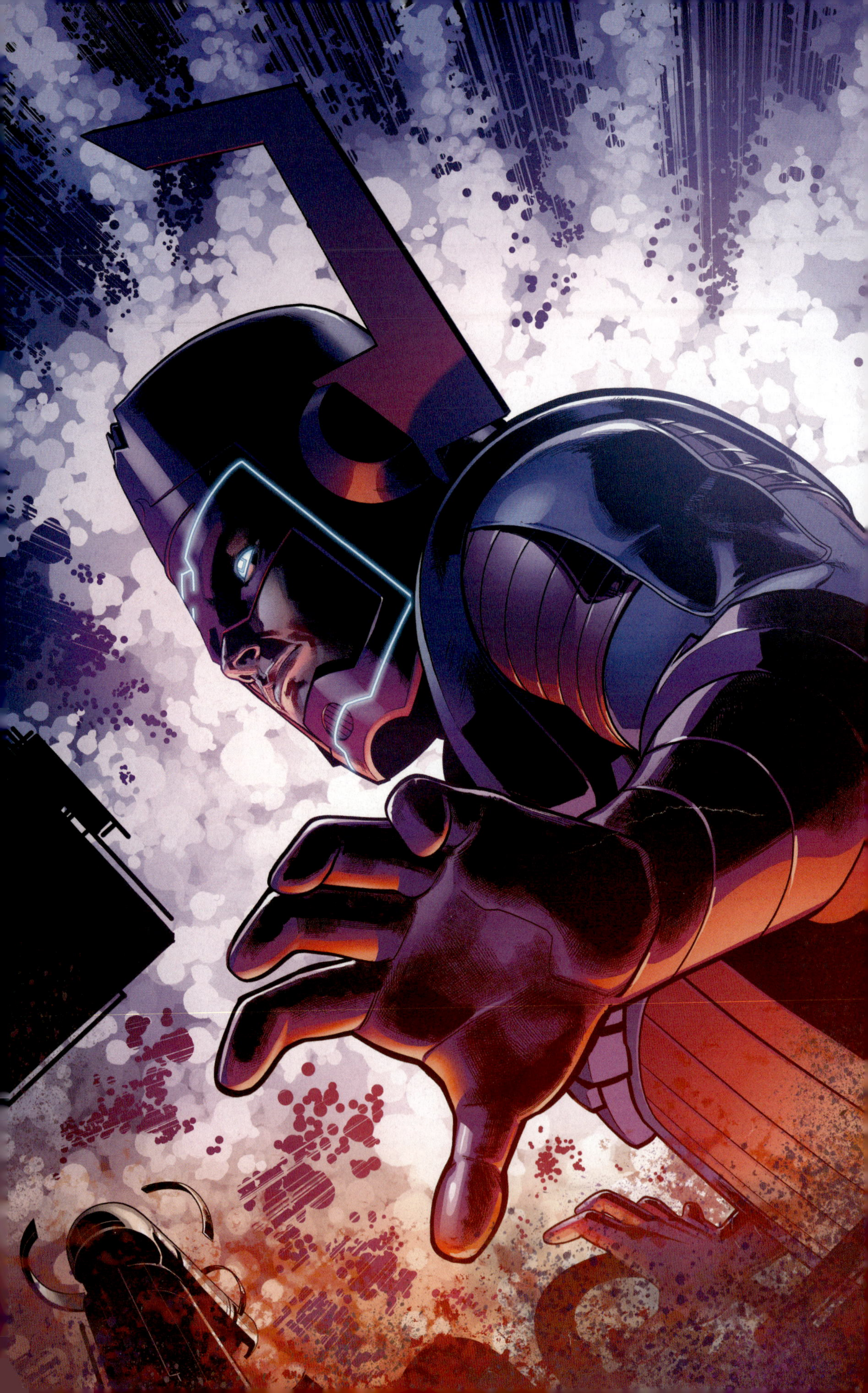

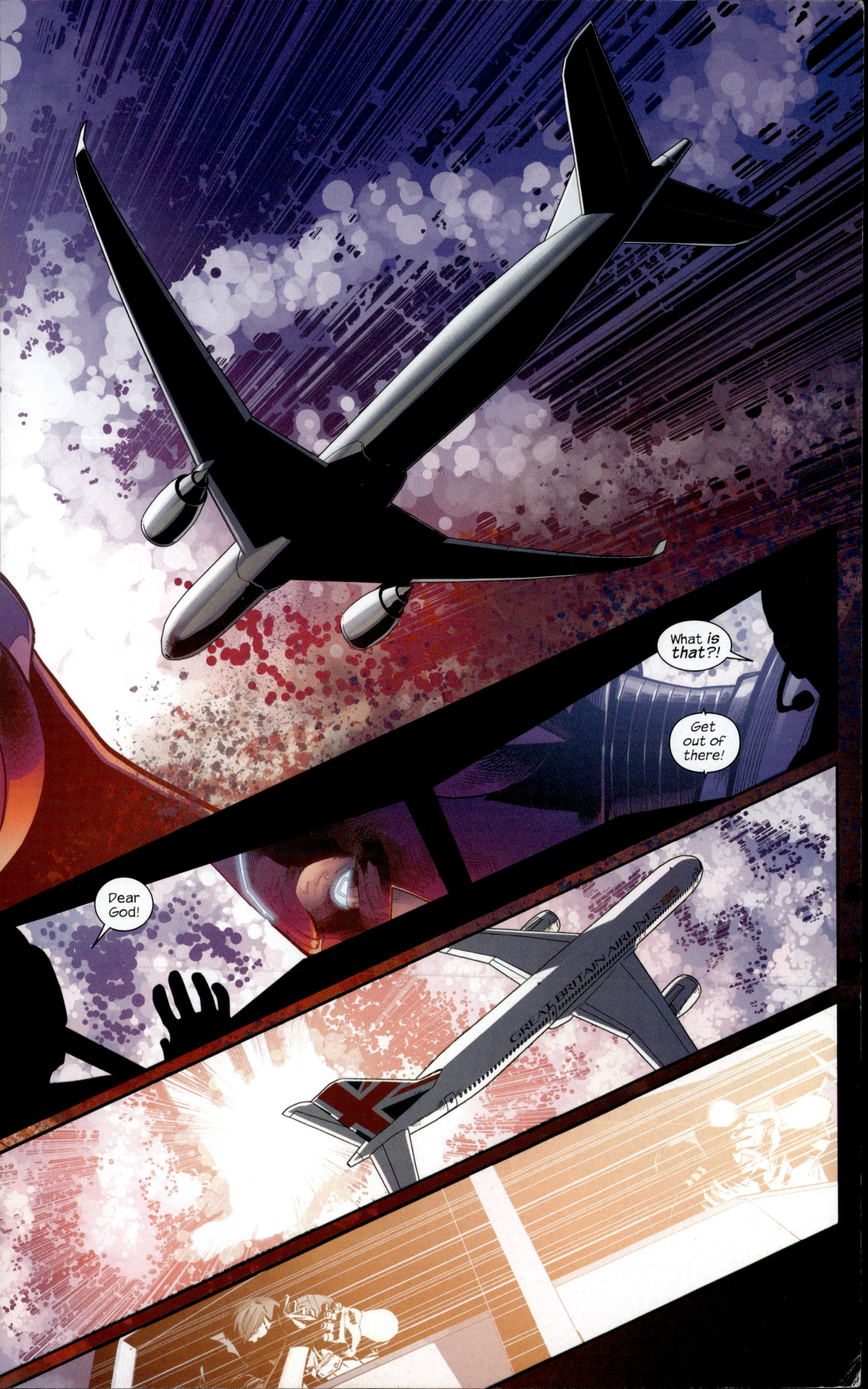
What is that?!
Get out of there!
Dear God!
GREAT BRITAIN AIRLINES

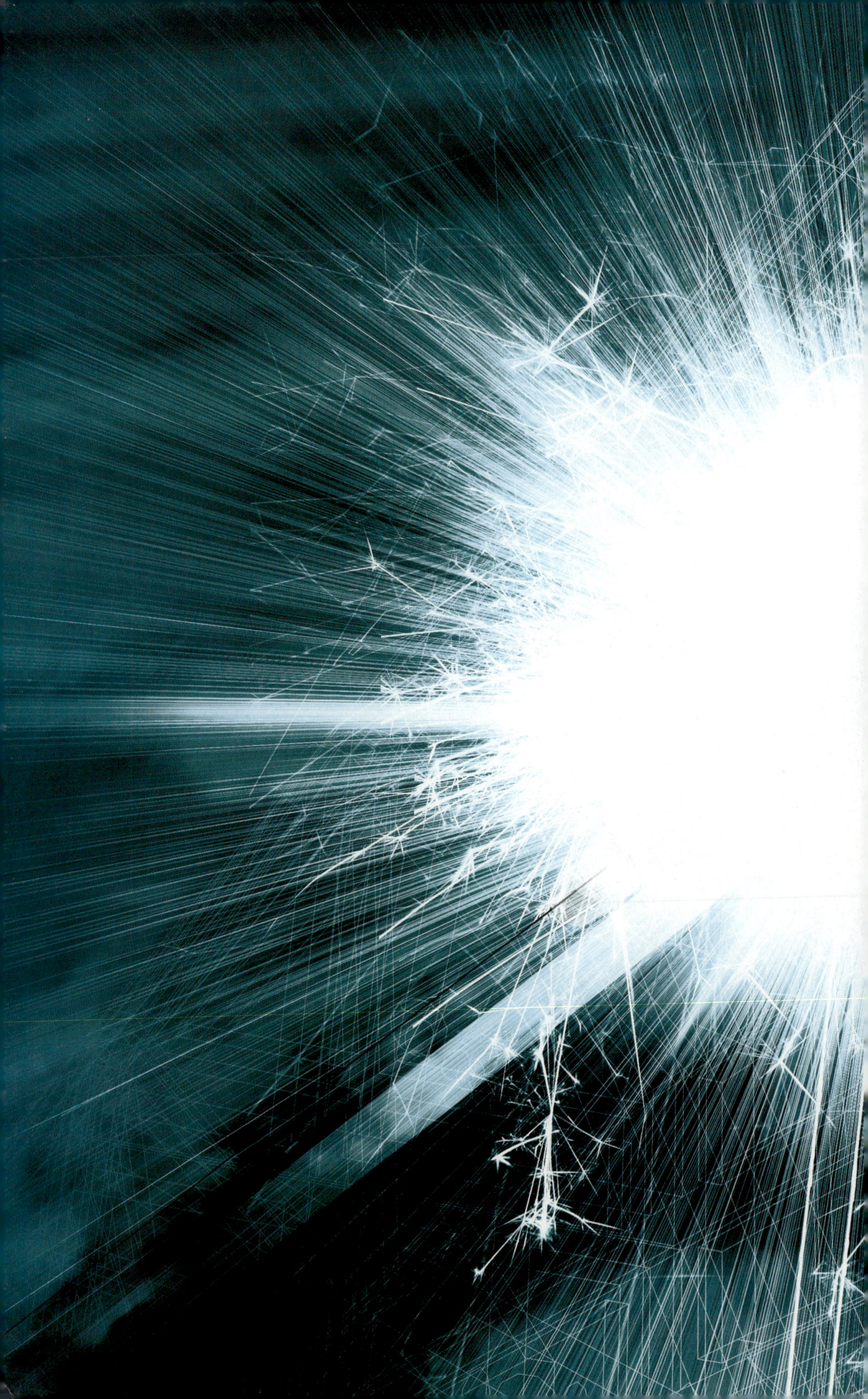

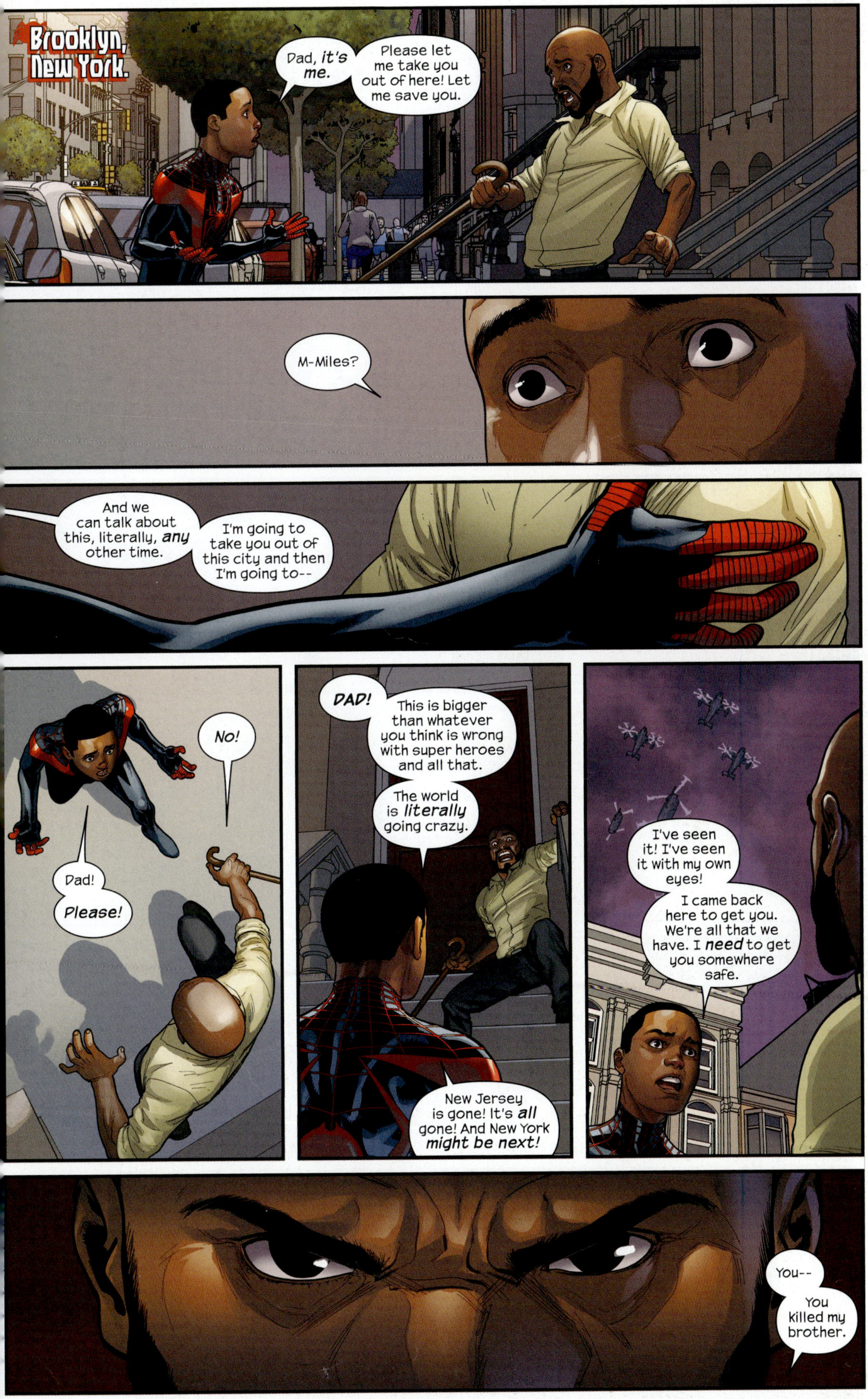

Brooklyn, New York.
Dad, *it's me.*
Please let me take you out of here! Let me save you.
M-Miles?
And we can talk about this, literally, *any* other time.
I'm going to take you out of this city and then I'm going to--
Dad!
Please!
No!
DAD!
This is bigger than whatever you think is wrong with super heroes and all that.
The world is *literally* going crazy.
New Jersey is gone! It's *all* gone! And New York *might be next!*
I've seen it! I've seen it with my own eyes!
I came back here to get you. We're all that we have. I *need* to get you somewhere safe.
You--
You killed my brother.

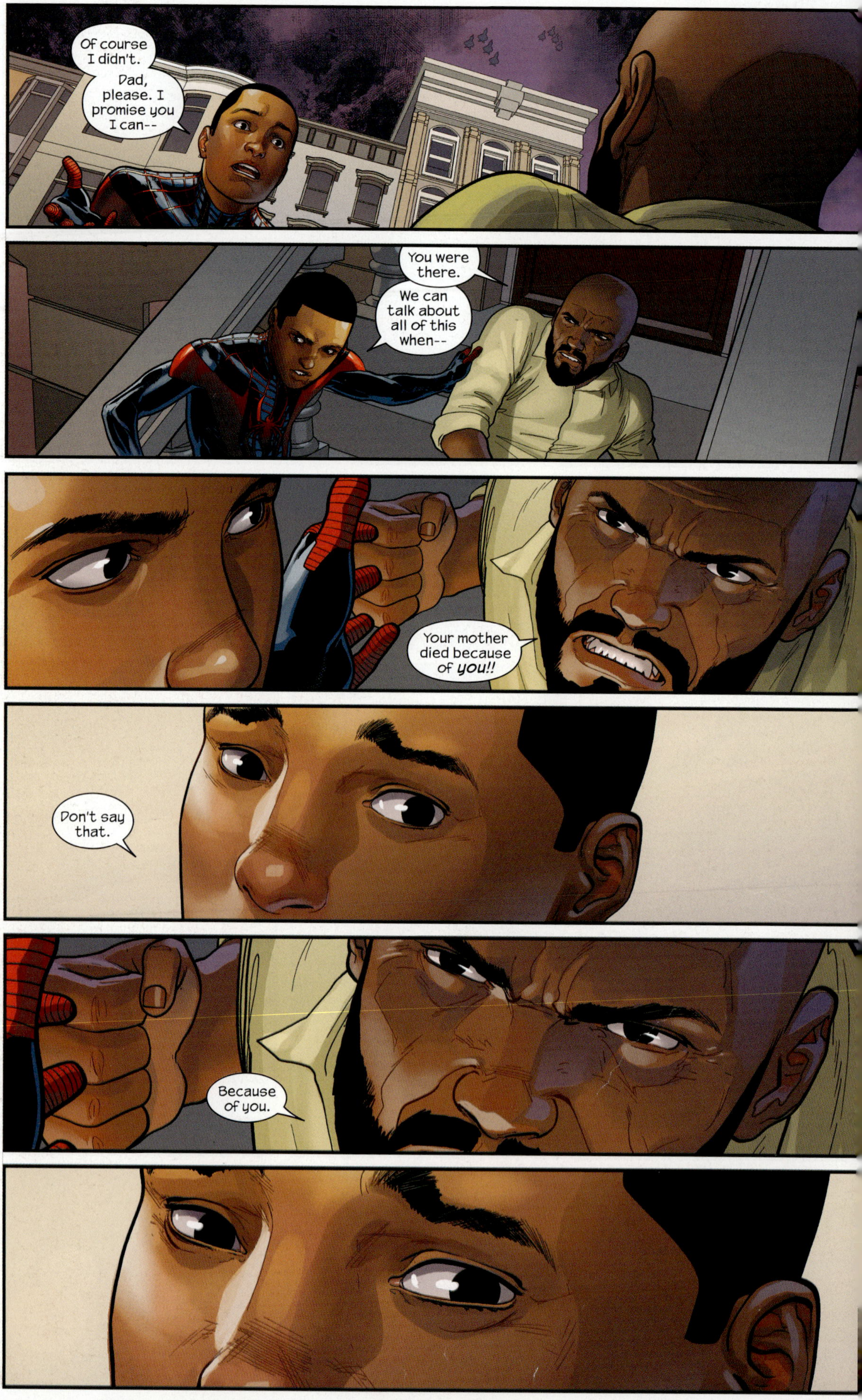
Of course I didn't.
Dad, please. I promise you I can--
You were there.
We can talk about all of this when--
Your mother died because of *you!!*
Don't say that.
Because of you.

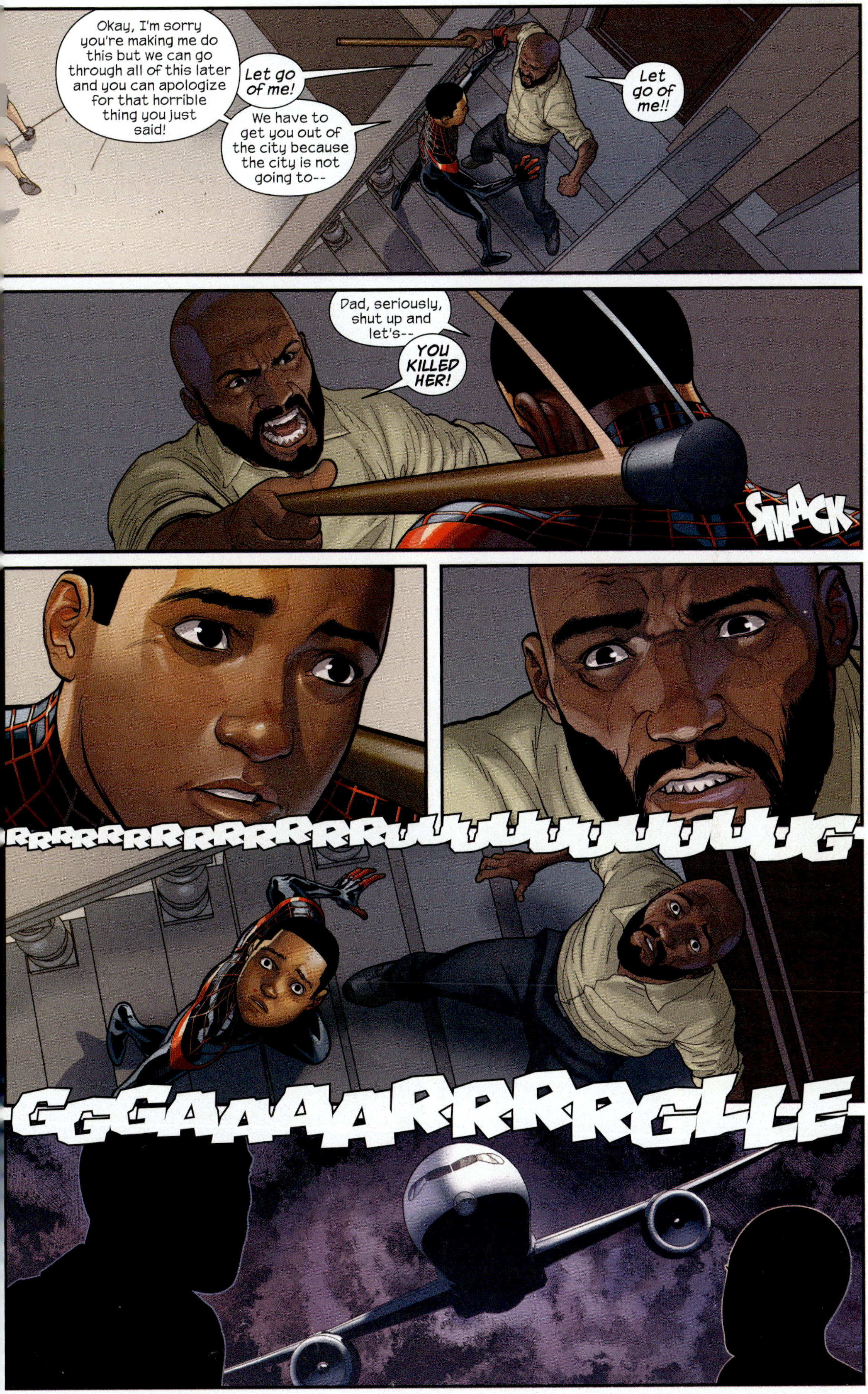

Okay, I'm sorry you're making me do this but we can go through all of this later and you can apologize for that horrible thing you just said!
Let go of me!
We have to get you out of the city because the city is not going to--
Let go of me!!
Dad, seriously, shut up and let's--
YOU KILLED HER!
SMACK
RRRRRRRRRRRRRRRUUUUUUUUUUUG-
GGGAAAARRRRGLLE-

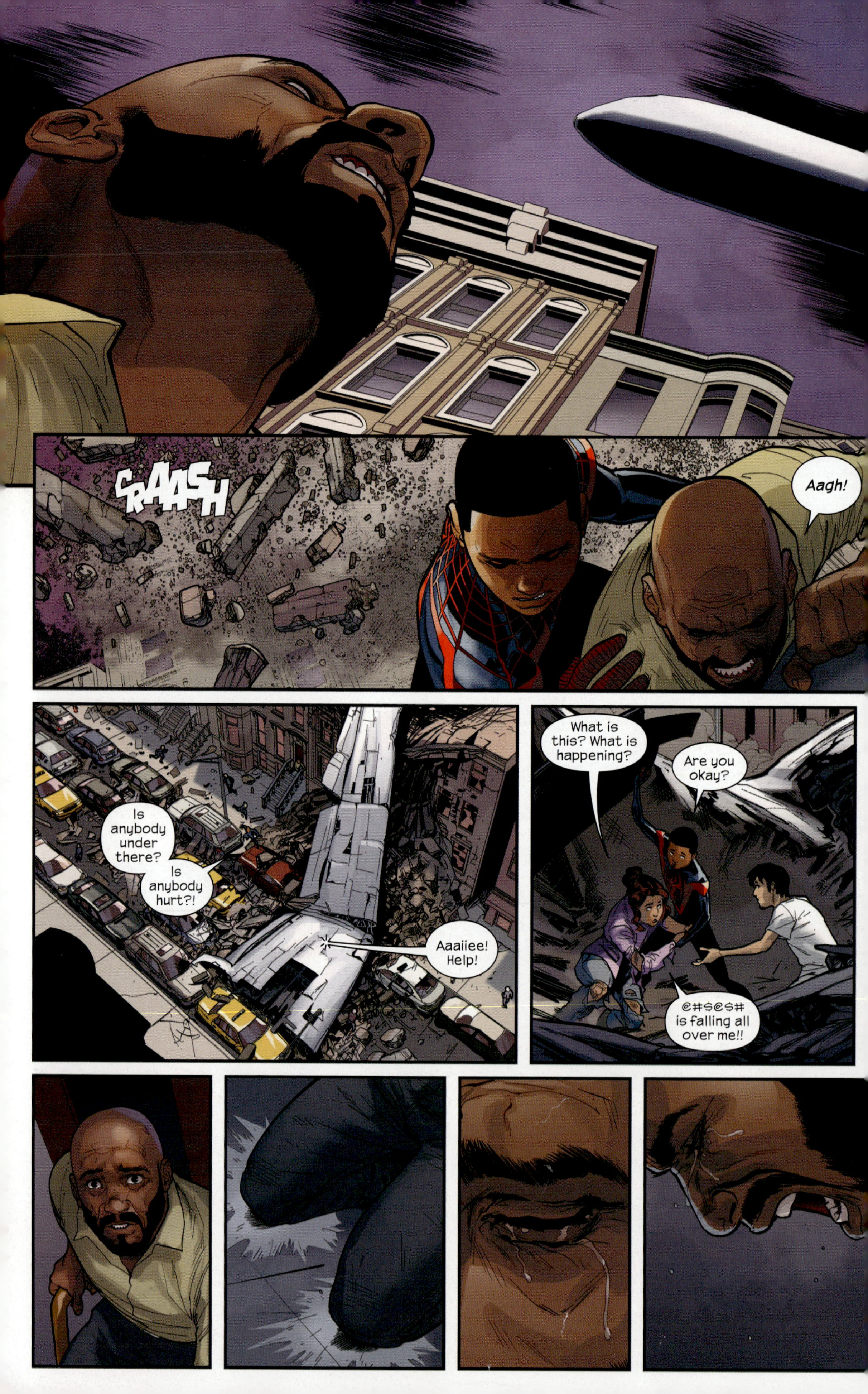
CRAASH
Aagh!
Is anybody under there?
Is anybody hurt?!
Aaaiiee! Help!
What is this? What is happening?
Are you okay?
@#$@$# is falling all over me!!

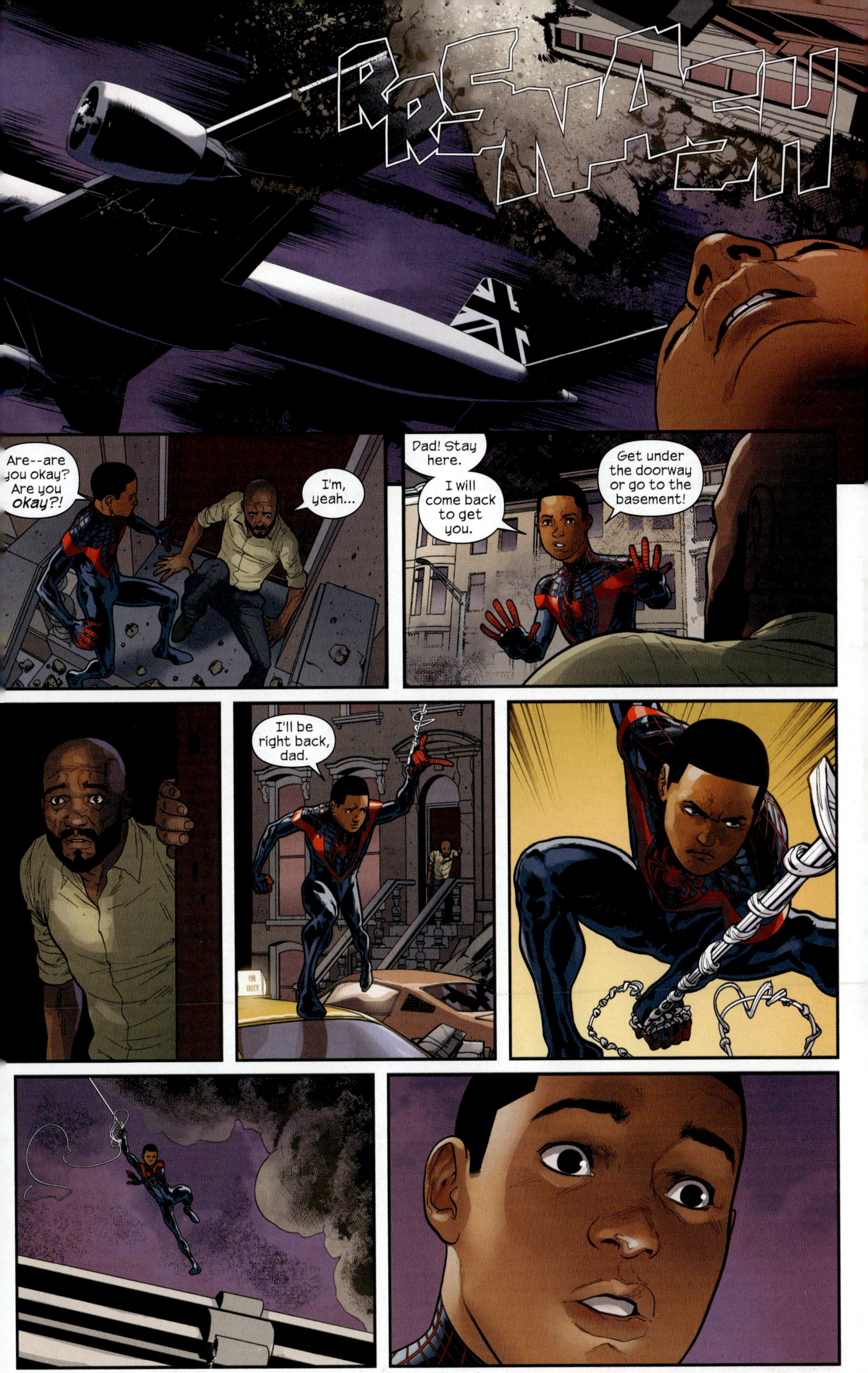

RRRSHWAAASH
Are--are you okay? Are you *okay*?!
I'm, yeah...
Dad! Stay here.
I will come back to get you.
Get under the doorway or go to the basement!
I'll be right back, dad.

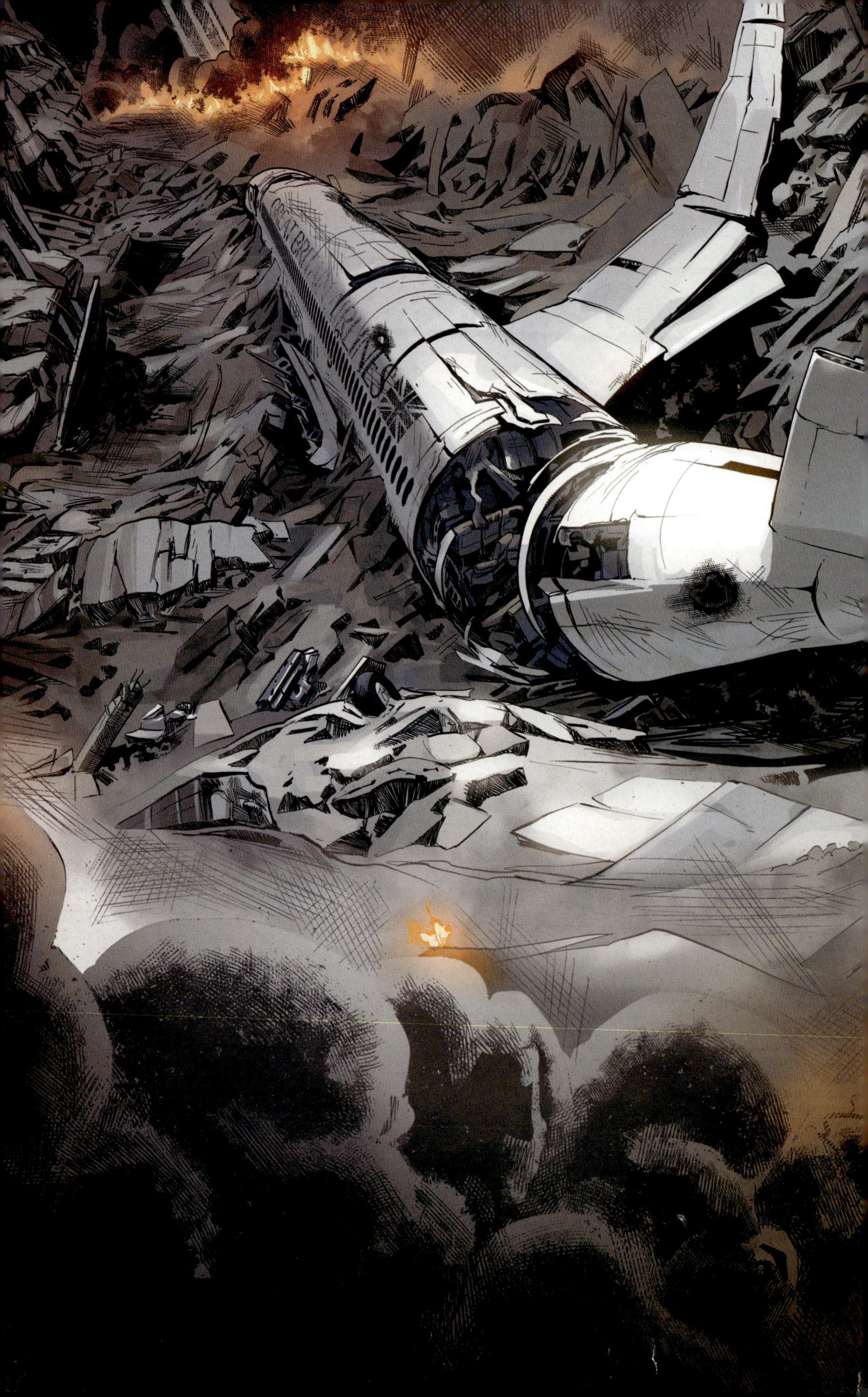

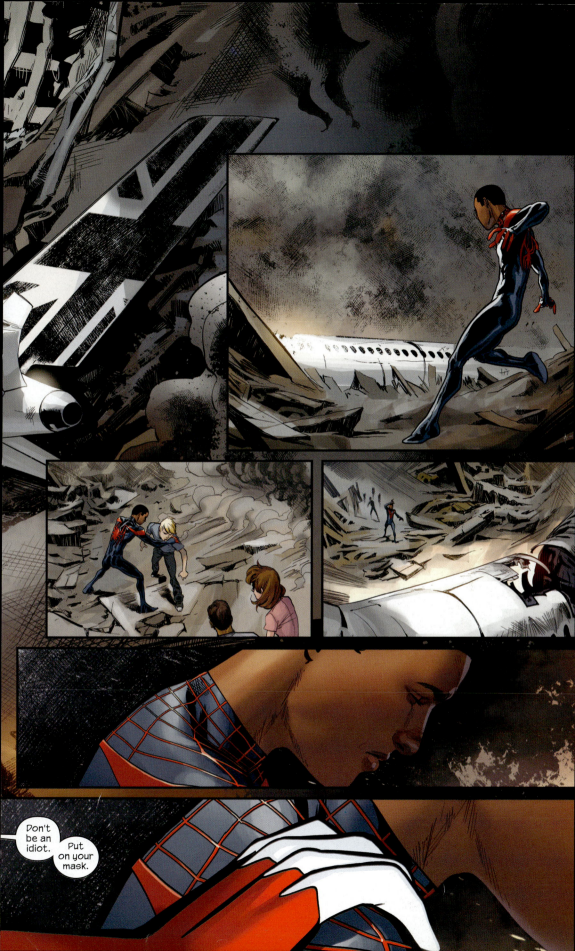

Don't be an idiot. Put on your mask.

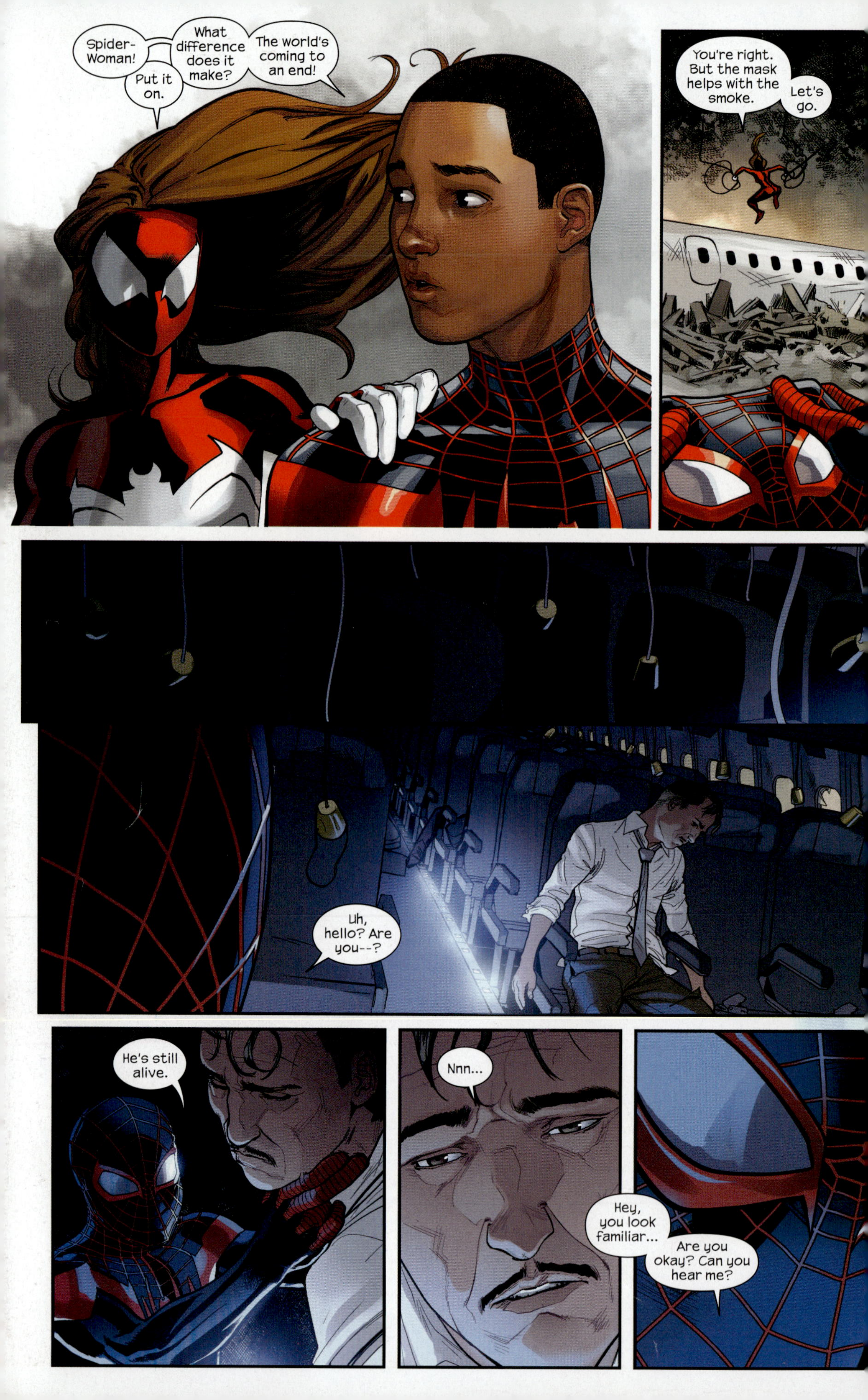
Spider-Woman!
Put it on.
What difference does it make?
The world's coming to an end!
You're right. But the mask helps with the smoke.
Let's go.
Uh, hello? Are you--?
He's still alive.
Nnn...
Hey, you look familiar...
Are you okay? Can you hear me?

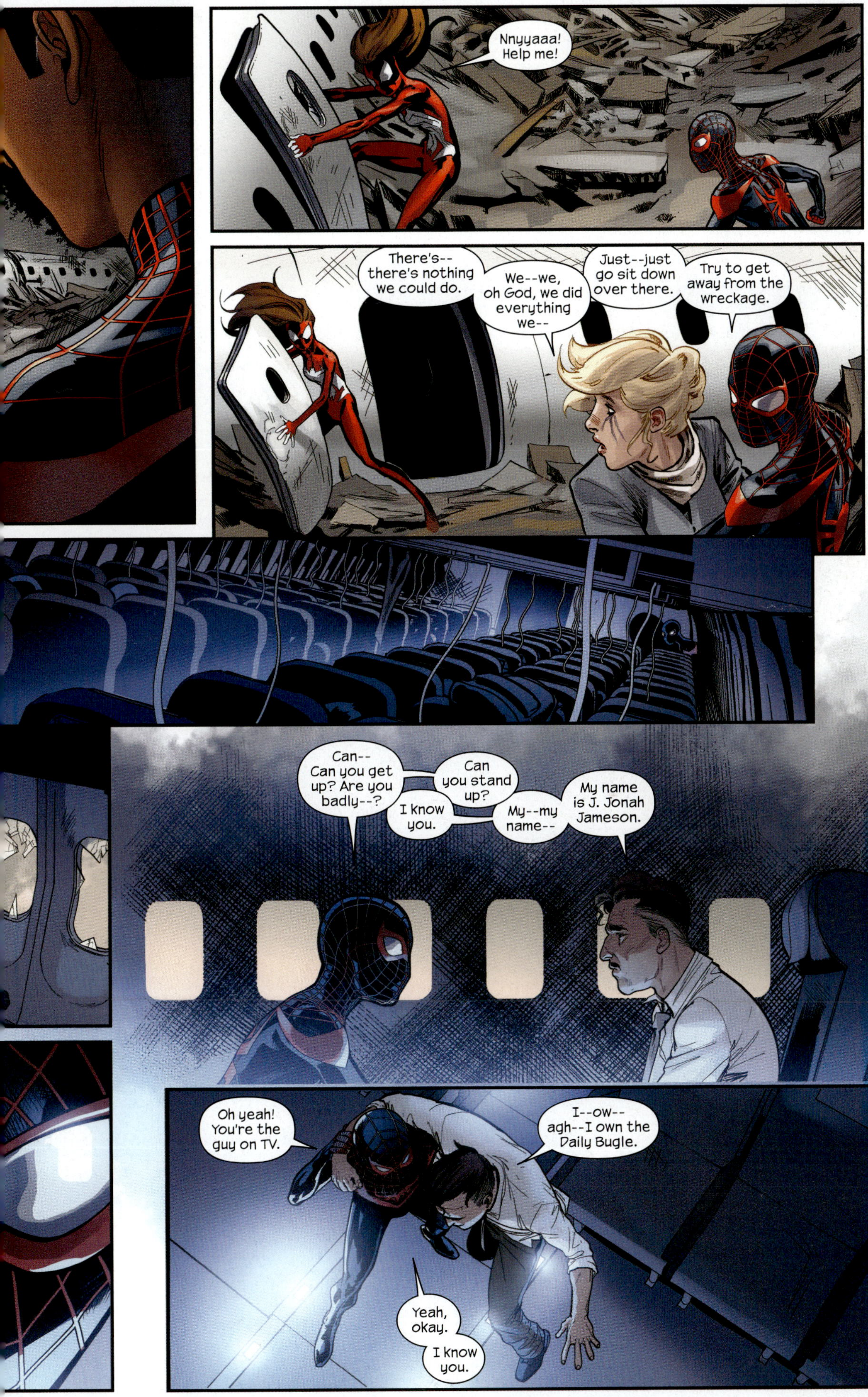
Nnyyaaa! Help me!
There's-- there's nothing we could do.
We--we, oh God, we did everything we--
Just--just go sit down over there.
Try to get away from the wreckage.
Can-- Can you get up? Are you badly--?
Can you stand up?
I know you.
My--my name--
My name is J. Jonah Jameson.
Oh yeah! You're the guy on TV.
I--ow-- agh--I own the Daily Bugle.
Yeah, okay.
I know you.

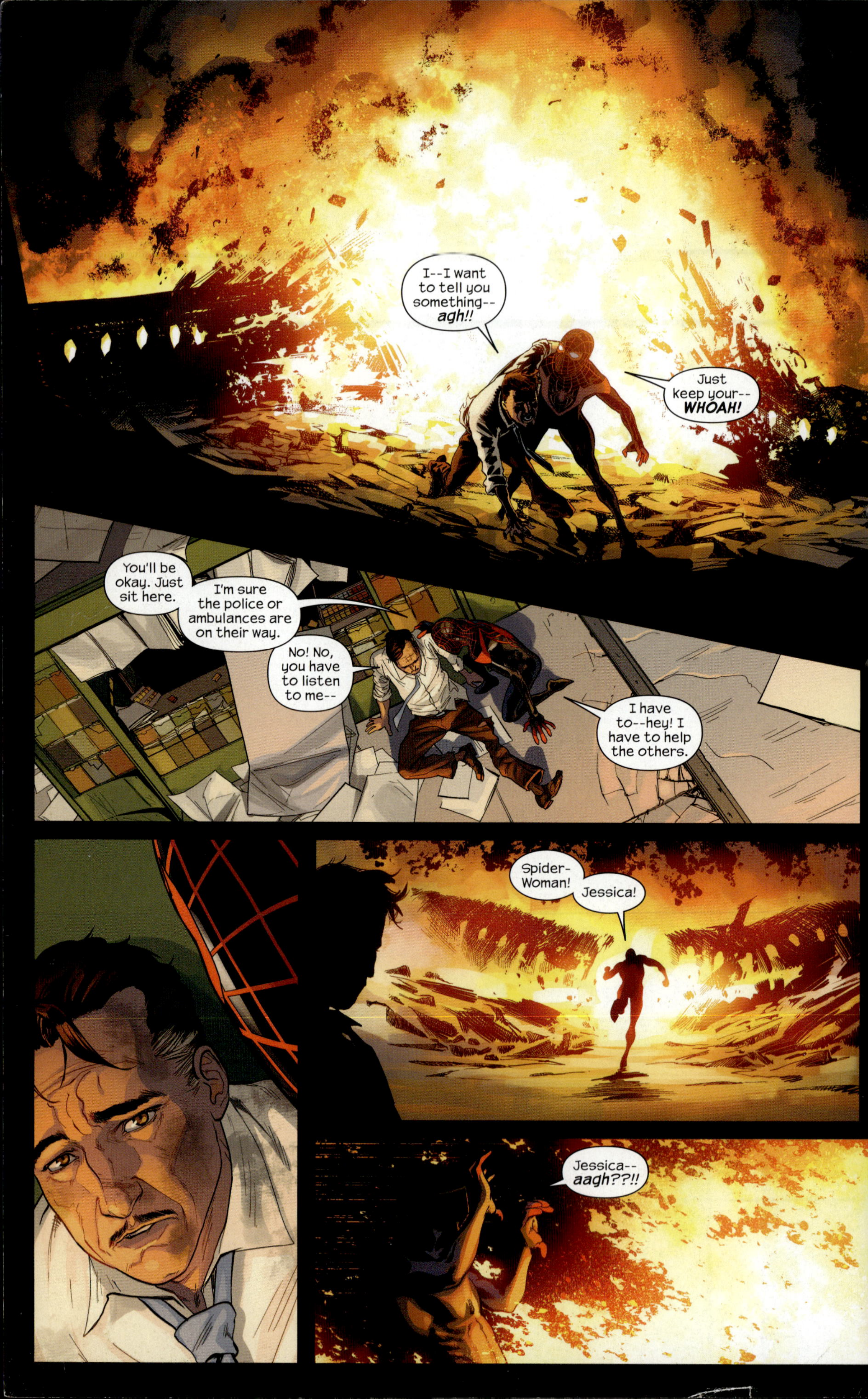
I--I want to tell you something-- agh!!
Just keep your-- WHOAH!
You'll be okay. Just sit here.
I'm sure the police or ambulances are on their way.
No! No, you have to listen to me--
I have to--hey! I have to help the others.
Spider-Woman!
Jessica!
Jessica-- aagh??!!

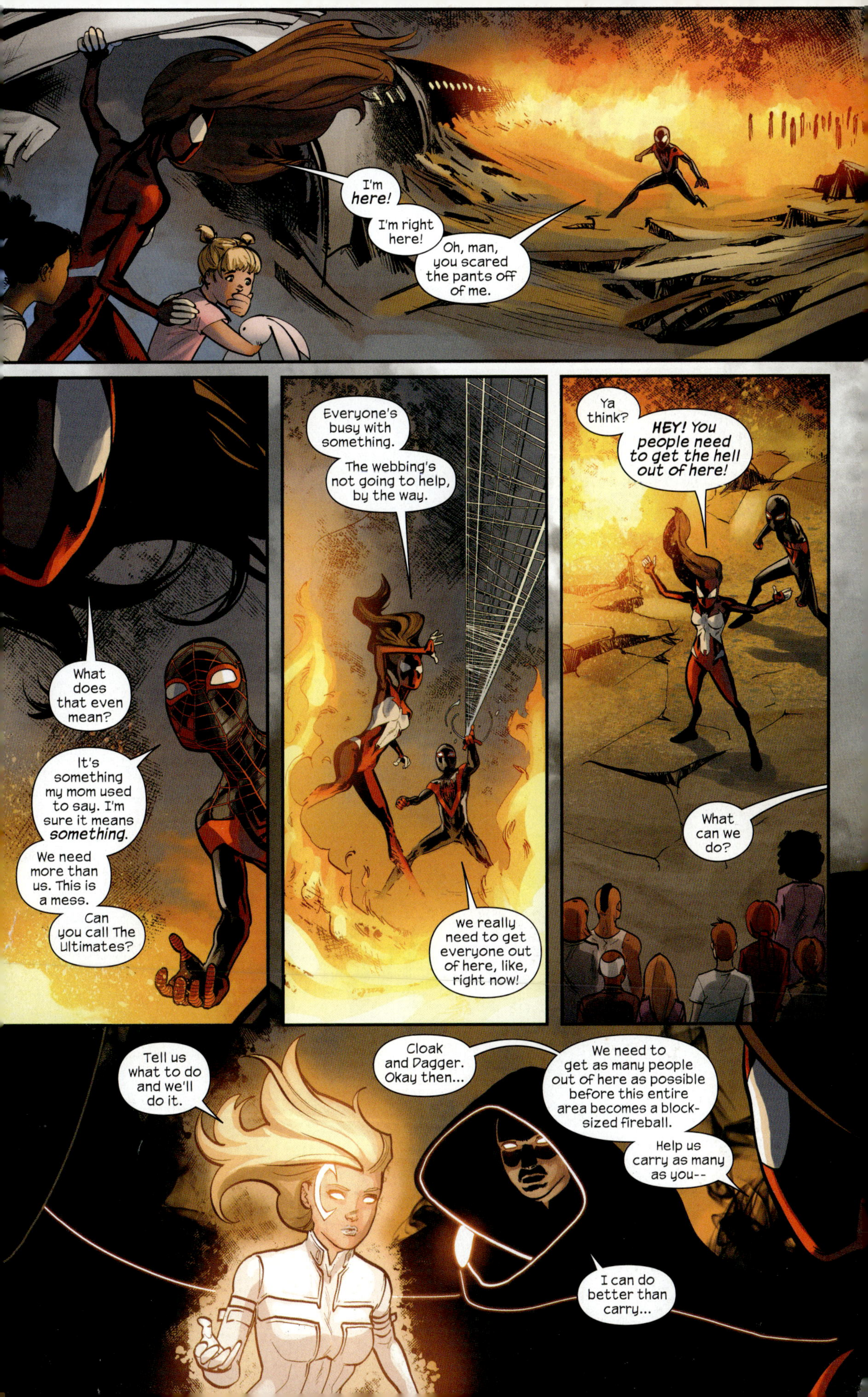
I'm *here!*
I'm right here!
Oh, man, you scared the pants off of me.
What does that even mean?
It's something my mom used to say. I'm sure it means *something.*
We need more than us. This is a mess.
Can you call The Ultimates?
Everyone's busy with something.
The webbing's not going to help, by the way.
We really need to get everyone out of here, like, right now!
Ya think?
***HEY!* You people need to get the hell out of here!**
What can we do?
Tell us what to do and we'll do it.
Cloak and Dagger. Okay then...
We need to get as many people out of here as possible before this entire area becomes a block-sized fireball.
Help us carry as many as you--
I can do better than carry...

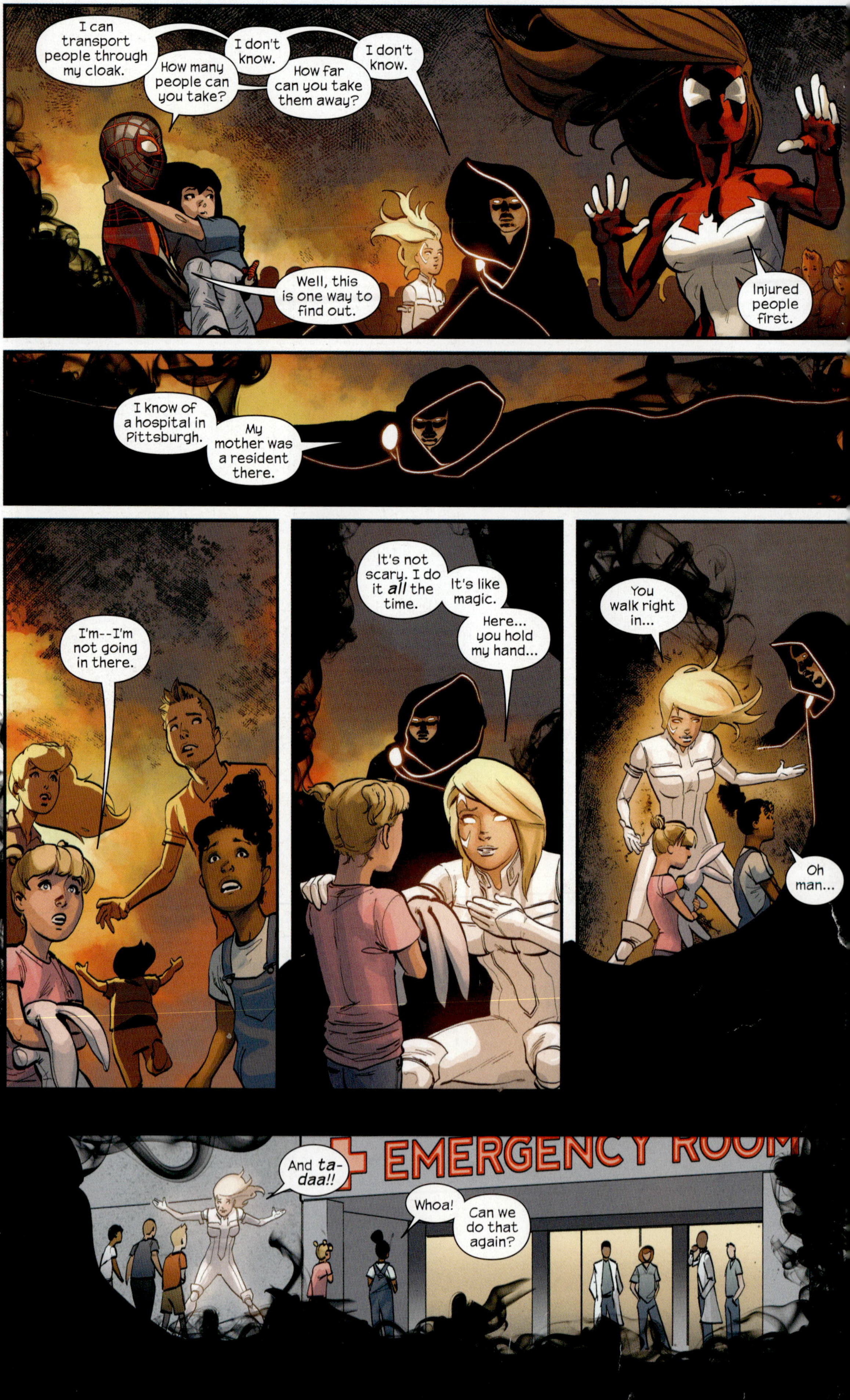
I can transport people through my cloak.
How many people can you take?
I don't know.
How far can you take them away?
I don't know.
Well, this is one way to find out.
Injured people first.
I know of a hospital in Pittsburgh.
My mother was a resident there.
I'm--I'm not going in there.
It's not scary. I do it *all* the time.
It's like magic.
Here... you hold my hand...
You walk right in...
Oh man...
EMERGENCY ROOM
And *ta-daa!!*
Whoa!
Can we do that again?

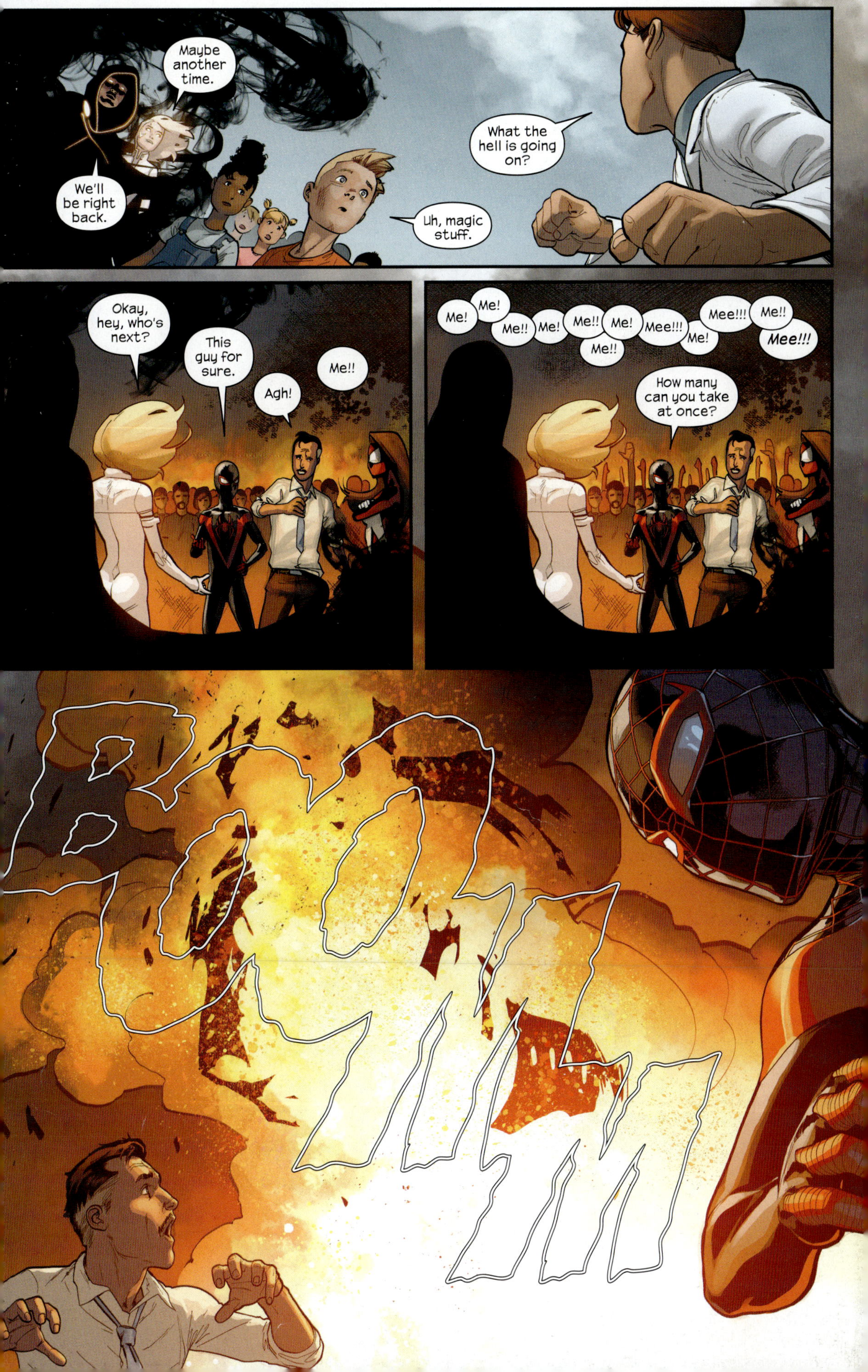

Maybe another time.
We'll be right back.
What the hell is going on?
Uh, magic stuff.
Okay, hey, who's next?
This guy for sure.
Agh!
Me!!
Me!
Me!
Me!!
Me!
Me!!
Me!!
Me!
Mee!!!
Me!
Mee!!!
Me!!
Mee!!!
How many can you take at once?

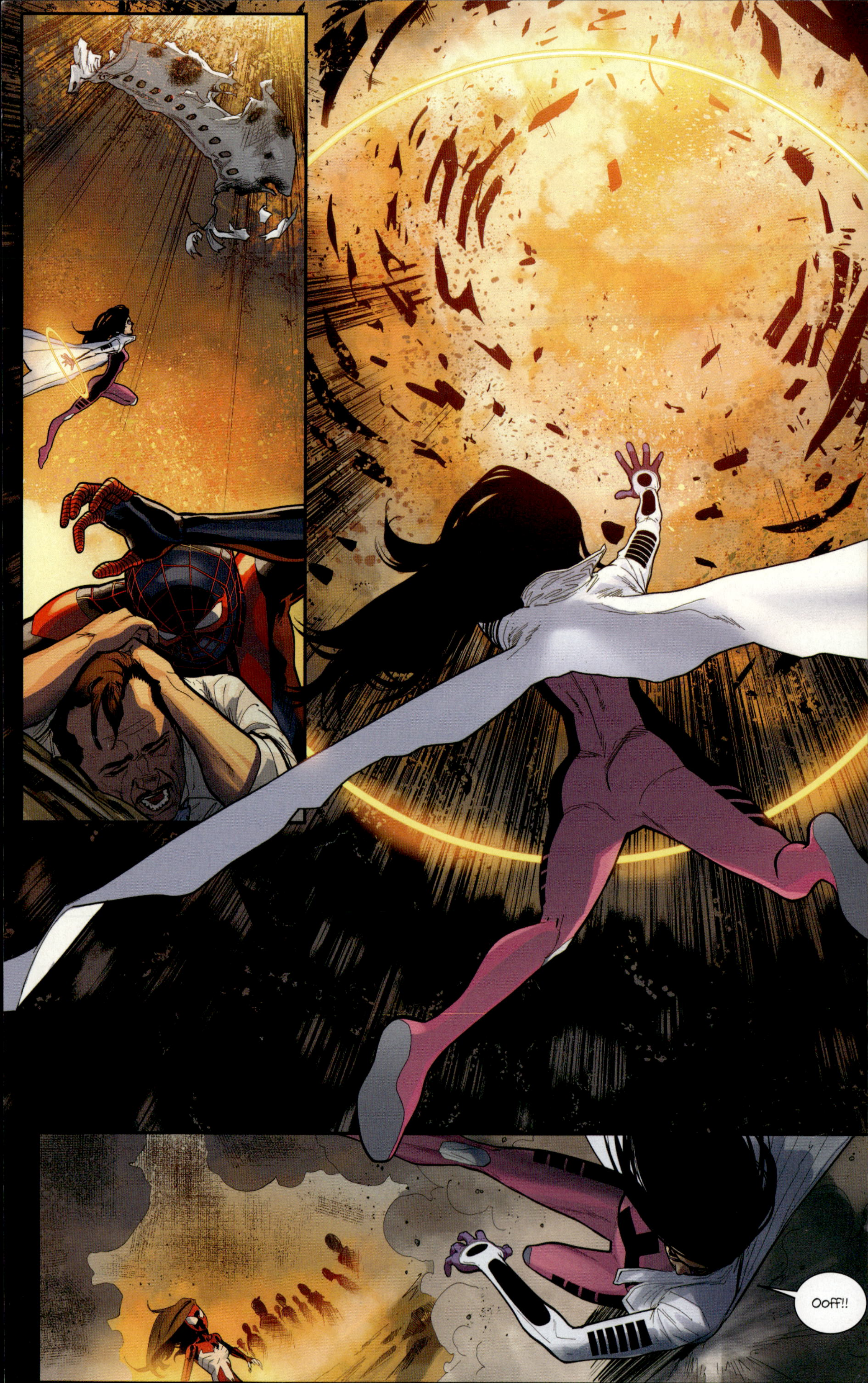
Ooff!!

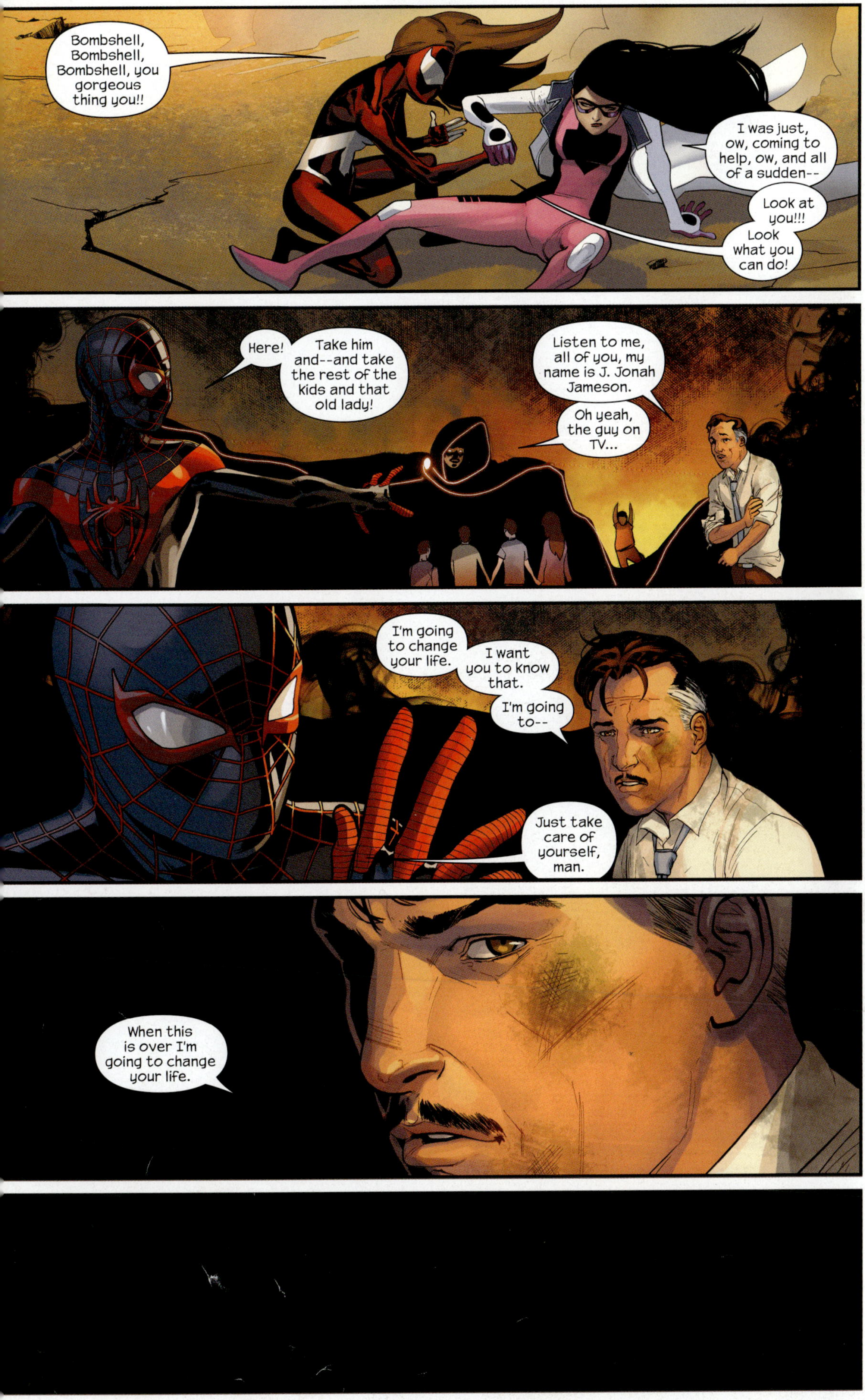
Bombshell, Bombshell, Bombshell, you gorgeous thing you!!
I was just, ow, coming to help, ow, and all of a sudden--
Look at you!!!
Look what you can do!
Here!
Take him and--and take the rest of the kids and that old lady!
Listen to me, all of you, my name is J. Jonah Jameson.
Oh yeah, the guy on TV...
I'm going to change your life.
I want you to know that.
I'm going to--
Just take care of yourself, man.
When this is over I'm going to change your life.

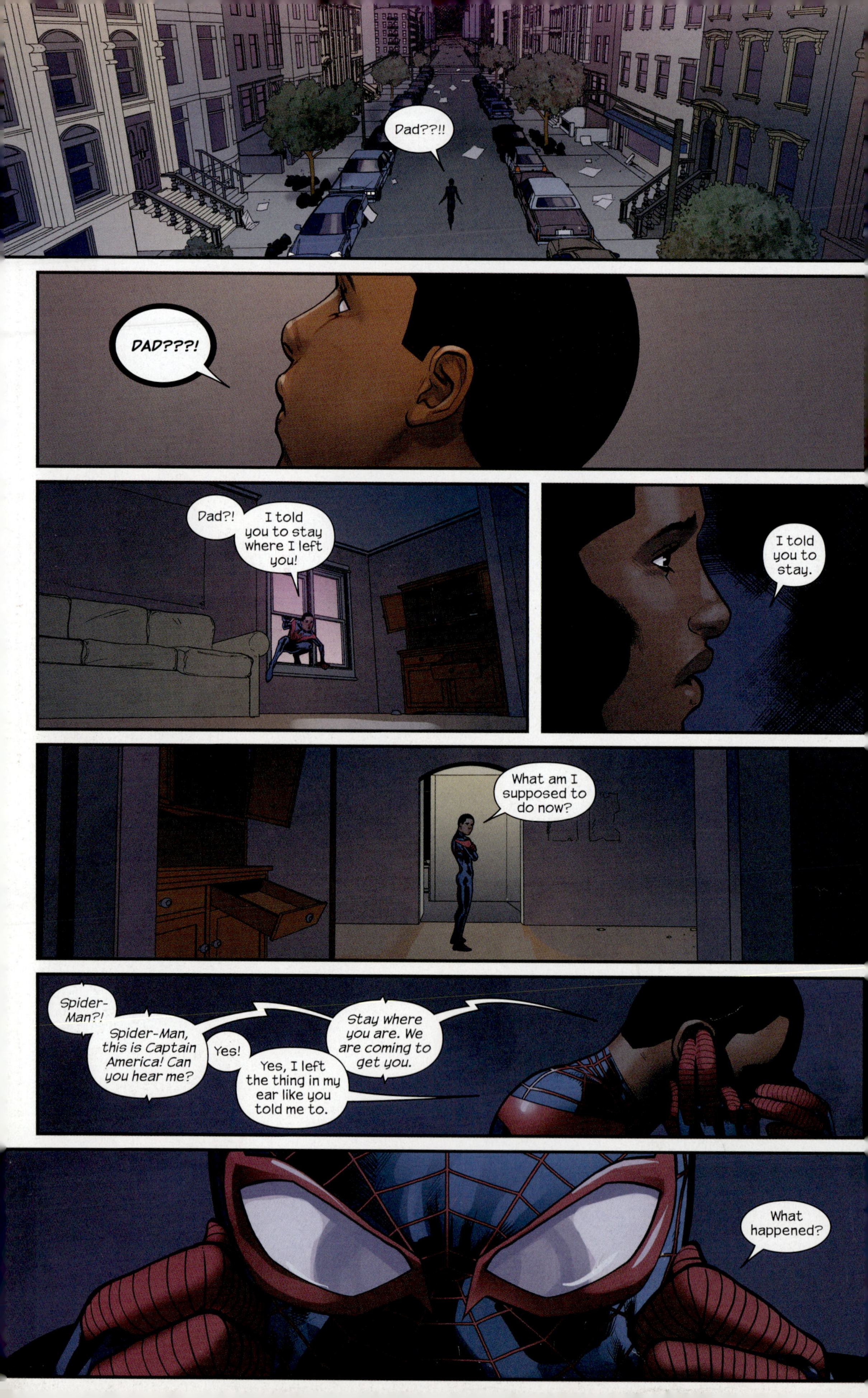
Dad??!!
DAD???!
Dad?!
I told you to stay where I left you!
I told you to stay.
What am I supposed to do now?
Spider-Man?!
Spider-Man, this is Captain America! Can you hear me?
Yes!
Yes, I left the thing in my ear like you told me to.
Stay where you are. We are coming to get you.
What happened?

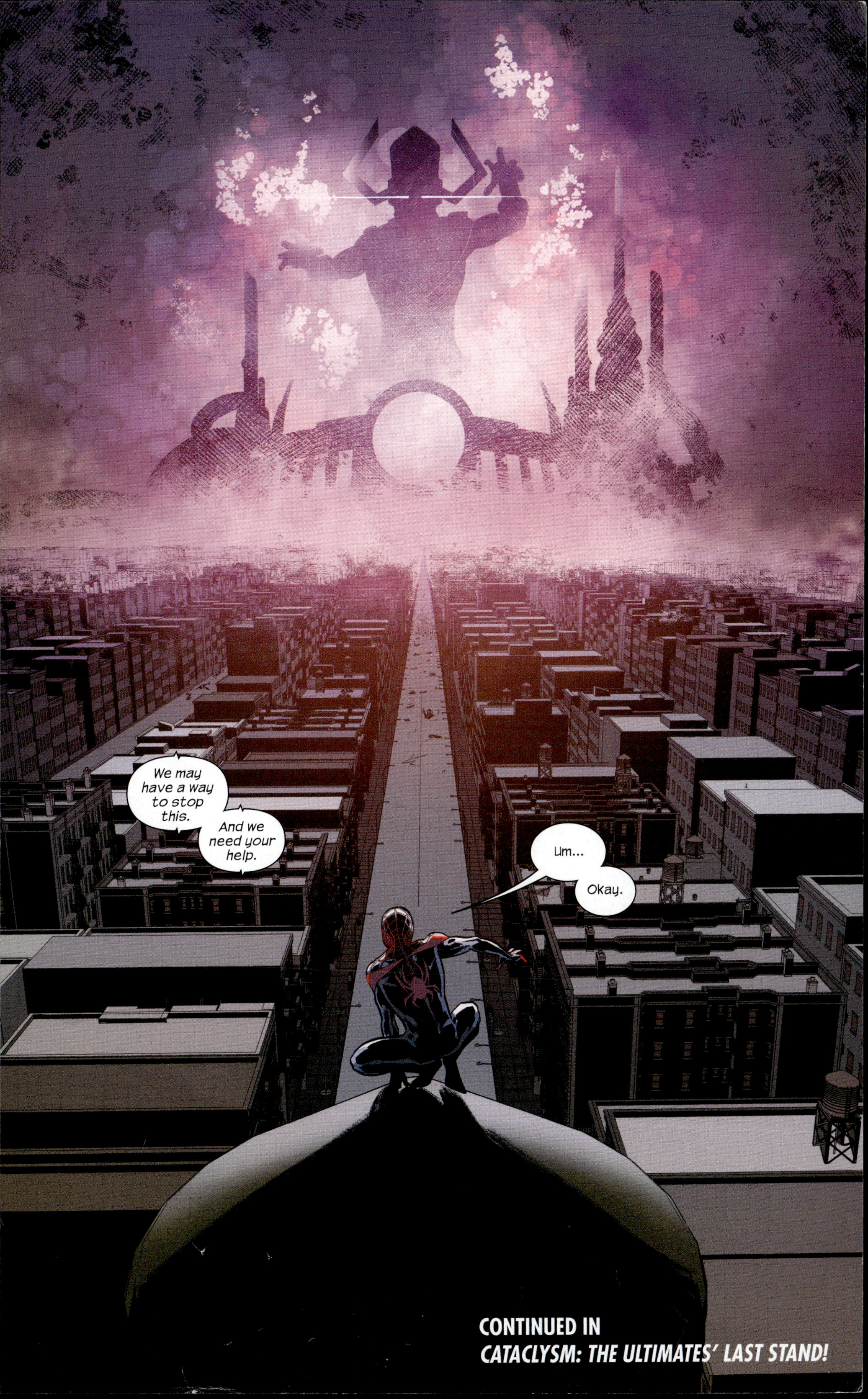

We may have a way to stop this.
And we need your help.
Um...
Okay.
CONTINUED IN
CATACLYSM: THE ULTIMATES' LAST STAND!

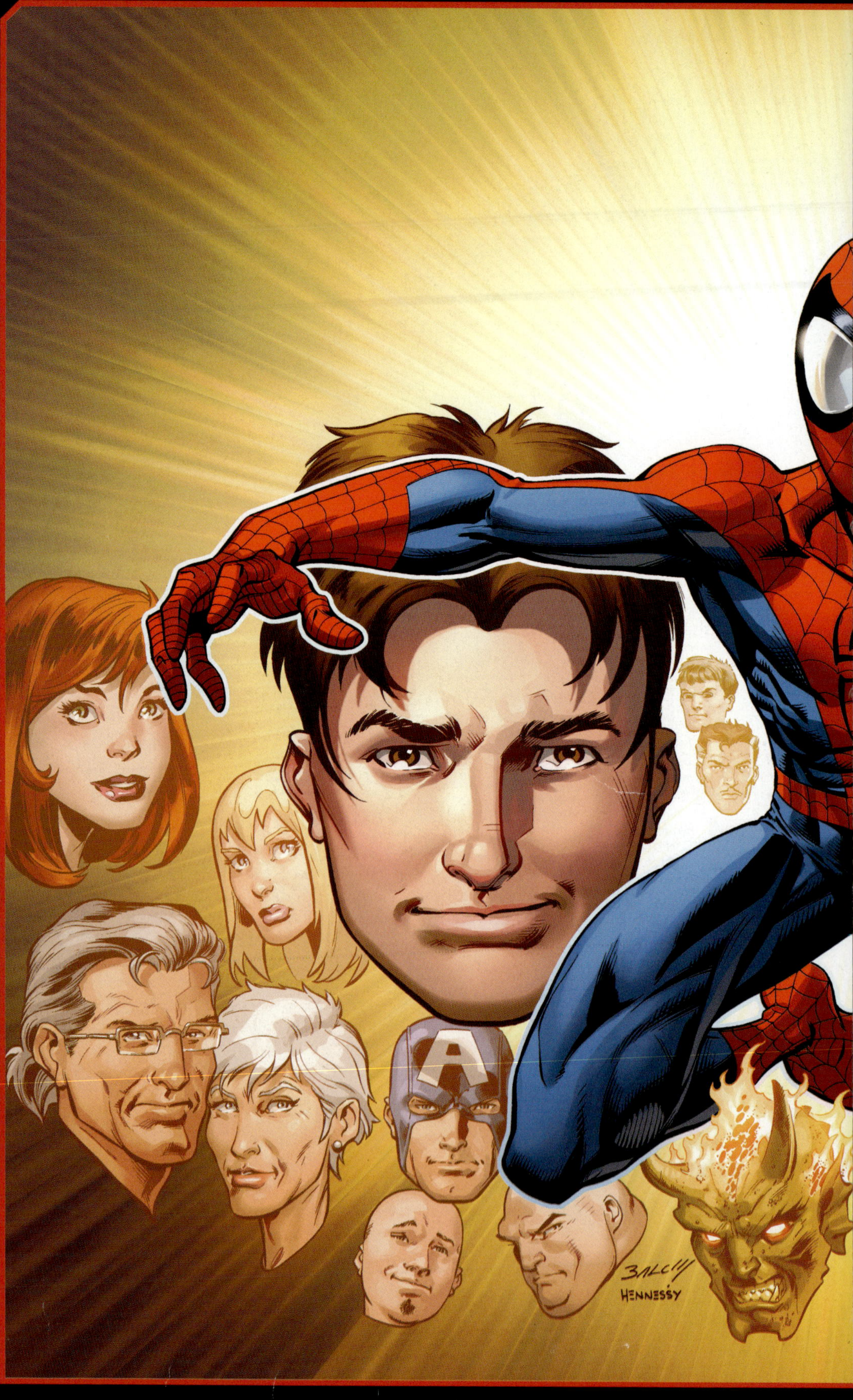
BAGLEY
HENNESSY

ULTIMATE SPIDER-MAN #200

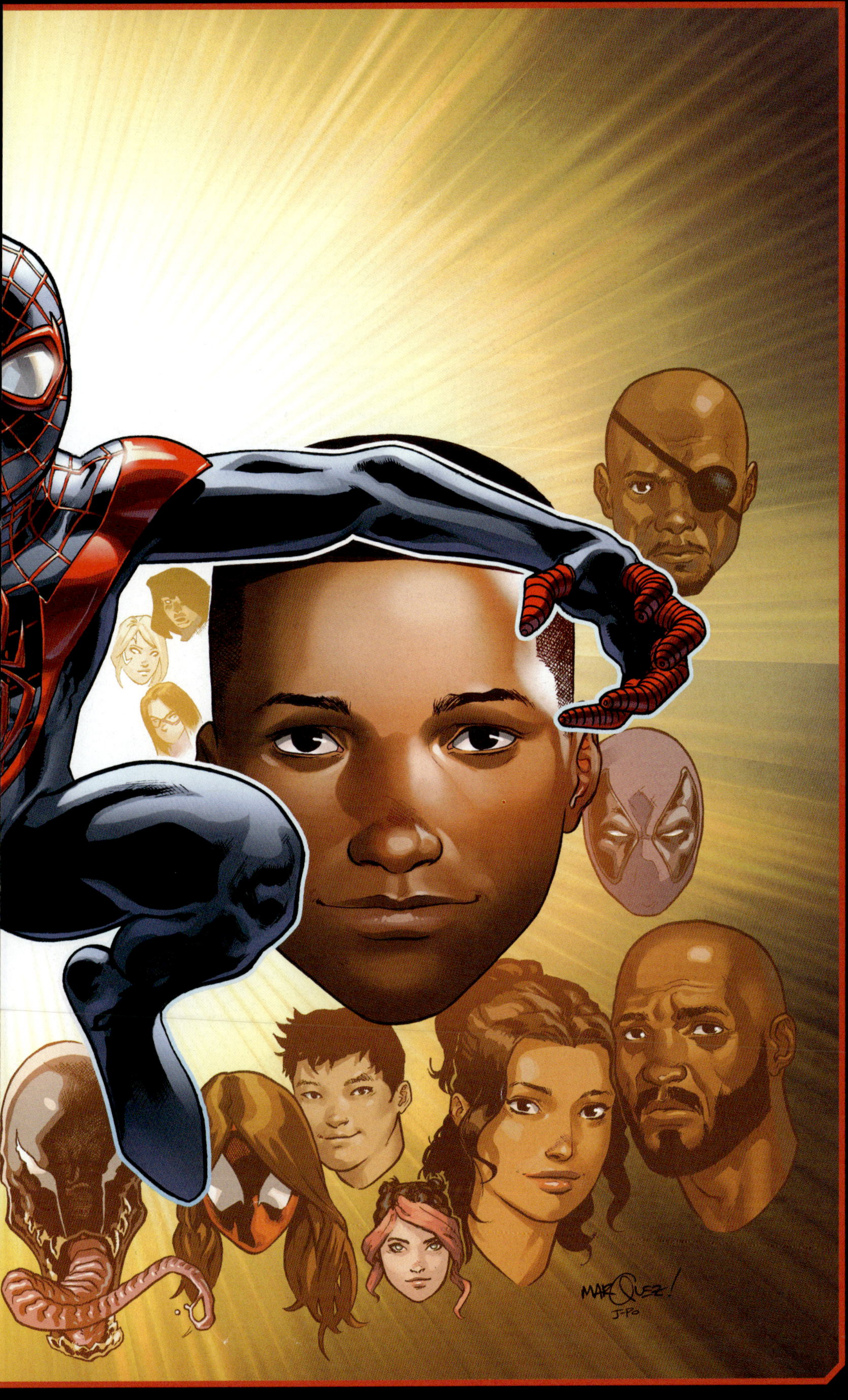

ULTIMATE SPIDER-MAN #200 VARIANT BY DAVID MARQUEZ & JUSTIN PONSOR

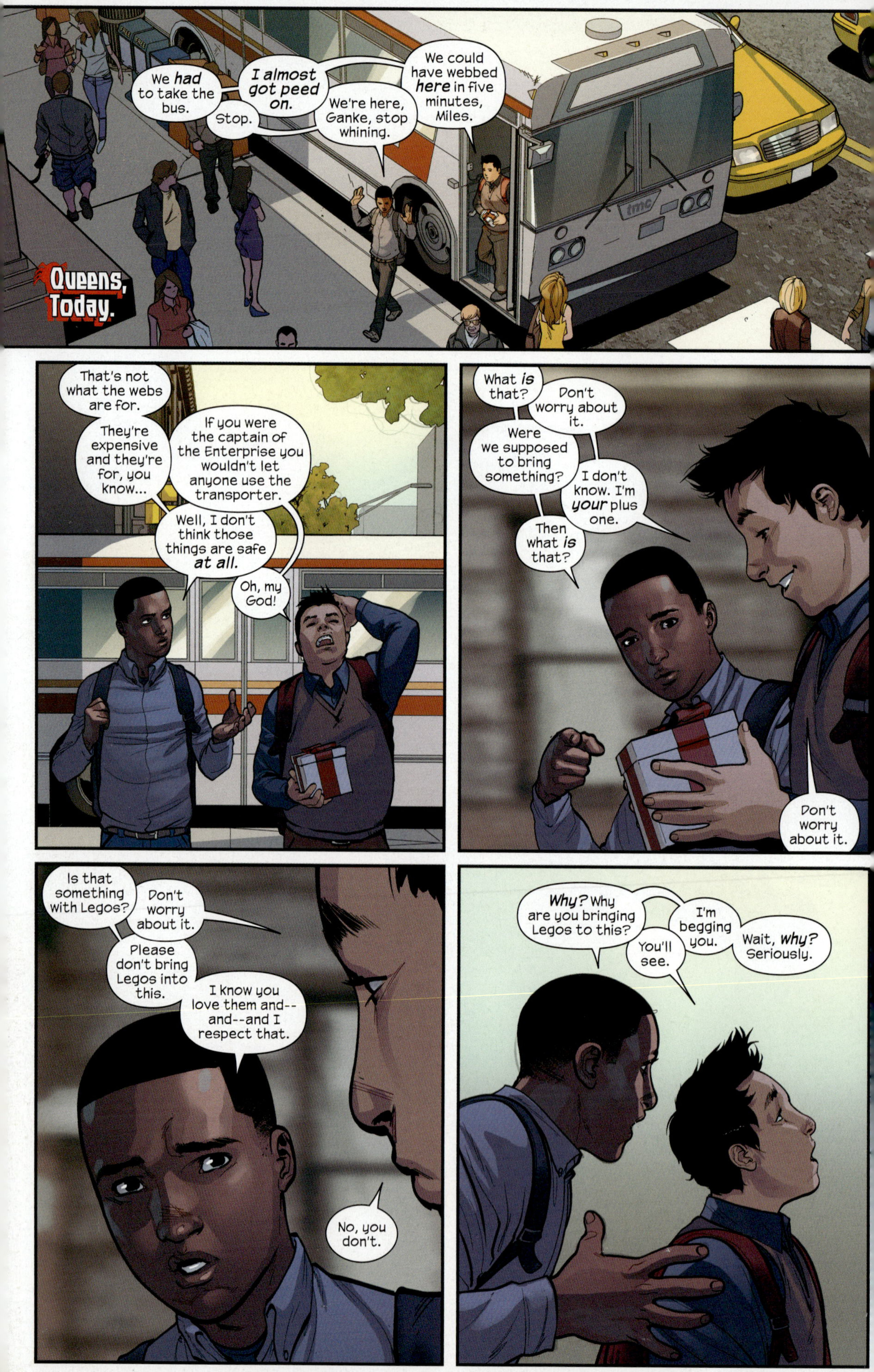
Queens, Today.
We had to take the bus.
I almost got peed on.
Stop.
We're here, Ganke, stop whining.
We could have webbed here in five minutes, Miles.
That's not what the webs are for.
They're expensive and they're for, you know...
If you were the captain of the Enterprise you wouldn't let anyone use the transporter.
Well, I don't think those things are safe at all.
Oh, my God!
What is that?
Don't worry about it.
Were we supposed to bring something?
I don't know. I'm your plus one.
Then what is that?
Don't worry about it.
Is that something with Legos?
Don't worry about it.
Please don't bring Legos into this.
I know you love them and--and--and I respect that.
No, you don't.
Why? Why are you bringing Legos to this?
I'm begging you.
You'll see.
Wait, why? Seriously.

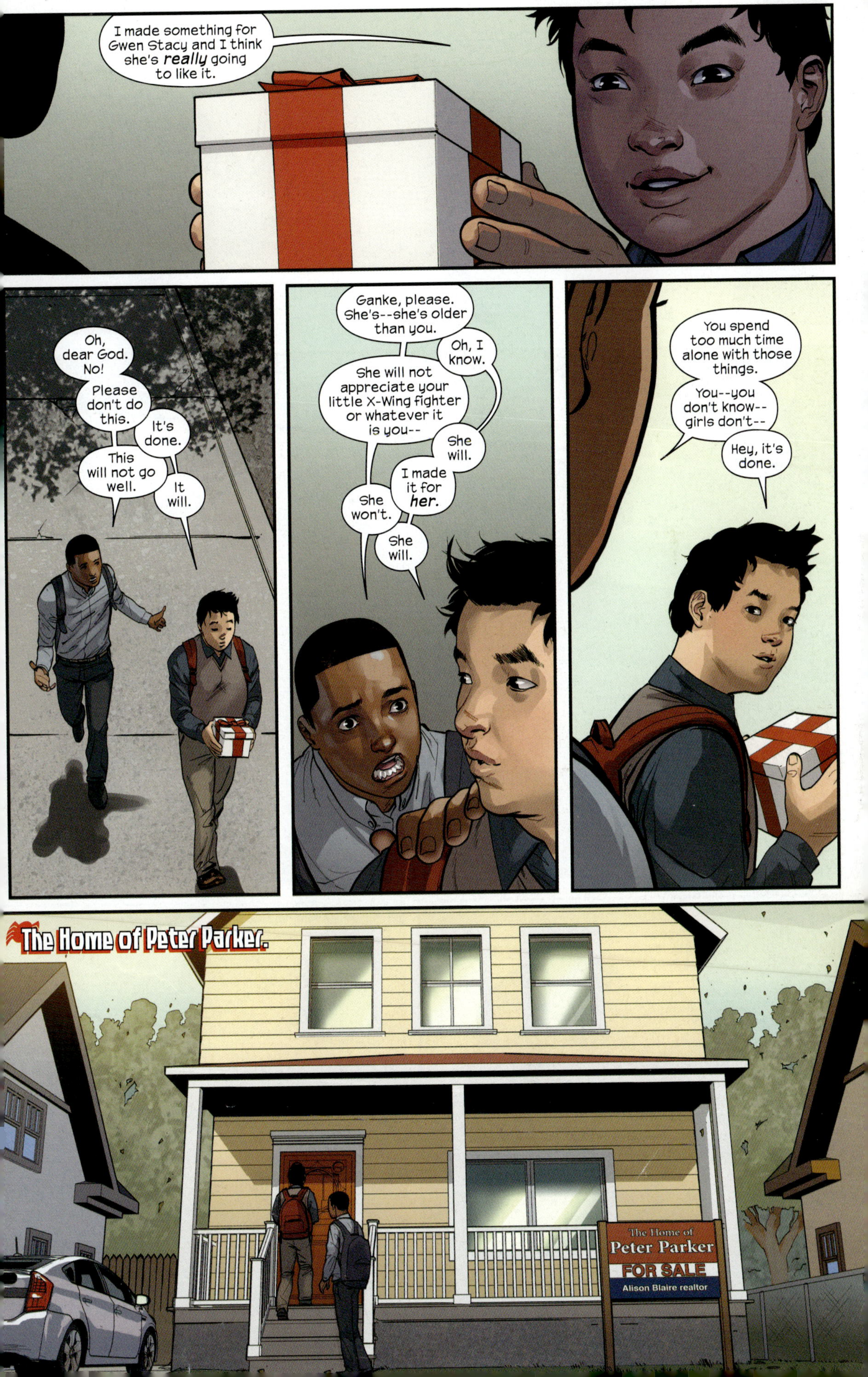
I made something for Gwen Stacy and I think she's *really* going to like it.
Oh, dear God. No!
Please don't do this.
It's done.
This will not go well.
It will.
Ganke, please. She's--she's older than you.
Oh, I know.
She will not appreciate your little X-Wing fighter or whatever it is you--
She will.
I made it for *her*.
She won't.
She will.
You spend too much time alone with those things.
You--you don't know--girls don't--
Hey, it's done.
The Home of Peter Parker.
The Home of
Peter Parker
FOR SALE
Alison Blaire realtor

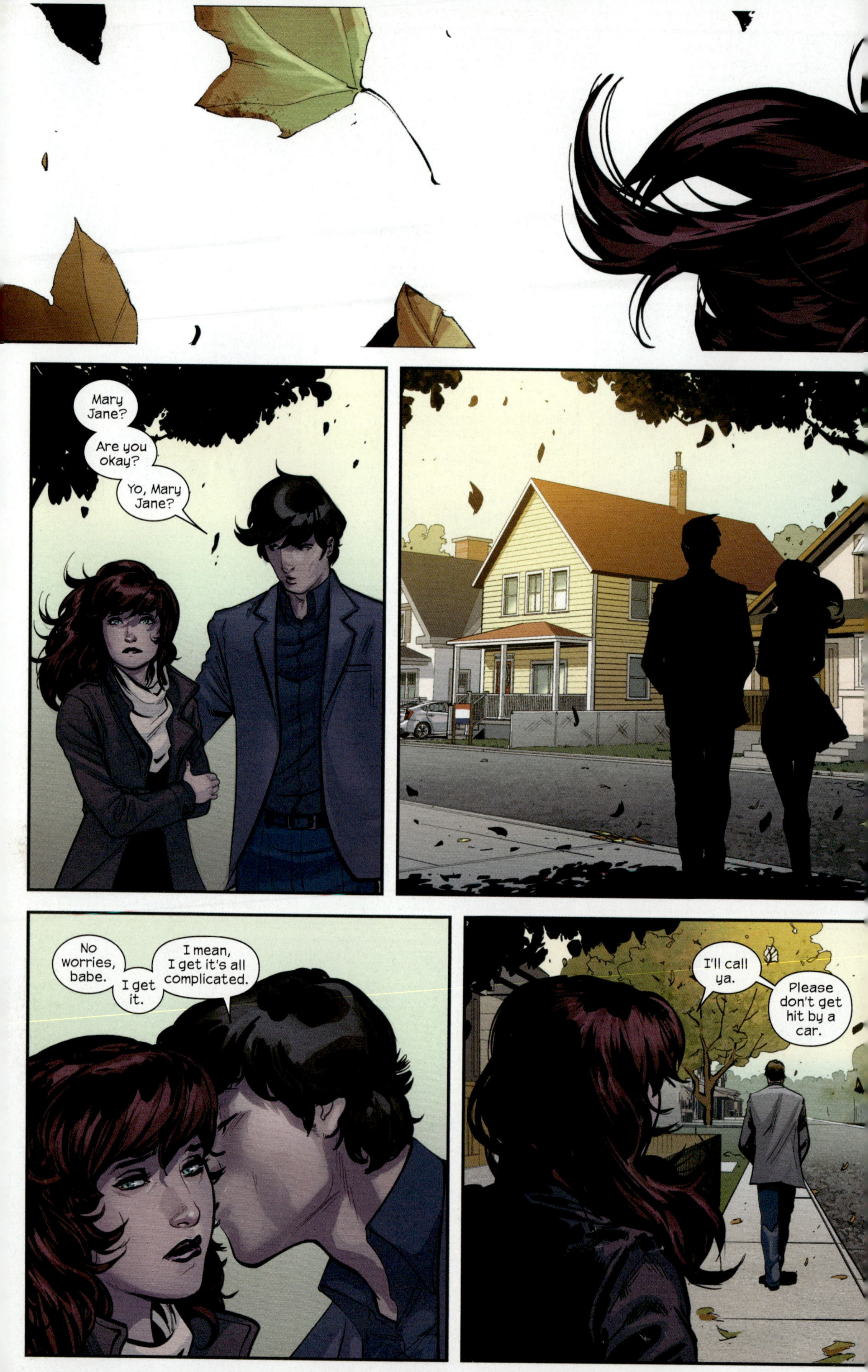
Mary Jane?
Are you okay?
Yo, Mary Jane?
No worries, babe.
I get it.
I mean, I get it's all complicated.
I'll call ya.
Please don't get hit by a car.

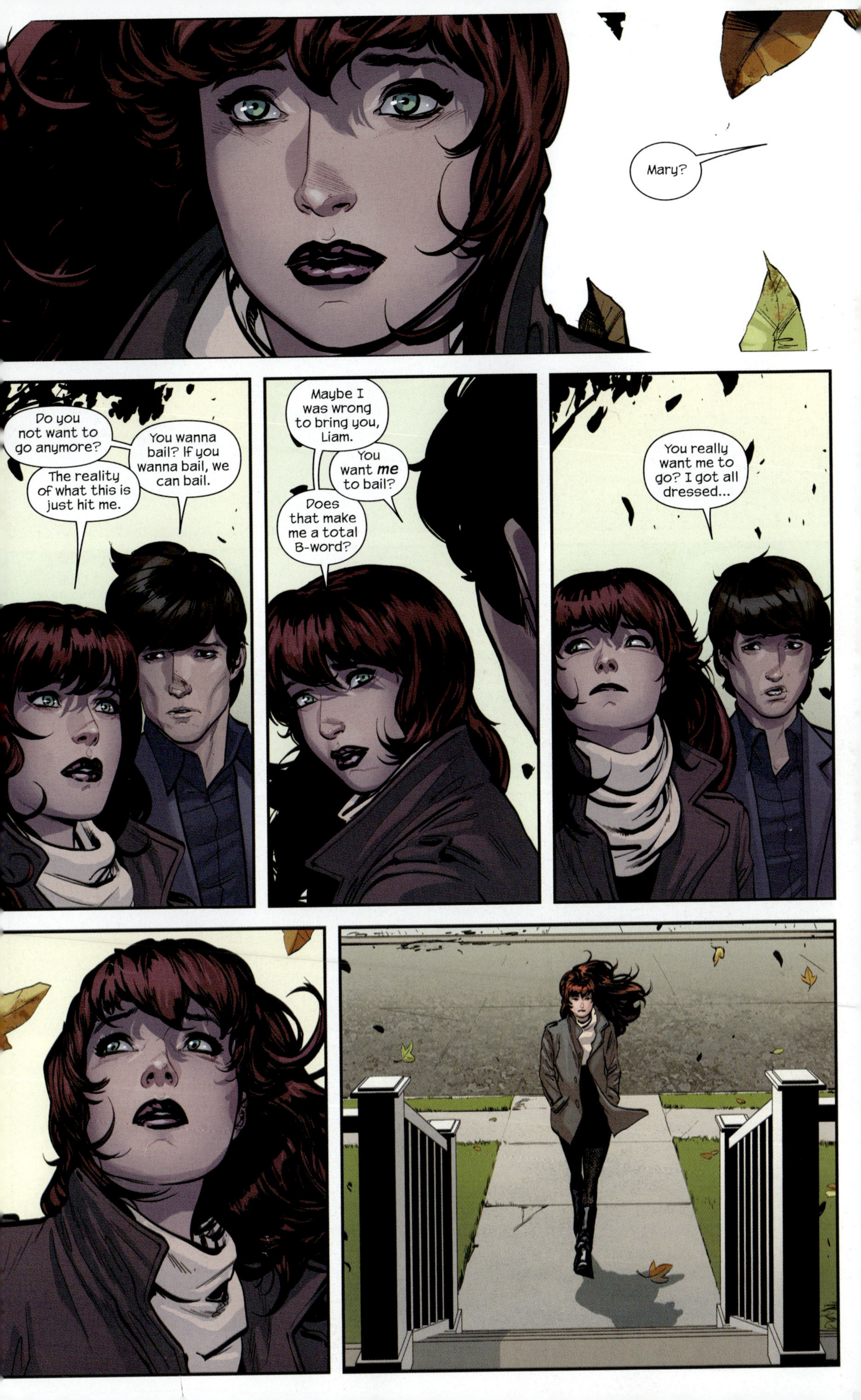

Mary?
Do you not want to go anymore?
You wanna bail? If you wanna bail, we can bail.
The reality of what this is just hit me.
Maybe I was wrong to bring you, Liam.
You want *me* to bail?
Does that make me a total B-word?
You really want me to go? I got all dressed...

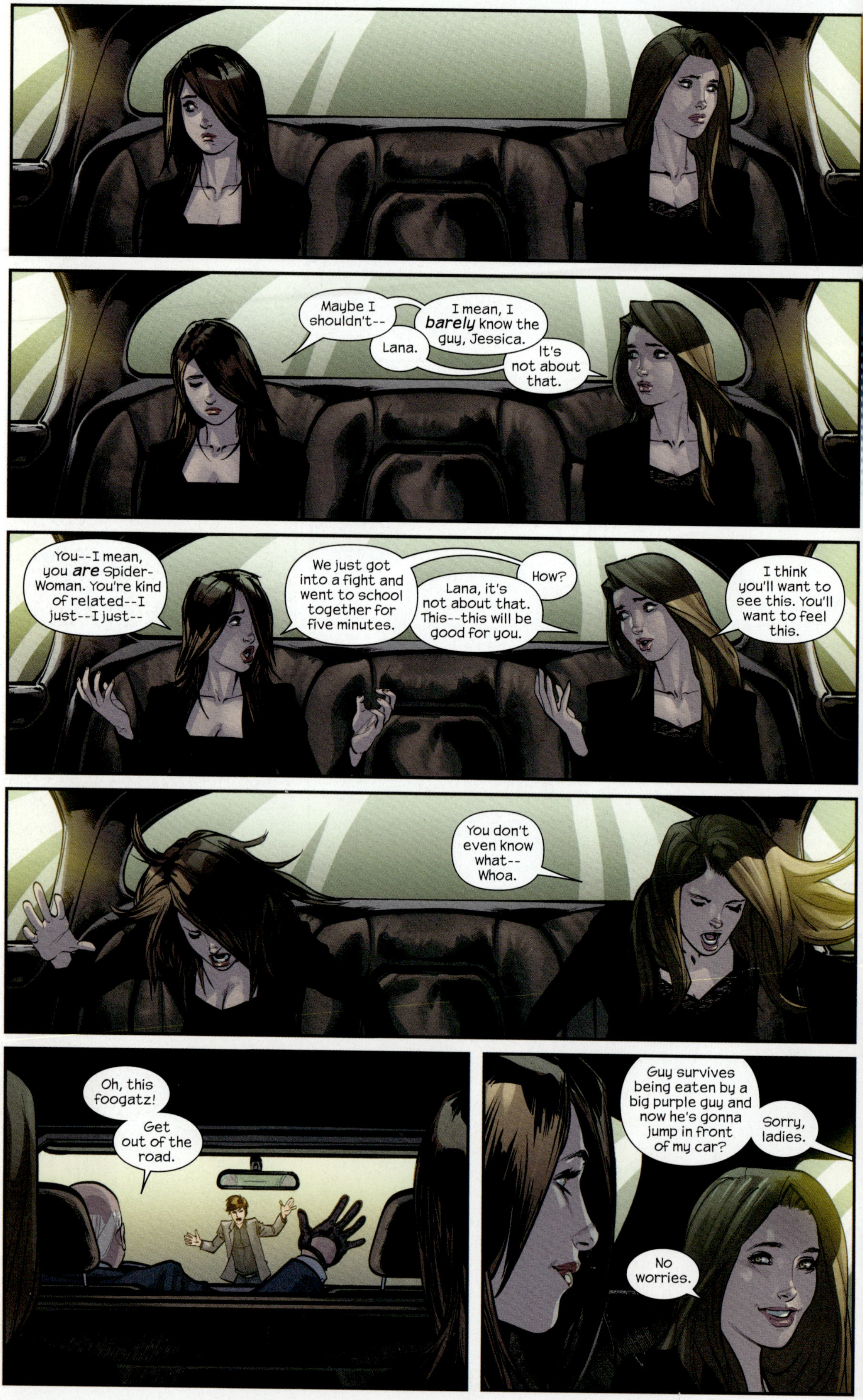
Maybe I shouldn't--
Lana.
I mean, I *barely* know the guy, Jessica.
It's not about that.
You--I mean, you *are* Spider-Woman. You're kind of related--I just--I just--
We just got into a fight and went to school together for five minutes.
How?
Lana, it's not about that. This--this will be good for you.
I think you'll want to see this. You'll want to feel this.
You don't even know what-- Whoa.
Oh, this foogatz!
Get out of the road.
Guy survives being eaten by a big purple guy and now he's gonna jump in front of my car?
Sorry, ladies.
No worries.

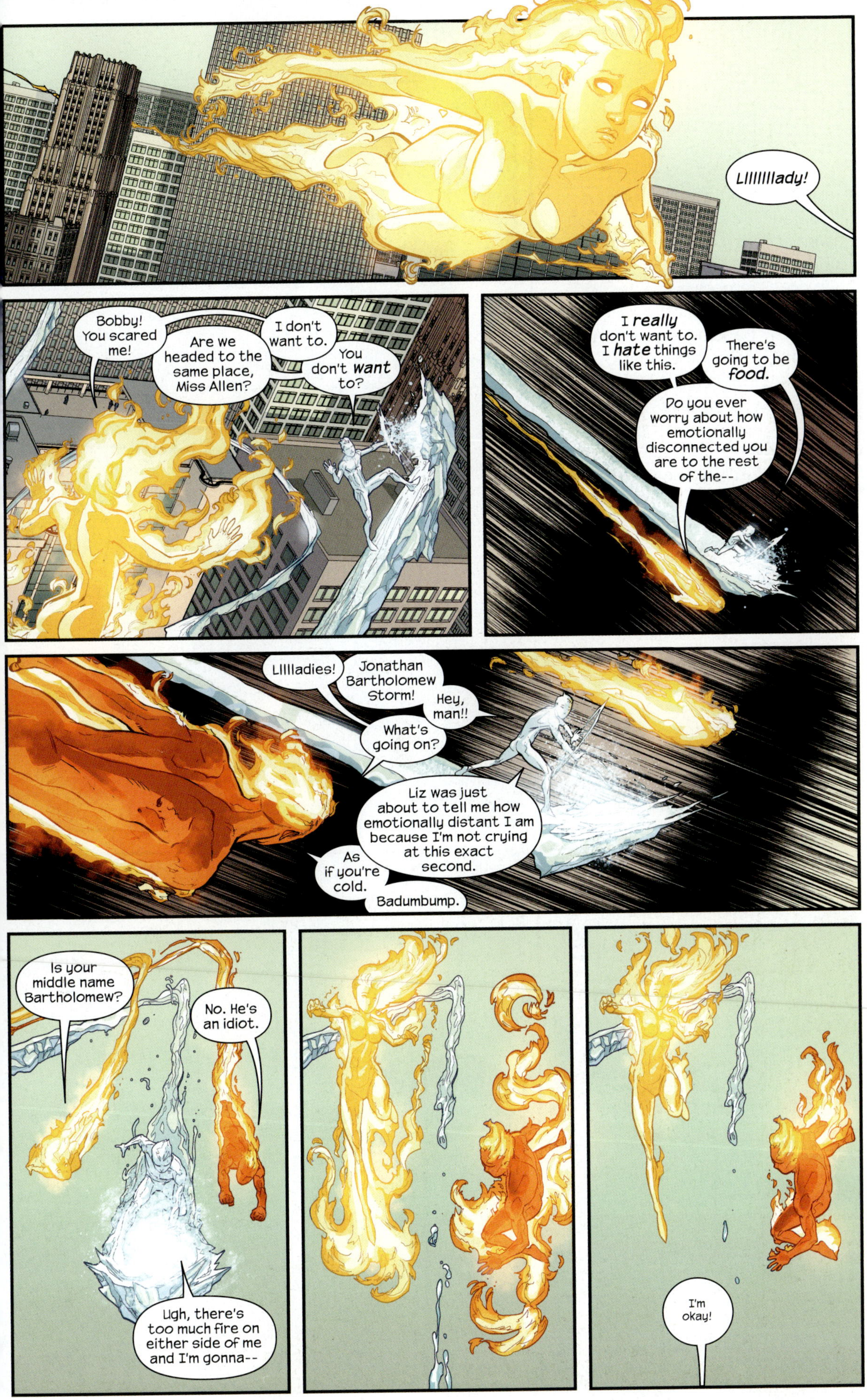

Lllllllady!
Bobby! You scared me!
Are we headed to the same place, Miss Allen?
I don't want to.
You don't *want* to?
I *really* don't want to. I *hate* things like this.
There's going to be *food.*
Do you ever worry about how emotionally disconnected you are to the rest of the--
Lllladies!
Jonathan Bartholomew Storm!
Hey, man!!
What's going on?
Liz was just about to tell me how emotionally distant I am because I'm not crying at this exact second.
As if you're cold.
Badumbump.
Is your middle name Bartholomew?
No. He's an idiot.
Ugh, there's too much fire on either side of me and I'm gonna--
I'm okay!

From:
silverhippy@jeemail.com
Subject:
a celebration of Peter Parker

To commemorate the second anniversary of our dear Peter's untimely passing we are having a small get-together at the house. This is a celebration of his life, not a mourning of his passing.

There will be food, drink and friends. I truly believe Peter would want us to do this and would want you there. I hope to see you there.

Please RSVP.
May Parker

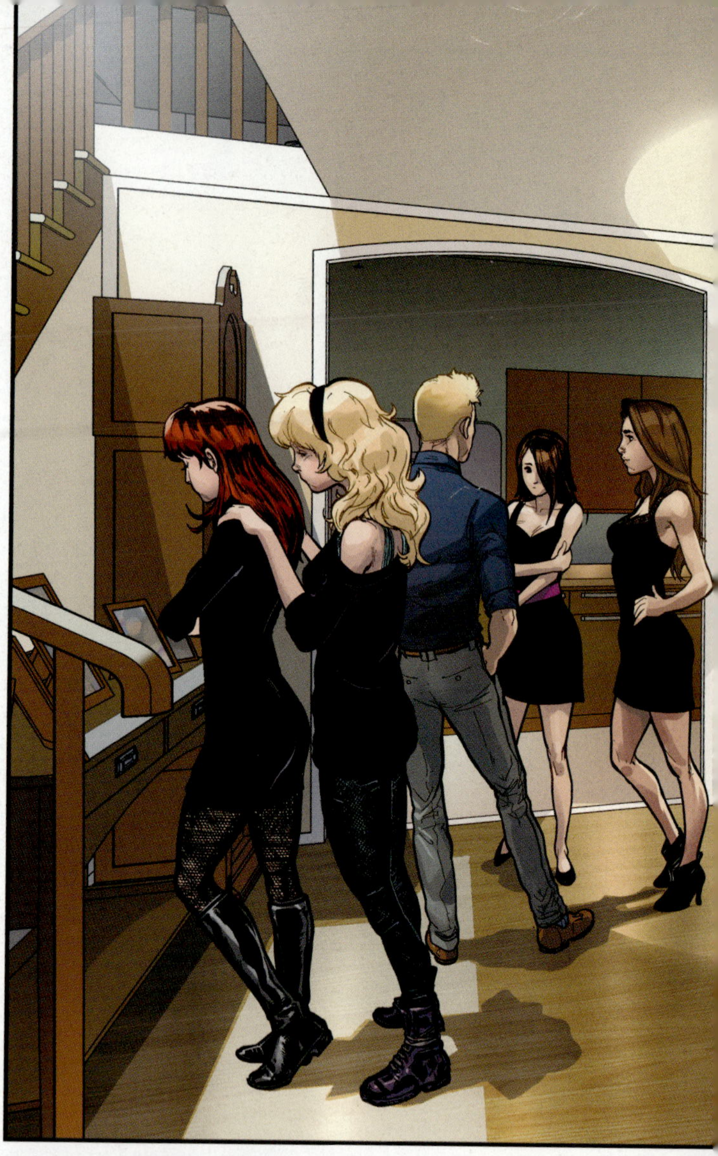

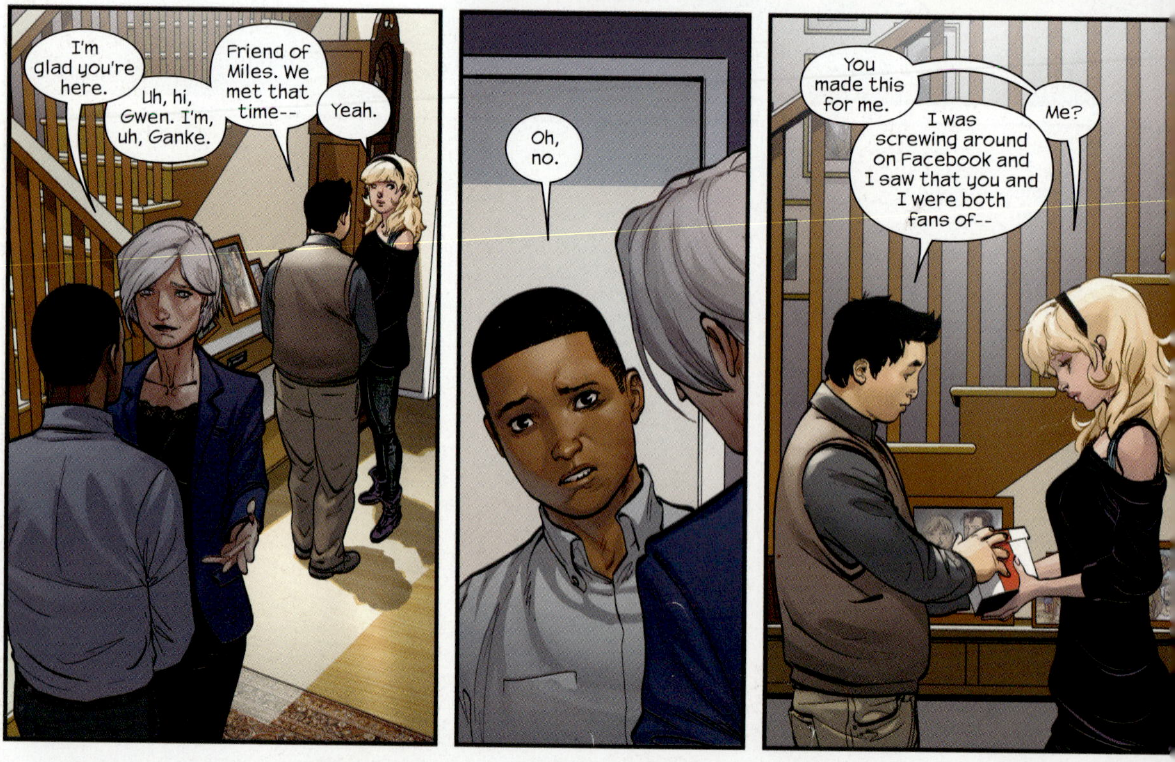
I'm glad you're here.
Uh, hi, Gwen. I'm, uh, Ganke.
Friend of Miles. We met that time--
Yeah.
Oh, no.
You made this for me.
Me?
I was screwing around on Facebook and I saw that you and I were both fans of--

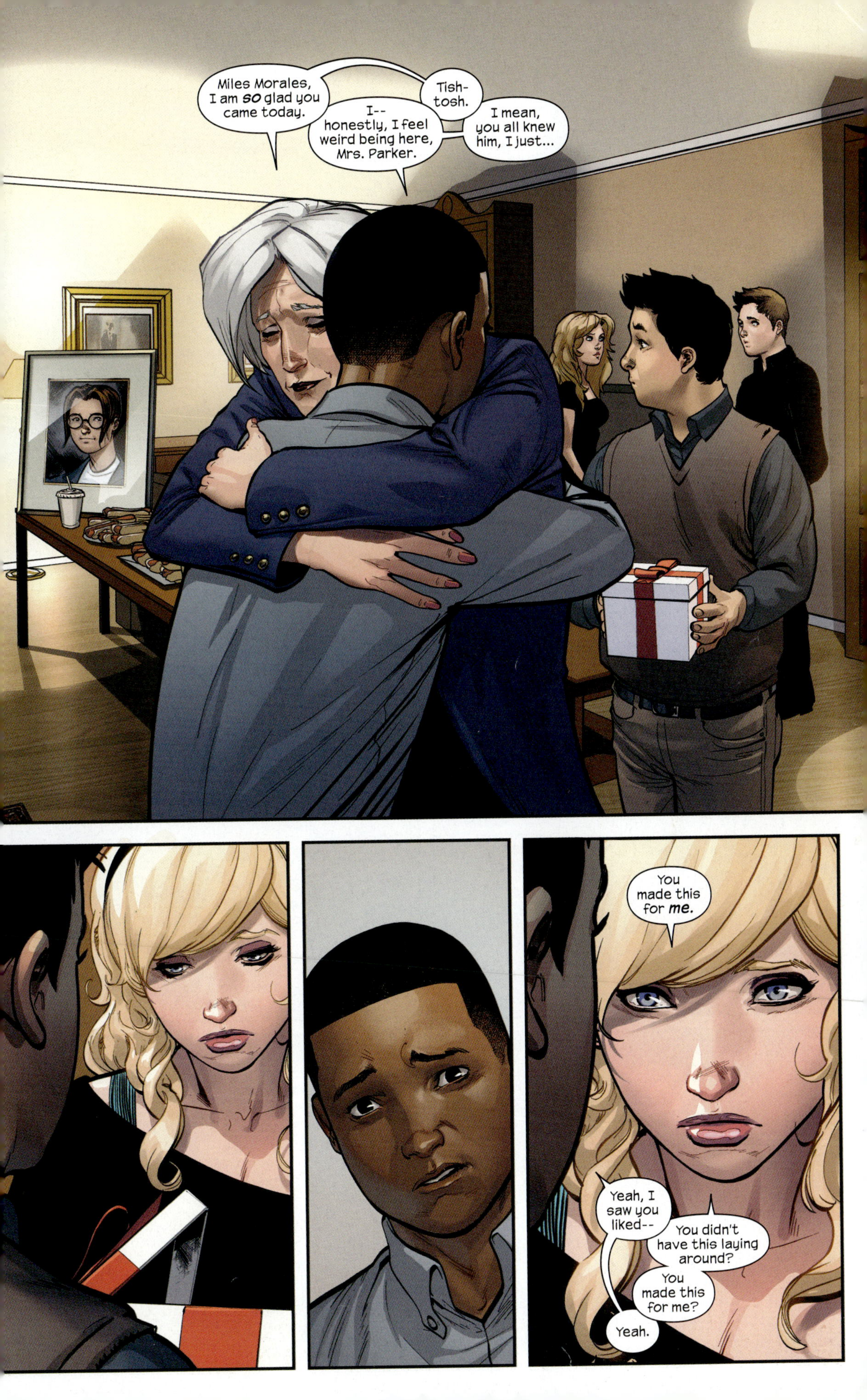
Miles Morales, I am SO glad you came today.
Tish-tosh.
I-- honestly, I feel weird being here, Mrs. Parker.
I mean, you all knew him, I just...
You made this for me.
Yeah, I saw you liked--
You didn't have this laying around?
You made this for me?
Yeah.

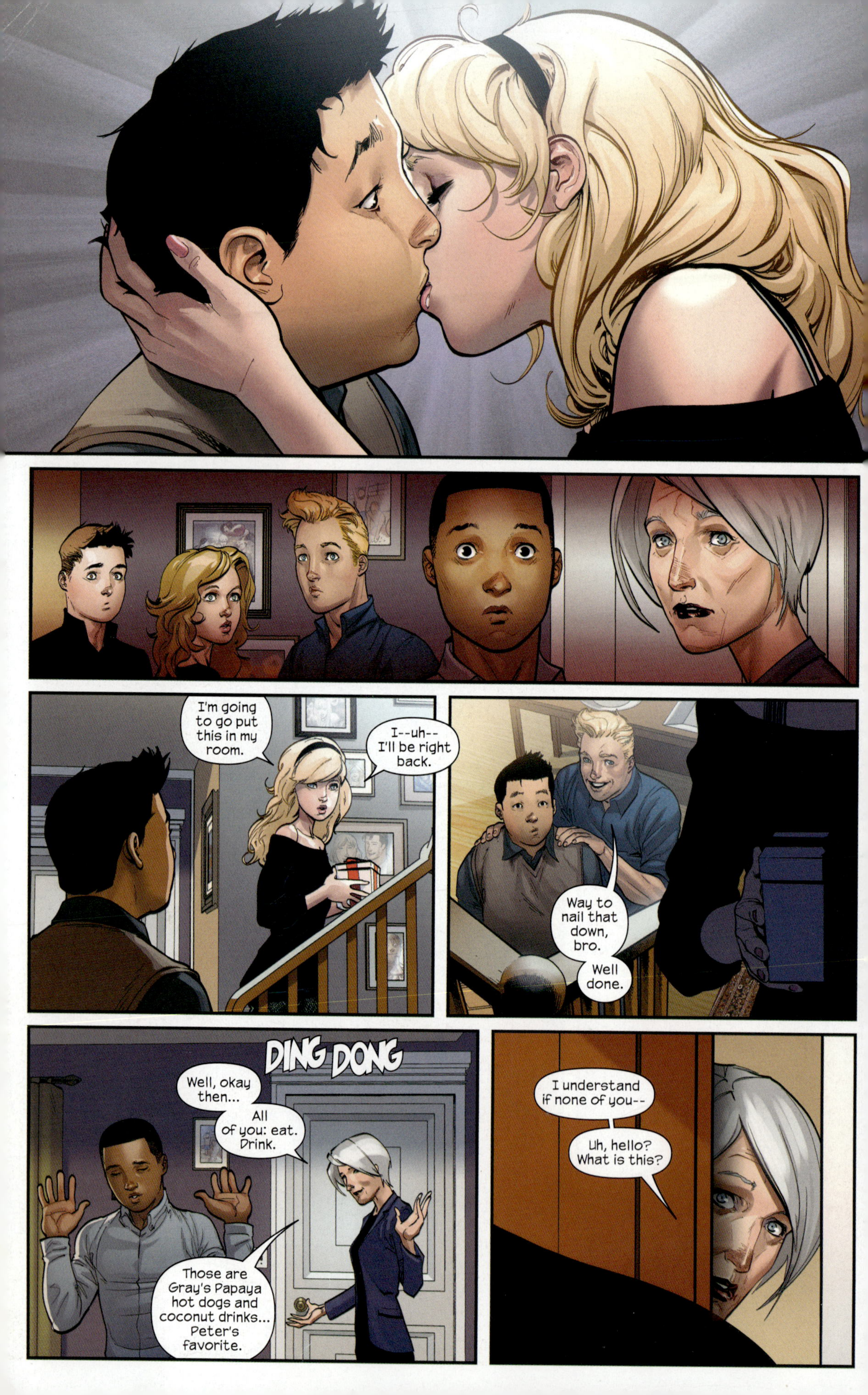
I'm going to go put this in my room.
I--uh-- I'll be right back.
Way to nail that down, bro.
Well done.
DING DONG
Well, okay then...
All of you: eat. Drink.
Those are Gray's Papaya hot dogs and coconut drinks... Peter's favorite.
I understand if none of you--
Uh, hello? What is this?

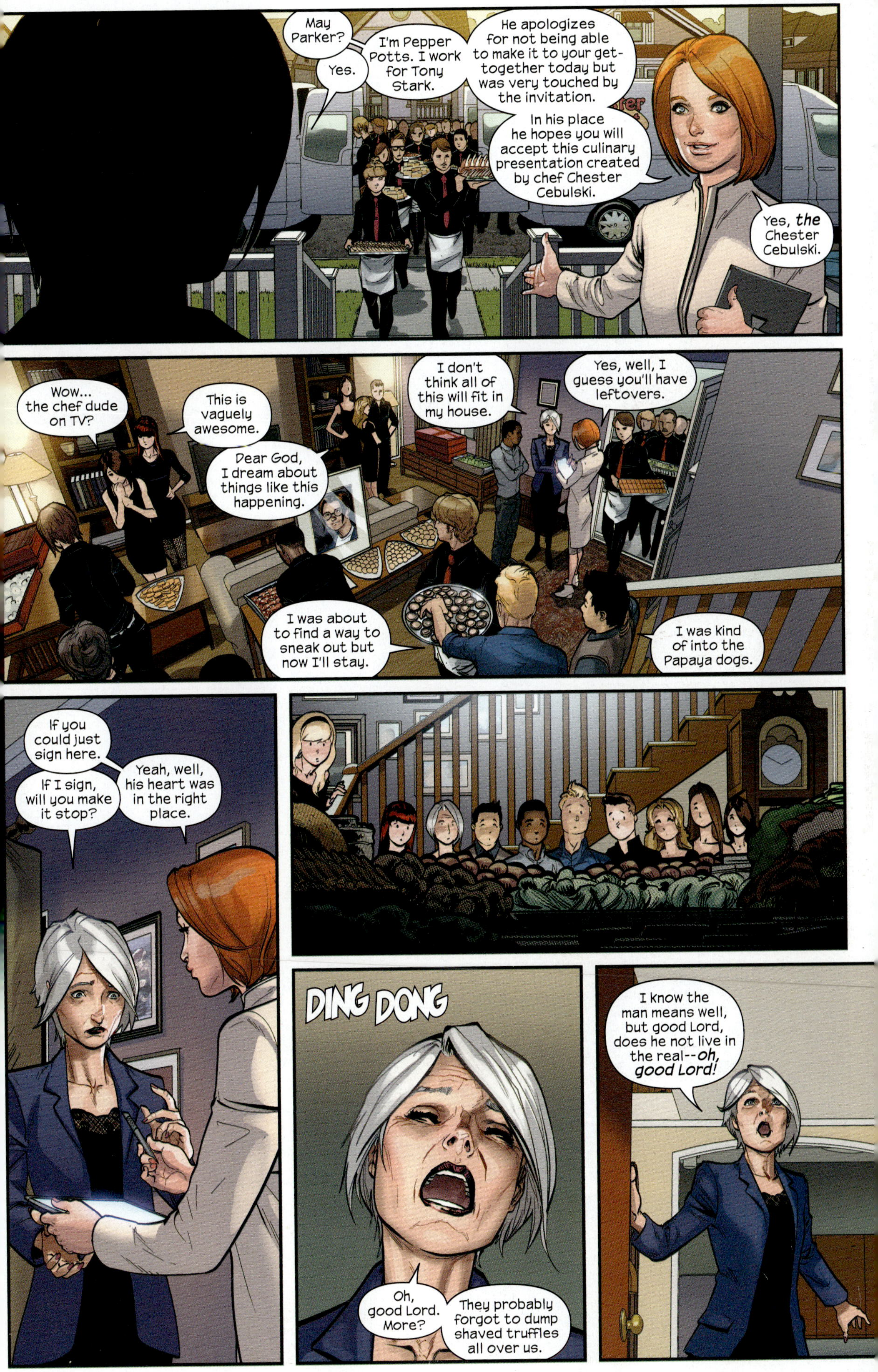
May Parker?
Yes.
I'm Pepper Potts. I work for Tony Stark.
He apologizes for not being able to make it to your get-together today but was very touched by the invitation.
In his place he hopes you will accept this culinary presentation created by chef Chester Cebulski.
Yes, the Chester Cebulski.
Wow... the chef dude on TV?
This is vaguely awesome.
Dear God, I dream about things like this happening.
I don't think all of this will fit in my house.
Yes, well, I guess you'll have leftovers.
I was about to find a way to sneak out but now I'll stay.
I was kind of into the Papaya dogs.
If you could just sign here.
If I sign, will you make it stop?
Yeah, well, his heart was in the right place.
DING DONG
Oh, good Lord. More?
They probably forgot to dump shaved truffles all over us.
I know the man means well, but good Lord, does he not live in the real--oh, good Lord!

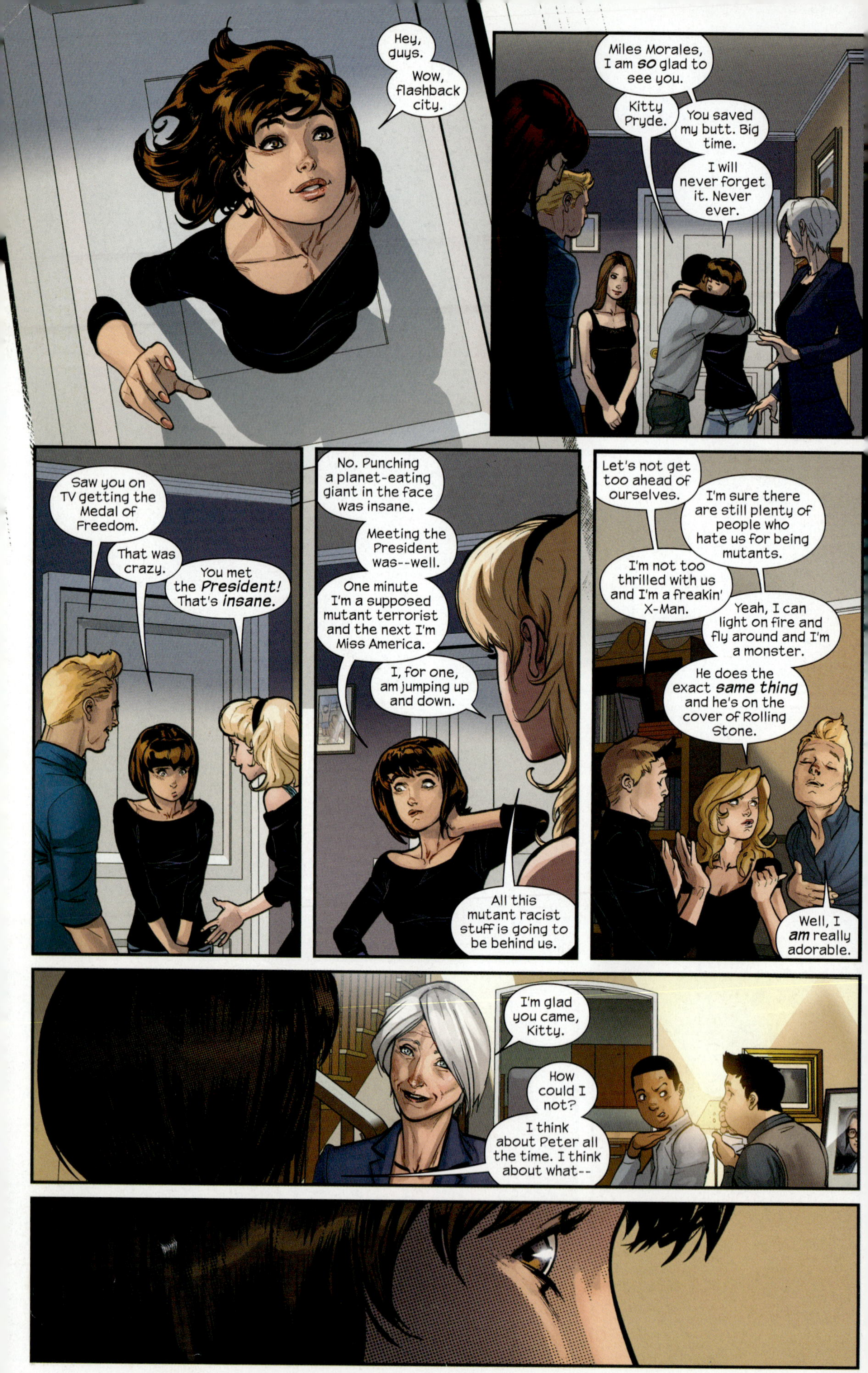
Hey, guys.
Wow, flashback city.
Miles Morales, I am *SO* glad to see you.
Kitty Pryde.
You saved my butt. Big time.
I will never forget it. Never ever.
Saw you on TV getting the Medal of Freedom.
That was crazy.
You met the *President!* That's *insane.*
No. Punching a planet-eating giant in the face was insane.
Meeting the President was--well.
One minute I'm a supposed mutant terrorist and the next I'm Miss America.
I, for one, am jumping up and down.
All this mutant racist stuff is going to be behind us.
Let's not get too ahead of ourselves.
I'm sure there are still plenty of people who hate us for being mutants.
I'm not too thrilled with us and I'm a freakin' X-Man.
Yeah, I can light on fire and fly around and I'm a monster.
He does the exact *same thing* and he's on the cover of Rolling Stone.
Well, I *am* really adorable.
I'm glad you came, Kitty.
How could I not?
I think about Peter all the time. I think about what--

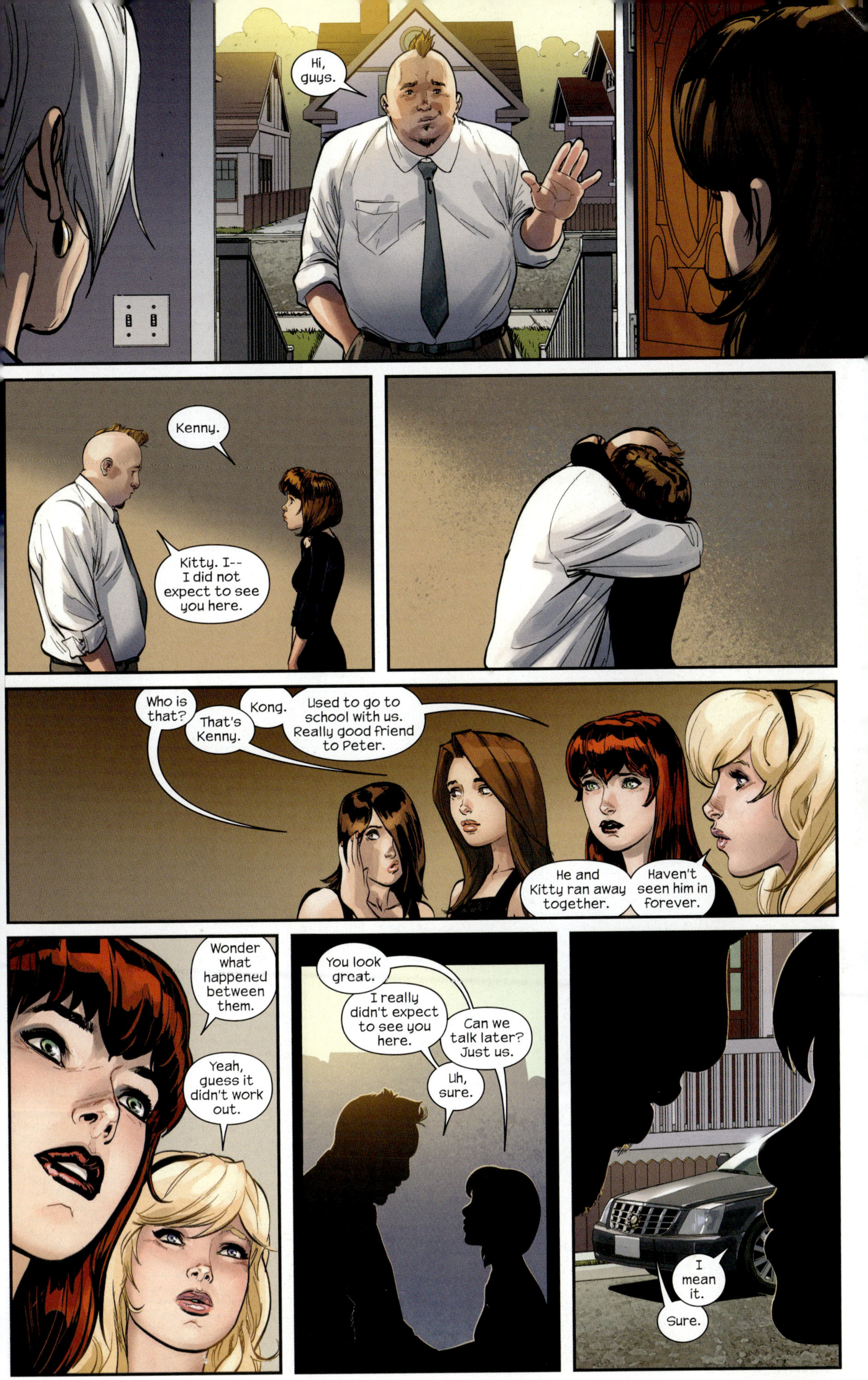
Hi, guys.
Kenny.
Kitty. I-- I did not expect to see you here.
Who is that?
That's Kenny.
Kong.
Used to go to school with us. Really good friend to Peter.
He and Kitty ran away together.
Haven't seen him in forever.
Wonder what happened between them.
Yeah, guess it didn't work out.
You look great.
I really didn't expect to see you here.
Can we talk later? Just us.
Uh, sure.
I mean it.
Sure.

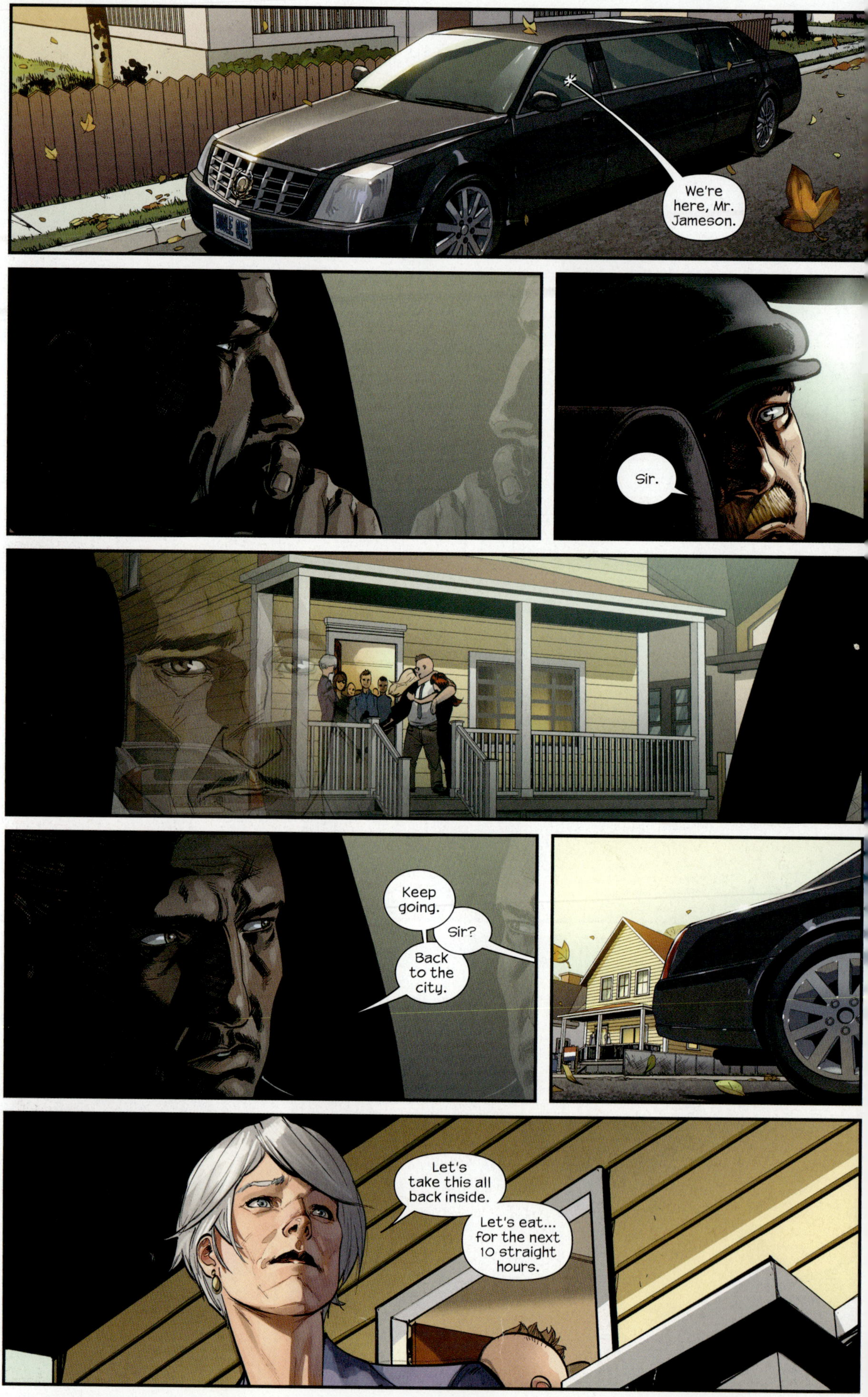

We're here, Mr. Jameson.
Sir.
Keep going.
Sir?
Back to the city.
Let's take this all back inside.
Let's eat... for the next 10 straight hours.

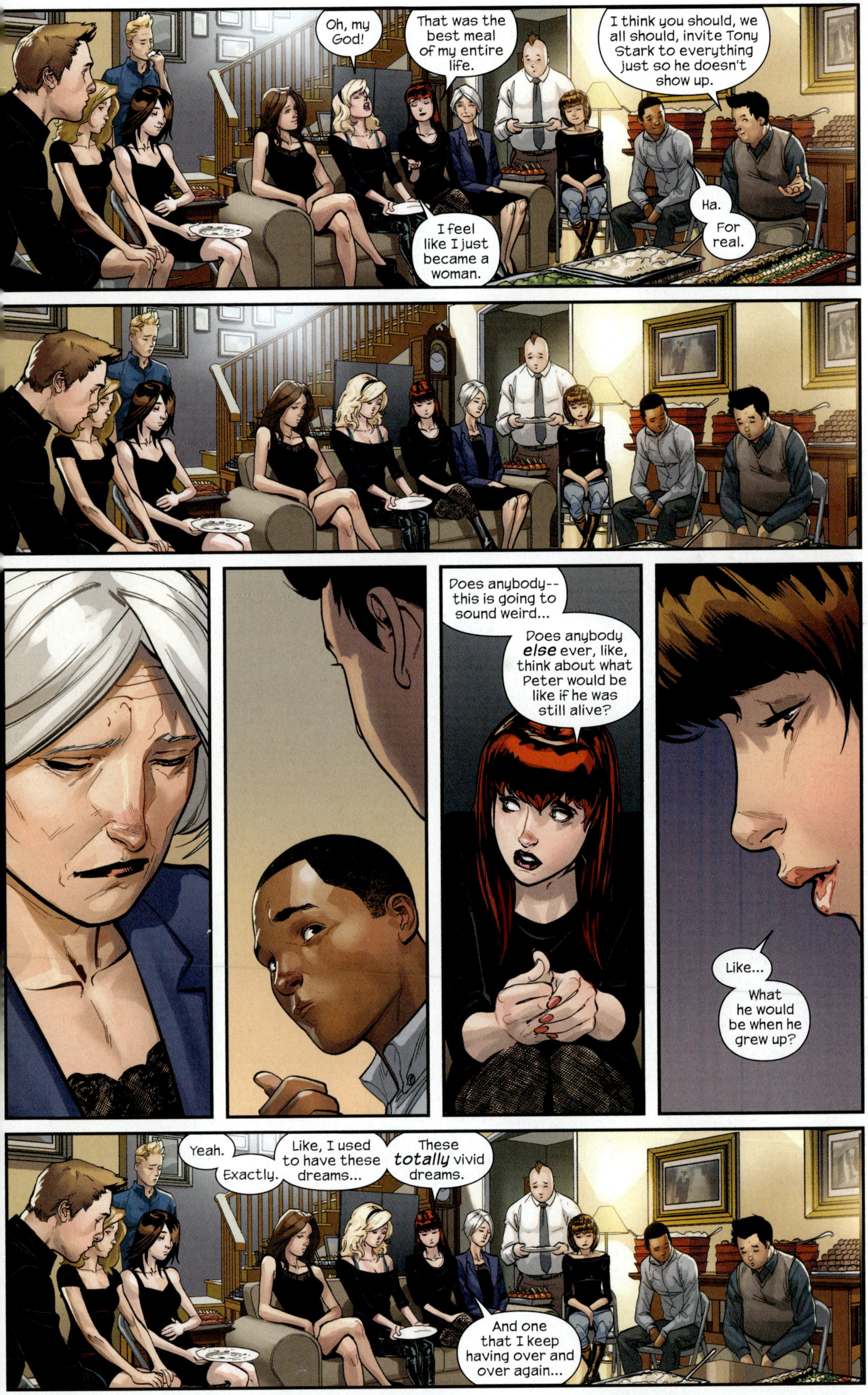
Oh, my God!
That was the best meal of my entire life.
I feel like I just became a woman.
I think you should, we all should, invite Tony Stark to everything just so he doesn't show up.
Ha.
For real.
Does anybody-- this is going to sound weird...
Does anybody *else* ever, like, think about what Peter would be like if he was still alive?
Like...
What he would be when he grew up?
Yeah.
Exactly.
Like, I used to have these dreams...
These *totally* vivid dreams.
And one that I keep having over and over again...

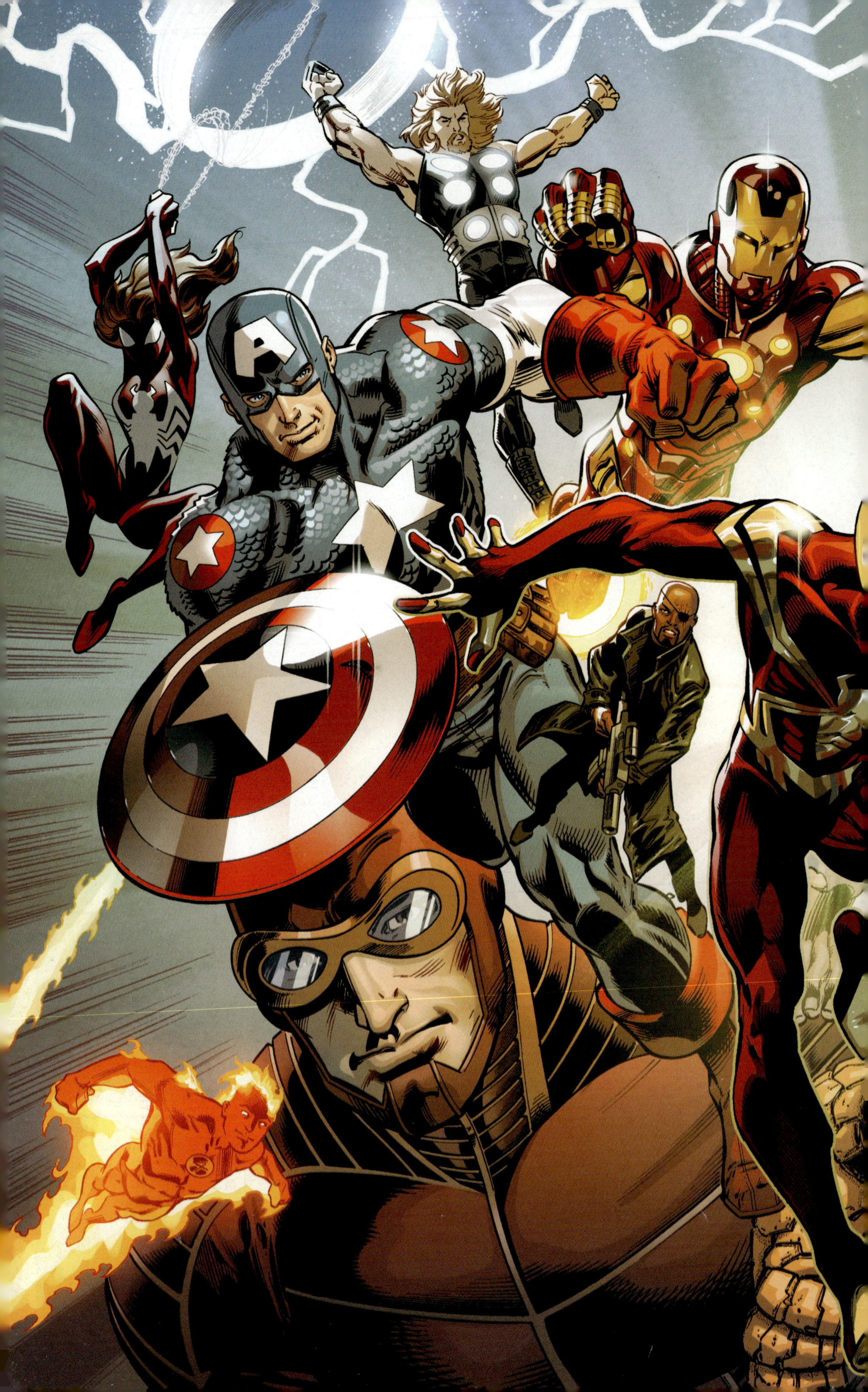

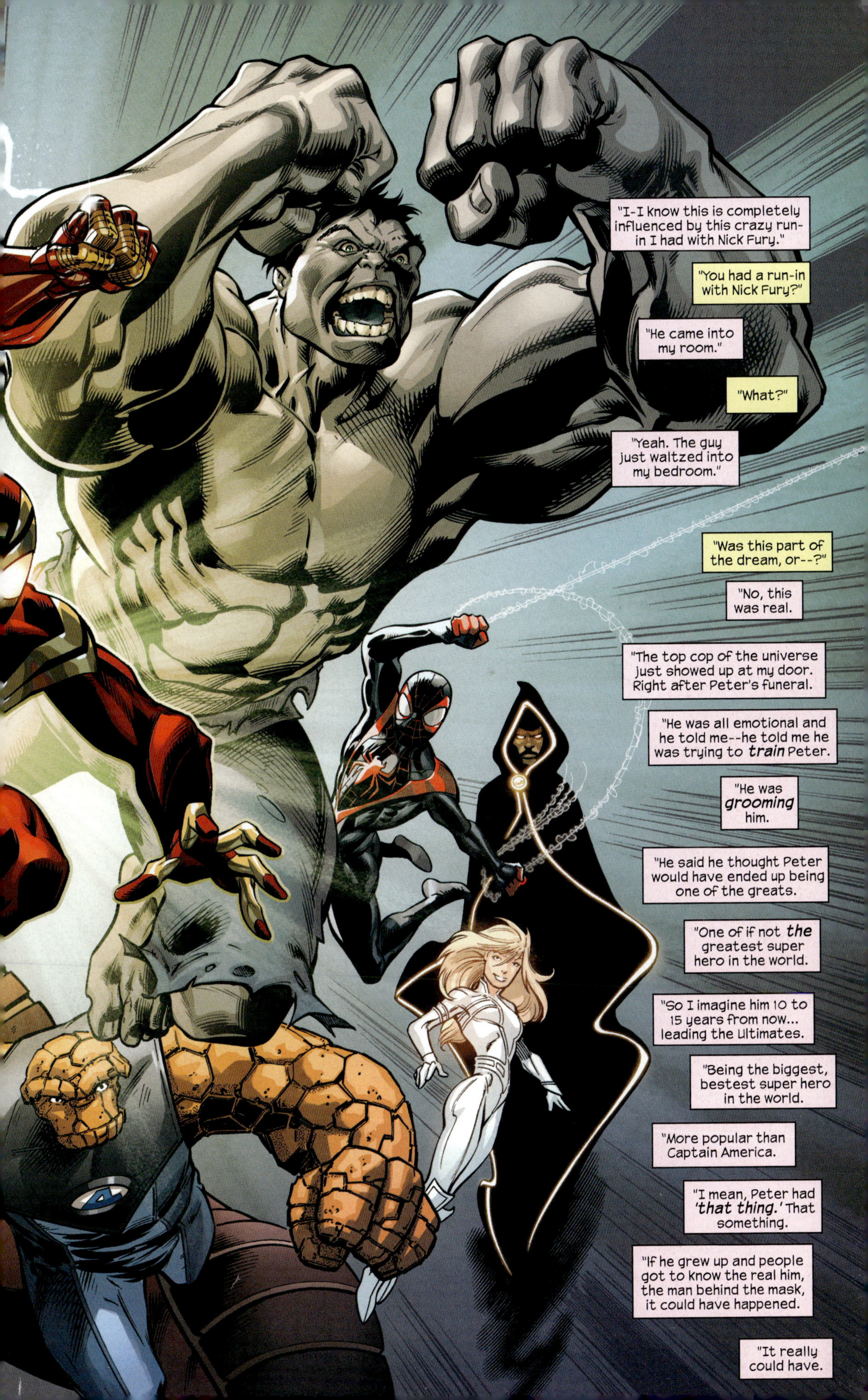
"I-I know this is completely influenced by this crazy run-in I had with Nick Fury."
"You had a run-in with Nick Fury?"
"He came into my room."
"What?"
"Yeah. The guy just waltzed into my bedroom."
"Was this part of the dream, or--?"
"No, this was real.
"The top cop of the universe just showed up at my door. Right after Peter's funeral.
"He was all emotional and he told me--he told me he was trying to *train* Peter.
"He was *grooming* him.
"He said he thought Peter would have ended up being one of the greats.
"One of if not *the* greatest super hero in the world.
"So I imagine him 10 to 15 years from now... leading the Ultimates.
"Being the biggest, bestest super hero in the world.
"More popular than Captain America.
"I mean, Peter had *'that thing.'* That something.
"If he grew up and people got to know the real him, the man behind the mask, it could have happened.
"It really could have.

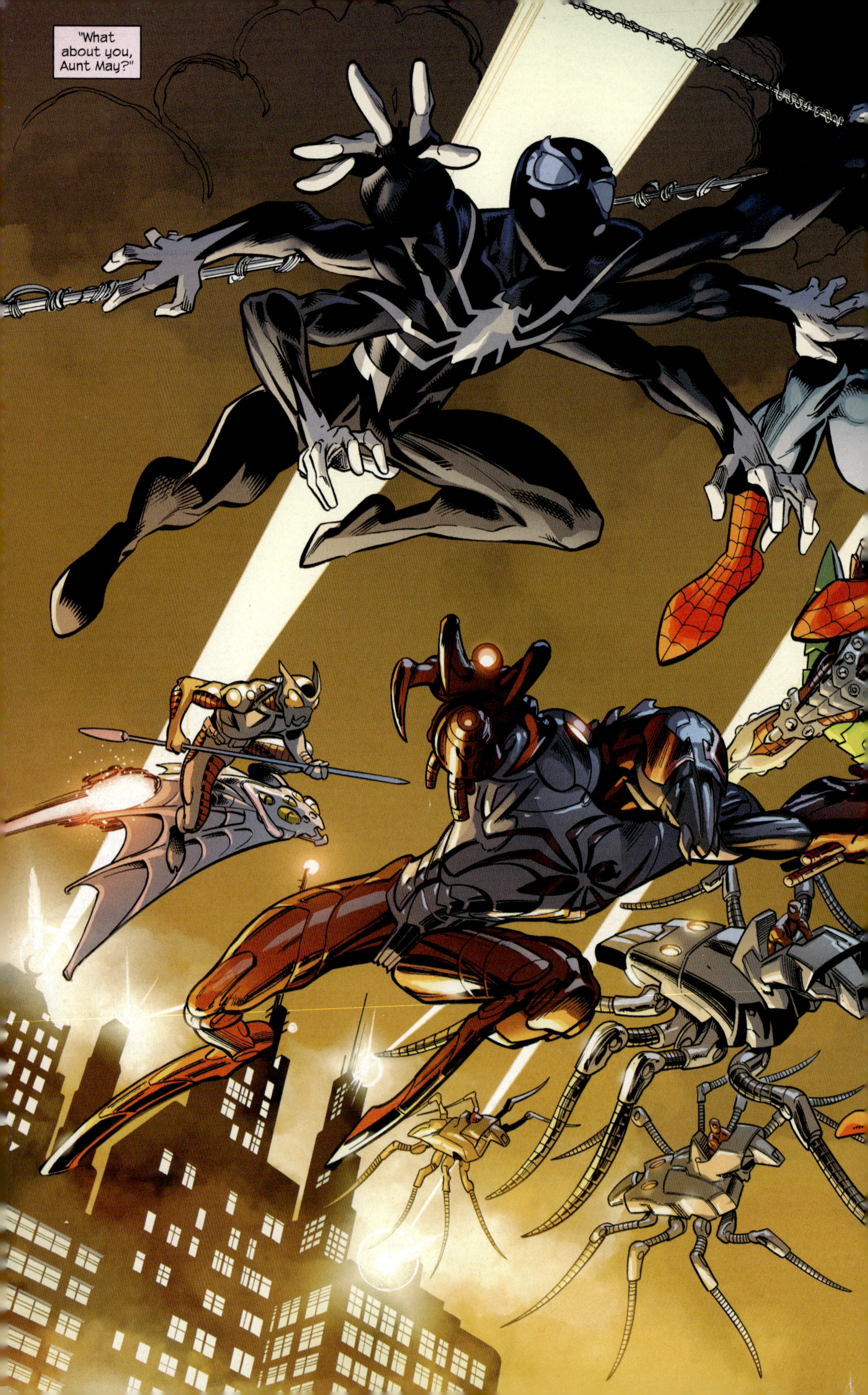
"What about you, Aunt May?"

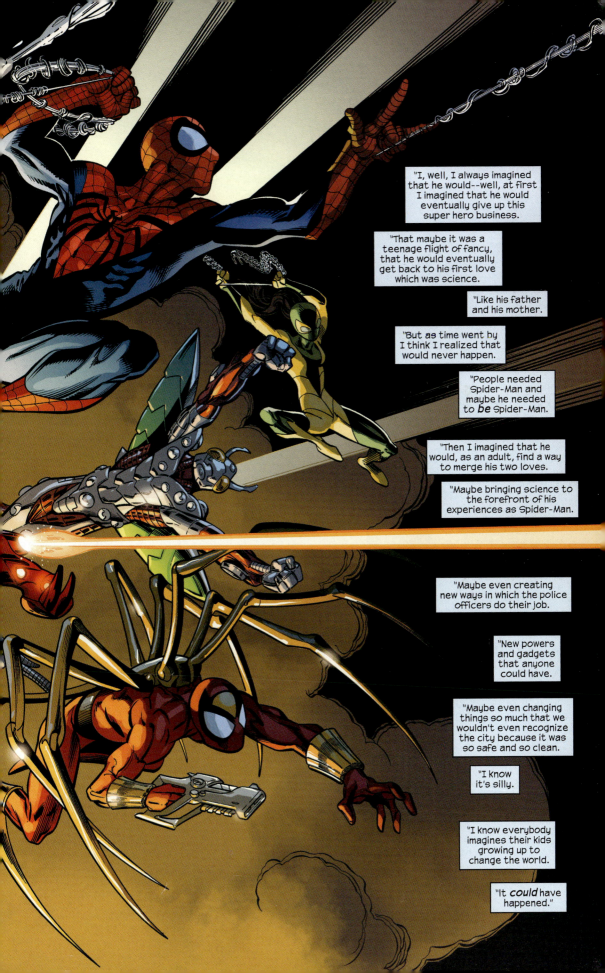

"I, well, I always imagined that he would--well, at first I imagined that he would eventually give up this super hero business.

"That maybe it was a teenage flight of fancy, that he would eventually get back to his first love which was science.

"Like his father and his mother.

"But as time went by I think I realized that would never happen.

"People needed Spider-Man and maybe he needed to *be* Spider-Man.

"Then I imagined that he would, as an adult, find a way to merge his two loves.

"Maybe bringing science to the forefront of his experiences as Spider-Man.

"Maybe even creating new ways in which the police officers do their job.

"New powers and gadgets that anyone could have.

"Maybe even changing things so much that we wouldn't even recognize the city because it was so safe and so clean.

"I know it's silly.

"I know everybody imagines their kids growing up to change the world.

"It *could* have happened."

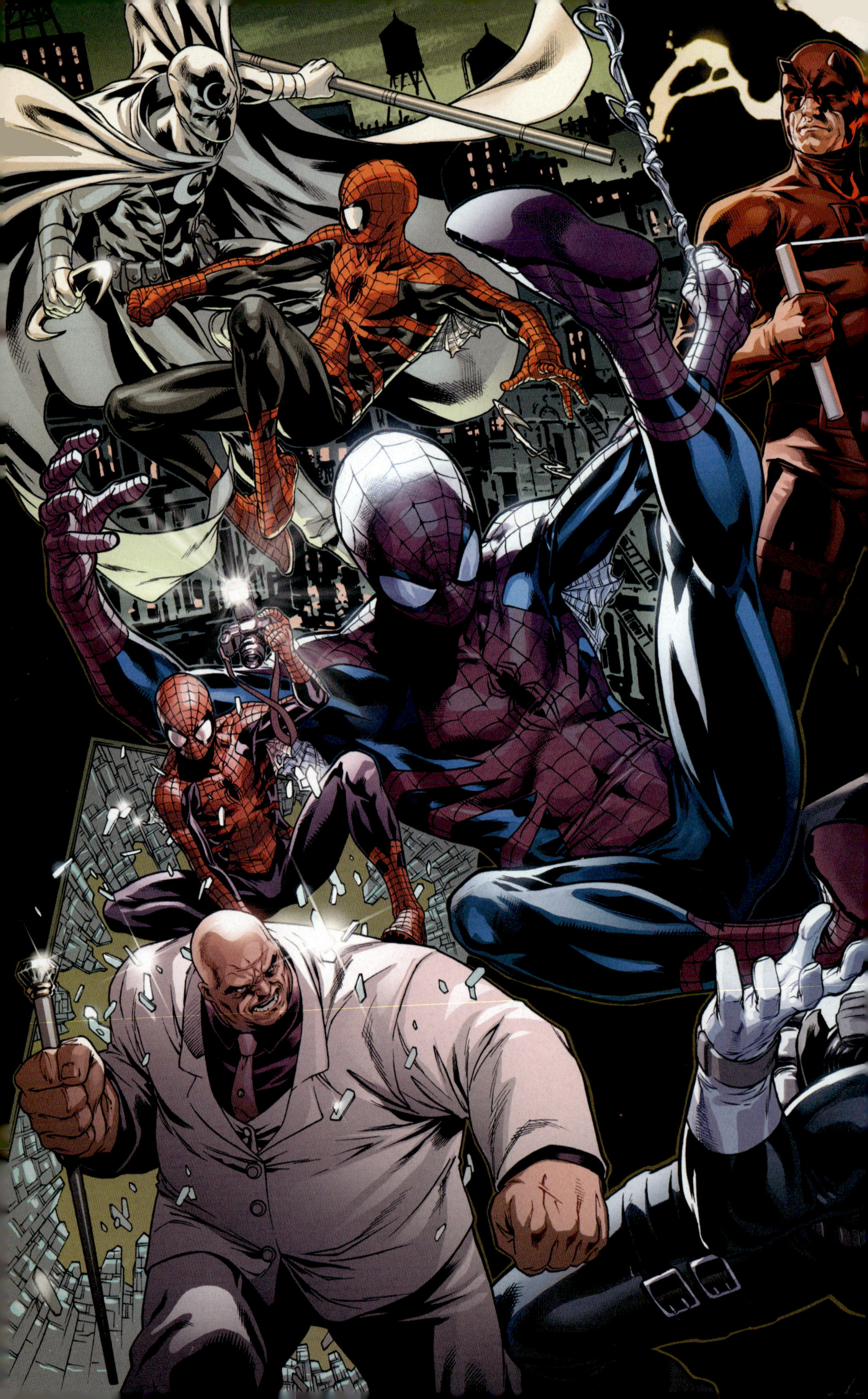

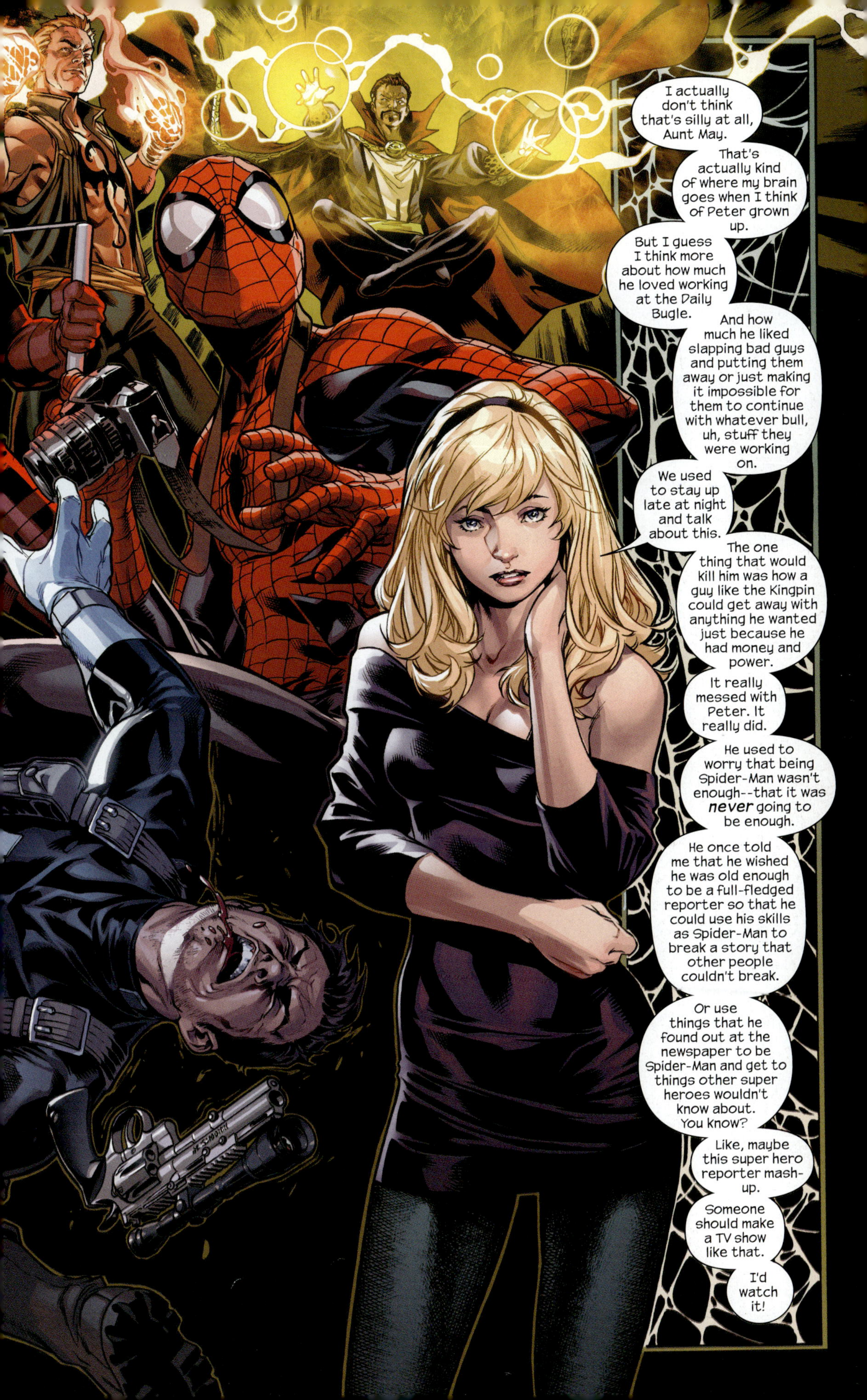
I actually don't think that's silly at all, Aunt May.
That's actually kind of where my brain goes when I think of Peter grown up.
But I guess I think more about how much he loved working at the Daily Bugle.
And how much he liked slapping bad guys and putting them away or just making it impossible for them to continue with whatever bull, uh, stuff they were working on.
We used to stay up late at night and talk about this.
The one thing that would kill him was how a guy like the Kingpin could get away with anything he wanted just because he had money and power.
It really messed with Peter. It really did.
He used to worry that being Spider-Man wasn't enough--that it was *never* going to be enough.
He once told me that he wished he was old enough to be a full-fledged reporter so that he could use his skills as Spider-Man to break a story that other people couldn't break.
Or use things that he found out at the newspaper to be Spider-Man and get to things other super heroes wouldn't know about. You know?
Like, maybe this super hero reporter mash-up.
Someone should make a TV show like that.
I'd watch it!

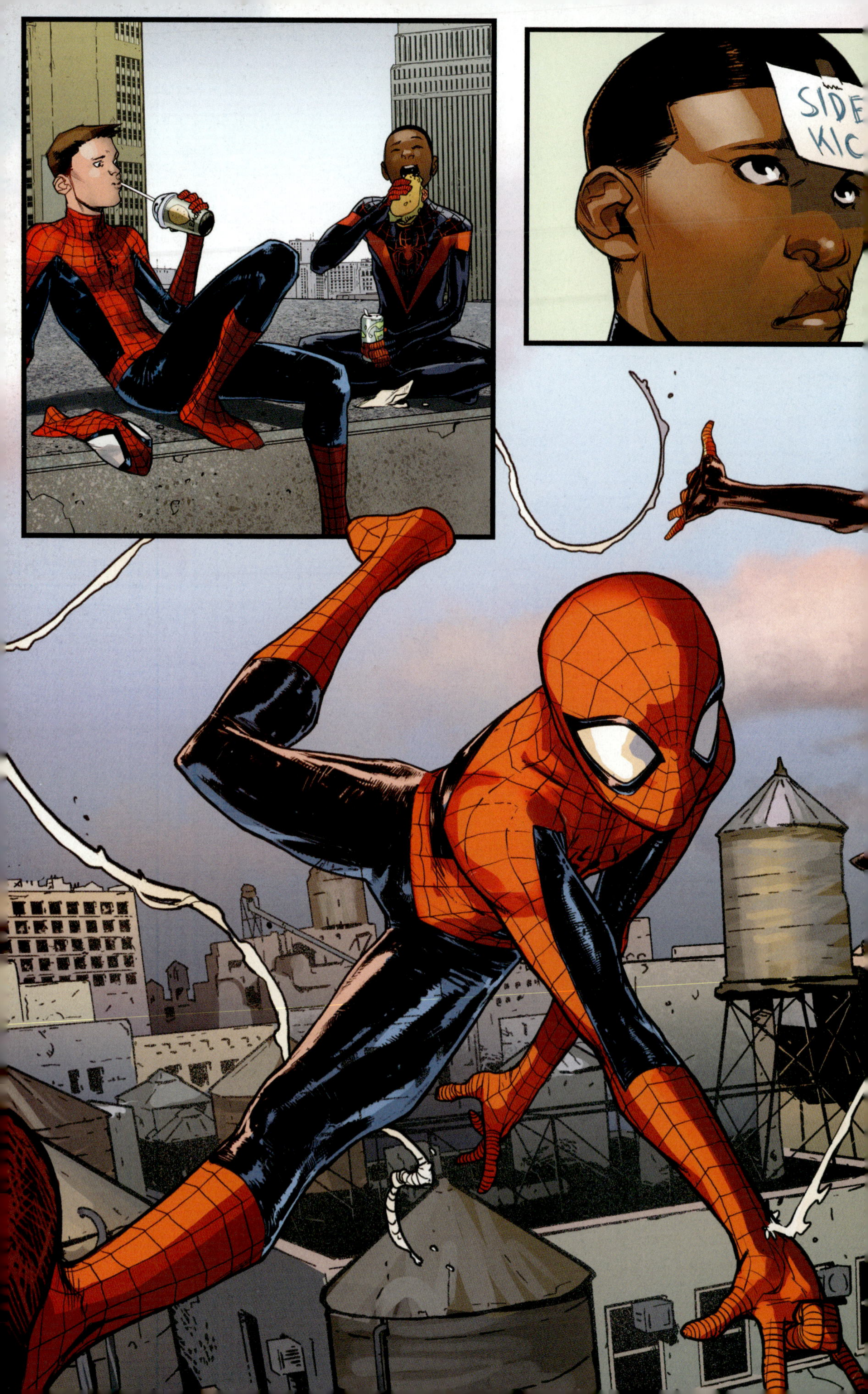
SIDE
KIC

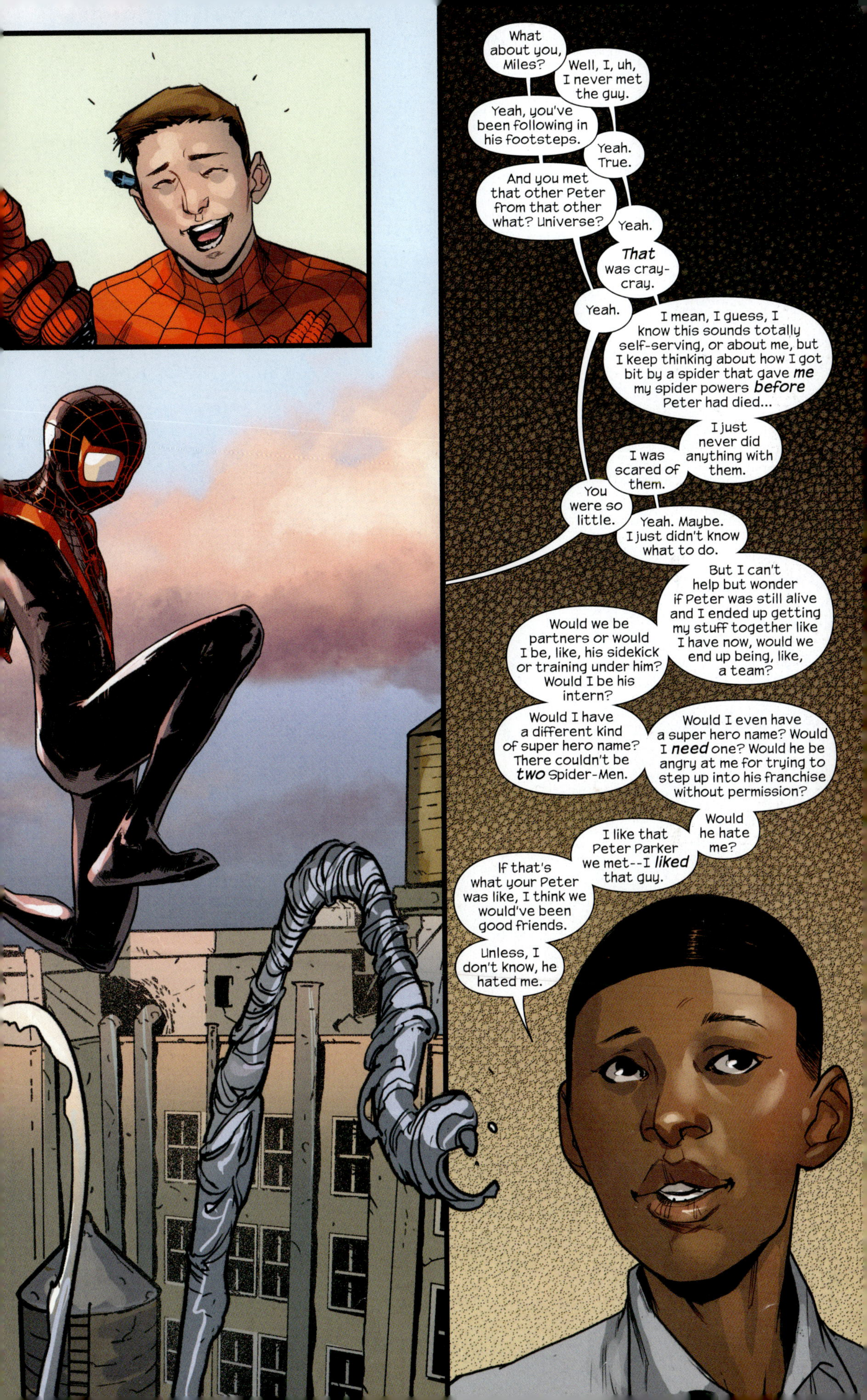
What about you, Miles?
Well, I, uh, I never met the guy.
Yeah, you've been following in his footsteps.
Yeah. True.
And you met that other Peter from that other what? Universe?
Yeah.
That was cray-cray.
Yeah.
I mean, I guess, I know this sounds totally self-serving, or about me, but I keep thinking about how I got bit by a spider that gave me my spider powers before Peter had died...
I just never did anything with them.
I was scared of them.
You were so little.
Yeah. Maybe. I just didn't know what to do.
But I can't help but wonder if Peter was still alive and I ended up getting my stuff together like I have now, would we end up being, like, a team?
Would we be partners or would I be, like, his sidekick or training under him? Would I be his intern?
Would I have a different kind of super hero name? There couldn't be two Spider-Men.
Would I even have a super hero name? Would I need one? Would he be angry at me for trying to step up into his franchise without permission?
Would he hate me?
I like that Peter Parker we met--I liked that guy.
If that's what your Peter was like, I think we would've been good friends.
Unless, I don't know, he hated me.

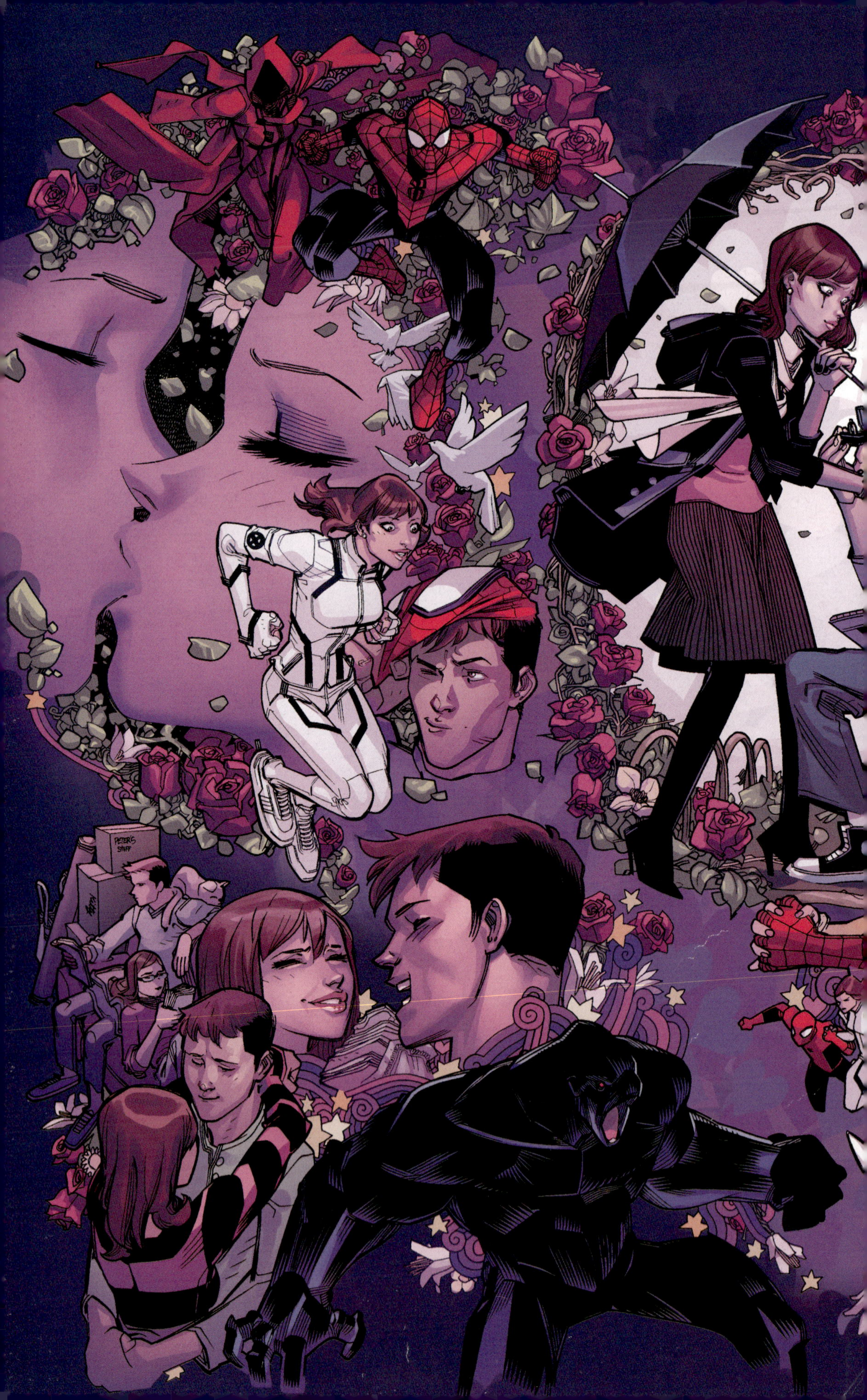
PETER'S STUFF

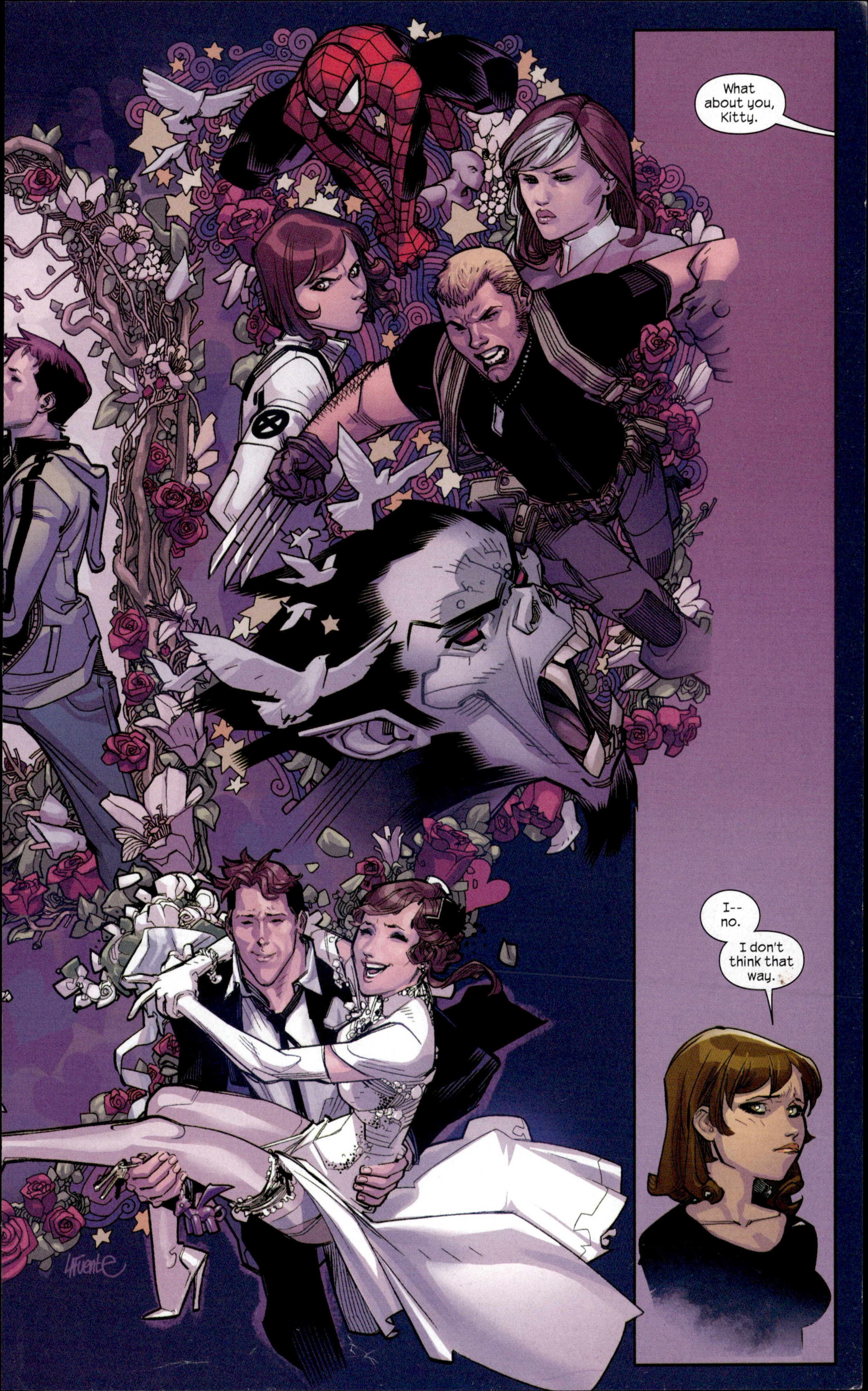

What about you, Kitty.
I-- no.
I don't think that way.

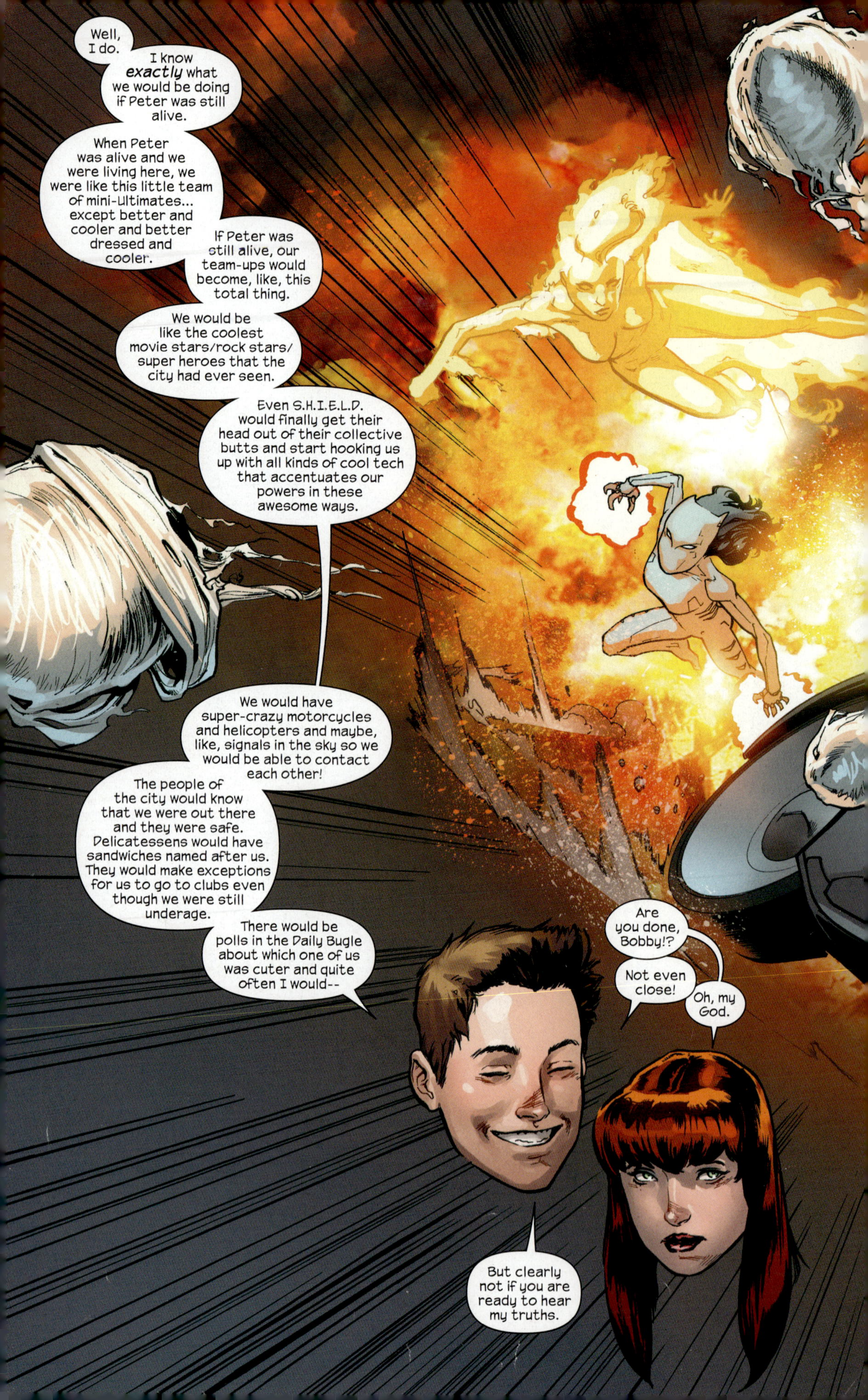
Well, I do.
I know *exactly* what we would be doing if Peter was still alive.
When Peter was alive and we were living here, we were like this little team of mini-Ultimates... except better and cooler and better dressed and cooler.
If Peter was still alive, our team-ups would become, like, this total thing.
We would be like the coolest movie stars/rock stars/ super heroes that the city had ever seen.
Even S.H.I.E.L.D. would finally get their head out of their collective butts and start hooking us up with all kinds of cool tech that accentuates our powers in these awesome ways.
We would have super-crazy motorcycles and helicopters and maybe, like, signals in the sky so we would be able to contact each other!
The people of the city would know that we were out there and they were safe. Delicatessens would have sandwiches named after us. They would make exceptions for us to go to clubs even though we were still underage.
There would be polls in the Daily Bugle about which one of us was cuter and quite often I would--
Are you done, Bobby!?
Not even close!
Oh, my God.
But clearly not if you are ready to hear my truths.

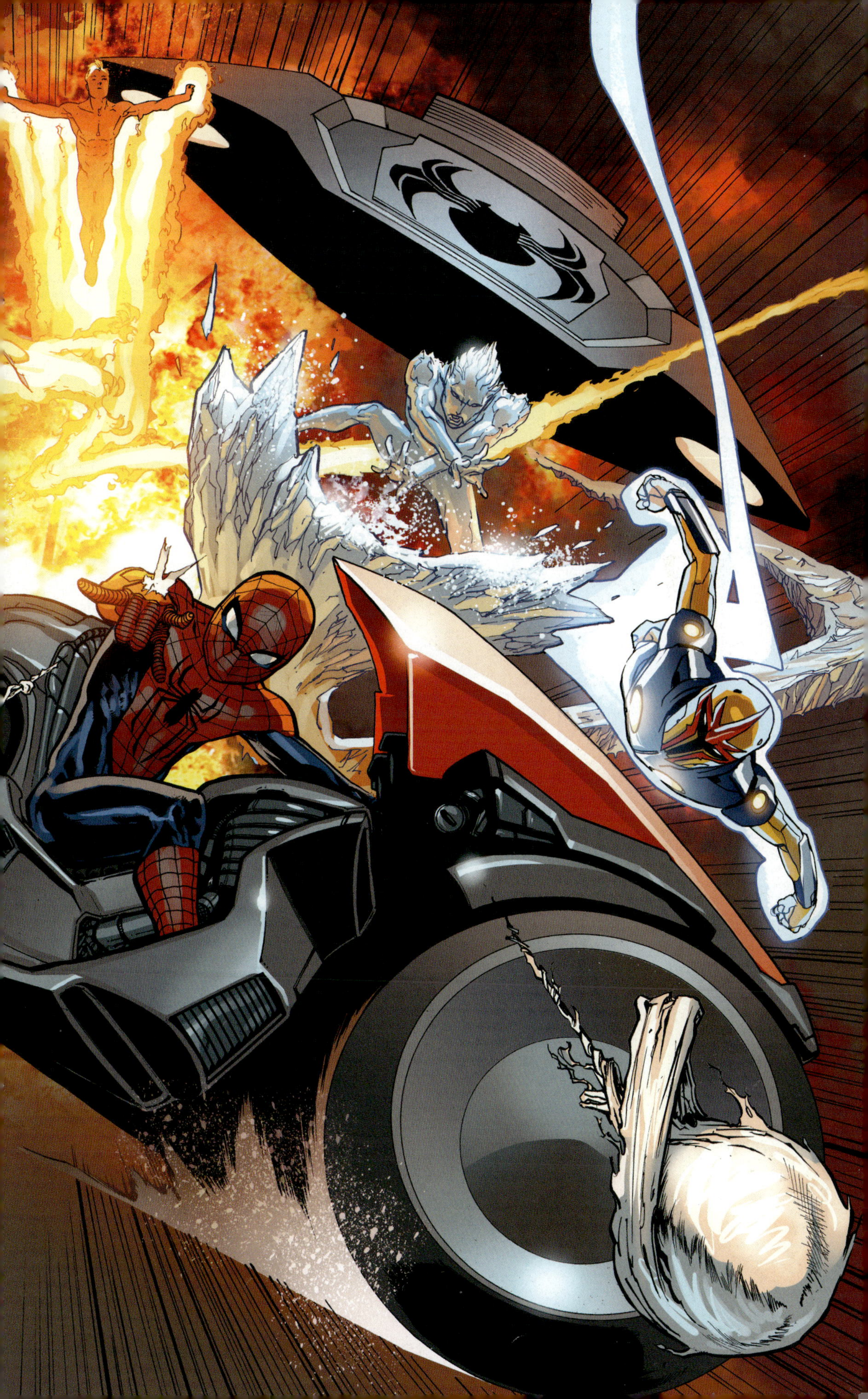

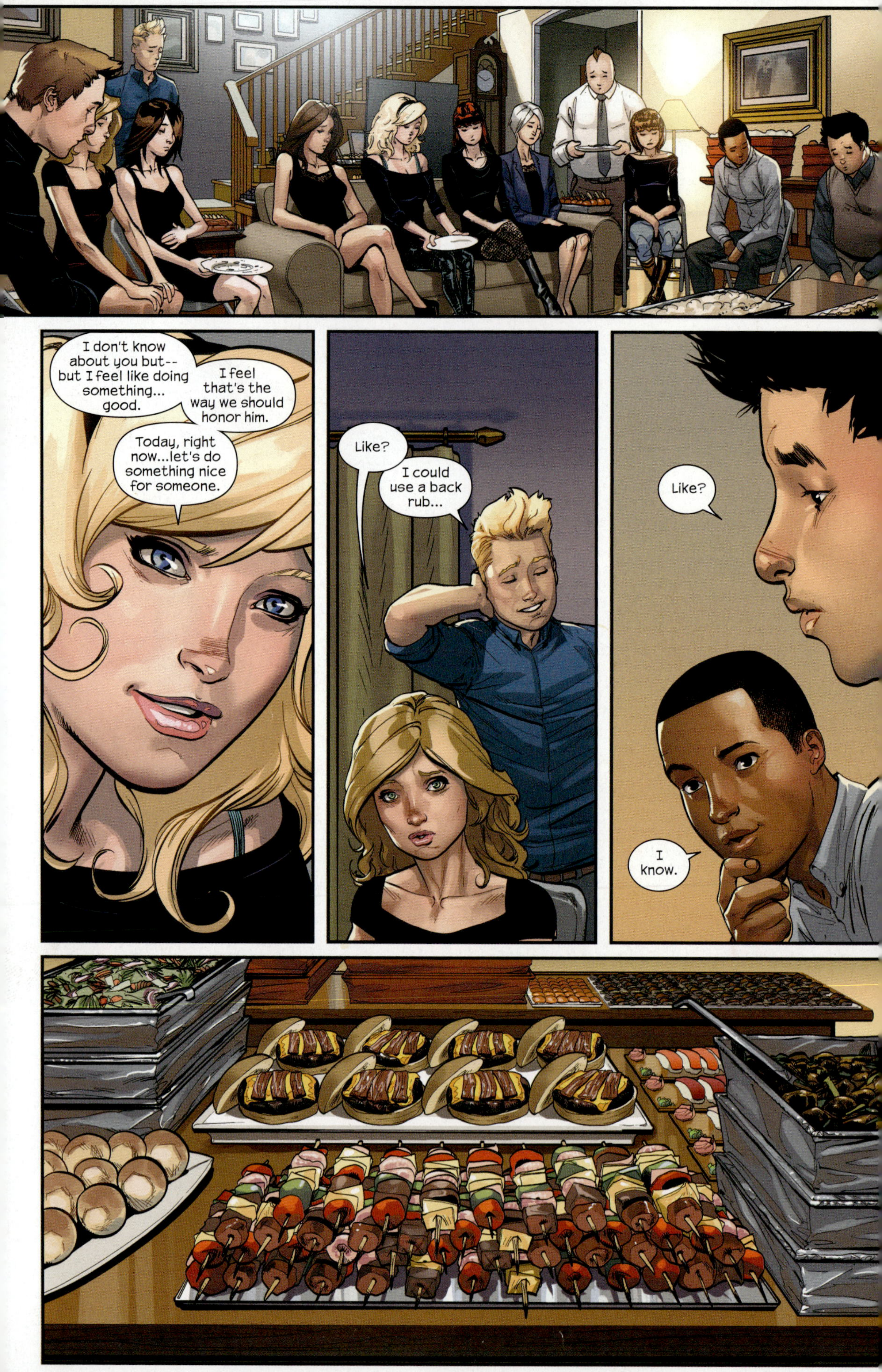
I don't know about you but-- but I feel like doing something... good.
I feel that's the way we should honor him.
Today, right now...let's do something nice for someone.
Like?
I could use a back rub...
Like?
I know.

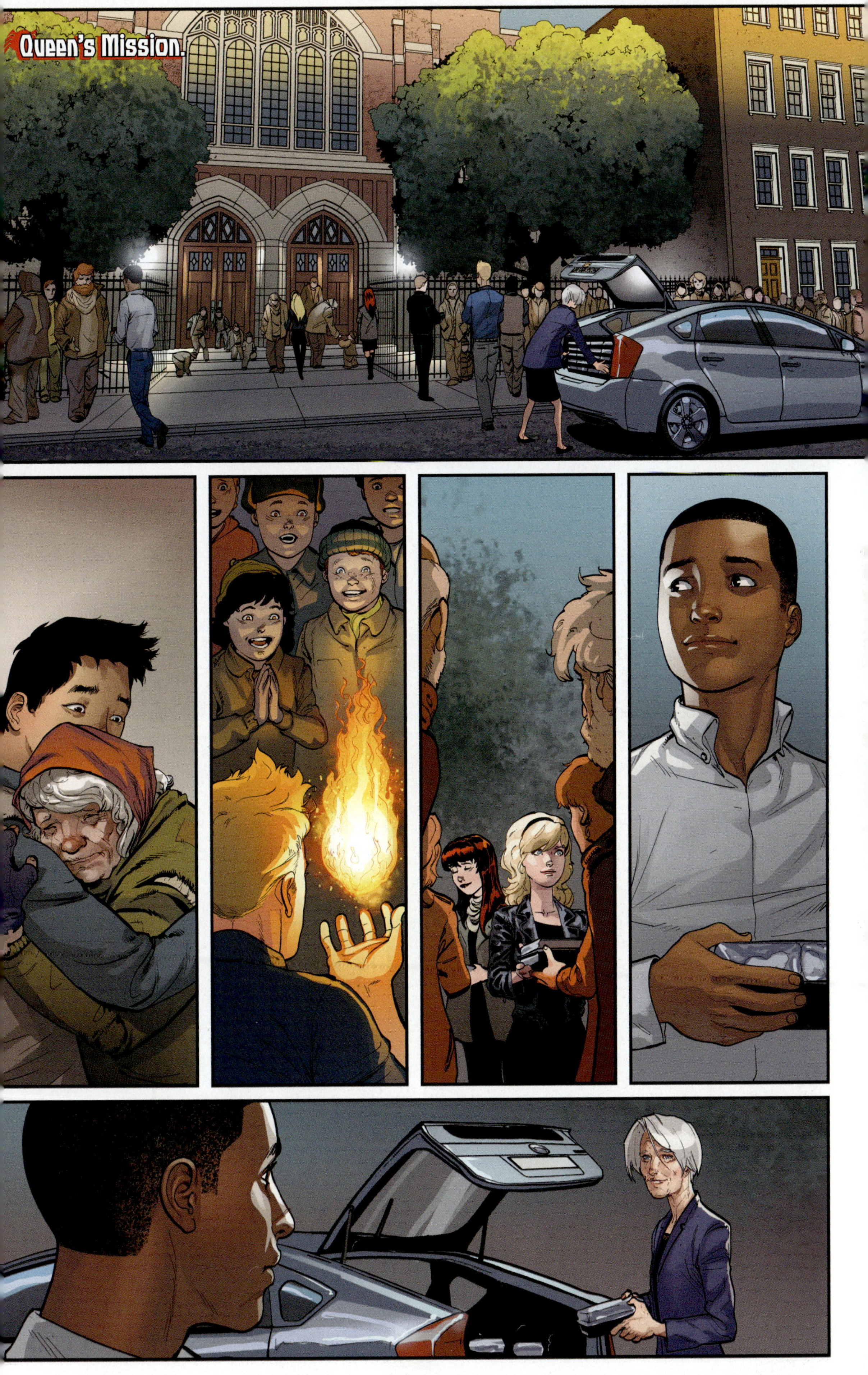
Queen's Mission.

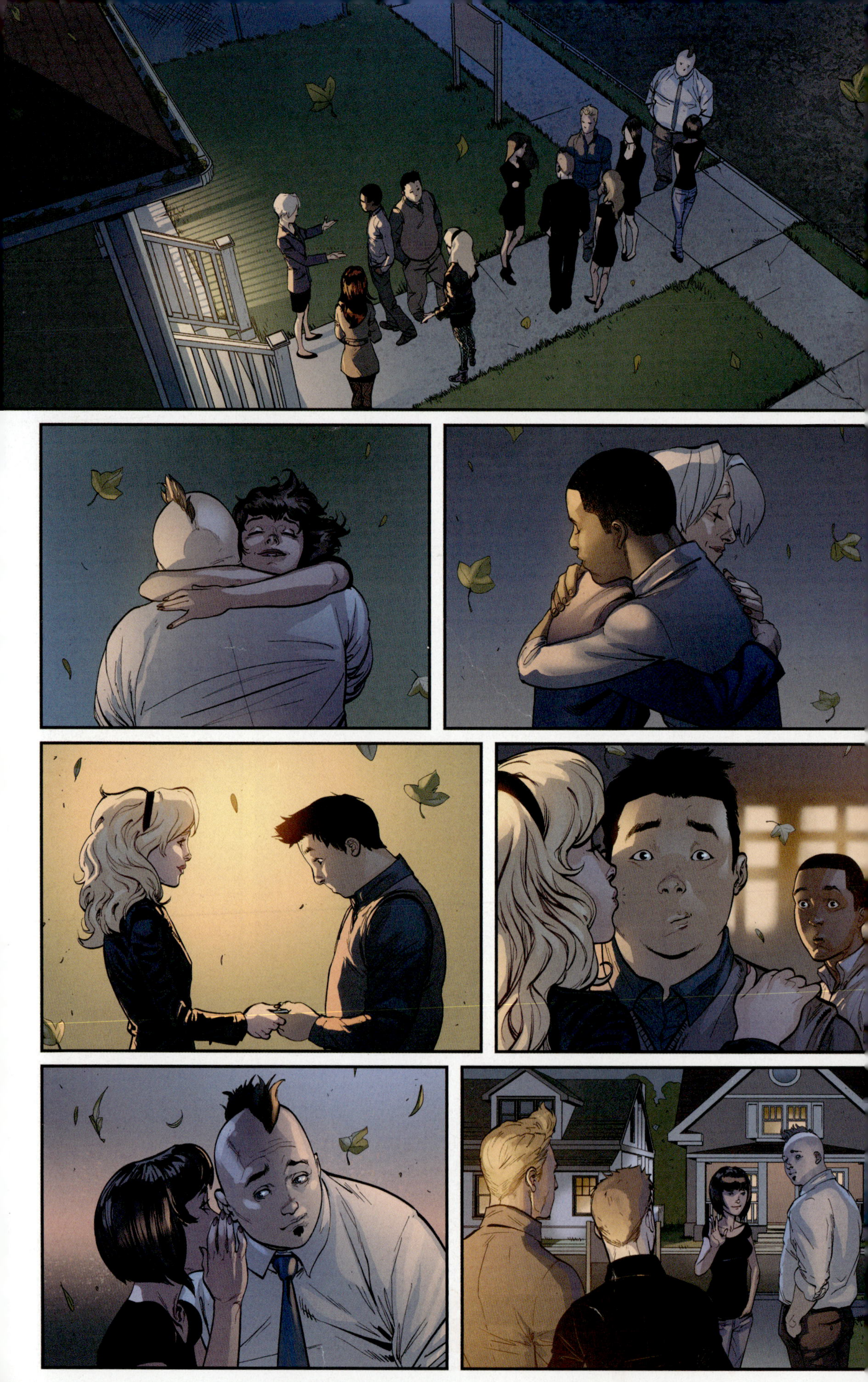

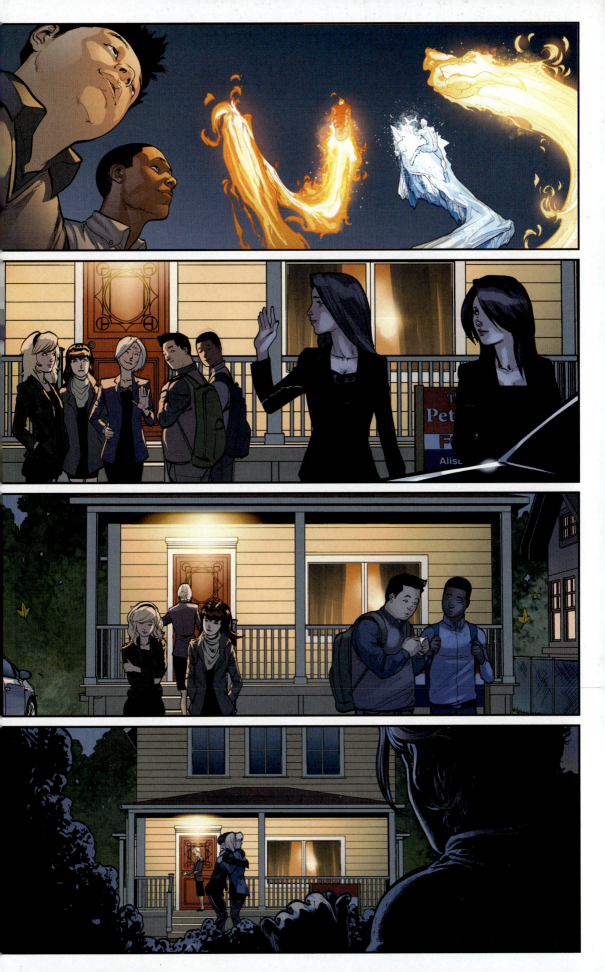

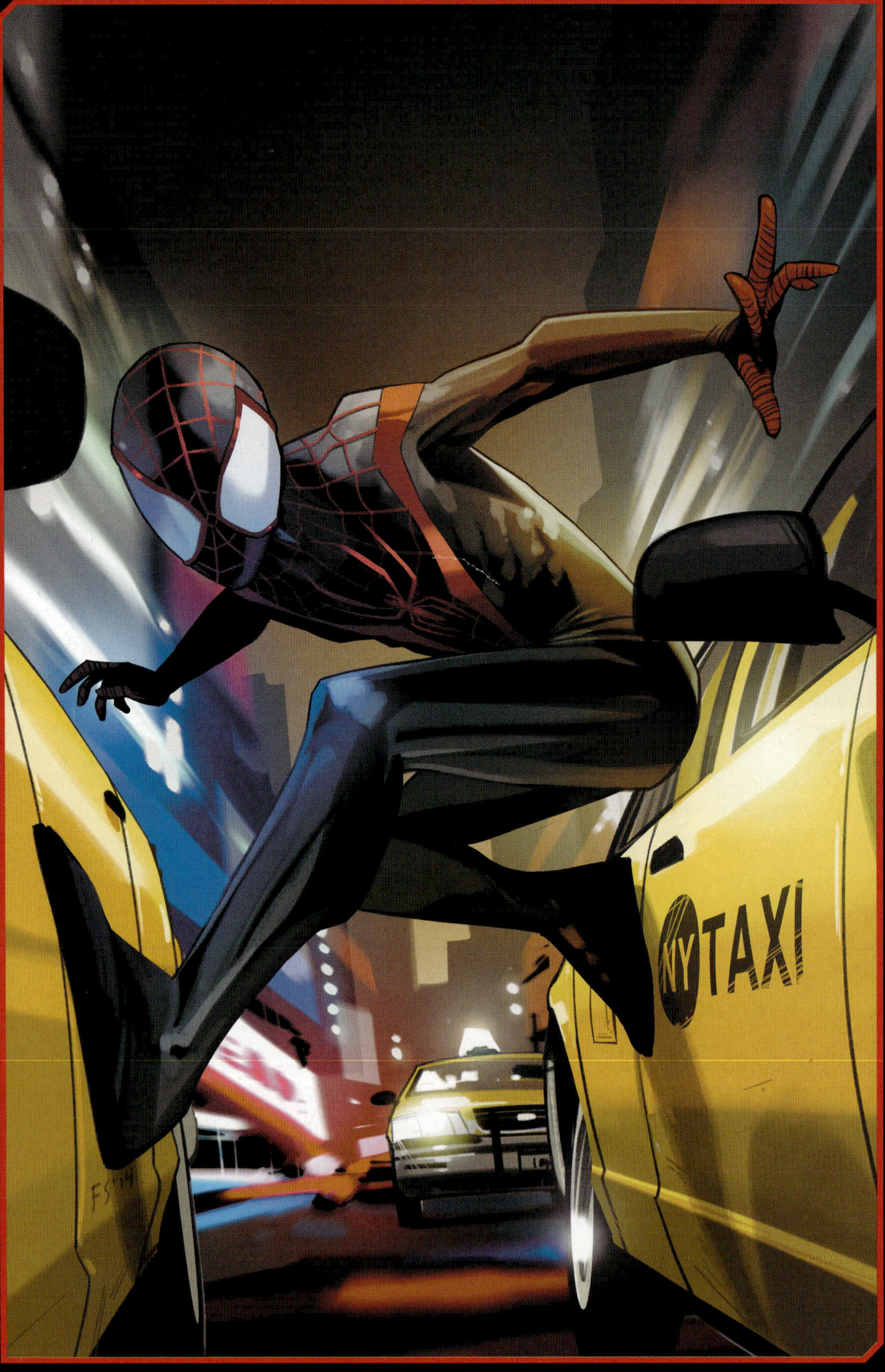
NY TAXI
FS'14

MILES MORALES: ULTIMATE SPIDER-MAN #1 VARIANT BY FIONA STAPLES

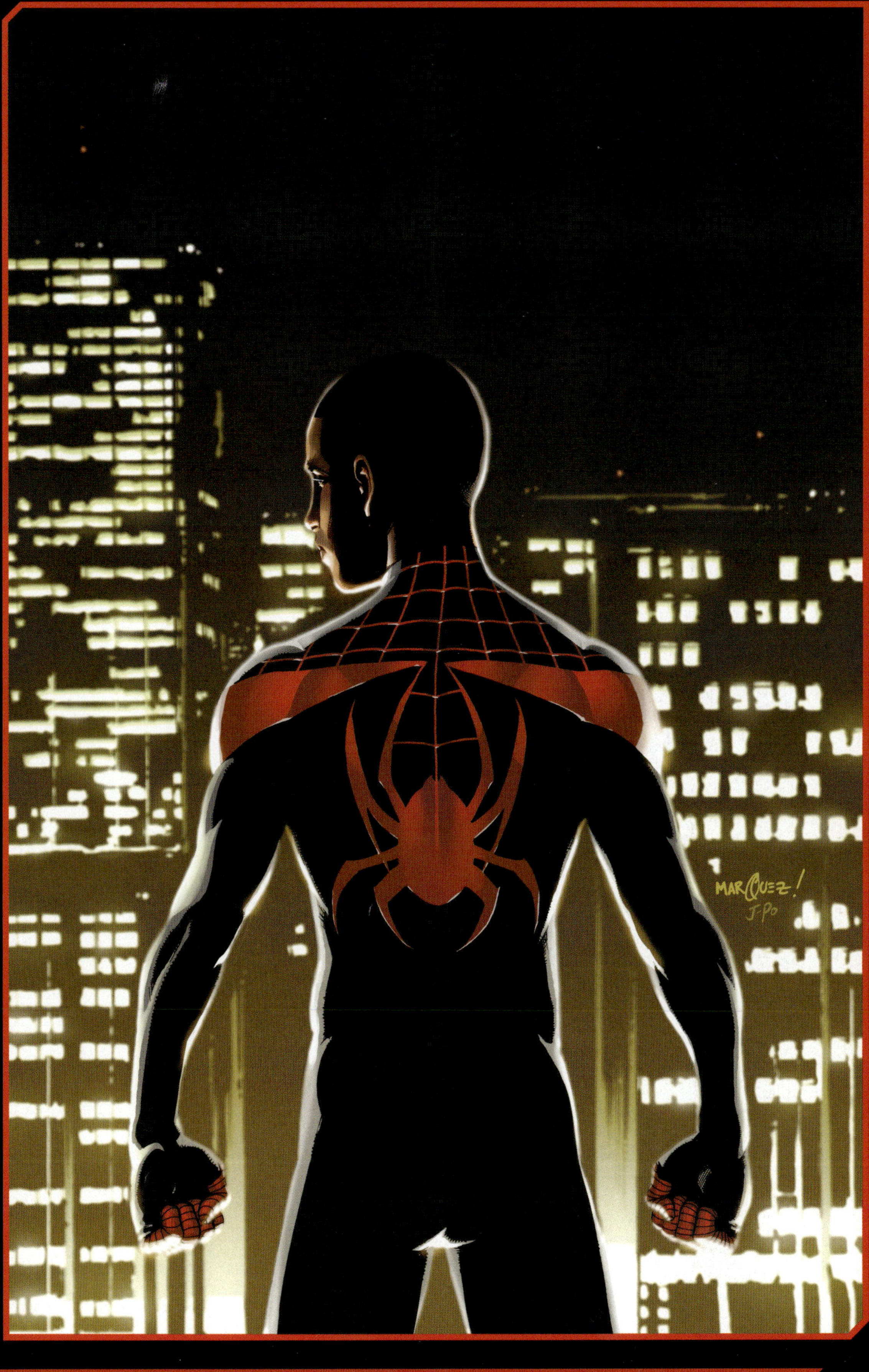
MARQUEZ!
J-Po

MILES MORALES: ULTIMATE SPIDER-MAN #1

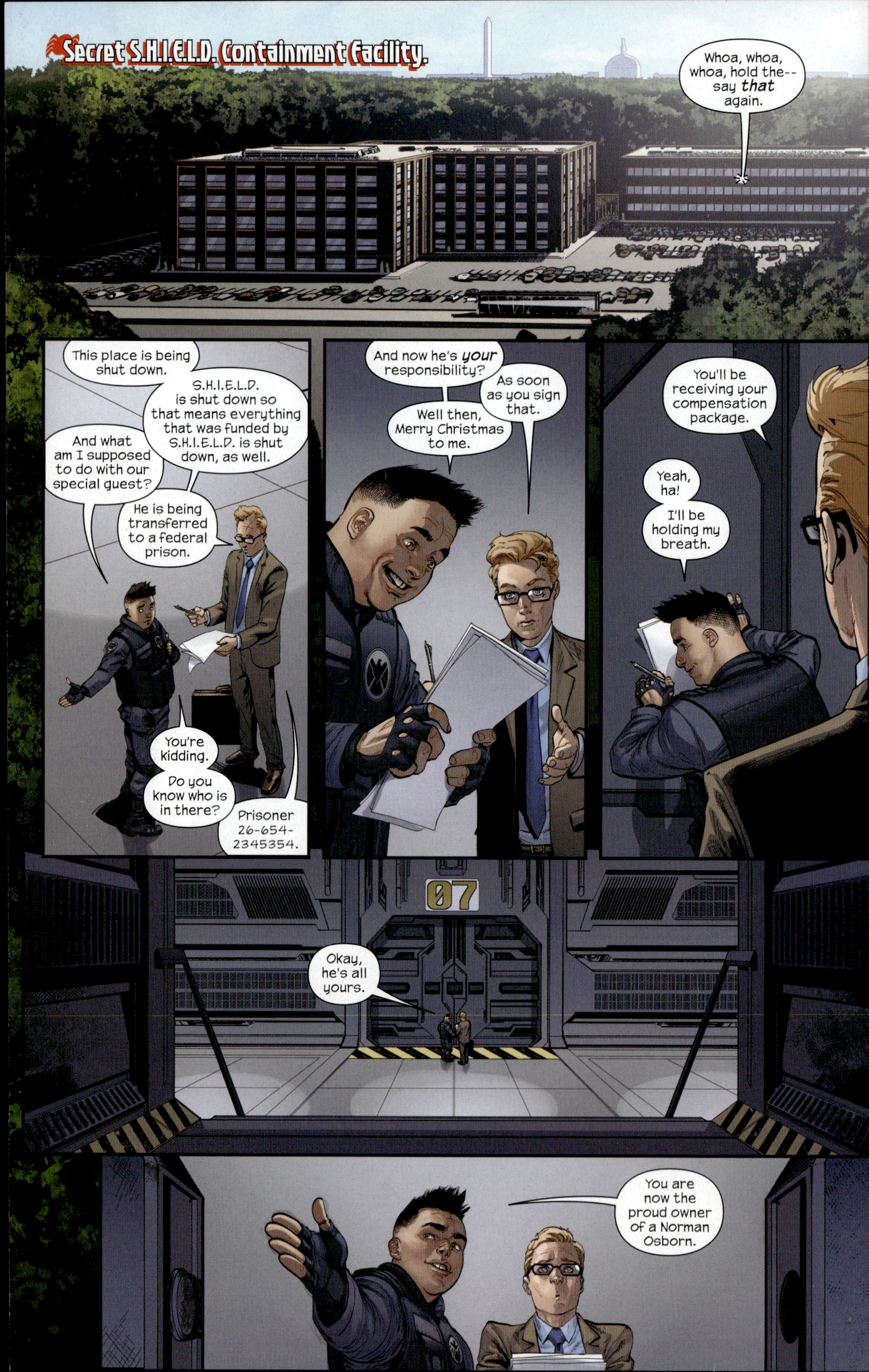
Secret S.H.I.E.L.D. Containment Facility.
Whoa, whoa, whoa, hold the-- say *that* again.
This place is being shut down.
S.H.I.E.L.D. is shut down so that means everything that was funded by S.H.I.E.L.D. is shut down, as well.
And what am I supposed to do with our special guest?
He is being transferred to a federal prison.
You're kidding.
Do you know who is in there?
Prisoner 26-654-2345354.
And now he's *your* responsibility?
Well then, Merry Christmas to me.
As soon as you sign that.
You'll be receiving your compensation package.
Yeah, ha!
I'll be holding my breath.
07
Okay, he's all yours.
You are now the proud owner of a Norman Osborn.

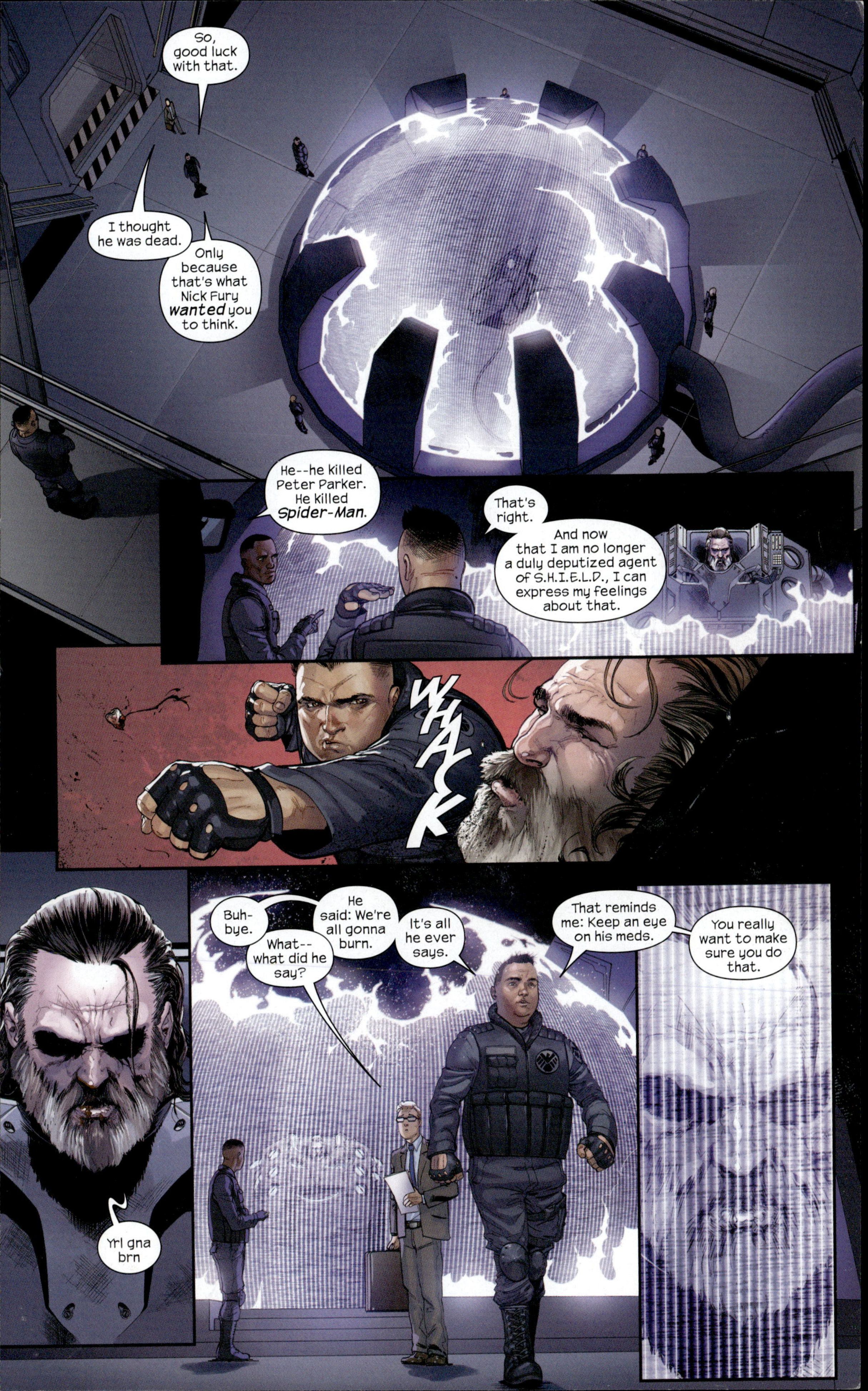
So, good luck with that.
I thought he was dead.
Only because that's what Nick Fury *wanted* you to think.
He--he killed Peter Parker. He killed *Spider-Man*.
That's right.
And now that I am no longer a duly deputized agent of S.H.I.E.L.D., I can express my feelings about that.
WHACK
Yrl gna brn
Buh-bye.
What--what did he say?
He said: We're all gonna burn.
It's all he ever says.
That reminds me: Keep an eye on his meds.
You really want to make sure you do that.

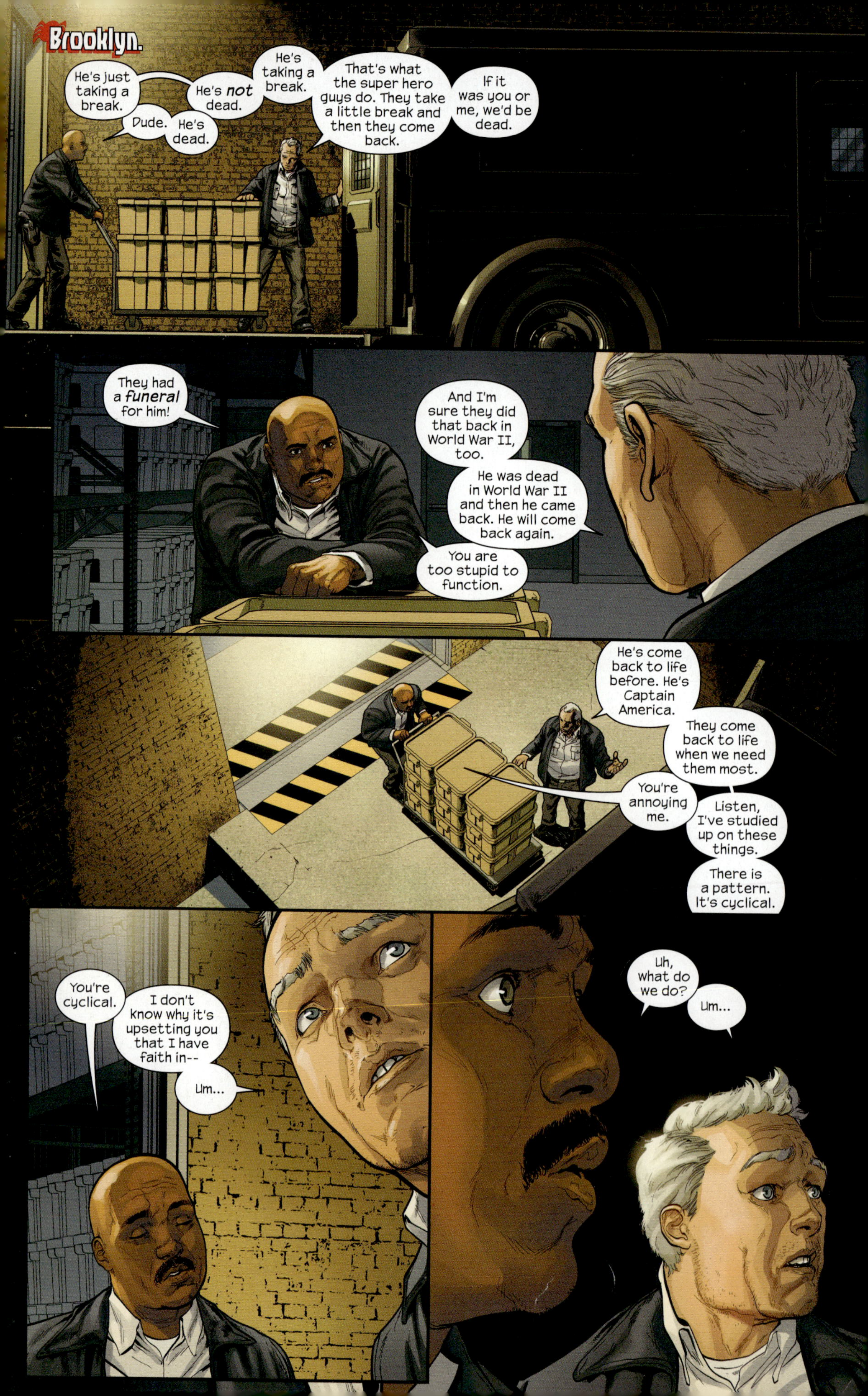
Brooklyn.
He's just taking a break.
Dude. He's dead.
He's not dead.
He's taking a break.
That's what the super hero guys do. They take a little break and then they come back.
If it was you or me, we'd be dead.
They had a funeral for him!
And I'm sure they did that back in World War II, too.
He was dead in World War II and then he came back. He will come back again.
You are too stupid to function.
He's come back to life before. He's Captain America.
They come back to life when we need them most.
You're annoying me.
Listen, I've studied up on these things.
There is a pattern. It's cyclical.
You're cyclical.
I don't know why it's upsetting you that I have faith in--
Um...
Uh, what do we do?
Um...

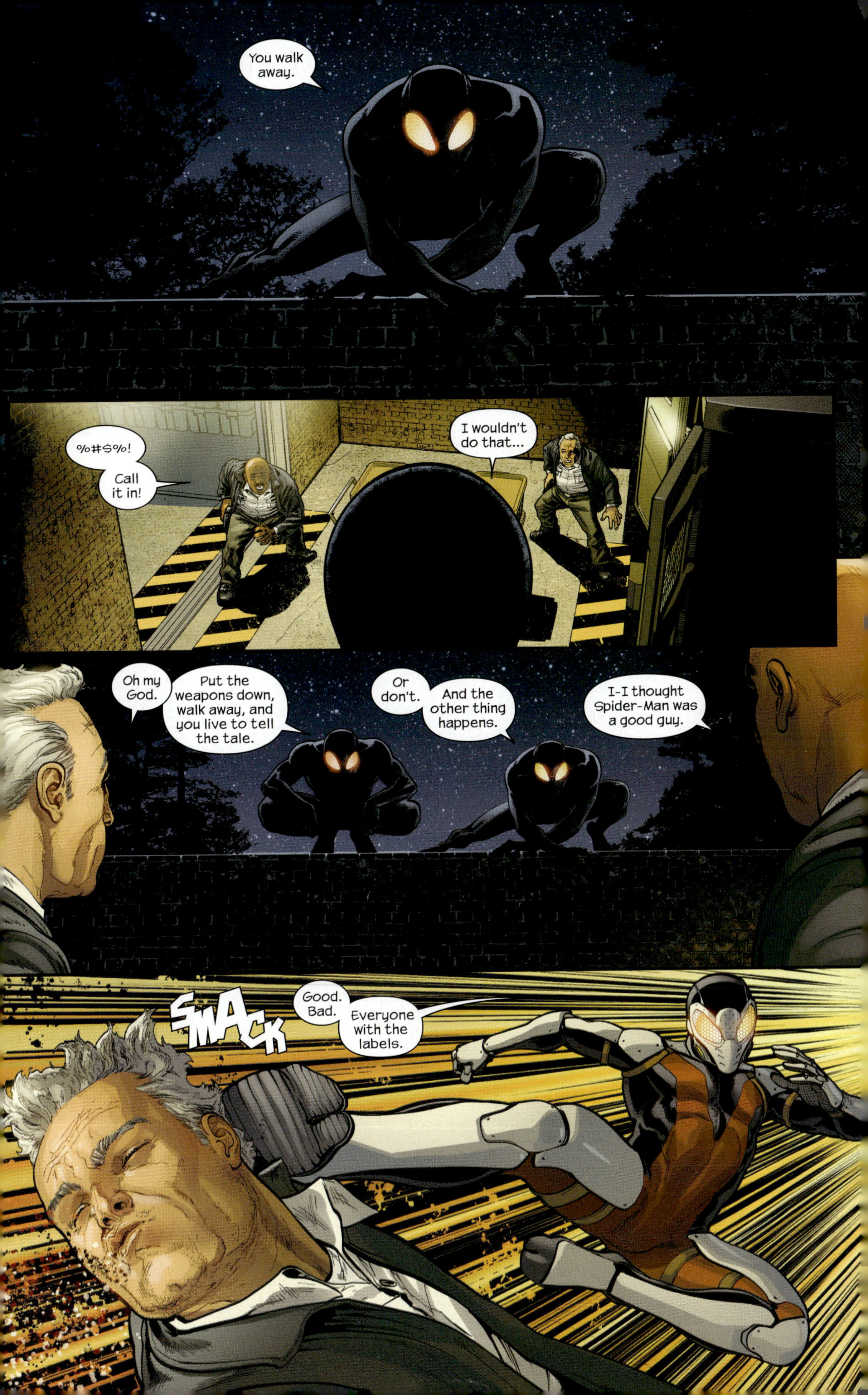
You walk away.
%#$%!
Call it in!
I wouldn't do that...
Oh my God.
Put the weapons down, walk away, and you live to tell the tale.
Or don't.
And the other thing happens.
I-I thought Spider-Man was a good guy.
SMACK
Good. Bad.
Everyone with the labels.

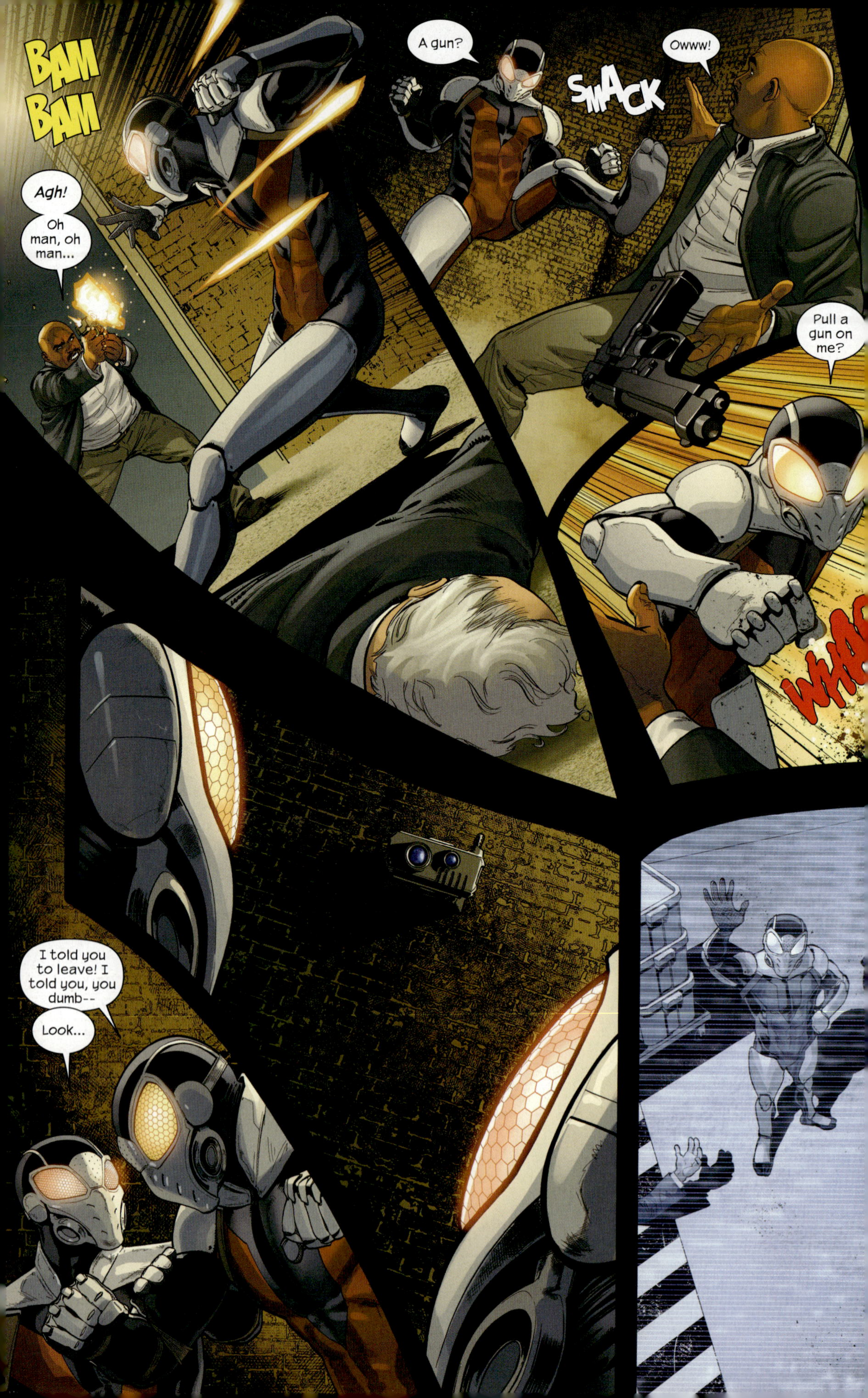
BAM
BAM
Agh!
Oh man, oh man...
A gun?
SMACK
Owww!
Pull a gun on me?
I told you to leave! I told you, you dumb--
Look...

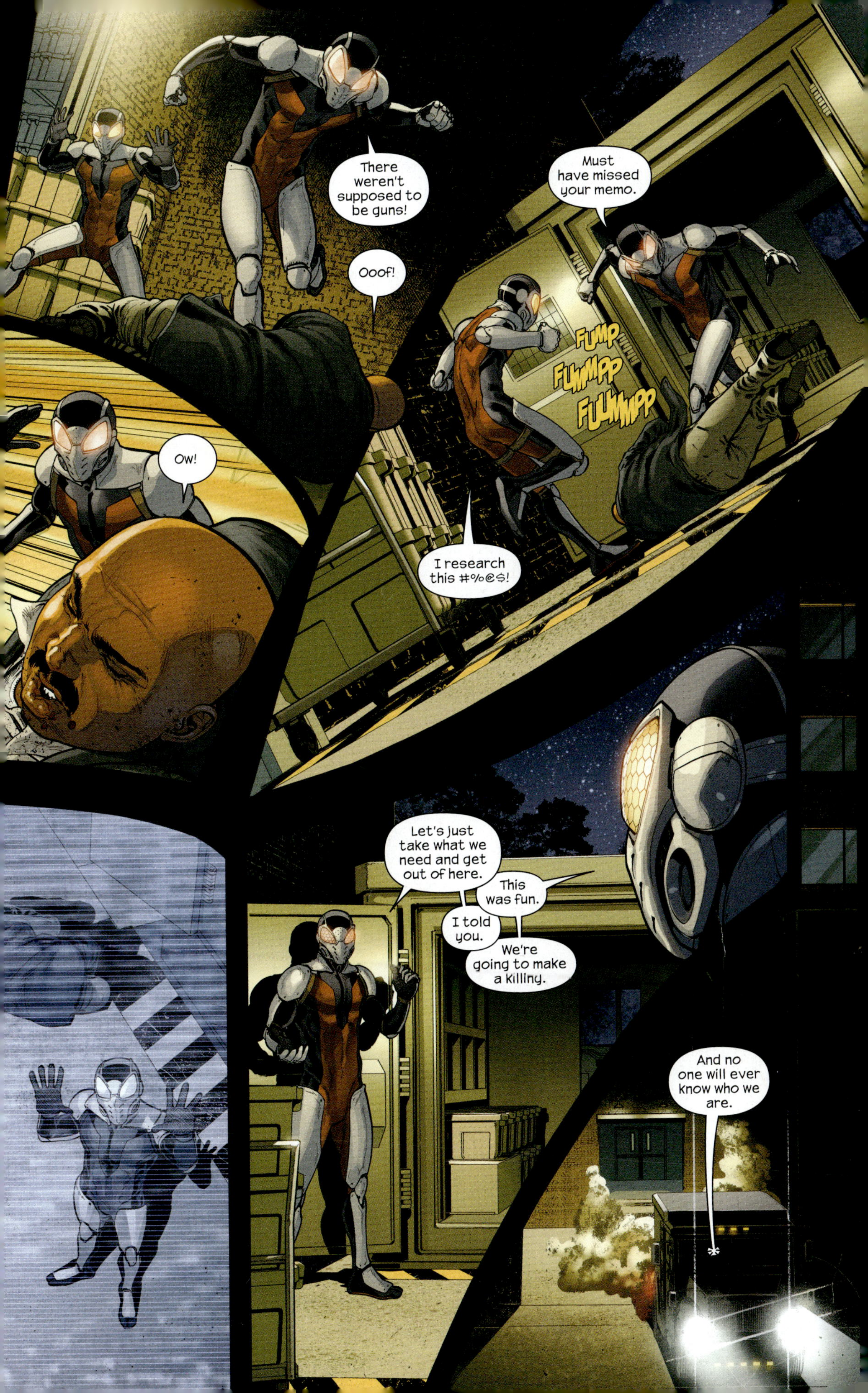
There weren't supposed to be guns!
Must have missed your memo.
Ooof!
FUMP
FUMMPP
FUMMPP
Ow!
I research this #%@$!
Let's just take what we need and get out of here.
This was fun.
I told you.
We're going to make a killing.
And no one will ever know who we are.

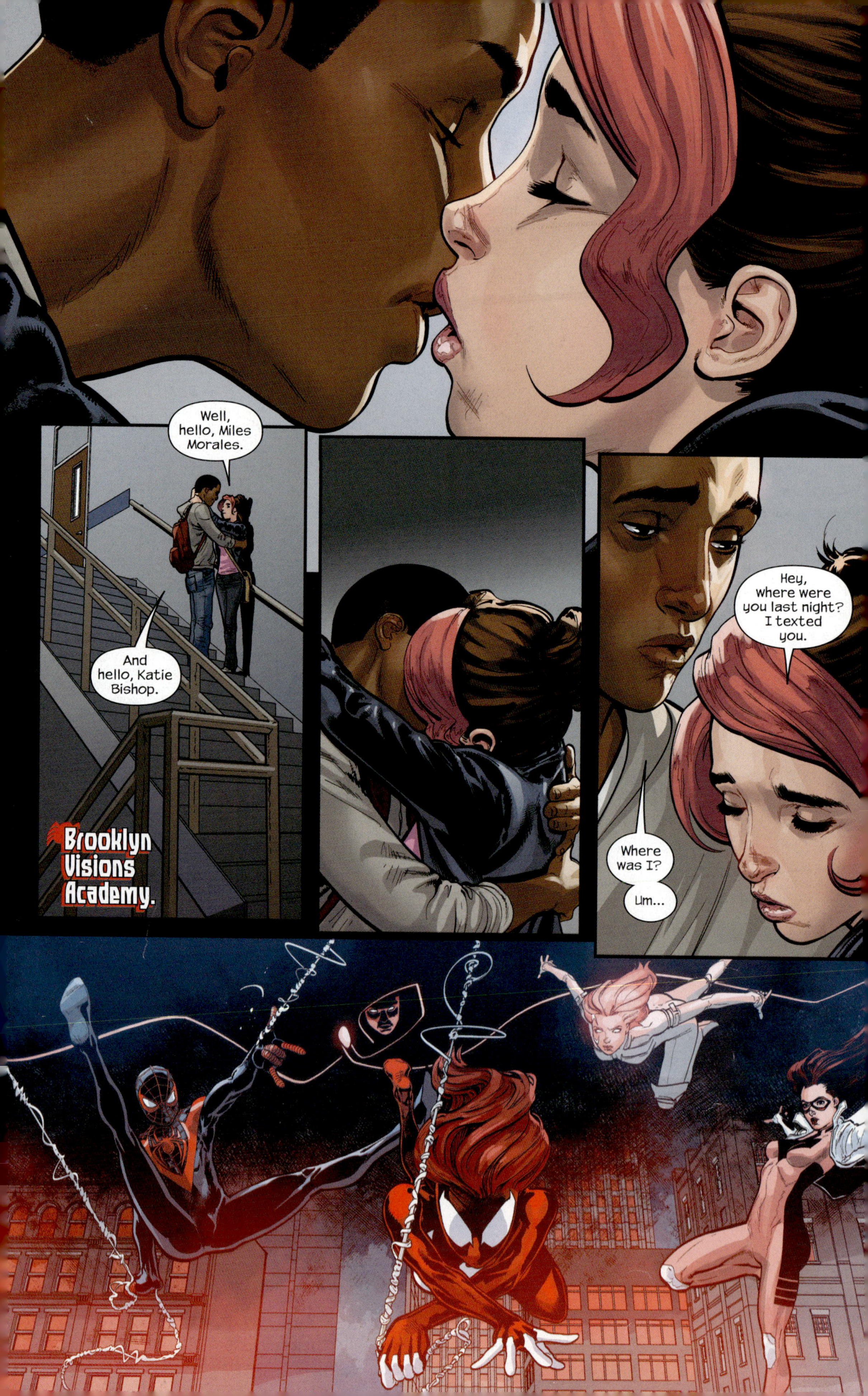
Well, hello, Miles Morales.
And hello, Katie Bishop.
Brooklyn Visions Academy.
Hey, where were you last night? I texted you.
Where was I?
Um...

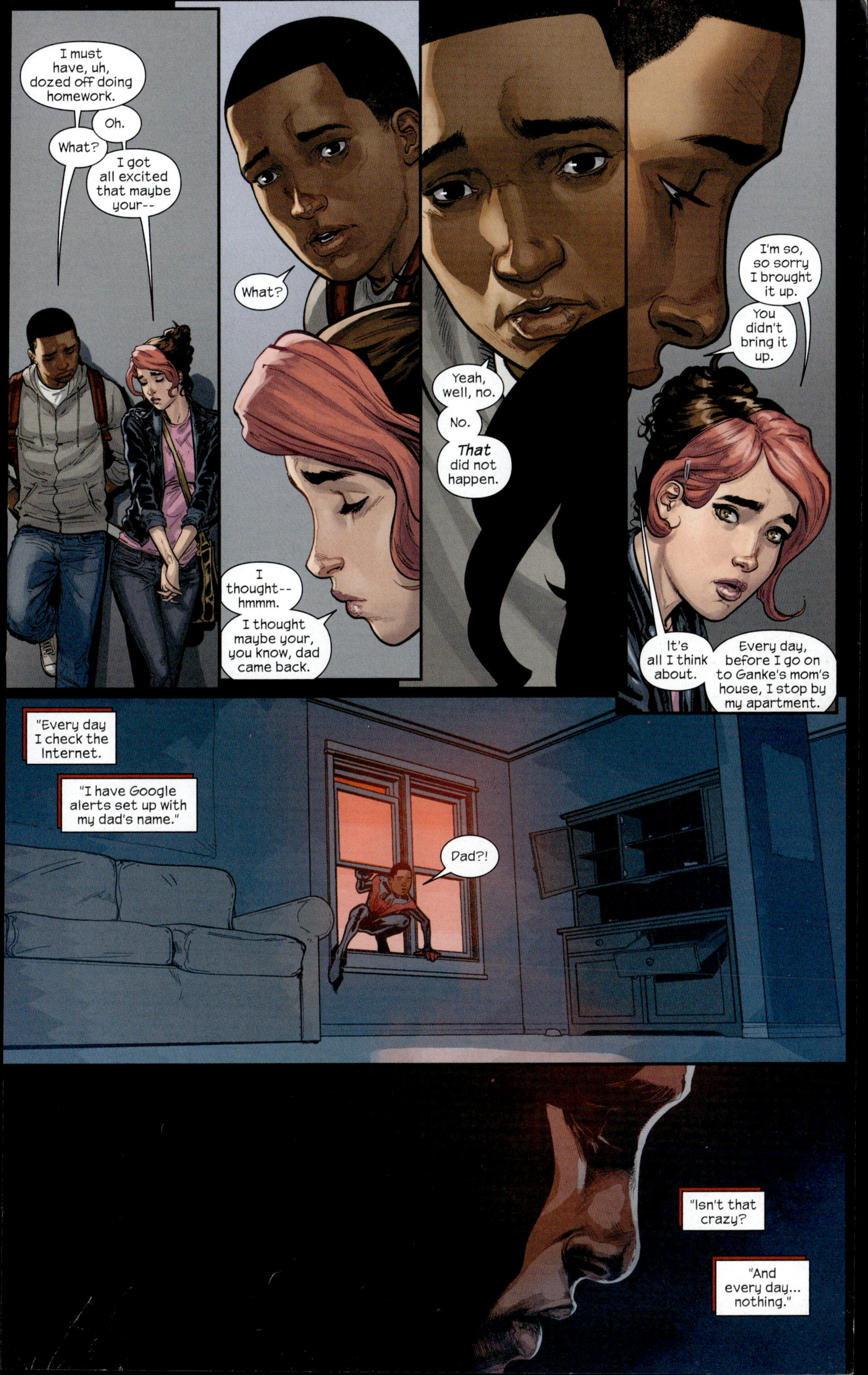
I must have, uh, dozed off doing homework.
Oh.
What?
I got all excited that maybe your--
What?
I thought--hmmm.
I thought maybe your, you know, dad came back.
Yeah, well, no.
No.
That did not happen.
I'm so, so sorry I brought it up.
You didn't bring it up.
It's all I think about.
Every day, before I go on to Ganke's mom's house, I stop by my apartment.
"Every day I check the Internet.
"I have Google alerts set up with my dad's name."
Dad?!
"Isn't that crazy?
"And every day... nothing."

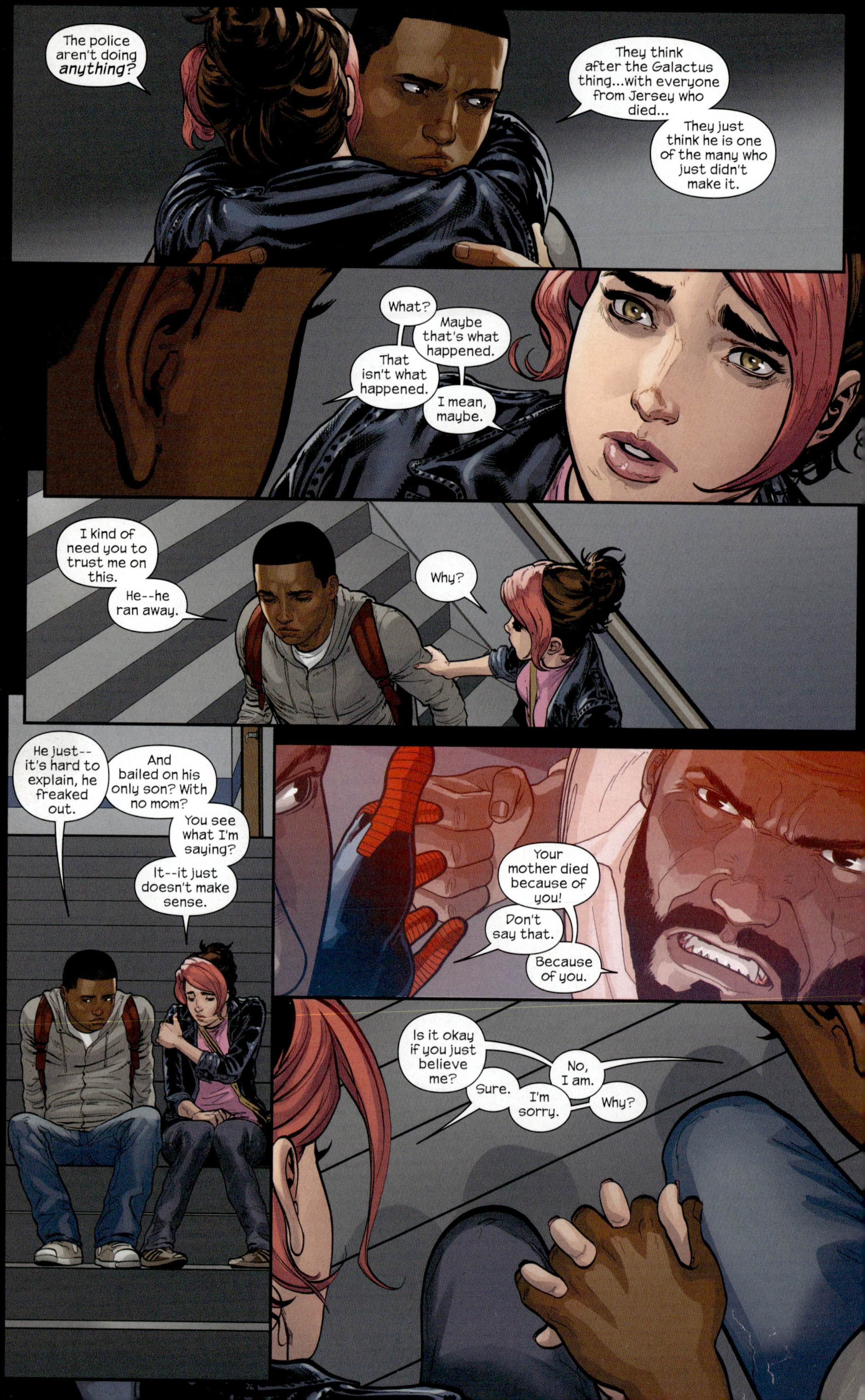

The police aren't doing *anything?*
They think after the Galactus thing...with everyone from Jersey who died...
They just think he is one of the many who just didn't make it.
What?
Maybe that's what happened.
That isn't what happened.
I mean, maybe.
I kind of need you to trust me on this.
He--he ran away.
Why?
He just-- it's hard to explain, he freaked out.
And bailed on his only son? With no mom?
You see what I'm saying?
It--it just doesn't make sense.
Your mother died because of you!
Don't say that.
Because of you.
Is it okay if you just believe me?
Sure.
No, I am.
I'm sorry.
Why?

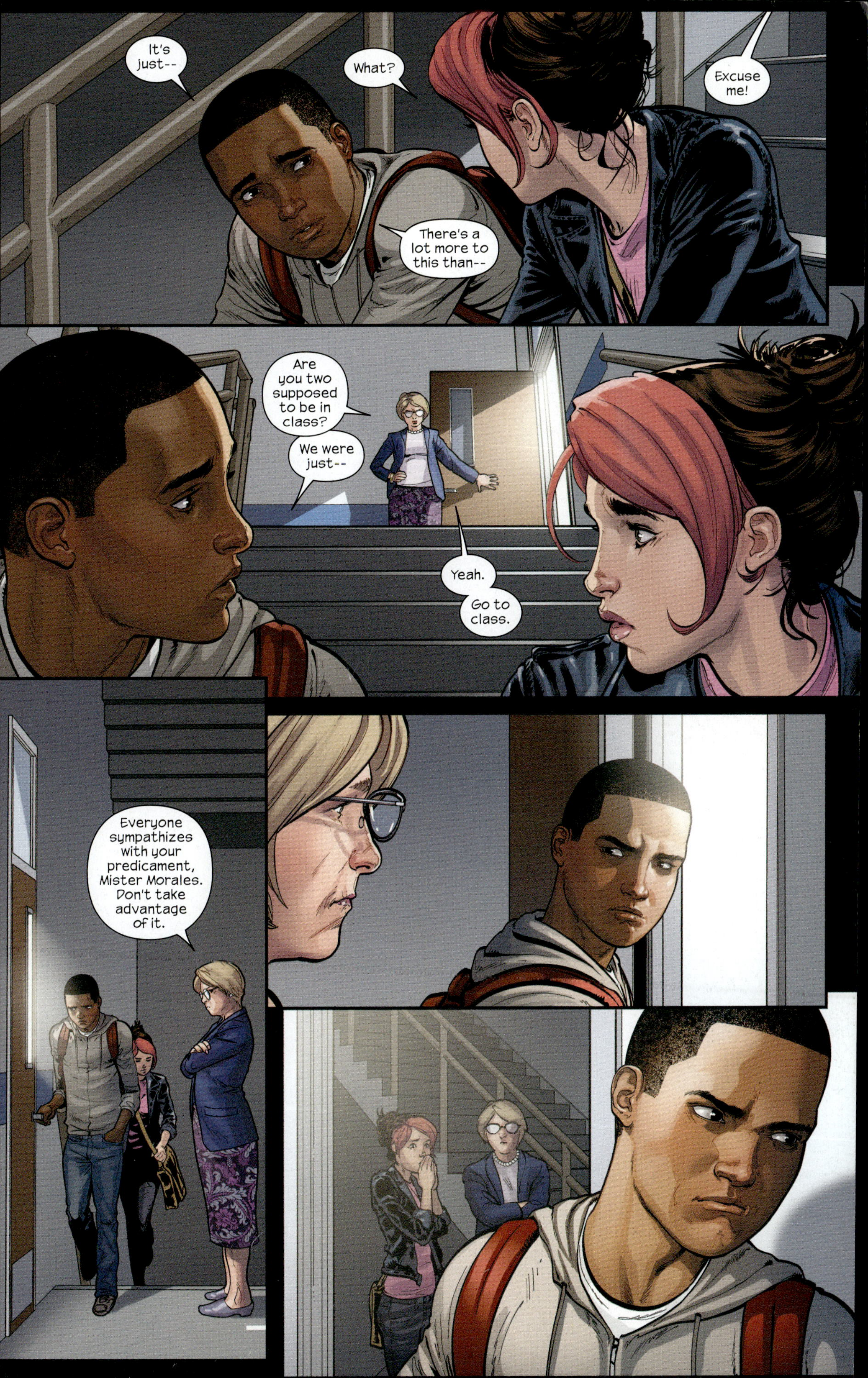
It's just--
What?
Excuse me!
There's a lot more to this than--
Are you two supposed to be in class?
We were just--
Yeah.
Go to class.
Everyone sympathizes with your predicament, Mister Morales. Don't take advantage of it.

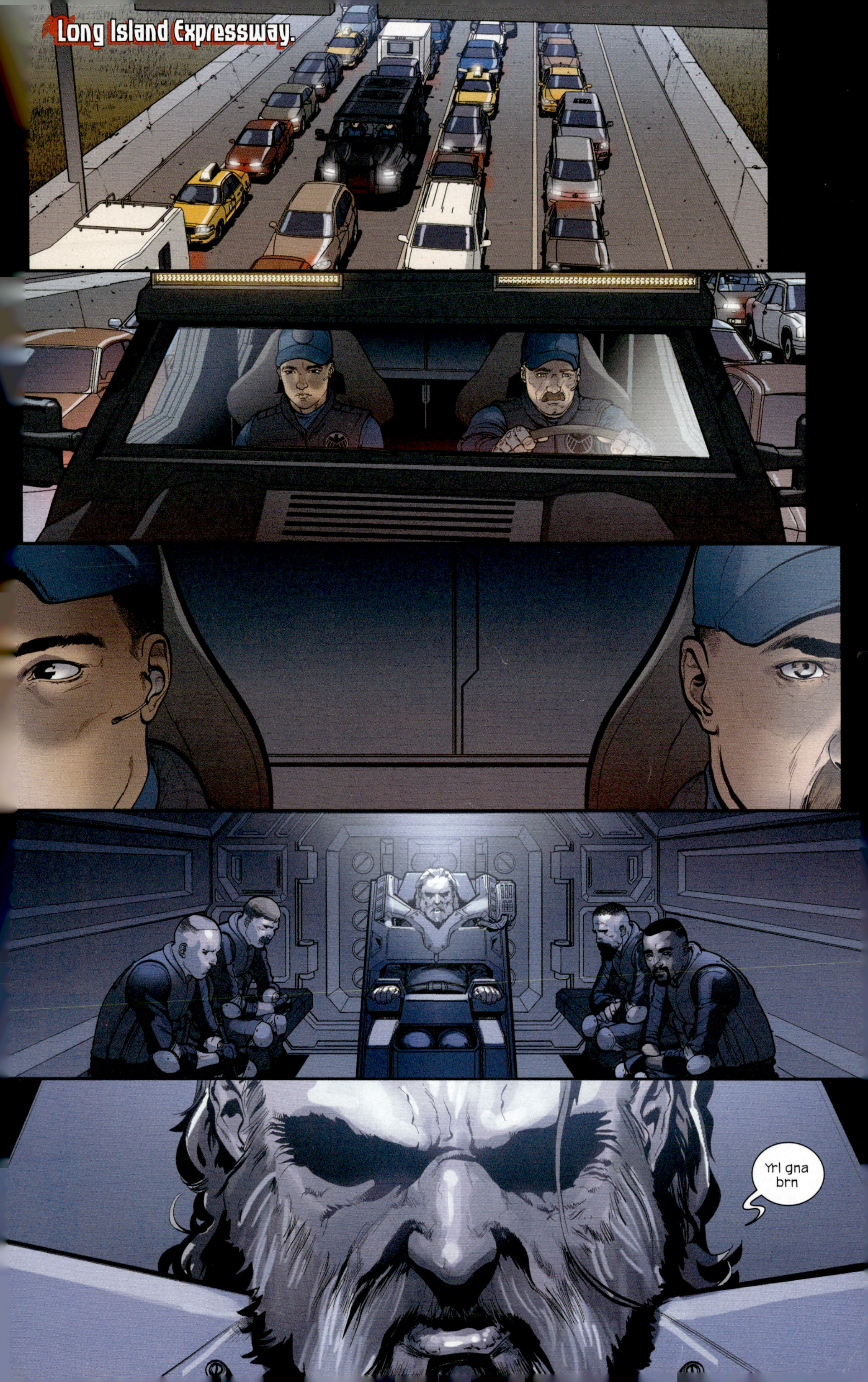
Long Island Expressway.
Yrl gna brn

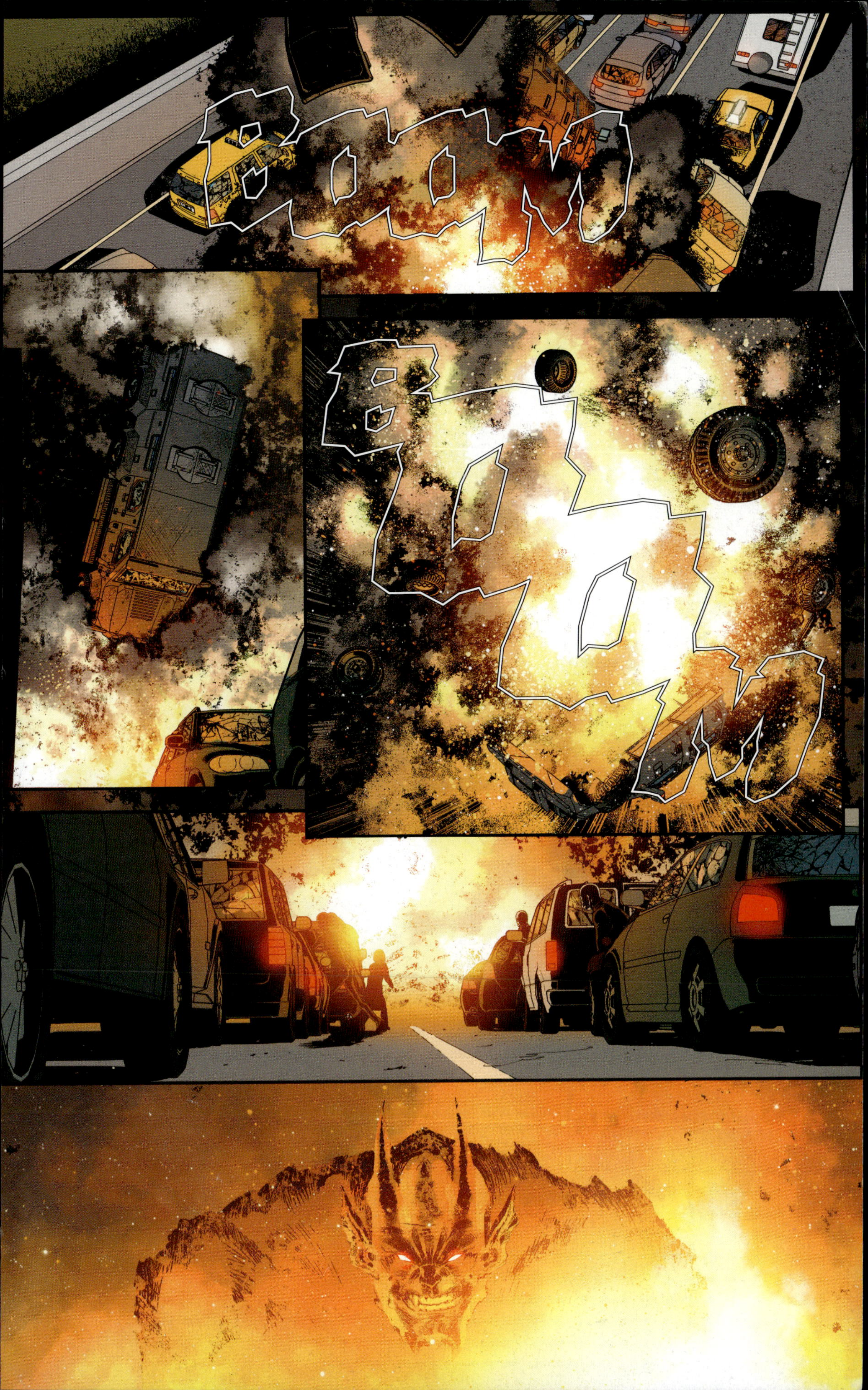
BOOM
BOOM

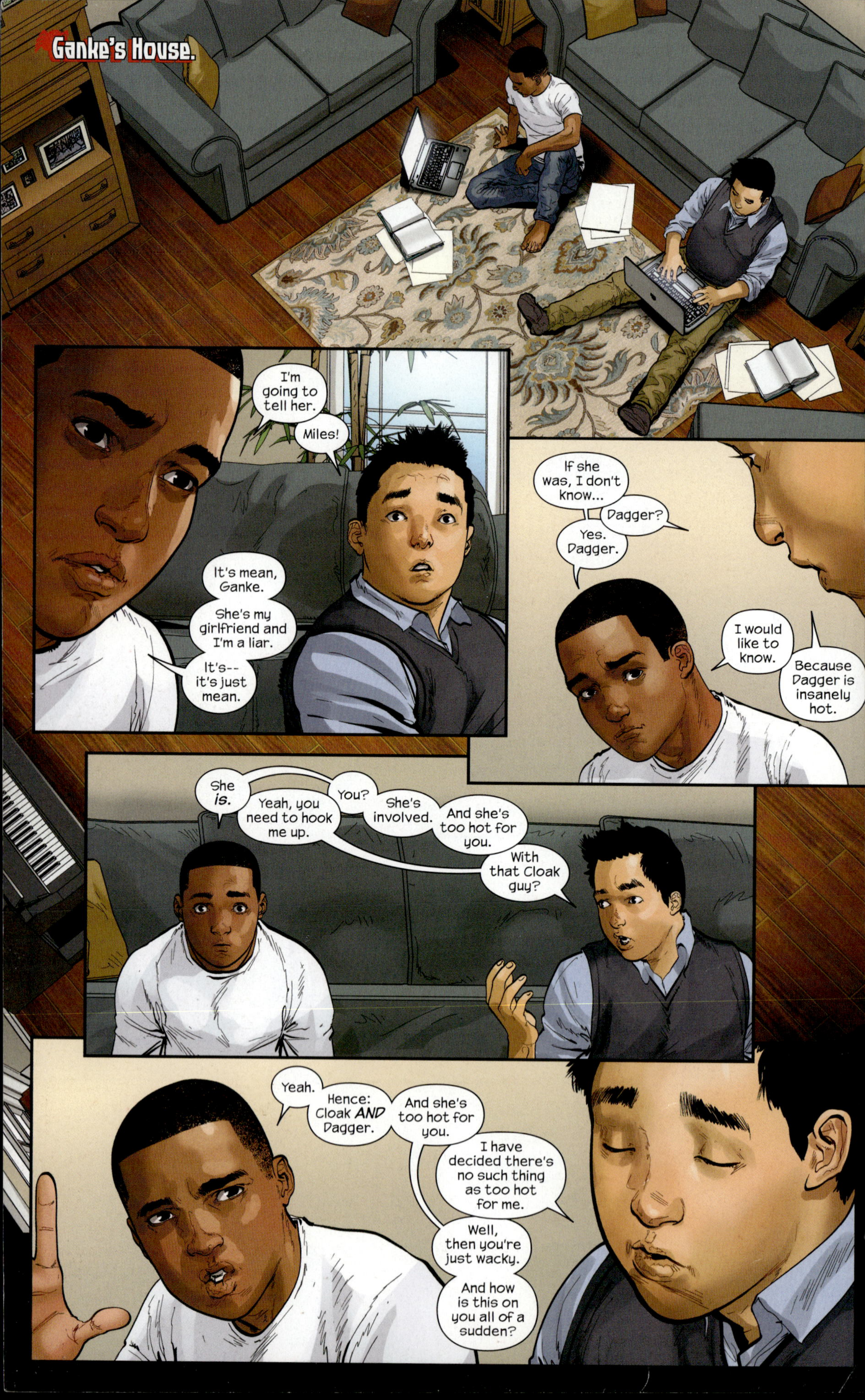
Ganke's House.
I'm going to tell her.
Miles!
It's mean, Ganke.
She's my girlfriend and I'm a liar.
It's-- it's just mean.
If she was, I don't know...
Dagger?
Yes. Dagger.
I would like to know.
Because Dagger is insanely hot.
She *is.*
Yeah, you need to hook me up.
You?
She's involved.
And she's too hot for you.
With that Cloak guy?
Yeah.
Hence: Cloak **AND** Dagger.
And she's too hot for you.
I have decided there's no such thing as too hot for me.
Well, then you're just wacky.
And how is this on you all of a sudden?

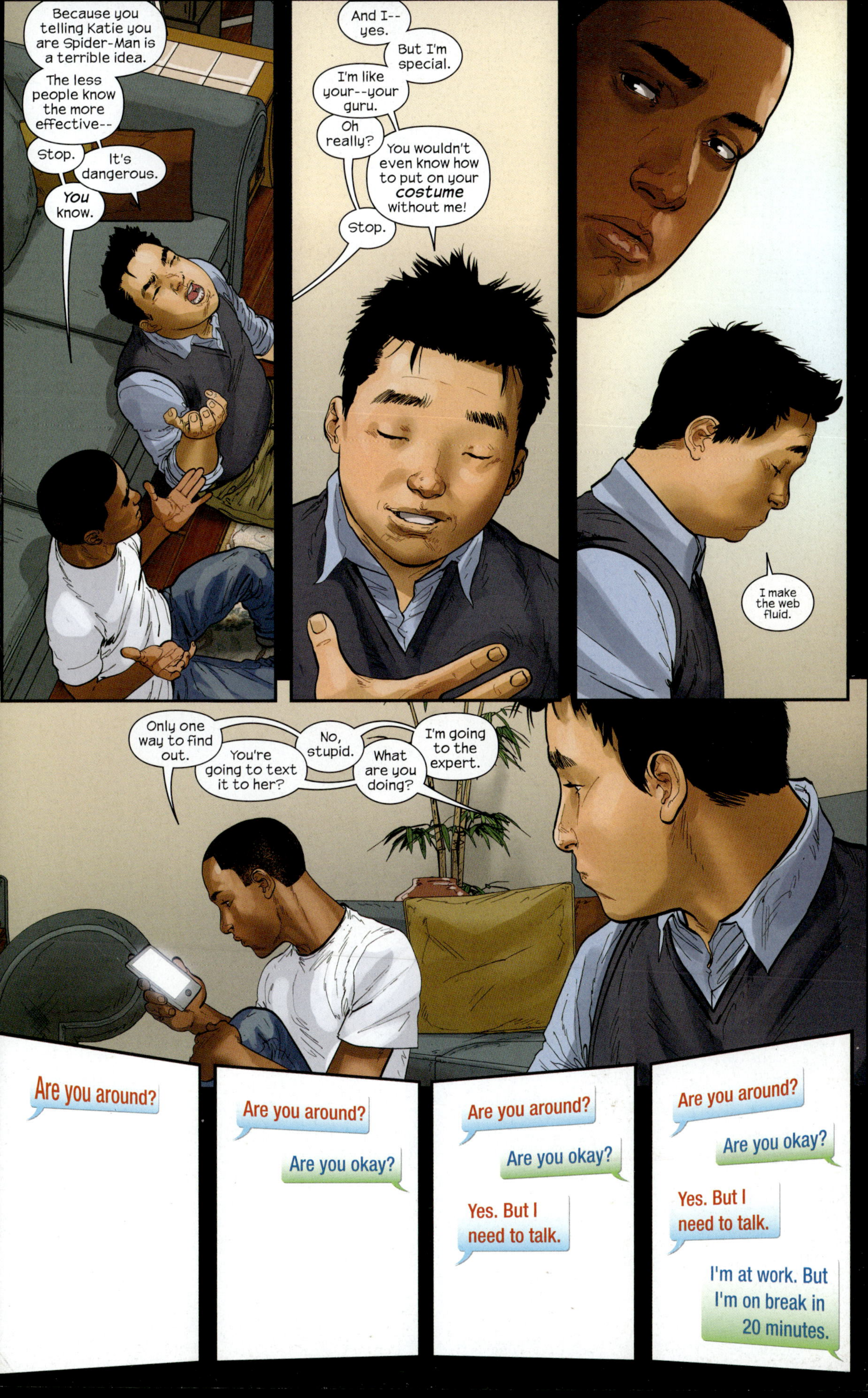
Because you telling Katie you are Spider-Man is a terrible idea.
The less people know the more effective--
Stop.
It's dangerous.
You know.
And I-- yes.
But I'm special.
I'm like your--your guru.
Oh really?
You wouldn't even know how to put on your *costume* without me!
Stop.
I make the web fluid.
Only one way to find out.
You're going to text it to her?
No, stupid.
What are you doing?
I'm going to the expert.
Are you around?
Are you around?
Are you okay?
Are you around?
Are you okay?
Yes. But I need to talk.
Are you around?
Are you okay?
Yes. But I need to talk.
I'm at work. But I'm on break in 20 minutes.

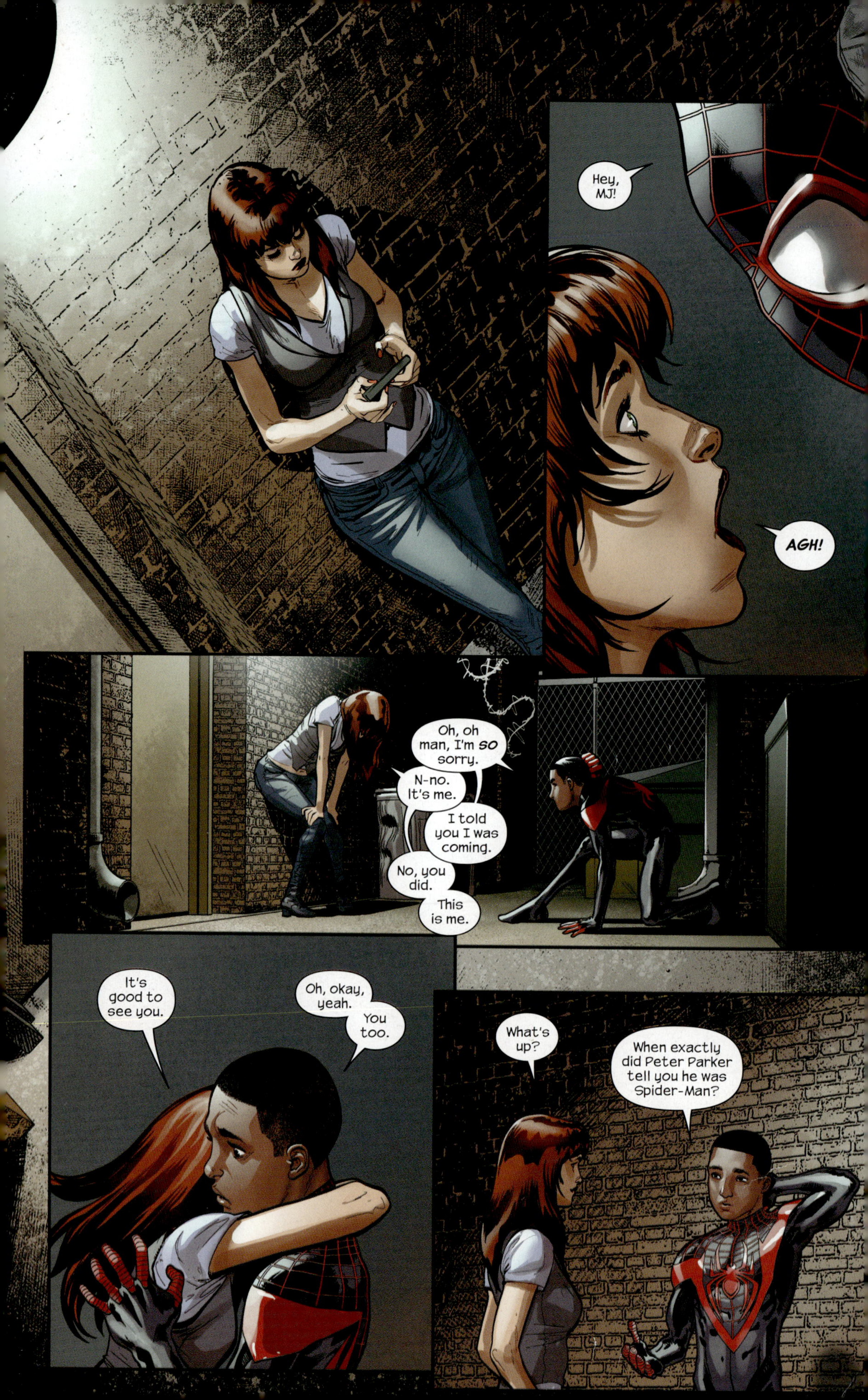
Hey, MJ!
AGH!
Oh, oh man, I'm SO sorry.
N-no. It's me.
I told you I was coming.
No, you did.
This is me.
It's good to see you.
Oh, okay, yeah.
You too.
What's up?
When exactly did Peter Parker tell you he was Spider-Man?

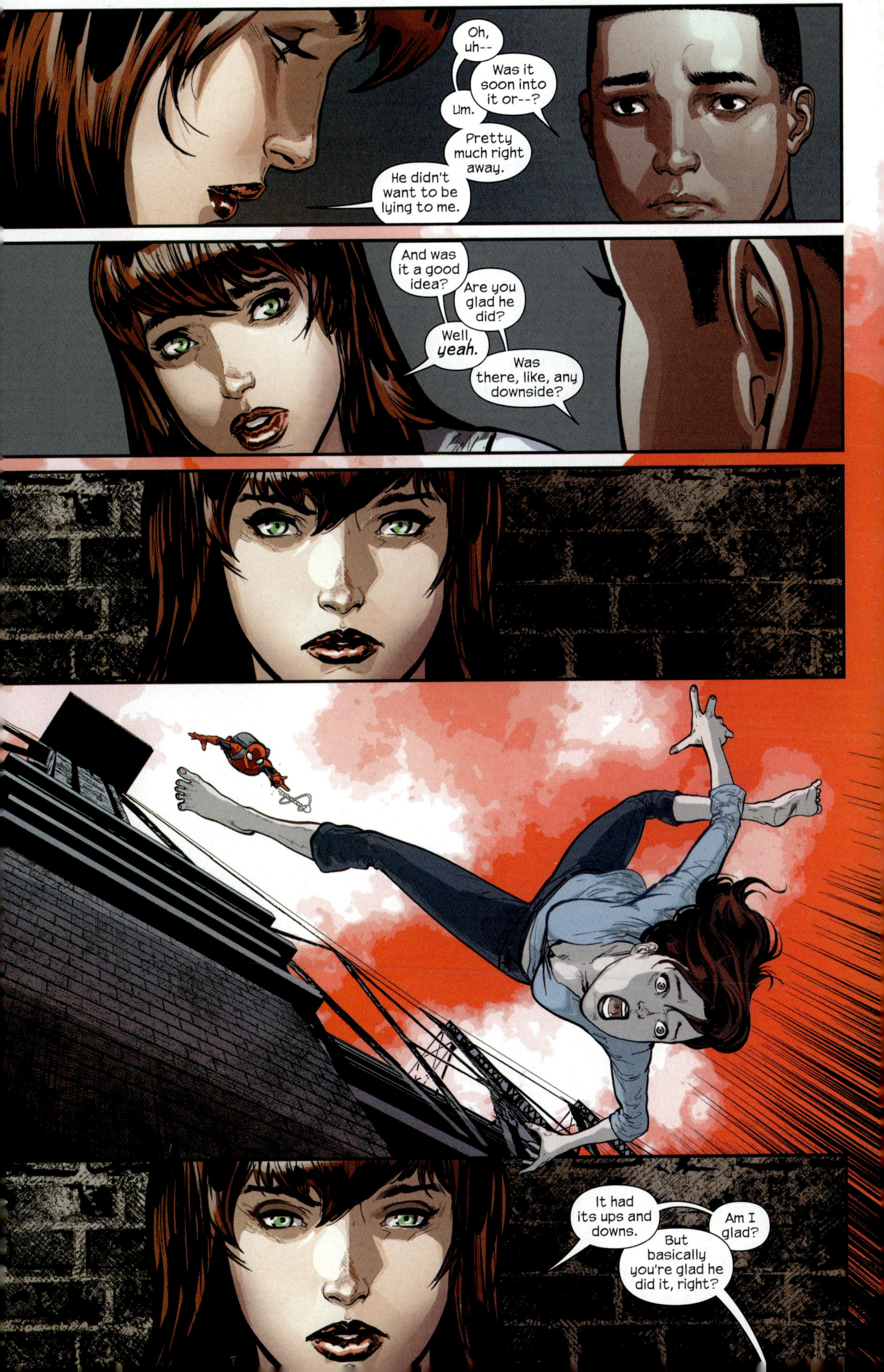
Oh, uh--
Was it soon into it or--?
Um.
Pretty much right away.
He didn't want to be lying to me.
And was it a good idea?
Are you glad he did?
Well, *yeah.*
Was there, like, any downside?
It had its ups and downs.
Am I glad?
But basically you're glad he did it, right?

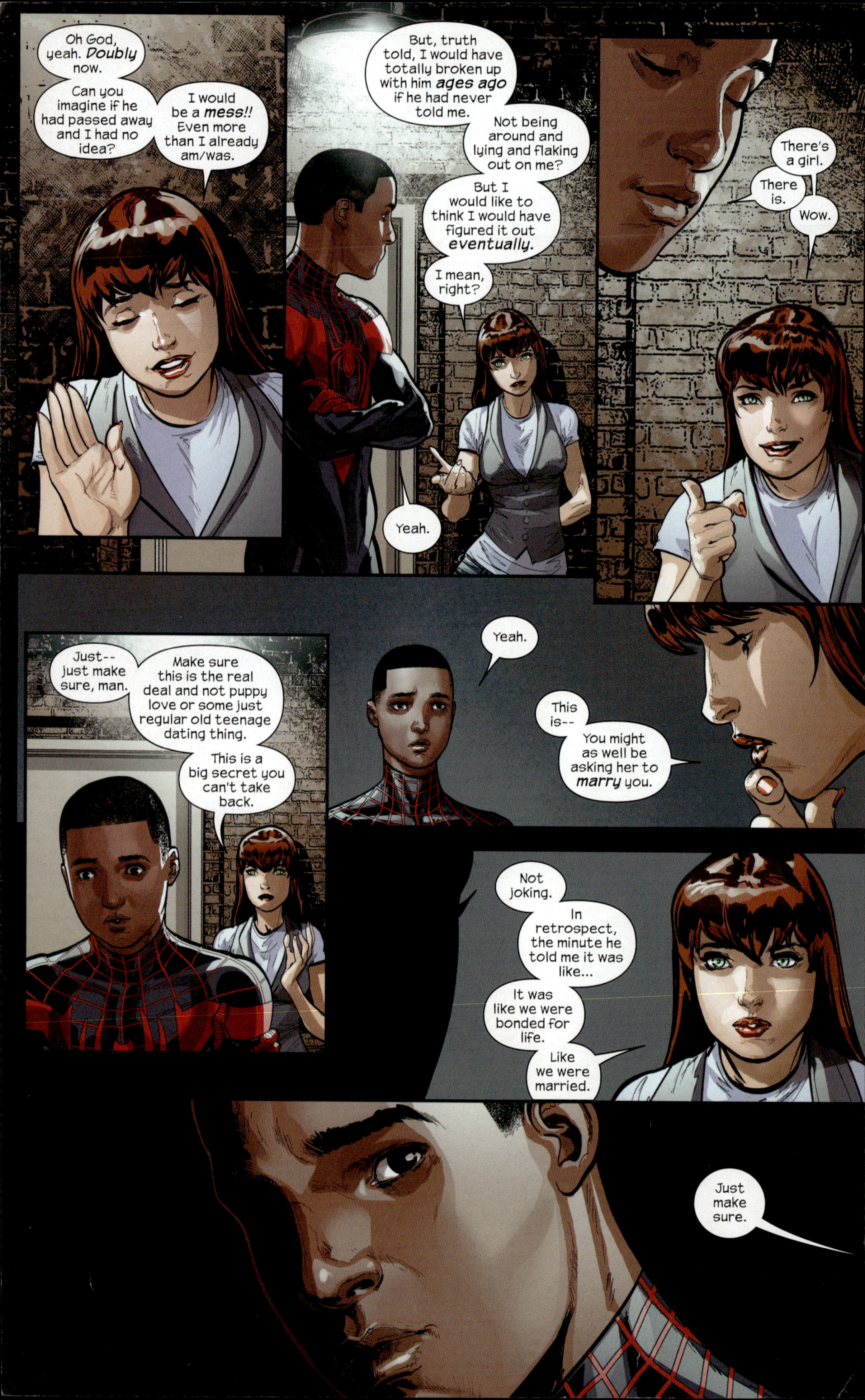
Oh God, yeah. *Doubly* now.
Can you imagine if he had passed away and I had no idea?
I would be a ***mess!!*** Even more than I already am/was.
But, truth told, I would have totally broken up with him ***ages ago*** if he had never told me.
Not being around and lying and flaking out on me?
But I would like to think I would have figured it out ***eventually.***
I mean, right?
Yeah.
There's a girl.
There is.
Wow.
Just-- just make sure, man.
Make sure this is the real deal and not puppy love or some just regular old teenage dating thing.
This is a big secret you can't take back.
Yeah.
This is--
You might as well be asking her to ***marry*** you.
Not joking.
In retrospect, the minute he told me it was like...
It was like we were bonded for life.
Like we were married.
Just make sure.

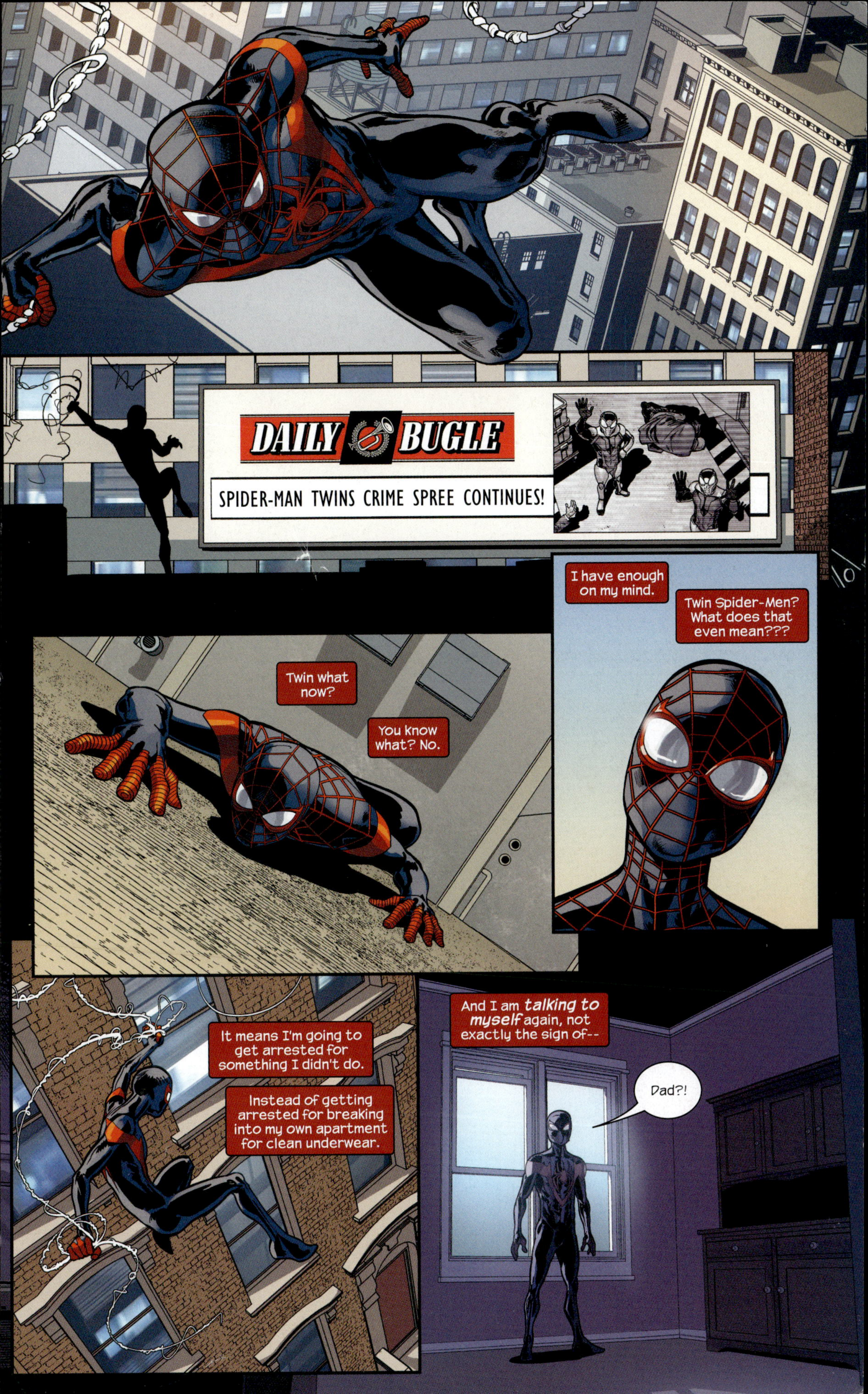
DAILY BUGLE
SPIDER-MAN TWINS CRIME SPREE CONTINUES!
Twin what now?
You know what? No.
I have enough on my mind.
Twin Spider-Men? What does that even mean???
It means I'm going to get arrested for something I didn't do.
Instead of getting arrested for breaking into my own apartment for clean underwear.
And I am *talking to myself* again, not exactly the sign of--
Dad?!

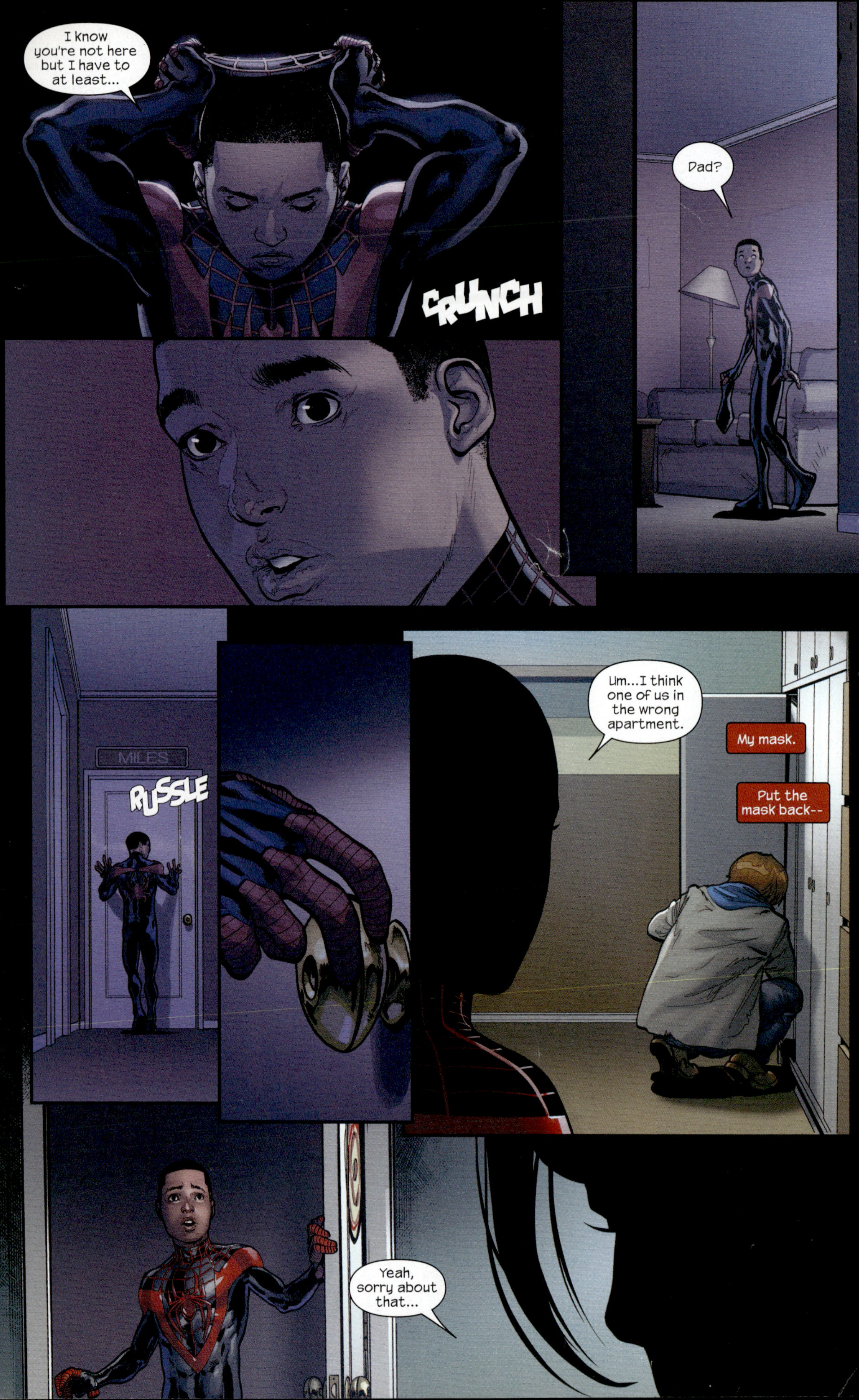
I know you're not here but I have to at least...
CRUNCH
Dad?
MILES
RUSSLE
Um...I think one of us in the wrong apartment.
My mask.
Put the mask back--
Yeah, sorry about that...

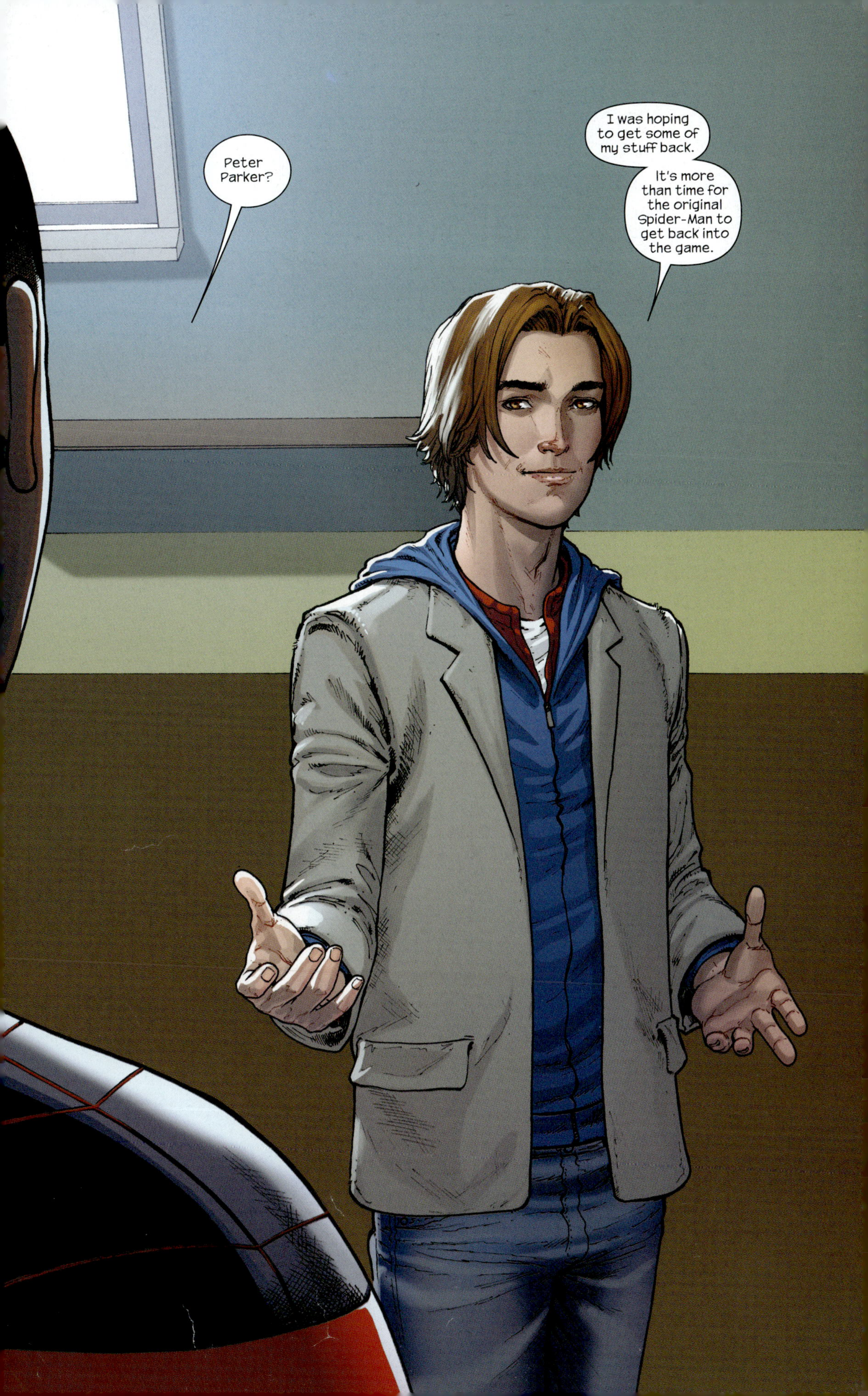
Peter Parker?
I was hoping to get some of my stuff back.
It's more than time for the original Spider-Man to get back into the game.

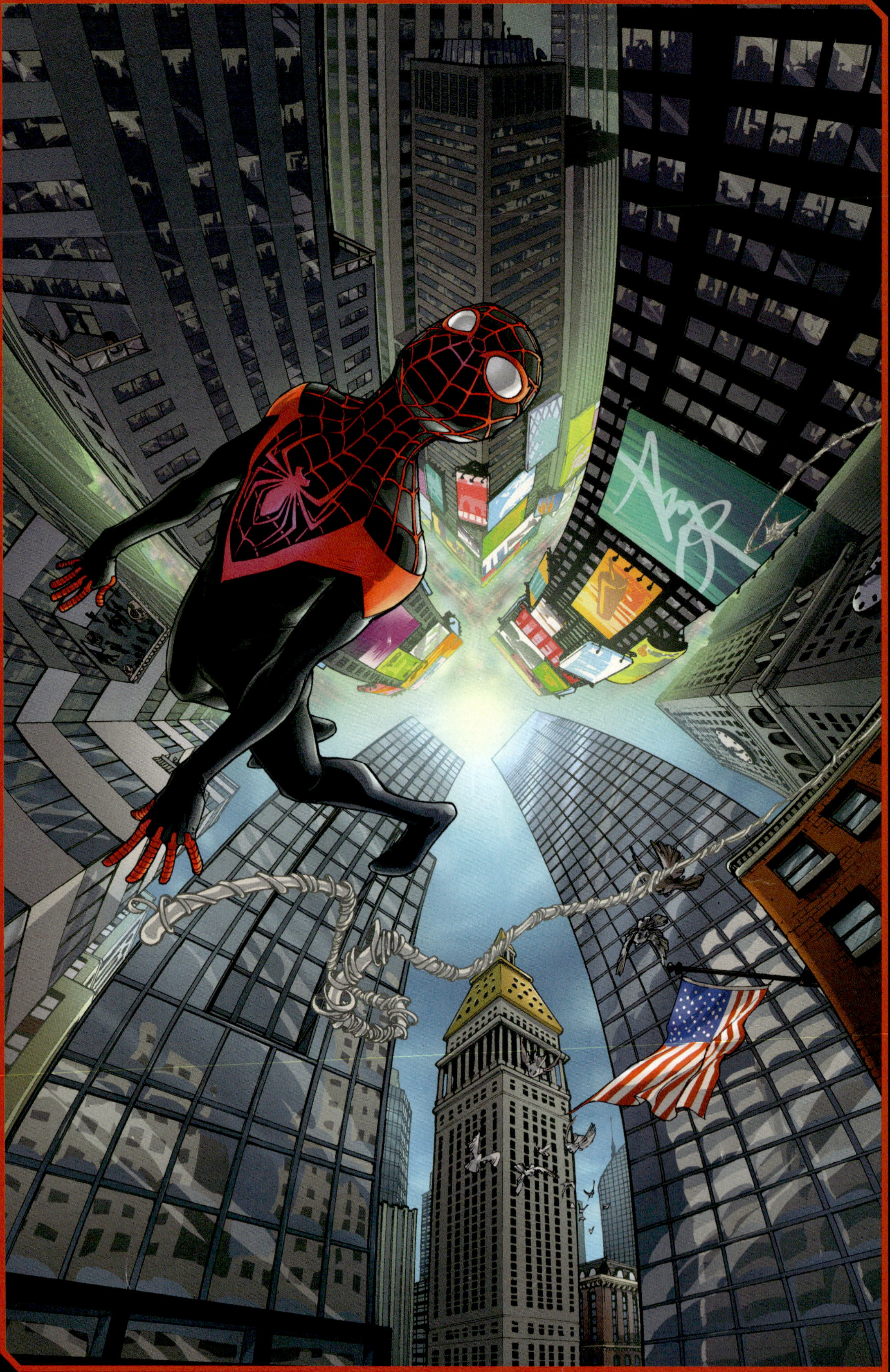

MILES MORALES: ULTIMATE SPIDER-MAN #2 VARIANT BY AMY REEDER

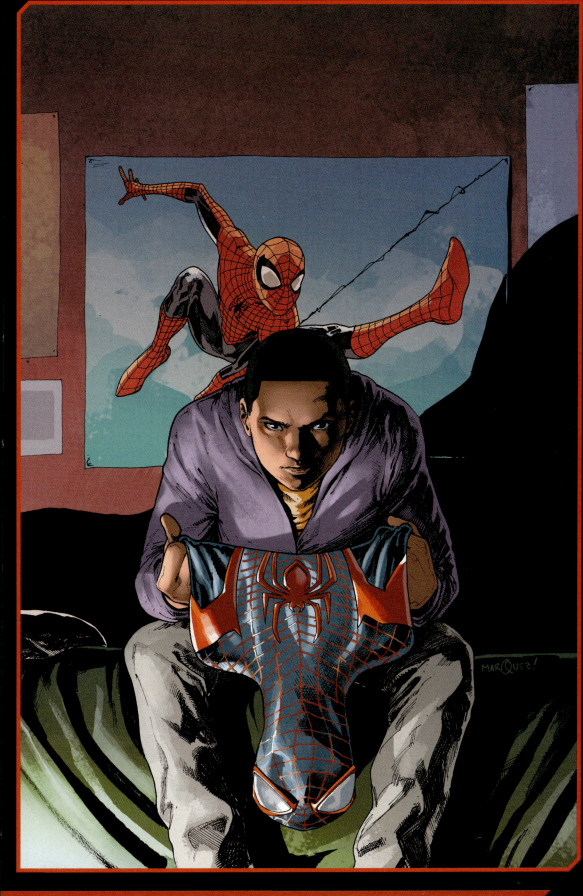

MILES MORALES: ULTIMATE SPIDER-MAN #2

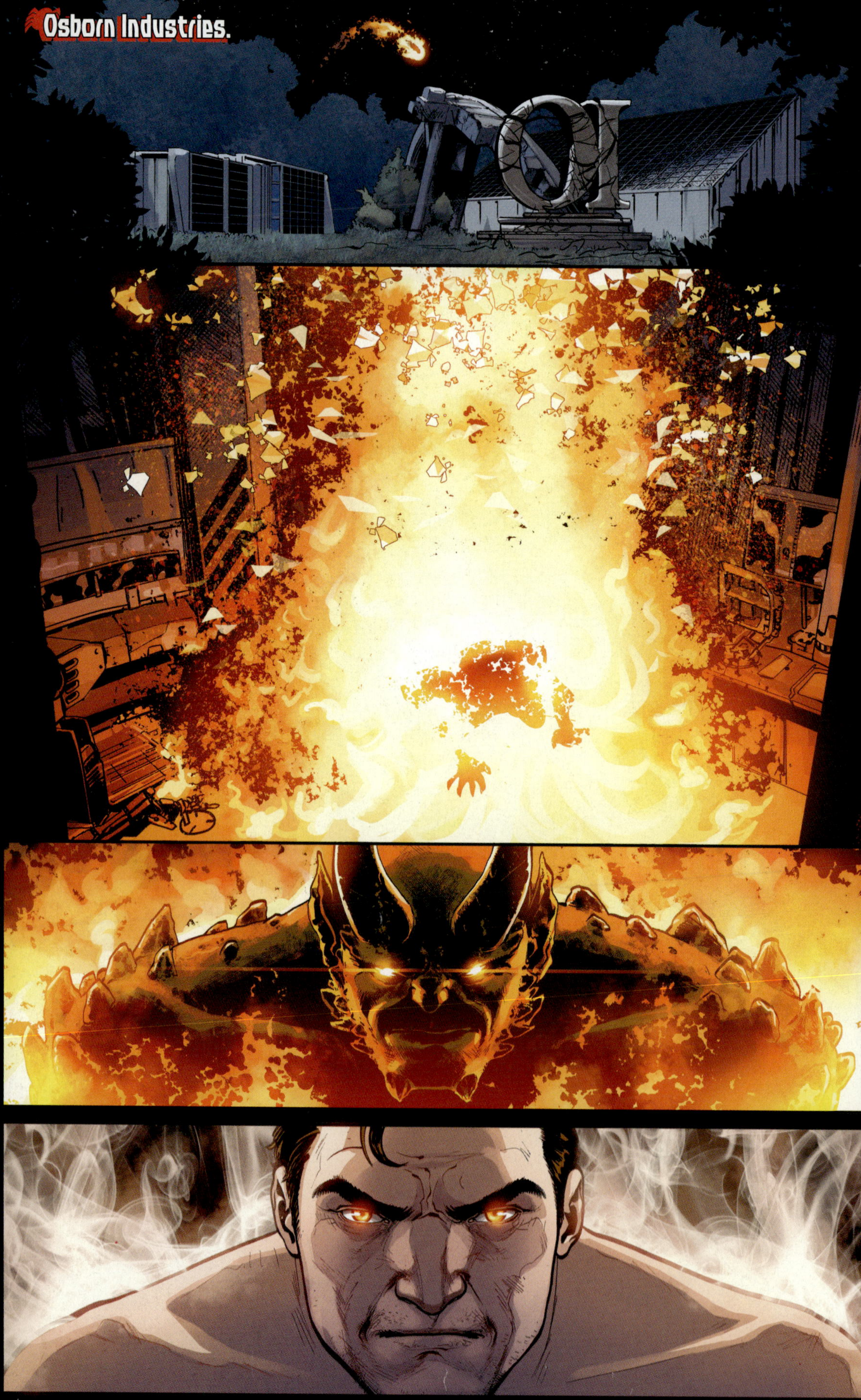
Osborn Industries.

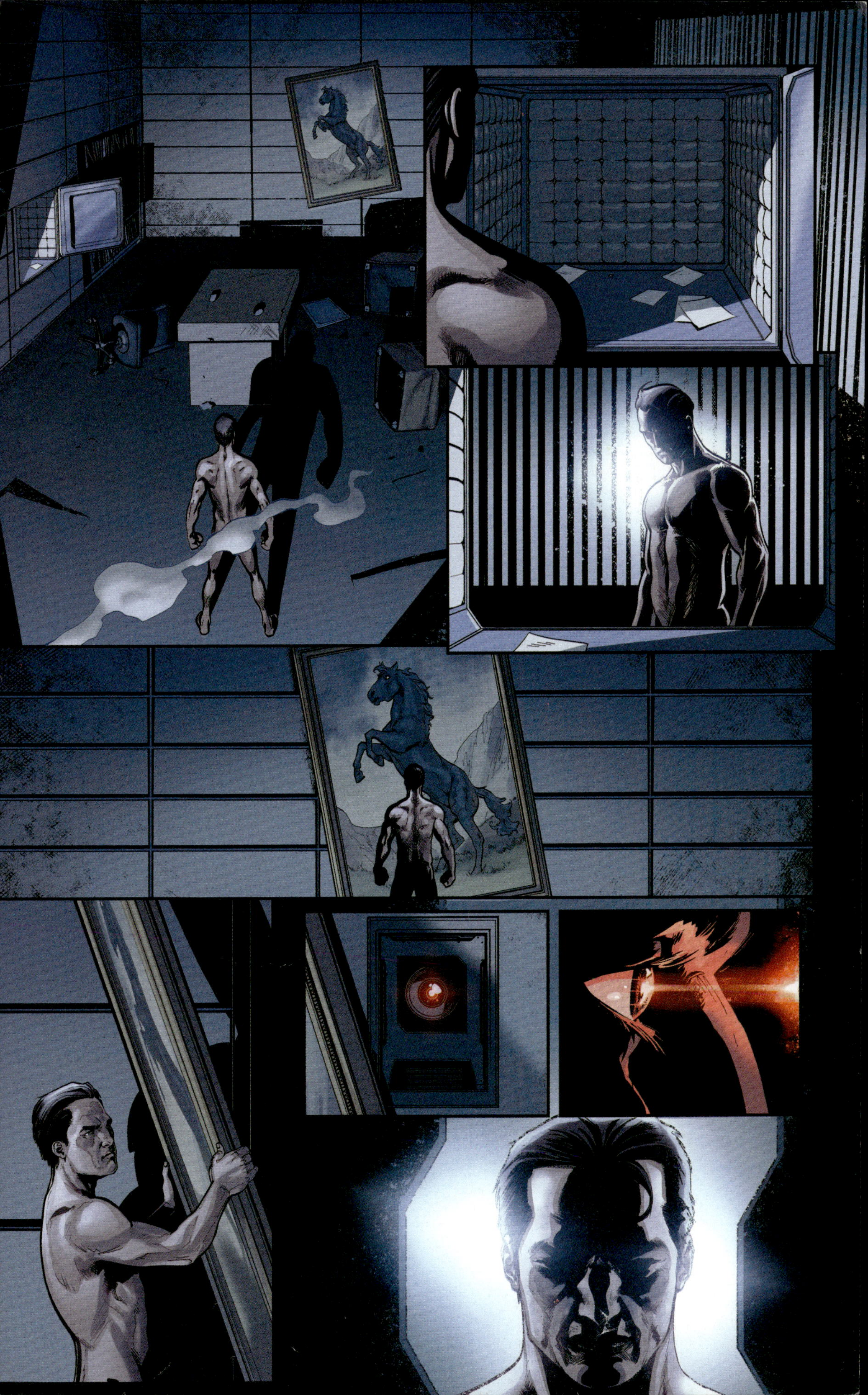

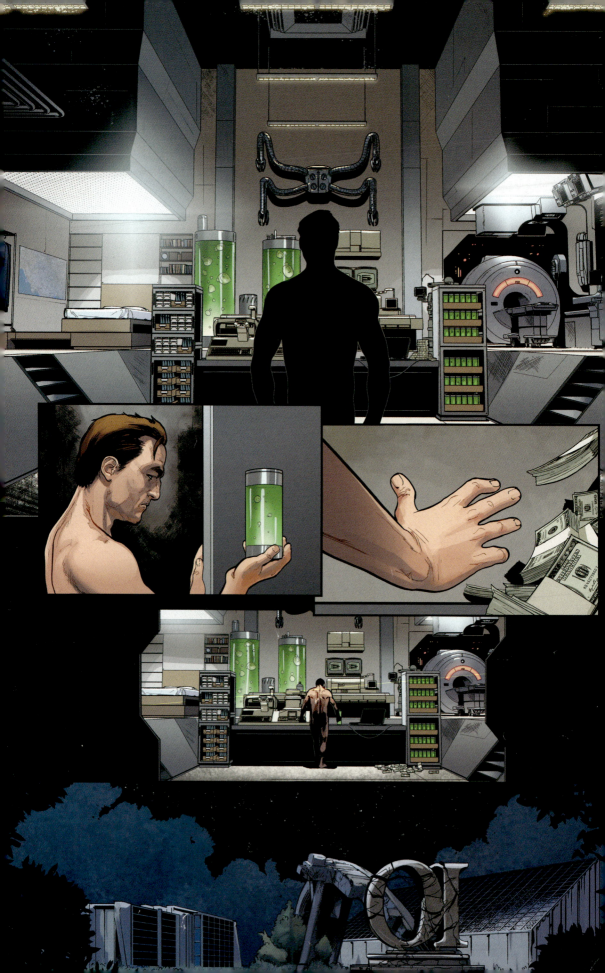

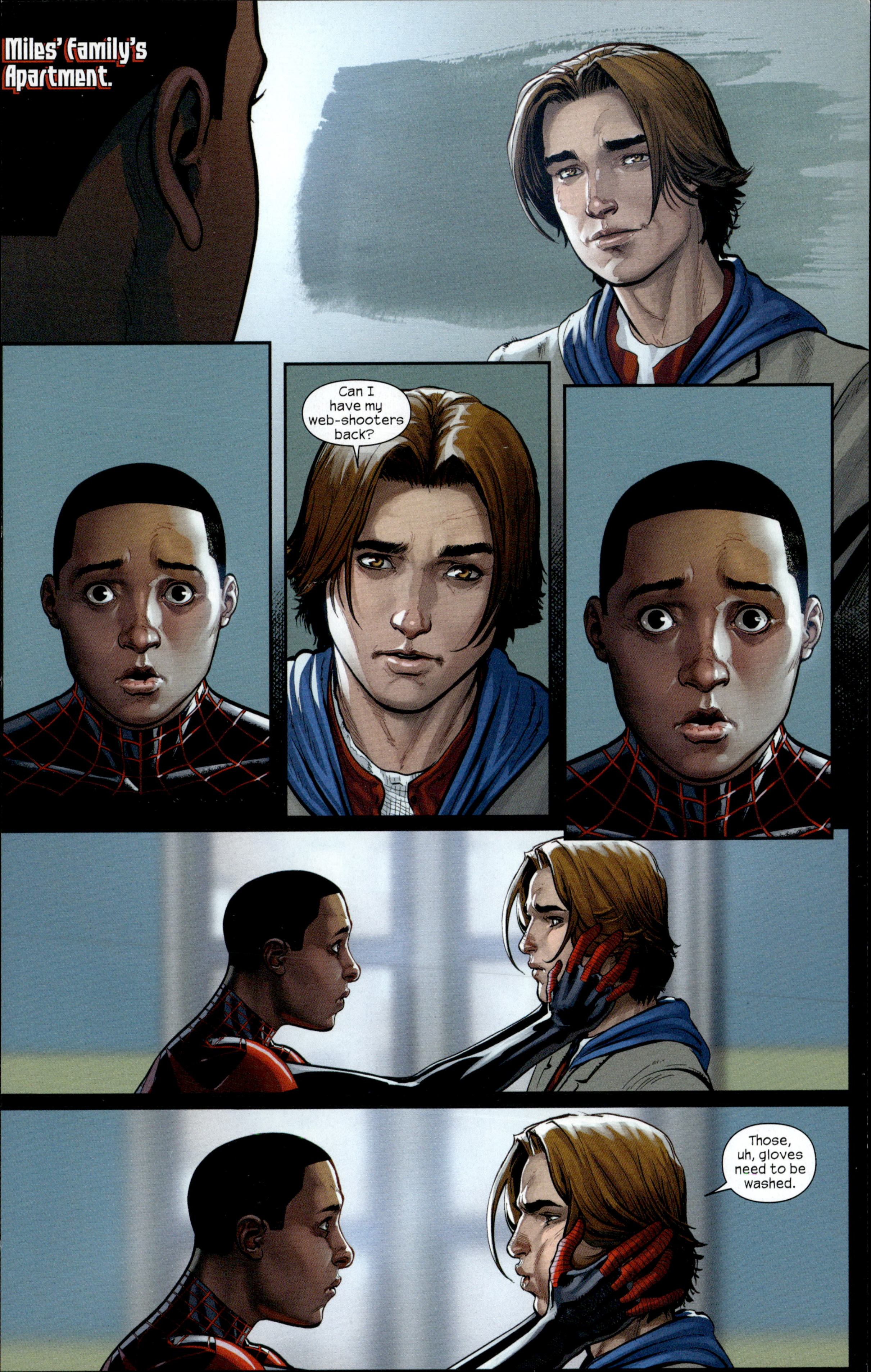
Miles' Family's Apartment.
Can I have my web-shooters back?
Those, uh, gloves need to be washed.

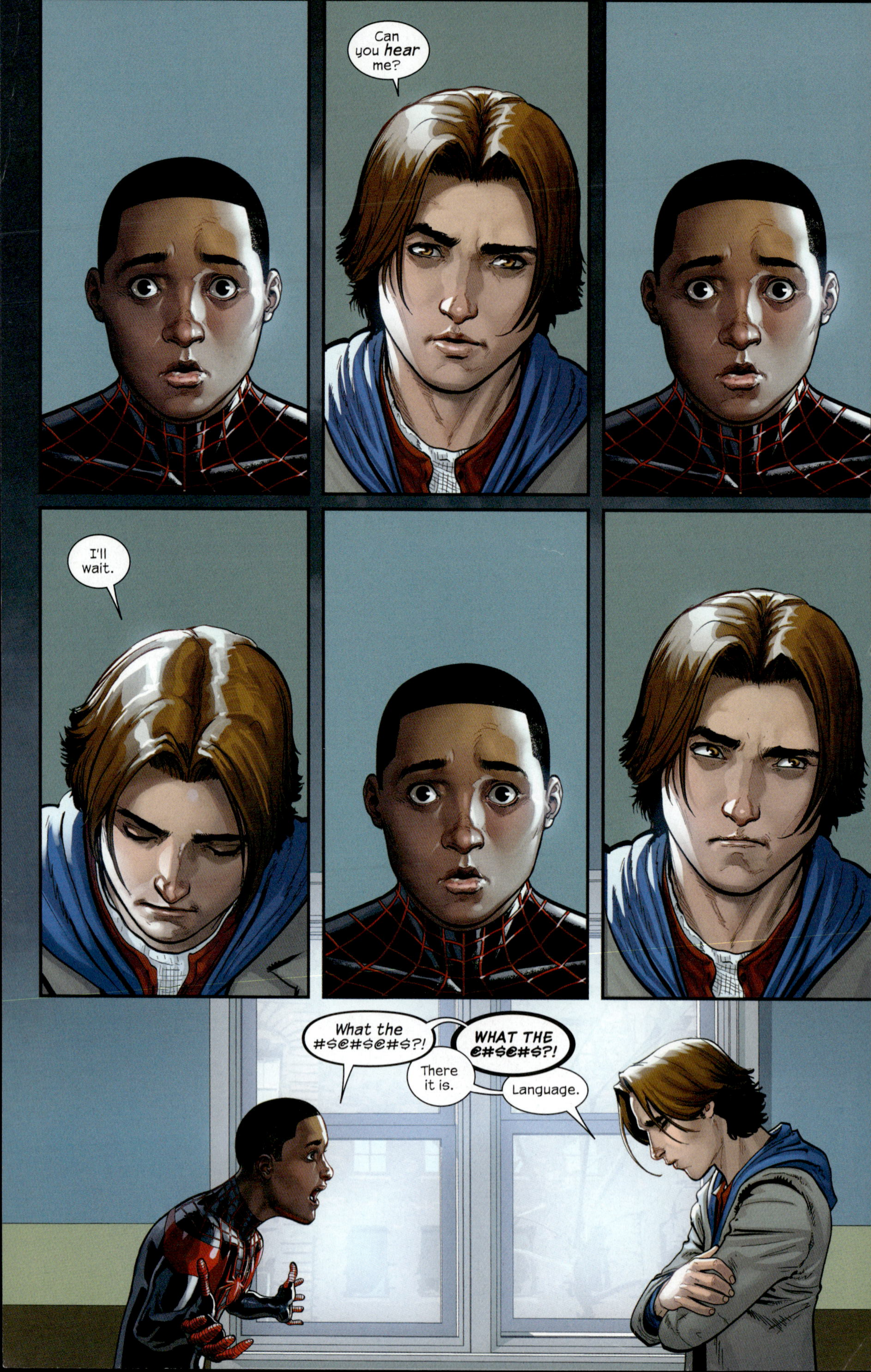
Can you hear me?
I'll wait.
What the #$@#$@#$?!
WHAT THE @#$@#$?!
There it is.
Language.

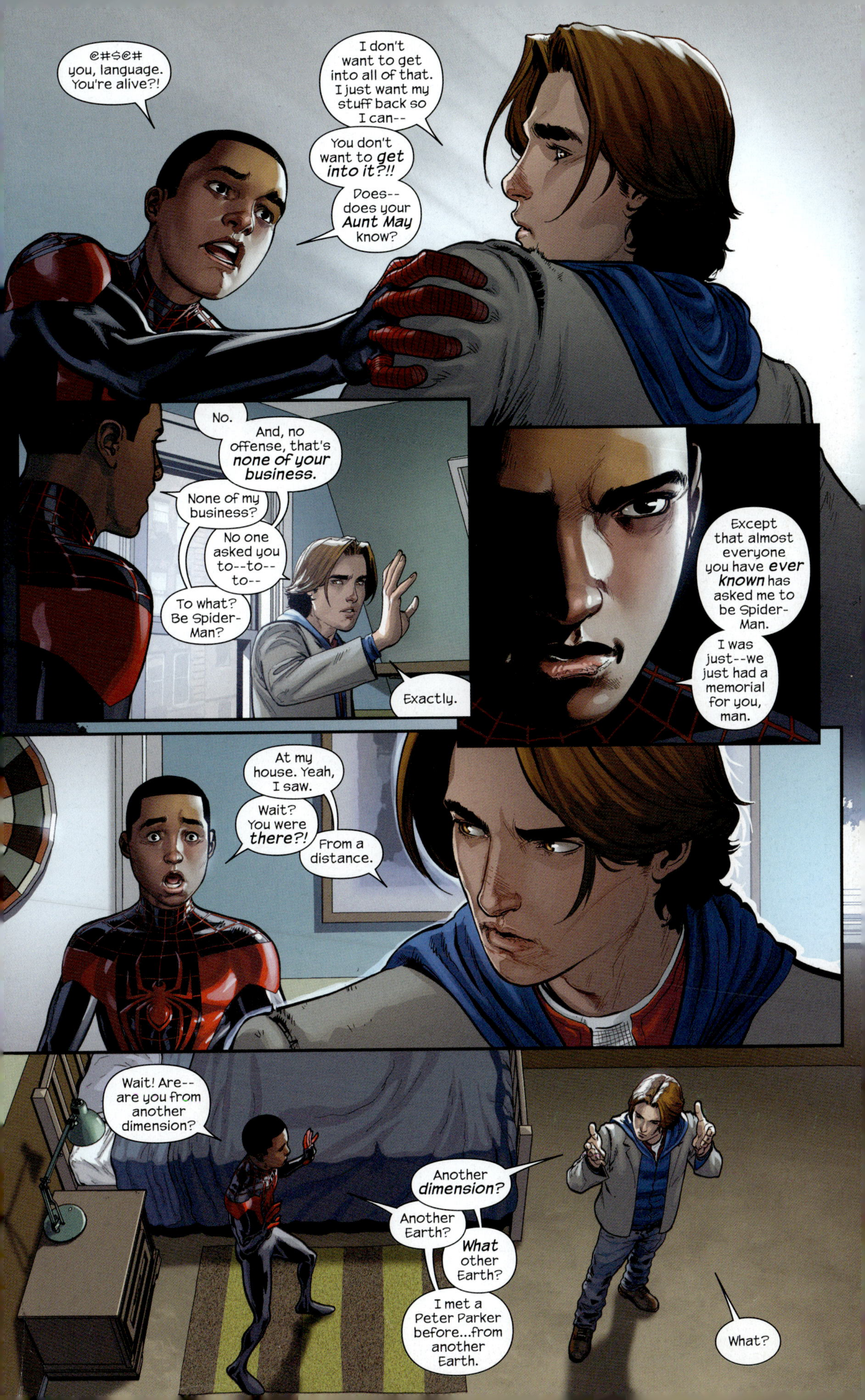

@#$@# you, language. You're alive?!
I don't want to get into all of that. I just want my stuff back so I can--
You don't want to get into it?!!
Does-- does your Aunt May know?
No.
And, no offense, that's none of your business.
None of my business?
No one asked you to--to-- to--
To what? Be Spider-Man?
Exactly.
Except that almost everyone you have ever known has asked me to be Spider-Man.
I was just--we just had a memorial for you, man.
At my house. Yeah, I saw.
Wait? You were there?!
From a distance.
Wait! Are-- are you from another dimension?
Another dimension?
Another Earth?
What other Earth?
I met a Peter Parker before...from another Earth.
What?

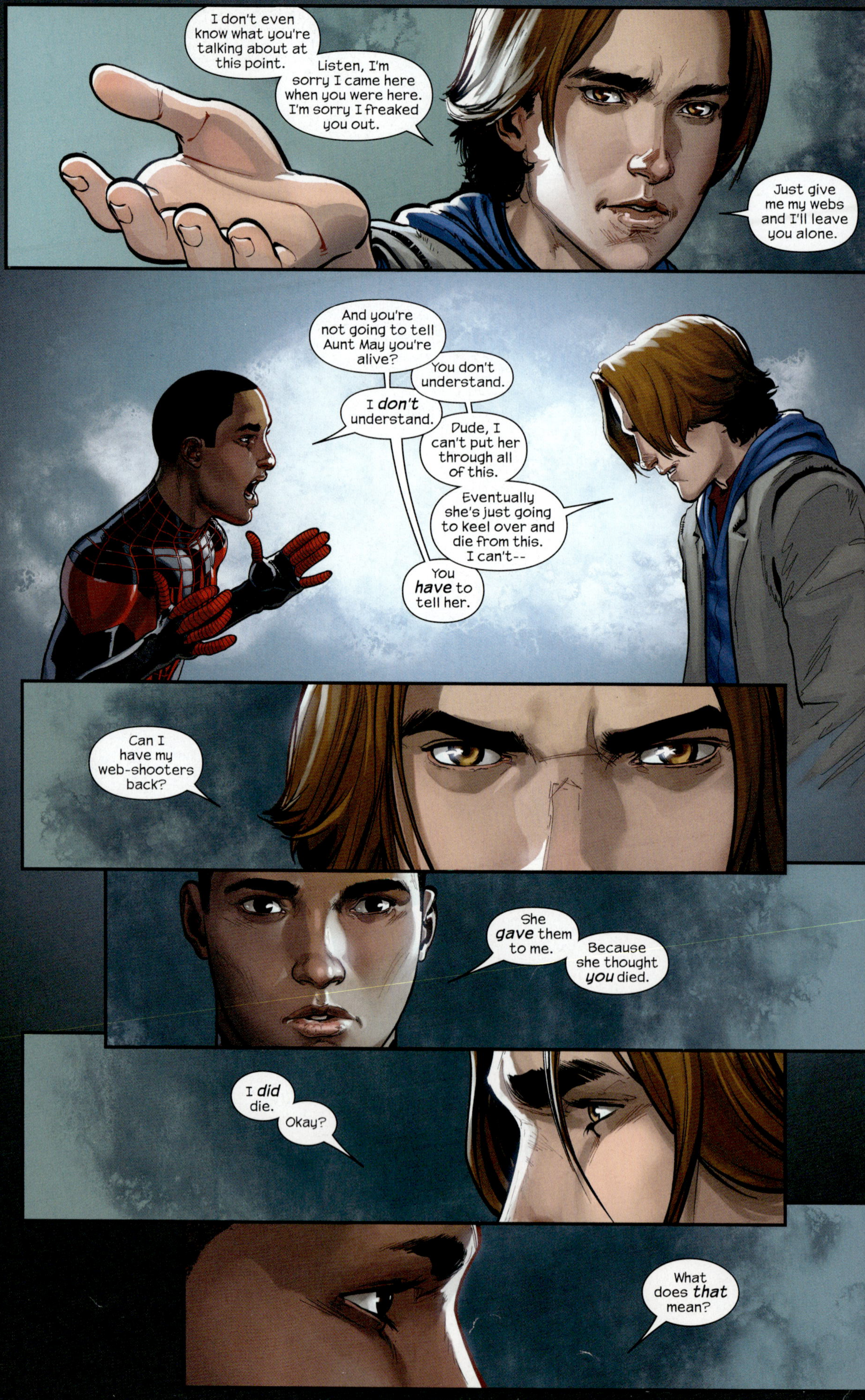

I don't even know what you're talking about at this point.
Listen, I'm sorry I came here when you were here. I'm sorry I freaked you out.
Just give me my webs and I'll leave you alone.
And you're not going to tell Aunt May you're alive?
You don't understand.
I *don't* understand.
Dude, I can't put her through all of this.
Eventually she's just going to keel over and die from this. I can't--
You *have* to tell her.
Can I have my web-shooters back?
She *gave* them to me.
Because she thought *you* died.
I *did* die.
Okay?
What does *that* mean?

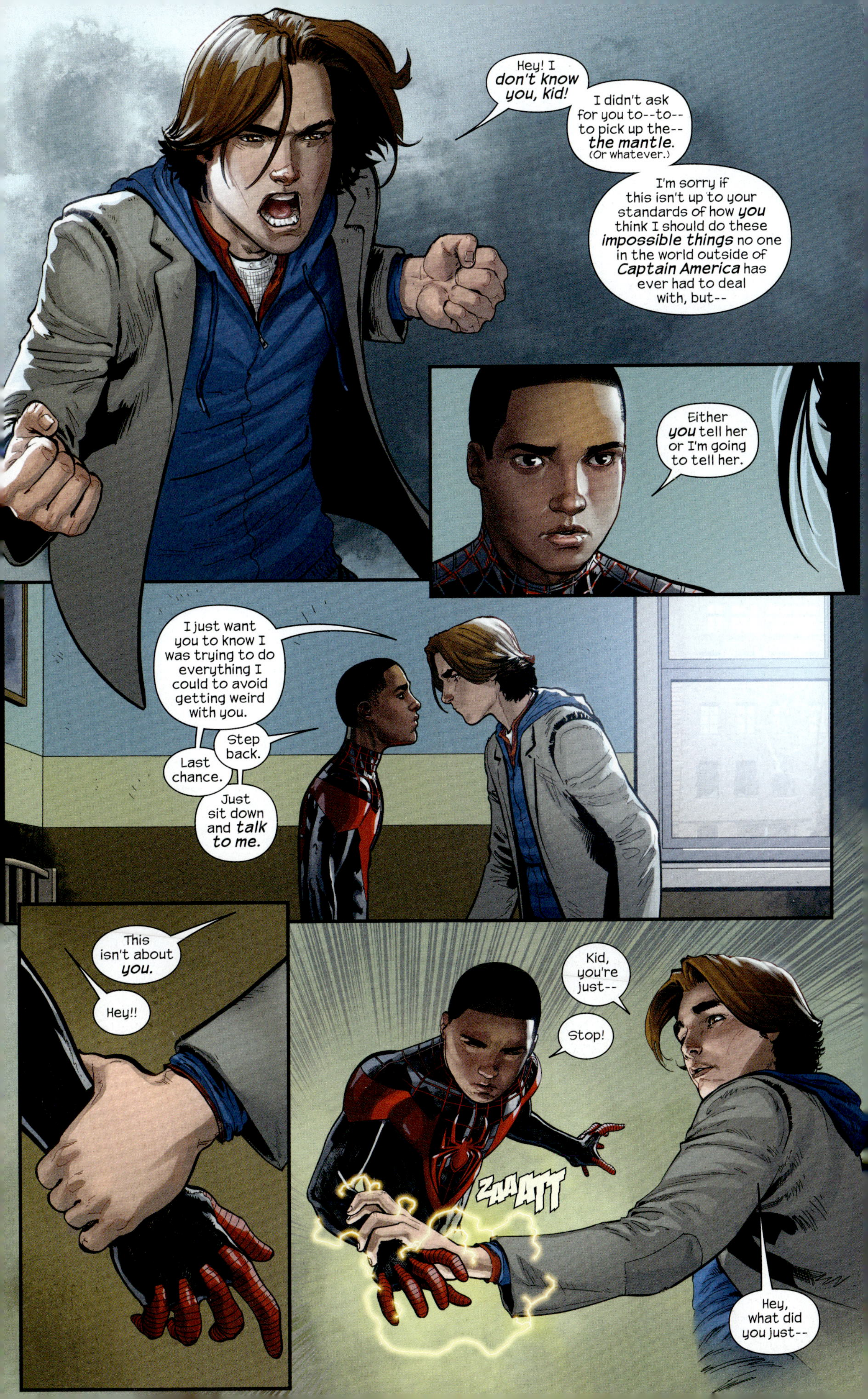
Hey! I don't know you, kid!
I didn't ask for you to--to--to pick up the--the mantle. (Or whatever.)
I'm sorry if this isn't up to your standards of how you think I should do these impossible things no one in the world outside of Captain America has ever had to deal with, but--
Either you tell her or I'm going to tell her.
I just want you to know I was trying to do everything I could to avoid getting weird with you.
Step back.
Last chance.
Just sit down and talk to me.
This isn't about you.
Hey!!
Kid, you're just--
Stop!
ZAAATT
Hey, what did you just--

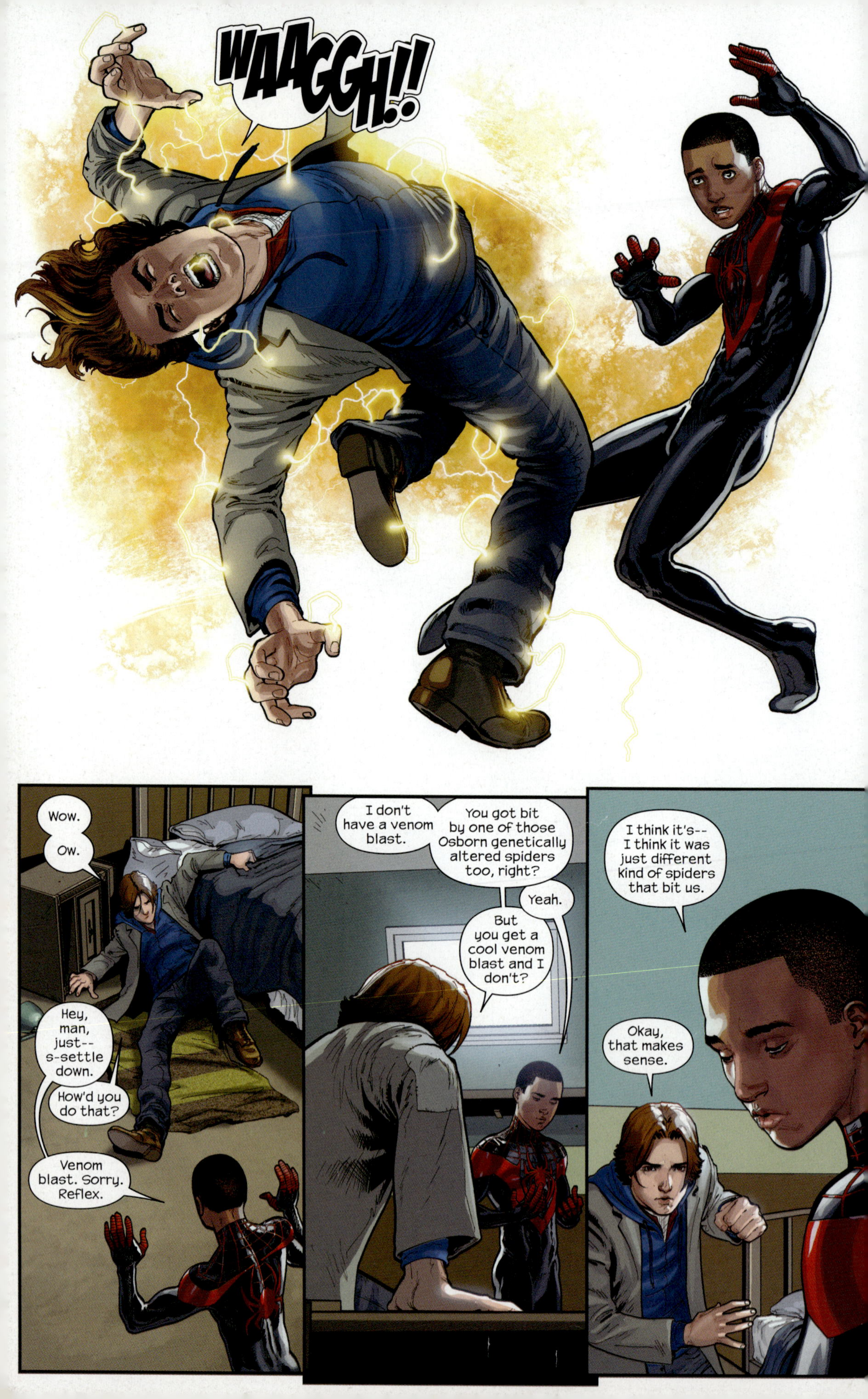
WAAGGH!!
Wow.
Ow.
Hey, man, just-- s-settle down.
How'd you do that?
Venom blast. Sorry. Reflex.
I don't have a venom blast.
You got bit by one of those Osborn genetically altered spiders too, right?
Yeah.
But you get a cool venom blast and I don't?
I think it's-- I think it was just different kind of spiders that bit us.
Okay, that makes sense.

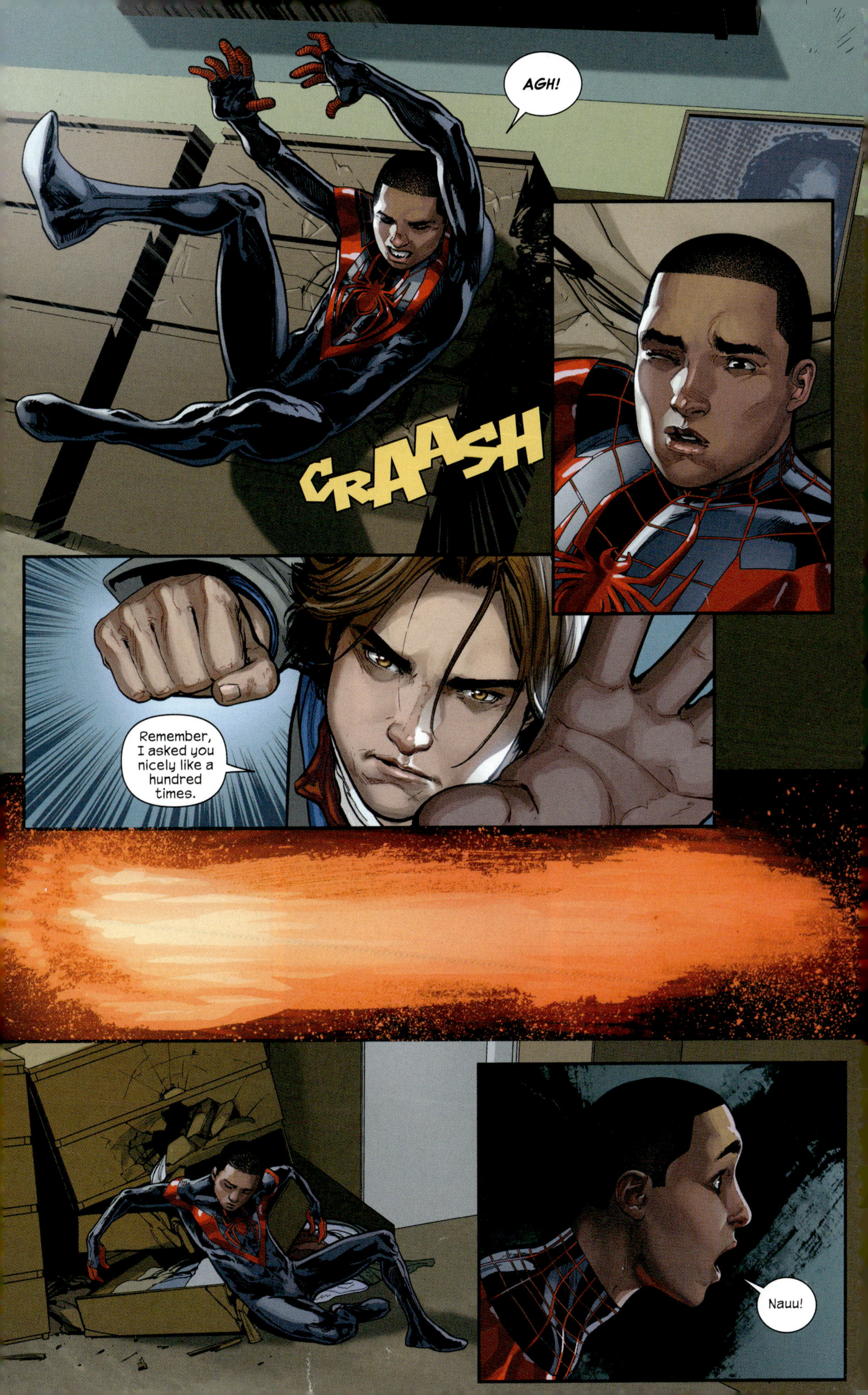
AGH!
CRAAASH
Remember, I asked you nicely like a hundred times.
Nauu!

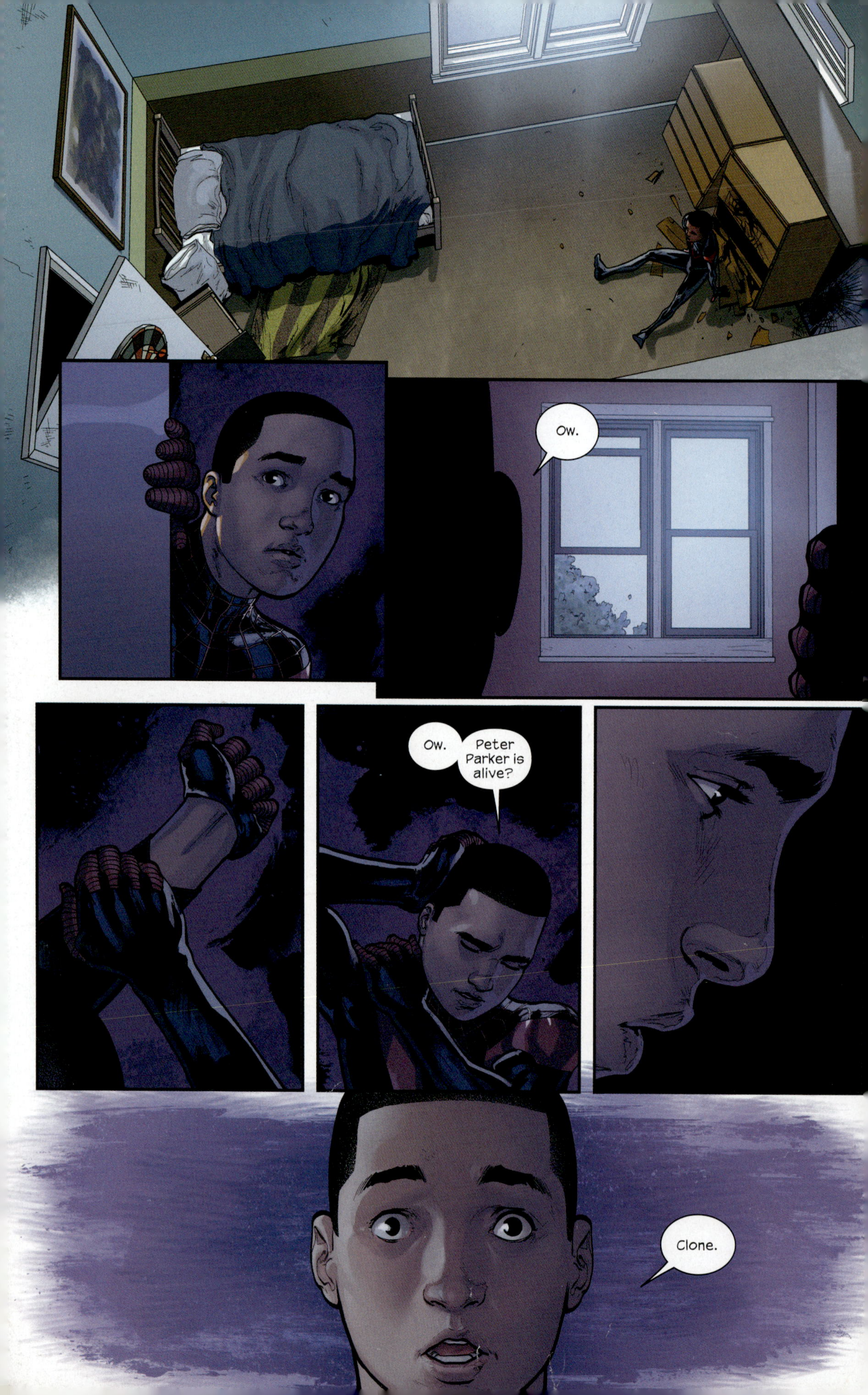
Ow.
Ow.
Peter Parker is alive?
Clone.

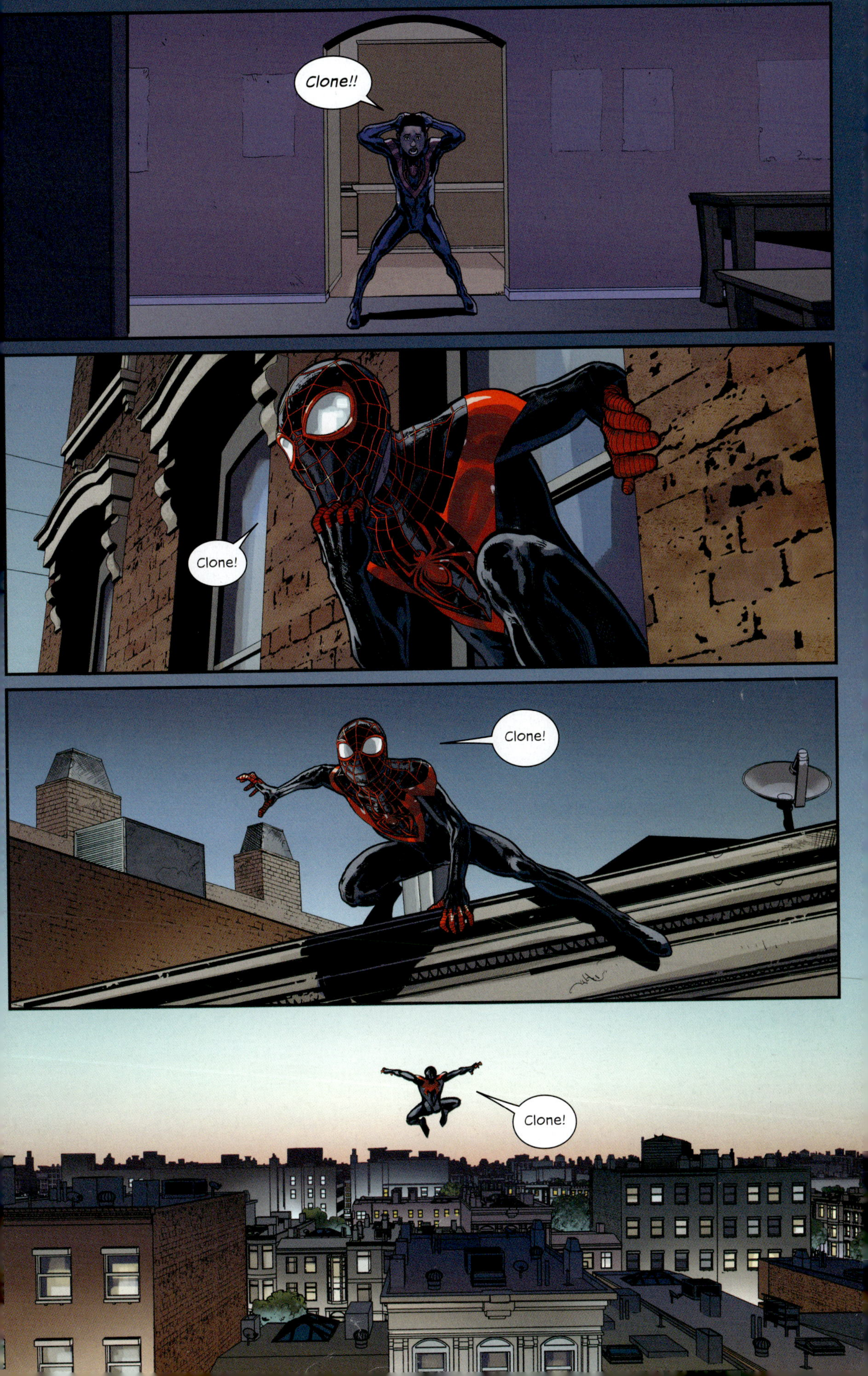
Clone!!
Clone!
Clone!
Clone!

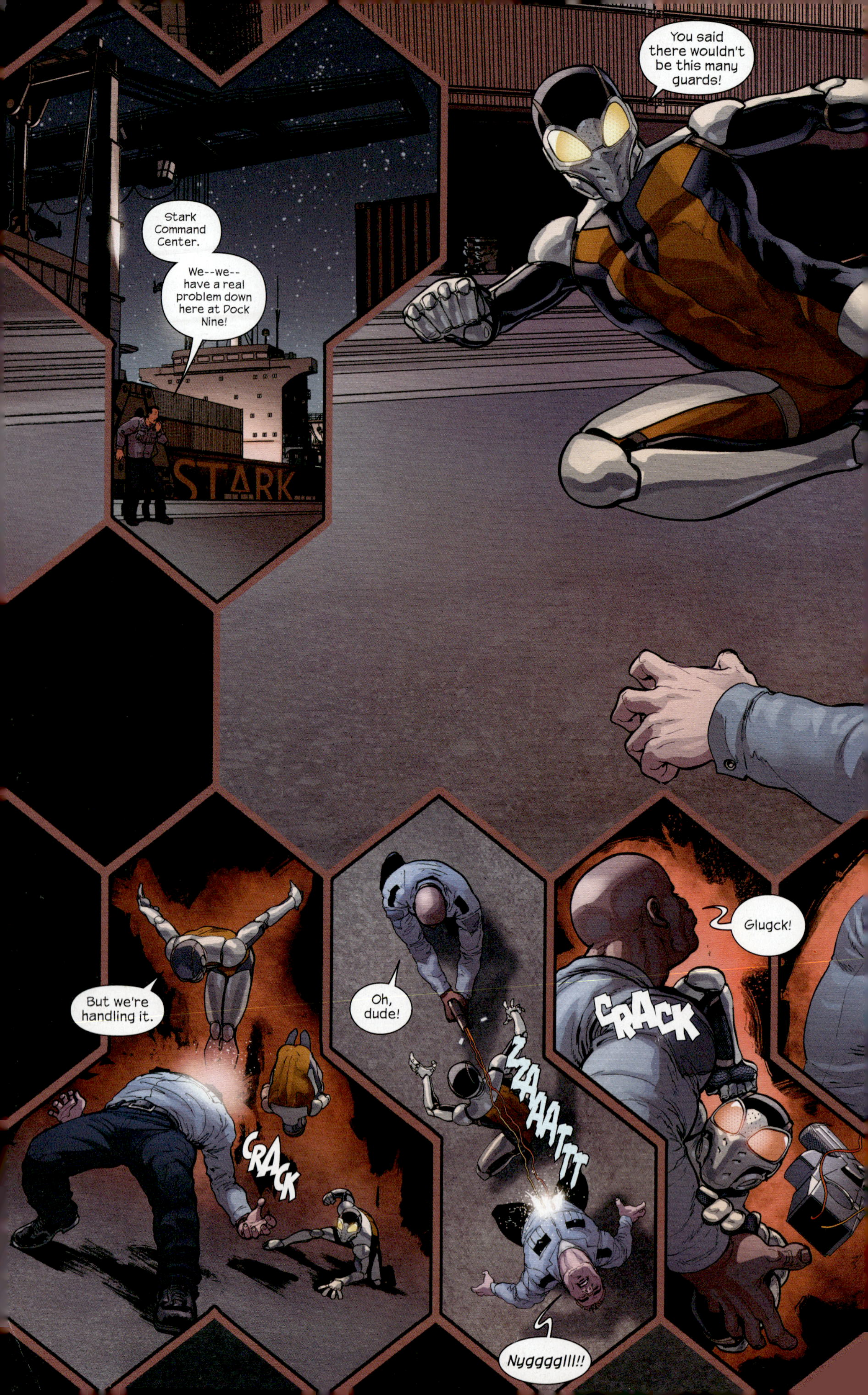
Stark Command Center.
We--we-- have a real problem down here at Dock Nine!
STARK
You said there wouldn't be this many guards!
But we're handling it.
CRACK
Oh, dude!
ZZAAAATTTT
Nygggglll!!
Glugck!
CRACK

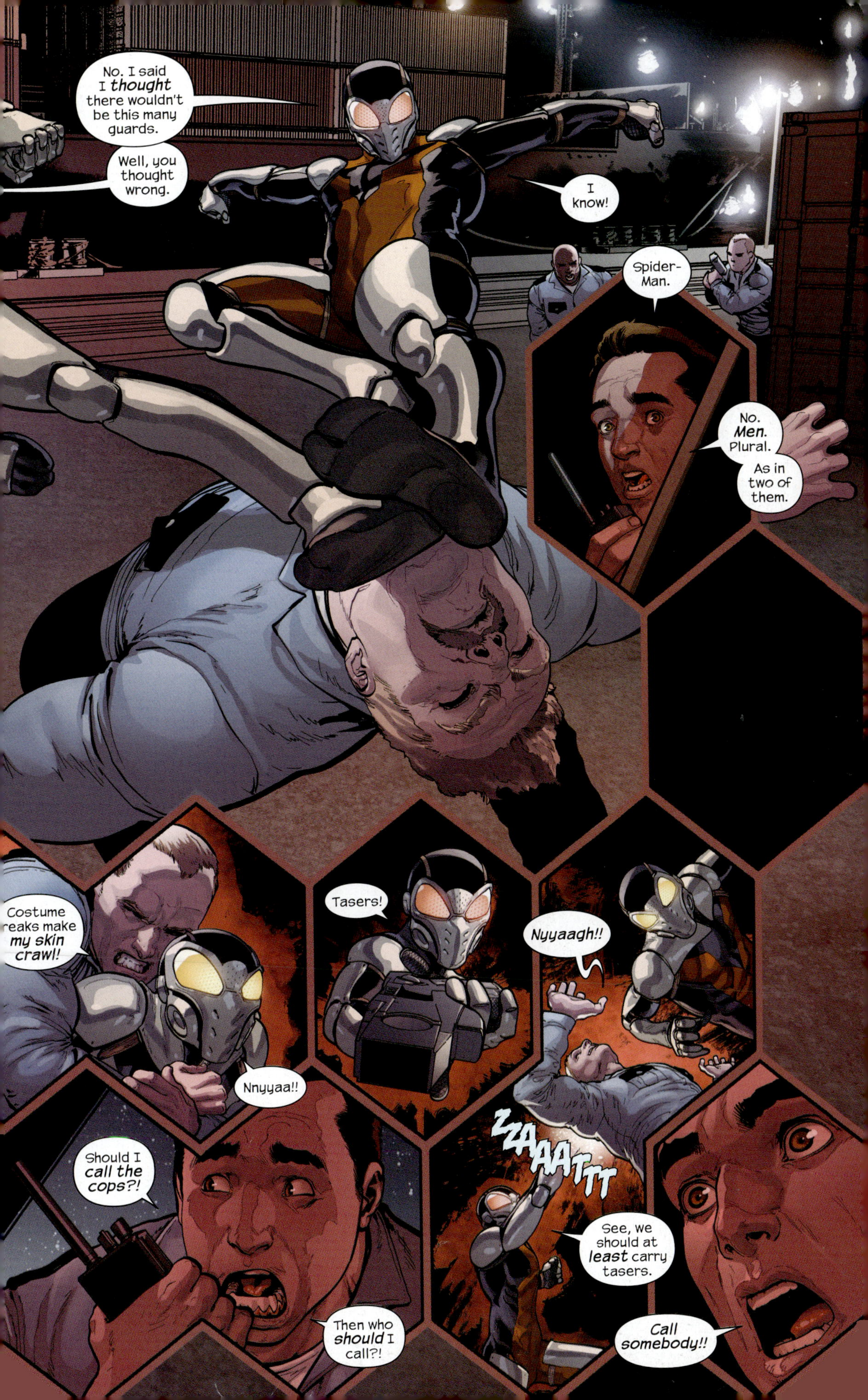

No. I said I *thought* there wouldn't be this many guards.
Well, you thought wrong.
I know!
Spider-Man.
No. *Men*. Plural.
As in two of them.
Costume freaks make *my skin crawl!*
Nnyyaa!!
Tasers!
Nyyaagh!!
Should I *call the cops?!*
Then who *should* I call?!
ZZAAATTT
See, we should at *least* carry tasers.
Call somebody!!

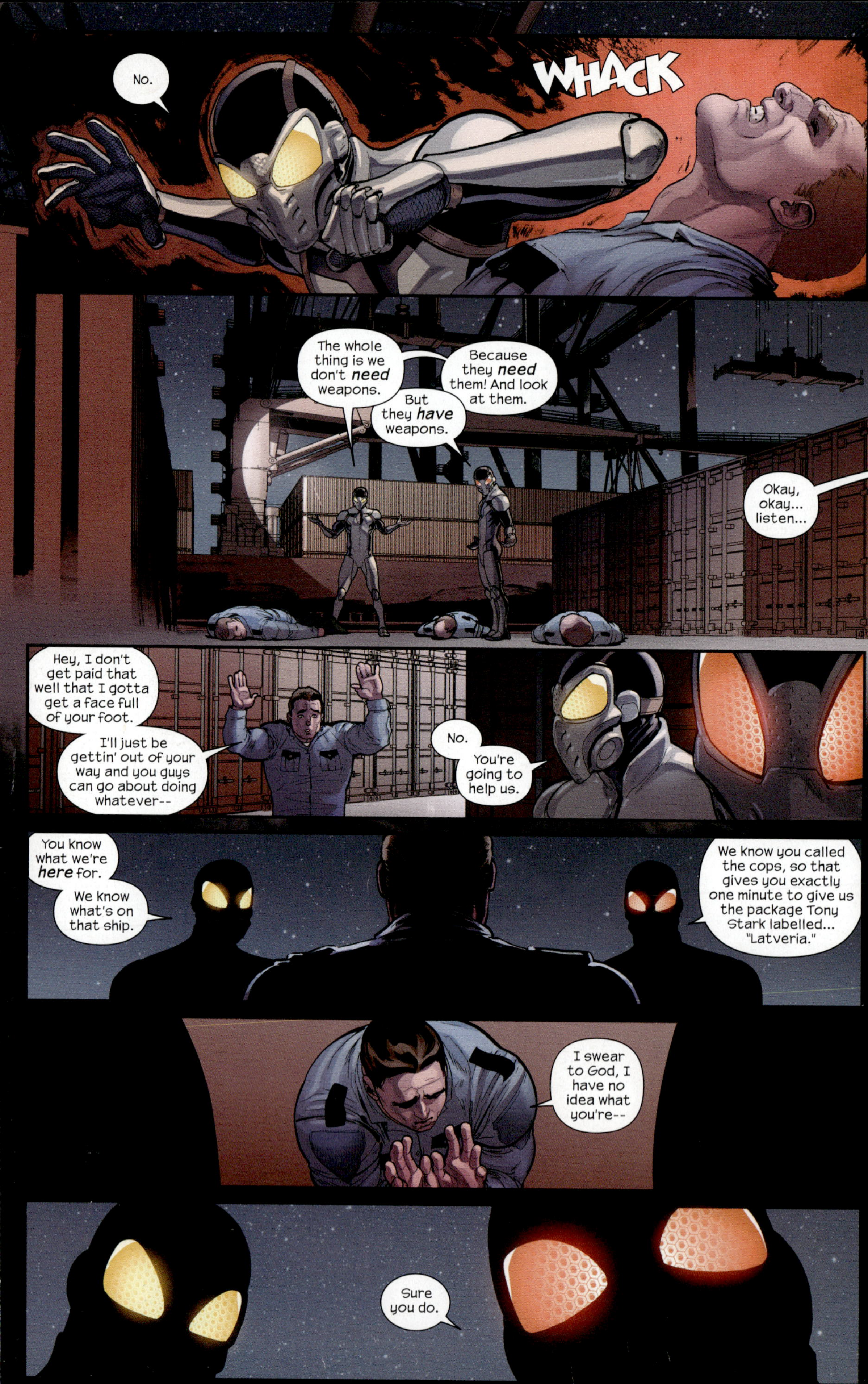

No.
WHACK
The whole thing is we don't *need* weapons.
Because they *need* them! And look at them.
But they *have* weapons.
Okay, okay... listen...
Hey, I don't get paid that well that I gotta get a face full of your foot.
I'll just be gettin' out of your way and you guys can go about doing whatever--
No.
You're going to help us.
You know what we're *here* for.
We know what's on that ship.
We know you called the cops, so that gives you exactly one minute to give us the package Tony Stark labelled... "Latveria."
I swear to God, I have no idea what you're--
Sure you do.

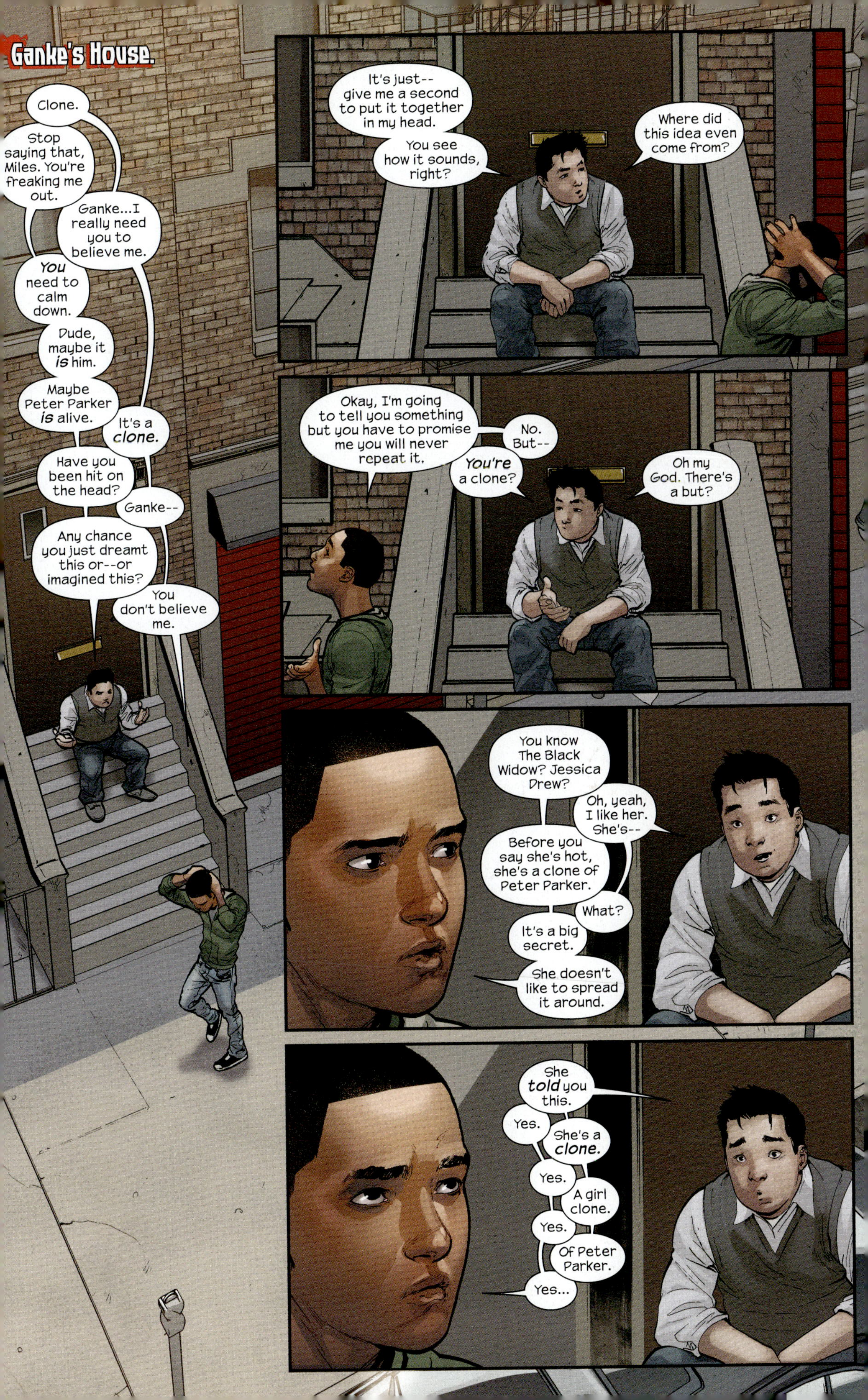
Ganke's House.
Clone.
Stop saying that, Miles. You're freaking me out.
Ganke...I really need you to believe me.
You need to calm down.
Dude, maybe it is him.
Maybe Peter Parker is alive.
It's a clone.
Have you been hit on the head?
Ganke--
Any chance you just dreamt this or--or imagined this?
You don't believe me.
It's just-- give me a second to put it together in my head.
You see how it sounds, right?
Where did this idea even come from?
Okay, I'm going to tell you something but you have to promise me you will never repeat it.
No. But--
You're a clone?
Oh my God. There's a but?
You know The Black Widow? Jessica Drew?
Oh, yeah, I like her. She's--
Before you say she's hot, she's a clone of Peter Parker.
What?
It's a big secret.
She doesn't like to spread it around.
She told you this.
Yes.
She's a clone.
Yes.
A girl clone.
Yes.
Of Peter Parker.
Yes...

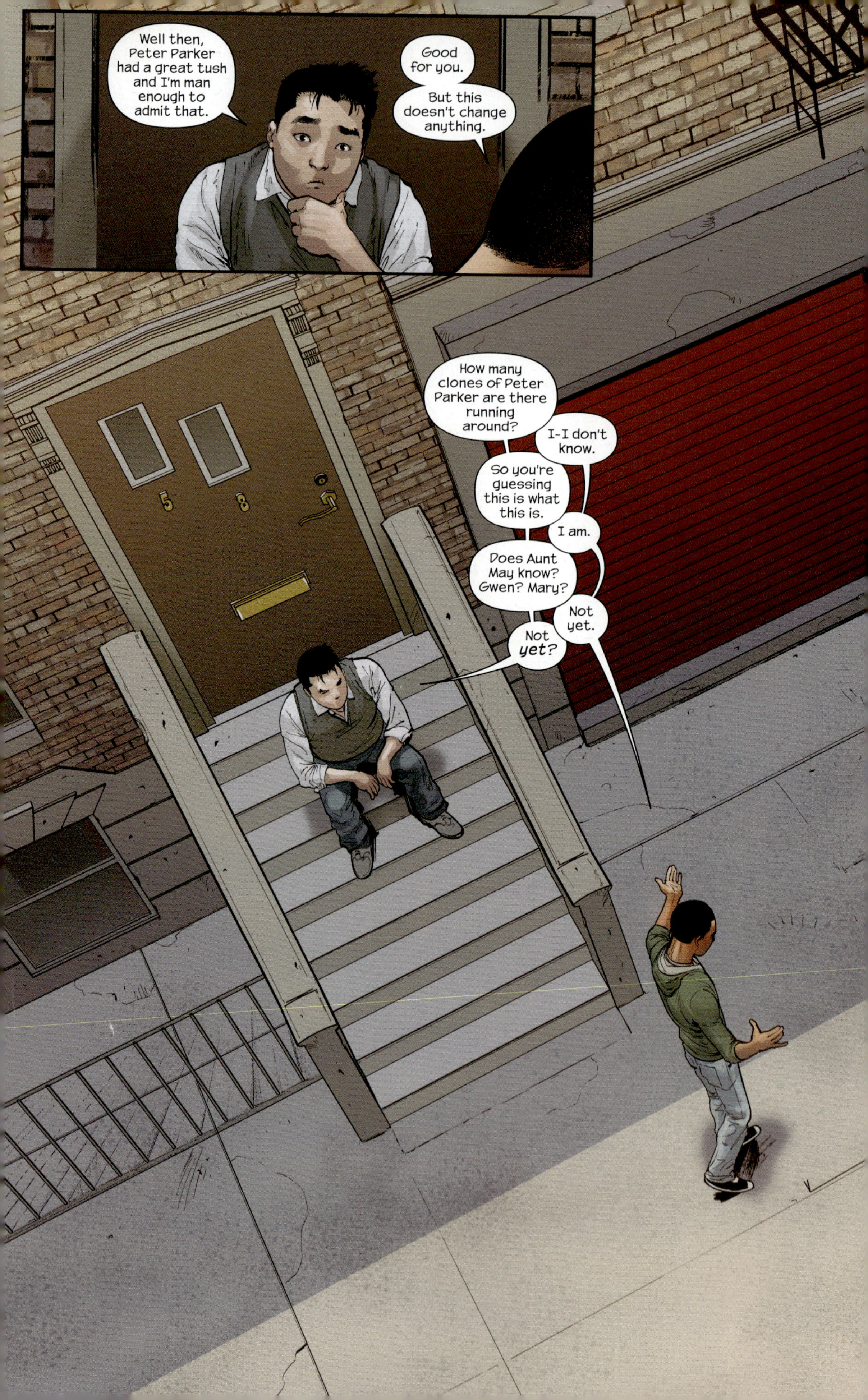
Well then, Peter Parker had a great tush and I'm man enough to admit that.
Good for you.
But this doesn't change anything.
How many clones of Peter Parker are there running around?
I-I don't know.
So you're guessing this is what this is.
I am.
Does Aunt May know? Gwen? Mary?
Not yet.
Not *yet*?

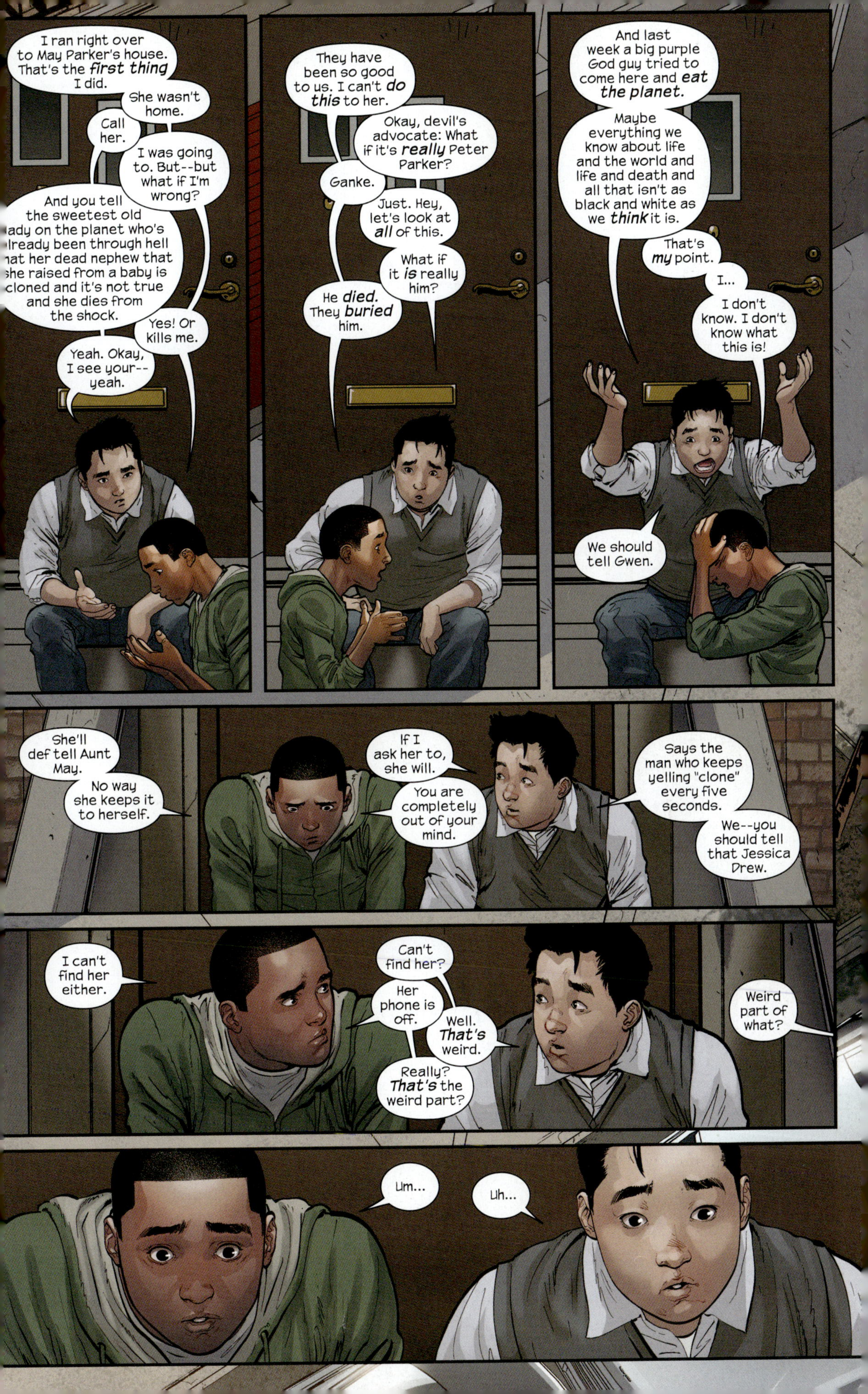
I ran right over to May Parker's house. That's the first thing I did.
She wasn't home.
Call her.
I was going to. But--but what if I'm wrong?
And you tell the sweetest old lady on the planet who's already been through hell that her dead nephew that she raised from a baby is cloned and it's not true and she dies from the shock.
Yes! Or kills me.
Yeah. Okay, I see your--yeah.
They have been so good to us. I can't do this to her.
Okay, devil's advocate: What if it's really Peter Parker?
Ganke.
Just. Hey, let's look at all of this.
What if it is really him?
He died. They buried him.
And last week a big purple God guy tried to come here and eat the planet.
Maybe everything we know about life and the world and life and death and all that isn't as black and white as we think it is.
That's my point.
I...
I don't know. I don't know what this is!
We should tell Gwen.
She'll def tell Aunt May.
No way she keeps it to herself.
If I ask her to, she will.
You are completely out of your mind.
Says the man who keeps yelling "clone" every five seconds.
We--you should tell that Jessica Drew.
I can't find her either.
Can't find her?
Her phone is off.
Well. That's weird.
Really? That's the weird part?
Weird part of what?
Um...
Uh...

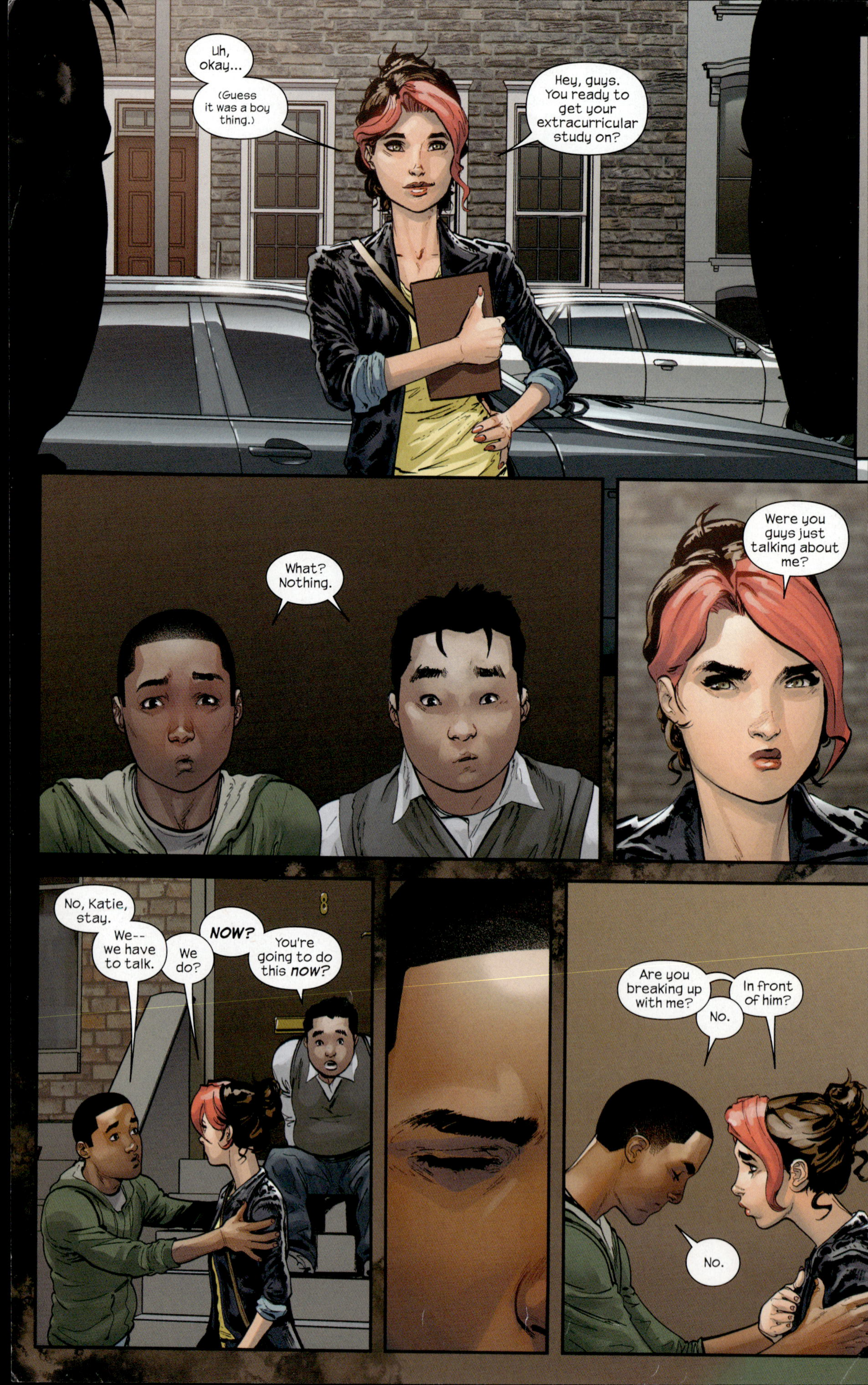
Uh, okay...
(Guess it was a boy thing.)
Hey, guys. You ready to get your extracurricular study on?
What? Nothing.
Were you guys just talking about me?
No, Katie, stay.
We-- we have to talk.
We do?
NOW?
You're going to do this NOW?
Are you breaking up with me?
No.
In front of him?
No.

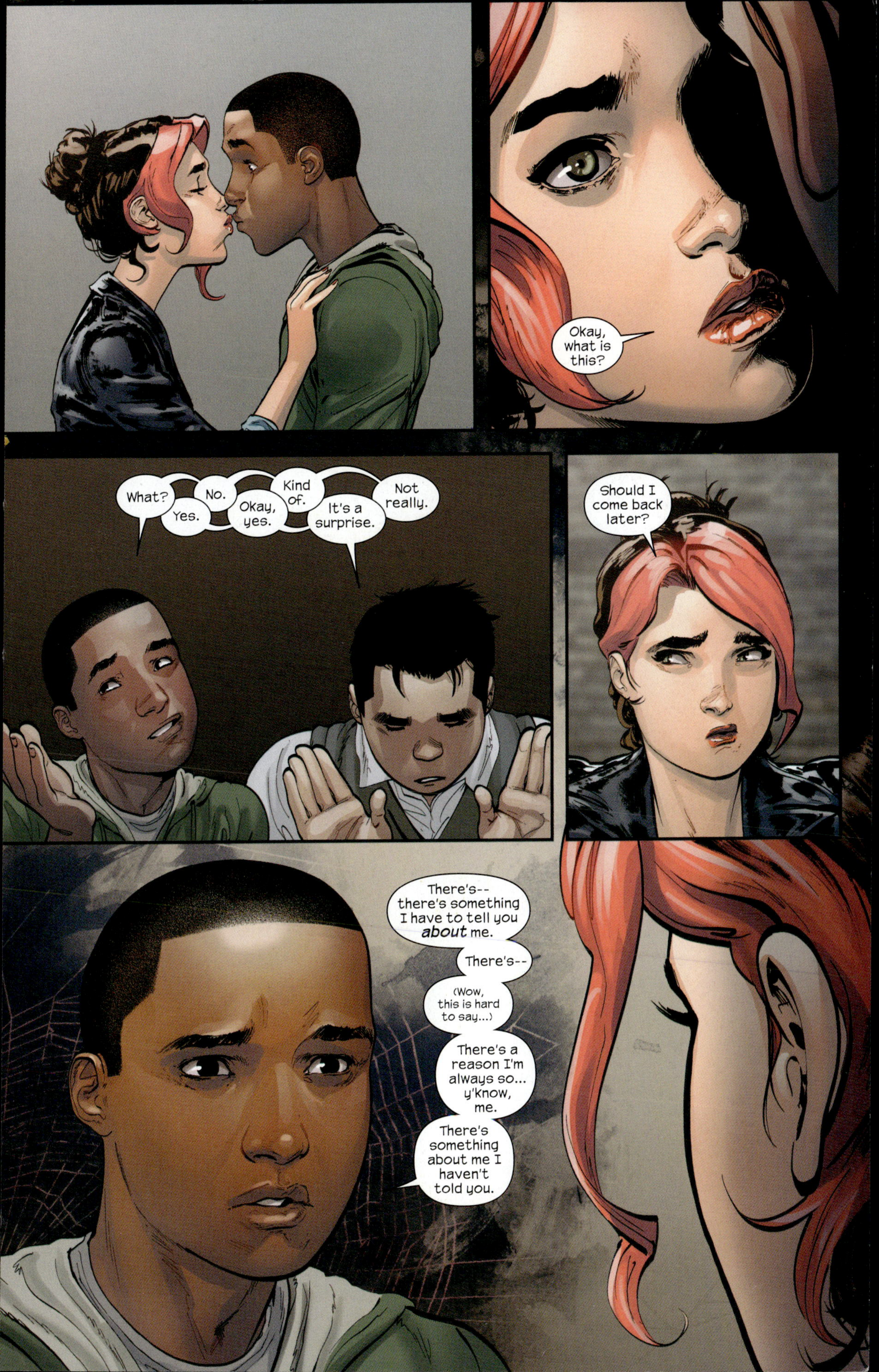
Okay, what is this?
What?
Yes.
No.
Okay, yes.
Kind of.
It's a surprise.
Not really.
Should I come back later?
There's-- there's something I have to tell you *about* me.
There's--
(Wow, this is hard to say...)
There's a reason I'm always so... y'know, me.
There's something about me I haven't told you.

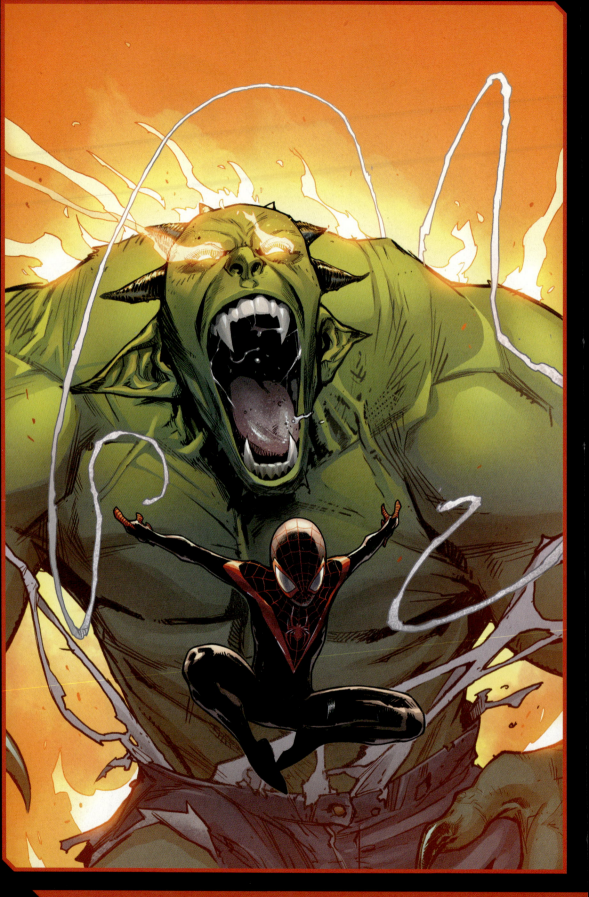

MILES MORALES: ULTIMATE SPIDER-MAN #3 VARIANT BY SARA PICHELLI & JUSTIN PONSOR

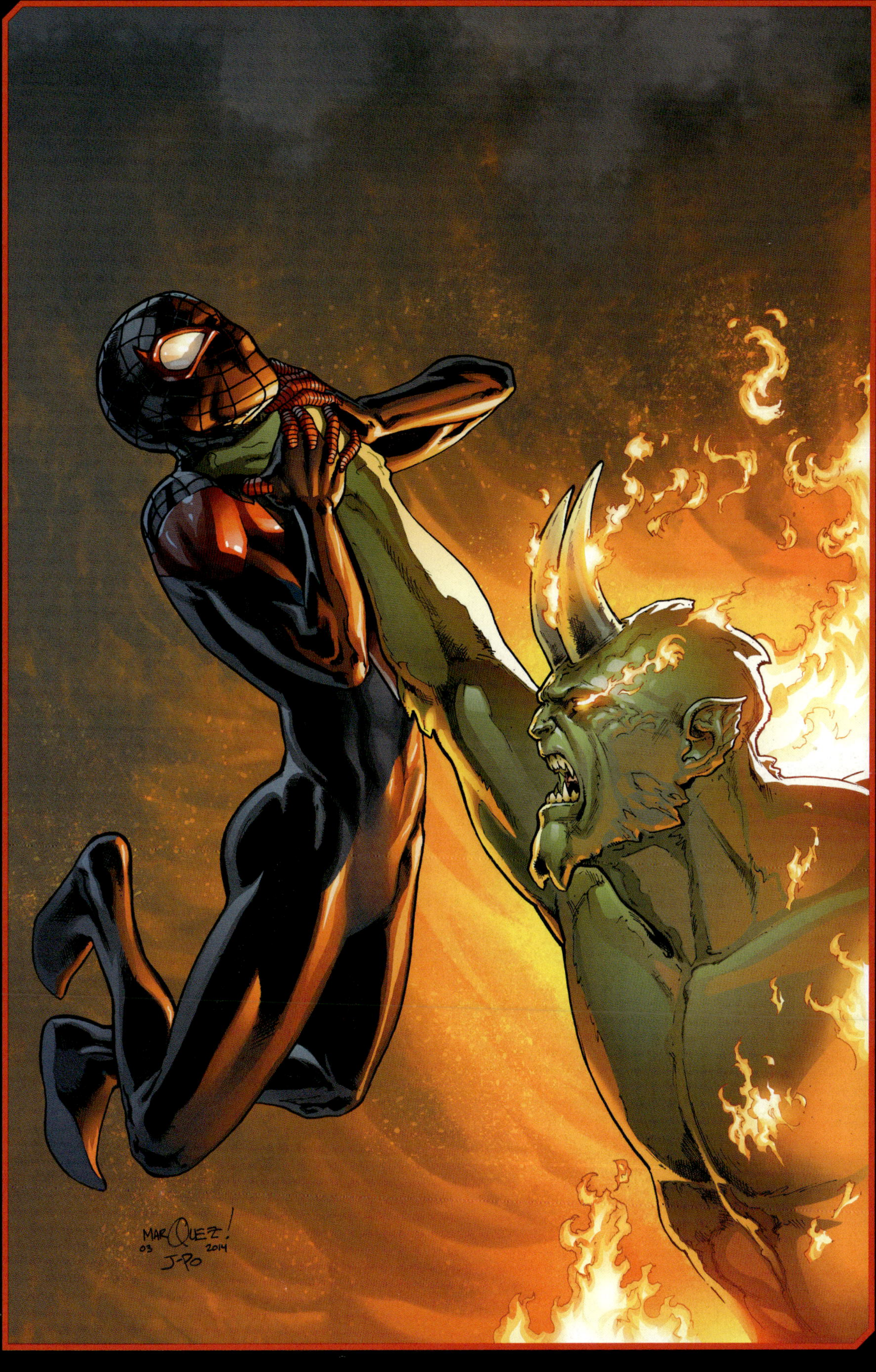
MARQUEZ!
03 2014
J-PO

MILES MORALES: ULTIMATE SPIDER-MAN #3

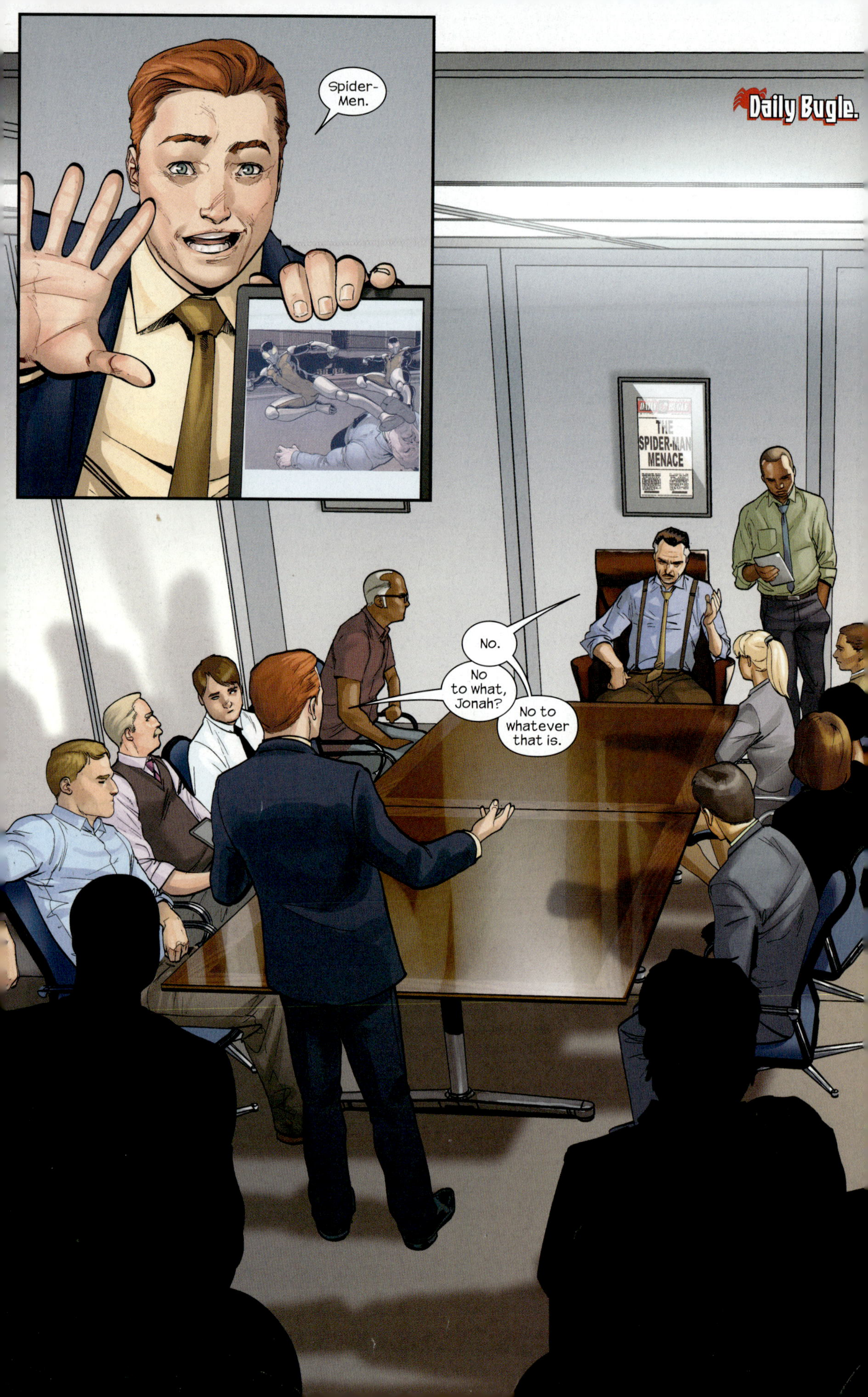
Daily Bugle.
Spider-Men.
THE SPIDER-MAN MENACE
No.
No to what, Jonah?
No to whatever that is.

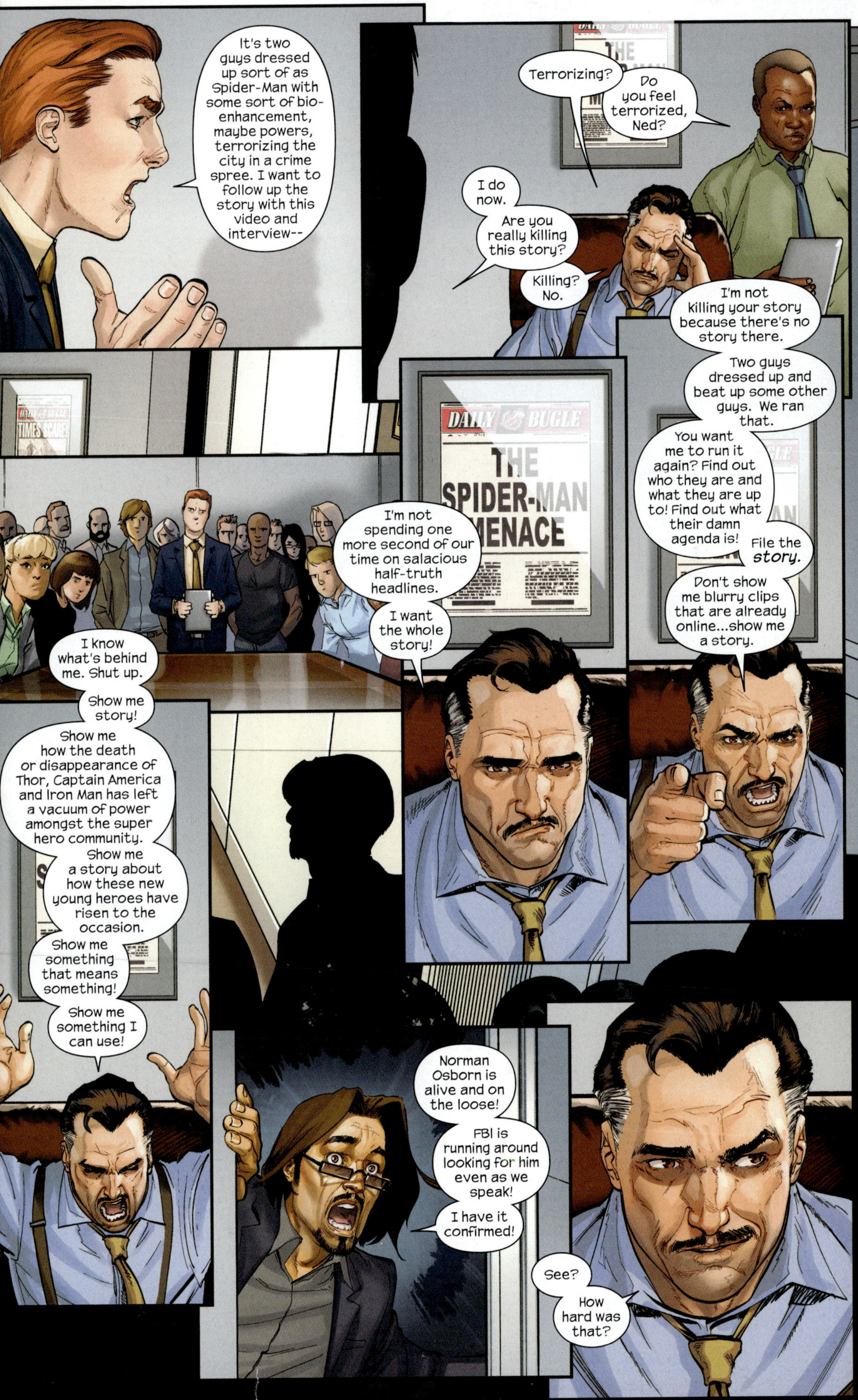
It's two guys dressed up sort of as Spider-Man with some sort of bio-enhancement, maybe powers, terrorizing the city in a crime spree. I want to follow up the story with this video and interview--
Terrorizing?
Do you feel terrorized, Ned?
I do now.
Are you really killing this story?
Killing? No.
I'm not killing your story because there's no story there.
Two guys dressed up and beat up some other guys. We ran that.
You want me to run it again? Find out who they are and what they are up to! Find out what their damn agenda is!
File the story.
Don't show me blurry clips that are already online...show me a story.
DAILY BUGLE
THE SPIDER-MAN MENACE
I'm not spending one more second of our time on salacious half-truth headlines.
I want the whole story!
TIMES SCARE
I know what's behind me. Shut up.
Show me story!
Show me how the death or disappearance of Thor, Captain America and Iron Man has left a vacuum of power amongst the super hero community.
Show me a story about how these new young heroes have risen to the occasion.
Show me something that means something!
Show me something I can use!
Norman Osborn is alive and on the loose!
FBI is running around looking for him even as we speak!
I have it confirmed!
See?
How hard was that?

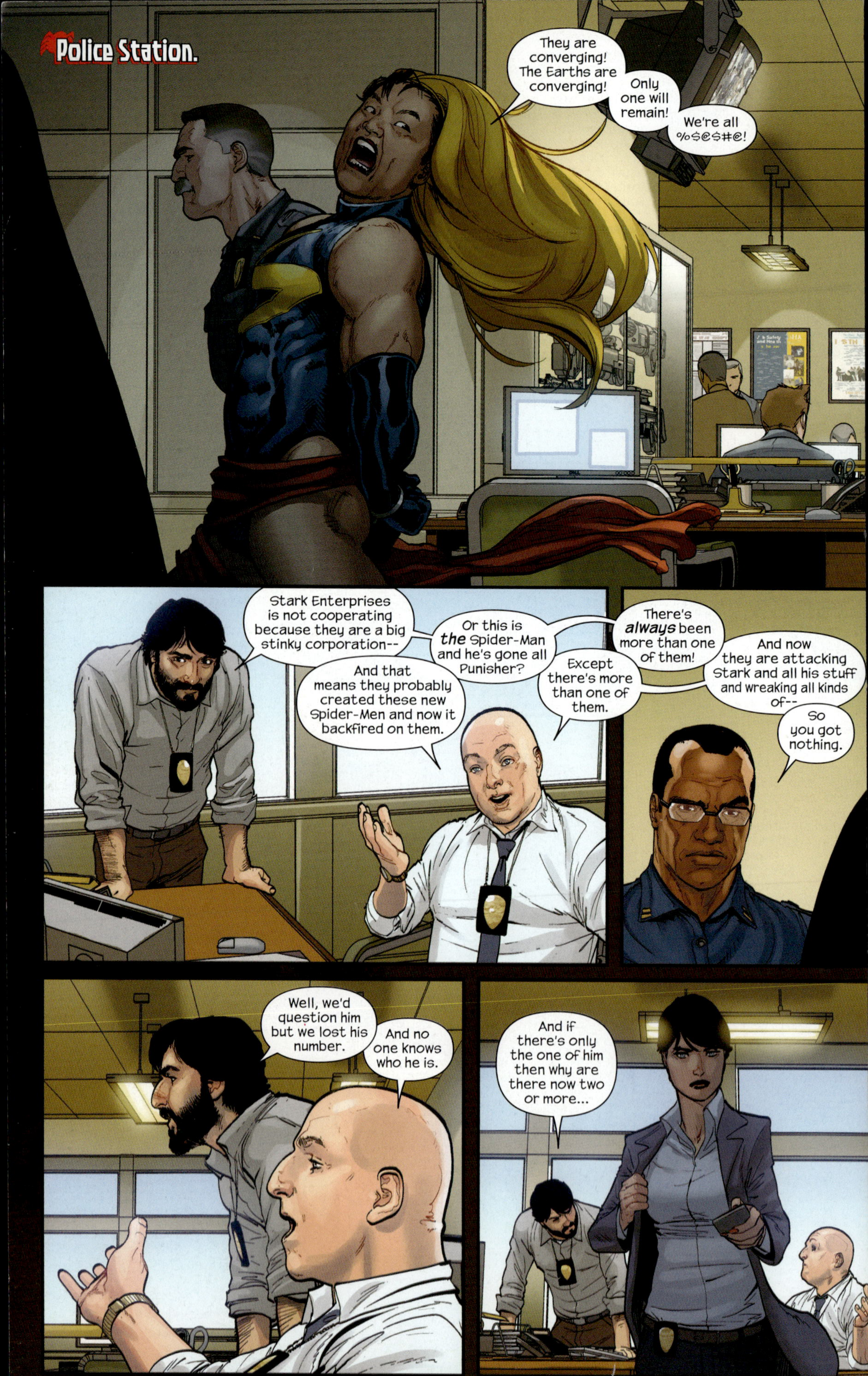

Police Station.
They are converging! The Earths are converging!
Only one will remain!
We're all %$@$#@!
Stark Enterprises is not cooperating because they are a big stinky corporation--
And that means they probably created these new Spider-Men and now it backfired on them.
Or this is *the* Spider-Man and he's gone all Punisher?
Except there's more than one of them.
There's *always* been more than one of them!
And now they are attacking Stark and all his stuff and wreaking all kinds of--
So you got nothing.
Well, we'd question him but we lost his number.
And no one knows who he is.
And if there's only the one of him then why are there now two or more...

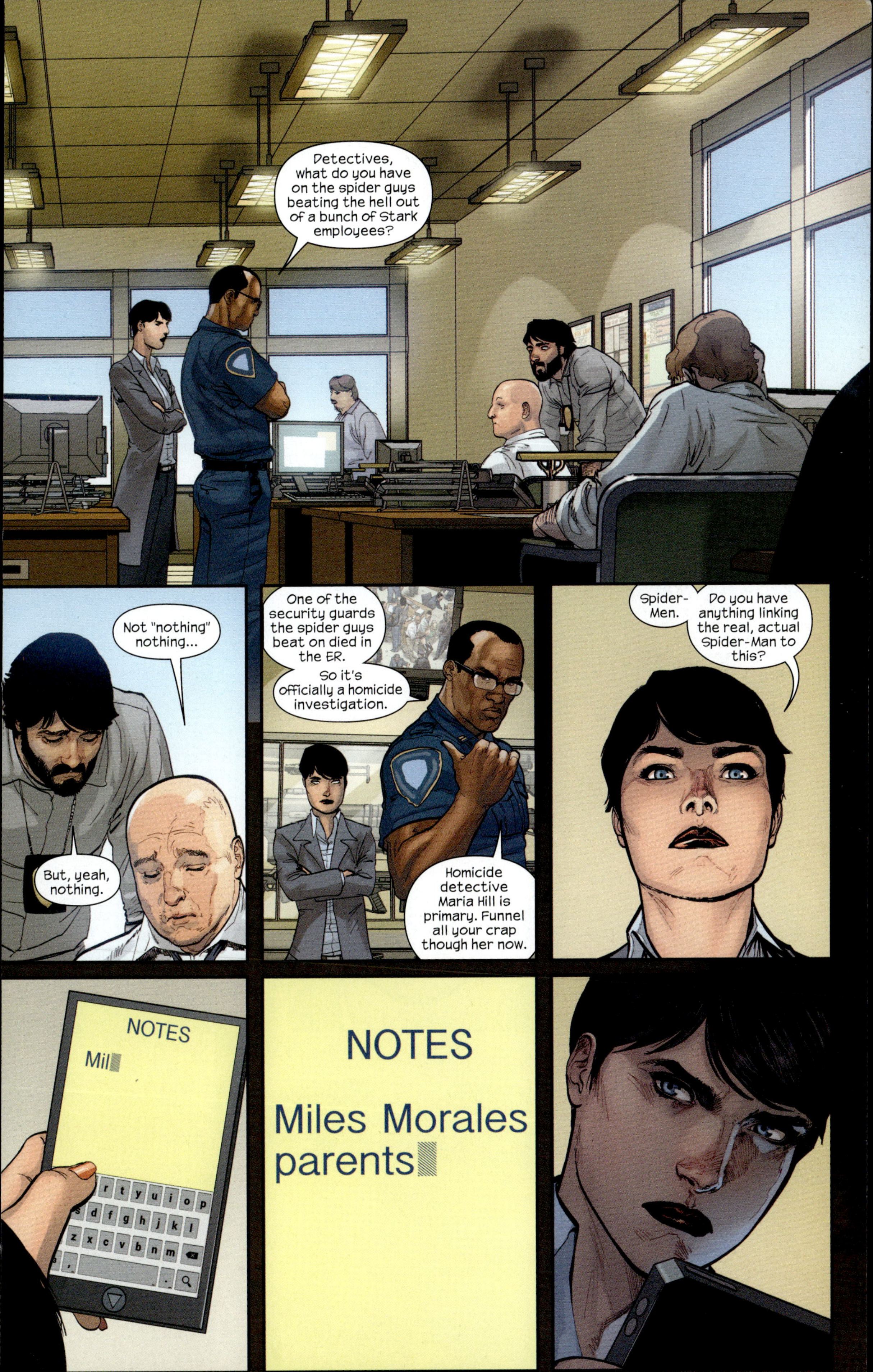
Detectives, what do you have on the spider guys beating the hell out of a bunch of Stark employees?
Not "nothing" nothing...
But, yeah, nothing.
One of the security guards the spider guys beat on died in the ER.
So it's officially a homicide investigation.
Homicide detective Maria Hill is primary. Funnel all your crap though her now.
Spider-Men.
Do you have anything linking the real, actual Spider-Man to this?
NOTES
Mil
NOTES
Miles Morales parents

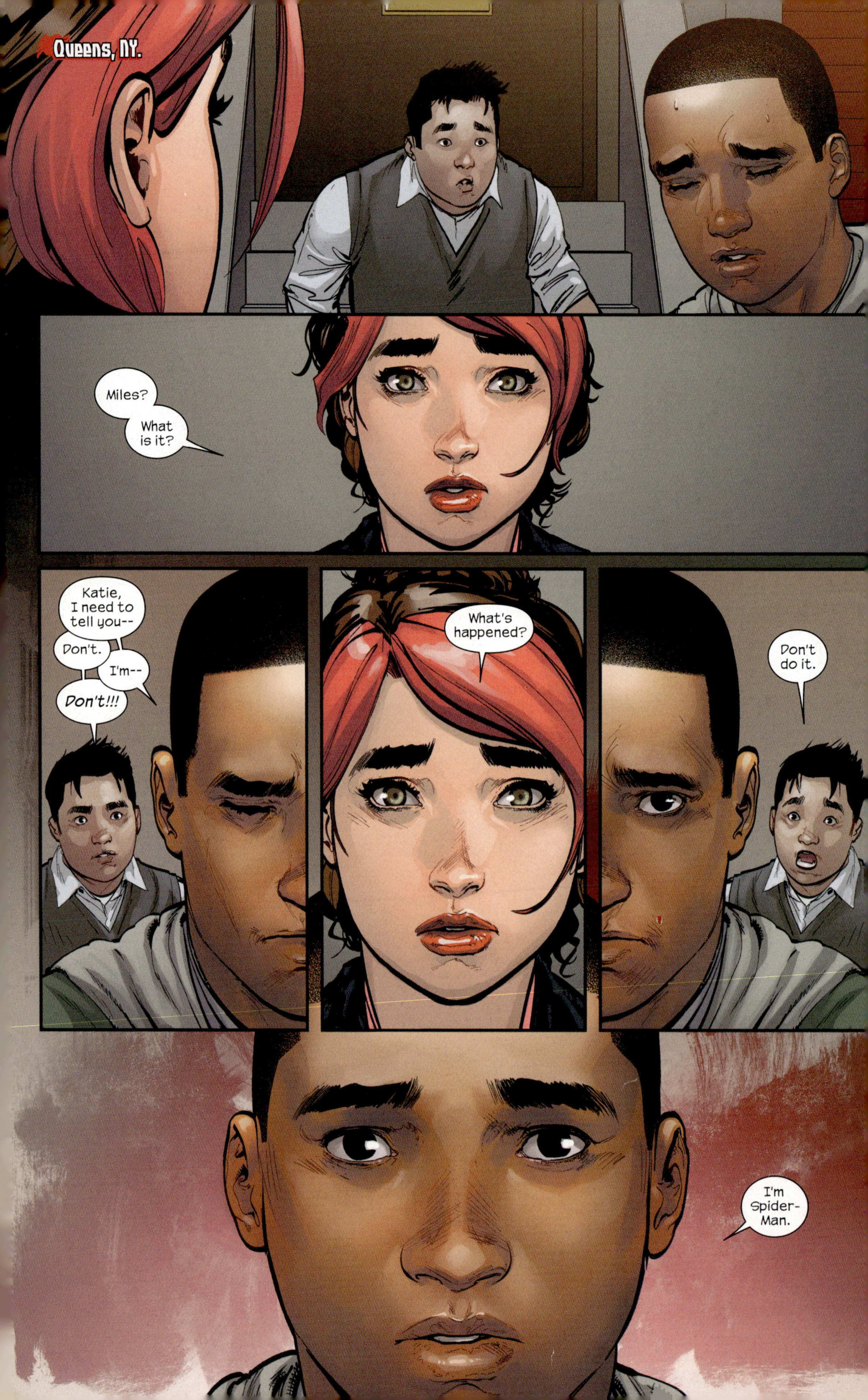
Queens, NY.
Miles?
What is it?
Katie, I need to tell you--
Don't.
I'm--
Don't!!!
What's happened?
Don't do it.
I'm Spider-Man.

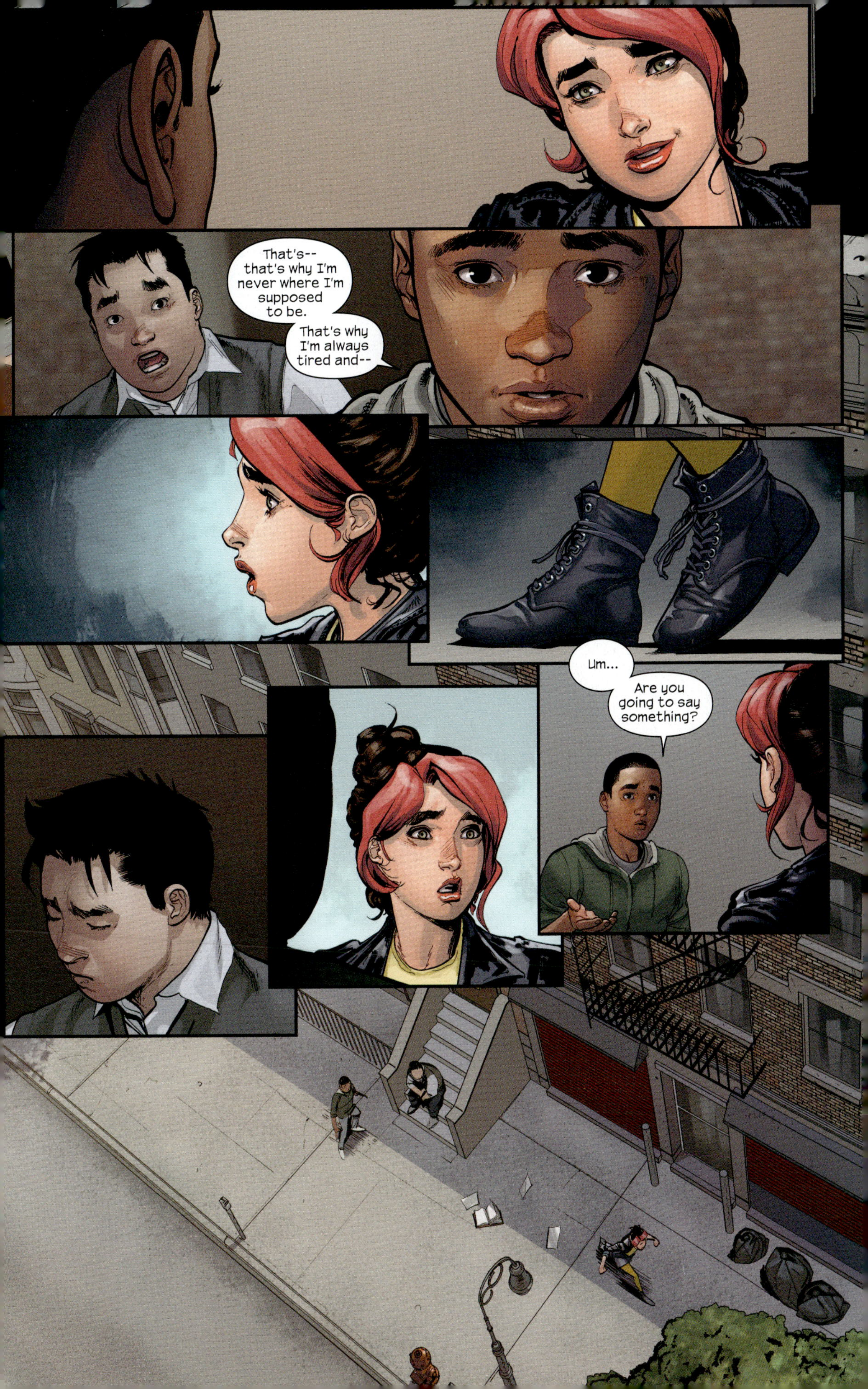
That's-- that's why I'm never where I'm supposed to be.
That's why I'm always tired and--
Um...
Are you going to say something?

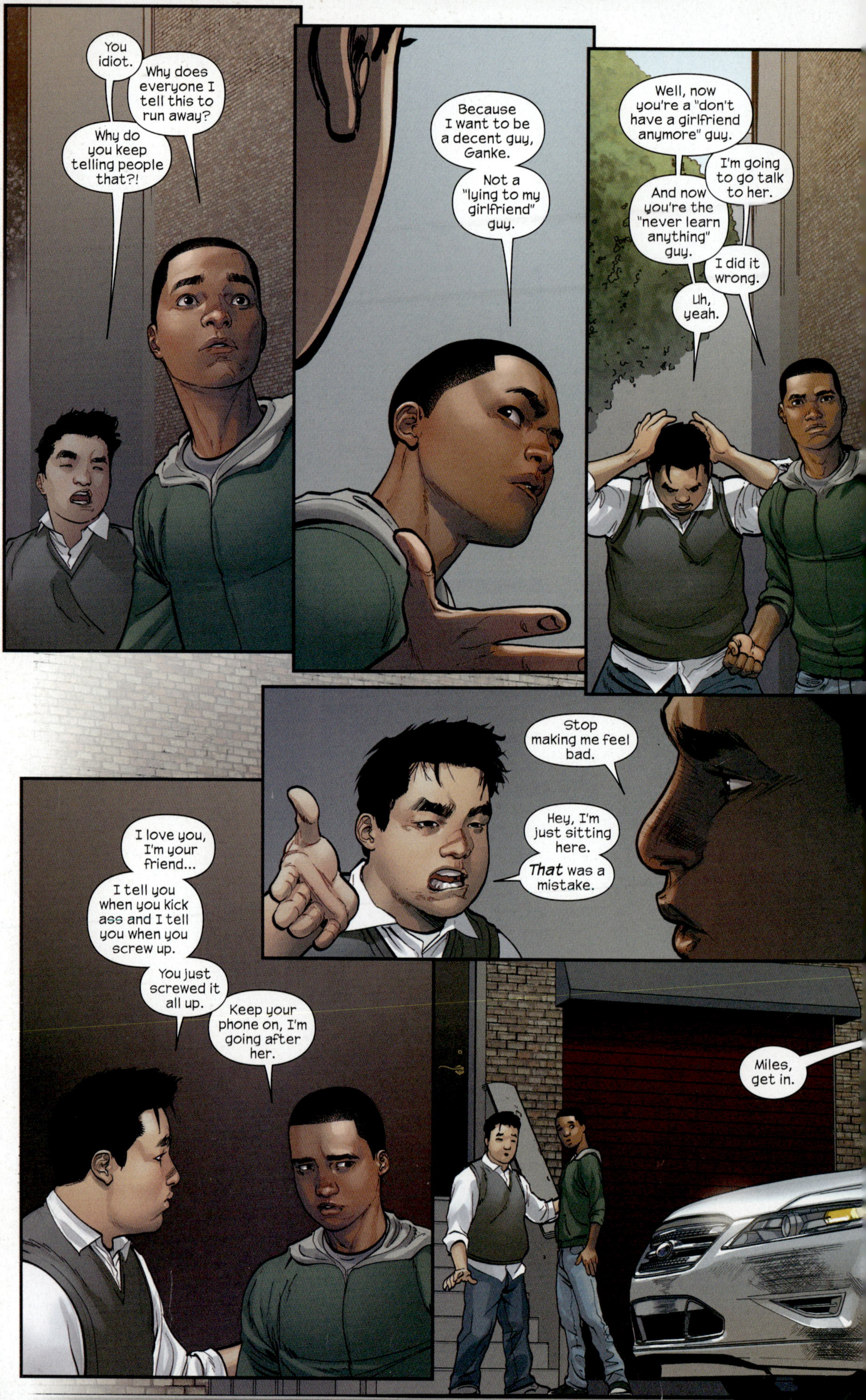
You idiot.
Why does everyone I tell this to run away?
Why do you keep telling people that?!
Because I want to be a decent guy, Ganke.
Not a "lying to my girlfriend" guy.
Well, now you're a "don't have a girlfriend anymore" guy.
I'm going to go talk to her.
And now you're the "never learn anything" guy.
I did it wrong.
Uh, yeah.
I love you, I'm your friend...
I tell you when you kick ass and I tell you when you screw up.
You just screwed it all up.
Keep your phone on, I'm going after her.
Stop making me feel bad.
Hey, I'm just sitting here.
That was a mistake.
Miles, get in.

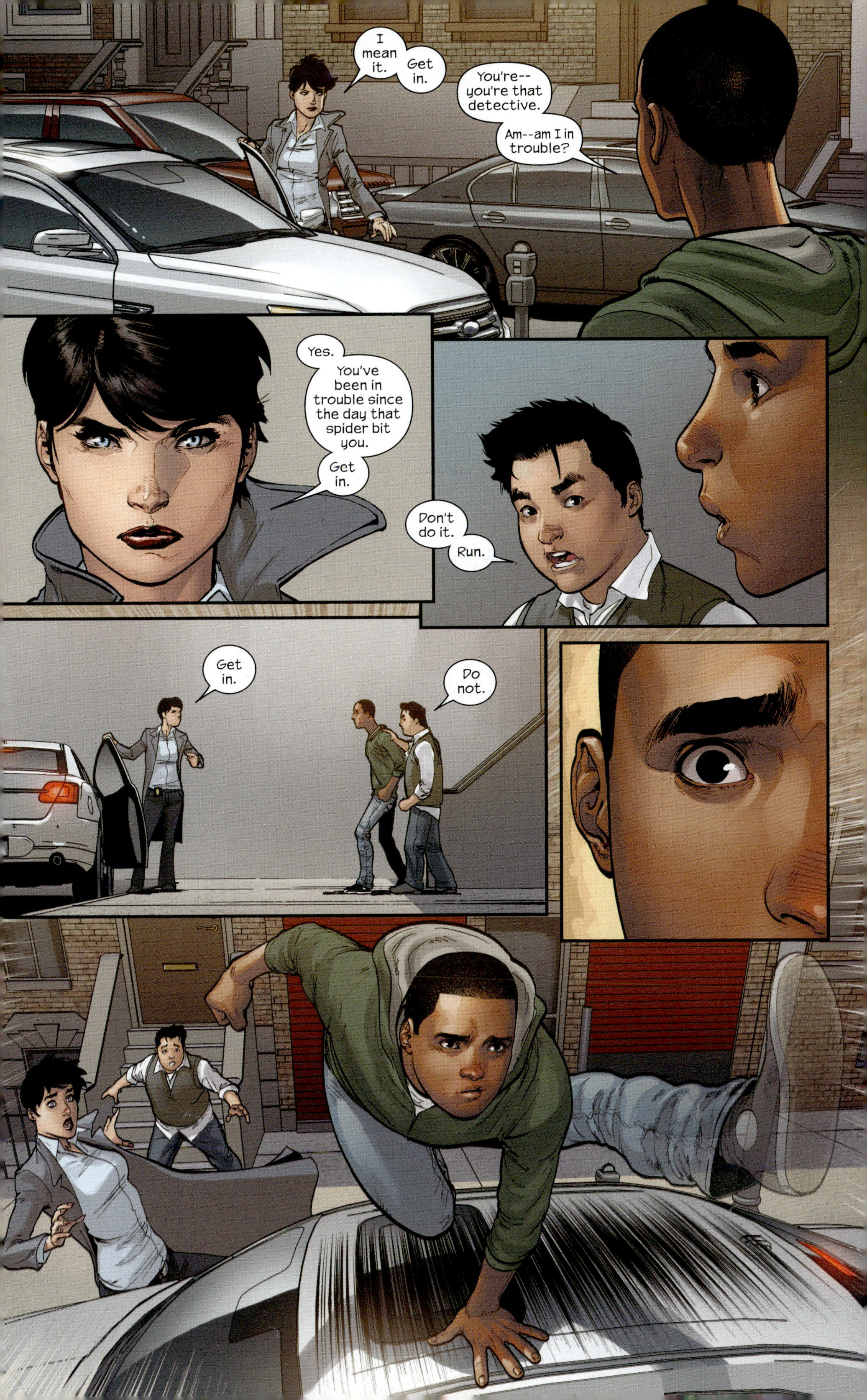
I mean it.
Get in.
You're-- you're that detective.
Am--am I in trouble?
Yes.
You've been in trouble since the day that spider bit you.
Get in.
Don't do it.
Run.
Get in.
Do not.

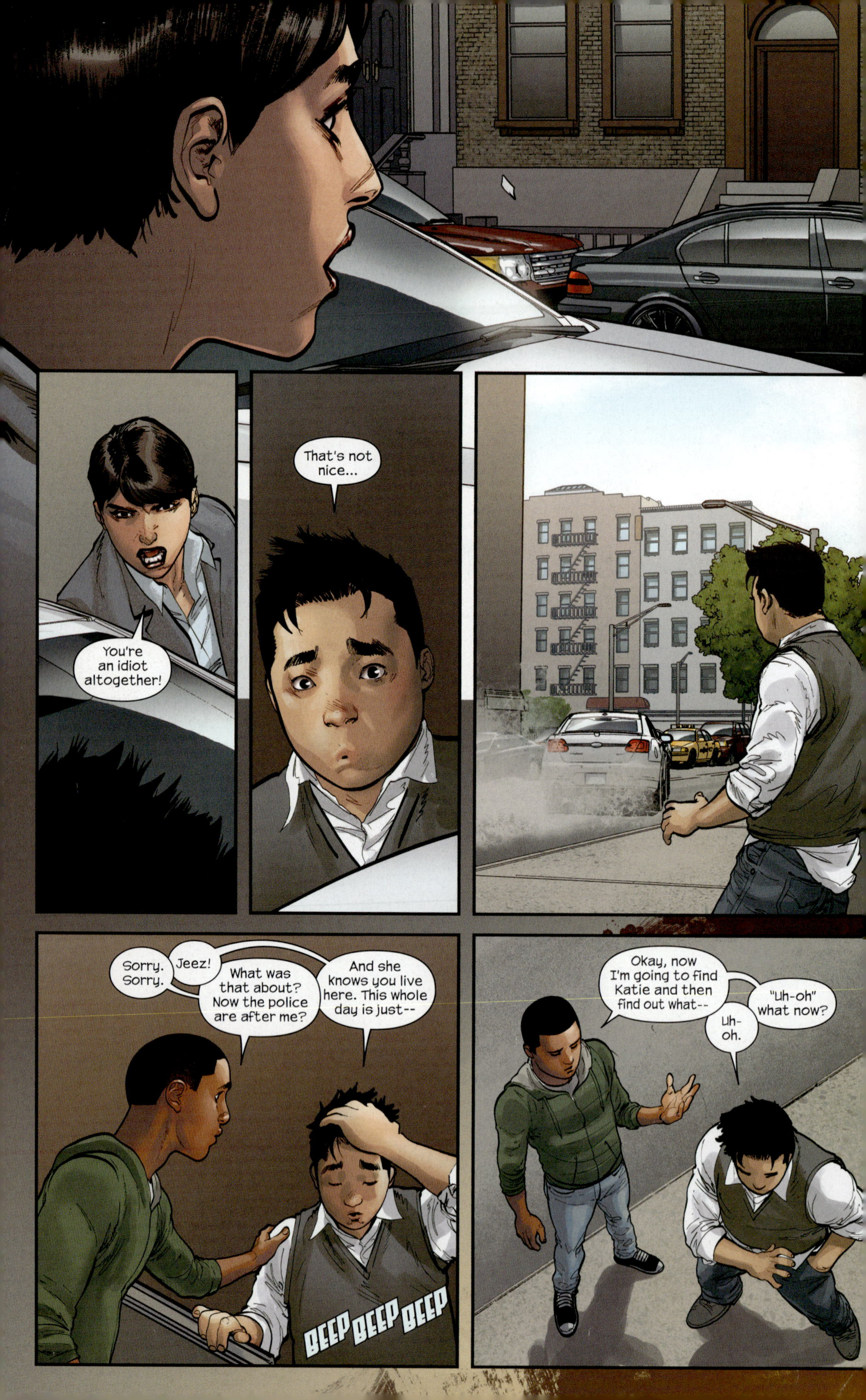
You're an idiot altogether!
That's not nice...
Sorry. Sorry.
Jeez!
What was that about? Now the police are after me?
And she knows you live here. This whole day is just--
BEEP BEEP BEEP
Okay, now I'm going to find Katie and then find out what--
Uh-oh.
"Uh-oh" what now?

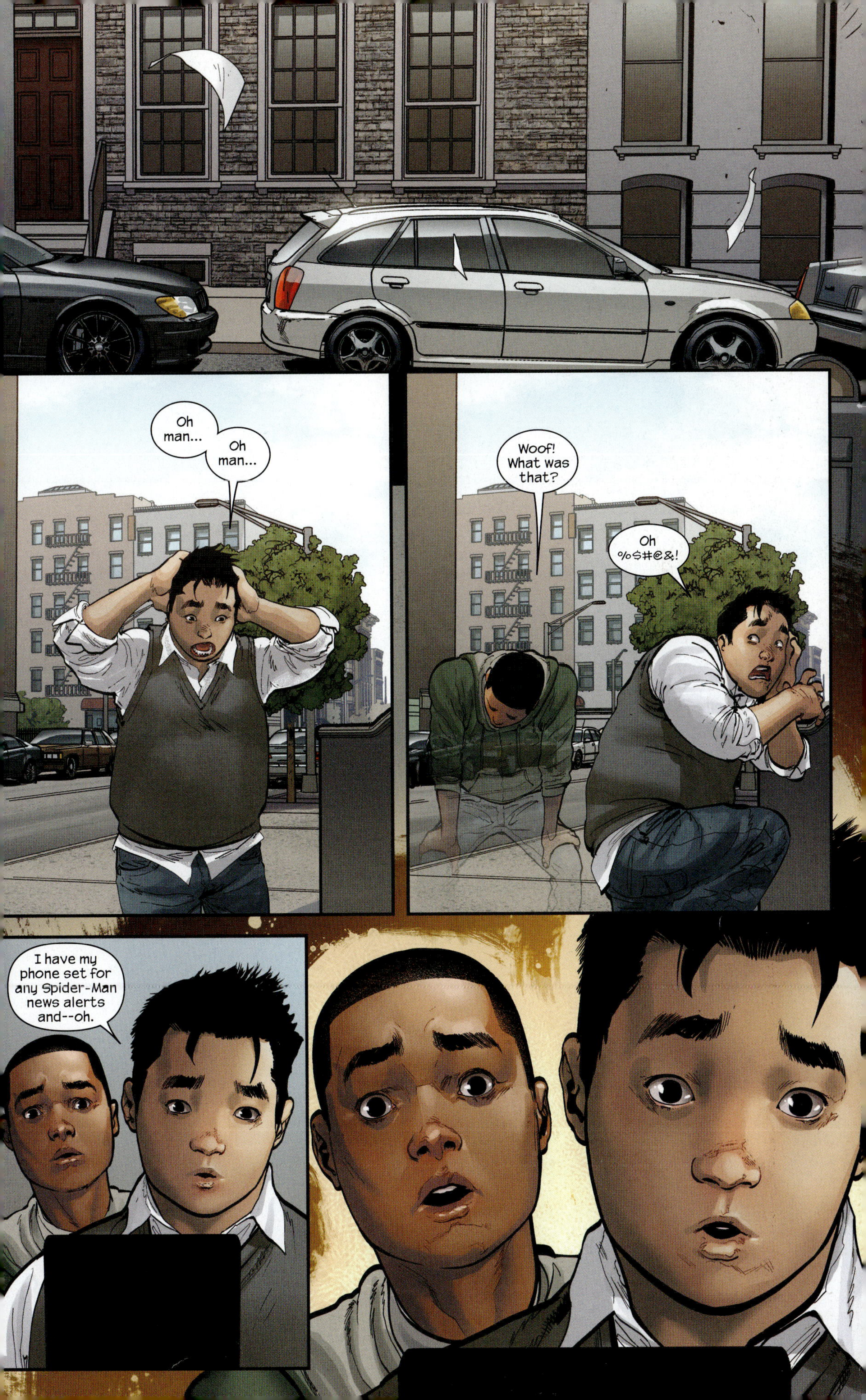
Oh man...
Oh man...
Woof! What was that?
Oh %$#@&!
I have my phone set for any Spider-Man news alerts and--oh.

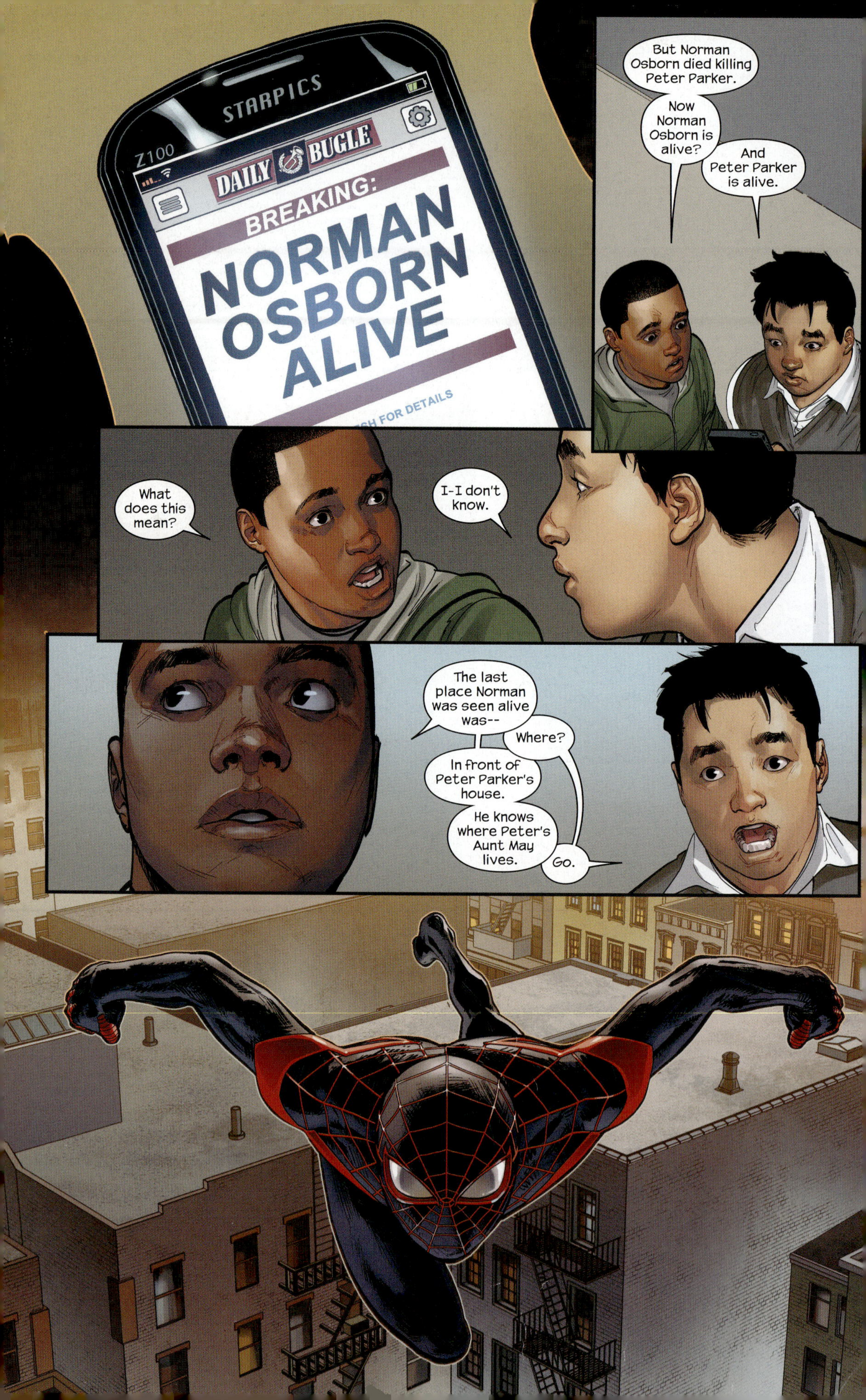
STARPICS
Z100
DAILY BUGLE
BREAKING:
NORMAN OSBORN ALIVE
FOR DETAILS
But Norman Osborn died killing Peter Parker.
Now Norman Osborn is alive?
And Peter Parker is alive.
What does this mean?
I-I don't know.
The last place Norman was seen alive was--
Where?
In front of Peter Parker's house.
He knows where Peter's Aunt May lives.
Go.

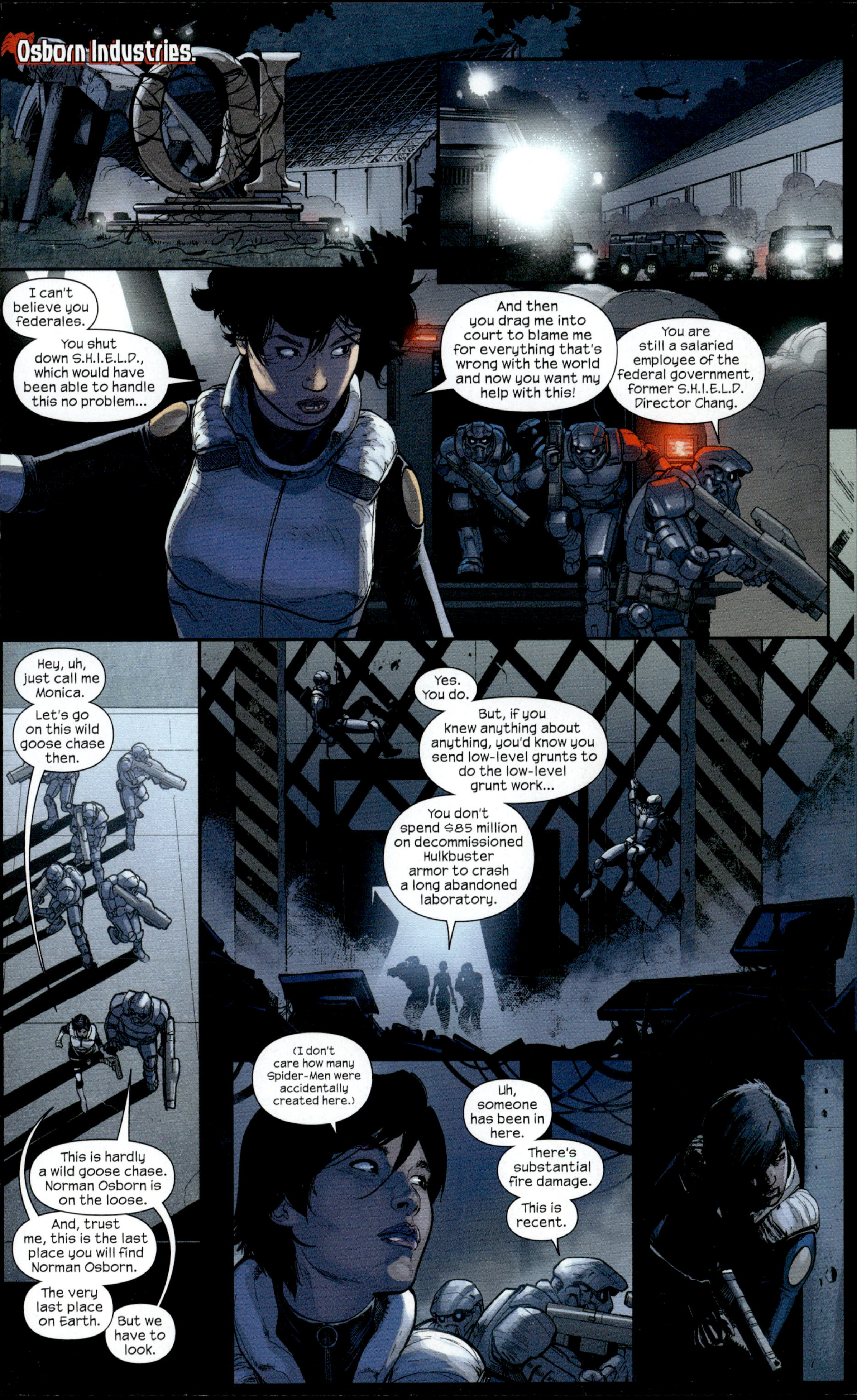
Osborn Industries.
I can't believe you federales.
You shut down S.H.I.E.L.D., which would have been able to handle this no problem...
And then you drag me into court to blame me for everything that's wrong with the world and now you want my help with this!
You are still a salaried employee of the federal government, former S.H.I.E.L.D. Director Chang.
Hey, uh, just call me Monica.
Let's go on this wild goose chase then.
Yes. You do.
But, if you knew anything about anything, you'd know you send low-level grunts to do the low-level grunt work...
You don't spend $85 million on decommissioned Hulkbuster armor to crash a long abandoned laboratory.
This is hardly a wild goose chase. Norman Osborn is on the loose.
And, trust me, this is the last place you will find Norman Osborn.
The very last place on Earth.
But we have to look.
(I don't care how many Spider-Men were accidentally created here.)
Uh, someone has been in here.
There's substantial fire damage.
This is recent.

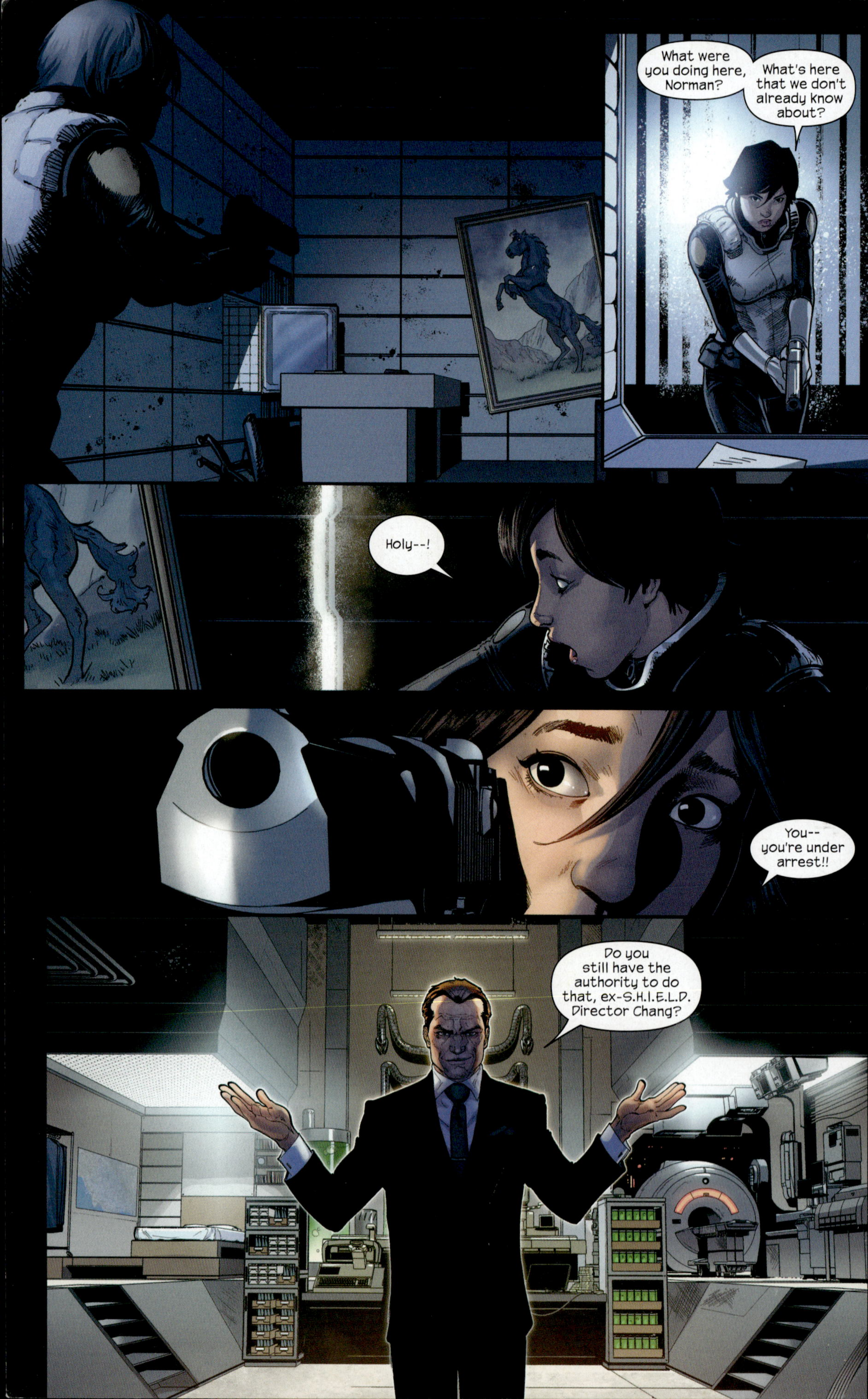
What were you doing here, Norman?
What's here that we don't already know about?
Holy--!
You-- you're under arrest!!
Do you still have the authority to do that, ex-S.H.I.E.L.D. Director Chang?

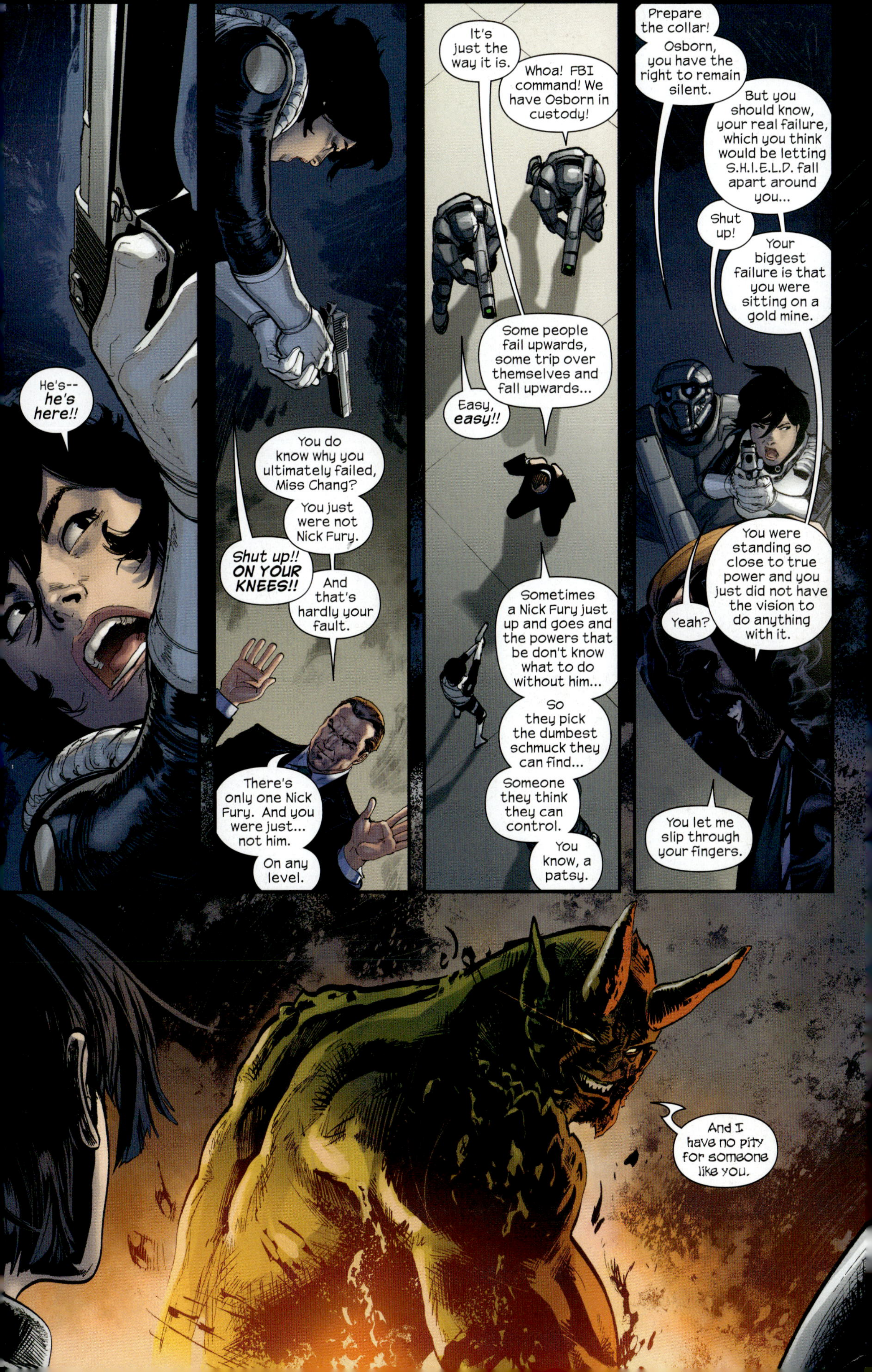
He's-- *he's here!!*
You do know why you ultimately failed, Miss Chang?
You just were not Nick Fury.
Shut up!! ON YOUR KNEES!!
And that's hardly your fault.
There's only one Nick Fury. And you were just... not him.
On any level.
It's just the way it is.
Whoa! FBI command! We have Osborn in custody!
Some people fail upwards, some trip over themselves and fall upwards...
Easy, *easy!!*
Sometimes a Nick Fury just up and goes and the powers that be don't know what to do without him...
So they pick the dumbest schmuck they can find...
Someone they think they can control.
You know, a patsy.
Prepare the collar!
Osborn, you have the right to remain silent.
But you should know, your real failure, which you think would be letting S.H.I.E.L.D. fall apart around you...
Shut up!
Your biggest failure is that you were sitting on a gold mine.
You were standing so close to true power and you just did not have the vision to do anything with it.
Yeah?
You let me slip through your fingers.
And I have no pity for someone like you.

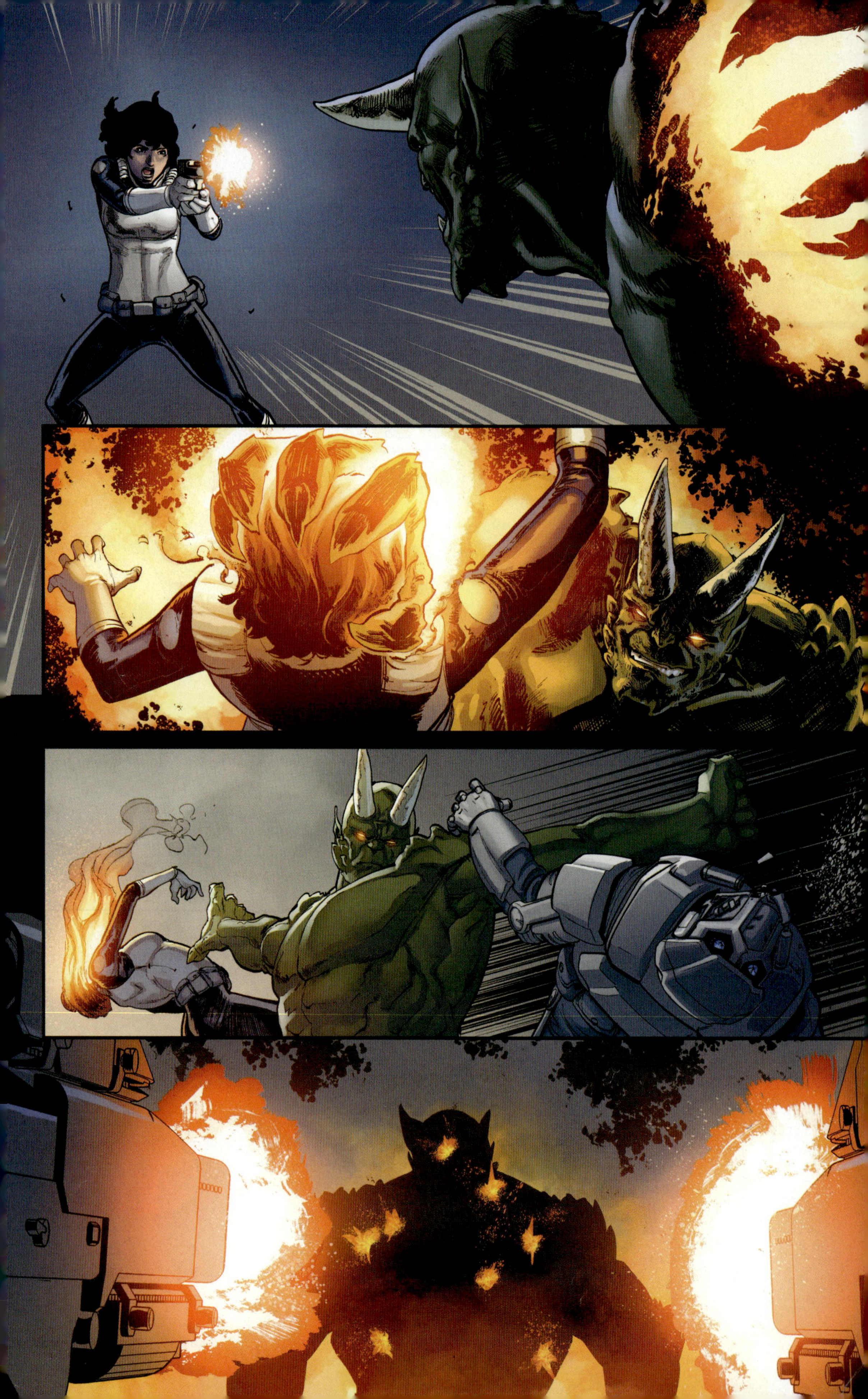

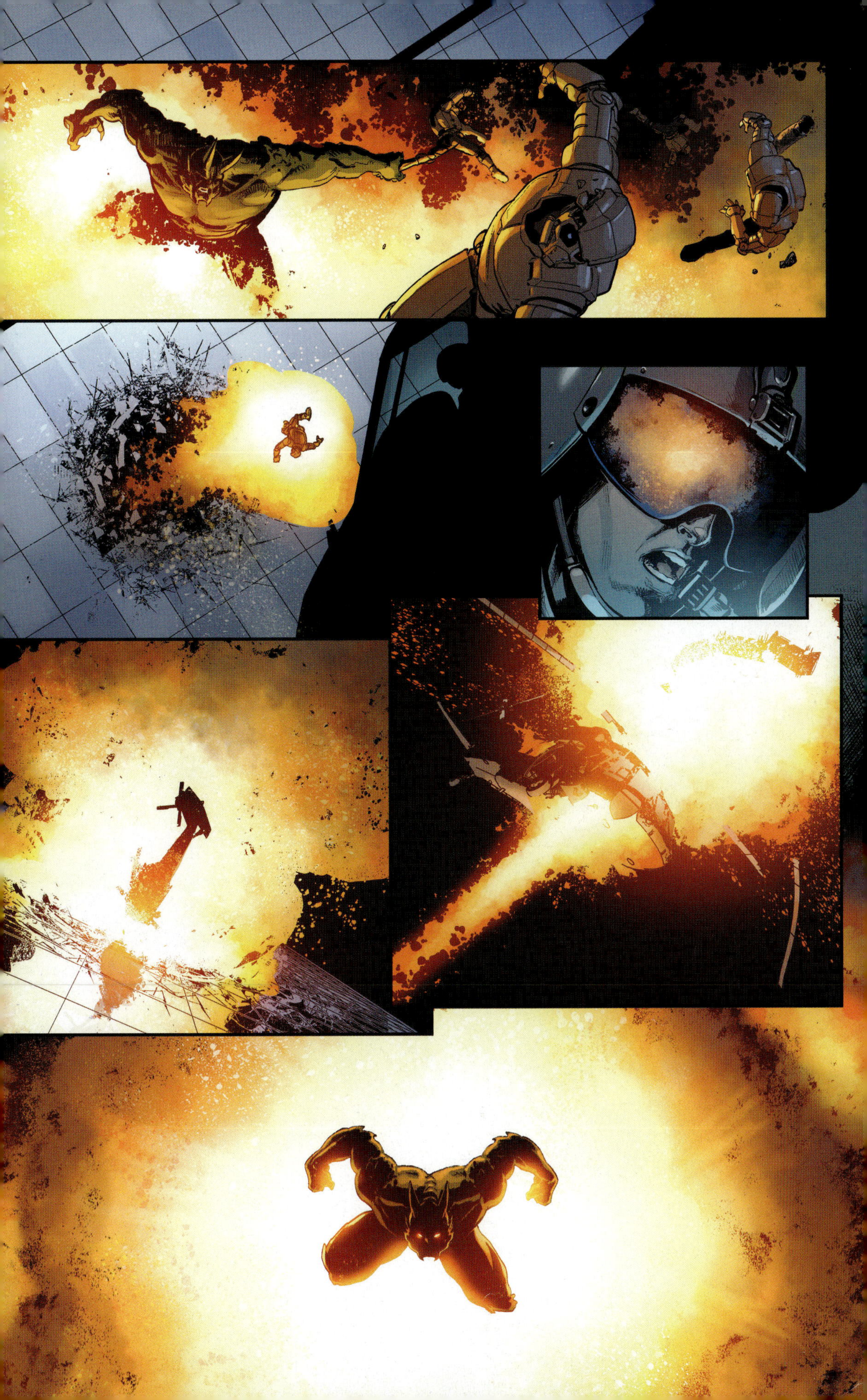

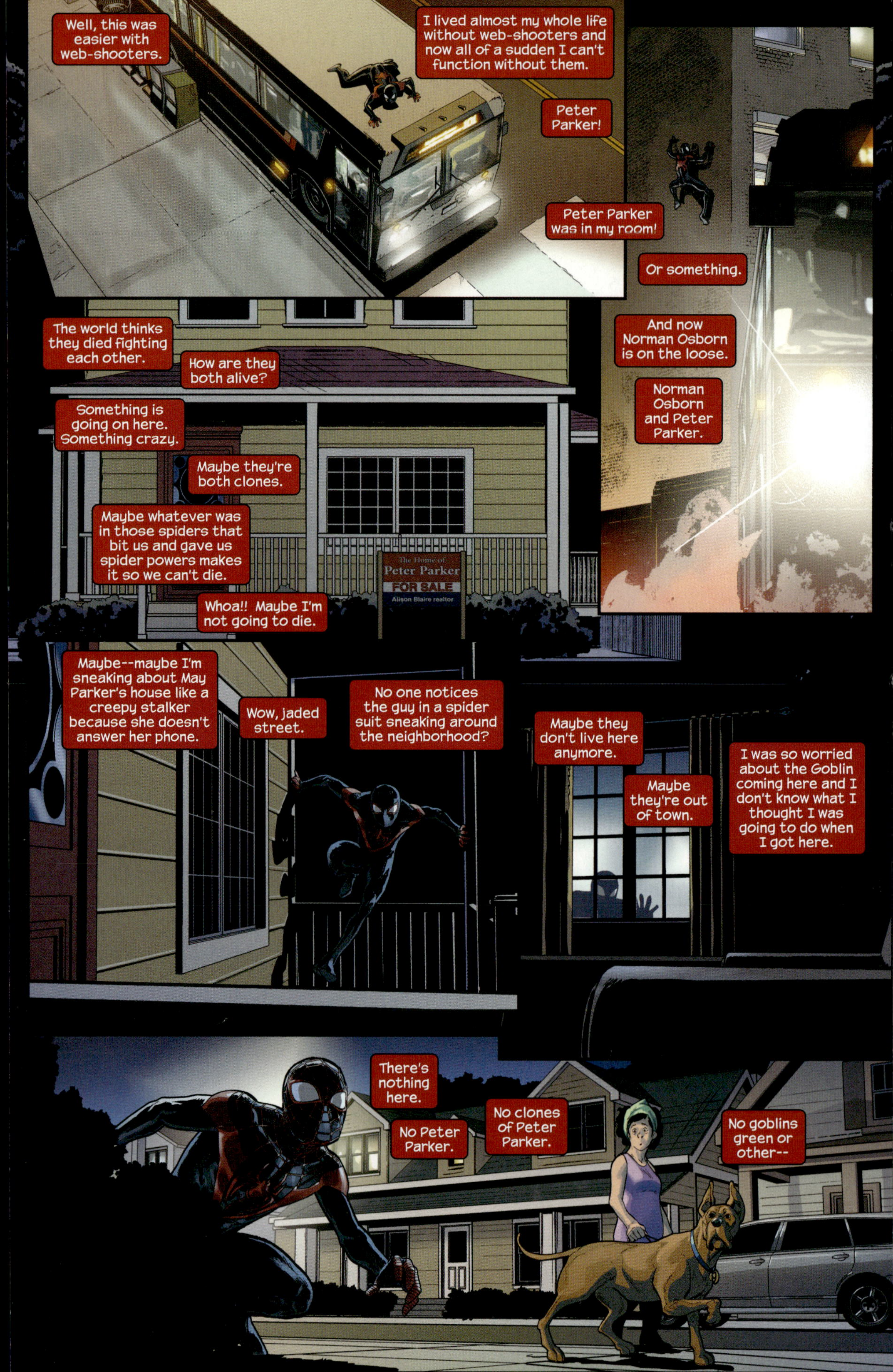

Well, this was easier with web-shooters.
I lived almost my whole life without web-shooters and now all of a sudden I can't function without them.
Peter Parker!
Peter Parker was in my room!
Or something.
And now Norman Osborn is on the loose.
Norman Osborn and Peter Parker.
The world thinks they died fighting each other.
How are they both alive?
Something is going on here. Something crazy.
Maybe they're both clones.
Maybe whatever was in those spiders that bit us and gave us spider powers makes it so we can't die.
The Home of Peter Parker
FOR SALE
Alison Blaire realtor
Whoa!! Maybe I'm not going to die.
Maybe--maybe I'm sneaking about May Parker's house like a creepy stalker because she doesn't answer her phone.
Wow, jaded street.
No one notices the guy in a spider suit sneaking around the neighborhood?
Maybe they don't live here anymore.
Maybe they're out of town.
I was so worried about the Goblin coming here and I don't know what I thought I was going to do when I got here.
There's nothing here.
No Peter Parker.
No clones of Peter Parker.
No goblins green or other--

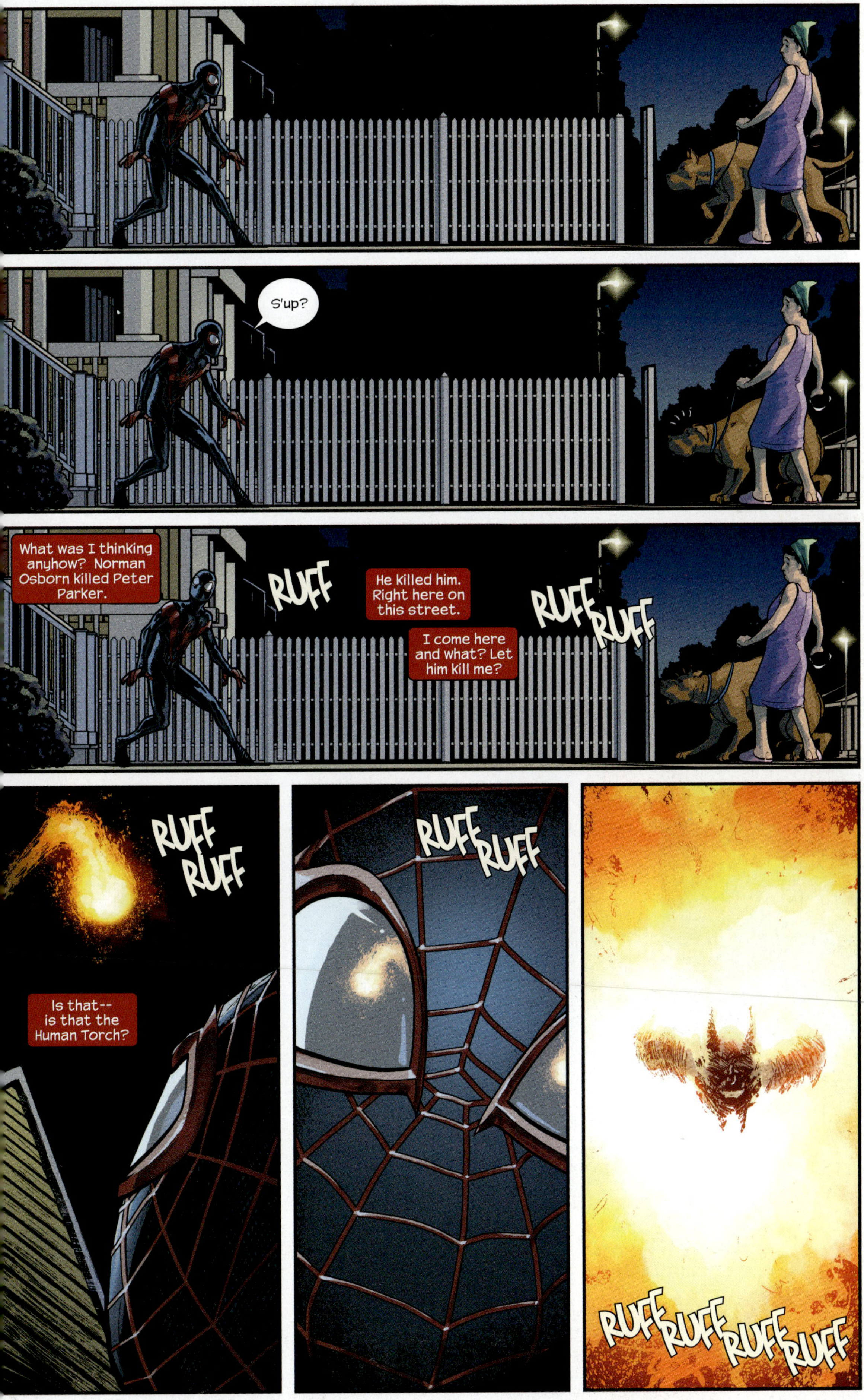
S'up?
What was I thinking anyhow? Norman Osborn killed Peter Parker.
RUFF
He killed him. Right here on this street.
I come here and what? Let him kill me?
RUFF RUFF
RUFF RUFF
Is that-- is that the Human Torch?
RUFF RUFF
RUFF RUFF RUFF RUFF

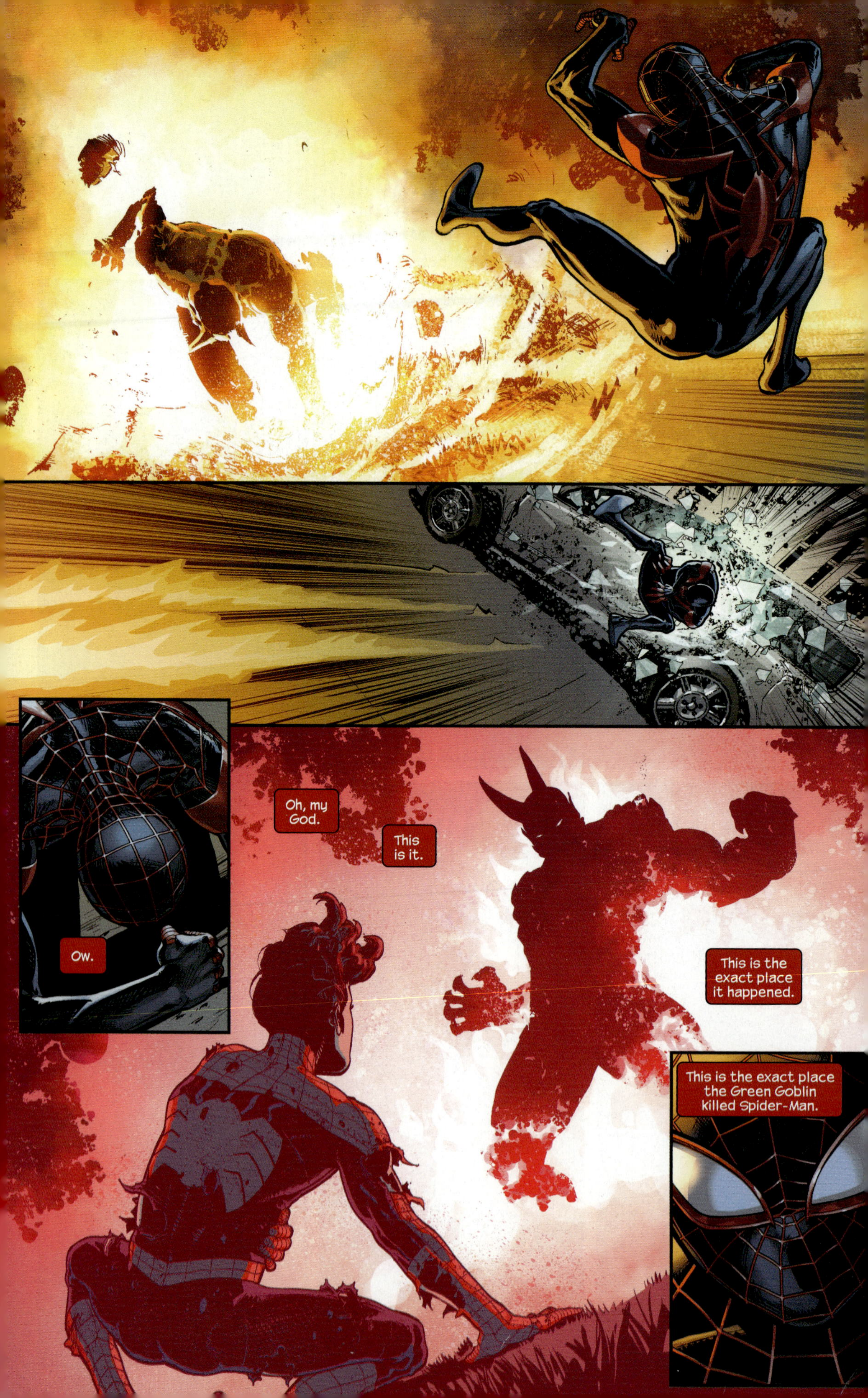
Ow.
Oh, my God.
This is it.
This is the exact place it happened.
This is the exact place the Green Goblin killed Spider-Man.

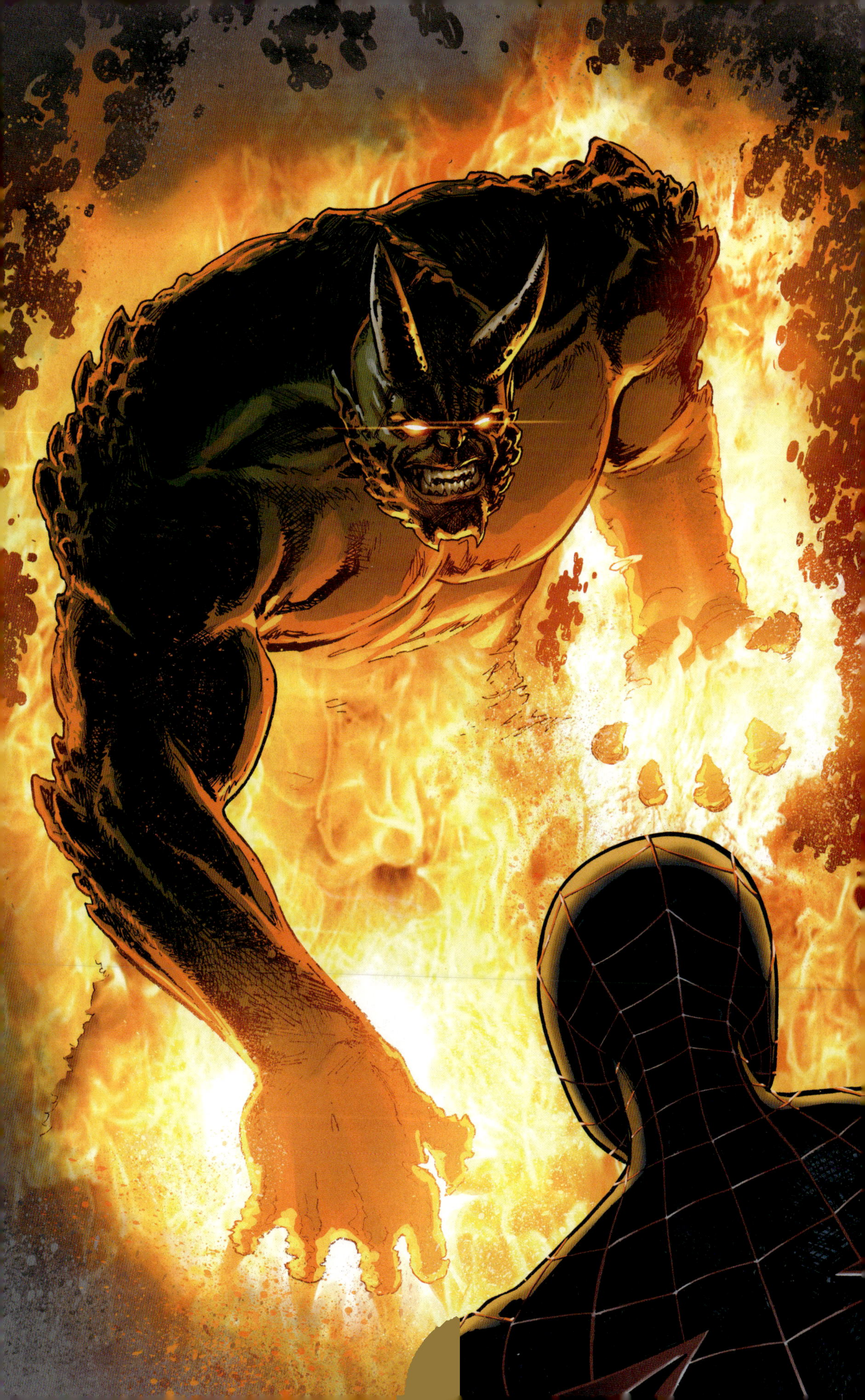

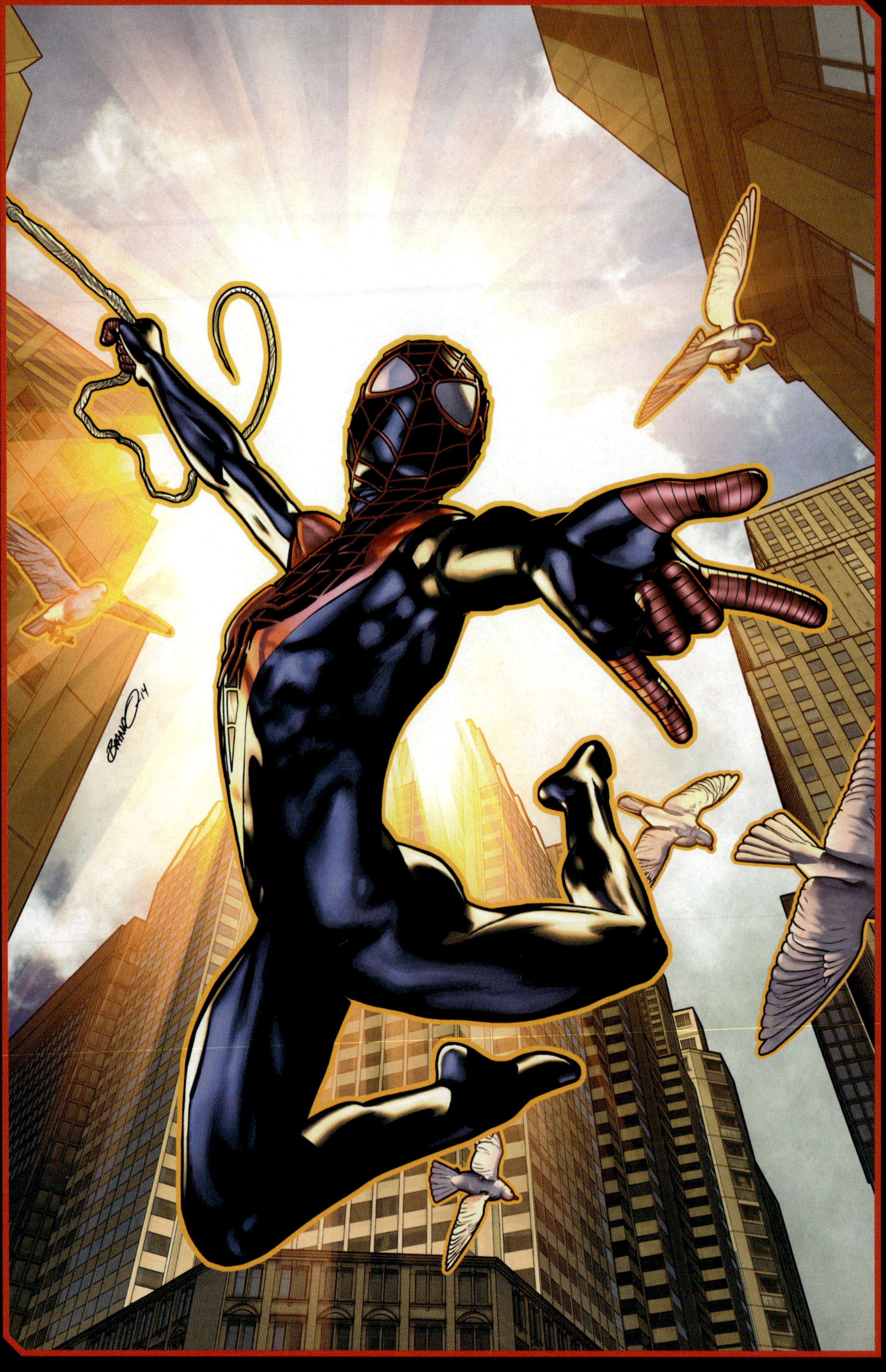
BRANDON '14

MILES MORALES: ULTIMATE SPIDER-MAN #1 VARIANT BY BRANDON PETERSON

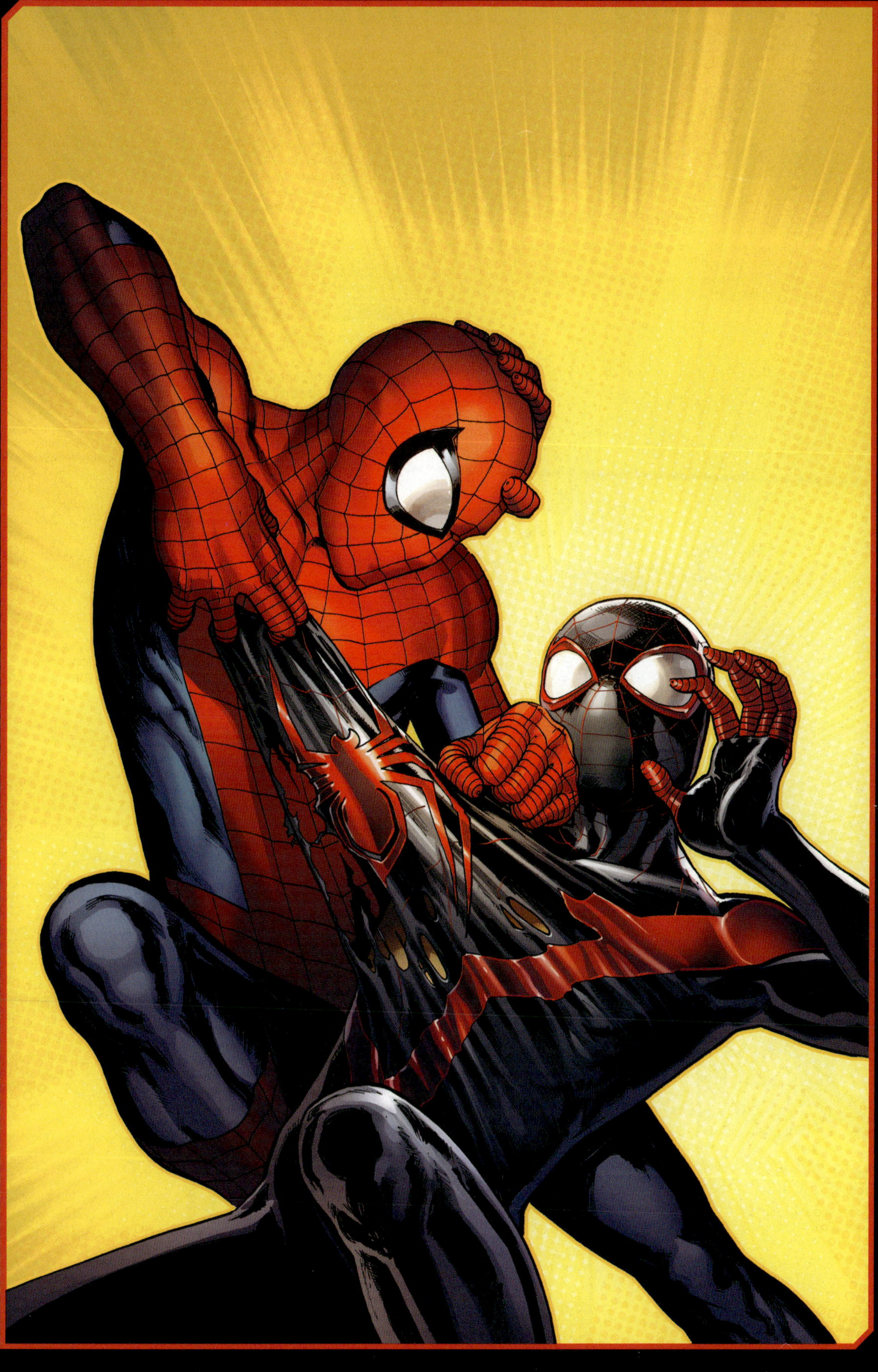

MILES MORALES: ULTIMATE SPIDER-MAN #4

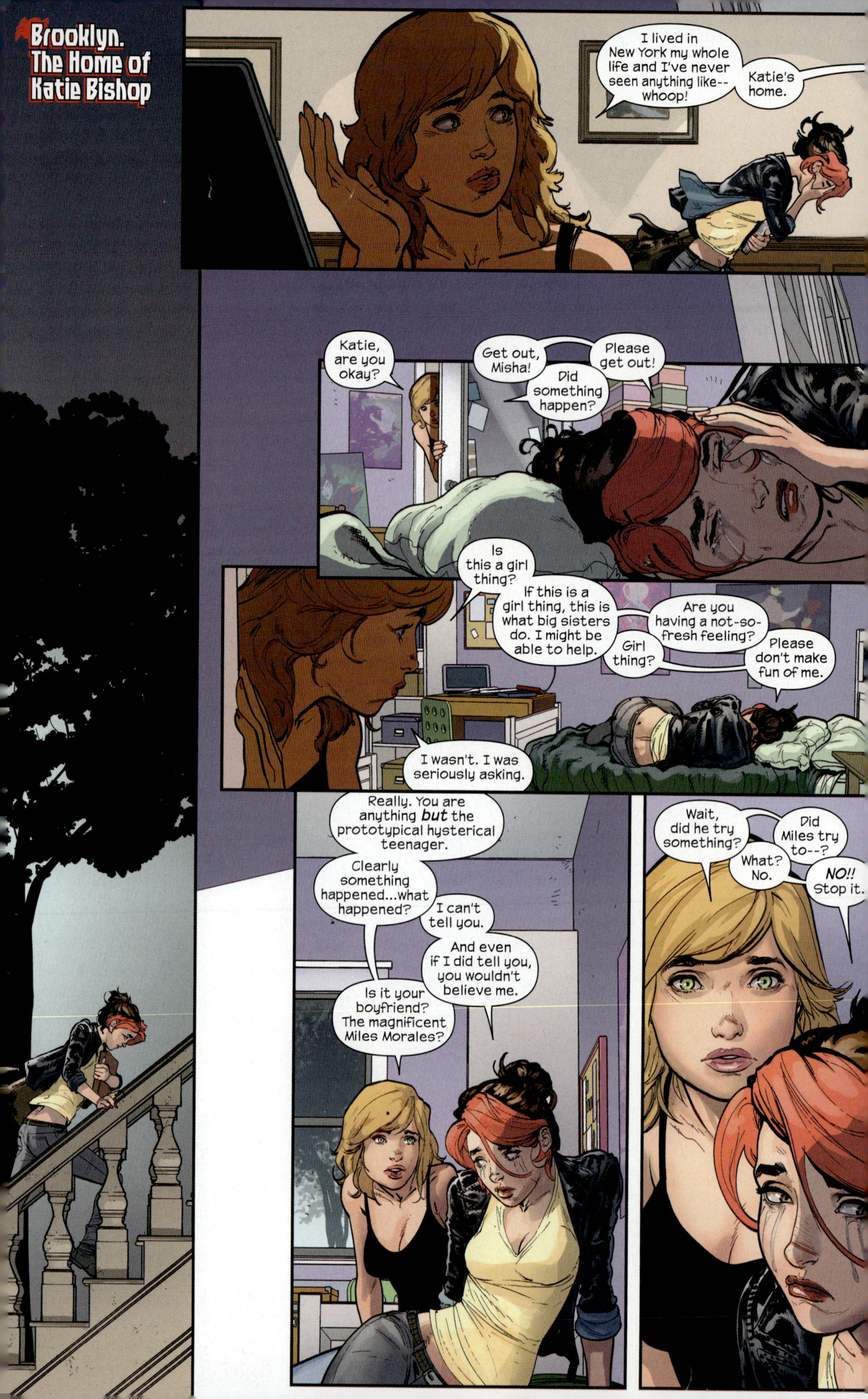
Brooklyn. The Home of Katie Bishop
I lived in New York my whole life and I've never seen anything like-- whoop!
Katie's home.
Katie, are you okay?
Get out, Misha!
Did something happen?
Please get out!
Is this a girl thing?
If this is a girl thing, this is what big sisters do. I might be able to help.
Girl thing?
Are you having a not-so-fresh feeling?
Please don't make fun of me.
I wasn't. I was seriously asking.
Really. You are anything **but** the prototypical hysterical teenager.
Clearly something happened...what happened?
I can't tell you.
And even if I did tell you, you wouldn't believe me.
Is it your boyfriend? The magnificent Miles Morales?
Wait, did he try something?
Did Miles try to--?
What? No.
NO!! Stop it.

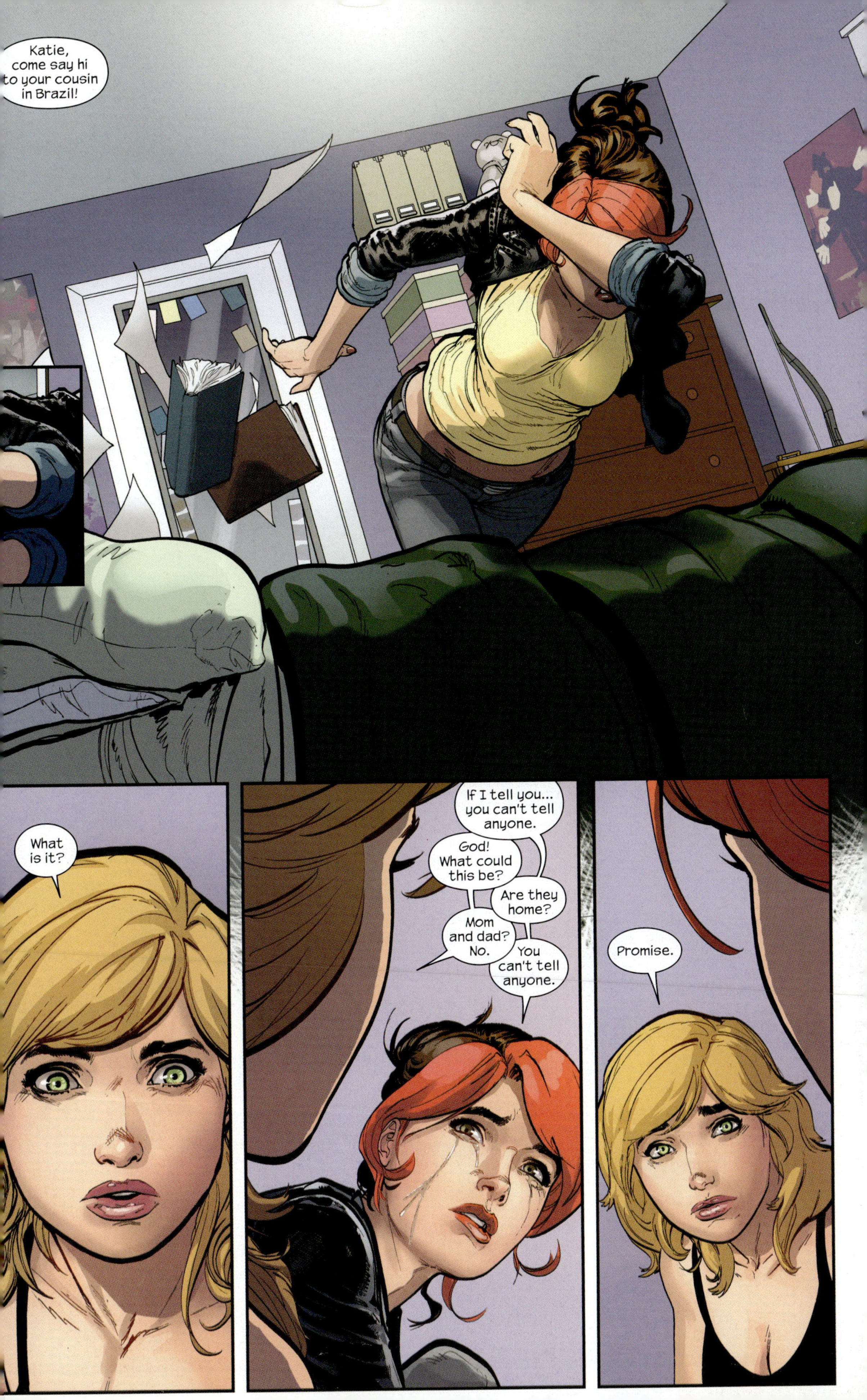
Katie, come say hi to your cousin in Brazil!
What is it?
If I tell you... you can't tell anyone.
God! What could this be?
Are they home?
Mom and dad? No.
You can't tell anyone.
Promise.

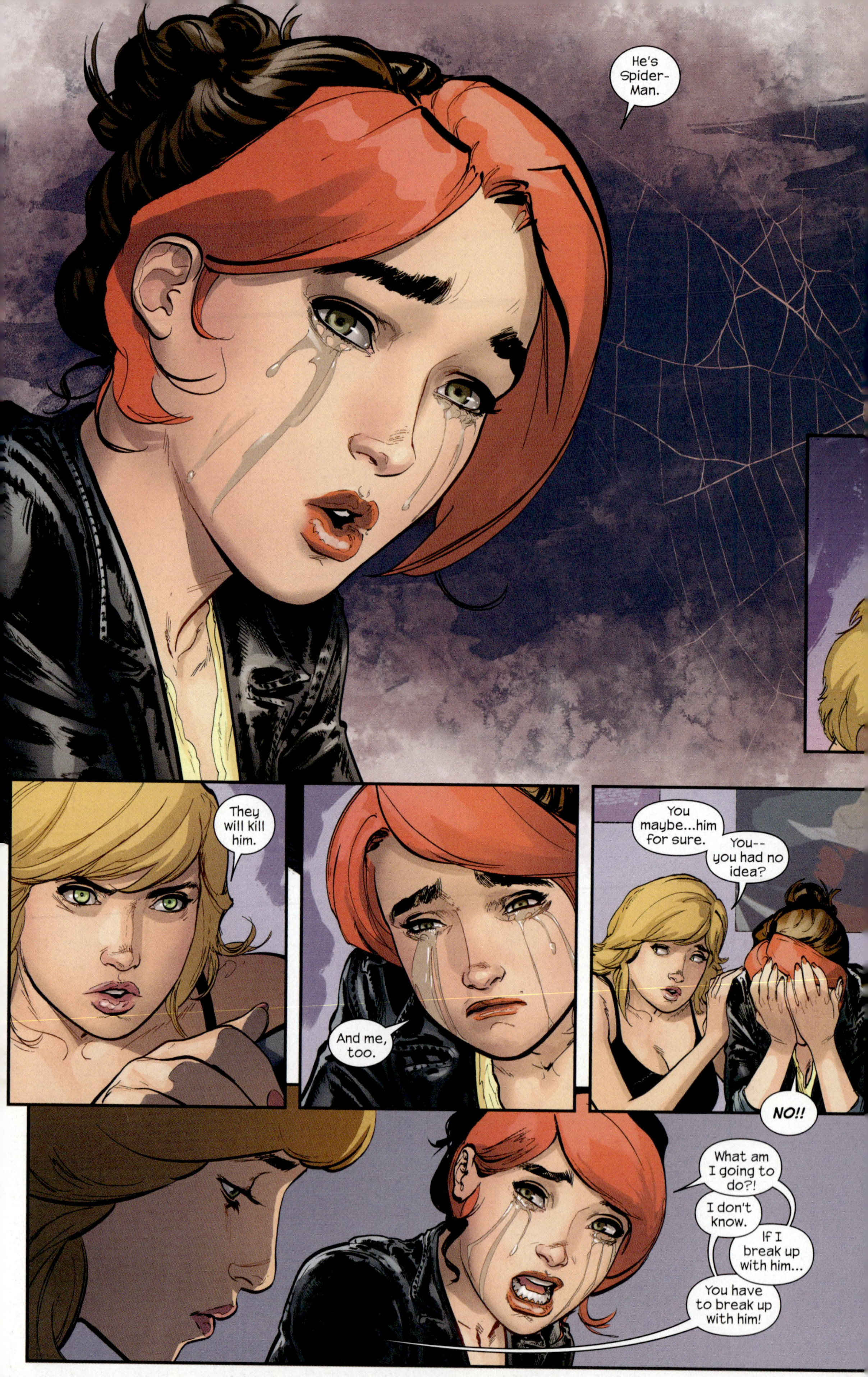
He's Spider-Man.
They will kill him.
And me, too.
You maybe...him for sure.
You--you had no idea?
NO!!
What am I going to do?!
I don't know.
If I break up with him...
You have to break up with him!

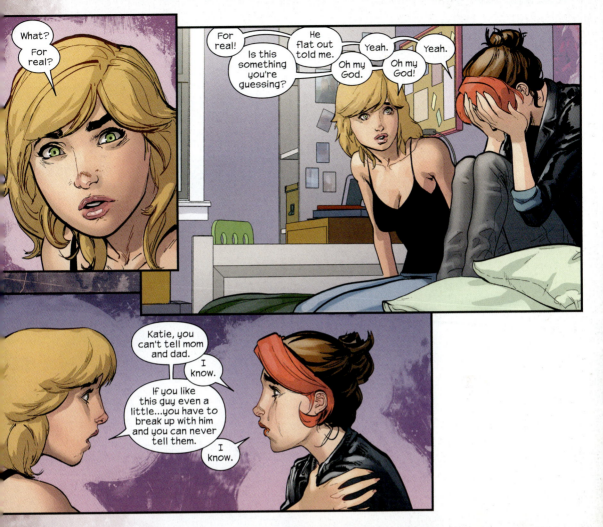

What? For real?

For real! Is this something you're guessing?

He flat out told me.

Yeah.

Oh my God.

Yeah.

Oh my God!

Katie, you can't tell mom and dad.

I know.

If you like this guy even a little...you have to break up with him and you can never tell them.

I know.

I don't want to break up with him and even if I do break up with him, he loves me as much as I love him and he's going to do something stupid to try to get me back!

He told you he was Spider-Man?

The new-ish Spider-Man?

Yes!

Why would he do that?

Because he *loves* me. Because he wanted to *trust* me. What-- what am I going to *do*?

Hope that a super villain kills him?

That-- that's an awful thing to say.

Hey! That's the best case scenario.

What?!

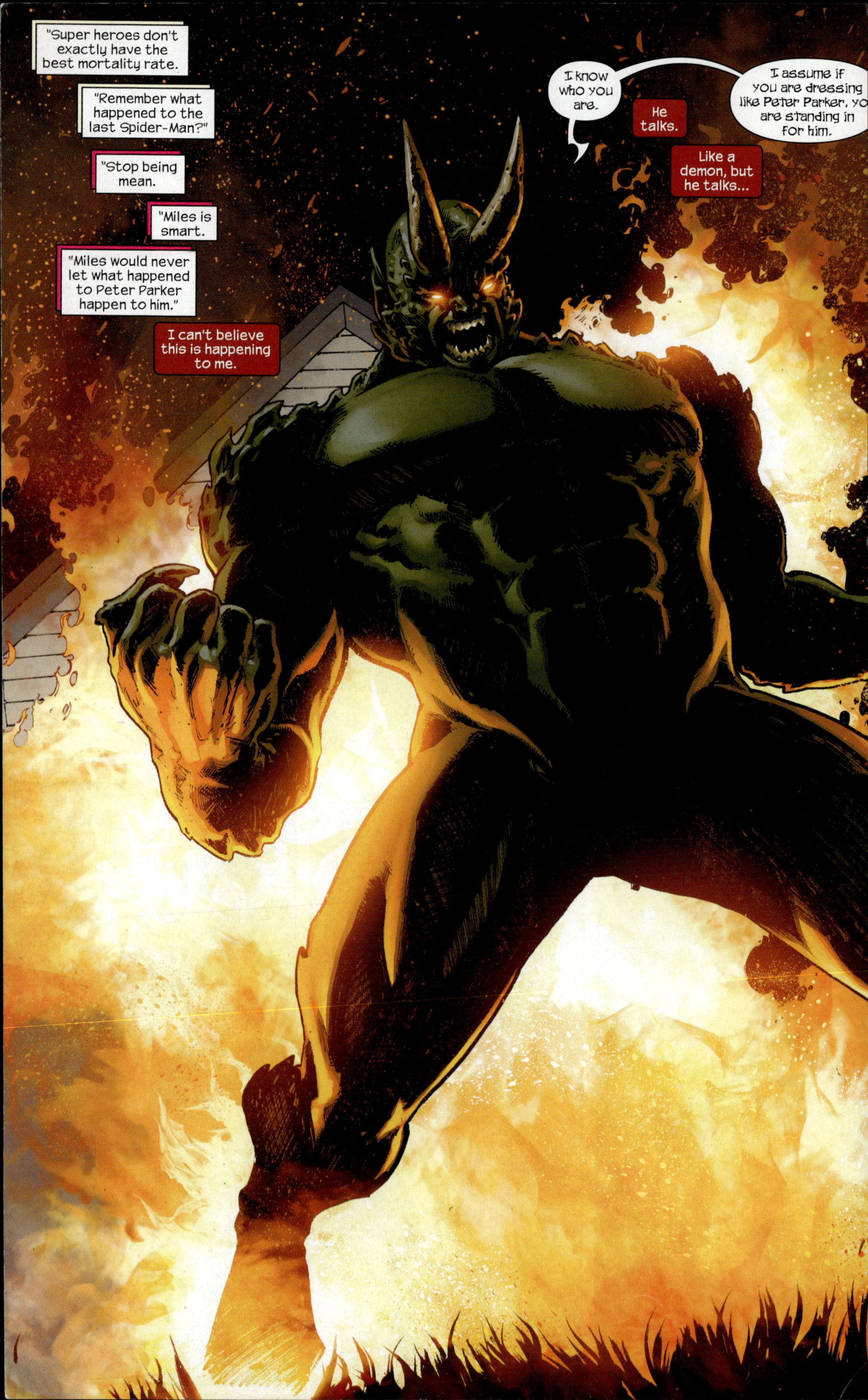
"Super heroes don't exactly have the best mortality rate.
"Remember what happened to the last Spider-Man?"
"Stop being mean.
"Miles is smart.
"Miles would never let what happened to Peter Parker happen to him."
I can't believe this is happening to me.
I know who you are.
I assume if you are dressing like Peter Parker, yo are standing in for him.
He talks.
Like a demon, but he talks...

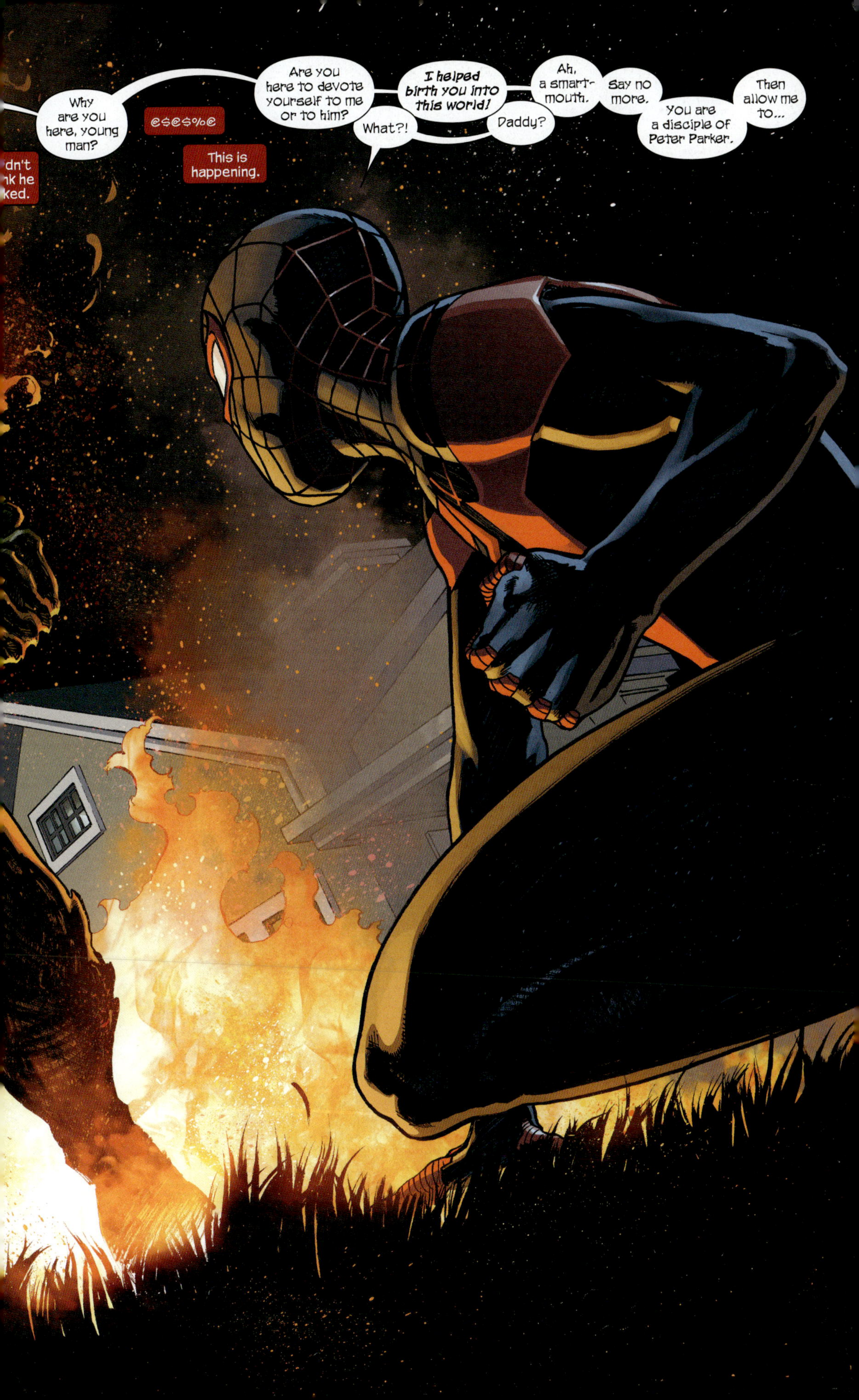
dn't nk he ked.
Why are you here, young man?
@$@$%@
This is happening.
Are you here to devote yourself to me or to him?
What?!
I helped birth you into this world!
Daddy?
Ah, a smart-mouth.
Say no more.
You are a disciple of Peter Parker.
Then allow me to...

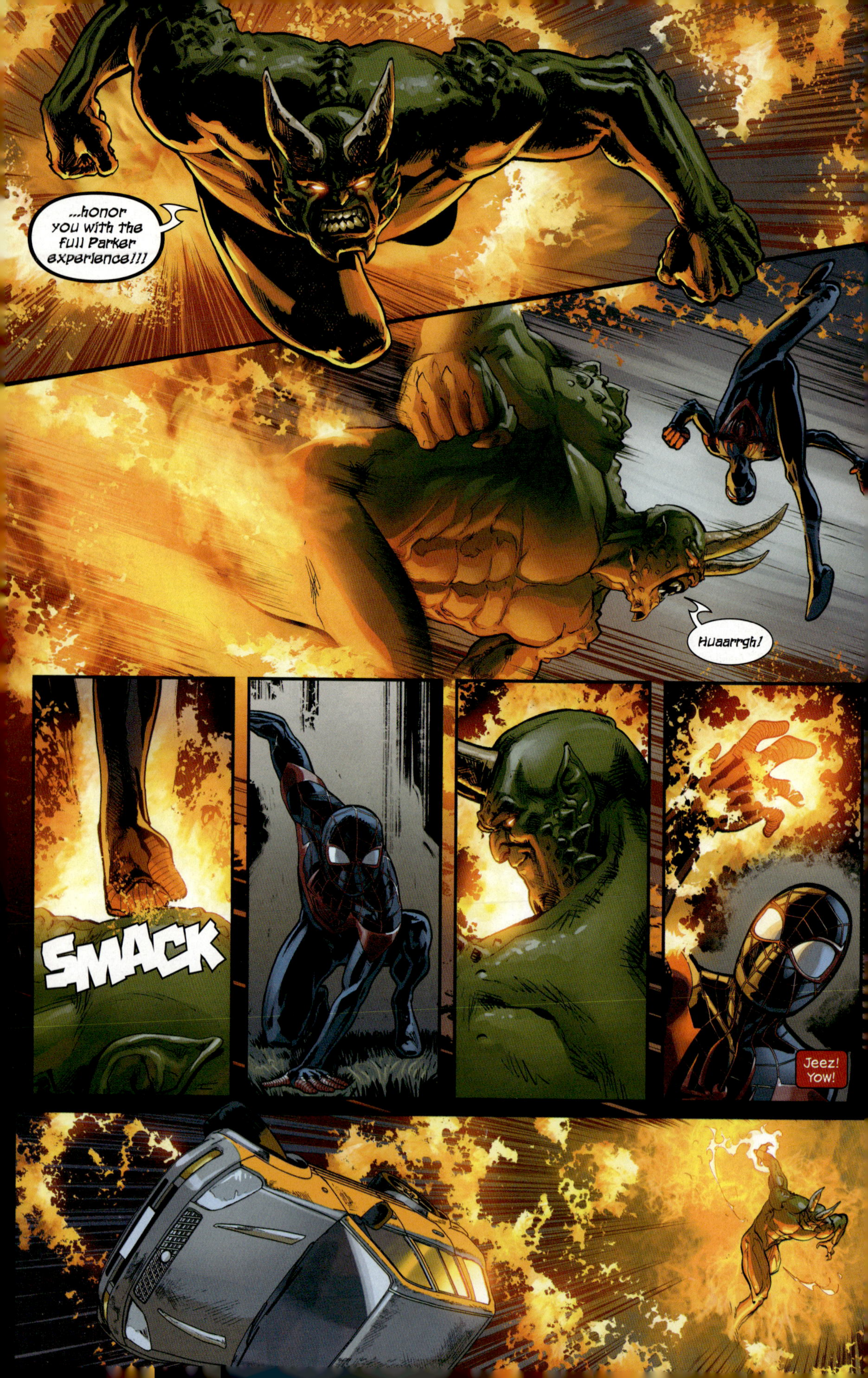
...honor you with the full Parker experience!!!
Huaarrgh!
SMACK
Jeez! Yow!

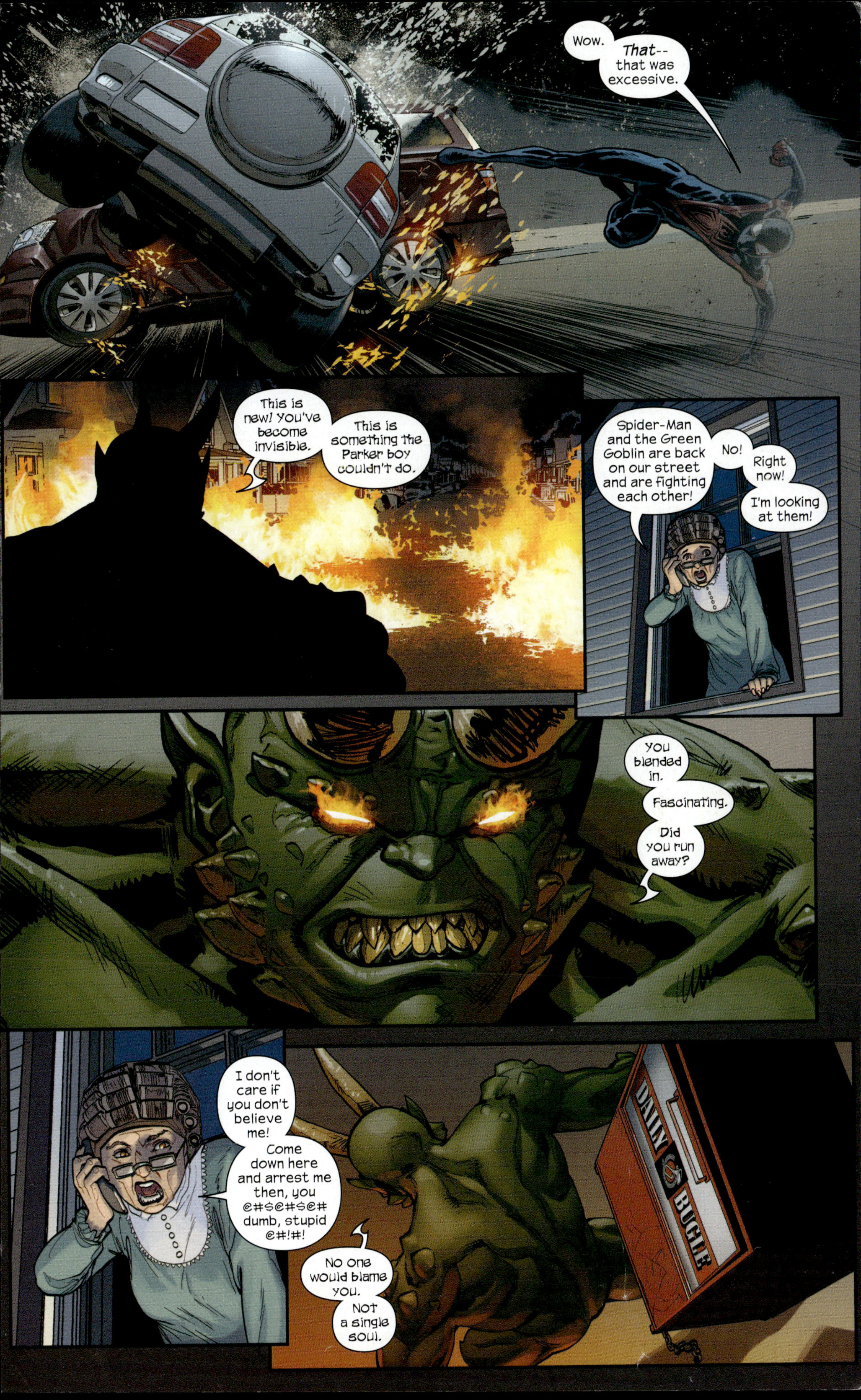
Wow.
That-- that was excessive.
This is new! You've become invisible.
This is something the Parker boy couldn't do.
Spider-Man and the Green Goblin are back on our street and are fighting each other!
No!
Right now!
I'm looking at them!
You blended in.
Fascinating.
Did you run away?
I don't care if you don't believe me!
Come down here and arrest me then, you @#$@#$@# dumb, stupid @#!#!
No one would blame you.
Not a single soul.
DAILY BUGLE

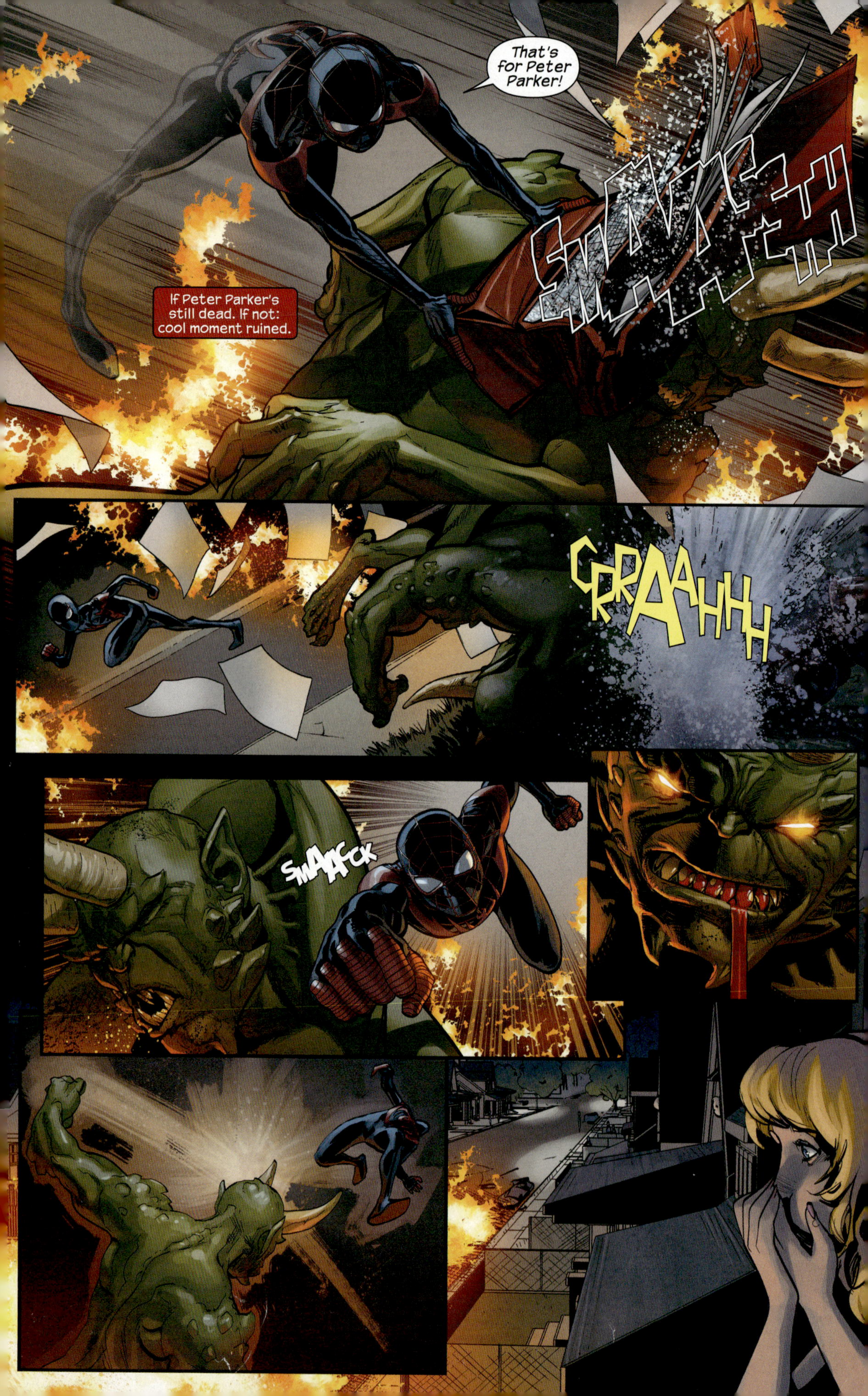
That's for Peter Parker!
SMAAASH
If Peter Parker's still dead. If not: cool moment ruined.
CRRAAHHH
SWAAACK

Numerous calls coming in from the Forest Hills neighborhood reporting Spider-Man--
And what may or may not be the Green Goblin--
Ganke, Best Friend.
Detective Maria Hill.
Ben Urich, Reporter.
The damage to the neighborhood is already severe.
If you are anywhere near this area, please stay in your home and stay off the streets.
FASHAAM
We are still waiting for confirmation that this is in fact Norman Osborn, once a well-respected member of the military-industrial complex and now--
Rumors of Osborn's escape from prison seem to be true.
Details are sketchy as to how this new Spider-Man and Osborn have come to find each other--
Neighborhood alerts! Super-power event sighting! Stay in your home! This is not a test.
Interestingly enough, this is exactly the location where Peter Parker last battled the Green Goblin and eventually lost his life.
J. Jonah Jameson, Daily Bugle Publisher.
Mary Jane Watson, Original Spider-Man Girlfriend.
Katie Bishop, Miles Morales' soon to be ex-girlfriend.
Aunt May and Gwen Stacy, Peter Parker's only remaining family.

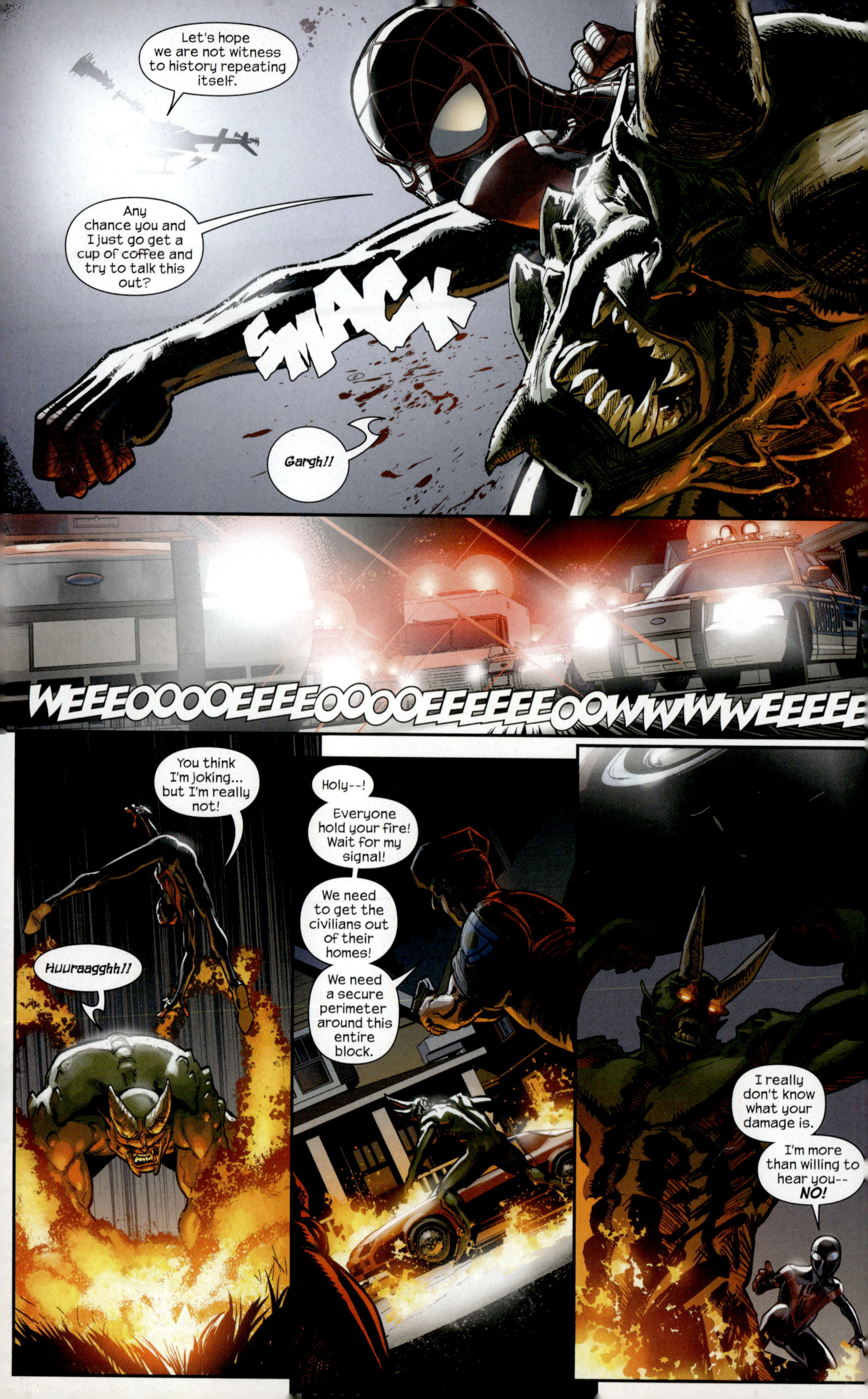
Let's hope we are not witness to history repeating itself.
Any chance you and I just go get a cup of coffee and try to talk this out?
SMACK
Gargh!!
WEEEOOOOEEEEOOOOEEEEEEOOWWWWEEEEE
You think I'm joking... but I'm really not!
Huuraagghh!!
Holy--!
Everyone hold your fire! Wait for my signal!
We need to get the civilians out of their homes!
We need a secure perimeter around this entire block.
I really don't know what your damage is.
I'm more than willing to hear you-- NO!

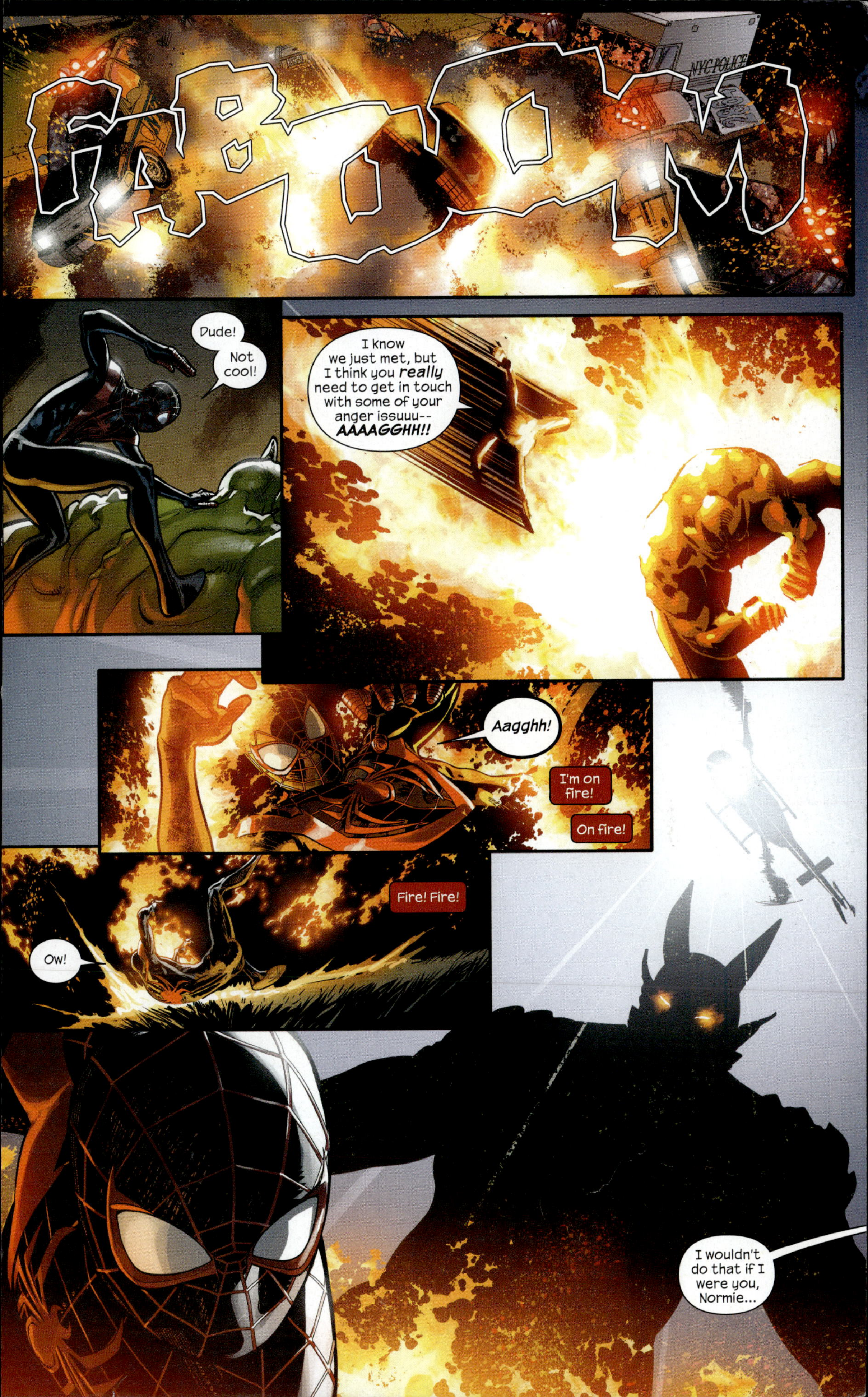
FRABOOOM
NYC POLICE
Dude!
Not cool!
I know we just met, but I think you *really* need to get in touch with some of your anger issuuu-- ***AAAAGGHH!!***
Aagghh!
I'm on fire!
On fire!
Fire! Fire!
Ow!
I wouldn't do that if I were you, Normie...

I mean, you can kill me all you want...
But if you lay one more hand on the president of my fan club, I'm going to have to smack the ugly right off of you.
And by the looks of you, that is going to take all night.
Boom!

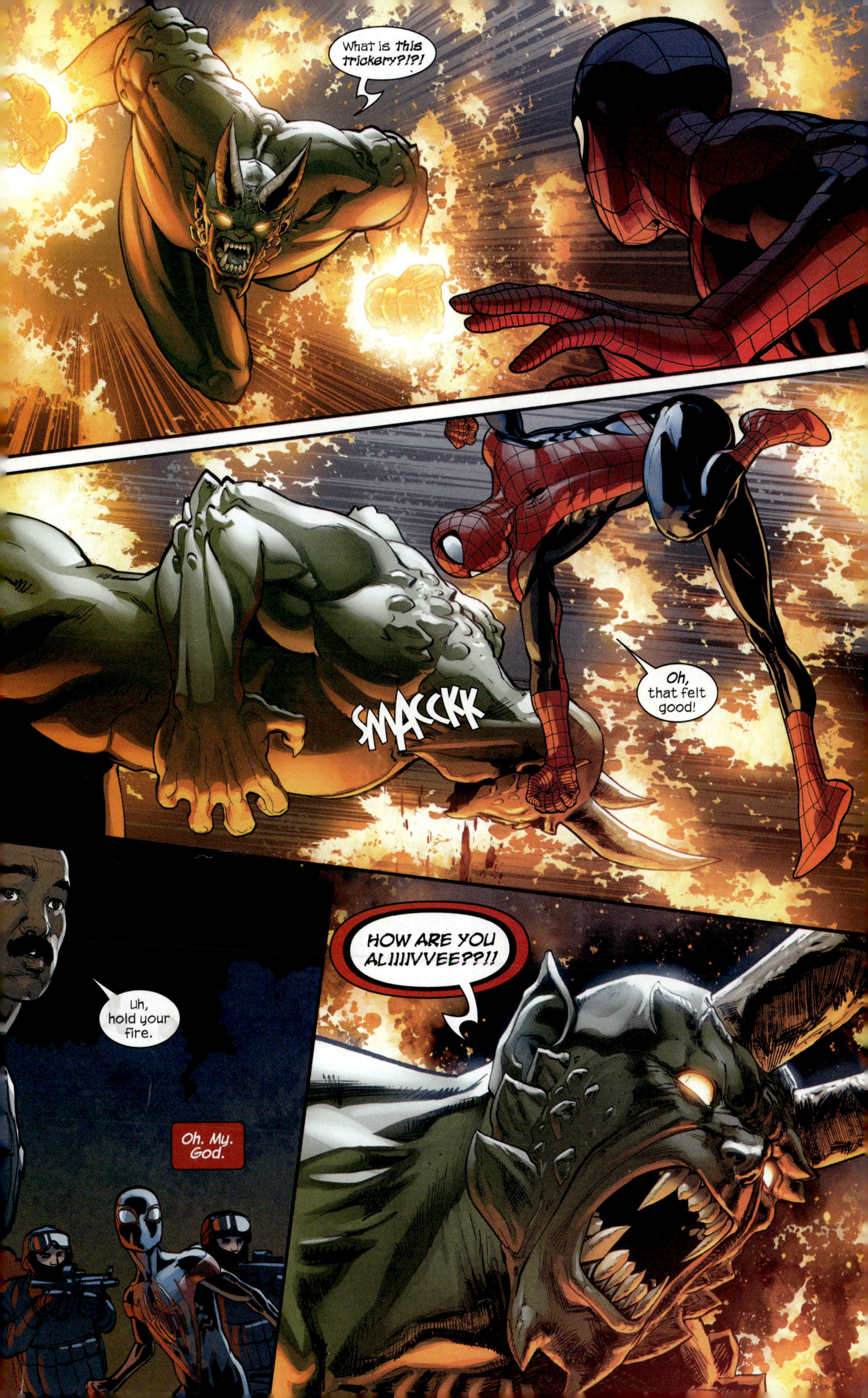

What is this trickery?!?!
SMACCKK
Oh, that felt good!
Uh, hold your fire.
Oh. My. God.
HOW ARE YOU ALIIIIVVEE??!!

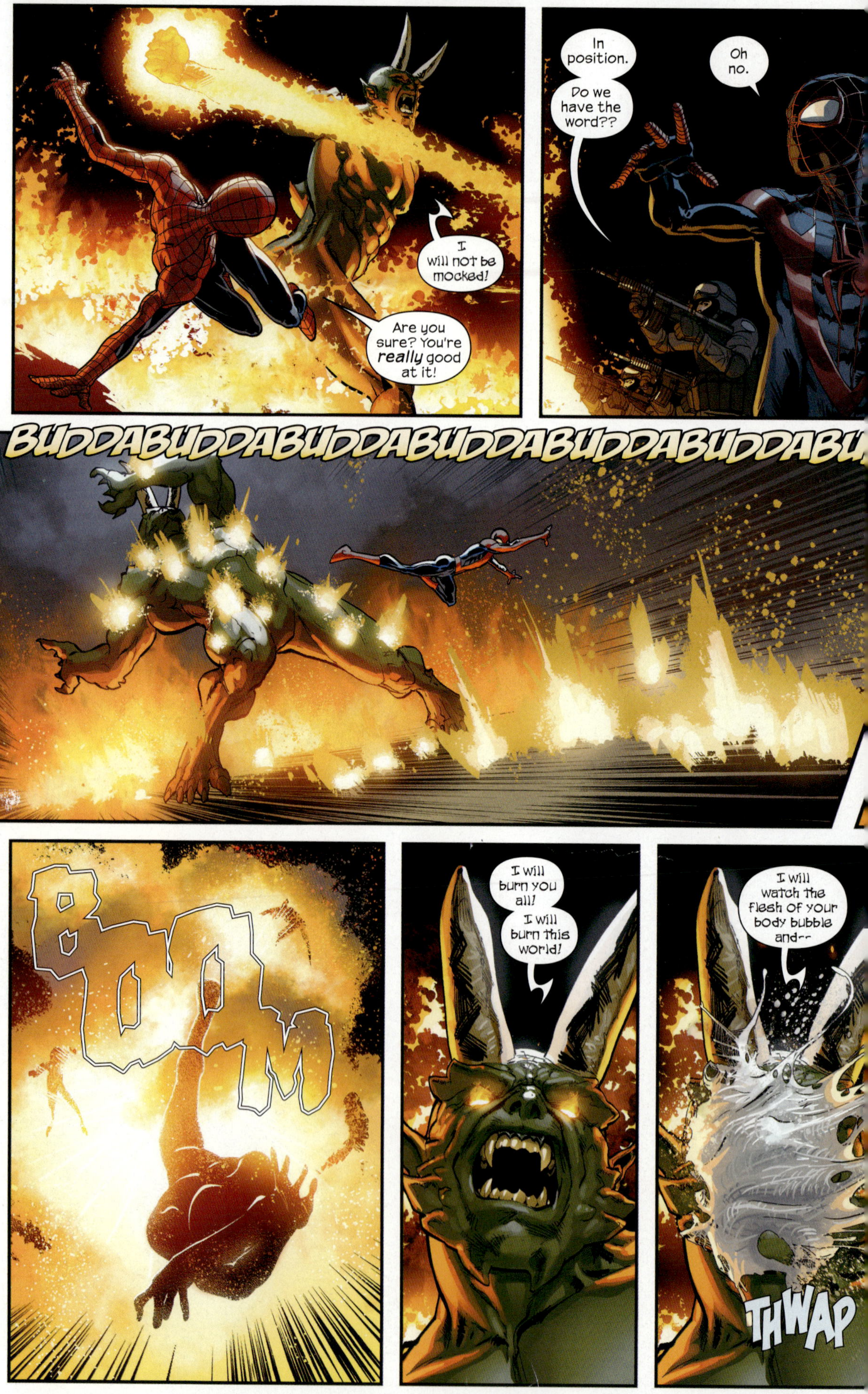
I will not be mocked!
Are you sure? You're really good at it!
In position.
Do we have the word??
Oh no.
BUDDABUDDABUDDABUDDABUDDABUDDABU
BOOM
I will burn you all!
I will burn this world!
I will watch the flesh of your body bubble and--
THWAP

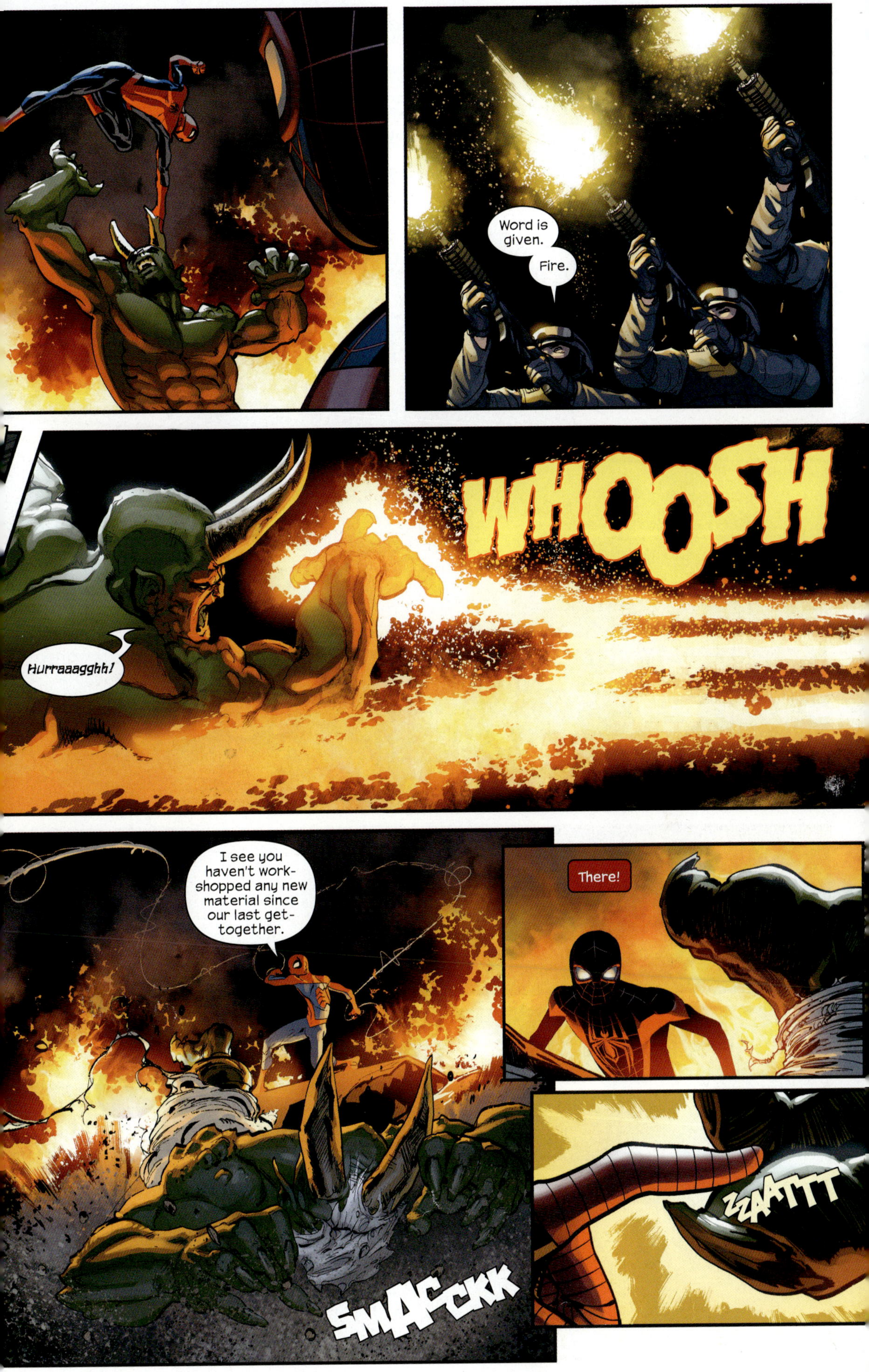
Word is given.
Fire.
WHOOSH
Hurraaagghh!
I see you haven't work-shopped any new material since our last get-together.
SMACCKK
There!
ZZAATTT

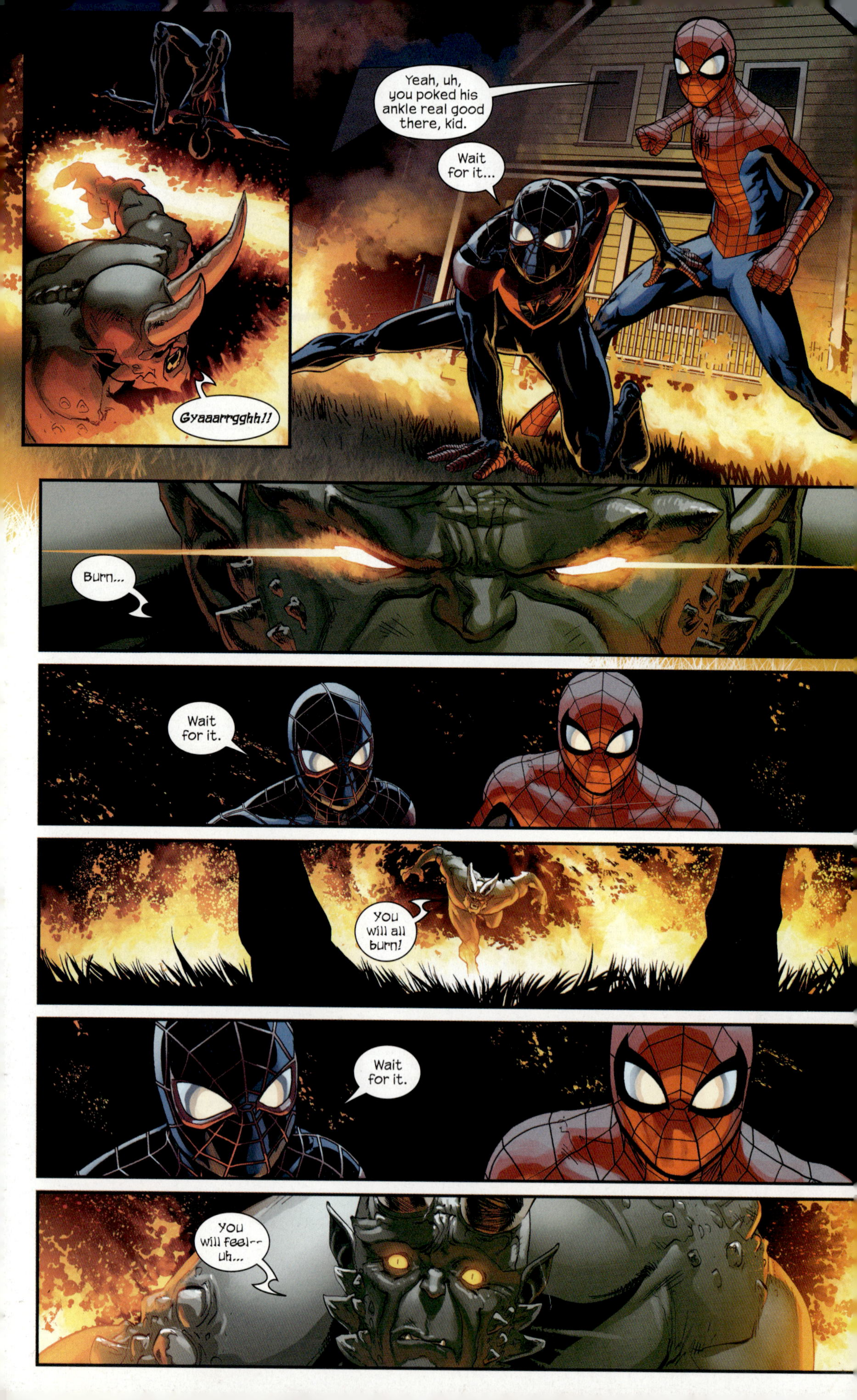
Gyaaarrgghh!!
Yeah, uh, you poked his ankle real good there, kid.
Wait for it...
Burn...
Wait for it.
You will all burn!
Wait for it.
You will feel-- uh...

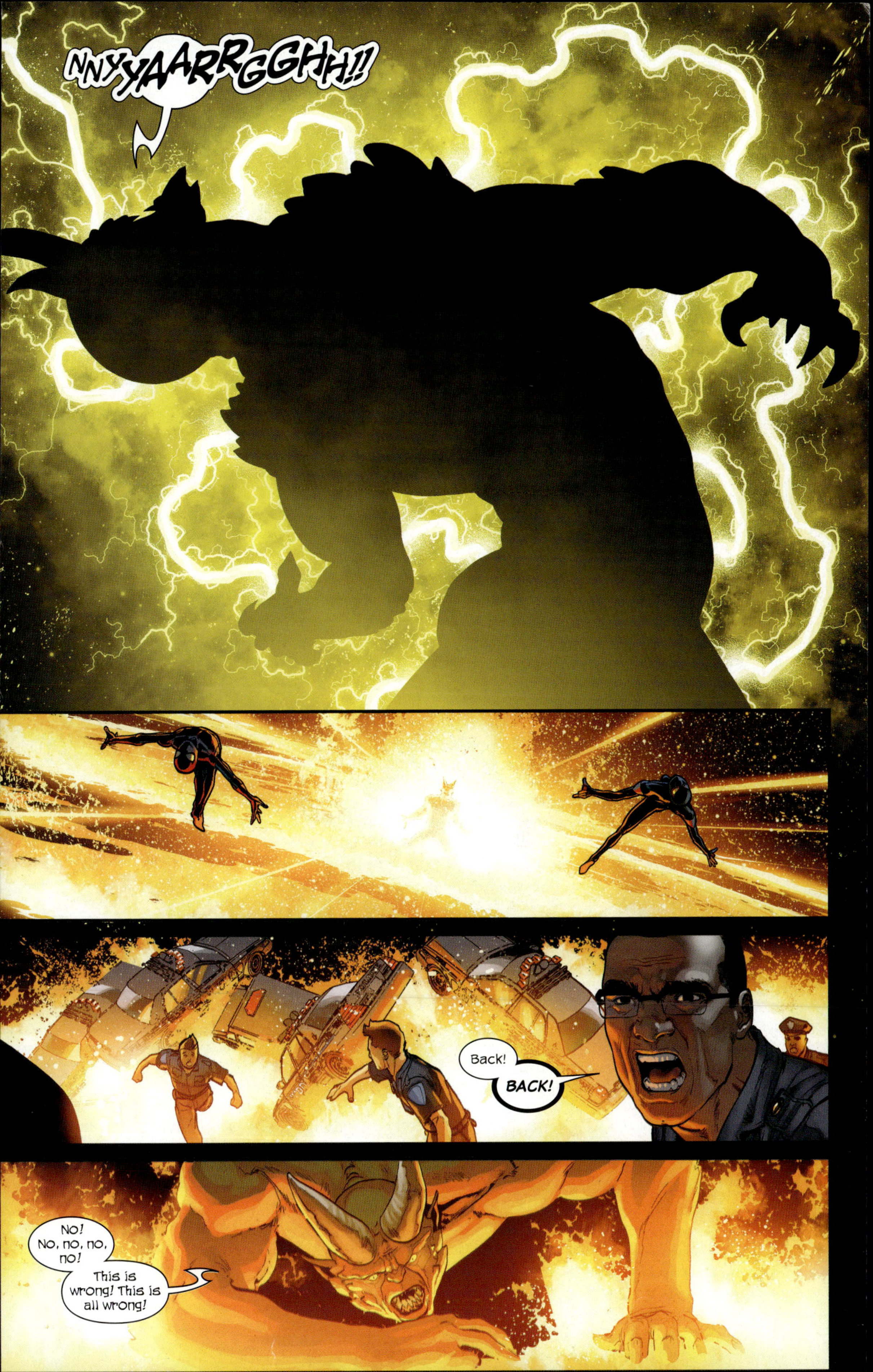
NNYYAARRGGHH!!
Back! BACK!
No! No, no, no, no!
This is wrong! This is all wrong!

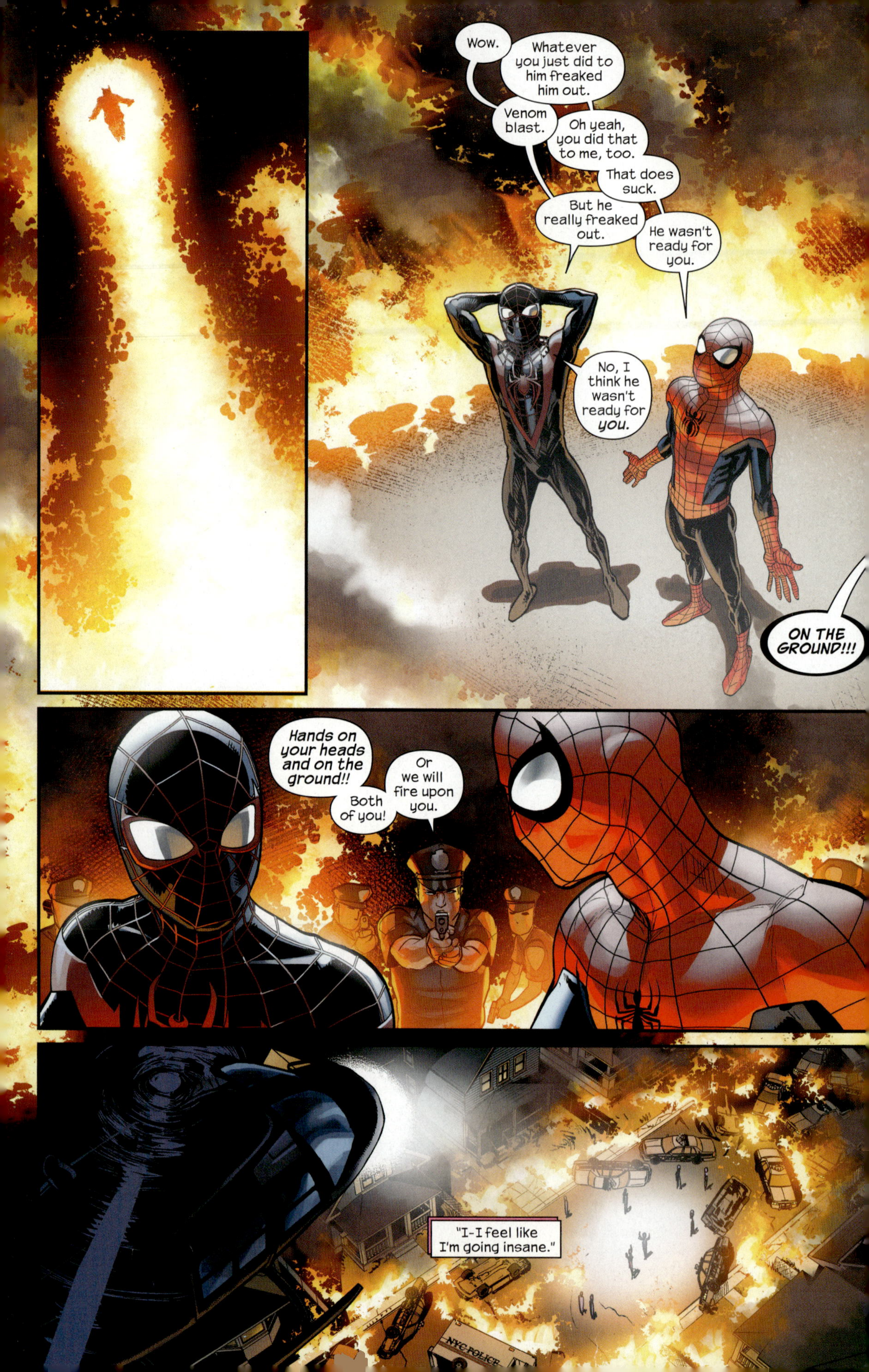
Wow.
Whatever you just did to him freaked him out.
Venom blast.
Oh yeah, you did that to me, too.
That does suck.
But he really freaked out.
He wasn't ready for you.
No, I think he wasn't ready for *you.*
ON THE GROUND!!!
Hands on your heads and on the ground!!
Both of you!
Or we will fire upon you.
"I-I feel like I'm going insane."
NYC POLICE

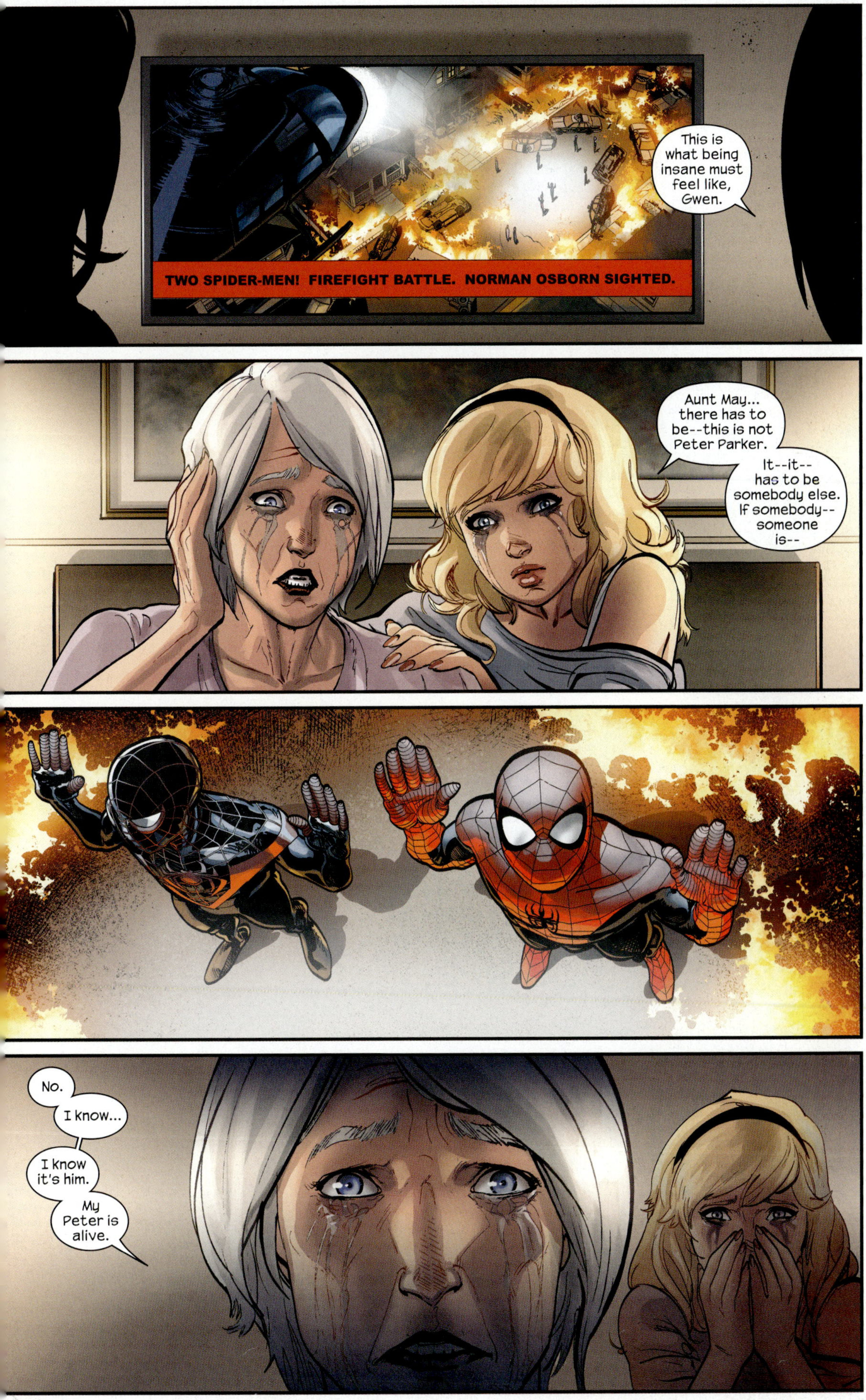
TWO SPIDER-MEN! FIREFIGHT BATTLE. NORMAN OSBORN SIGHTED.
This is what being insane must feel like, Gwen.
Aunt May... there has to be--this is not Peter Parker.
It--it--has to be somebody else. If somebody--someone is--
No.
I know...
I know it's him.
My Peter is alive.

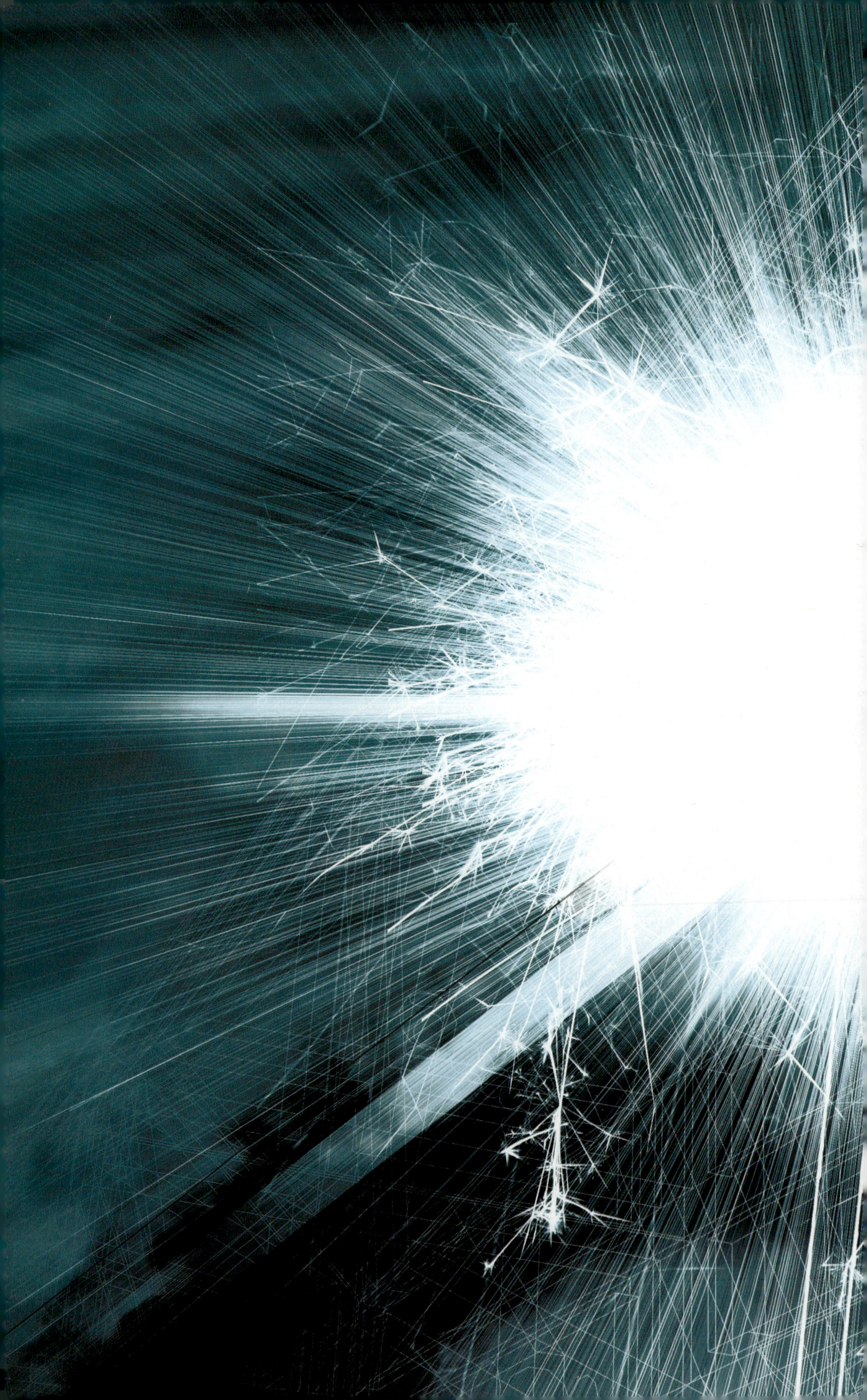

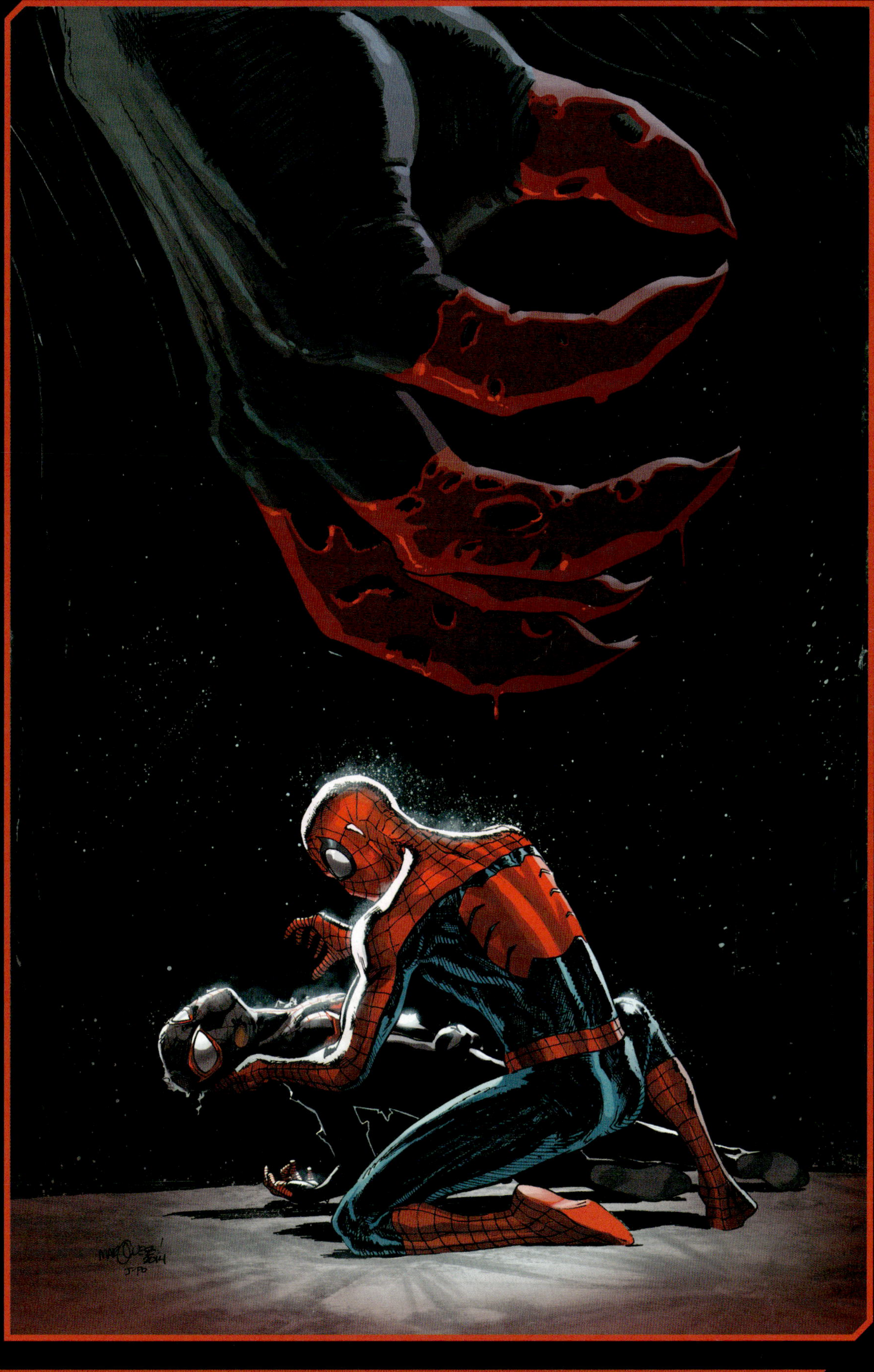

MILES MORALES: ULTIMATE SPIDER-MAN #5

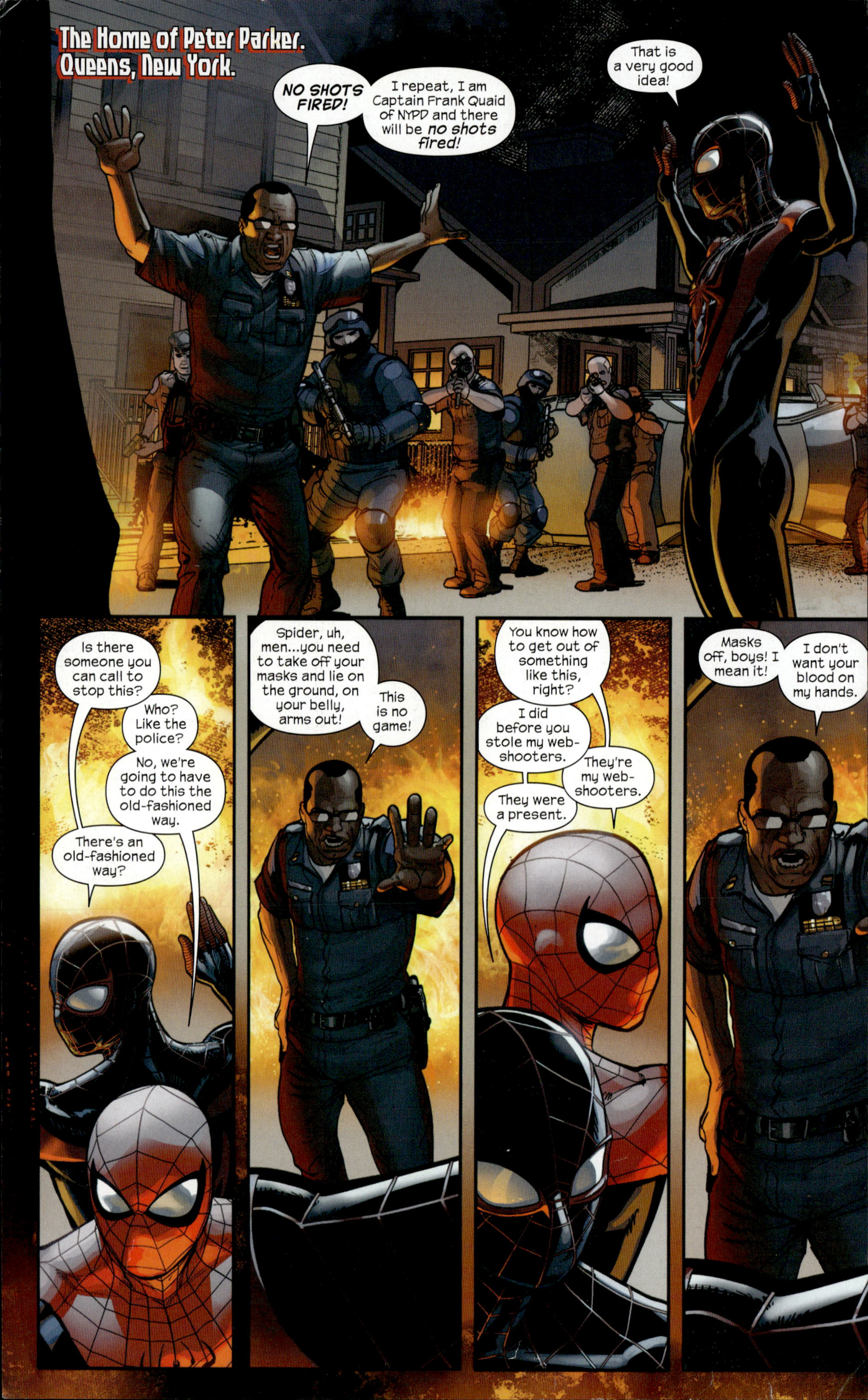
The Home of Peter Parker.
Queens, New York.
NO SHOTS FIRED!
I repeat, I am Captain Frank Quaid of NYPD and there will be no shots fired!
That is a very good idea!
Is there someone you can call to stop this?
Who? Like the police?
No, we're going to have to do this the old-fashioned way.
There's an old-fashioned way?
Spider, uh, men...you need to take off your masks and lie on the ground, on your belly, arms out!
This is no game!
You know how to get out of something like this, right?
I did before you stole my web-shooters.
They're my web-shooters.
They were a present.
Masks off, boys! I mean it!
I don't want your blood on my hands.

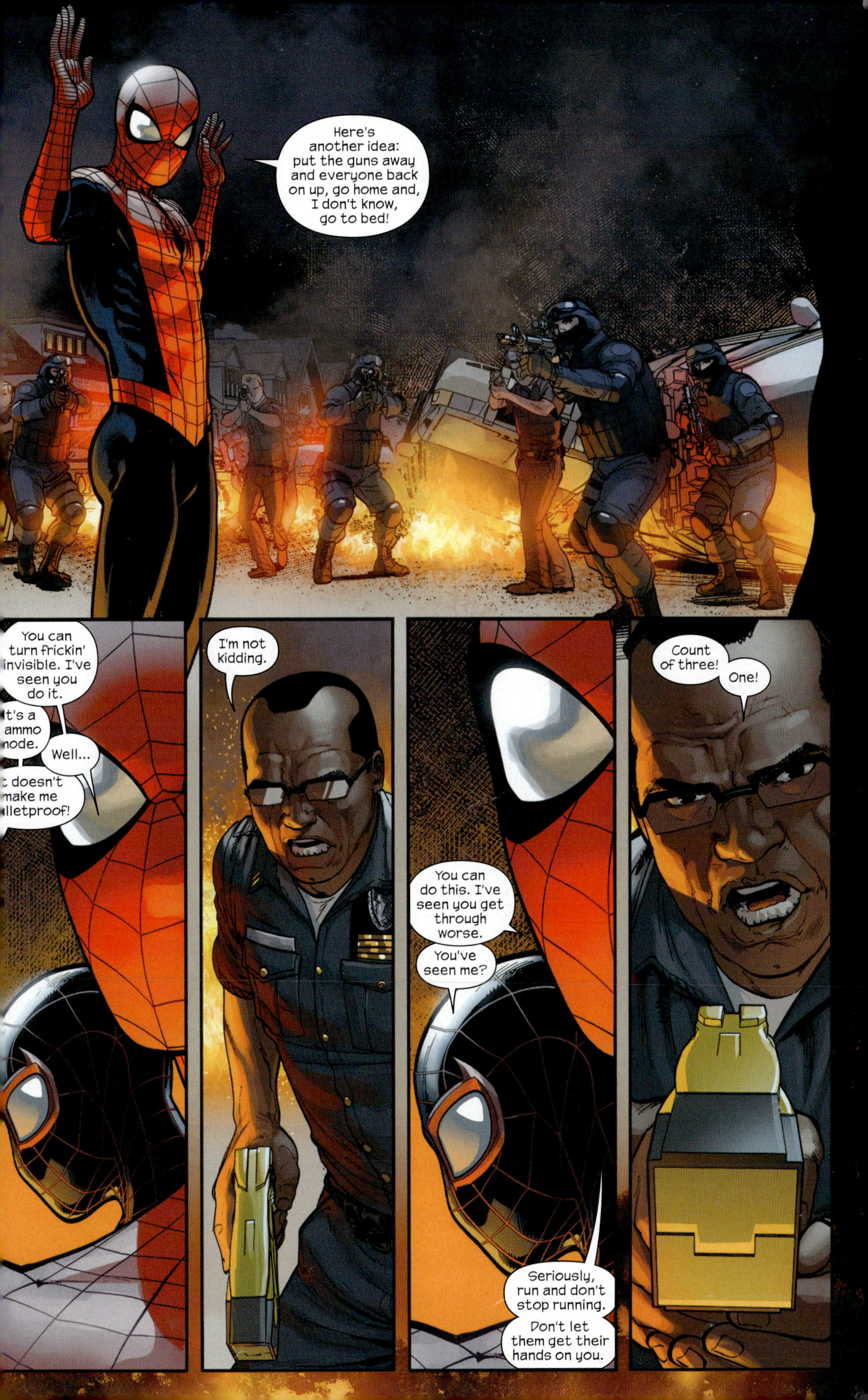

Here's another idea: put the guns away and everyone back on up, go home and, I don't know, go to bed!
You can turn frickin' invisible. I've seen you do it.
t's a ammo node.
Well...
doesn't make me lletproof!
I'm not kidding.
You can do this. I've seen you get through worse.
You've seen me?
Seriously, run and don't stop running.
Don't let them get their hands on you.
Count of three!
One!

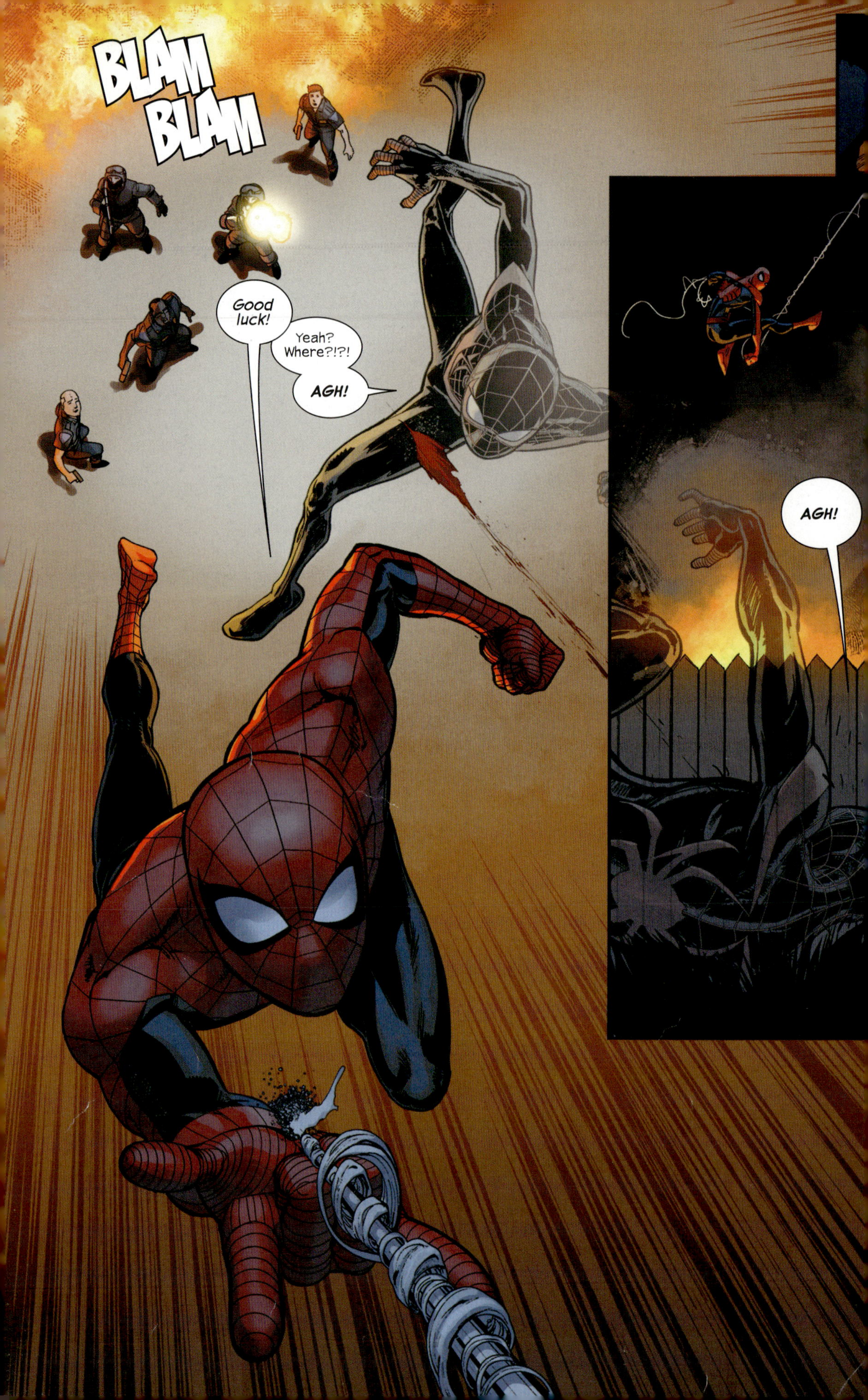
BLAM BLAM
Good luck!
Yeah? Where?!?!
AGH!
AGH!

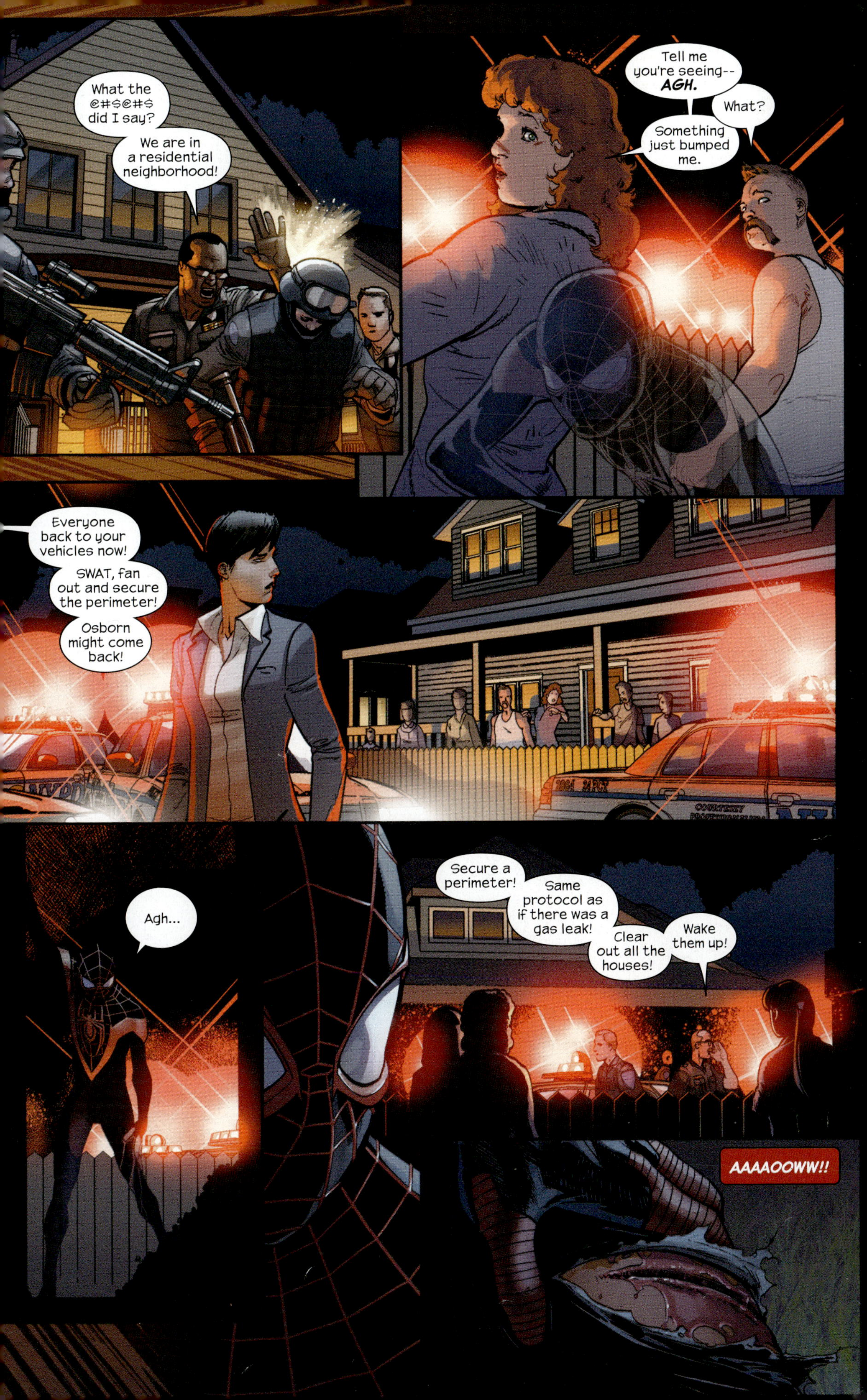
What the @#$@#$ did I say?
We are in a residential neighborhood!
Tell me you're seeing-- **AGH.**
What?
Something just bumped me.
Everyone back to your vehicles now!
SWAT, fan out and secure the perimeter!
Osborn might come back!
Agh...
Secure a perimeter!
Same protocol as if there was a gas leak!
Clear out all the houses!
Wake them up!
AAAAOOWW!!

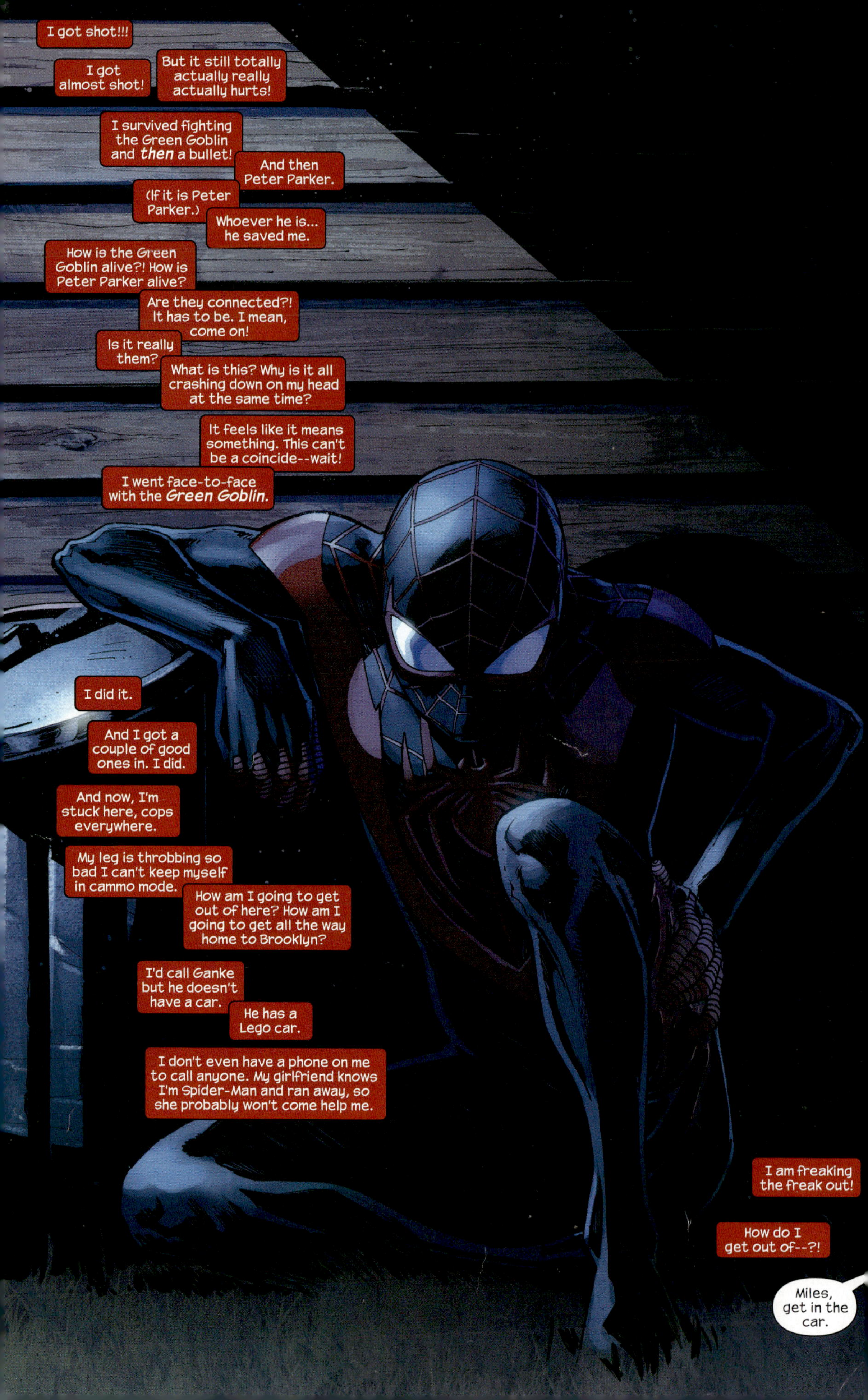
I got shot!!!
I got almost shot!
But it still totally actually really actually hurts!
I survived fighting the Green Goblin and *then* a bullet!
And then Peter Parker.
(If it is Peter Parker.)
Whoever he is... he saved me.
How is the Green Goblin alive?! How is Peter Parker alive?
Are they connected?! It has to be. I mean, come on!
Is it really them?
What is this? Why is it all crashing down on my head at the same time?
It feels like it means something. This can't be a coincide--wait!
I went face-to-face with the *Green Goblin.*
I did it.
And I got a couple of good ones in. I did.
And now, I'm stuck here, cops everywhere.
My leg is throbbing so bad I can't keep myself in cammo mode.
How am I going to get out of here? How am I going to get all the way home to Brooklyn?
I'd call Ganke but he doesn't have a car.
He has a Lego car.
I don't even have a phone on me to call anyone. My girlfriend knows I'm Spider-Man and ran away, so she probably won't come help me.
I am freaking the freak out!
How do I get out of--?!
Miles, get in the car.

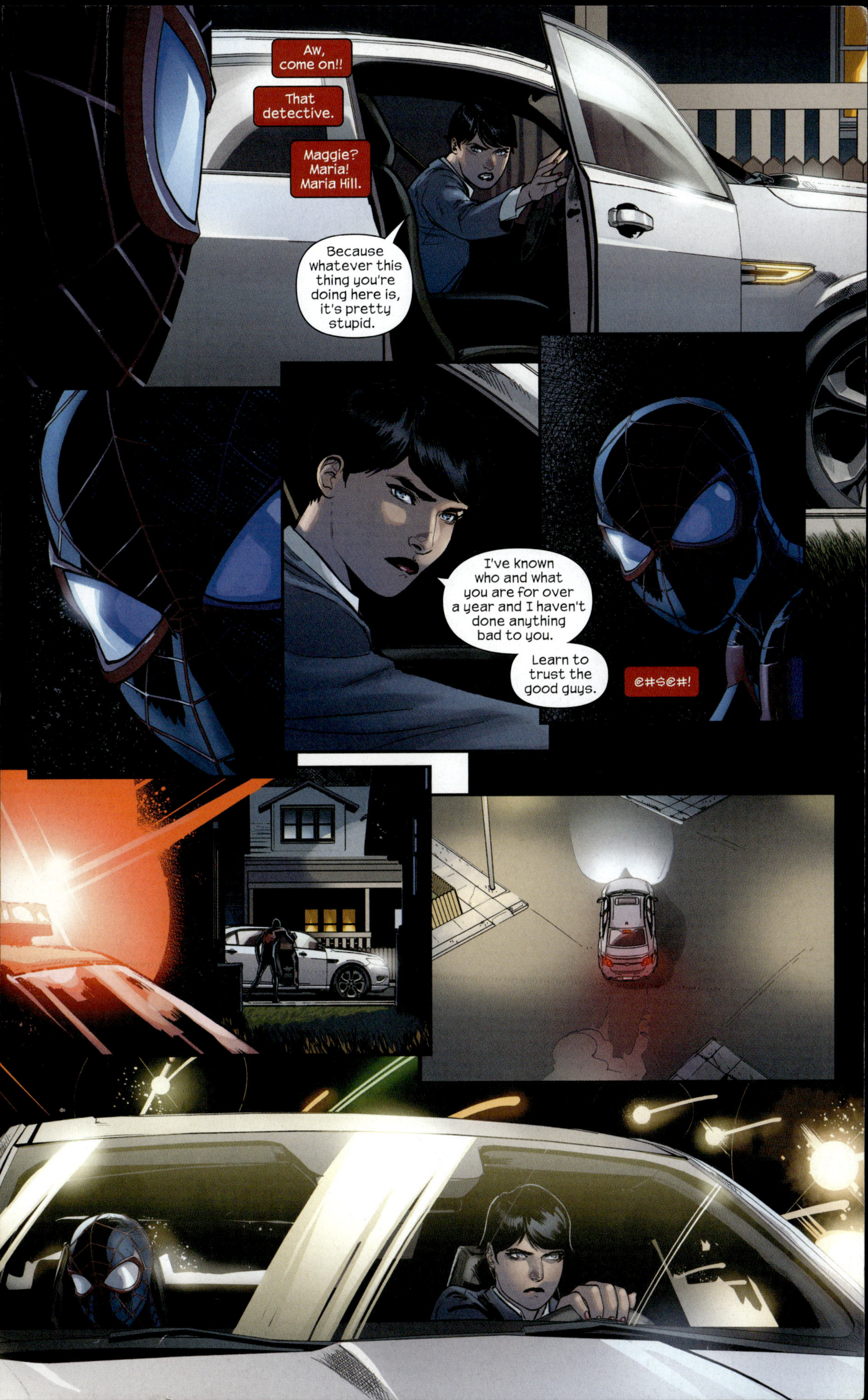
Aw, come on!!
That detective.
Maggie? Maria! Maria Hill.
Because whatever this thing you're doing here is, it's pretty stupid.
I've known who and what you are for over a year and I haven't done anything bad to you.
Learn to trust the good guys.
@#$@#!

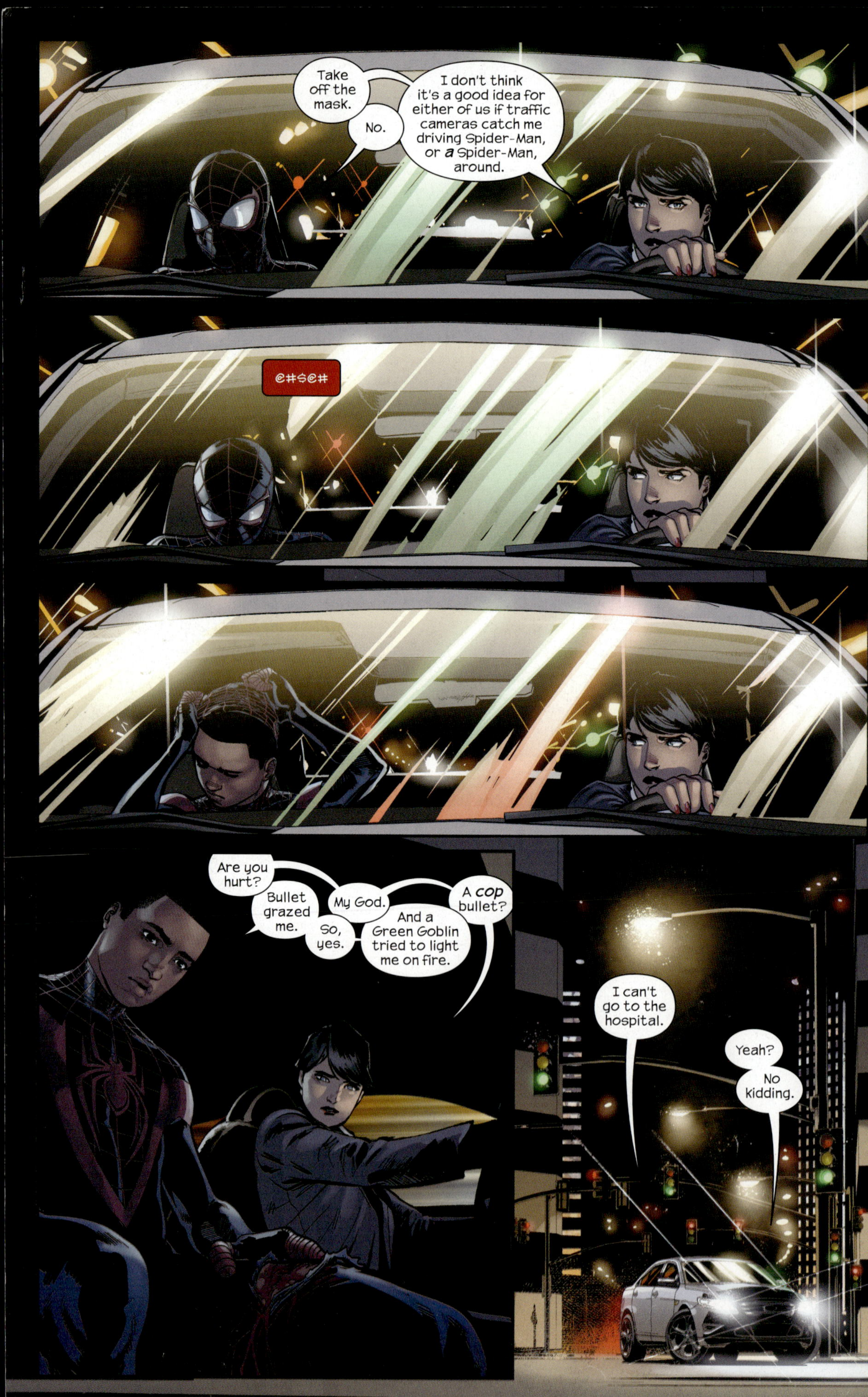
Take off the mask.
No.
I don't think it's a good idea for either of us if traffic cameras catch me driving Spider-Man, or a Spider-Man, around.
@#$@#
Are you hurt?
Bullet grazed me.
My God.
So, yes.
And a Green Goblin tried to light me on fire.
A cop bullet?
I can't go to the hospital.
Yeah?
No kidding.

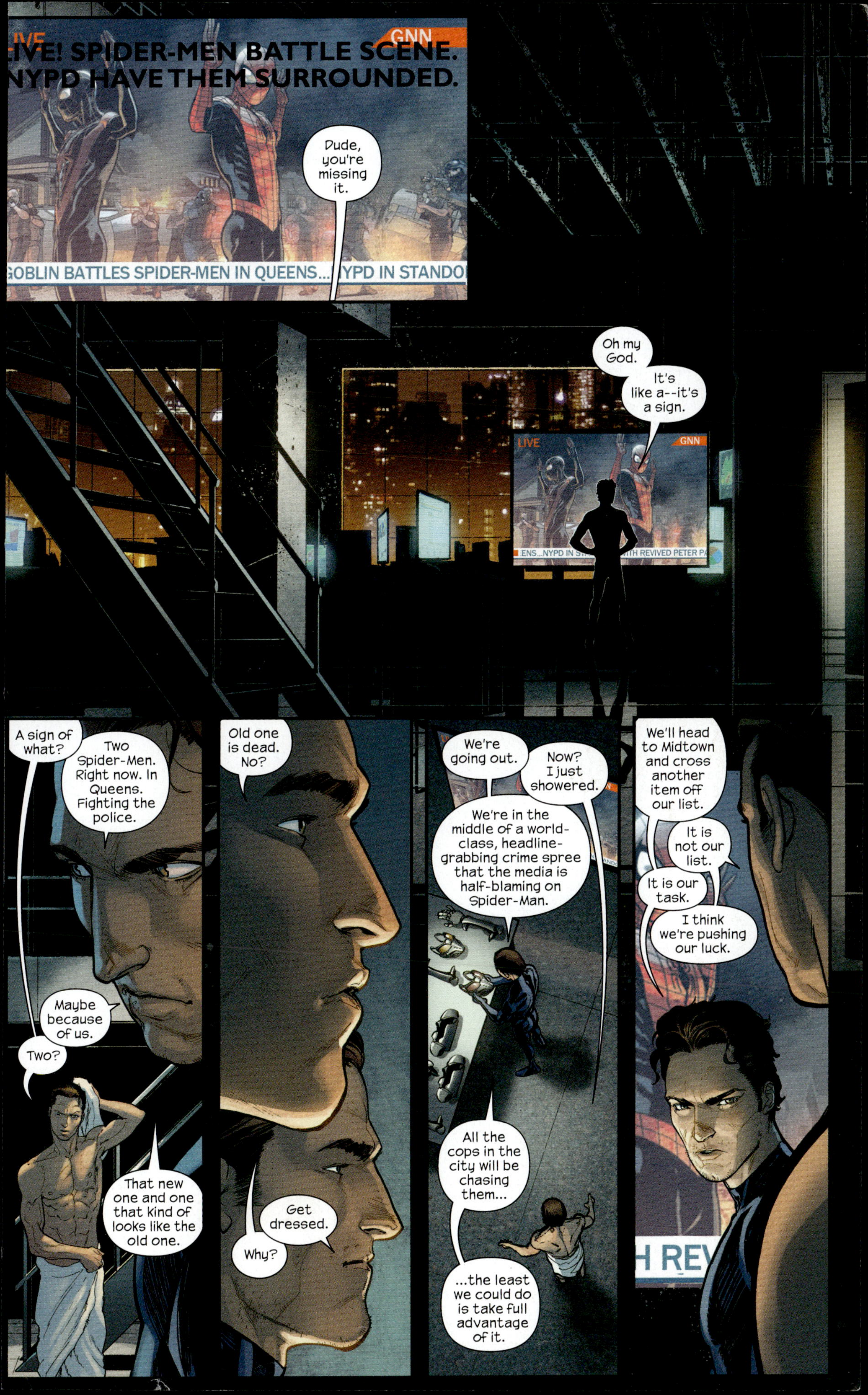
LIVE! SPIDER-MEN BATTLE SCENE.
NYPD HAVE THEM SURROUNDED.
GNN
GOBLIN BATTLES SPIDER-MEN IN QUEENS... NYPD IN STANDO
Dude, you're missing it.
Oh my God.
It's like a--it's a sign.
LIVE
GNN
ENS...NYPD IN ST
ITH REVIVED PETER PA
A sign of what?
Two Spider-Men. Right now. In Queens. Fighting the police.
Maybe because of us.
Two?
That new one and one that kind of looks like the old one.
Old one is dead. No?
Get dressed.
Why?
We're going out.
Now? I just showered.
We're in the middle of a world-class, headline-grabbing crime spree that the media is half-blaming on Spider-Man.
All the cops in the city will be chasing them...
...the least we could do is take full advantage of it.
We'll head to Midtown and cross another item off our list.
It is not our list.
It is our task.
I think we're pushing our luck.
H REV

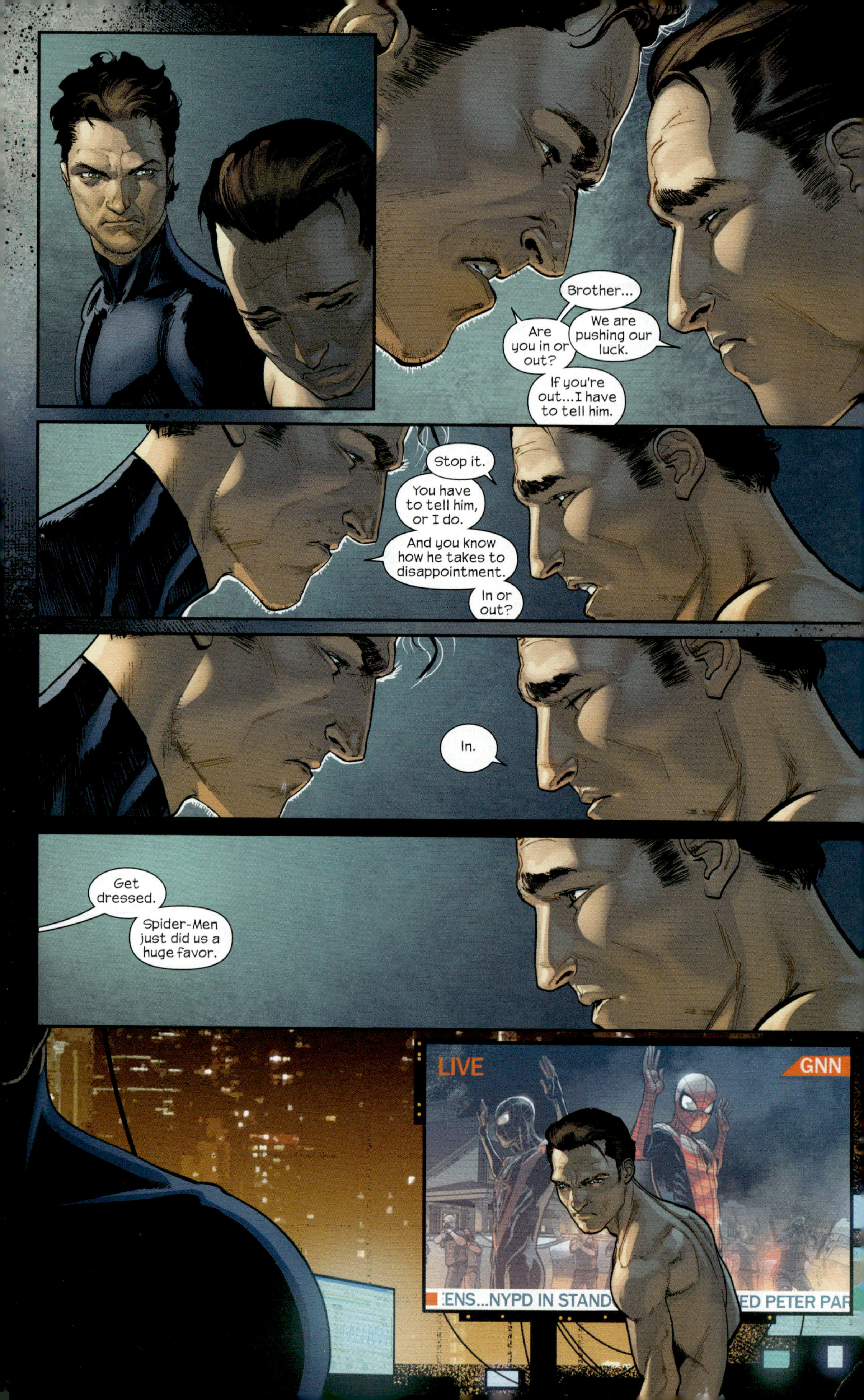
Brother...
Are you in or out?
We are pushing our luck.
If you're out...I have to tell him.
Stop it.
You have to tell him, or I do.
And you know how he takes to disappointment.
In or out?
In.
Get dressed.
Spider-Men just did us a huge favor.
LIVE
GNN
ENS...NYPD IN STAND
ED PETER PAR

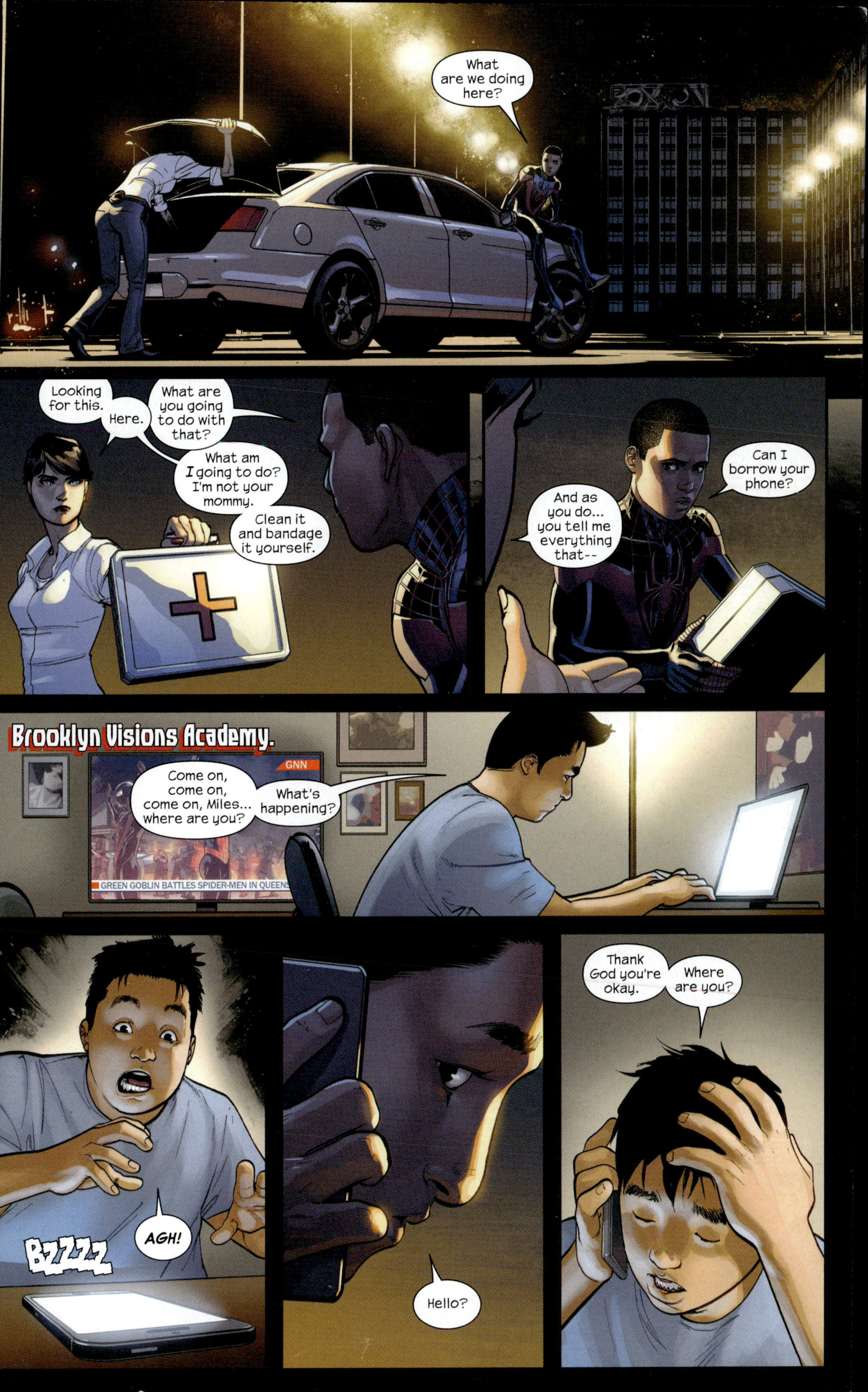
What are we doing here?
Looking for this.
Here.
What are you going to do with that?
What am I going to do? I'm not your mommy.
Clean it and bandage it yourself.
Can I borrow your phone?
And as you do... you tell me everything that--
Brooklyn Visions Academy.
GNN
GREEN GOBLIN BATTLES SPIDER-MEN IN QUEENS
Come on, come on, come on, Miles... where are you?
What's happening?
BZZZZ
AGH!
Hello?
Thank God you're okay.
Where are you?

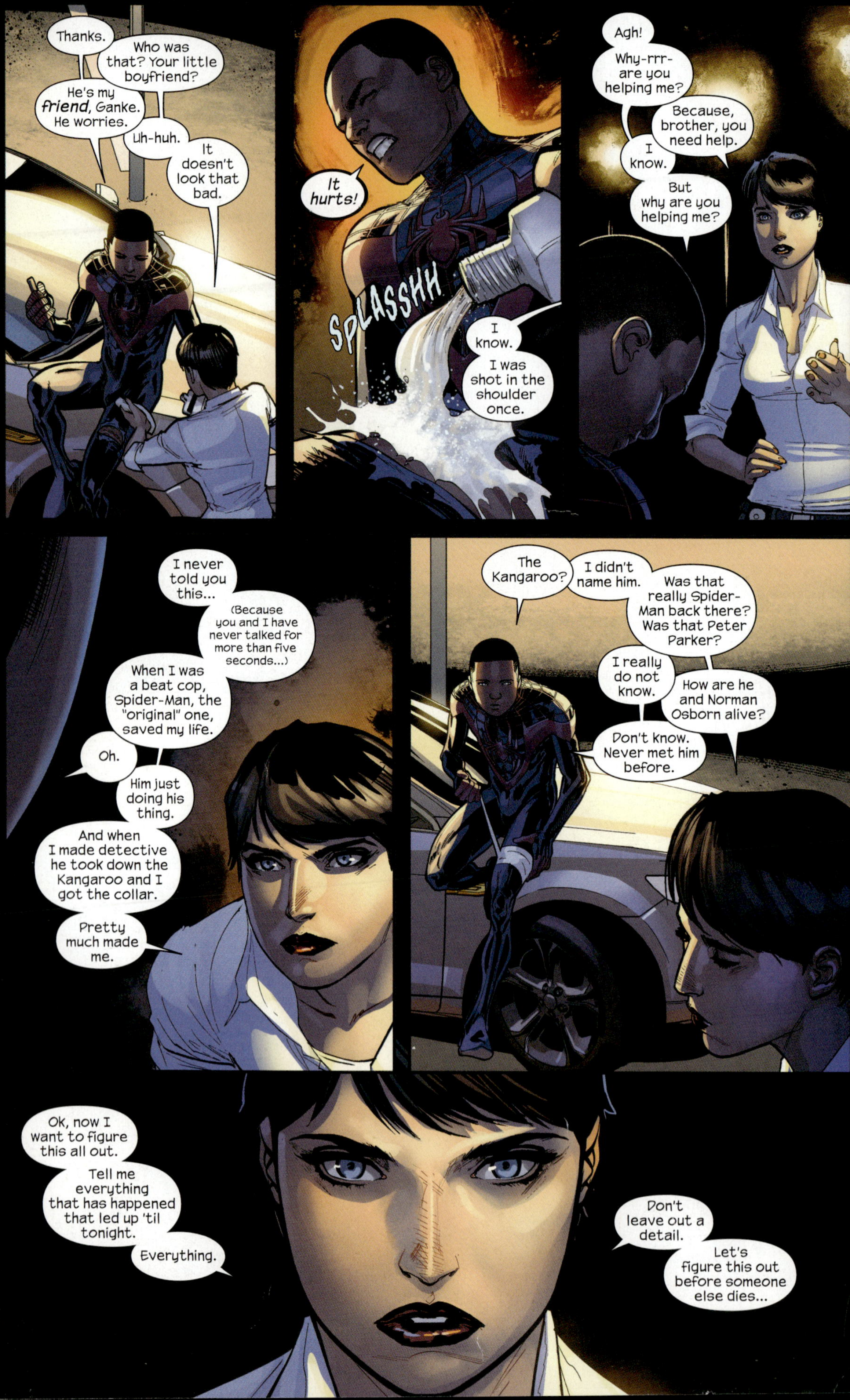
Thanks.
Who was that? Your little boyfriend?
He's my *friend*, Ganke. He worries.
Uh-huh.
It doesn't look that bad.
It hurts!
SPLASSHH
I know.
I was shot in the shoulder once.
Agh!
Why-rrr- are you helping me?
Because, brother, you need help.
I know.
But why are you helping me?
I never told you this...
(Because you and I have never talked for more than five seconds...)
When I was a beat cop, Spider-Man, the "original" one, saved my life.
Oh.
Him just doing his thing.
And when I made detective he took down the Kangaroo and I got the collar.
Pretty much made me.
The Kangaroo?
I didn't name him.
Was that really Spider-Man back there? Was that Peter Parker?
I really do not know.
How are he and Norman Osborn alive?
Don't know. Never met him before.
Ok, now I want to figure this all out.
Tell me everything that has happened that led up 'til tonight.
Everything.
Don't leave out a detail.
Let's figure this out before someone else dies...

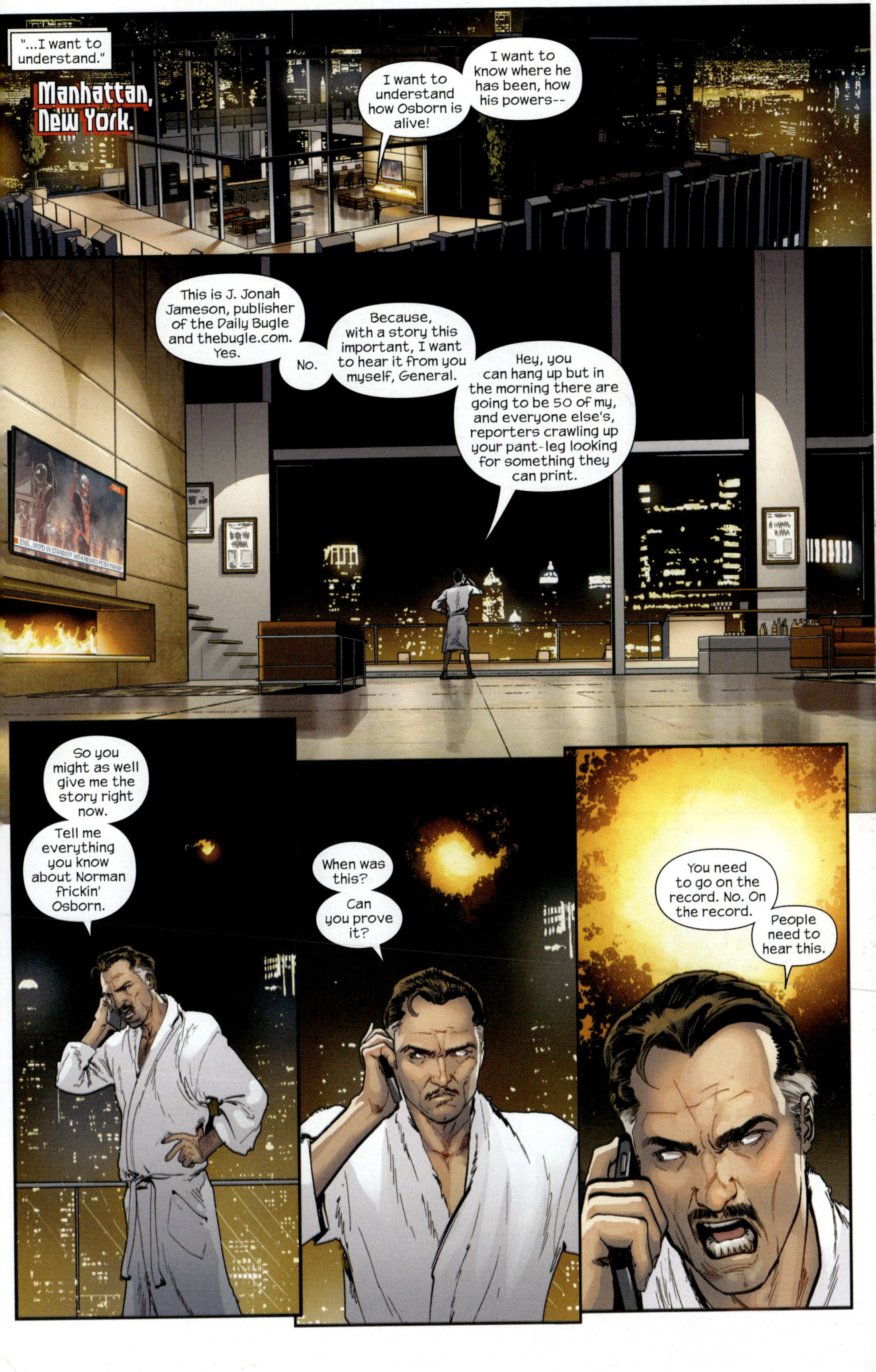
"...I want to understand."
Manhattan, New York.
I want to understand how Osborn is alive!
I want to know where he has been, how his powers--
This is J. Jonah Jameson, publisher of the Daily Bugle and thebugle.com. Yes.
No.
Because, with a story this important, I want to hear it from you myself, General.
Hey, you can hang up but in the morning there are going to be 50 of my, and everyone else's, reporters crawling up your pant-leg looking for something they can print.
So you might as well give me the story right now.
Tell me everything you know about Norman frickin' Osborn.
When was this?
Can you prove it?
You need to go on the record. No. On the record.
People need to hear this.

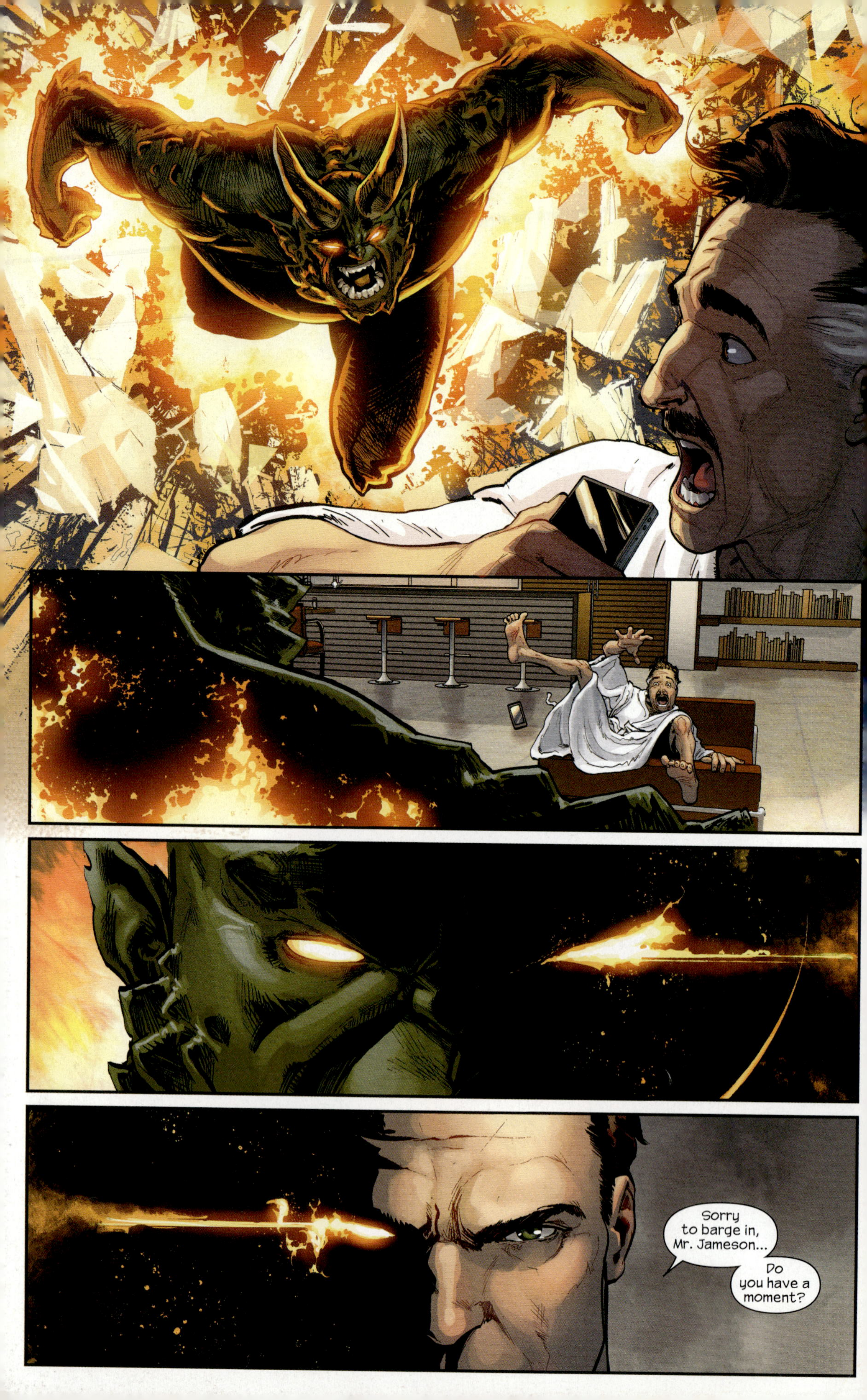
Sorry to barge in, Mr. Jameson...
Do you have a moment?

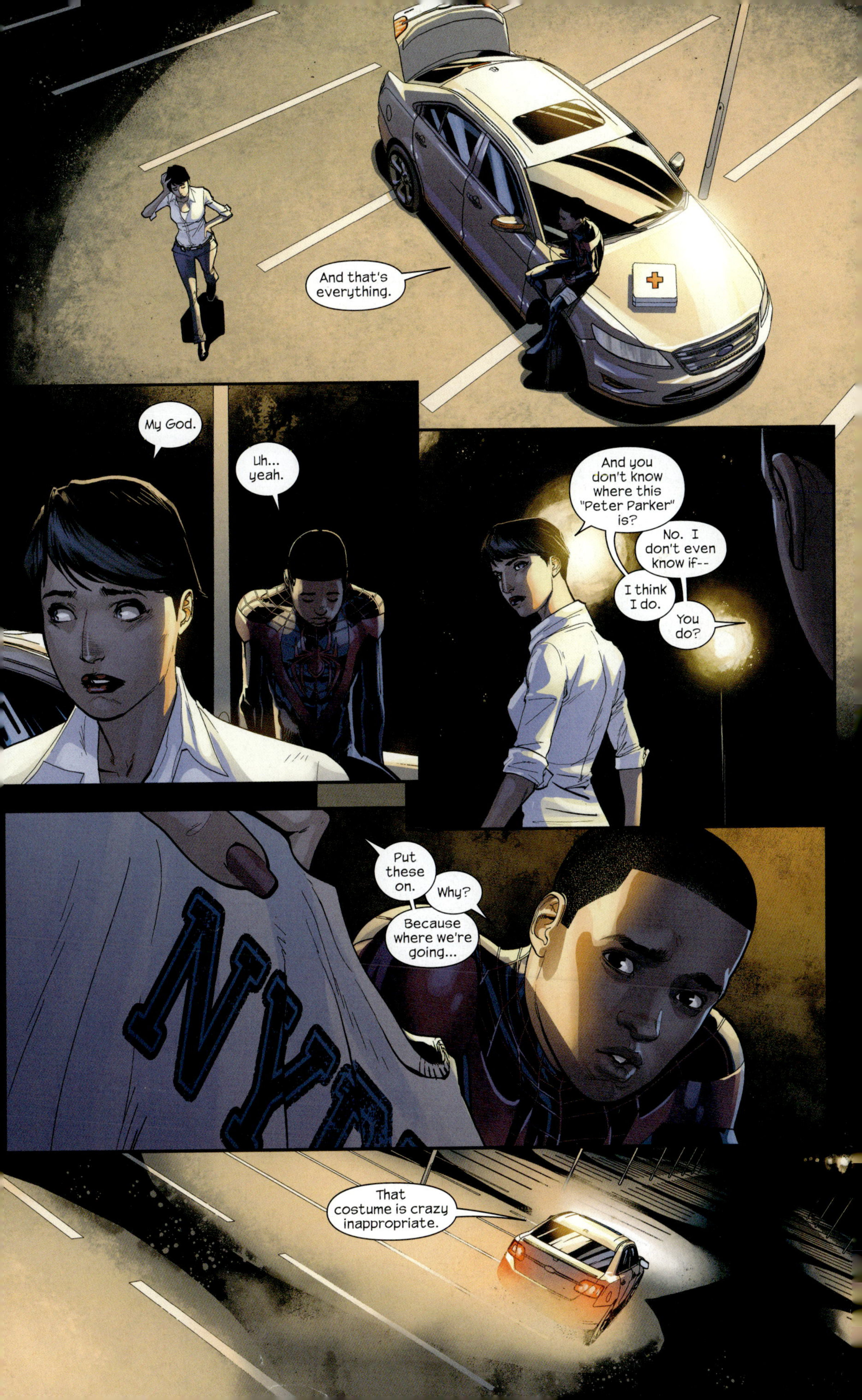
And that's everything.
My God.
Uh... yeah.
And you don't know where this "Peter Parker" is?
No. I don't even know if--
I think I do.
You do?
Put these on.
Why?
Because where we're going...
That costume is crazy inappropriate.

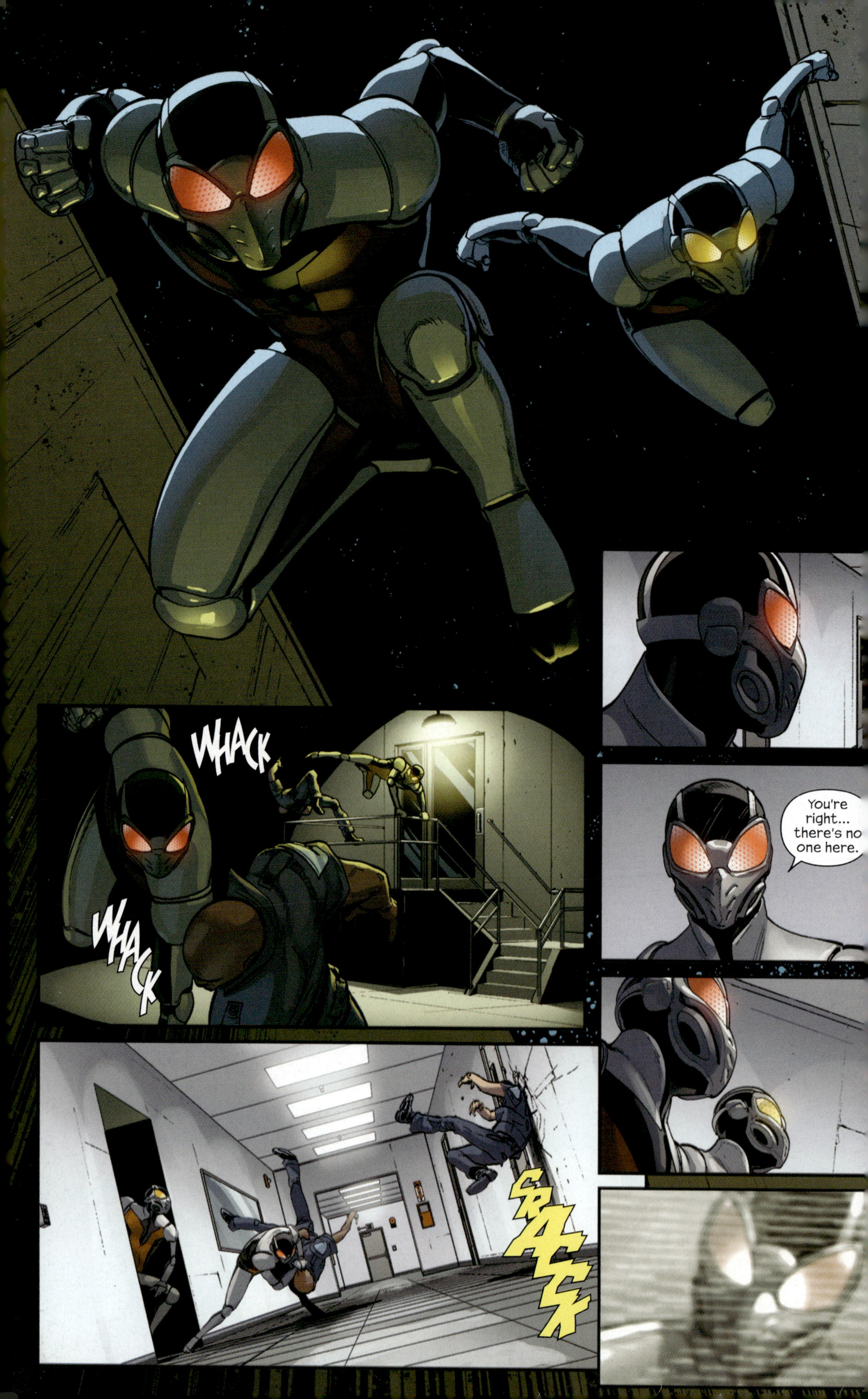
WHACK
WHACK
You're right... there's no one here.
CRACK

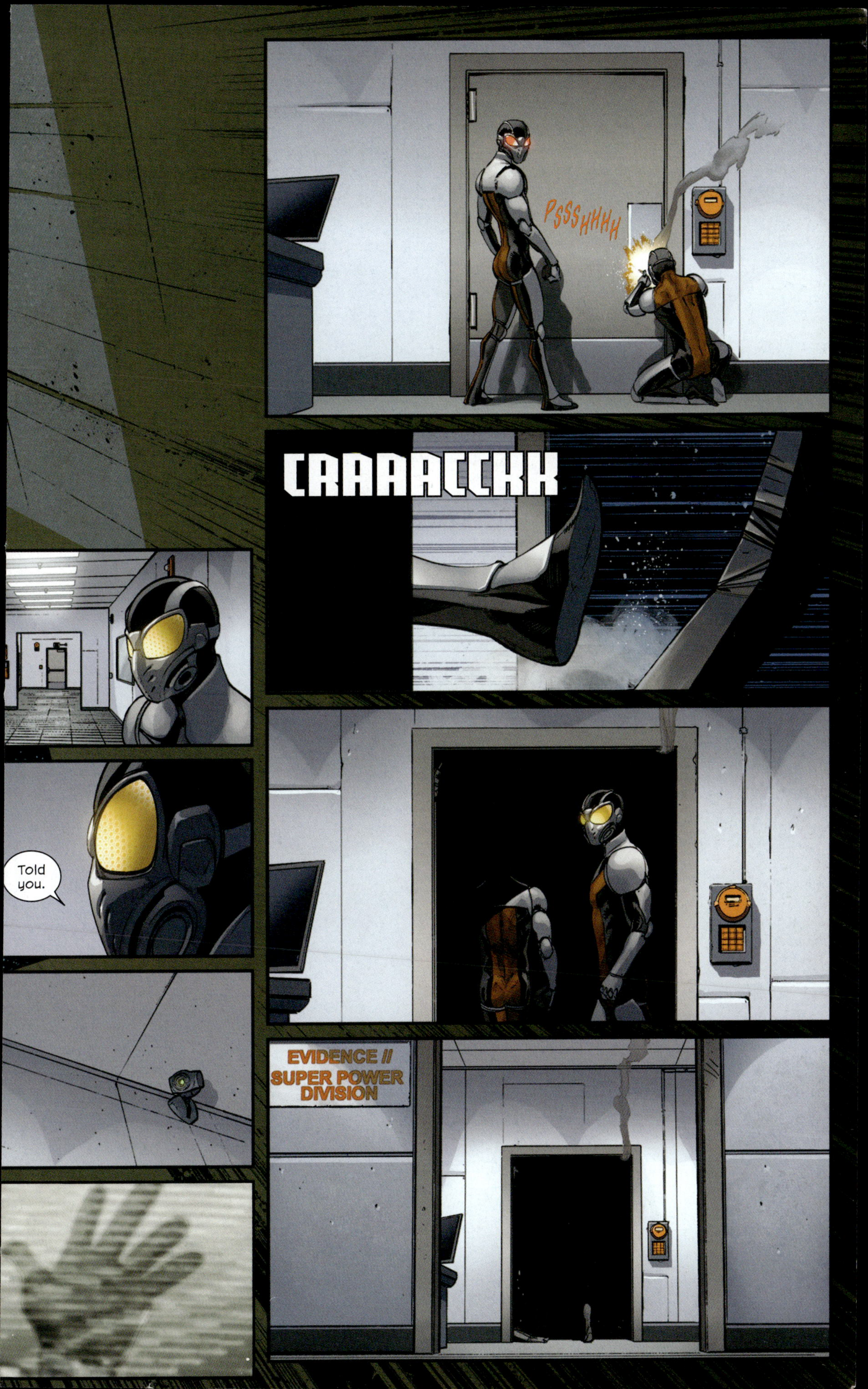
PSSSHHHH
CRAAACCKK
Told you.
EVIDENCE //
SUPER POWER
DIVISION

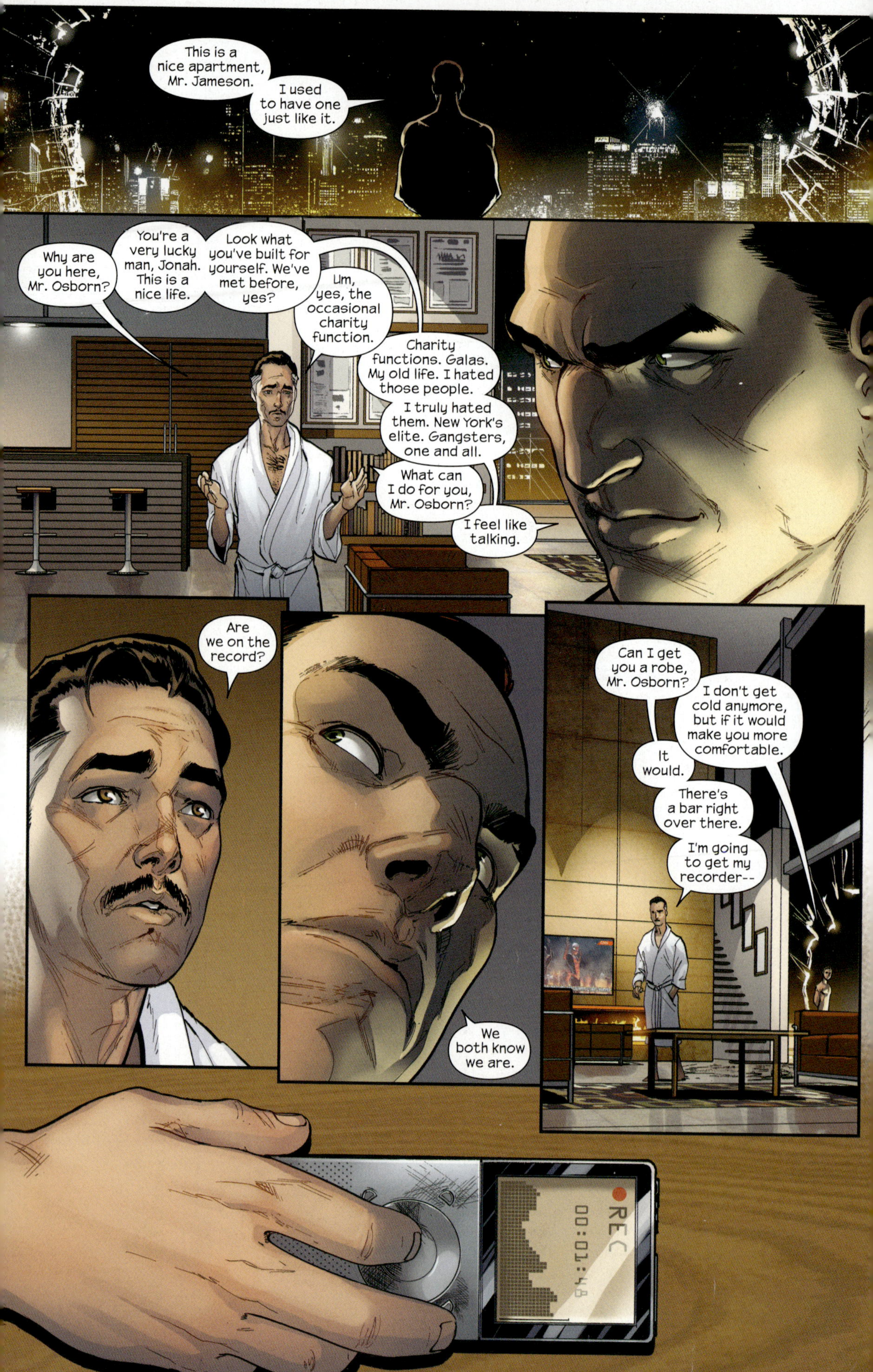

This is a nice apartment, Mr. Jameson.
I used to have one just like it.
Why are you here, Mr. Osborn?
You're a very lucky man, Jonah. This is a nice life.
Look what you've built for yourself. We've met before, yes?
Um, yes, the occasional charity function.
Charity functions. Galas. My old life. I hated those people.
I truly hated them. New York's elite. Gangsters, one and all.
What can I do for you, Mr. Osborn?
I feel like talking.
Are we on the record?
We both know we are.
Can I get you a robe, Mr. Osborn?
I don't get cold anymore, but if it would make you more comfortable.
It would.
There's a bar right over there.
I'm going to get my recorder--
REC
00:01:48

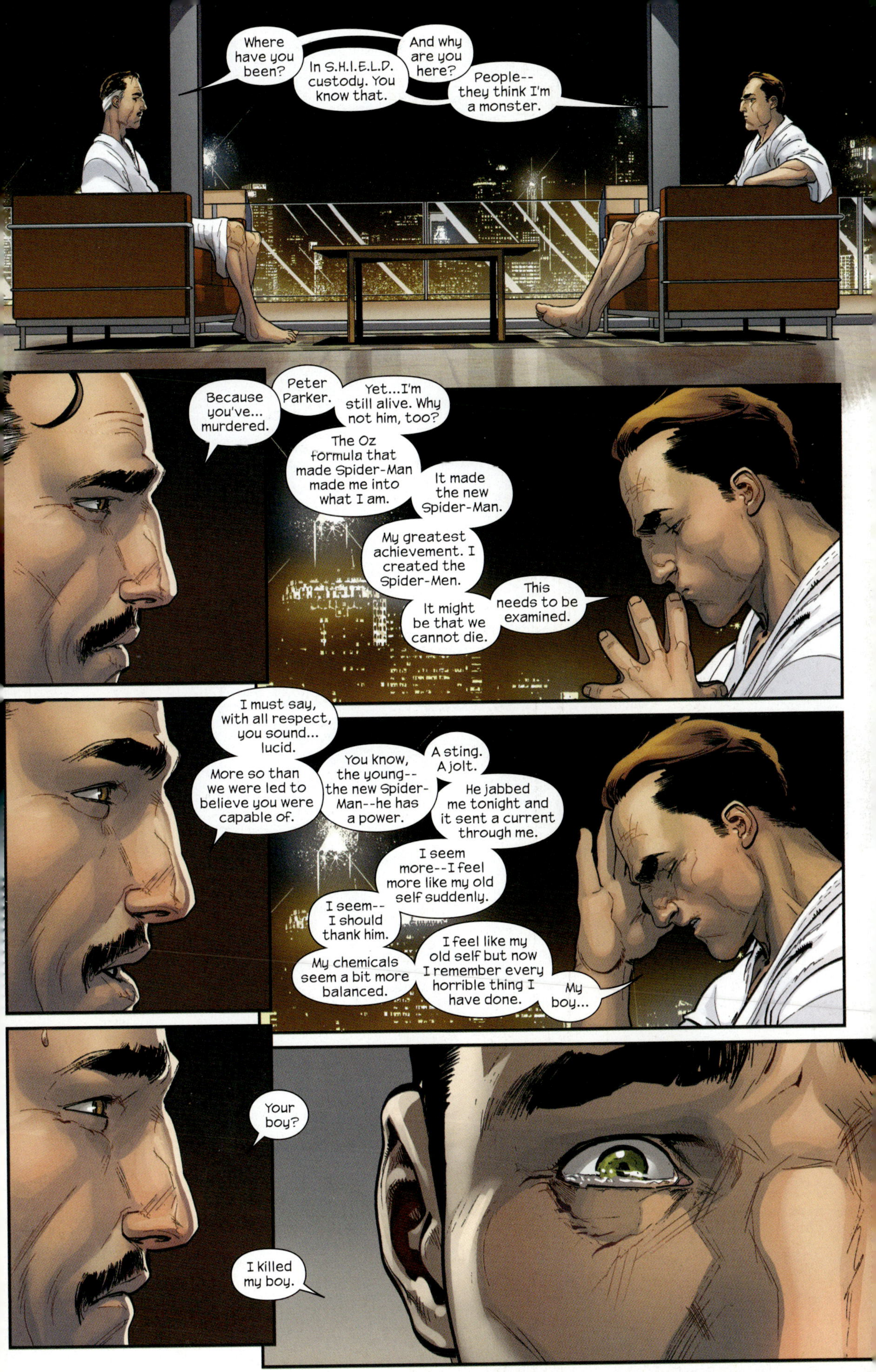
Where have you been?
And why are you here?
In S.H.I.E.L.D. custody. You know that.
People-- they think I'm a monster.
Because you've... murdered.
Peter Parker.
Yet...I'm still alive. Why not him, too?
The Oz formula that made Spider-Man made me into what I am.
It made the new Spider-Man.
My greatest achievement. I created the Spider-Men.
It might be that we cannot die.
This needs to be examined.
I must say, with all respect, you sound... lucid.
More so than we were led to believe you were capable of.
You know, the young-- the new Spider-Man--he has a power.
A sting. A jolt.
He jabbed me tonight and it sent a current through me.
I seem more--I feel more like my old self suddenly.
I seem-- I should thank him.
My chemicals seem a bit more balanced.
I feel like my old self but now I remember every horrible thing I have done.
My boy...
Your boy?
I killed my boy.

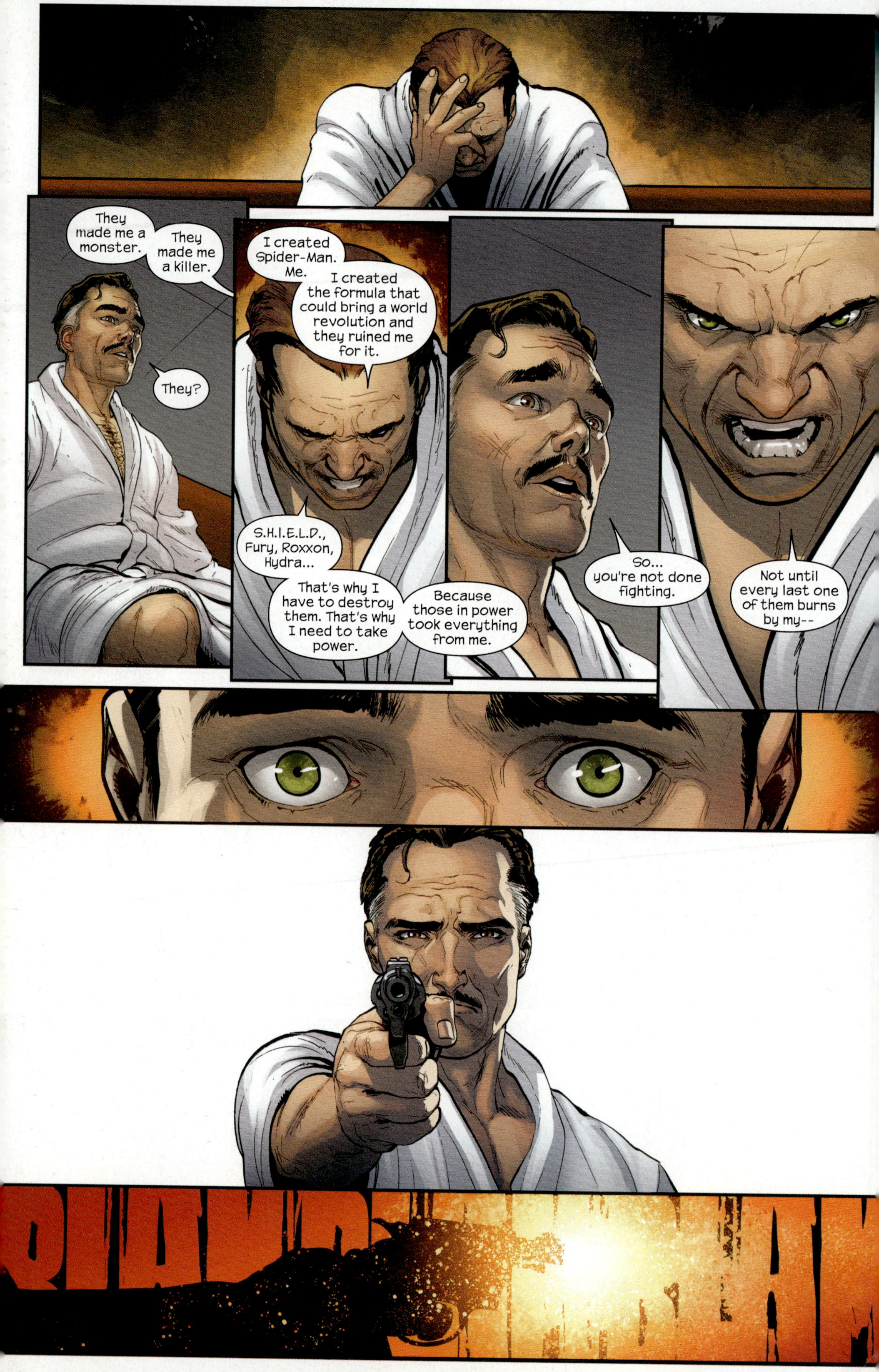
They made me a monster.
They made me a killer.
They?
I created Spider-Man. Me.
I created the formula that could bring a world revolution and they ruined me for it.
S.H.I.E.L.D., Fury, Roxxon, Hydra...
That's why I have to destroy them. That's why I need to take power.
Because those in power took everything from me.
So... you're not done fighting.
Not until every last one of them burns by my--

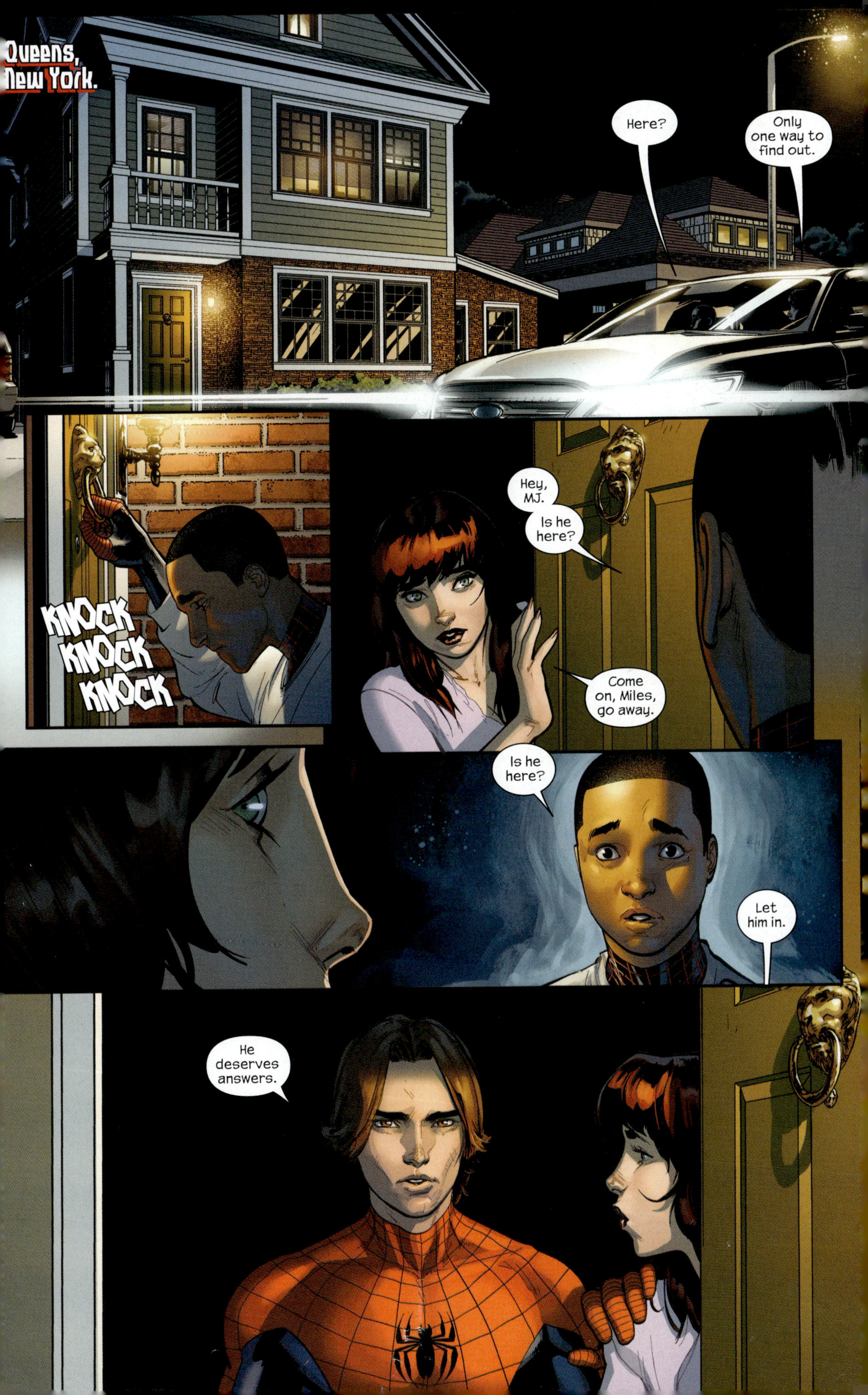
Queens, New York.
Here?
Only one way to find out.
KNOCK KNOCK KNOCK
Hey, MJ.
Is he here?
Come on, Miles, go away.
Is he here?
Let him in.
He deserves answers.

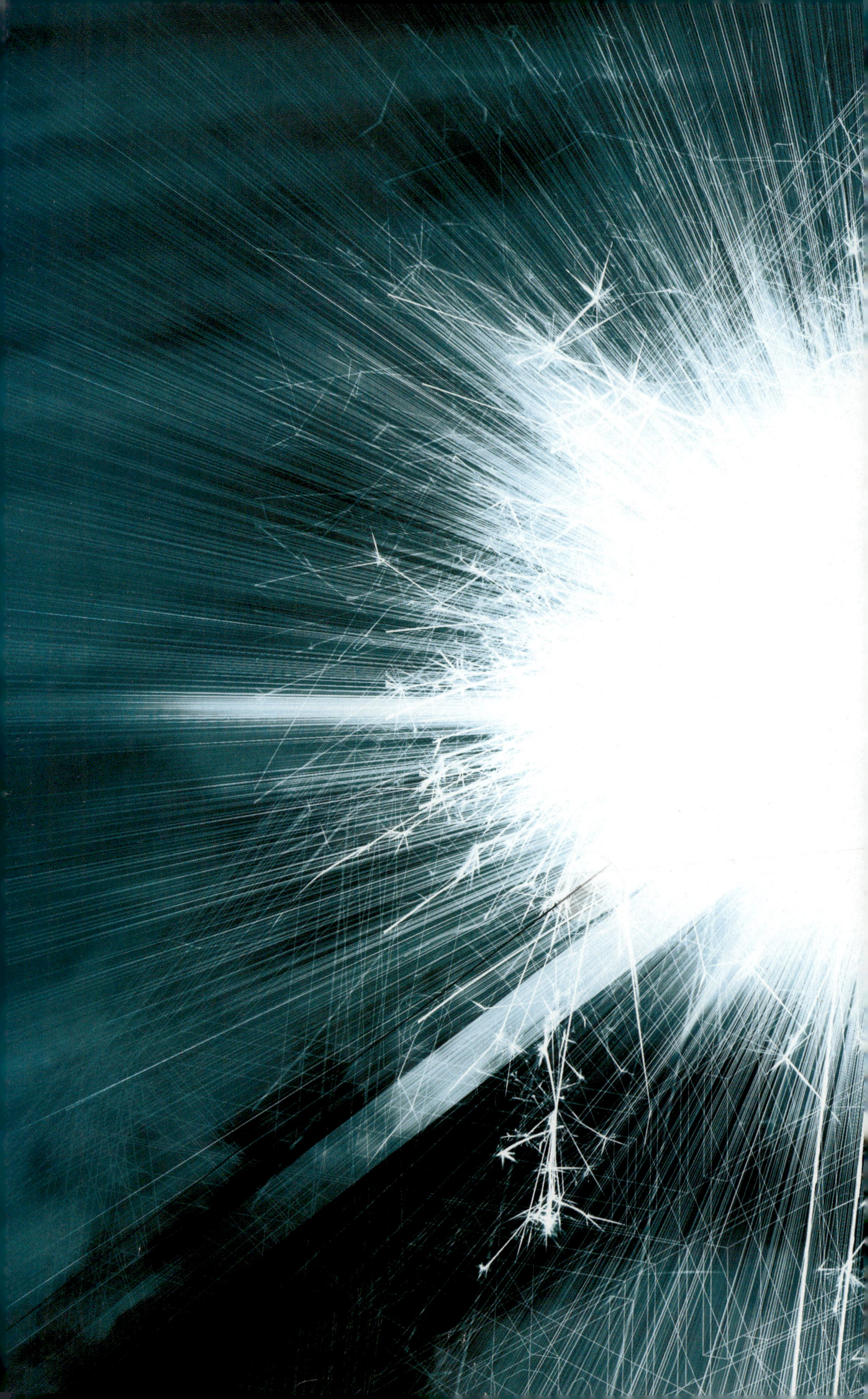

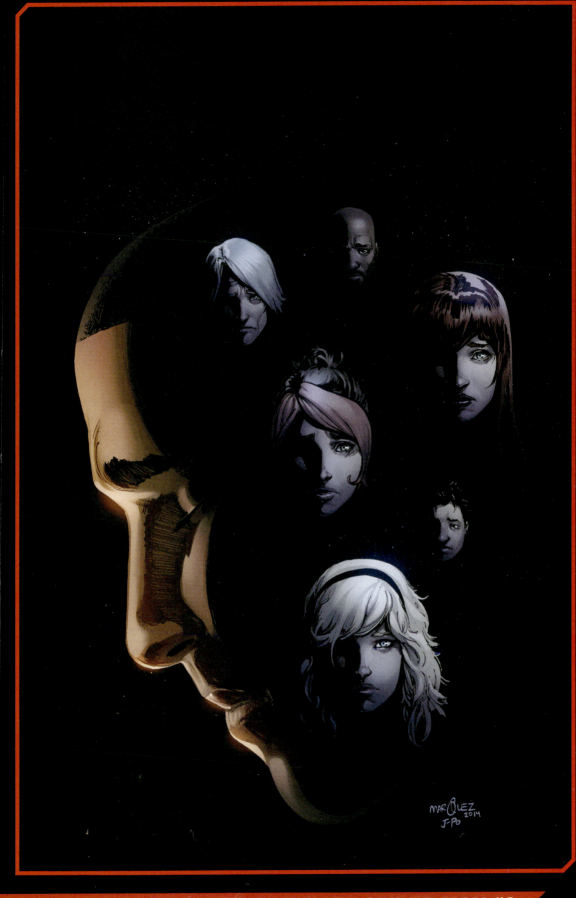

MILES MORALES: ULTIMATE SPIDER-MAN #6

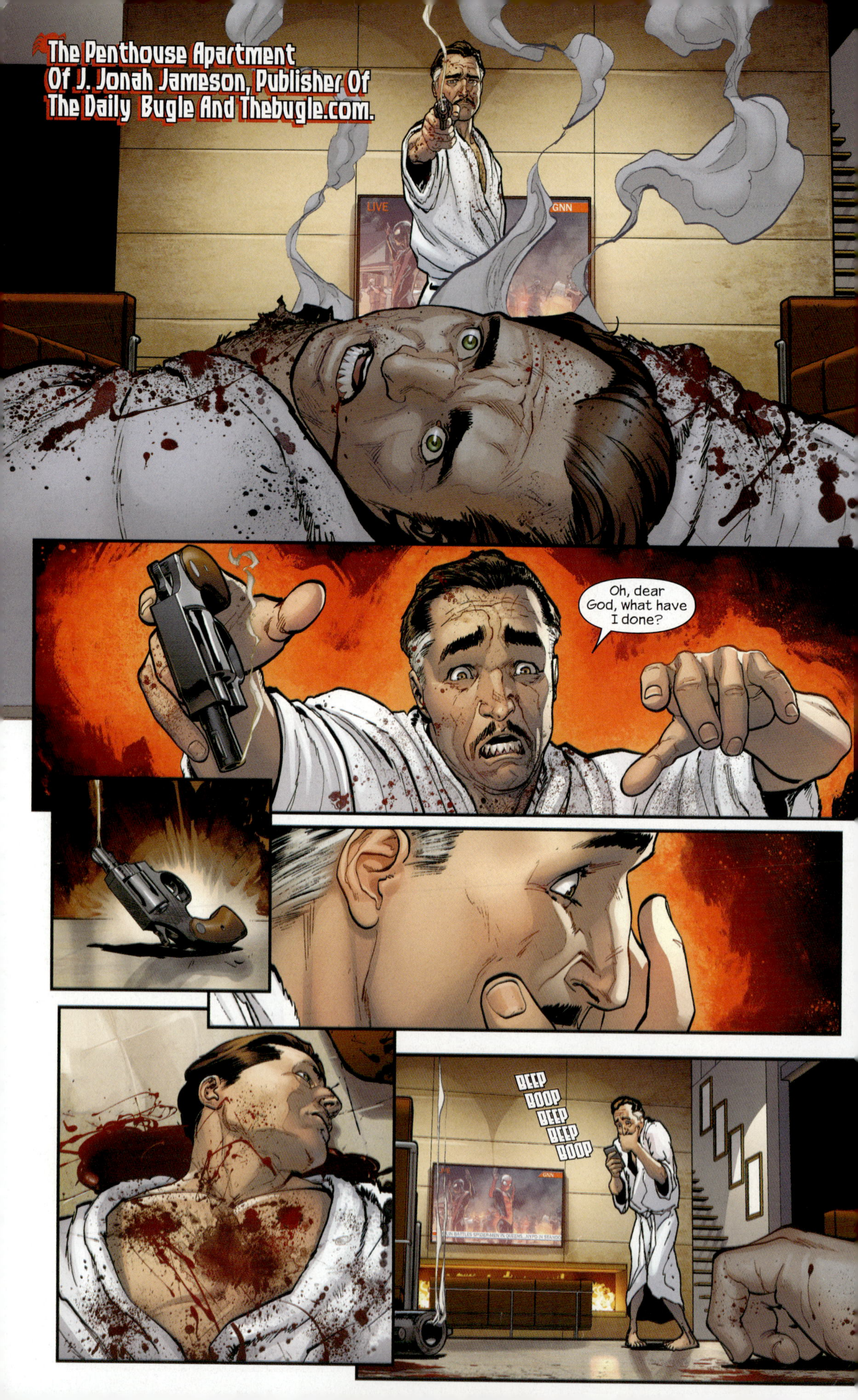
The Penthouse Apartment Of J. Jonah Jameson, Publisher Of The Daily Bugle And Thebugle.com.
LIVE
GNN
Oh, dear God, what have I done?
BEEP
BOOP
BEEP
BEEP
BOOP

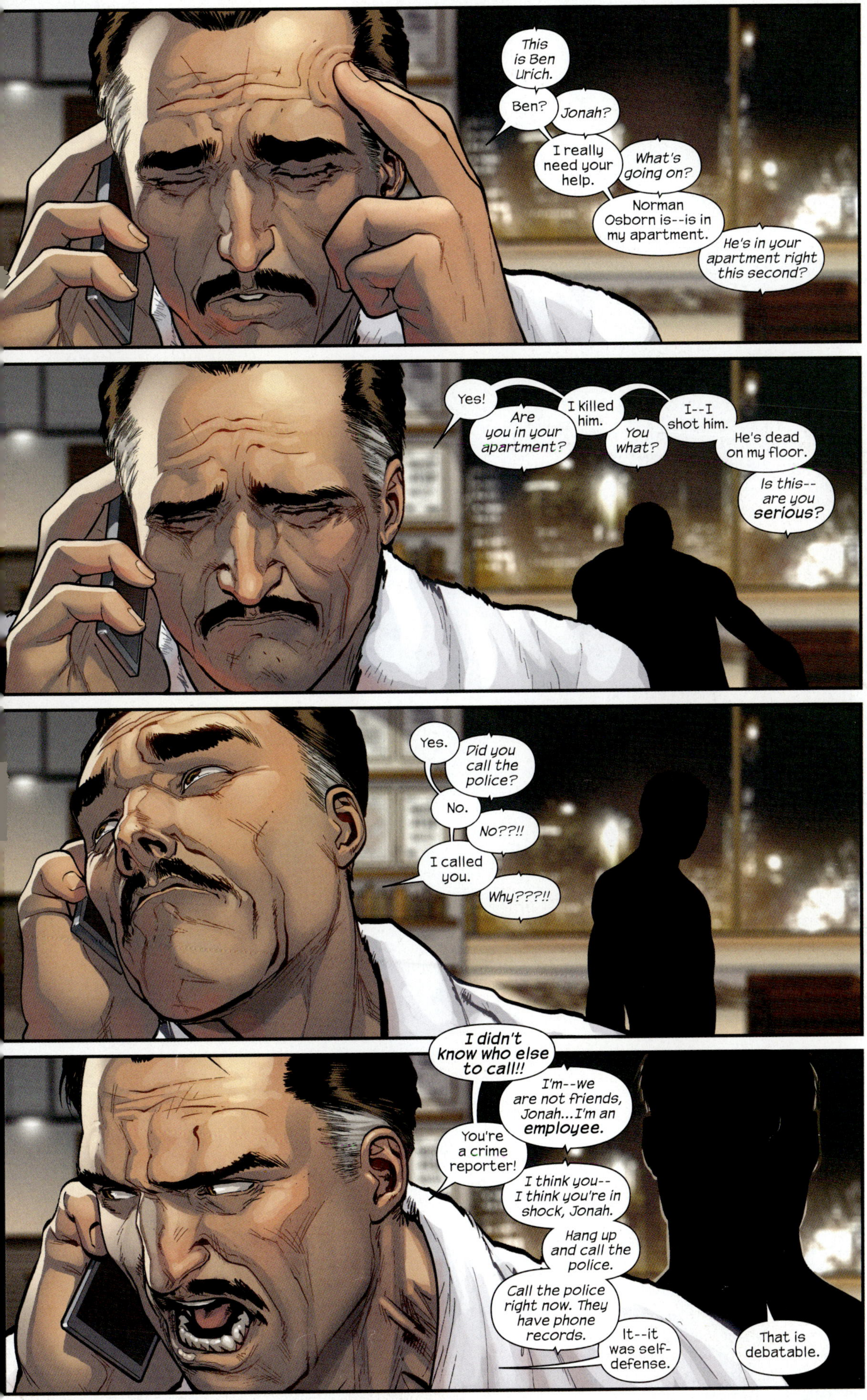
This is Ben Urich.
Ben?
Jonah?
I really need your help.
What's going on?
Norman Osborn is--is in my apartment.
He's in your apartment right this second?
Yes!
Are you in your apartment?
I killed him.
You what?
I--I shot him.
He's dead on my floor.
Is this--are you serious?
Yes.
Did you call the police?
No.
No??!!
I called you.
Why???!!
I didn't know who else to call!!
I'm--we are not friends, Jonah...I'm an employee.
You're a crime reporter!
I think you--I think you're in shock, Jonah.
Hang up and call the police.
Call the police right now. They have phone records.
It--it was self-defense.
That is debatable.

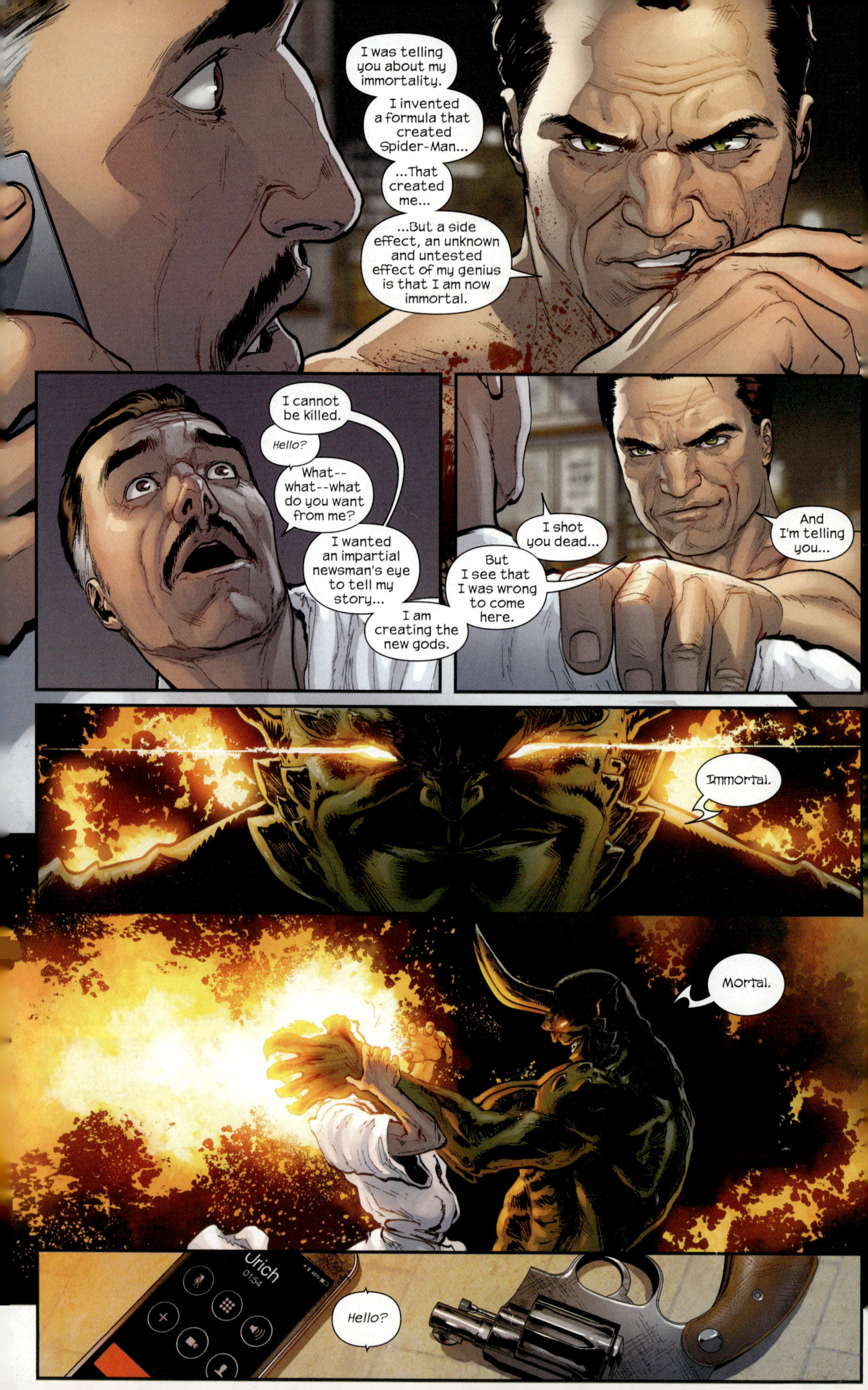

I was telling you about my immortality.
I invented a formula that created Spider-Man...
...That created me...
...But a side effect, an unknown and untested effect of my genius is that I am now immortal.
I cannot be killed.
Hello?
What--what--what do you want from me?
I wanted an impartial newsman's eye to tell my story...
I am creating the new gods.
I shot you dead...
And I'm telling you...
But I see that I was wrong to come here.
Immortal.
Mortal.
Urich
01:54
Hello?

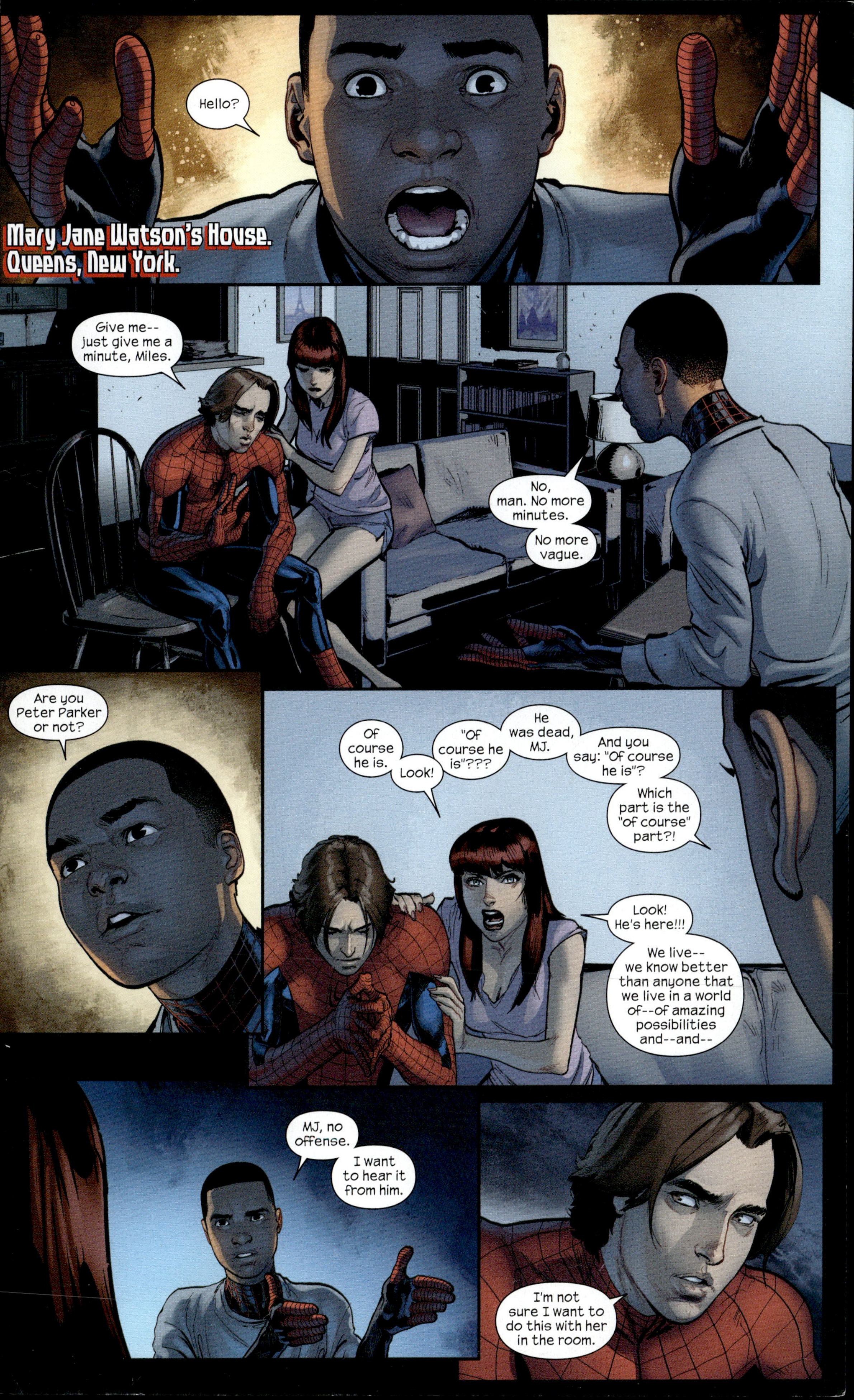
Hello?
Mary Jane Watson's House. Queens, New York.
Give me-- just give me a minute, Miles.
No, man. No more minutes.
No more vague.
Are you Peter Parker or not?
Of course he is.
Look!
"Of course he is"???
He was dead, MJ.
And you say: "Of course he is"?
Which part is the "of course" part?!
Look! He's here!!!
We live-- we know better than anyone that we live in a world of--of amazing possibilities and--and--
MJ, no offense.
I want to hear it from him.
I'm not sure I want to do this with her in the room.

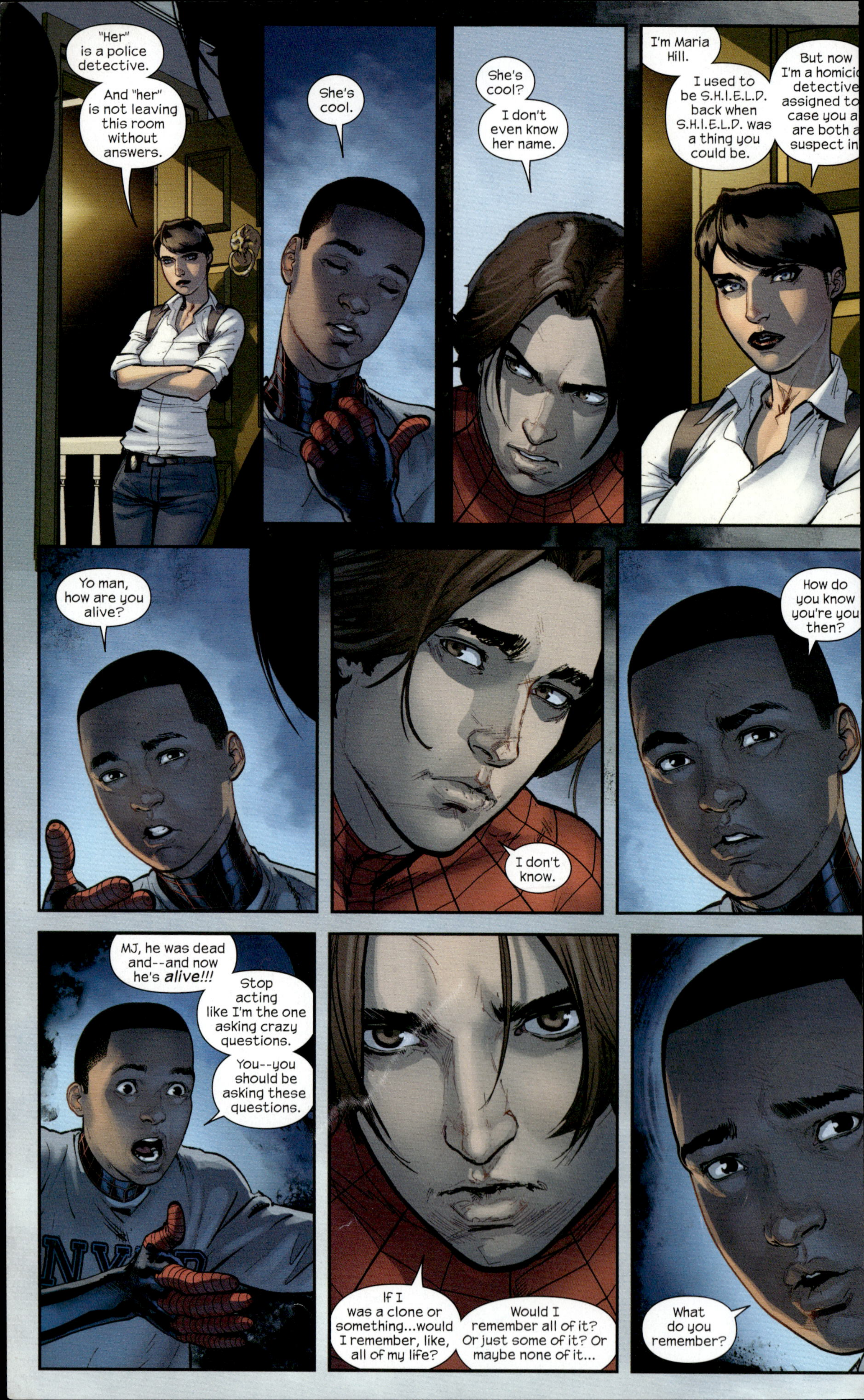

"Her" is a police detective.
And "her" is not leaving this room without answers.
She's cool.
She's cool?
I don't even know her name.
I'm Maria Hill.
I used to be S.H.I.E.L.D. back when S.H.I.E.L.D. was a thing you could be.
But now I'm a homicide detective assigned to case you are both a suspect in
Yo man, how are you alive?
I don't know.
How do you know you're you then?
MJ, he was dead and--and now he's *alive!!!*
Stop acting like I'm the one asking crazy questions.
You--you should be asking these questions.
If I was a clone or something...would I remember, like, all of my life?
Would I remember all of it? Or just some of it? Or maybe none of it...
What do you remember?

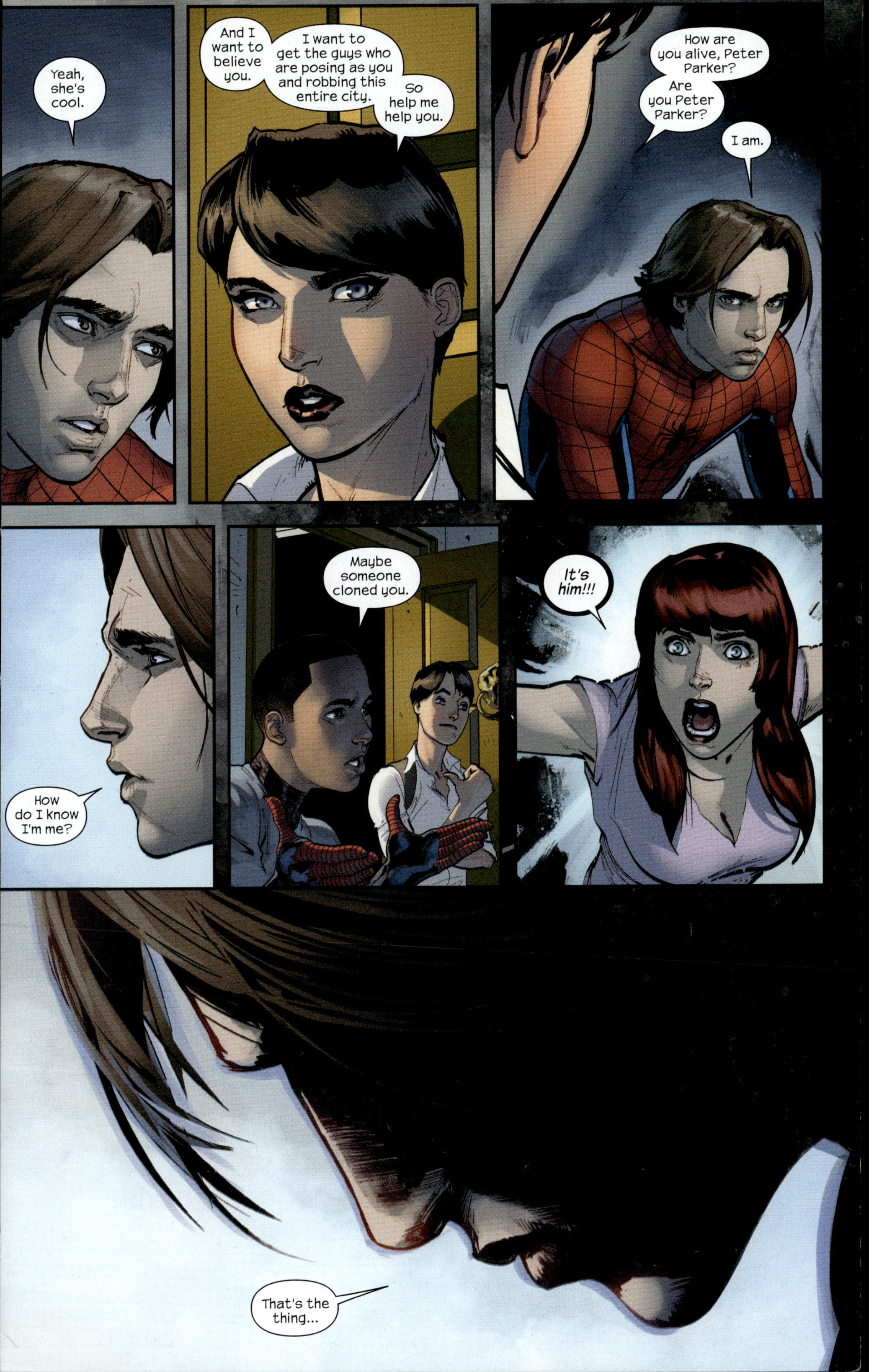
Yeah, she's cool.
And I want to believe you.
I want to get the guys who are posing as you and robbing this entire city.
So help me help you.
How are you alive, Peter Parker?
Are you Peter Parker?
I am.
How do I know I'm me?
Maybe someone cloned you.
It's him!!!
That's the thing...

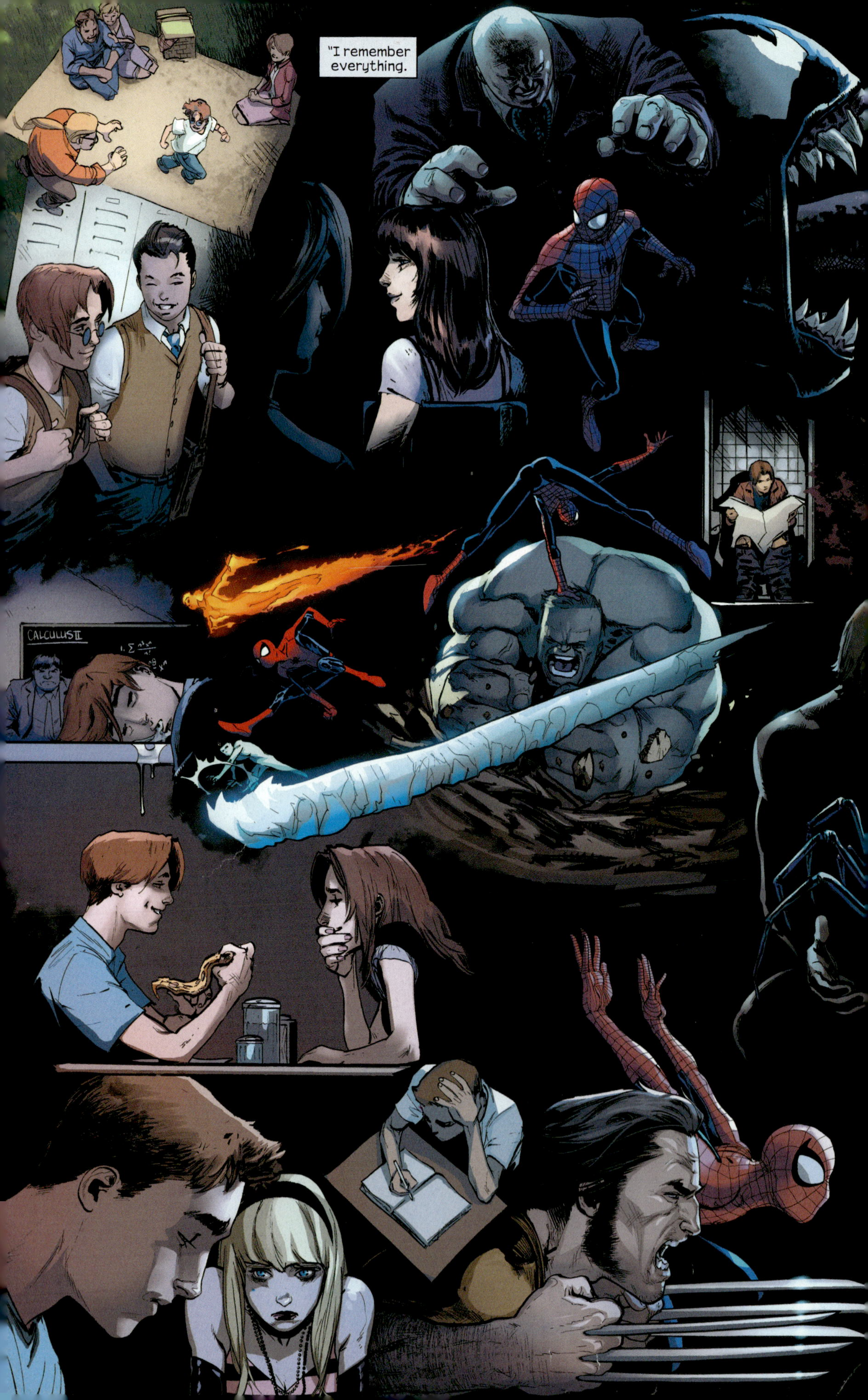
"I remember everything.
CALCULUS II

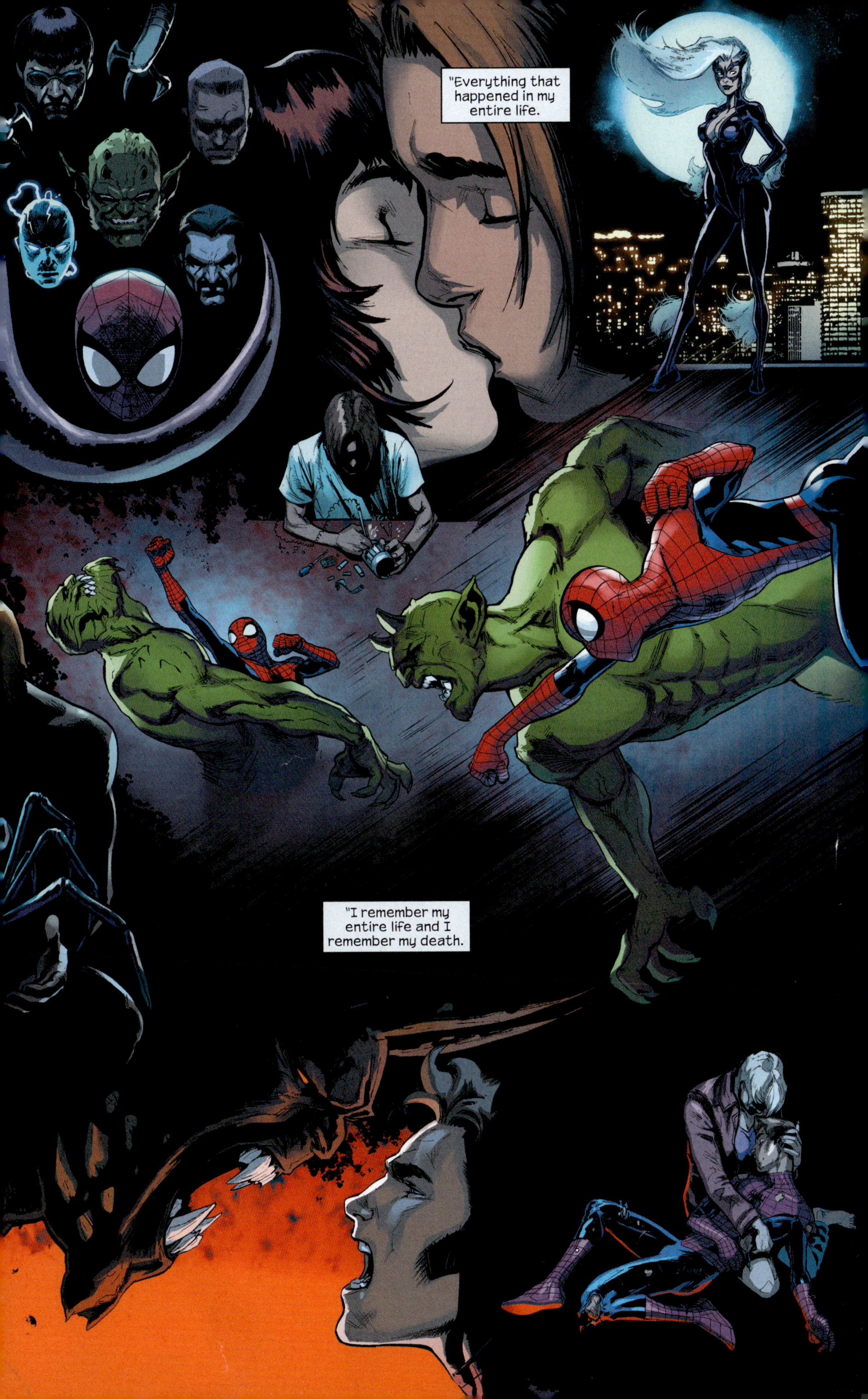
"Everything that happened in my entire life.
"I remember my entire life and I remember my death.

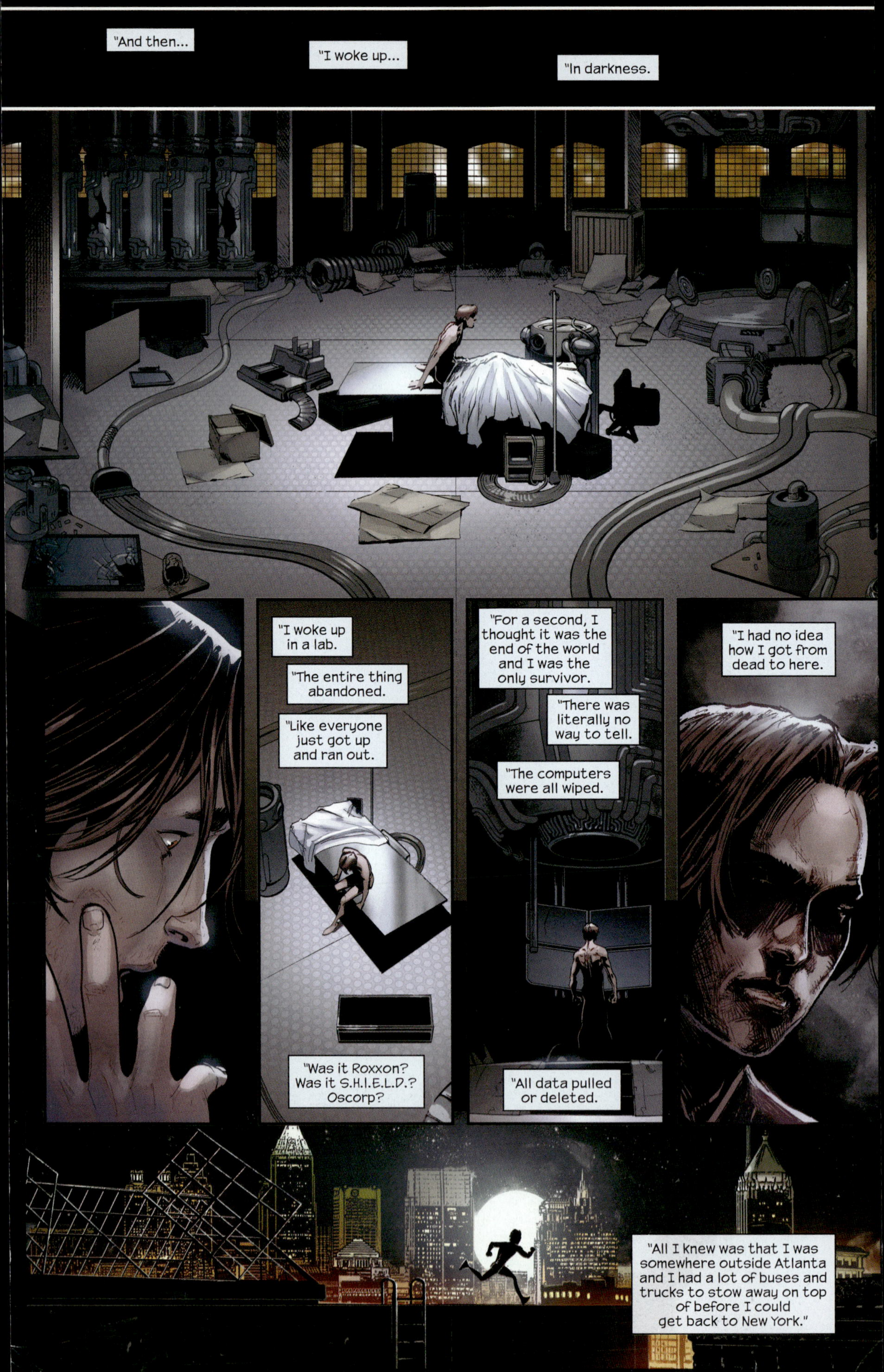
"And then...
"I woke up...
"In darkness.
"I woke up in a lab.
"The entire thing abandoned.
"Like everyone just got up and ran out.
"Was it Roxxon? Was it S.H.I.E.L.D.? Oscorp?
"For a second, I thought it was the end of the world and I was the only survivor.
"There was literally no way to tell.
"The computers were all wiped.
"All data pulled or deleted.
"I had no idea how I got from dead to here.
"All I knew was that I was somewhere outside Atlanta and I had a lot of buses and trucks to stow away on top of before I could get back to New York."

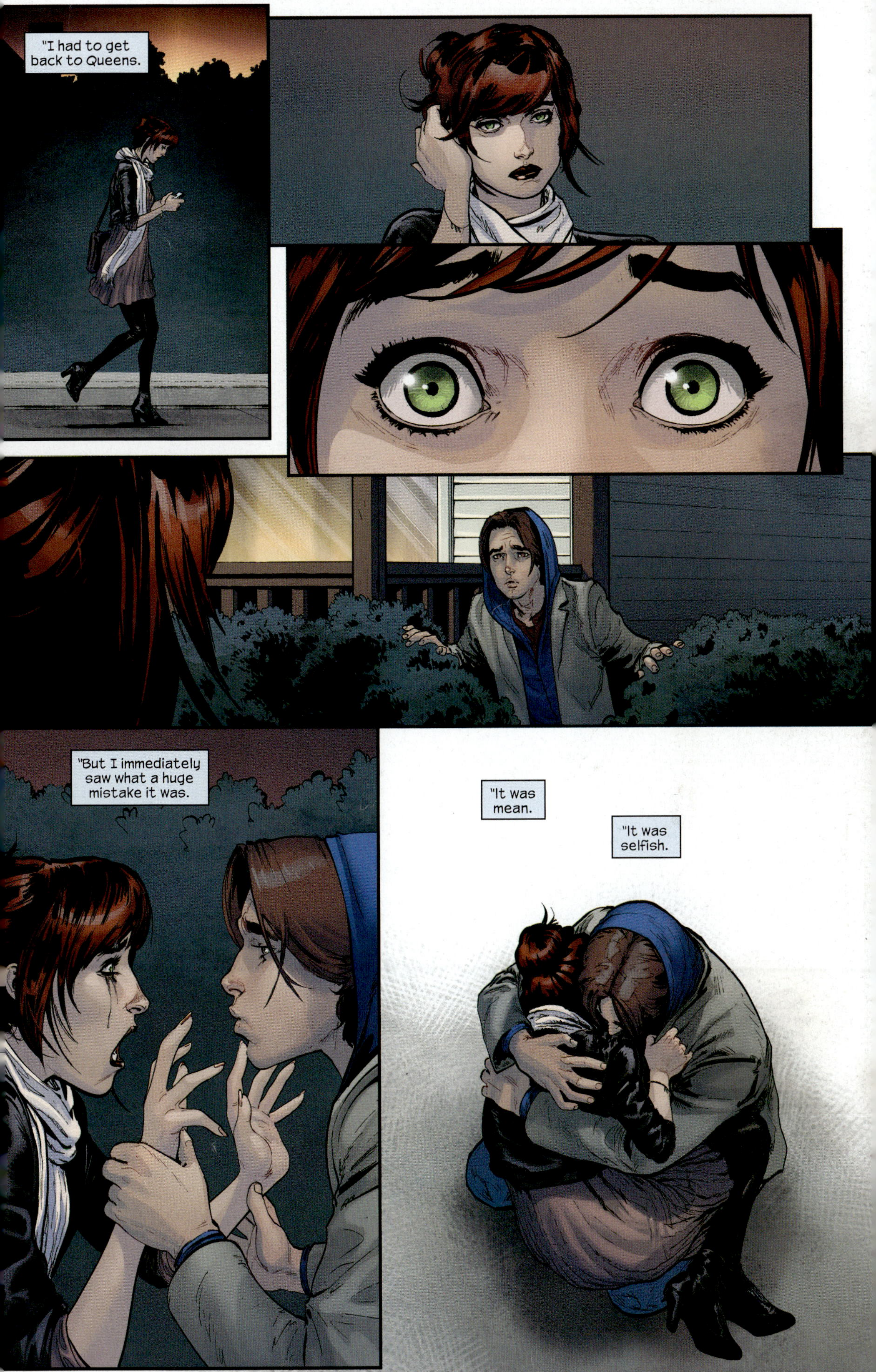
"I had to get back to Queens.
"But I immediately saw what a huge mistake it was.
"It was mean.
"It was selfish.

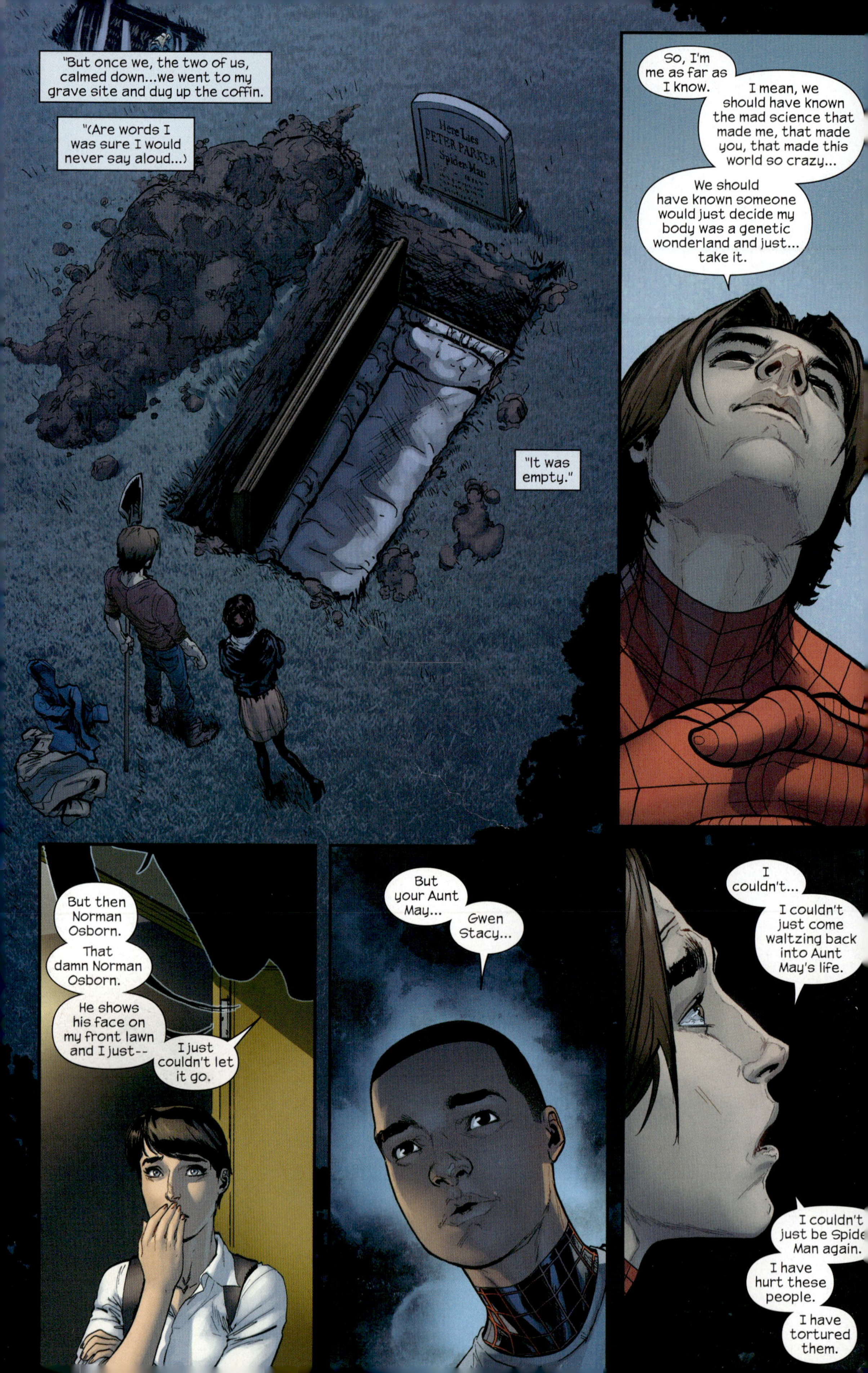
"But once we, the two of us, calmed down...we went to my grave site and dug up the coffin.
"(Are words I was sure I would never say aloud...)
Here Lies
PETER PARKER
Spider-Man
"It was empty."
So, I'm me as far as I know.
I mean, we should have known the mad science that made me, that made you, that made this world so crazy...
We should have known someone would just decide my body was a genetic wonderland and just... take it.
But then Norman Osborn.
That damn Norman Osborn.
He shows his face on my front lawn and I just--
I just couldn't let it go.
But your Aunt May...
Gwen Stacy...
I couldn't...
I couldn't just come waltzing back into Aunt May's life.
I couldn't just be Spide Man again.
I have hurt these people.
I have tortured them.

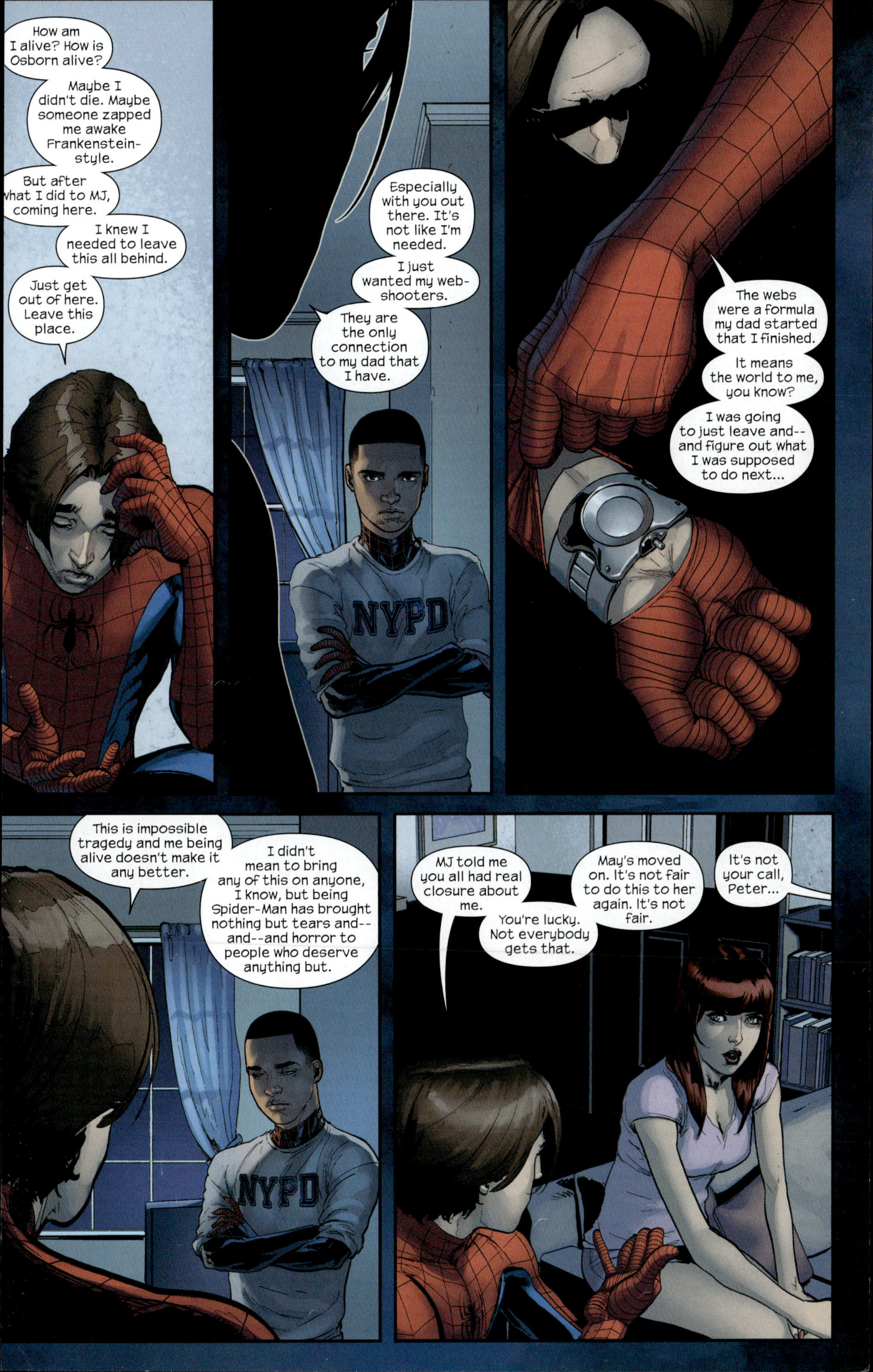

How am I alive? How is Osborn alive?
Maybe I didn't die. Maybe someone zapped me awake Frankenstein-style.
But after what I did to MJ, coming here.
I knew I needed to leave this all behind.
Just get out of here. Leave this place.
Especially with you out there. It's not like I'm needed.
I just wanted my web-shooters.
They are the only connection to my dad that I have.
The webs were a formula my dad started that I finished.
It means the world to me, you know?
I was going to just leave and--and figure out what I was supposed to do next...
This is impossible tragedy and me being alive doesn't make it any better.
I didn't mean to bring any of this on anyone, I know, but being Spider-Man has brought nothing but tears and--and--and horror to people who deserve anything but.
MJ told me you all had real closure about me.
You're lucky. Not everybody gets that.
May's moved on. It's not fair to do this to her again. It's not fair.
It's not your call, Peter...

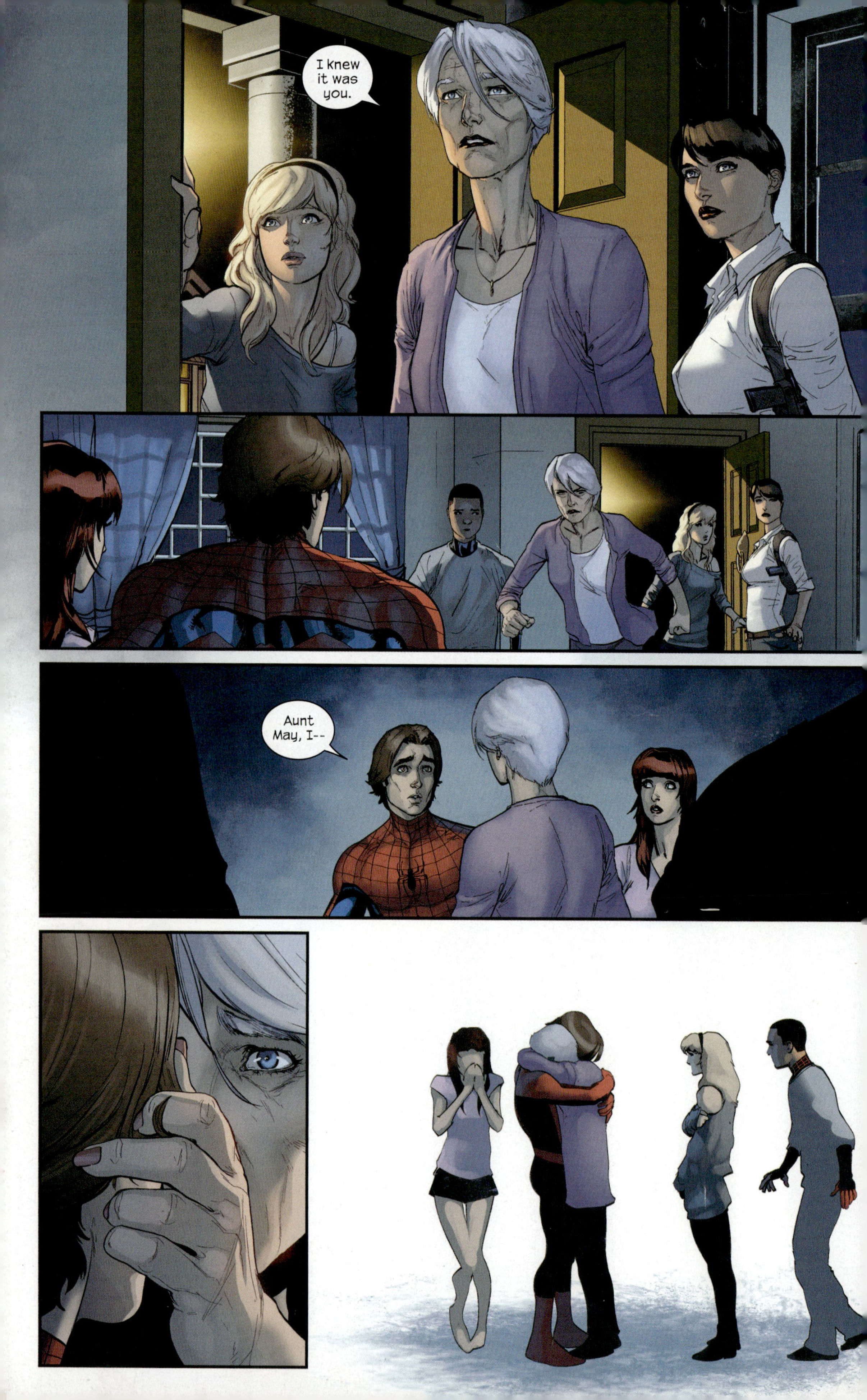
I knew it was you.
Aunt May, I--

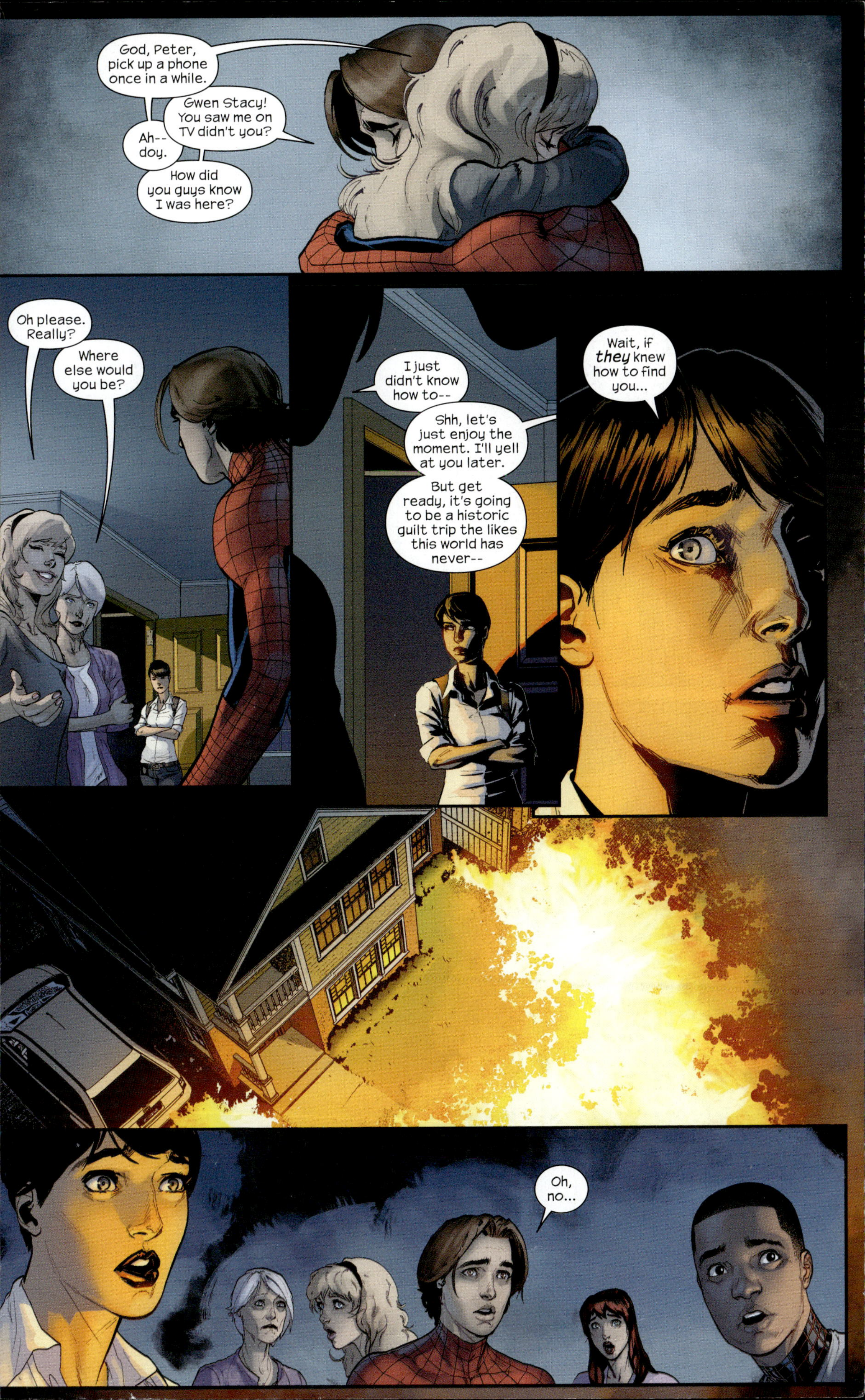

God, Peter, pick up a phone once in a while.
Ah--doy.
Gwen Stacy! You saw me on TV didn't you?
How did you guys know I was here?
Oh please. Really?
Where else would you be?
I just didn't know how to--
Shh, let's just enjoy the moment. I'll yell at you later.
But get ready, it's going to be a historic guilt trip the likes this world has never--
Wait, if *they* knew how to find you...
Oh, no...

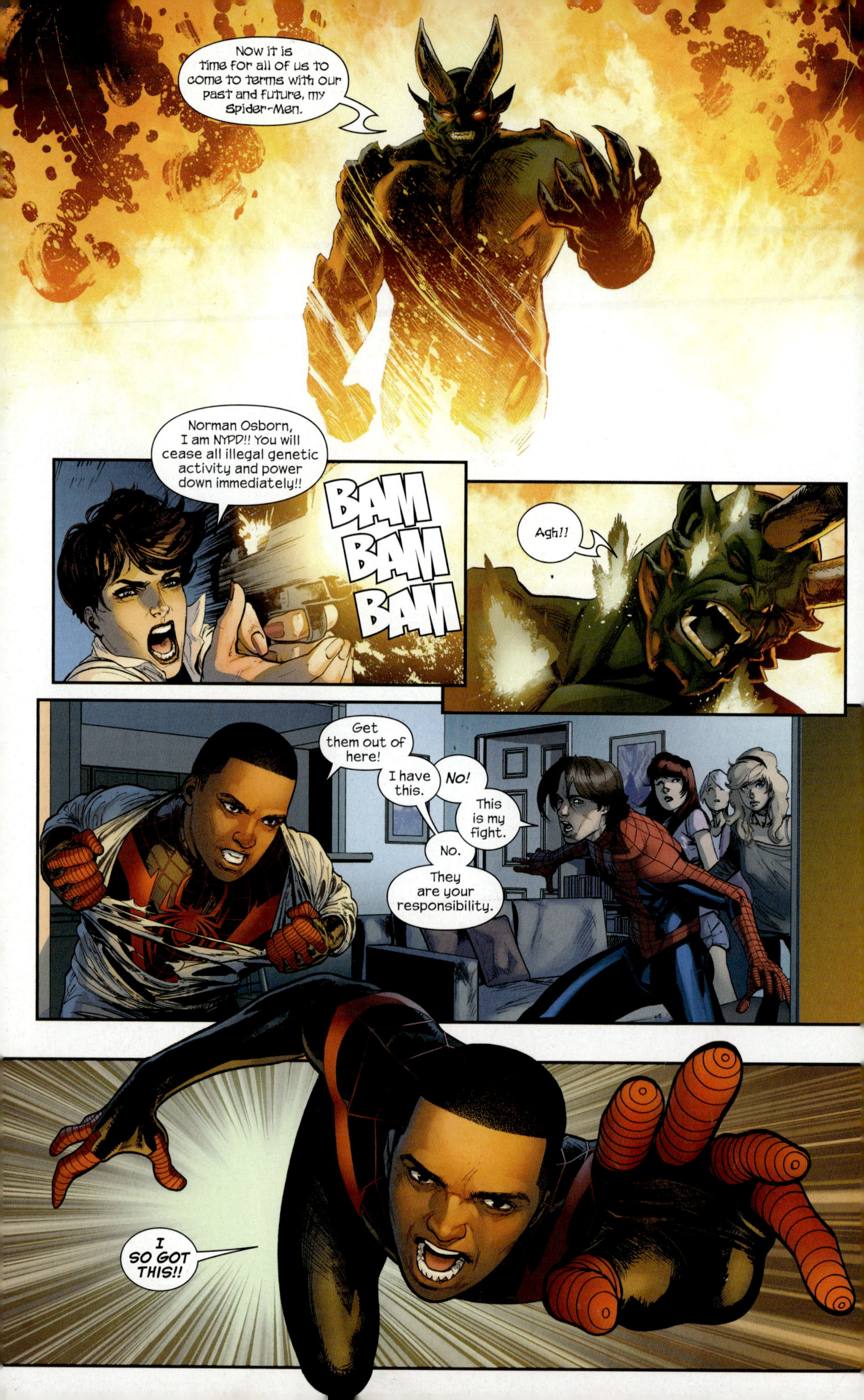
Now it is time for all of us to come to terms with our past and future, my Spider-Men.
Norman Osborn, I am NYPD!! You will cease all illegal genetic activity and power down immediately!!
BAM BAM BAM
Agh!!
Get them out of here!
I have this.
No!
This is my fight.
No.
They are your responsibility.
I SO GOT THIS!!

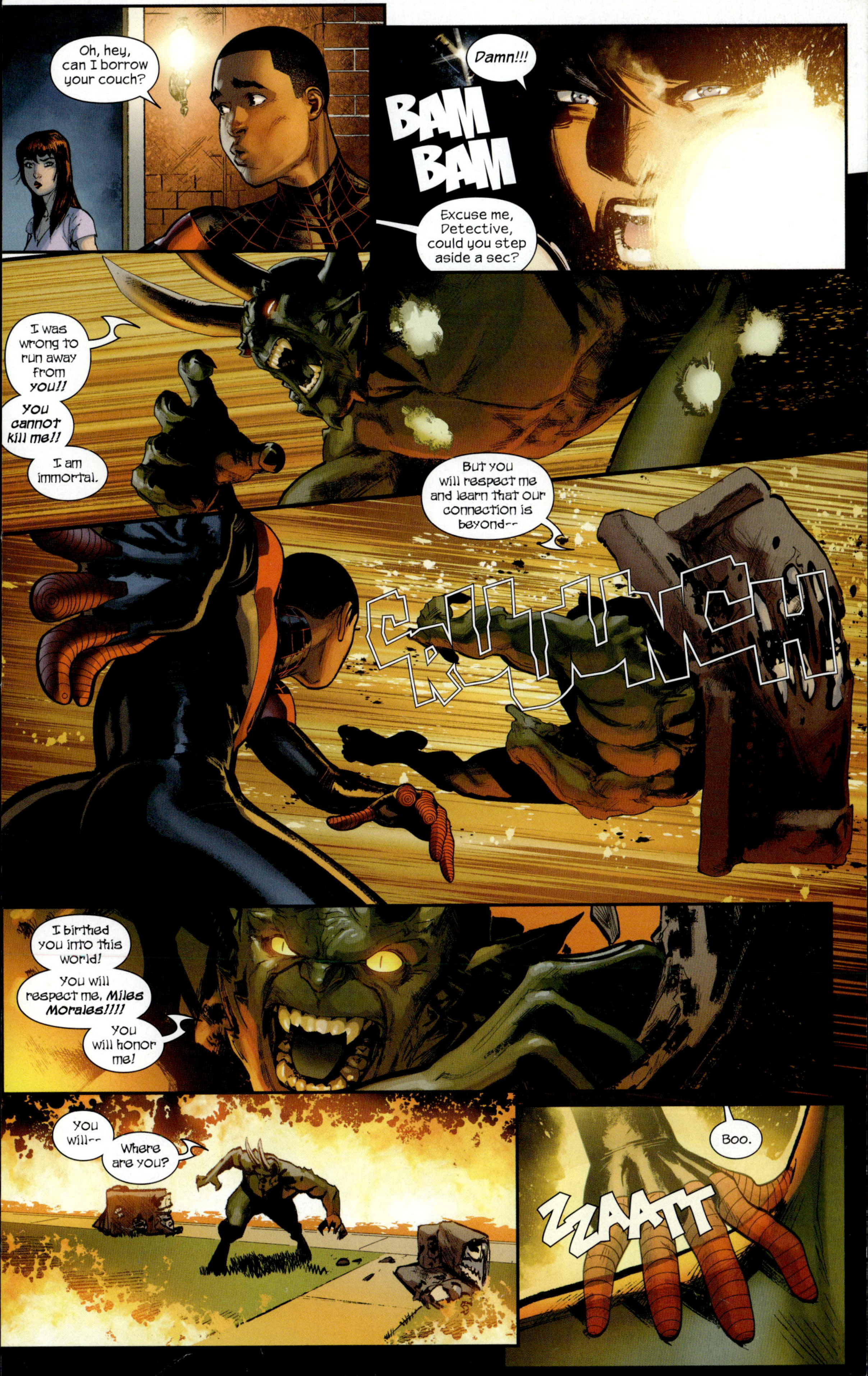
Oh, hey, can I borrow your couch?
Damn!!!
BAM BAM
Excuse me, Detective, could you step aside a sec?
I was wrong to run away from you!!
You cannot kill me!!
I am immortal.
But you will respect me and learn that our connection is beyond--
CRUNCH
I birthed you into this world!
You will respect me, Miles Morales!!!!
You will honor me!
You will--
Where are you?
Boo.
ZZAATT

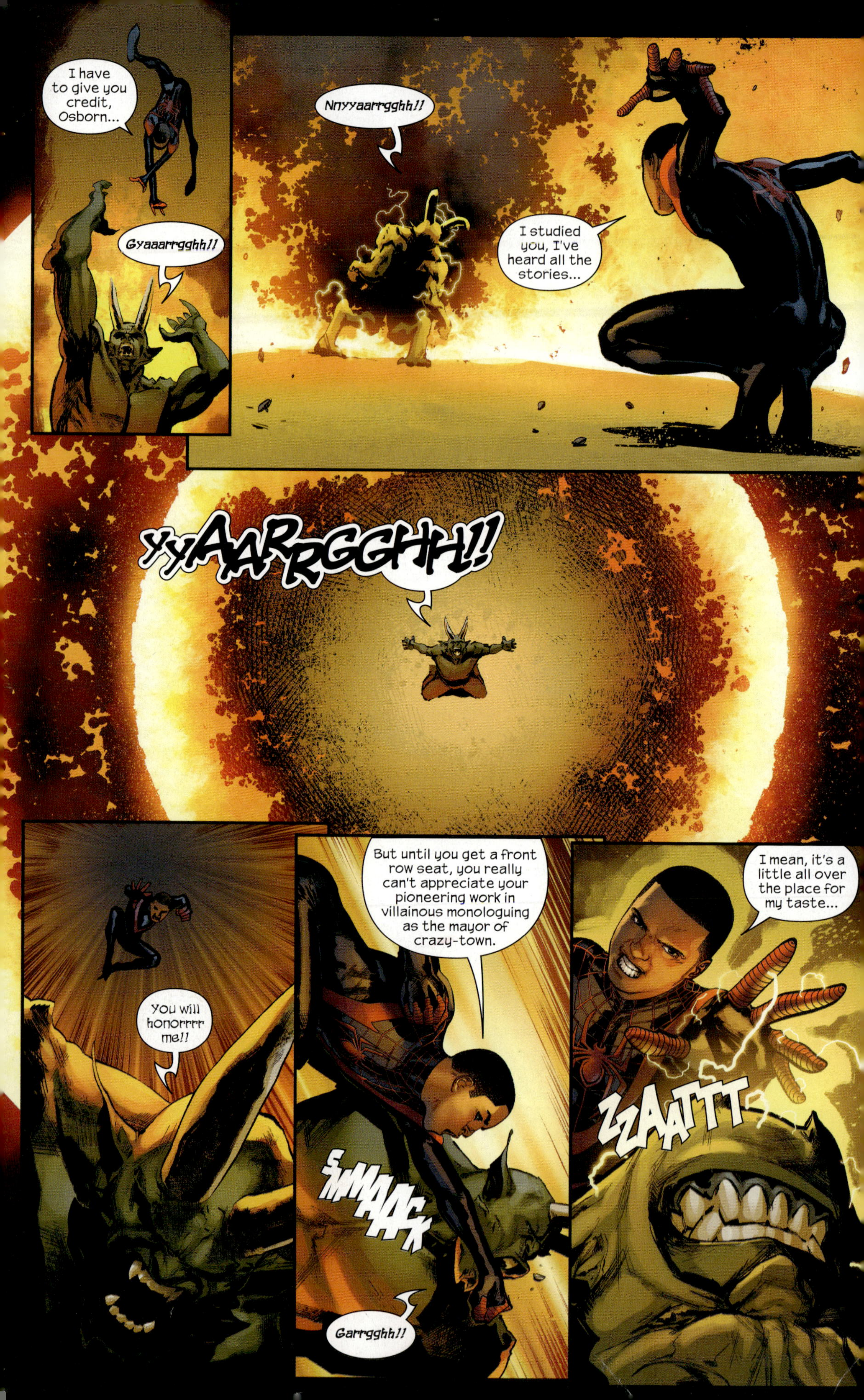

I have to give you credit, Osborn...
Gyaaarrgghh!!
Nnyyaarrgghh!!
I studied you, I've heard all the stories...
YYAARRGGHH!!
You will honorrrr me!!
But until you get a front row seat, you really can't appreciate your pioneering work in villainous monologuing as the mayor of crazy-town.
SMAACK
Garrgghh!!
I mean, it's a little all over the place for my taste...
ZZAATTT

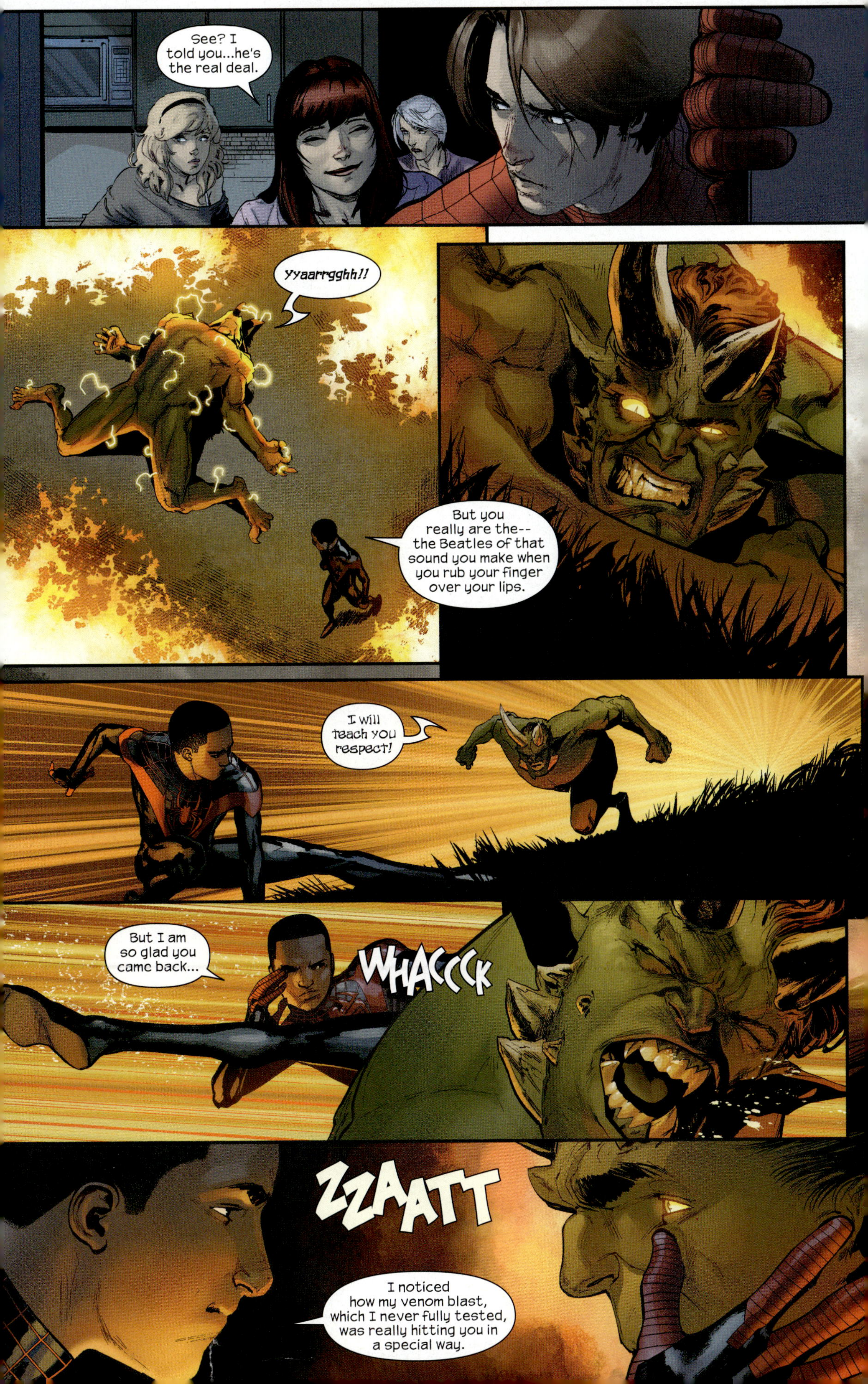
See? I told you...he's the real deal.
Yyaarrgghh!!
But you really are the-- the Beatles of that sound you make when you rub your finger over your lips.
I will teach you respect!
But I am so glad you came back...
WHACCCK
ZZAATT
I noticed how my venom blast, which I never fully tested, was really hitting you in a special way.

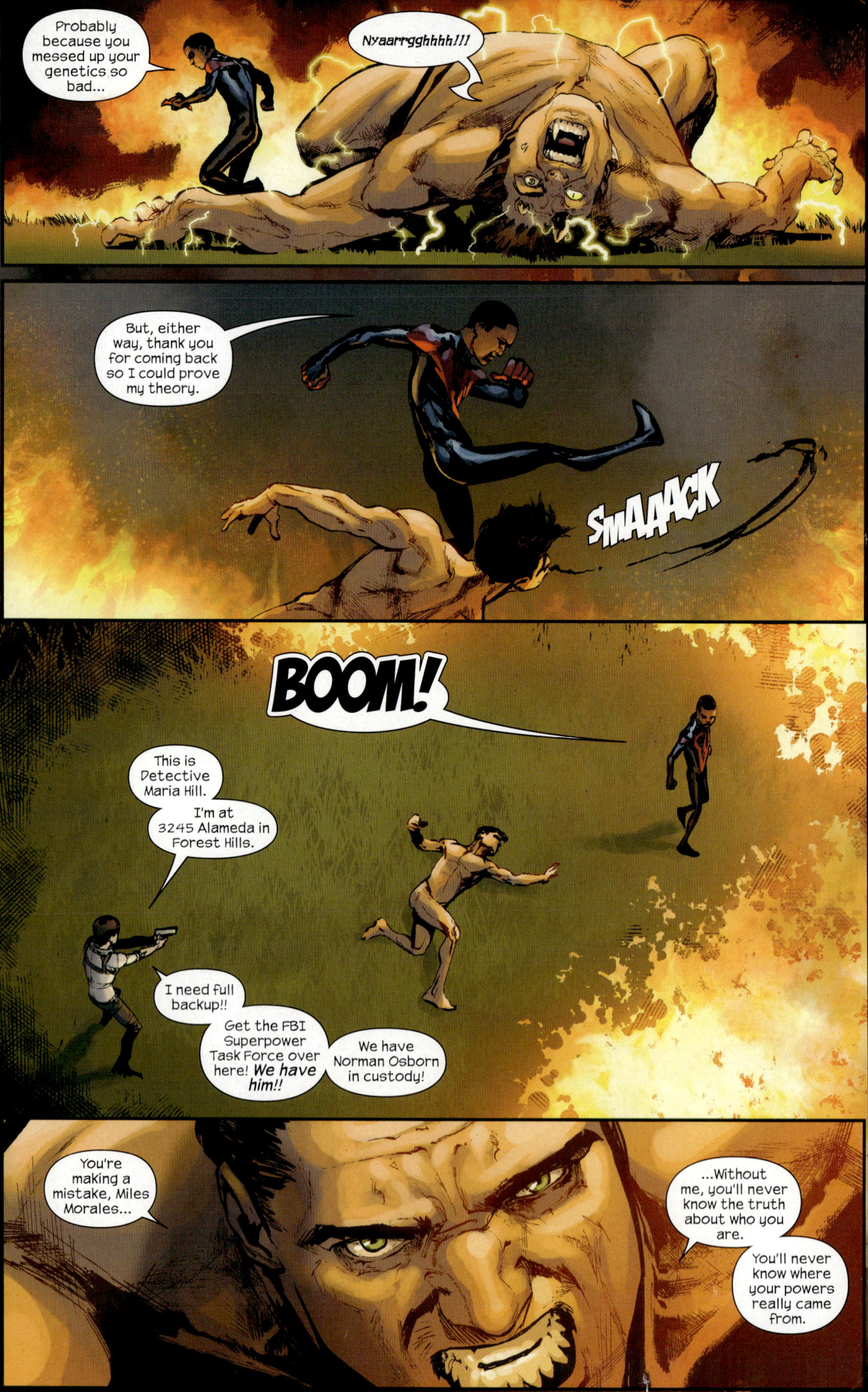
Probably because you messed up your genetics so bad...
Nyaarrgghhhh!!!
But, either way, thank you for coming back so I could prove my theory.
SMAAACK
BOOM!
This is Detective Maria Hill.
I'm at 3245 Alameda in Forest Hills.
I need full backup!!
Get the FBI Superpower Task Force over here! We have him!!
We have Norman Osborn in custody!
You're making a mistake, Miles Morales...
...Without me, you'll never know the truth about who you are.
You'll never know where your powers really came from.

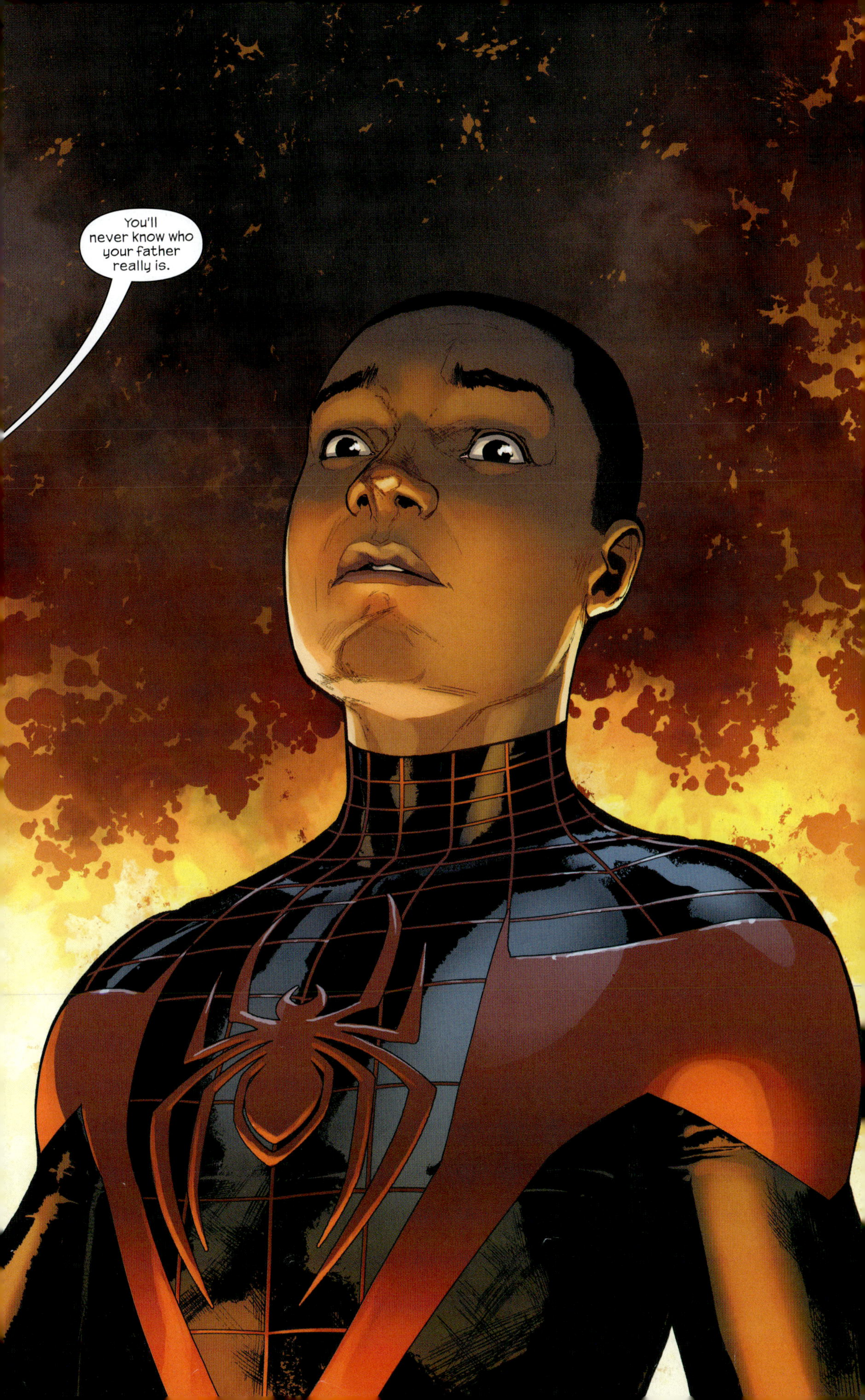
You'll never know who your father really is.

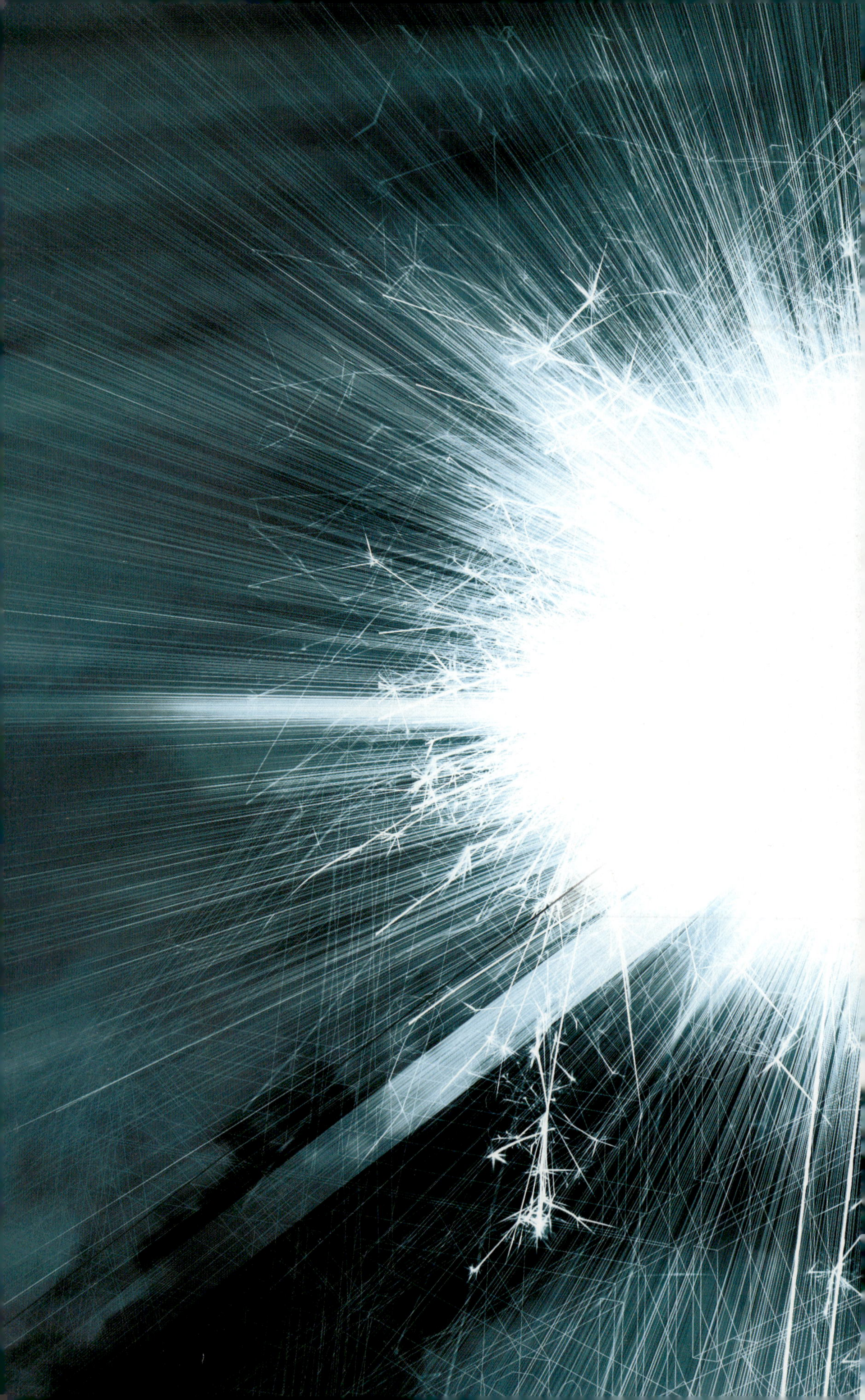

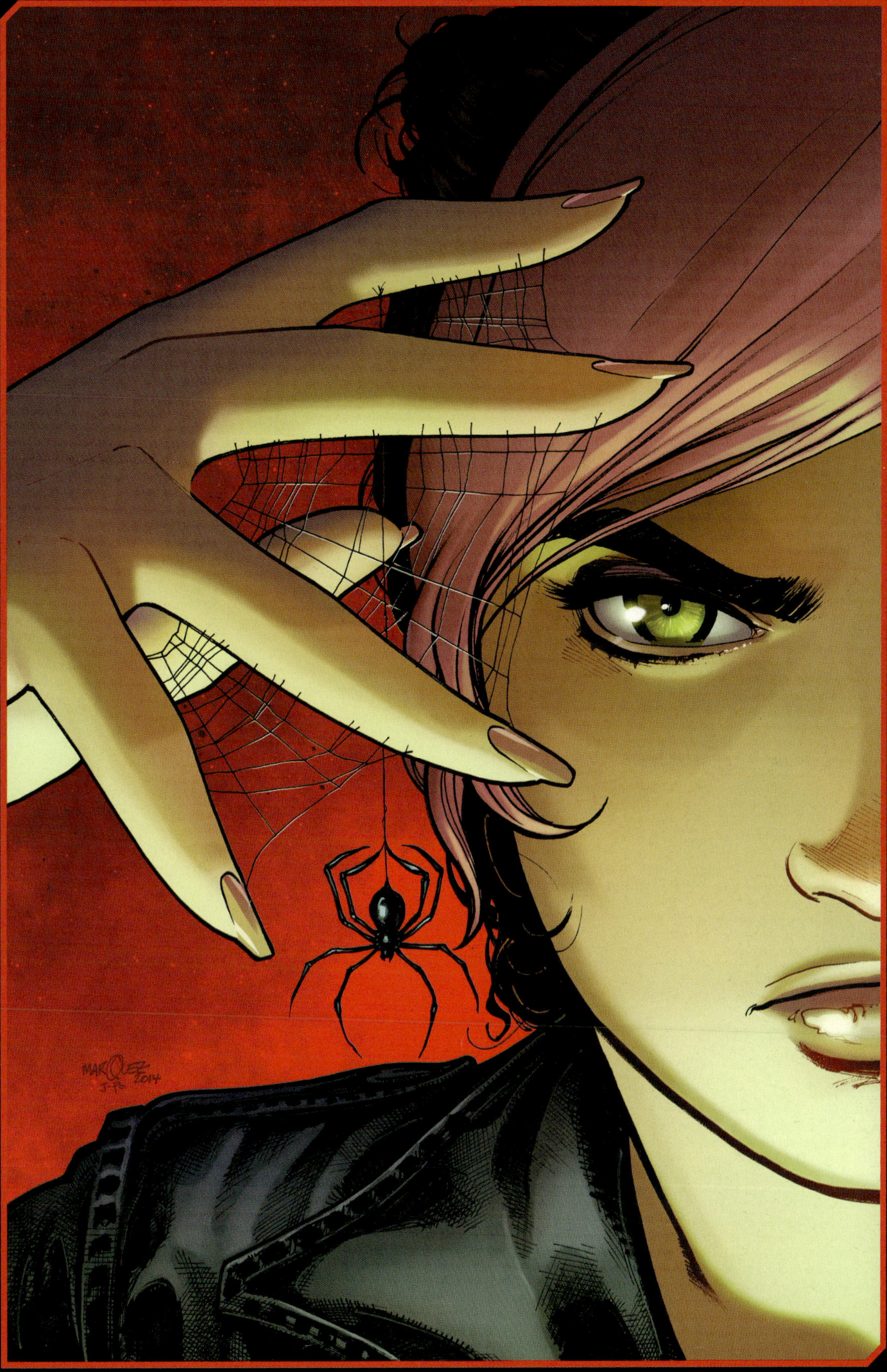

MILES MORALES: ULTIMATE SPIDER-MAN #7

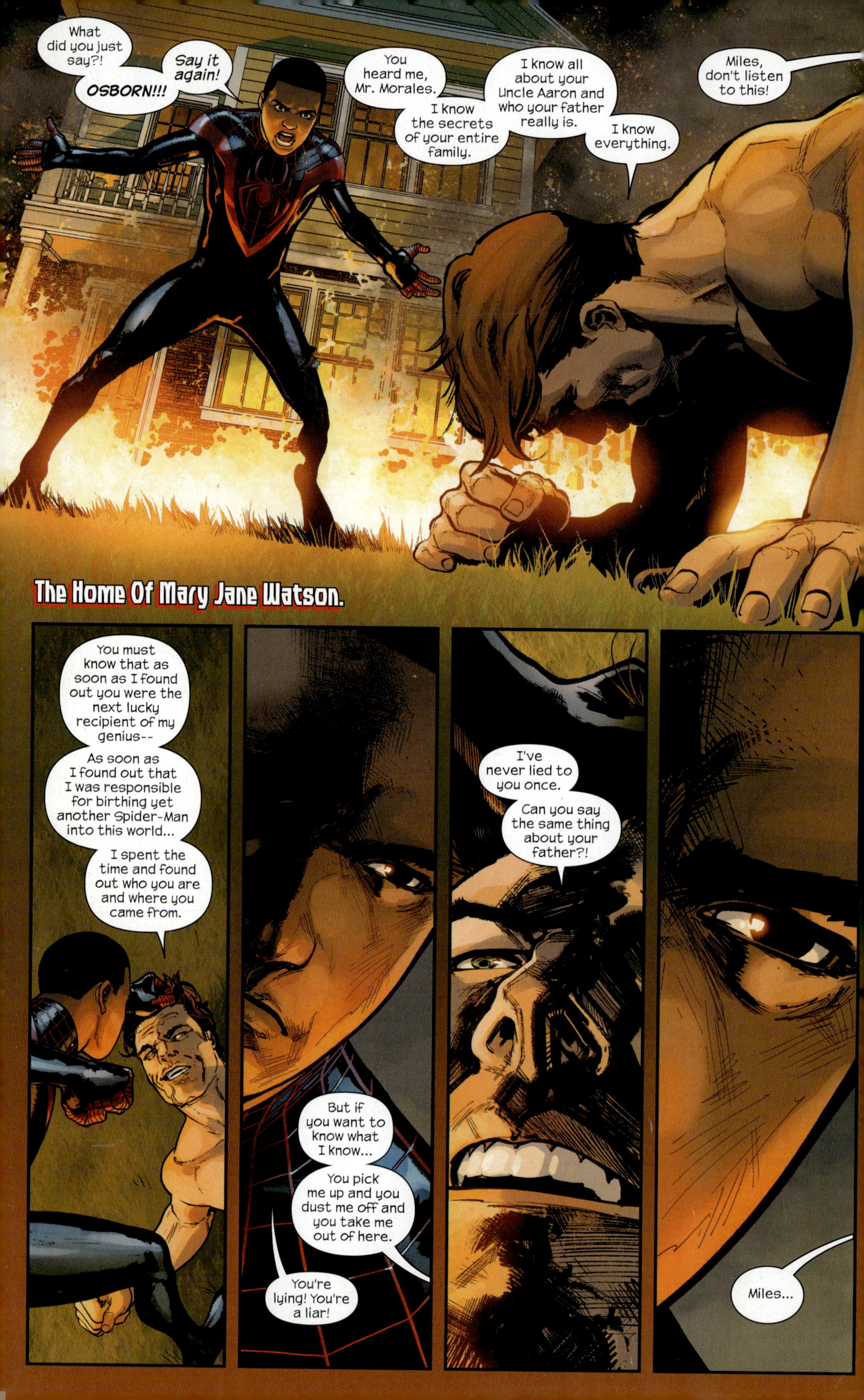
What did you just say?!
OSBORN!!!
Say it again!
You heard me, Mr. Morales.
I know the secrets of your entire family.
I know all about your Uncle Aaron and who your father really is.
I know everything.
Miles, don't listen to this!
The Home Of Mary Jane Watson.
You must know that as soon as I found out you were the next lucky recipient of my genius--
As soon as I found out that I was responsible for birthing yet another Spider-Man into this world...
I spent the time and found out who you are and where you came from.
But if you want to know what I know...
You pick me up and you dust me off and you take me out of here.
You're lying! You're a liar!
I've never lied to you once.
Can you say the same thing about your father?!
Miles...

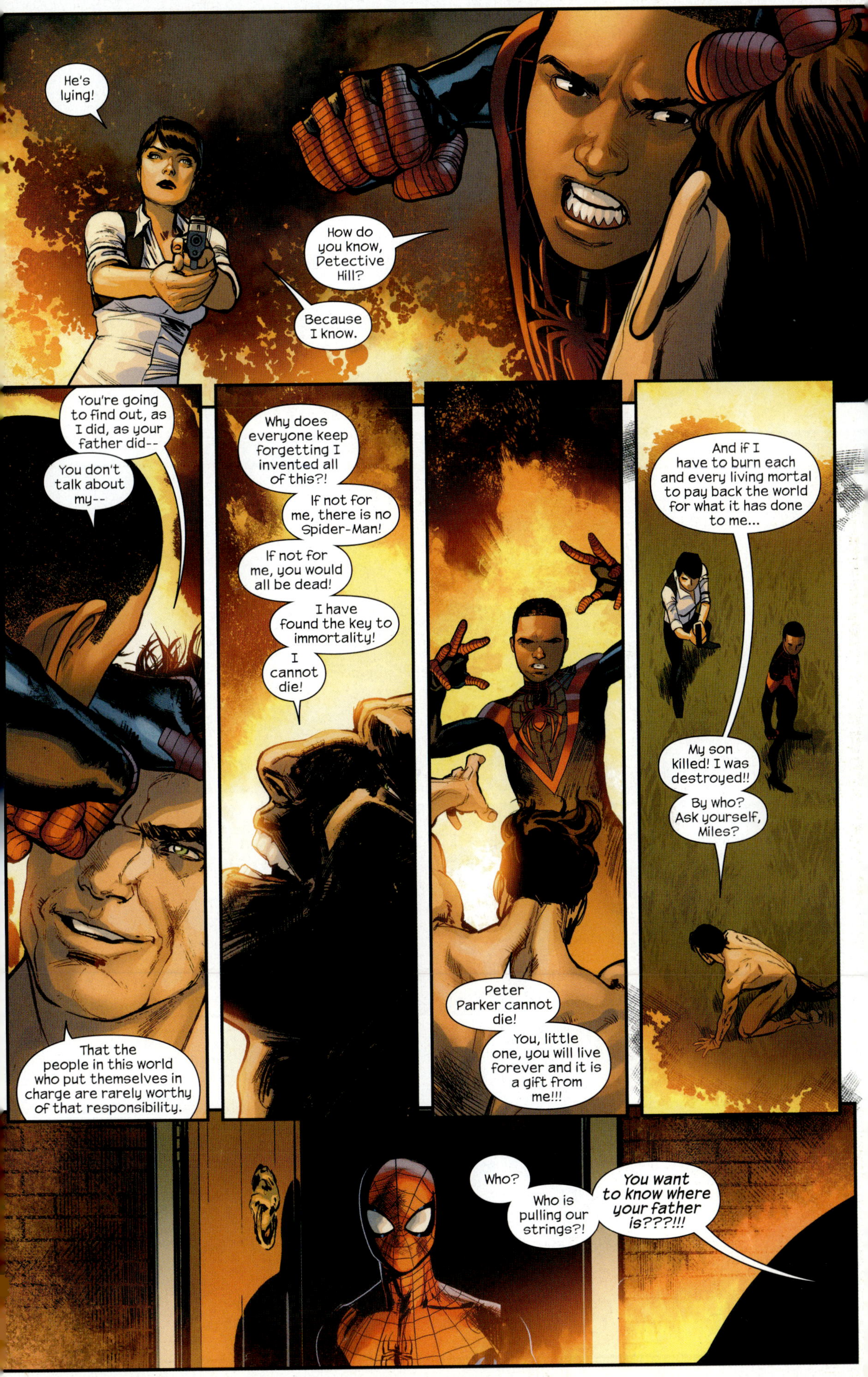
He's lying!
How do you know, Detective Hill?
Because I know.
You're going to find out, as I did, as your father did--
You don't talk about my--
That the people in this world who put themselves in charge are rarely worthy of that responsibility.
Why does everyone keep forgetting I invented all of this?!
If not for me, there is no Spider-Man!
If not for me, you would all be dead!
I have found the key to immortality!
I cannot die!
Peter Parker cannot die!
You, little one, you will live forever and it is a gift from me!!!
And if I have to burn each and every living mortal to pay back the world for what it has done to me...
My son killed! I was destroyed!!
By who? Ask yourself, Miles?
Who?
Who is pulling our strings?!
You want to know where your father is???!!!

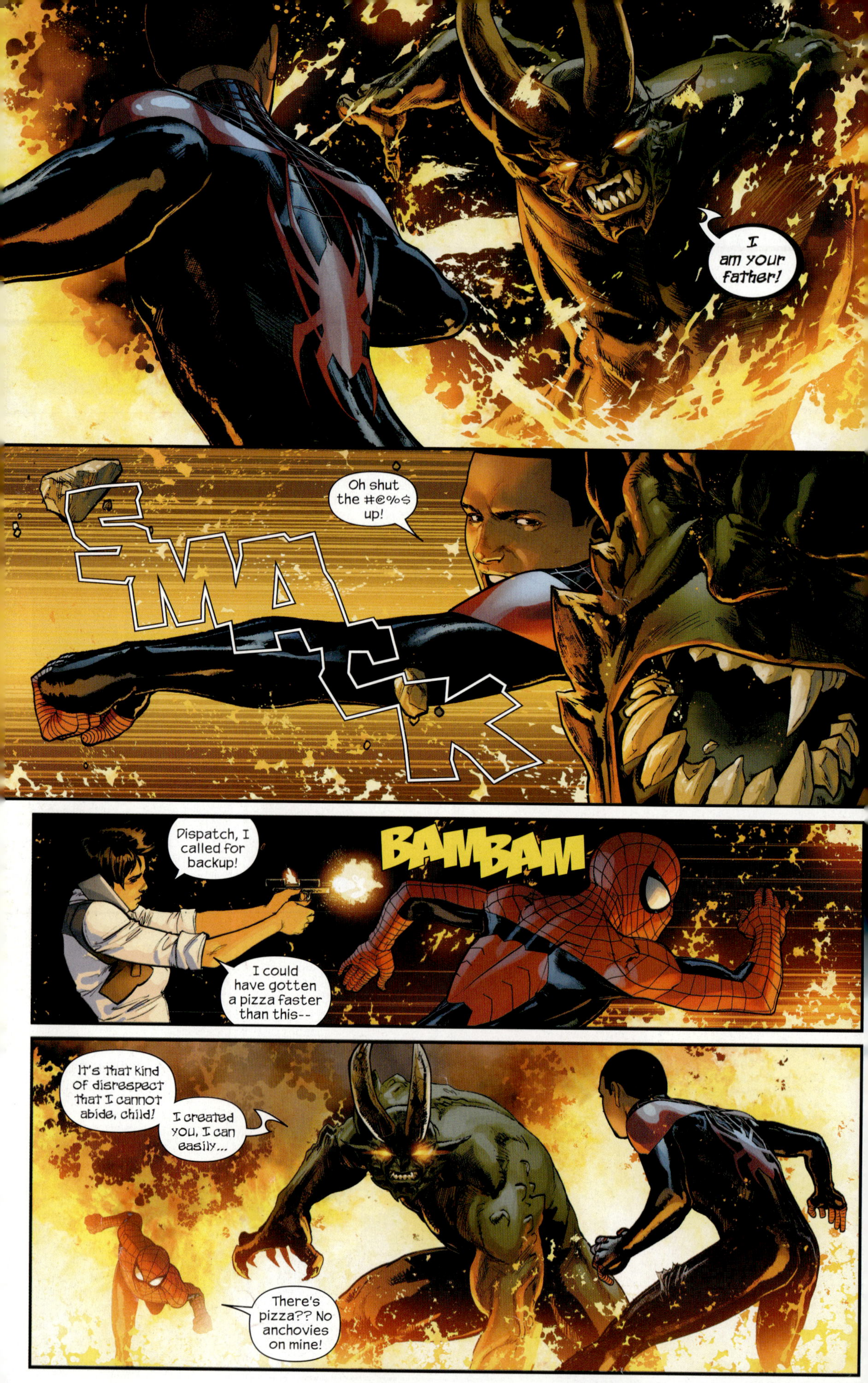
I am your father!
Oh shut the #@%$ up!
SMACK
Dispatch, I called for backup!
BAMBAM
I could have gotten a pizza faster than this--
It's that kind of disrespect that I cannot abide, child!
I created you, I can easily...
There's pizza?? No anchovies on mine!

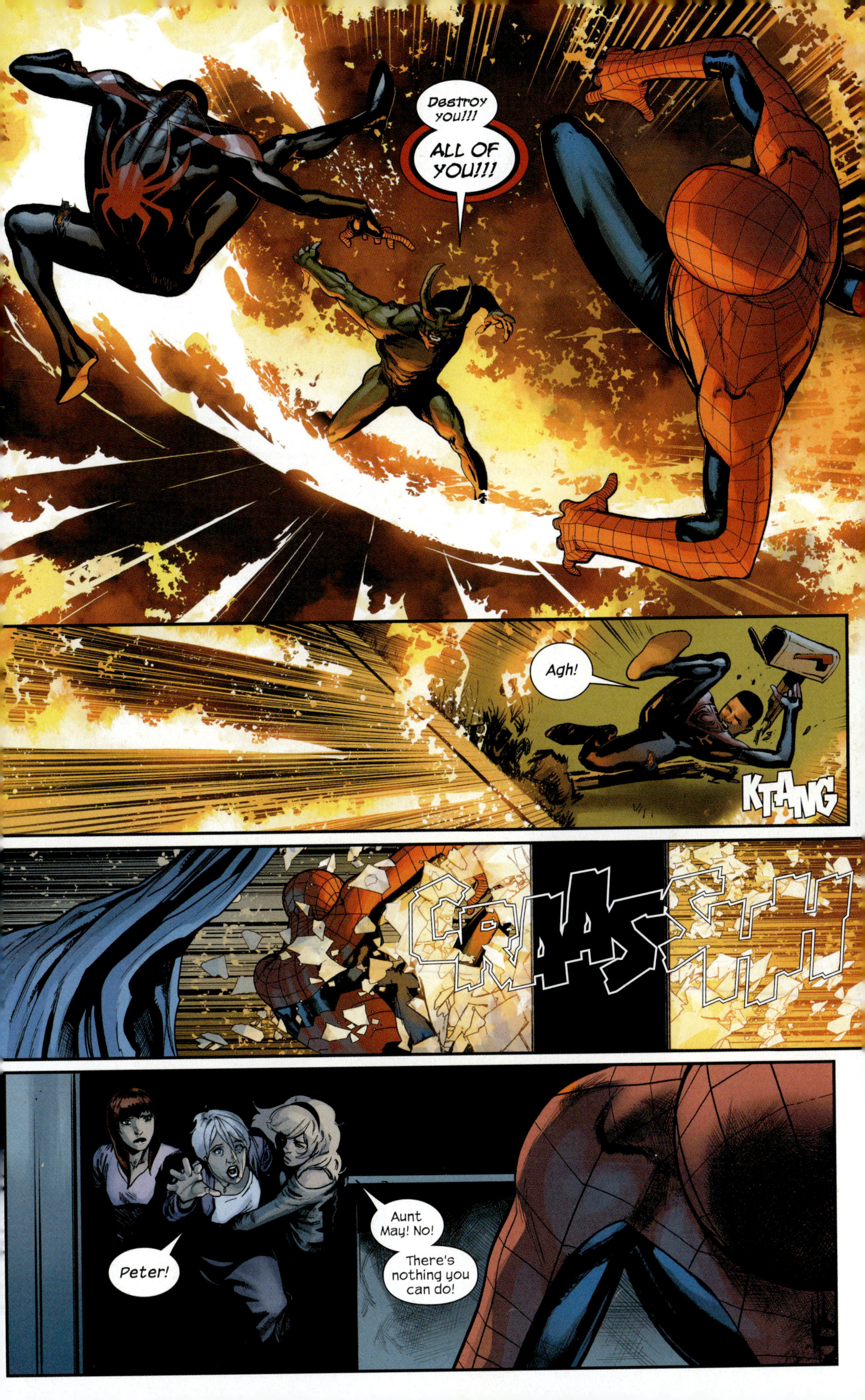

Destroy you!!!
ALL OF YOU!!!
Agh!
KTANG
CRAASSHH
Peter!
Aunt May! No!
There's nothing you can do!

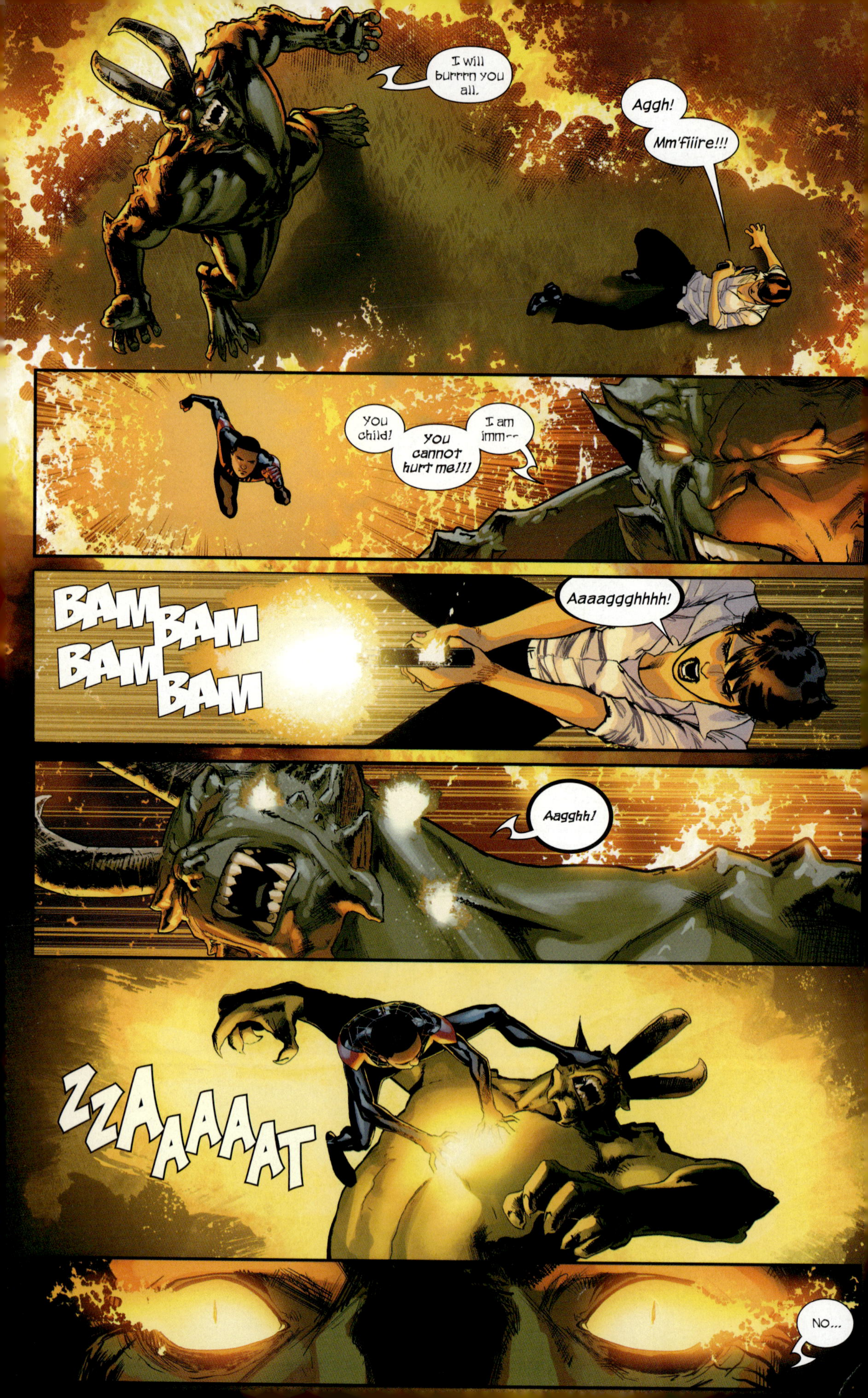
I will burrrn you all.
Aggh!
Mm'fiiire!!!
You child!
You cannot hurt me!!!
I am imm--
BAM BAM
BAM BAM
Aaaaggghhhh!
Aagghh!
ZZAAAAAT
NO...

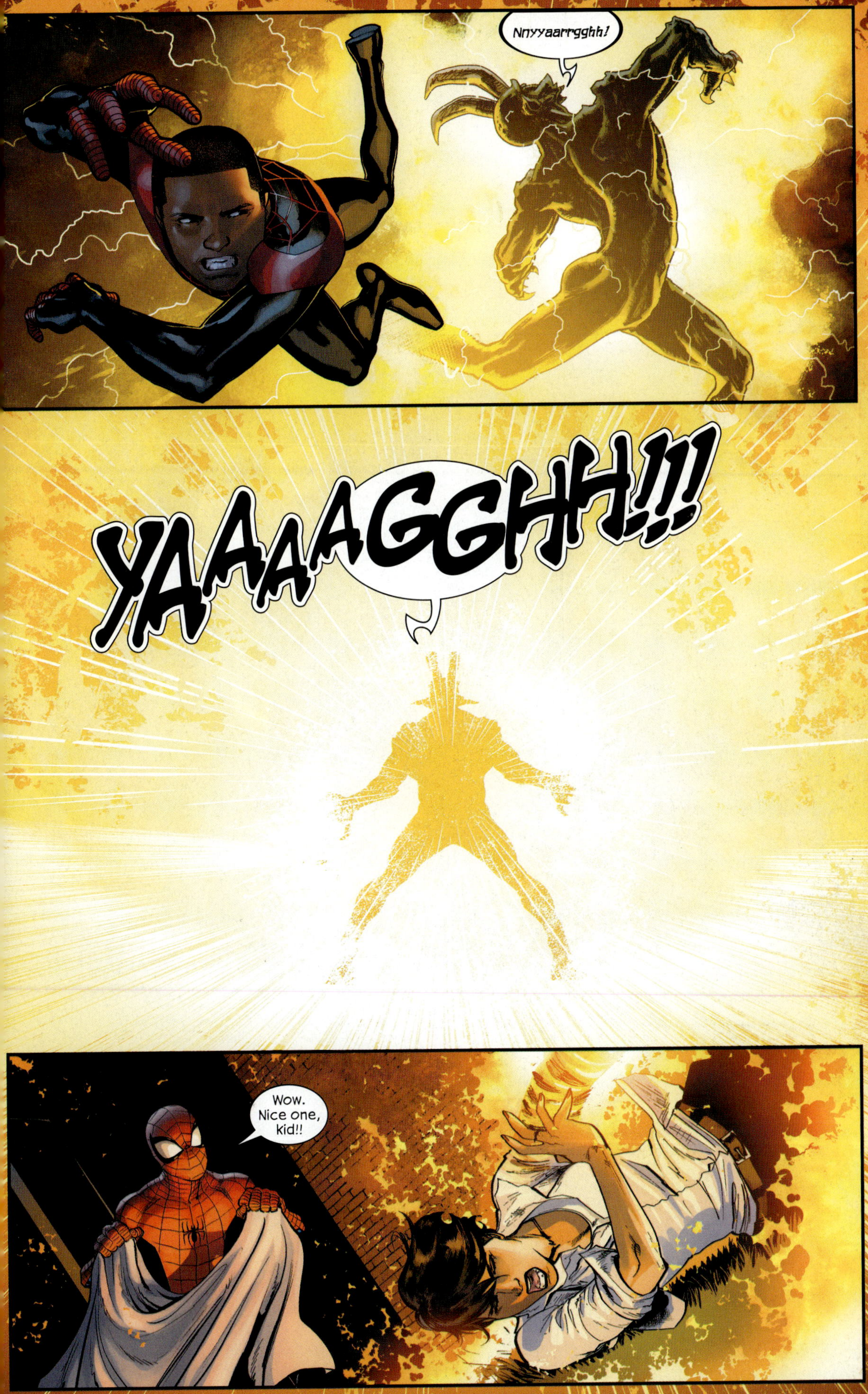
Nnyyaarrgghh!
YAAAAGGHH!!!
Wow. Nice one, kid!!

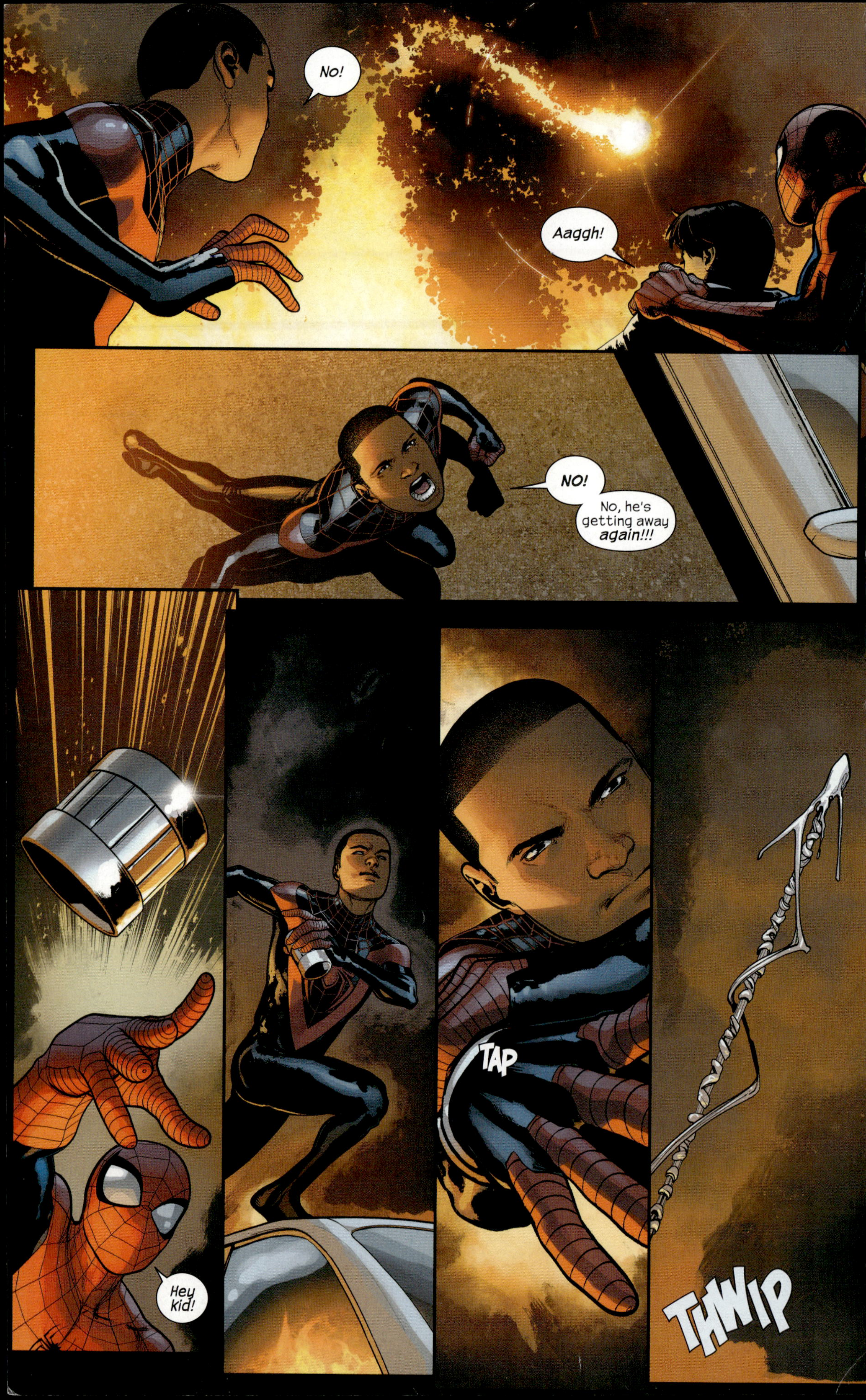
No!
Aaggh!
NO!
No, he's getting away again!!!
Hey kid!
TAP
THWIP

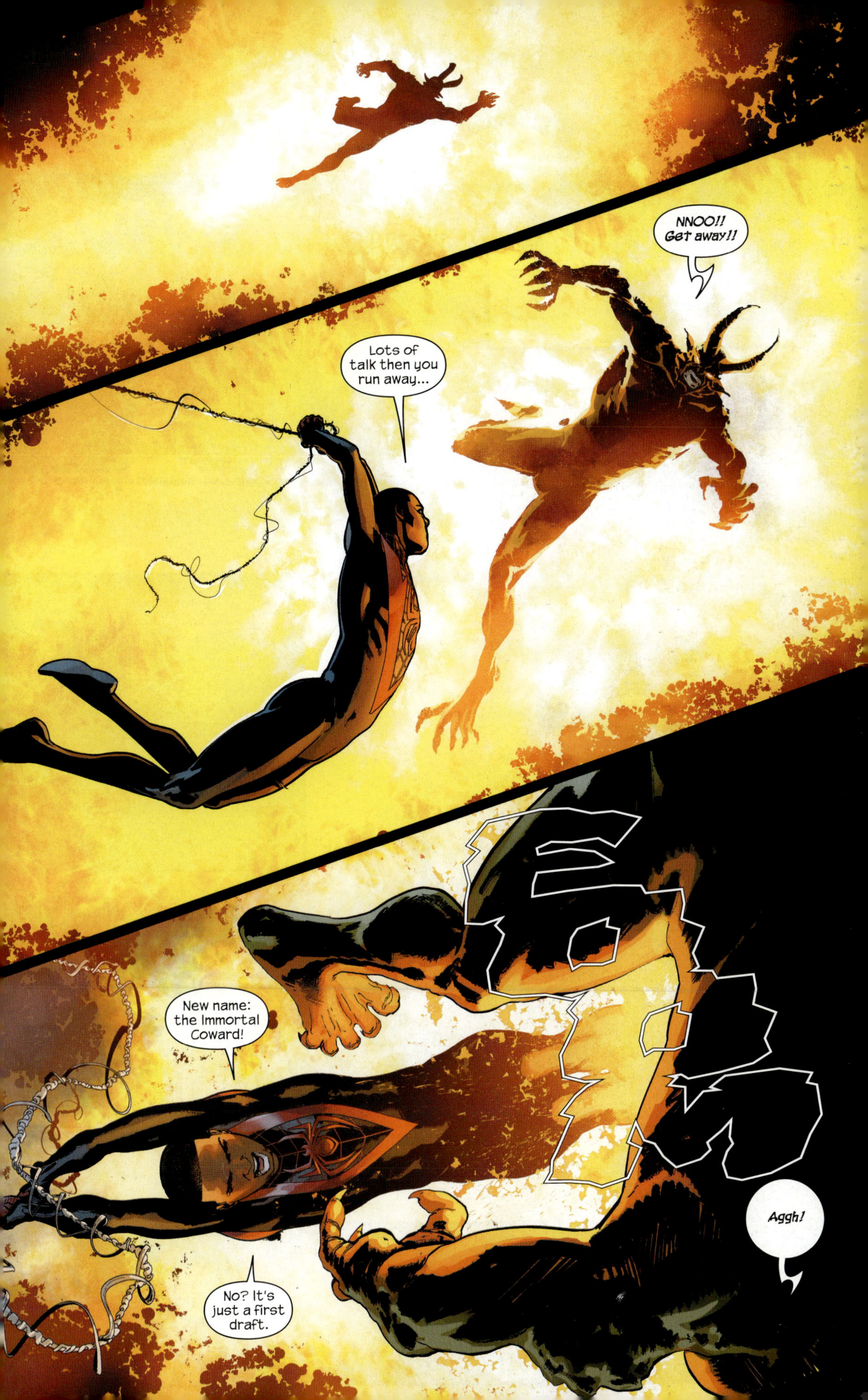
NNOO!! Get away!!
Lots of talk then you run away...
New name: the Immortal Coward!
No? It's just a first draft.
Aggh!

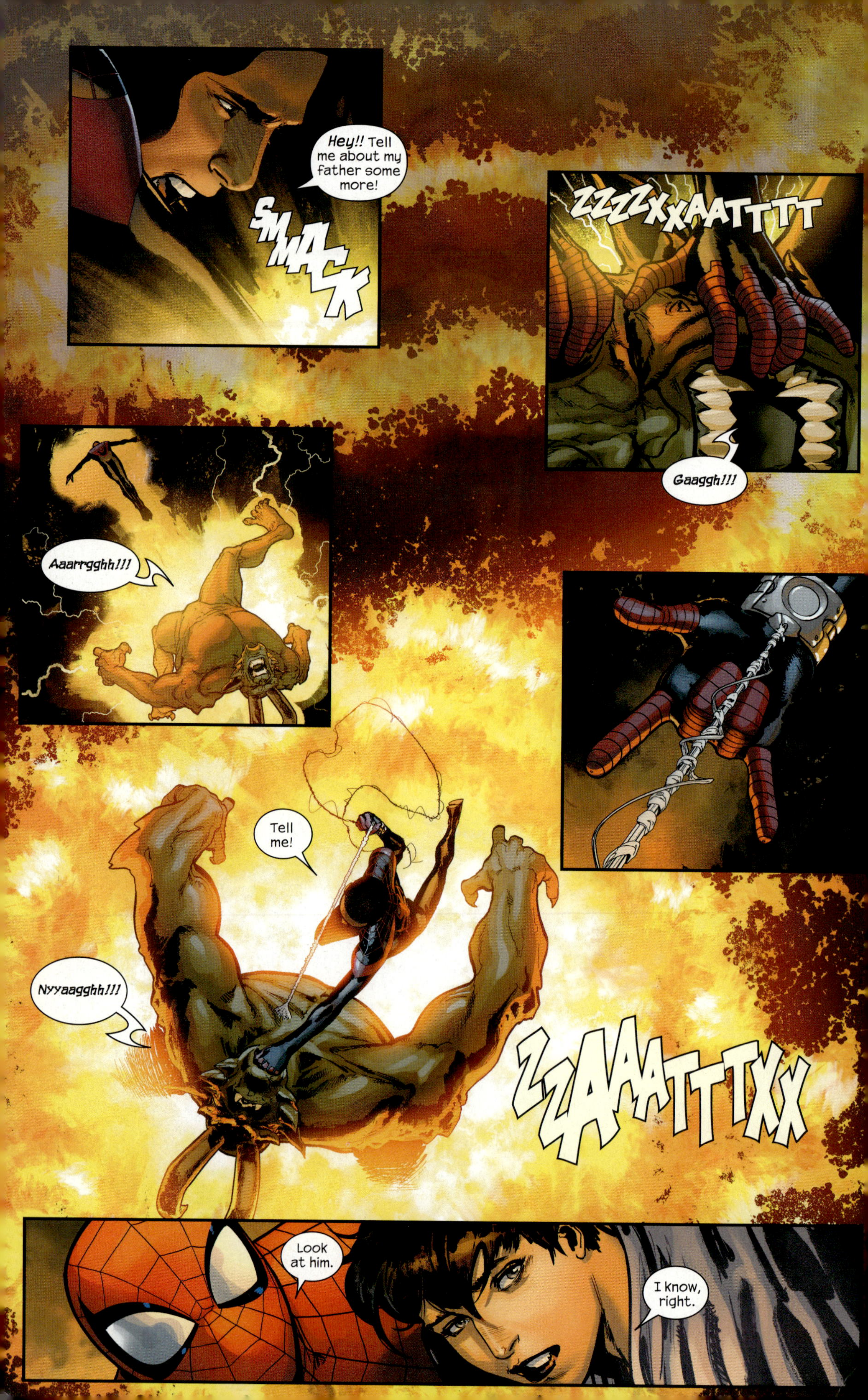
Hey!! Tell me about my father some more!
SMMACK
ZZZZXXAATTTTT
Gaaggh!!!
Aaarrgghh!!!
Tell me!
Nyyaagghh!!!
ZZAAAATTTXX
Look at him.
I know, right.

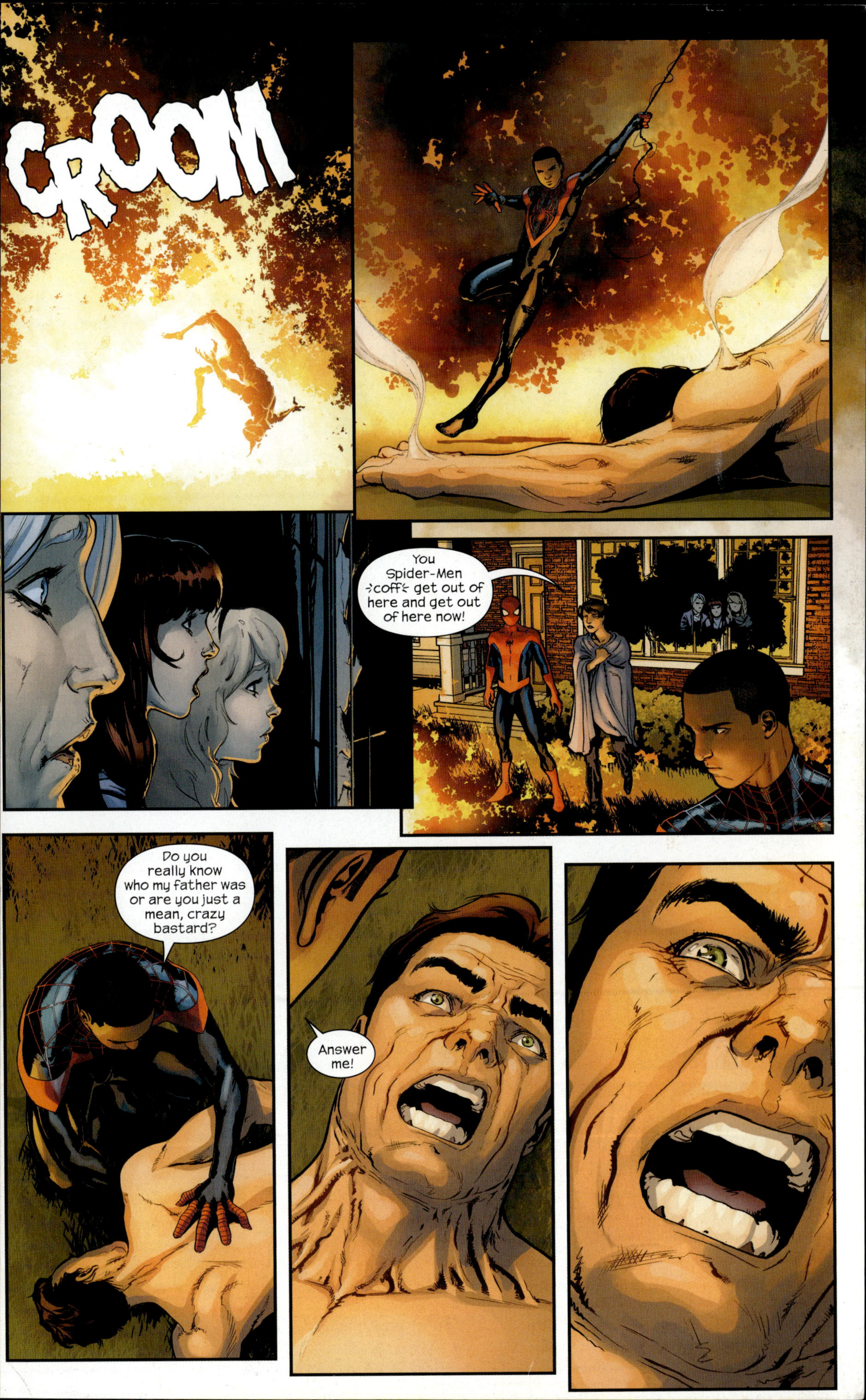
CROOM
You Spider-Men -coff- get out of here and get out of here now!
Do you really know who my father was or are you just a mean, crazy bastard?
Answer me!

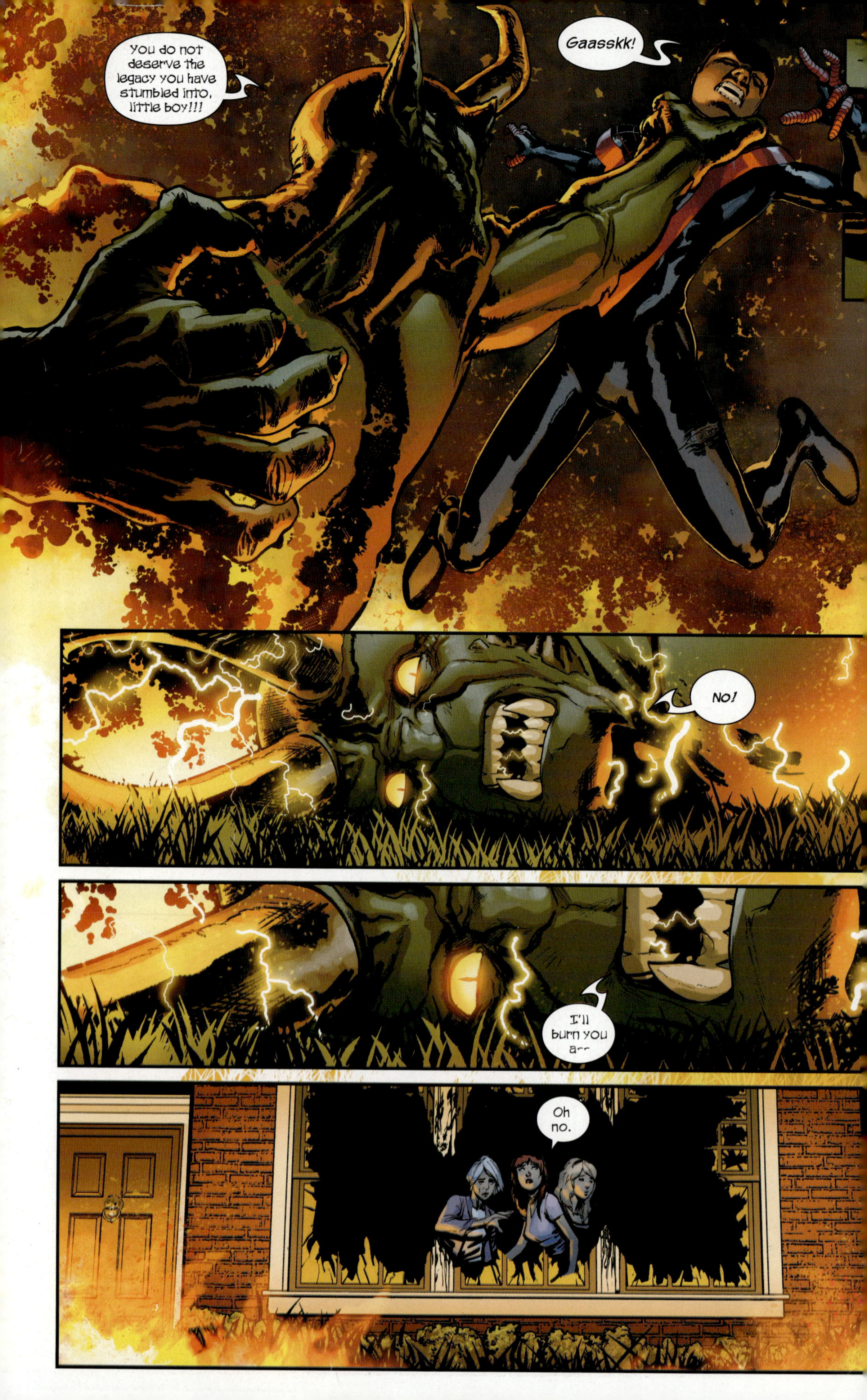
You do not deserve the legacy you have stumbled into, little boy!!!
Gaasskk!
NO!
I'll burn you a--
Oh no.

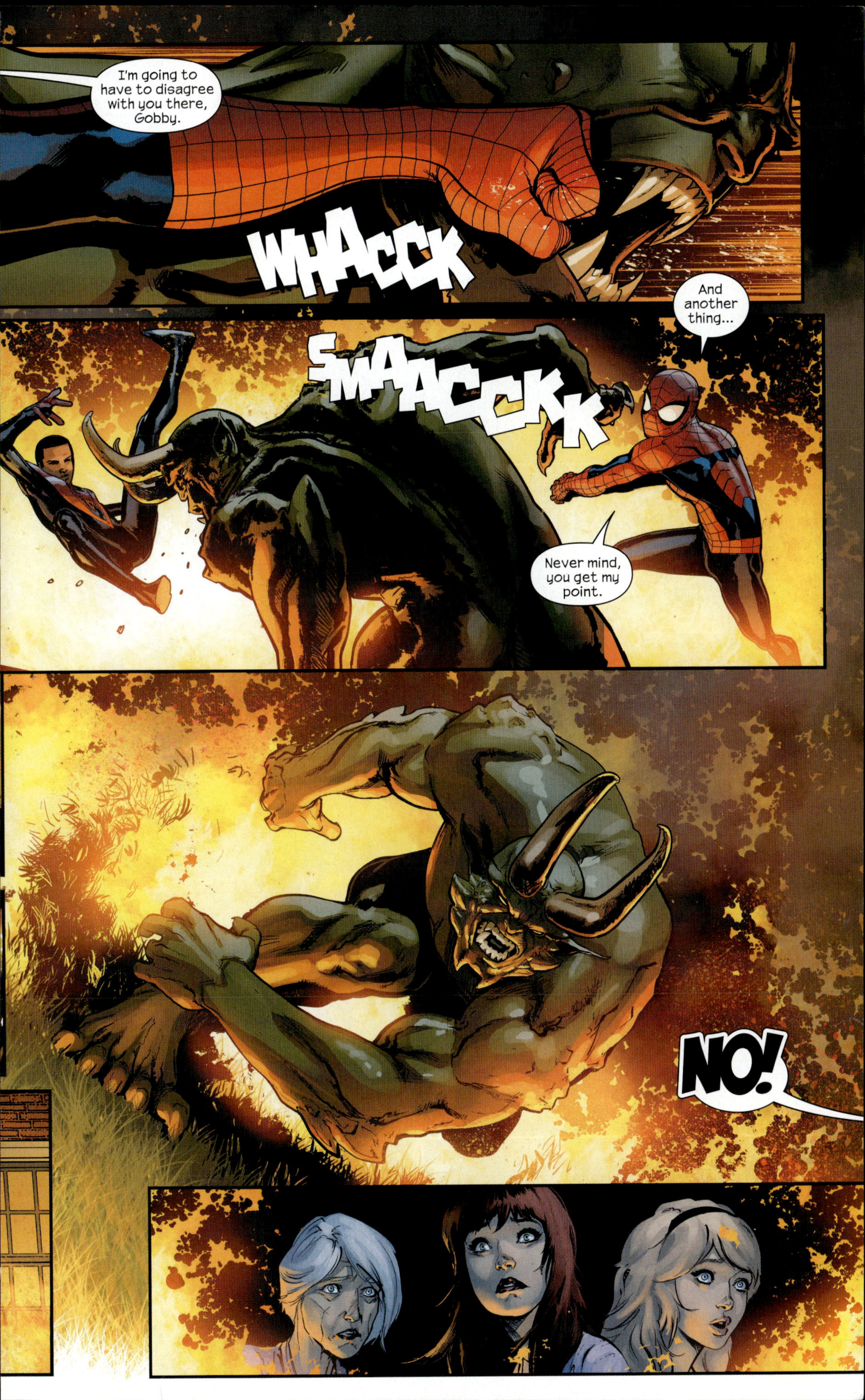
I'm going to have to disagree with you there, Gobby.
WHACCK
And another thing...
SMAACCKK
Never mind, you get my point.
NO!

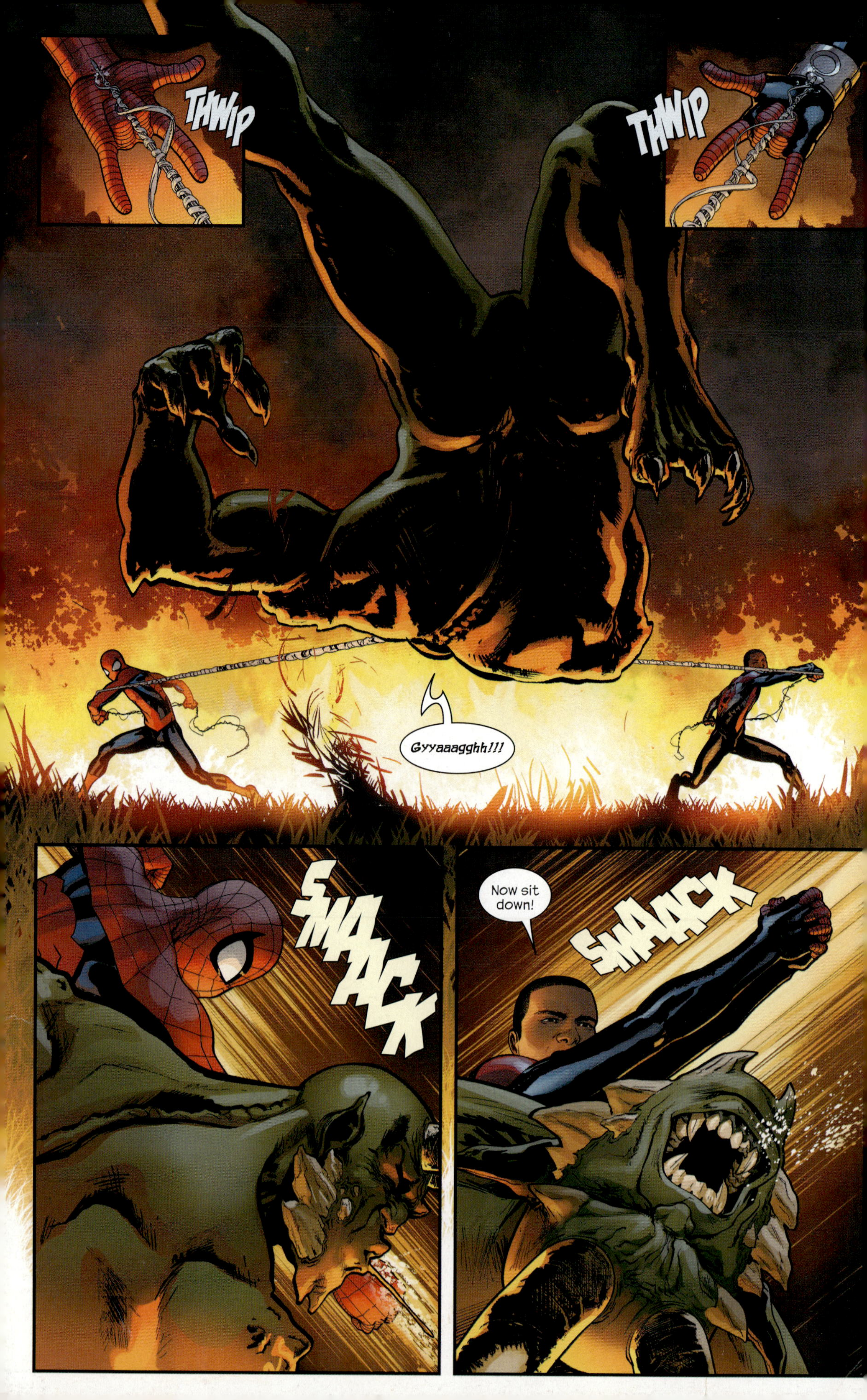
THWIP
THWIP
Gyyaaagghh!!!
SMACK
Now sit down!
SMAACK

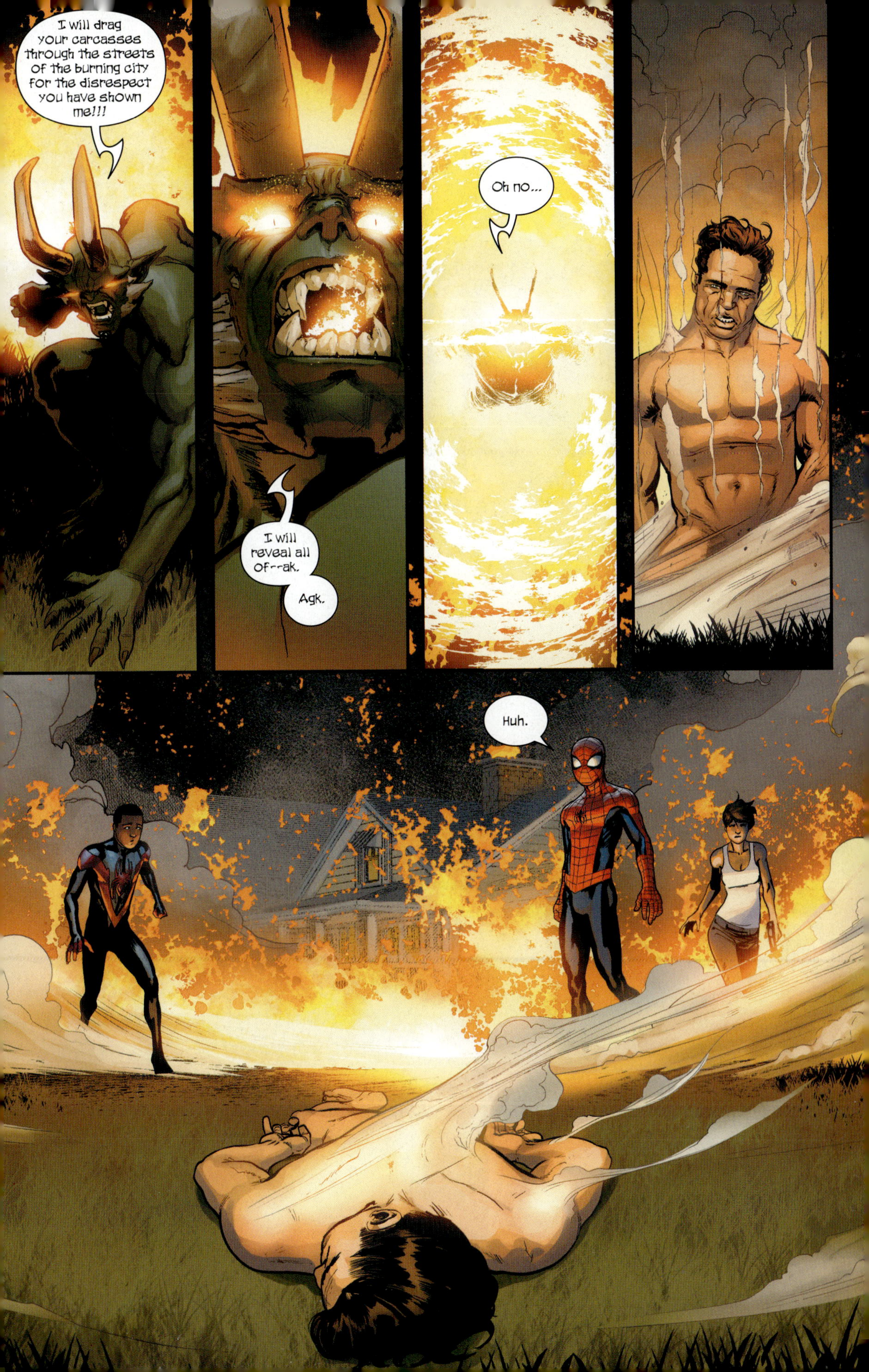
I will drag your carcasses through the streets of the burning city for the disrespect you have shown me!!!
I will reveal all of--ak.
Agk.
Oh no...
Huh.

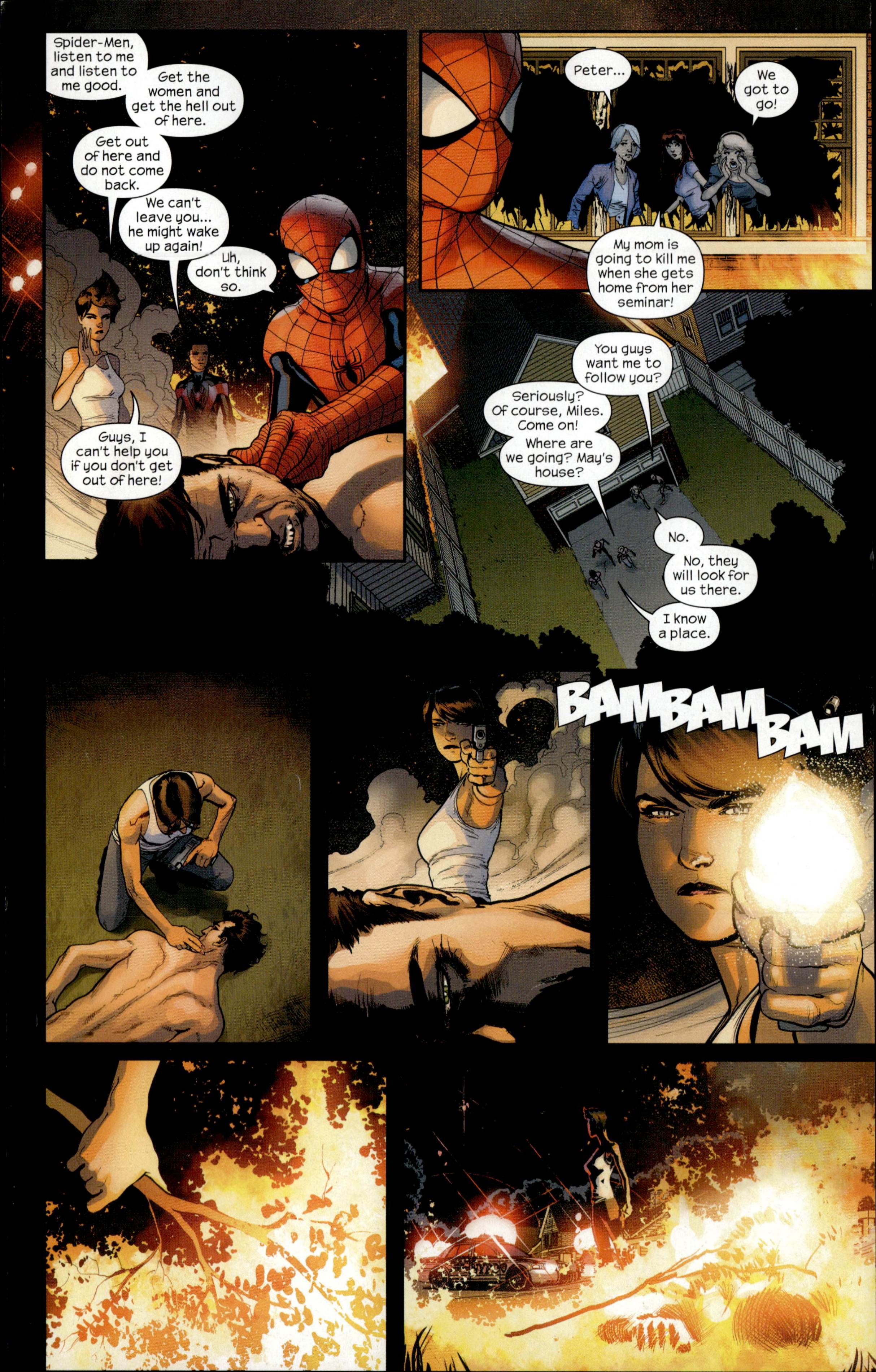

Spider-Men, listen to me and listen to me good.
Get the women and get the hell out of here.
Get out of here and do not come back.
We can't leave you... he might wake up again!
Uh, don't think so.
Guys, I can't help you if you don't get out of here!
Peter...
We got to go!
My mom is going to kill me when she gets home from her seminar!
You guys want me to follow you?
Seriously? Of course, Miles. Come on!
Where are we going? May's house?
No.
No, they will look for us there.
I know a place.
BAMBAMBAM

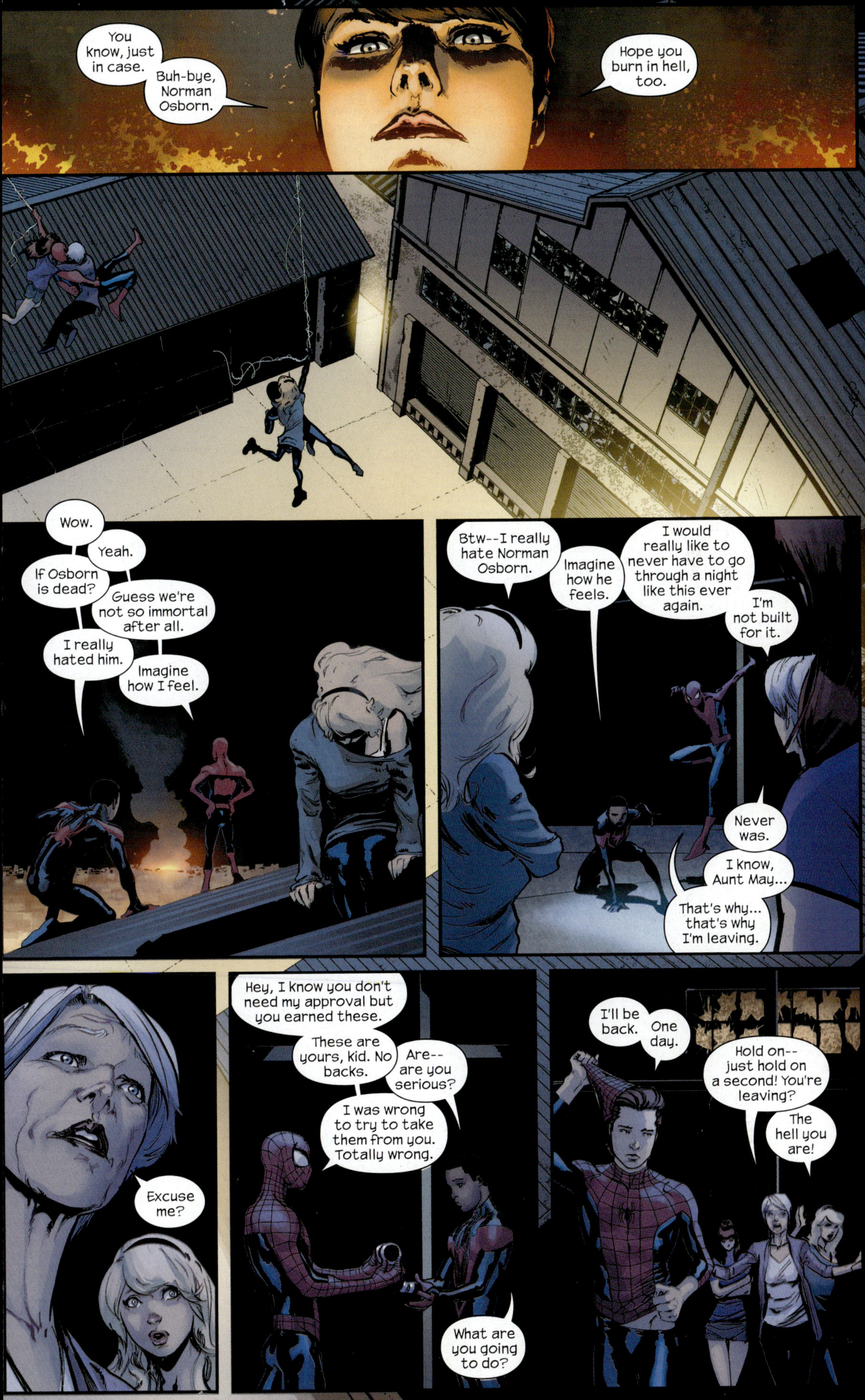

You know, just in case.
Buh-bye, Norman Osborn.
Hope you burn in hell, too.
Wow.
Yeah.
If Osborn is dead?
Guess we're not so immortal after all.
I really hated him.
Imagine how I feel.
Btw--I really hate Norman Osborn.
Imagine how he feels.
I would really like to never have to go through a night like this ever again.
I'm not built for it.
Never was.
I know, Aunt May...
That's why... that's why I'm leaving.
Excuse me?
Hey, I know you don't need my approval but you earned these.
These are yours, kid. No backs.
Are-- are you serious?
I was wrong to try to take them from you. Totally wrong.
What are you going to do?
I'll be back.
One day.
Hold on-- just hold on a second! You're leaving?
The hell you are!

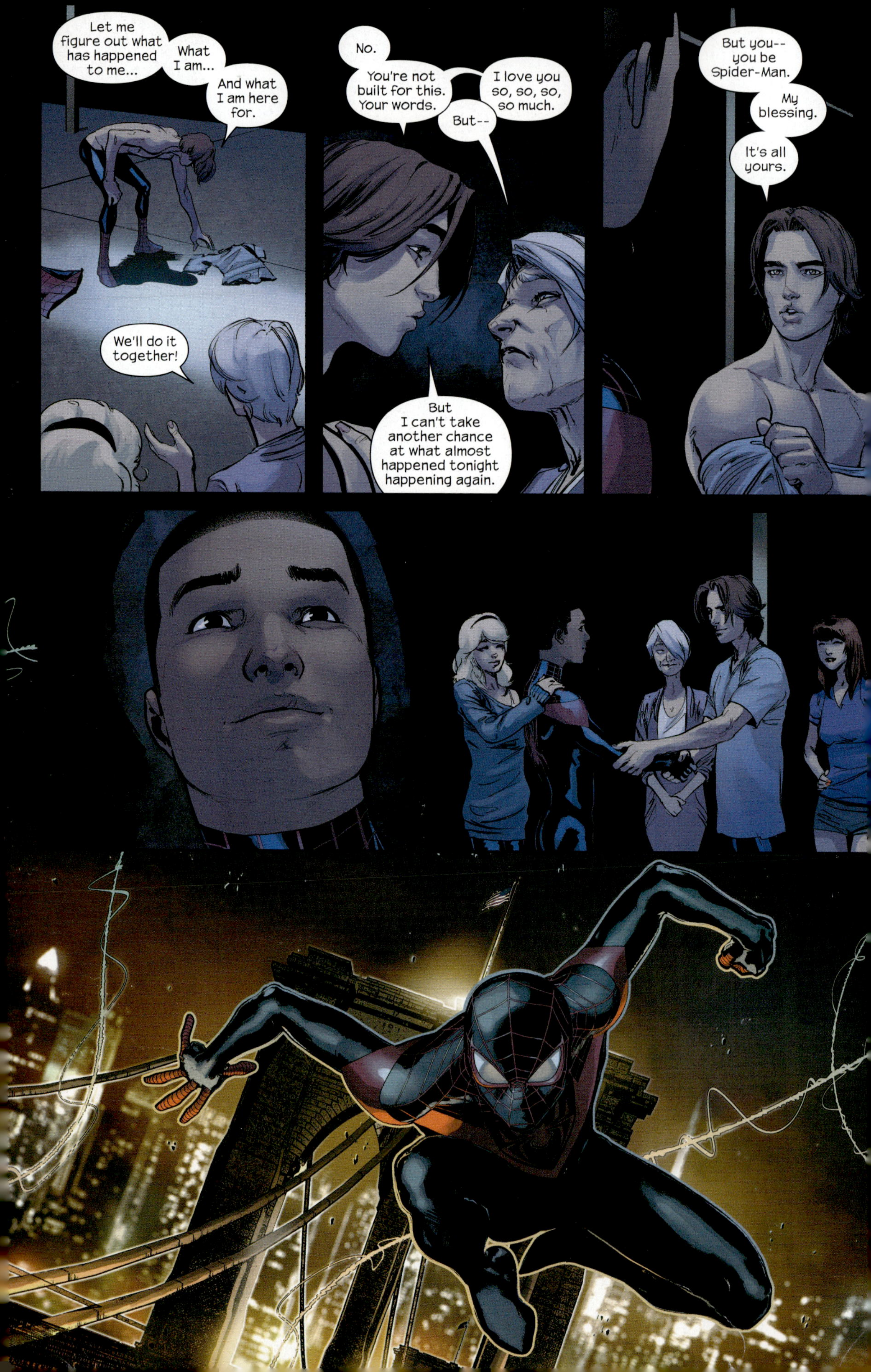
Let me figure out what has happened to me...
What I am...
And what I am here for.
We'll do it together!
No.
You're not built for this. Your words.
I love you so, so, so, so much.
But--
But I can't take another chance at what almost happened tonight happening again.
But you-- you be Spider-Man.
My blessing.
It's all yours.

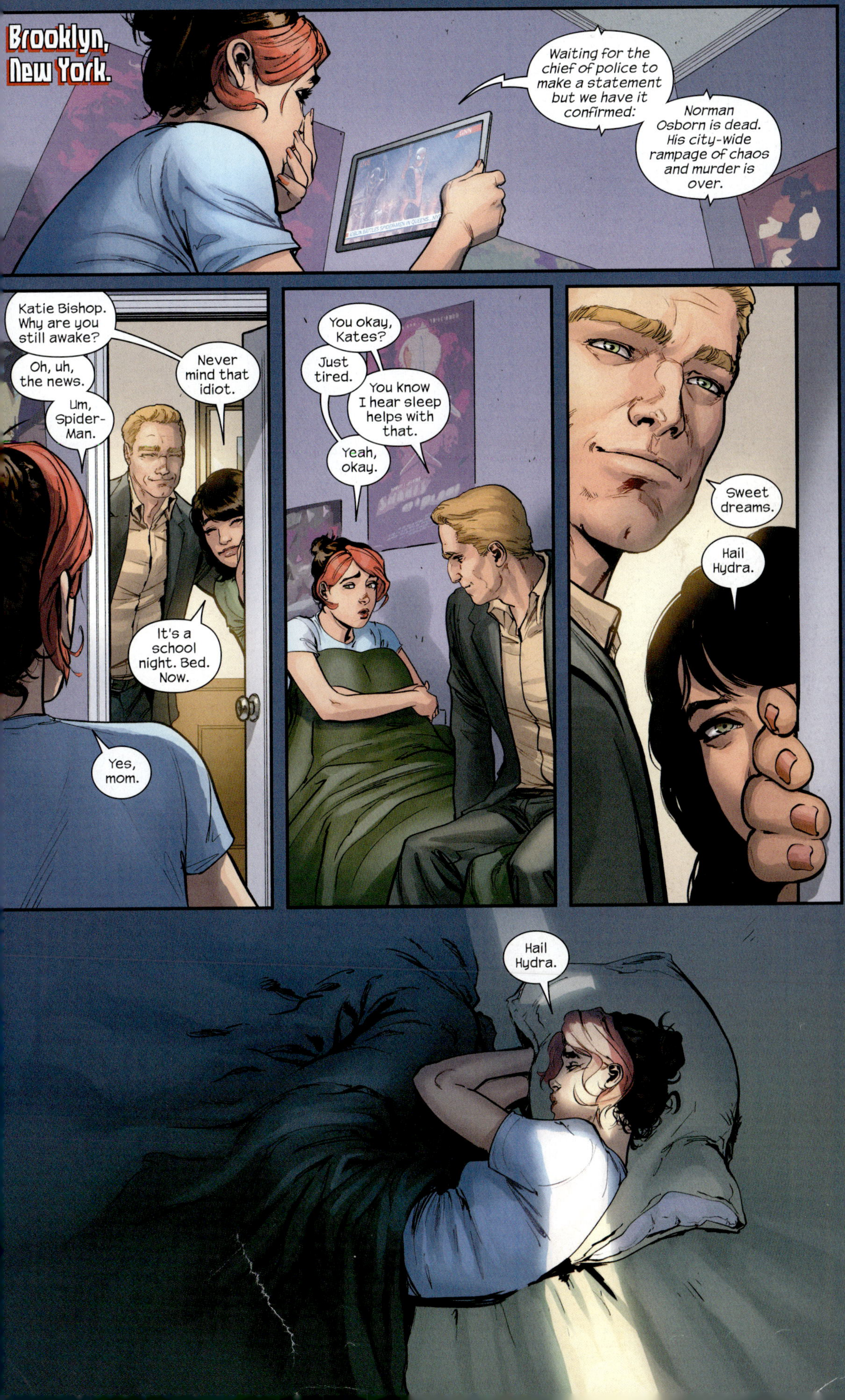
Brooklyn, New York.
Waiting for the chief of police to make a statement but we have it confirmed:
Norman Osborn is dead. His city-wide rampage of chaos and murder is over.
Katie Bishop. Why are you still awake?
Oh, uh, the news.
Um, Spider-Man.
Never mind that idiot.
It's a school night. Bed. Now.
Yes, mom.
You okay, Kates?
Just tired.
You know I hear sleep helps with that.
Yeah, okay.
Sweet dreams.
Hail Hydra.
Hail Hydra.

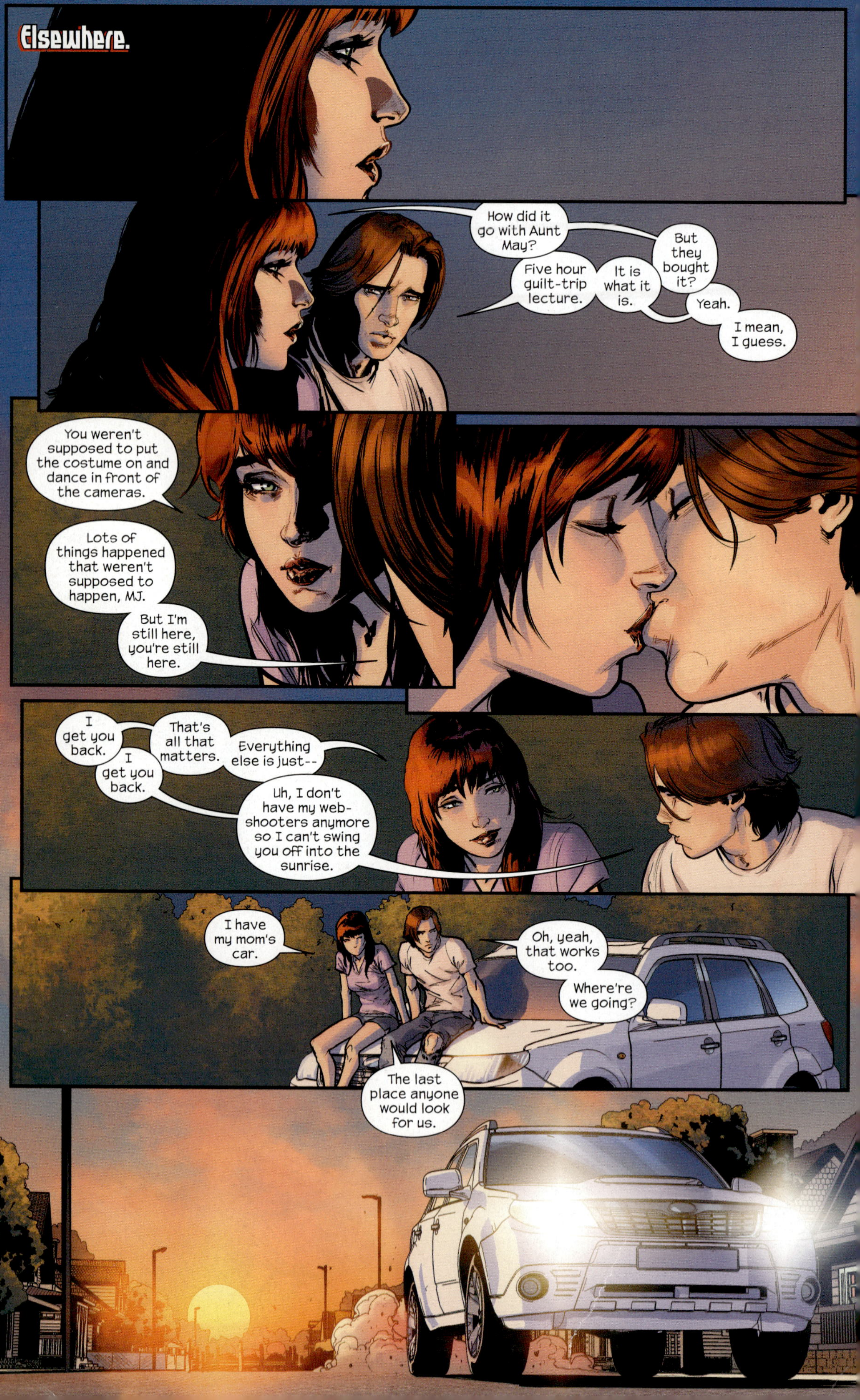

Elsewhere.
How did it go with Aunt May?
Five hour guilt-trip lecture.
It is what it is.
But they bought it?
Yeah.
I mean, I guess.
You weren't supposed to put the costume on and dance in front of the cameras.
Lots of things happened that weren't supposed to happen, MJ.
But I'm still here, you're still here.
I get you back.
That's all that matters.
Everything else is just--
I get you back.
Uh, I don't have my web-shooters anymore so I can't swing you off into the sunrise.
I have my mom's car.
Oh, yeah, that works too.
Where're we going?
The last place anyone would look for us.

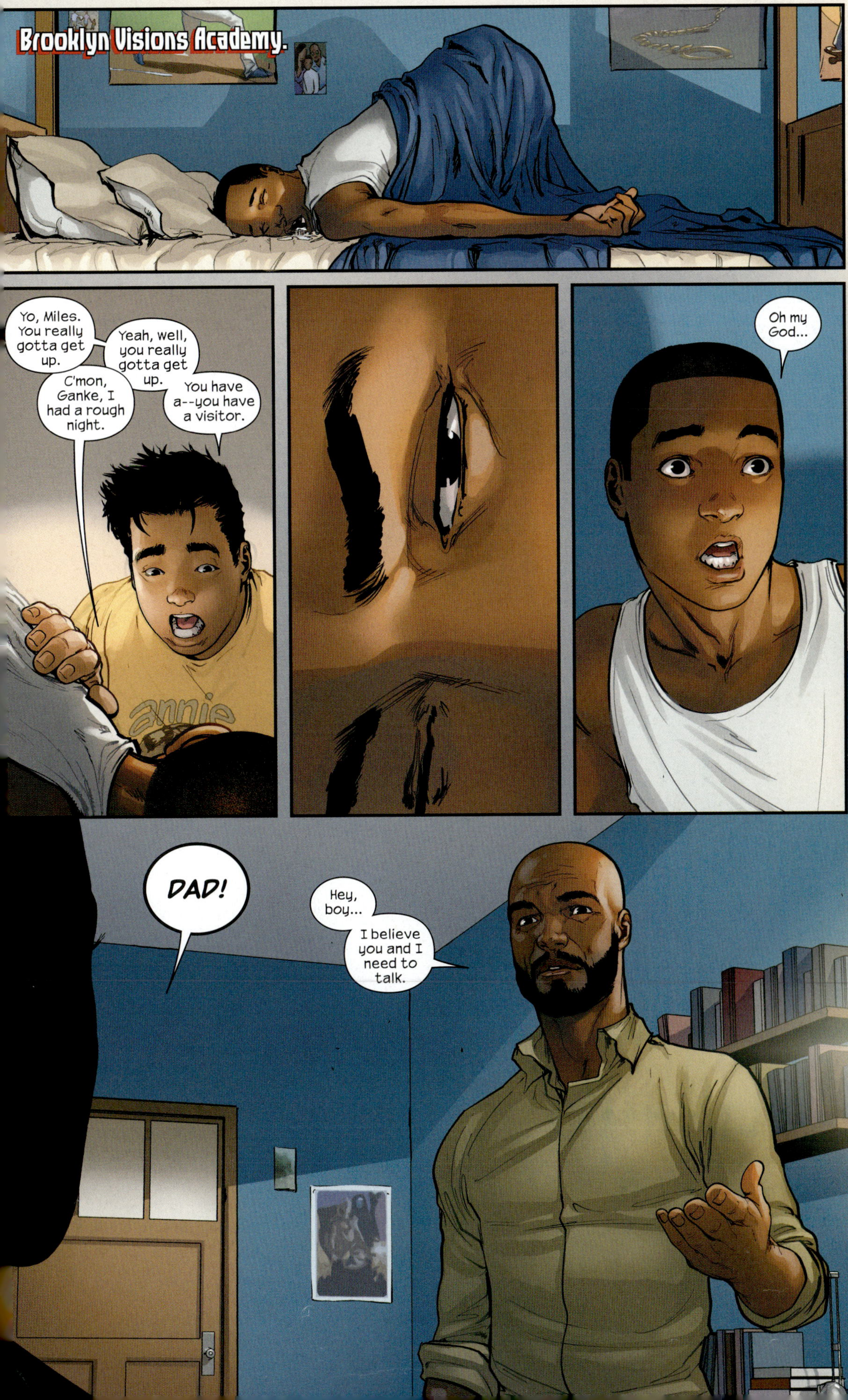
Brooklyn Visions Academy.
Yo, Miles. You really gotta get up.
C'mon, Ganke, I had a rough night.
Yeah, well, you really gotta get up.
You have a--you have a visitor.
Oh my God...
DAD!
Hey, boy...
I believe you and I need to talk.

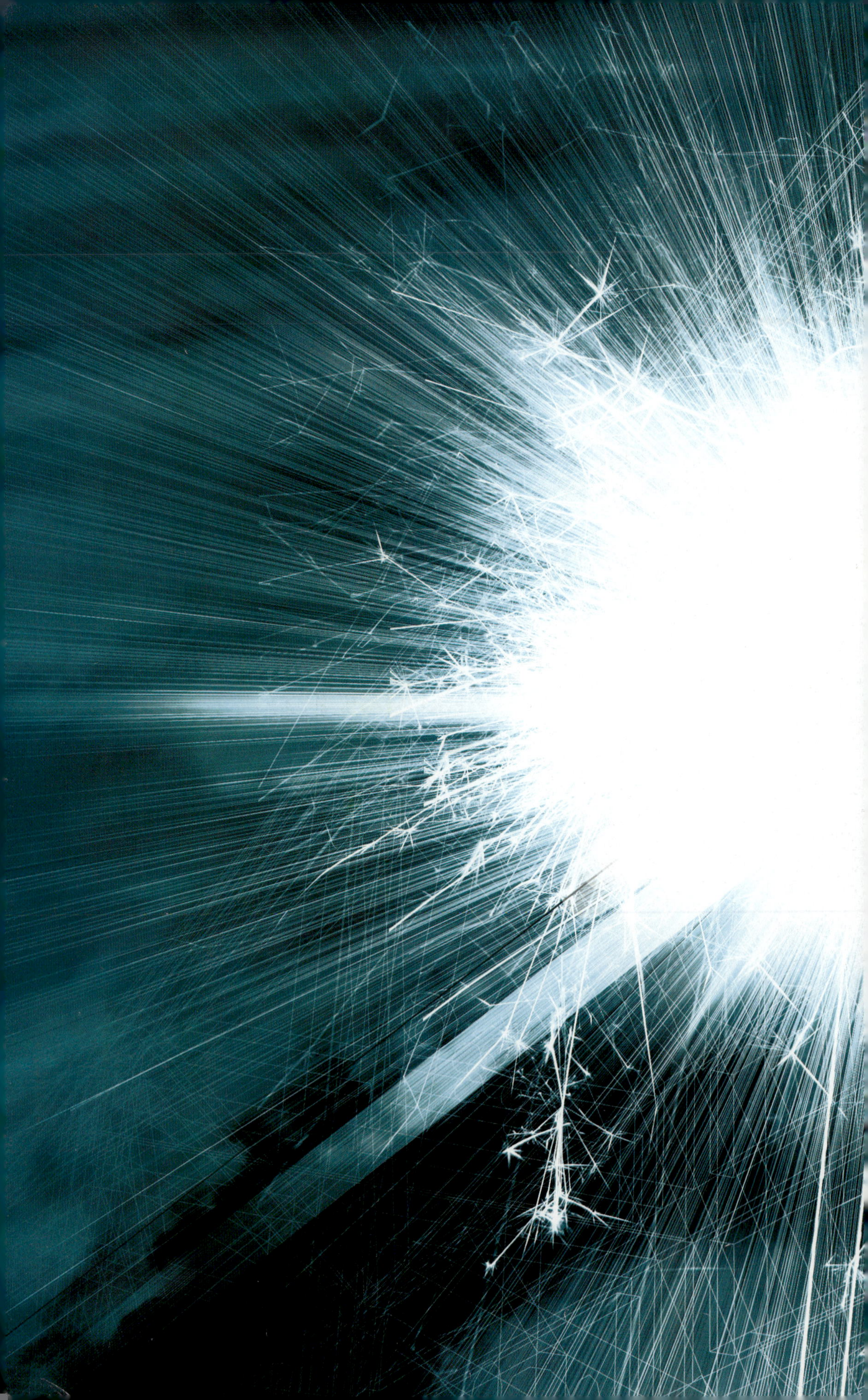

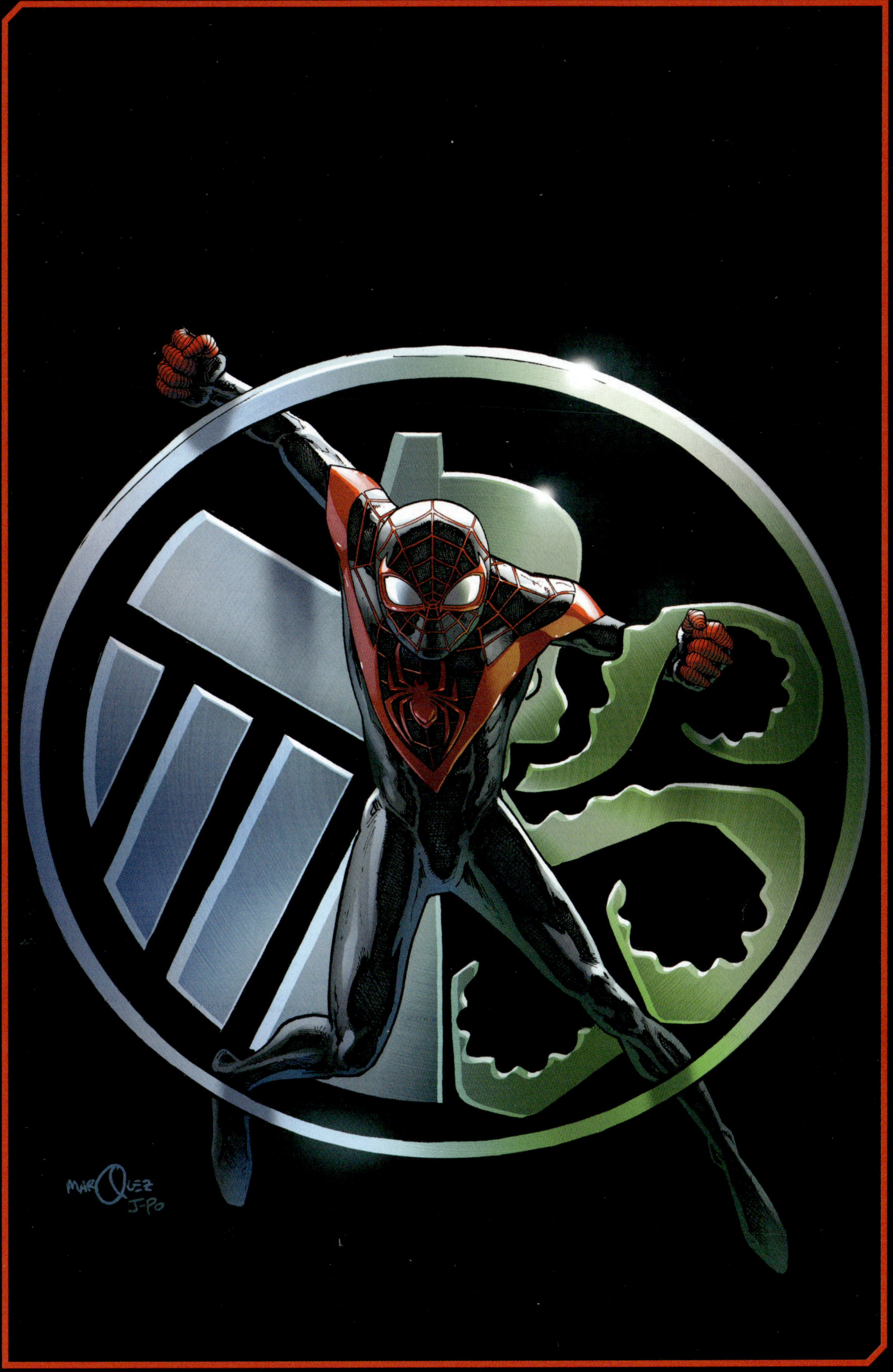

MILES MORALES: ULTIMATE SPIDER-MAN #8

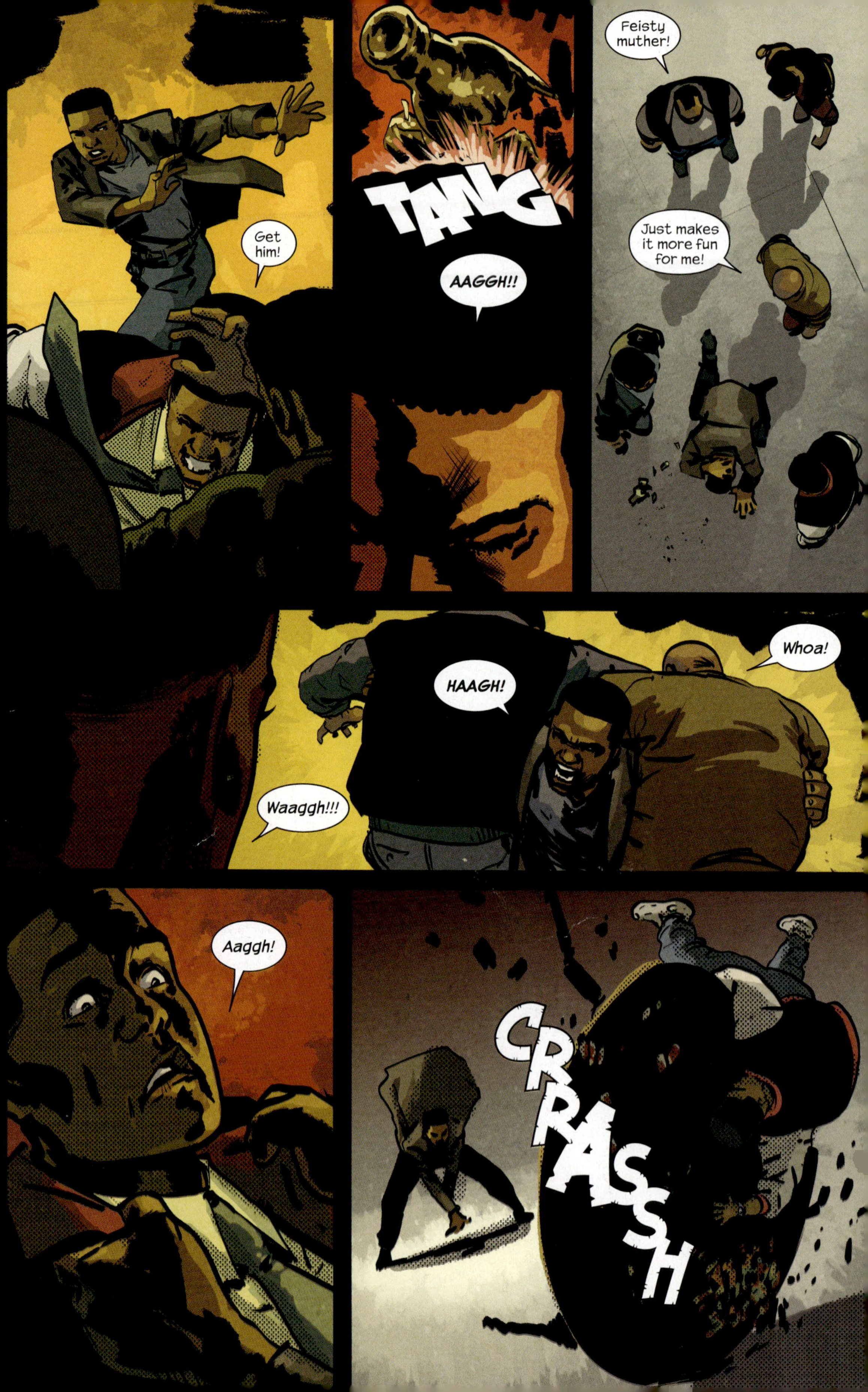
Get him!
TANG
AAGGH!!
Feisty muther!
Just makes it more fun for me!
HAAGH!
Whoa!
Waaggh!!!
Aaggh!
CRRASSH

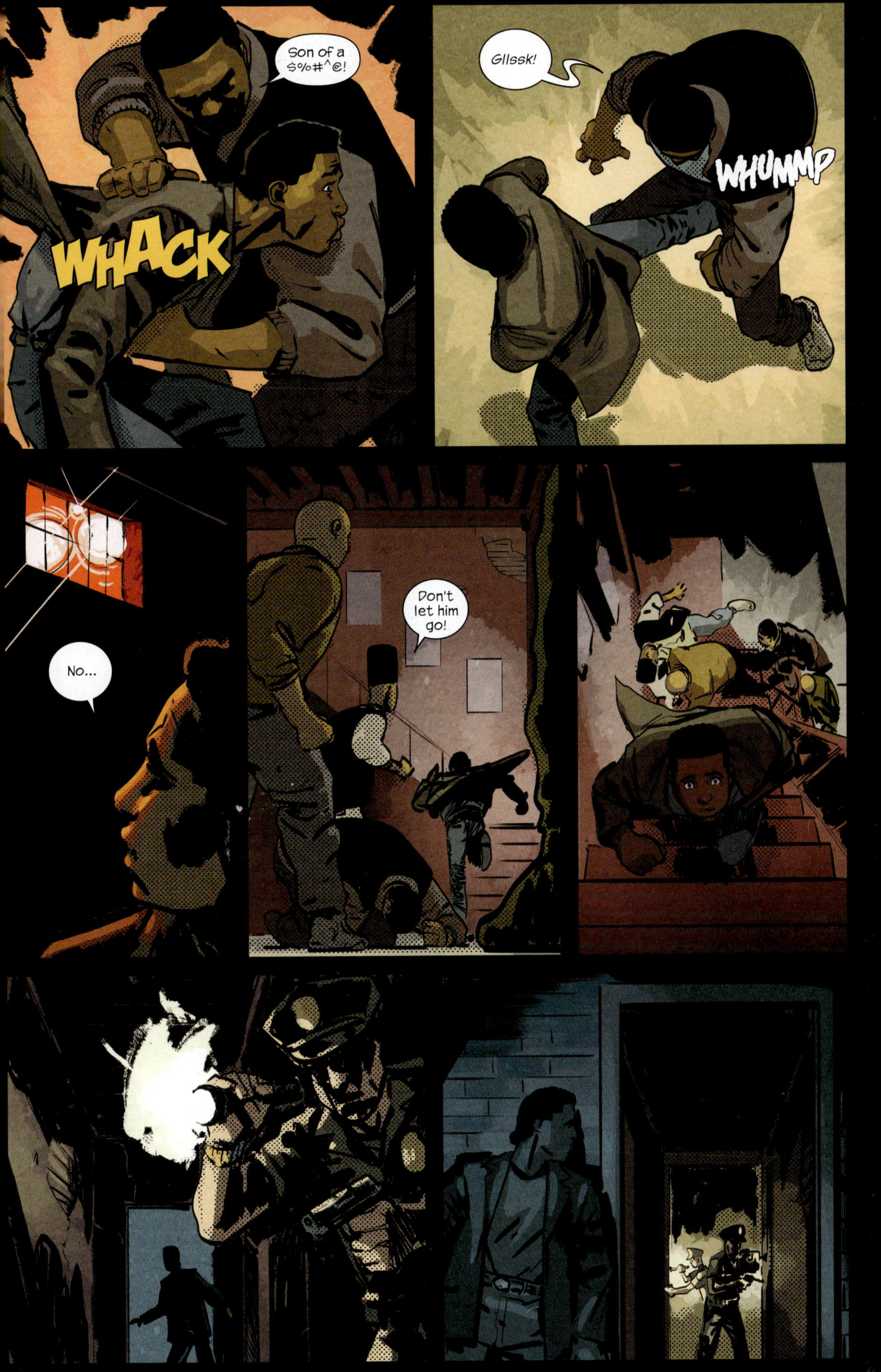
Son of a $%#^@!
WHACK
Gllssk!
WHUMMP
No...
Don't let him go!

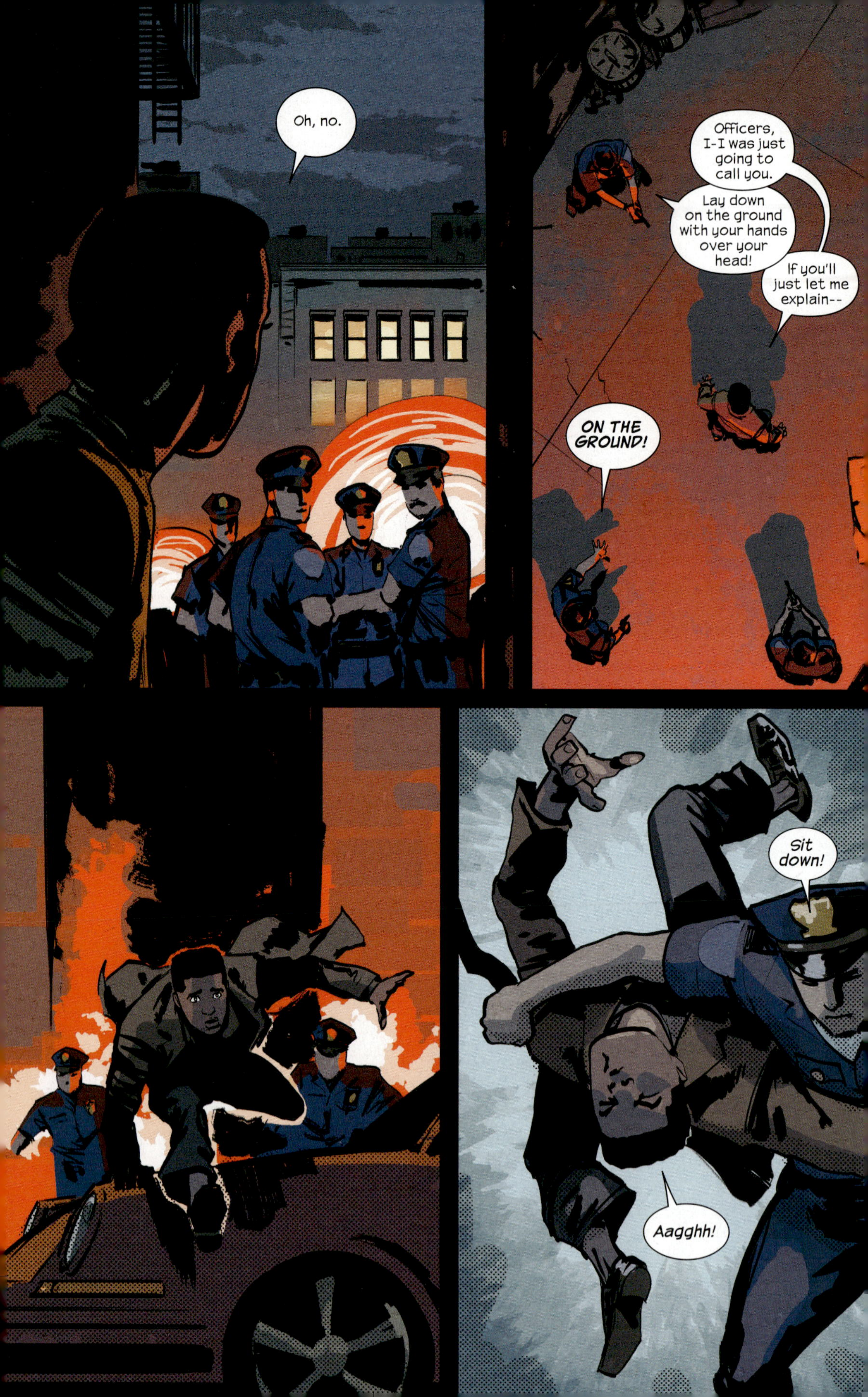
Oh, no.
Officers, I-I was just going to call you.
Lay down on the ground with your hands over your head!
If you'll just let me explain--
ON THE GROUND!
Sit down!
Aagghh!

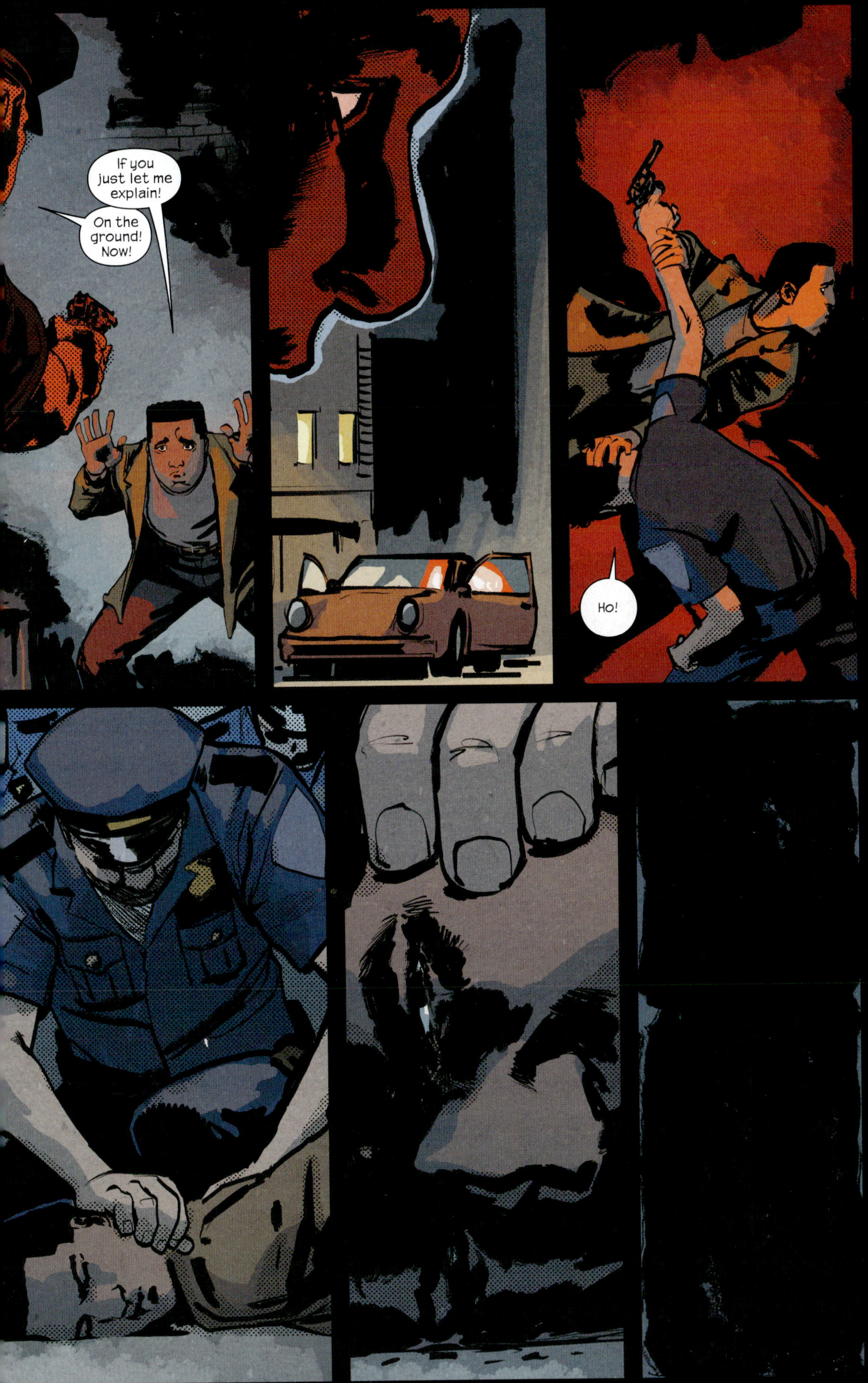
If you just let me explain!
On the ground! Now!
Ho!

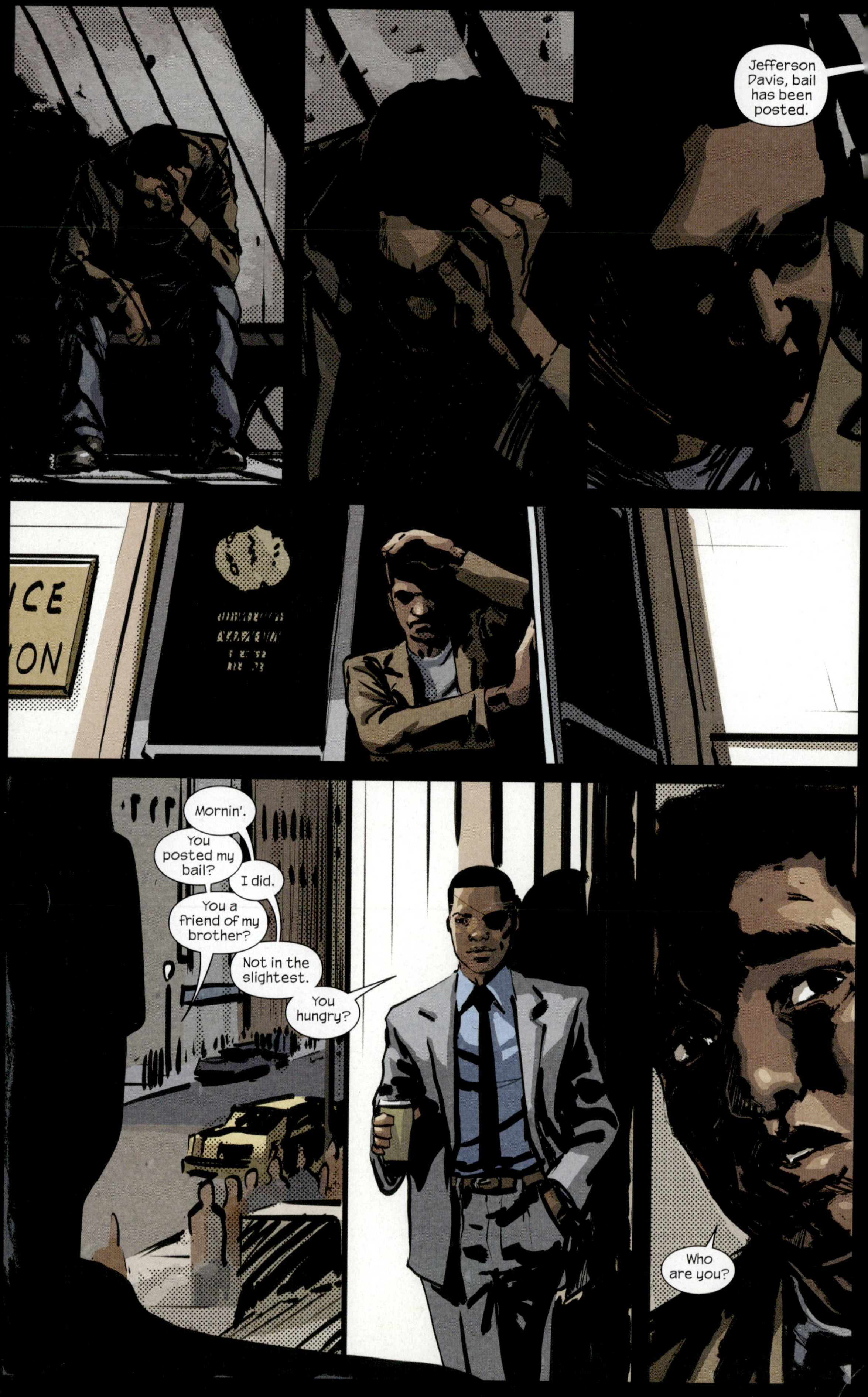

Jefferson Davis, bail has been posted.
ICE
ON
Mornin'.
You posted my bail?
I did.
You a friend of my brother?
Not in the slightest.
You hungry?
Who are you?

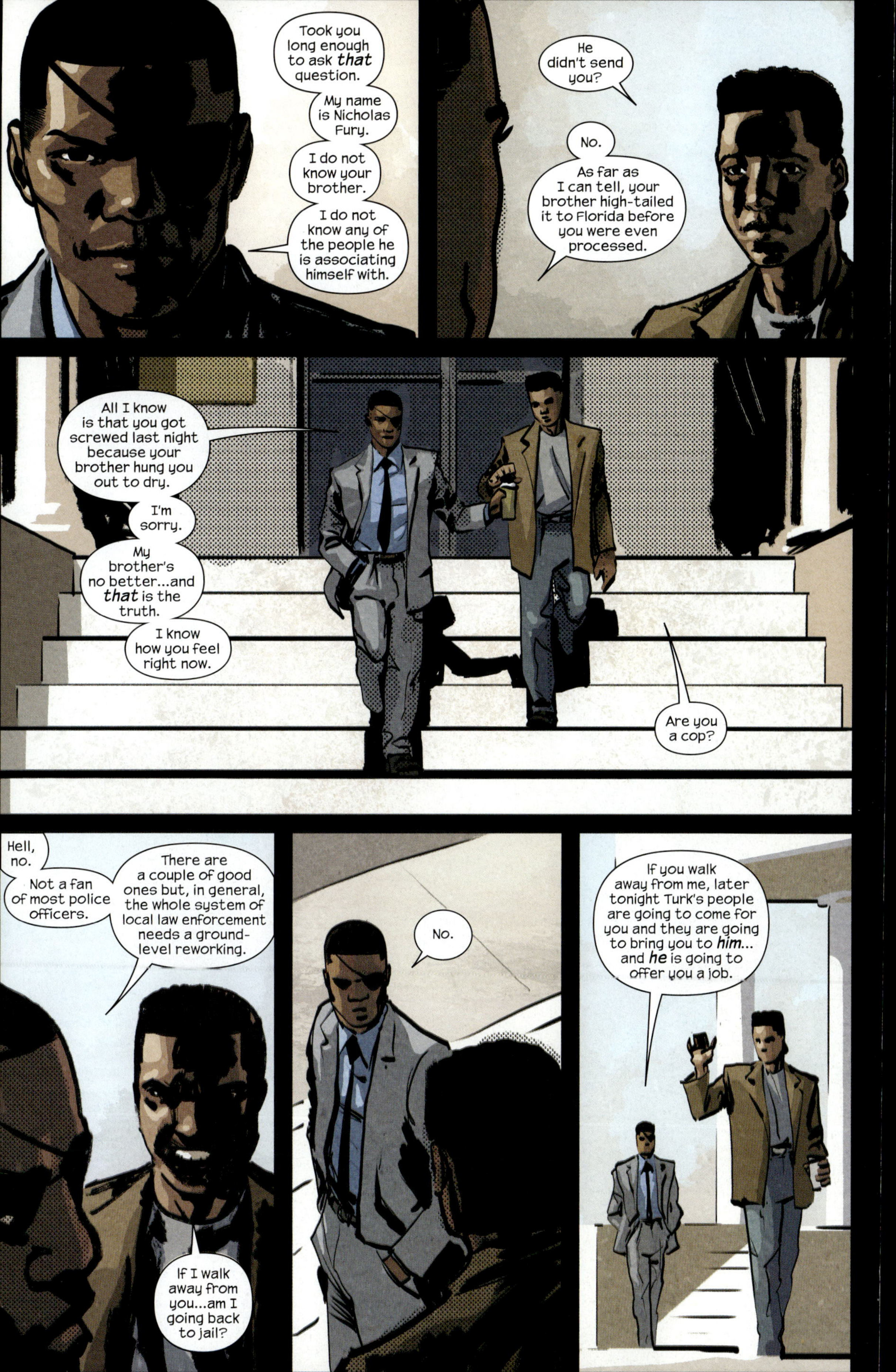
Took you long enough to ask *that* question.
My name is Nicholas Fury.
I do not know your brother.
I do not know any of the people he is associating himself with.
He didn't send you?
No.
As far as I can tell, your brother high-tailed it to Florida before you were even processed.
All I know is that you got screwed last night because your brother hung you out to dry.
I'm sorry.
My brother's no better...and *that* is the truth.
I know how you feel right now.
Are you a cop?
Hell, no.
Not a fan of most police officers.
There are a couple of good ones but, in general, the whole system of local law enforcement needs a ground-level reworking.
If I walk away from you...am I going back to jail?
No.
If you walk away from me, later tonight Turk's people are going to come for you and they are going to bring you to *him*... and *he* is going to offer you a job.

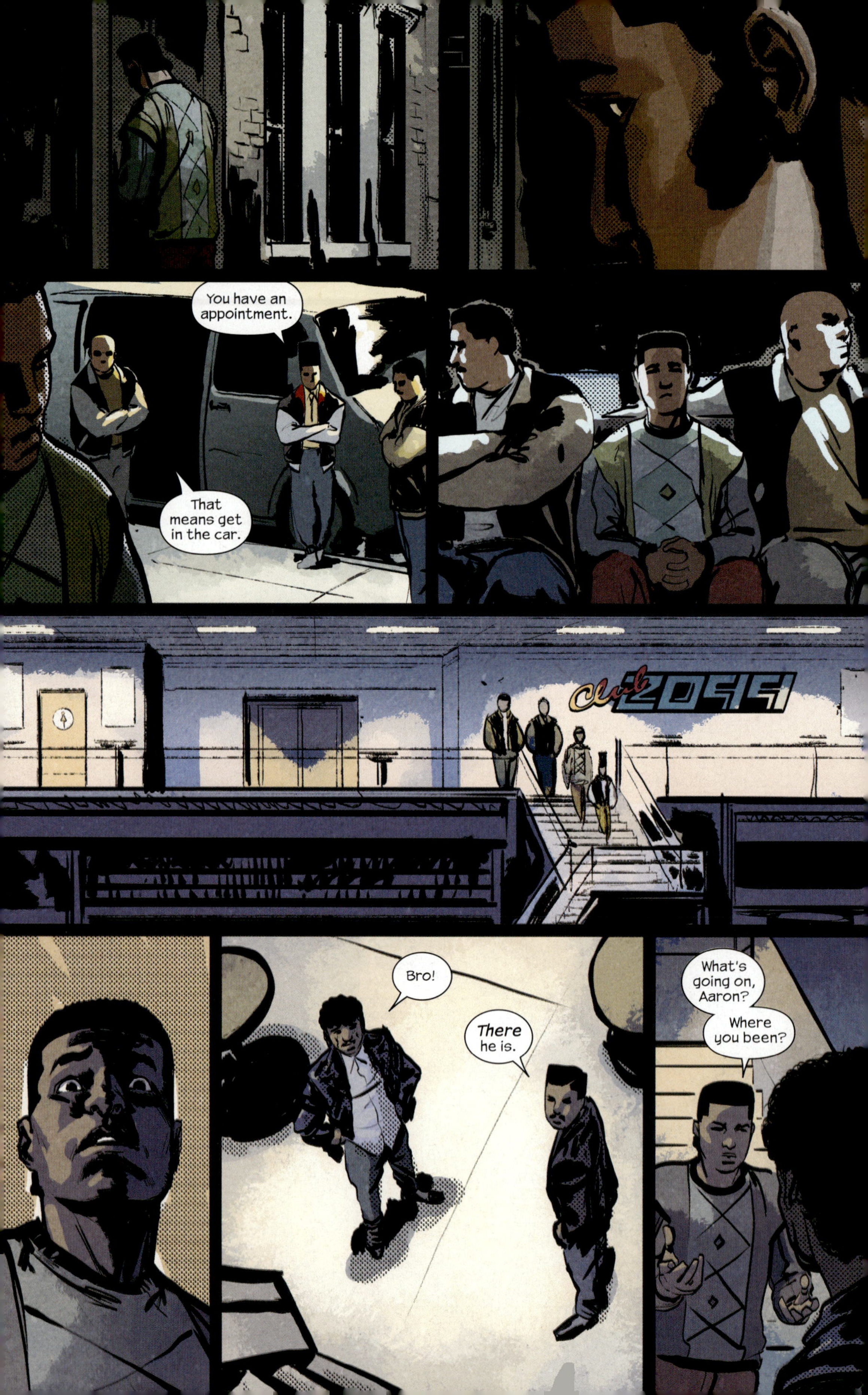
You have an appointment.
That means get in the car.
Club 2099
Bro!
There he is.
What's going on, Aaron?
Where you been?

"You will be so good at being bad that you are going to embolden this already emboldened bacteria in a suit.

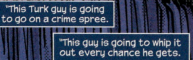

"This Turk guy is going to go on a crime spree.

"This guy is going to whip it out every chance he gets.

"All I care about is that with every bold move the word will get out: This weasel is dangerous.

"A certain kind of element will start coming out of the woodwork to challenge him or to attempt to negotiate with him.

"And of all these wannabe badasses there is one who is already watching Turk...

"Someone who is already looking for a time to make his play against your new boss...

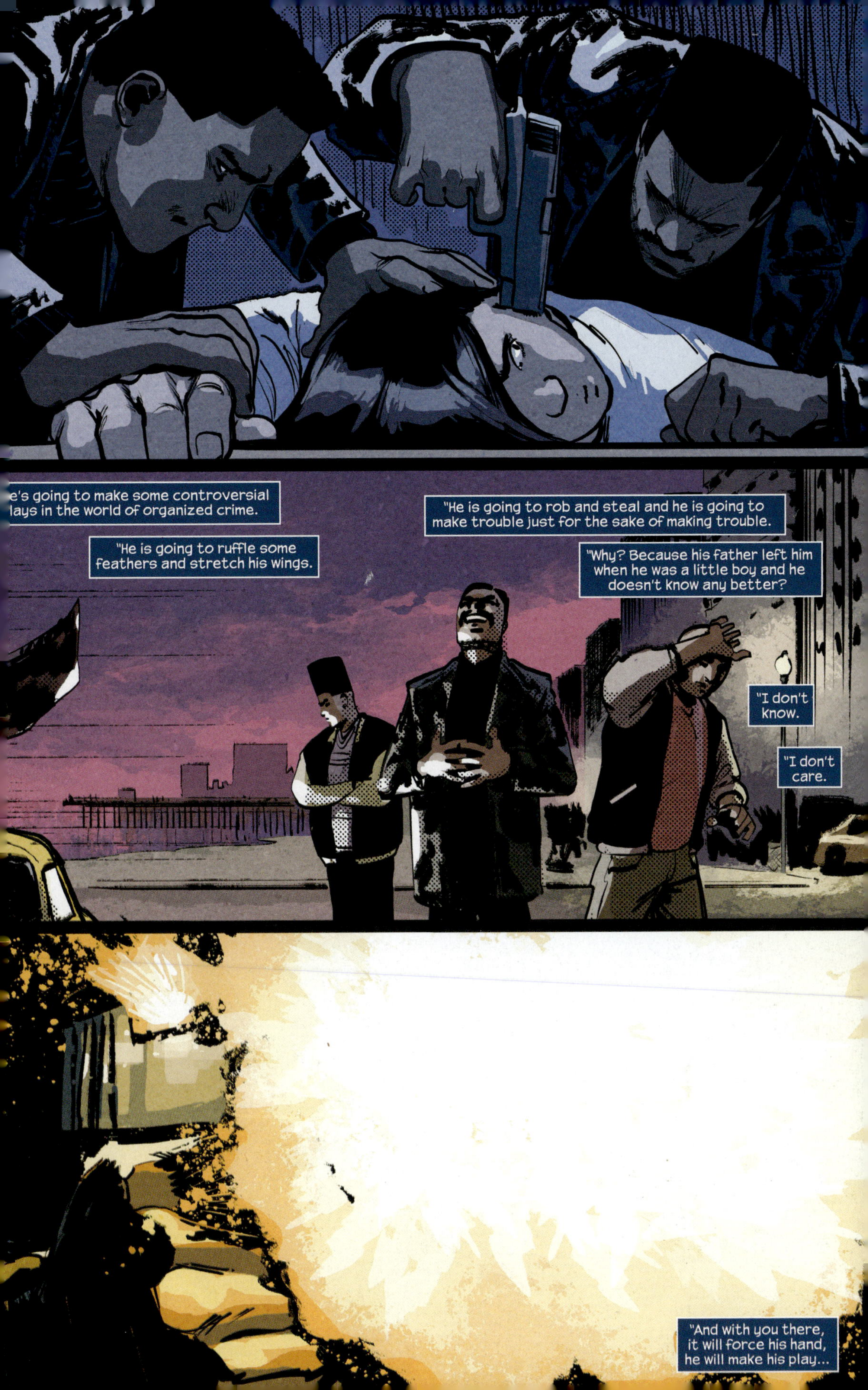
e's going to make some controversial
lays in the world of organized crime.
"He is going to ruffle some feathers and stretch his wings.
"He is going to rob and steal and he is going to make trouble just for the sake of making trouble.
"Why? Because his father left him when he was a little boy and he doesn't know any better?
"I don't know.
"I don't care.
"And with you there, it will force his hand, he will make his play...

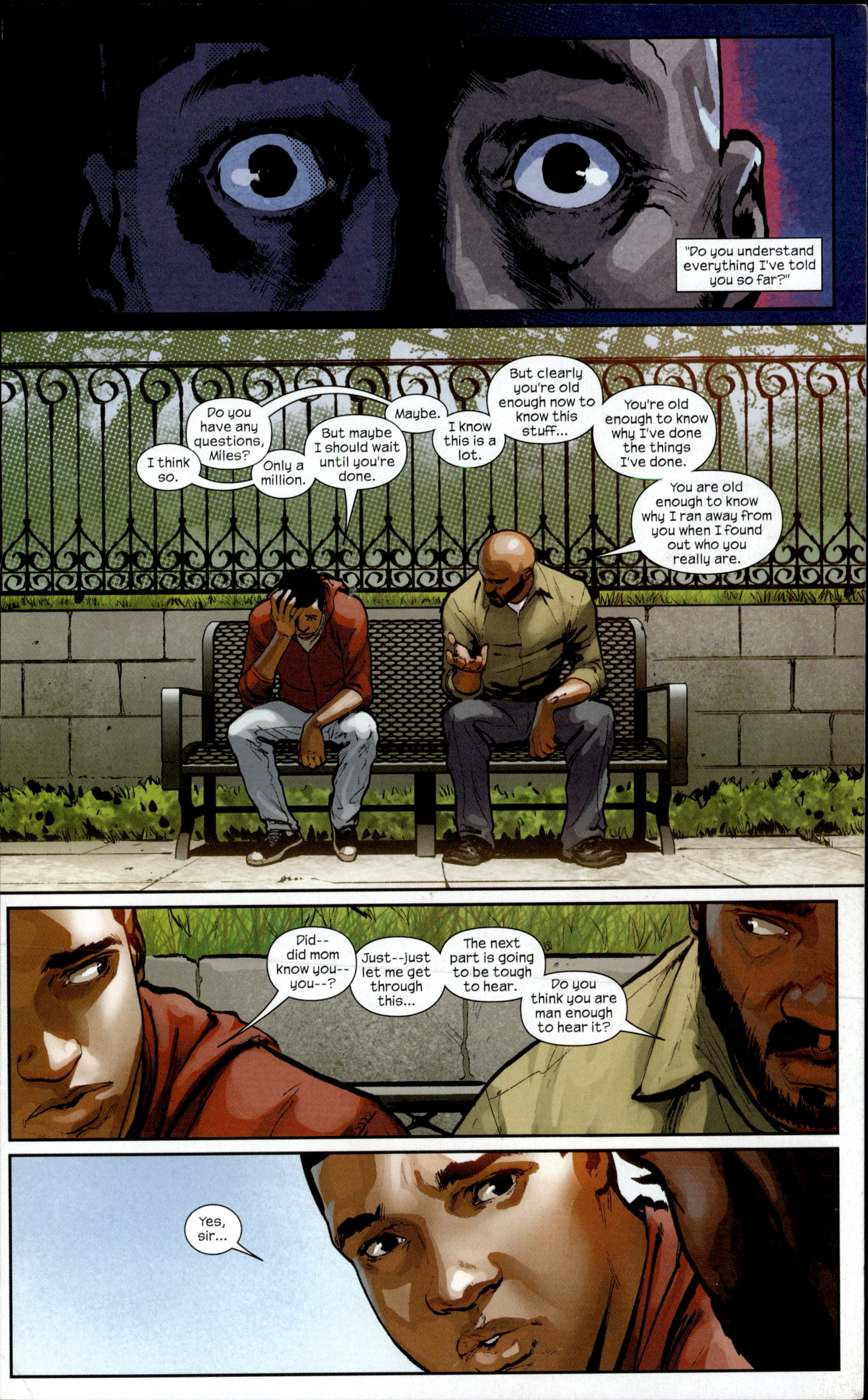

"Do you understand everything I've told you so far?"
Do you have any questions, Miles?
I think so.
Only a million.
But maybe I should wait until you're done.
Maybe.
I know this is a lot.
But clearly you're old enough now to know this stuff...
You're old enough to know why I've done the things I've done.
You are old enough to know why I ran away from you when I found out who you really are.
Did--did mom know you--you--?
Just--just let me get through this...
The next part is going to be tough to hear.
Do you think you are man enough to hear it?
Yes, sir...

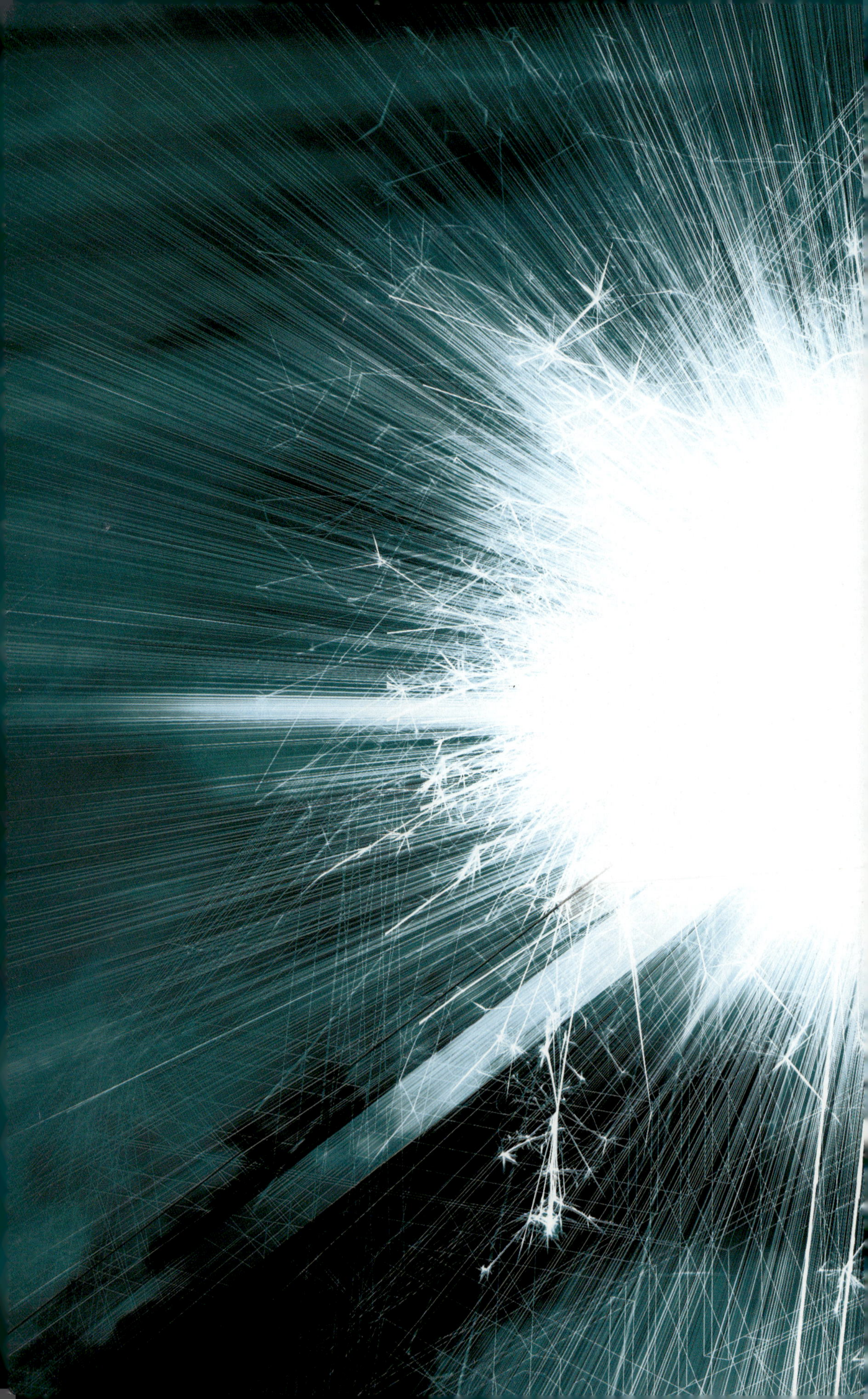

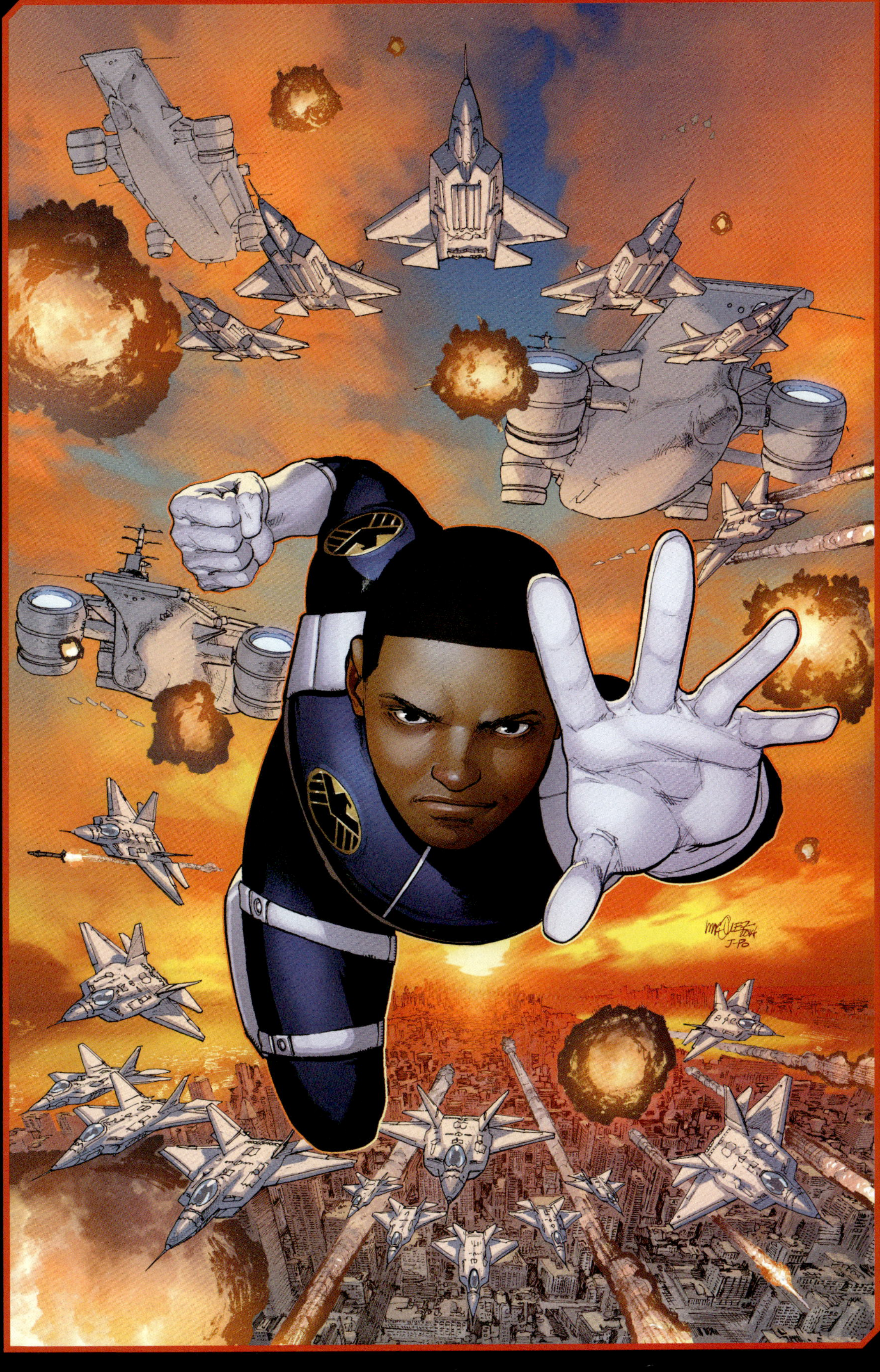

MILES MORALES: ULTIMATE SPIDER-MAN #9

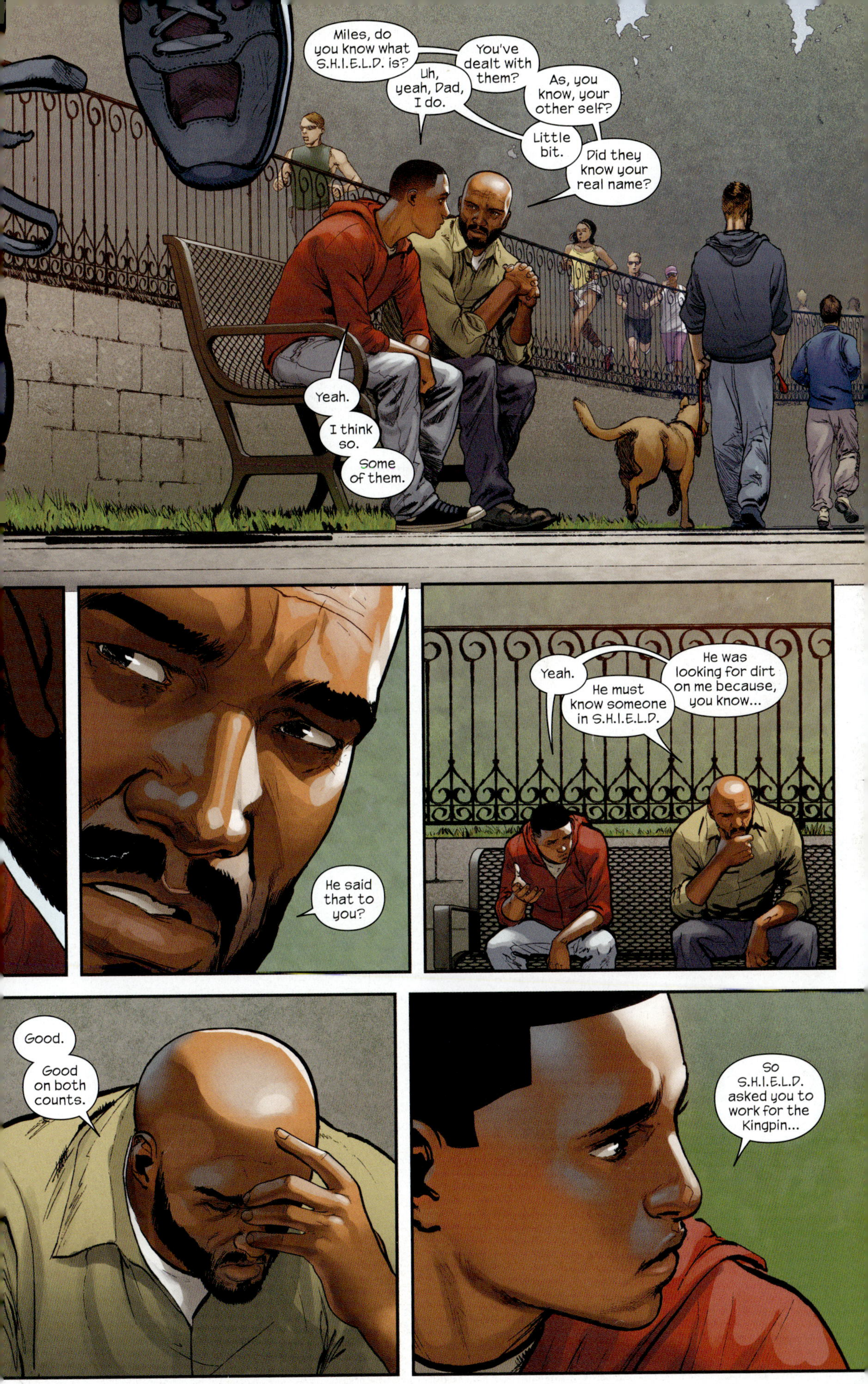
Miles, do you know what S.H.I.E.L.D. is?
Uh, yeah, Dad, I do.
You've dealt with them?
Little bit.
As, you know, your other self?
Did they know your real name?
Yeah.
I think so.
Some of them.
He said that to you?
Yeah.
He was looking for dirt on me because, you know...
He must know someone in S.H.I.E.L.D.
Good.
Good on both counts.
So S.H.I.E.L.D. asked you to work for the Kingpin...

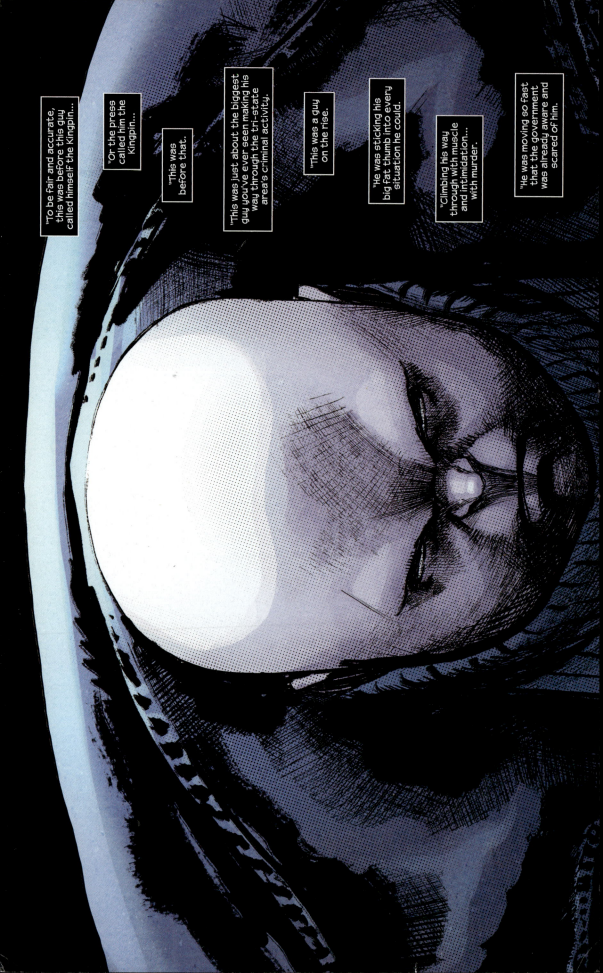

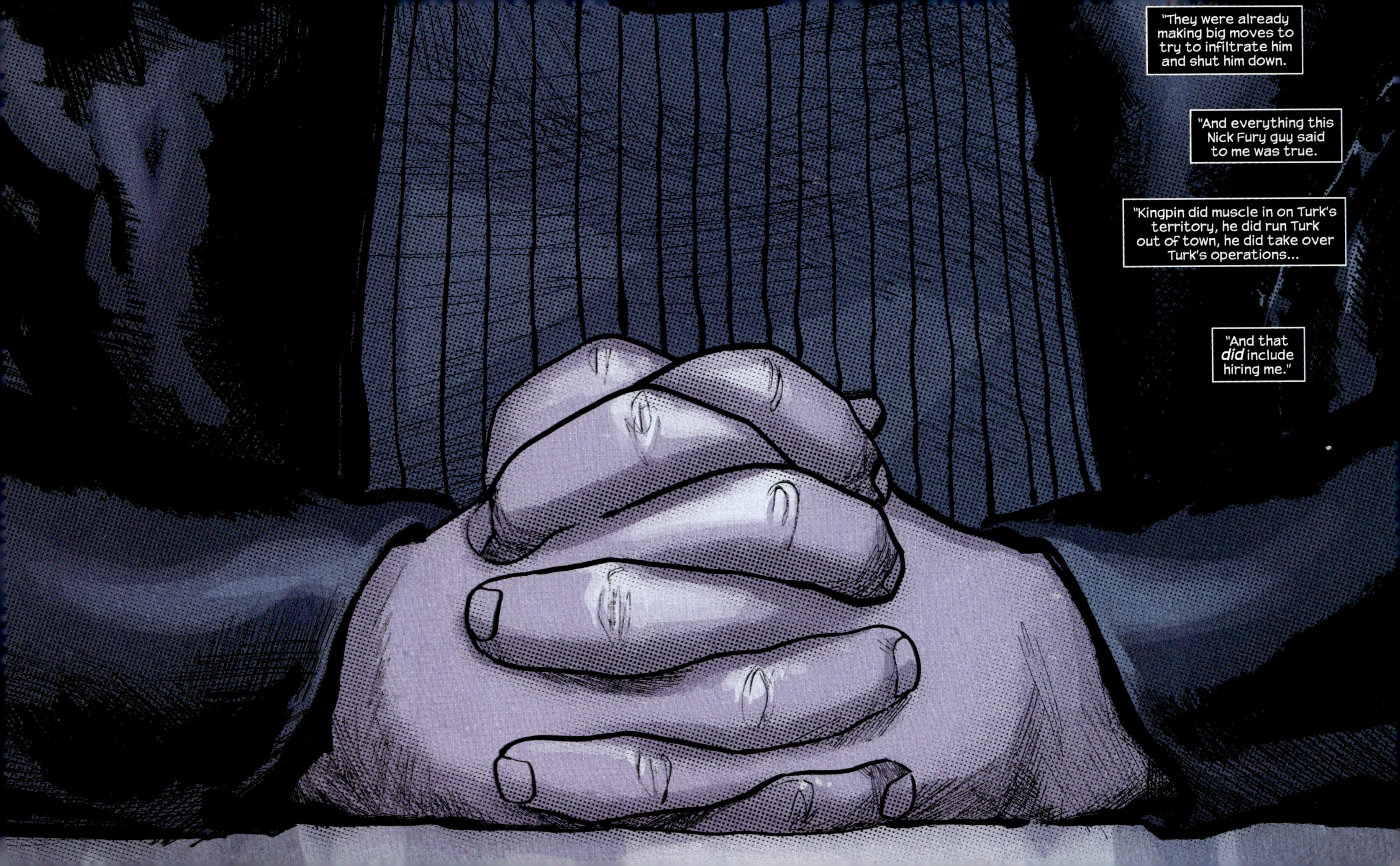
"They were already making big moves to try to infiltrate him and shut him down.
"And everything this Nick Fury guy said to me was true.
"Kingpin did muscle in on Turk's territory, he did run Turk out of town, he did take over Turk's operations...
"And that *did* include hiring me."

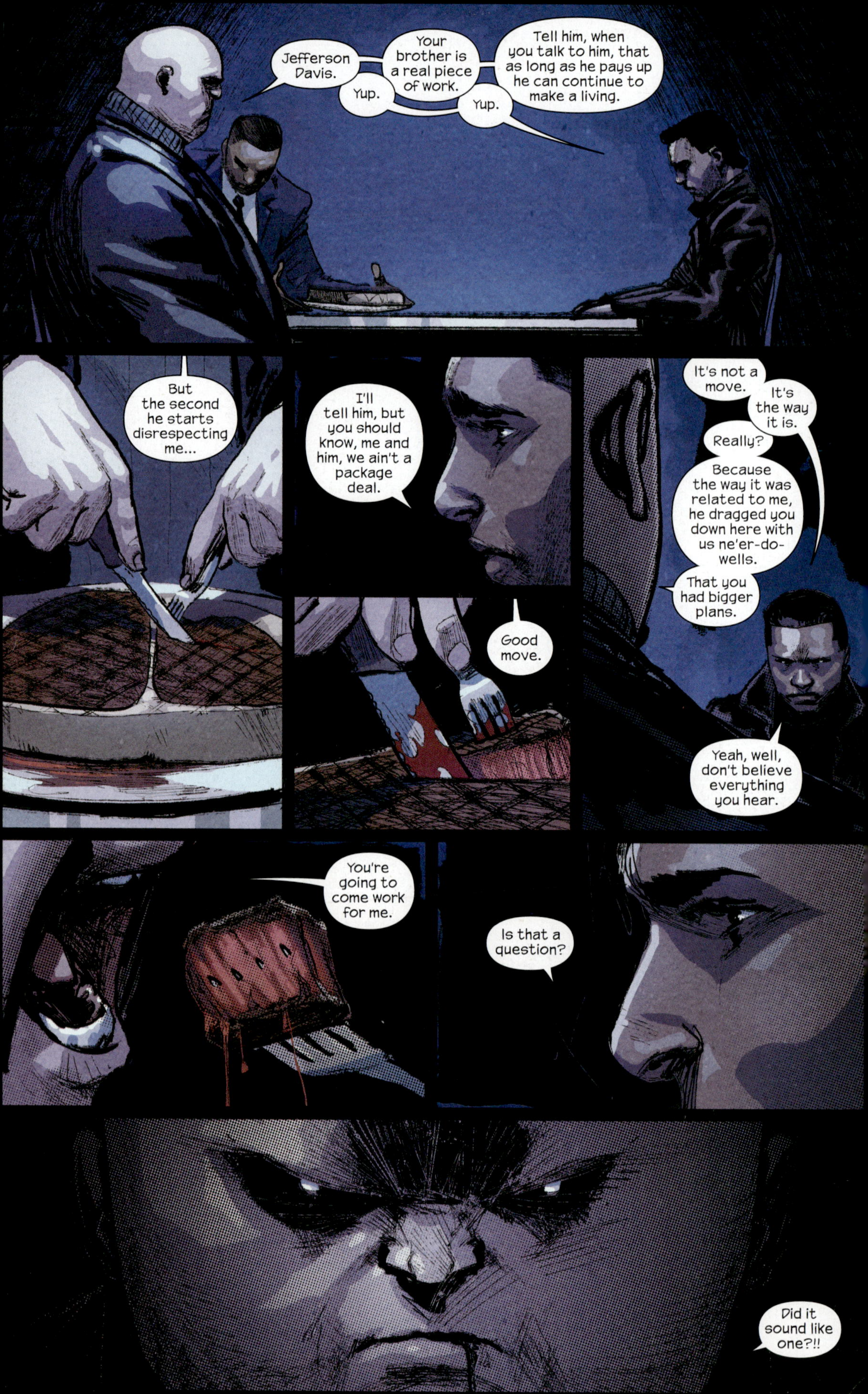
Jefferson Davis.
Your brother is a real piece of work.
Yup.
Tell him, when you talk to him, that as long as he pays up he can continue to make a living.
Yup.
But the second he starts disrespecting me...
I'll tell him, but you should know, me and him, we ain't a package deal.
Good move.
It's not a move.
It's the way it is.
Really?
Because the way it was related to me, he dragged you down here with us ne'er-do-wells.
That you had bigger plans.
Yeah, well, don't believe everything you hear.
You're going to come work for me.
Is that a question?
Did it sound like one?!!

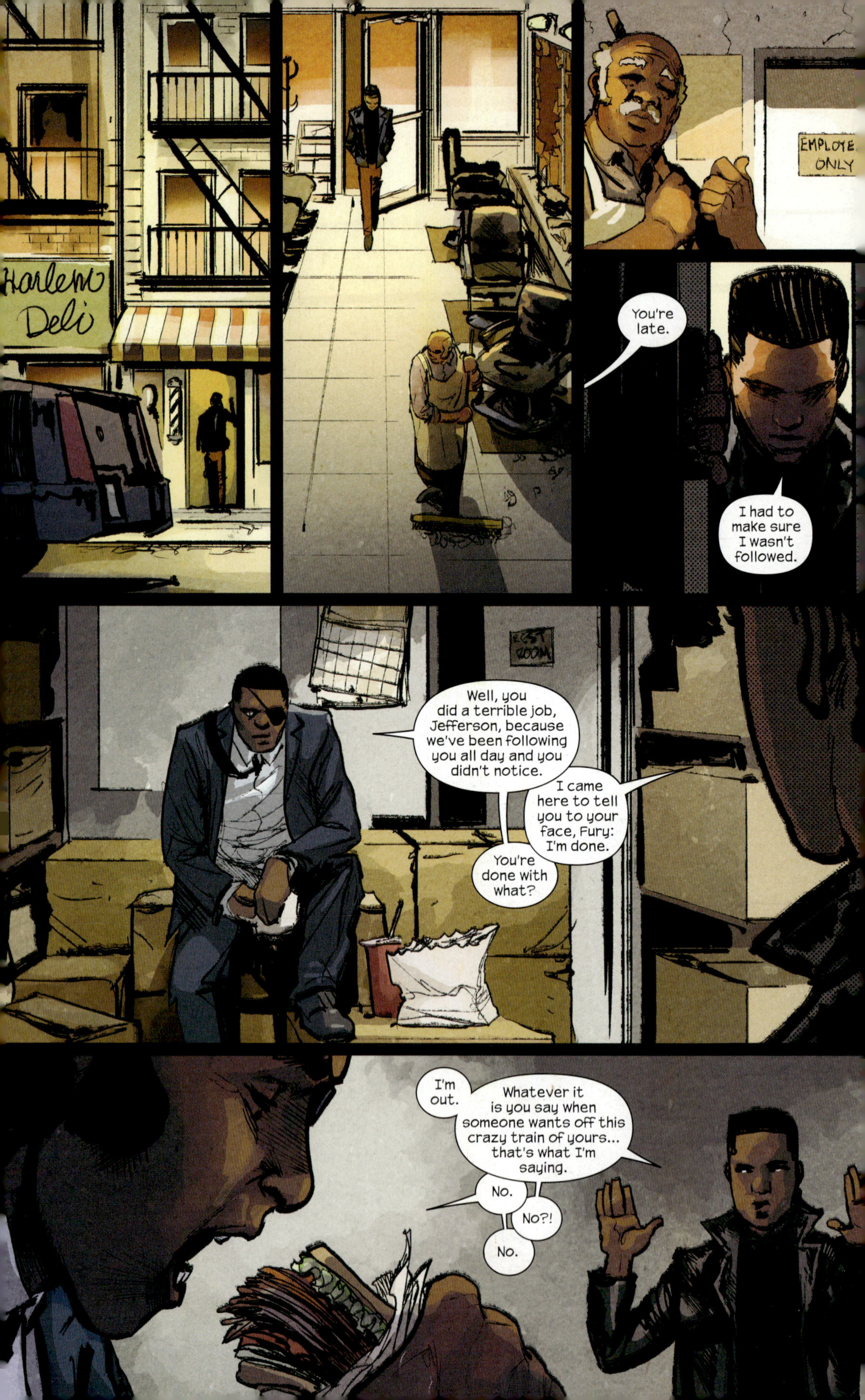
Harlem Deli
EMPLOYEE ONLY
You're late.
I had to make sure I wasn't followed.
REST ROOM
Well, you did a terrible job, Jefferson, because we've been following you all day and you didn't notice.
I came here to tell you to your face, Fury: I'm done.
You're done with what?
I'm out.
Whatever it is you say when someone wants off this crazy train of yours... that's what I'm saying.
No.
No?!
No.

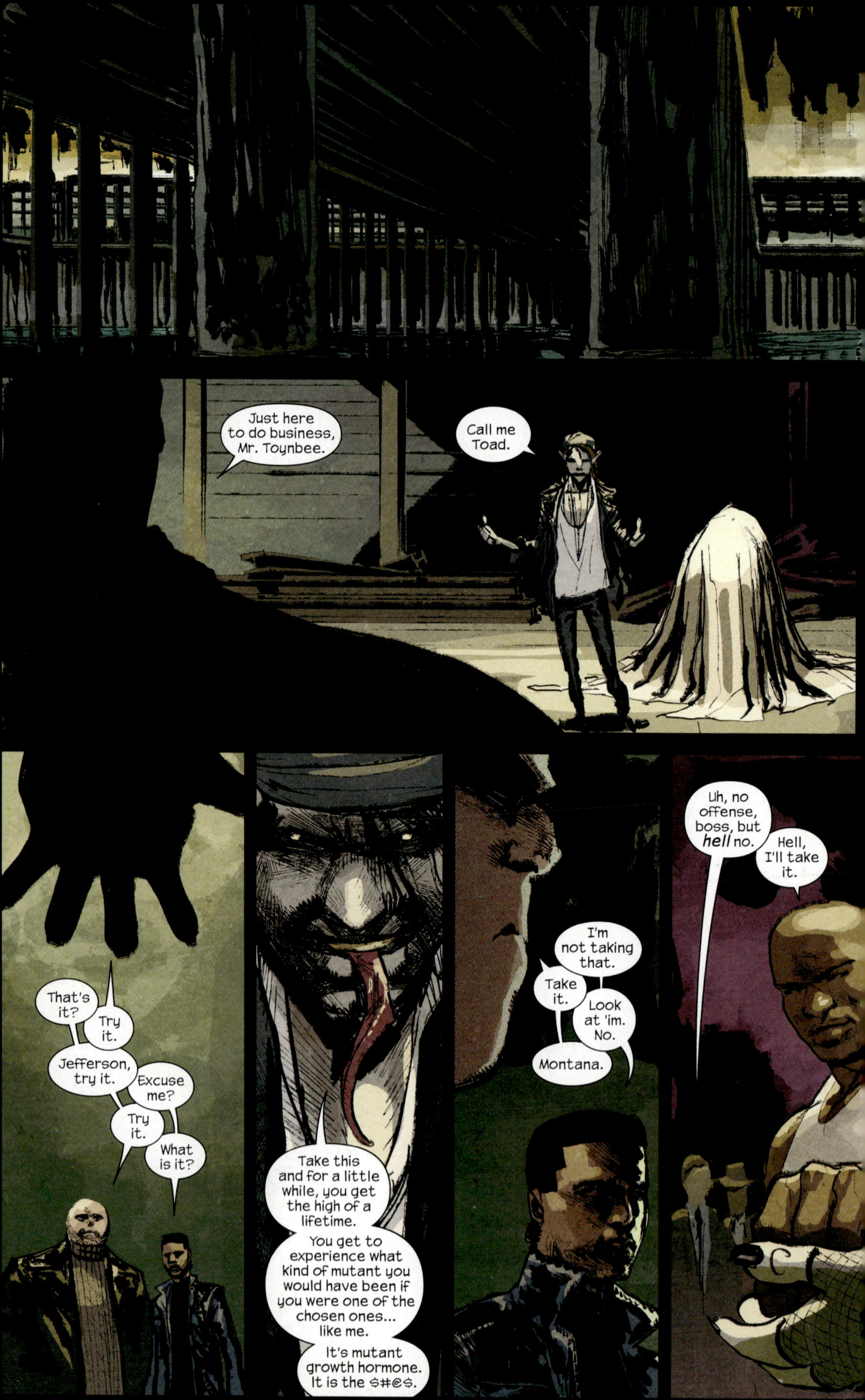
Just here to do business, Mr. Toynbee.
Call me Toad.
That's it?
Try it.
Jefferson, try it.
Excuse me?
Try it.
What is it?
Take this and for a little while, you get the high of a lifetime.
You get to experience what kind of mutant you would have been if you were one of the chosen ones... like me.
It's mutant growth hormone. It is the $#@$.
I'm not taking that.
Take it.
Look at 'im. No.
Montana.
Uh, no offense, boss, but *hell* no.
Hell, I'll take it.

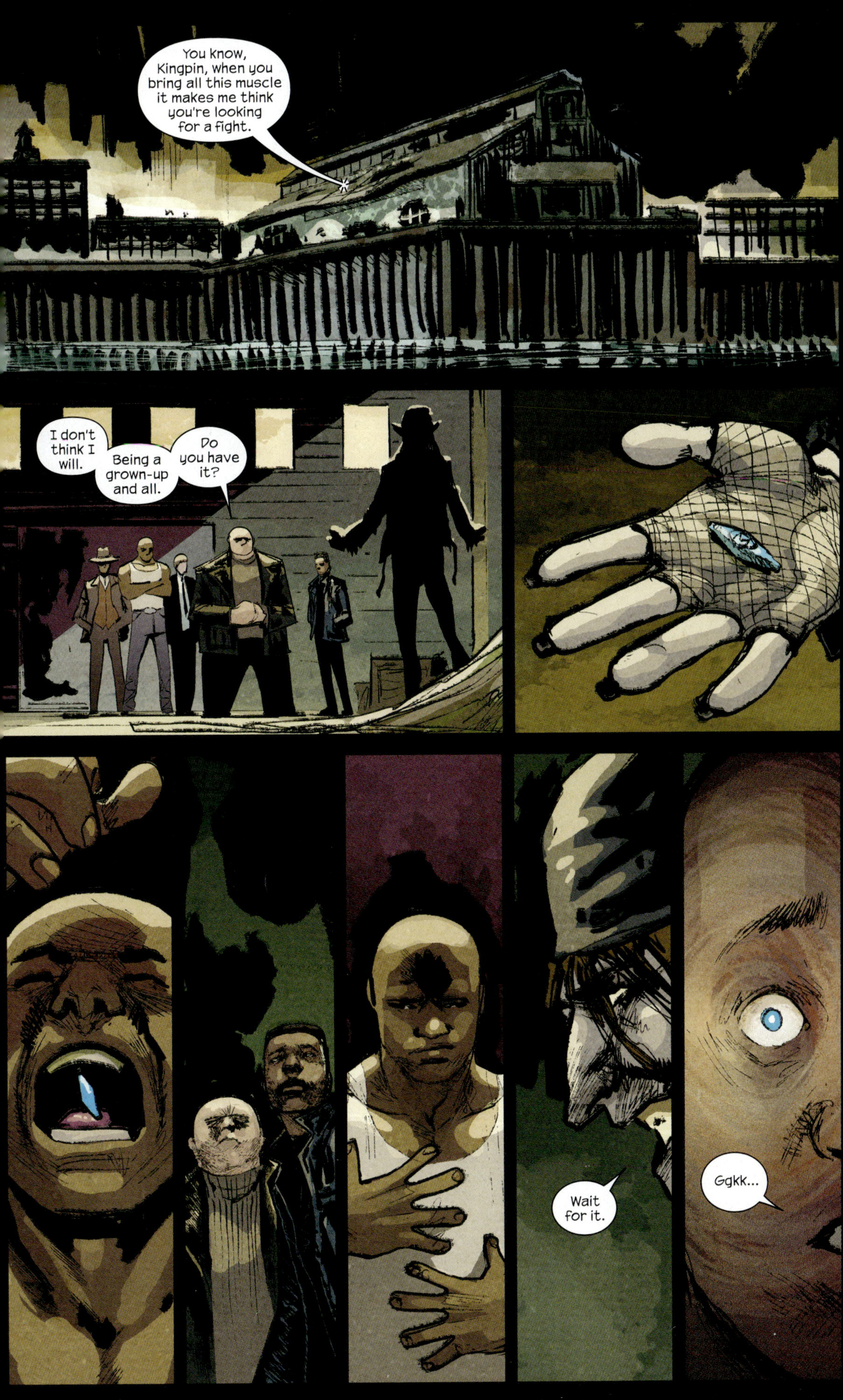
You know, Kingpin, when you bring all this muscle it makes me think you're looking for a fight.
I don't think I will.
Being a grown-up and all.
Do you have it?
Wait for it.
Ggkk...

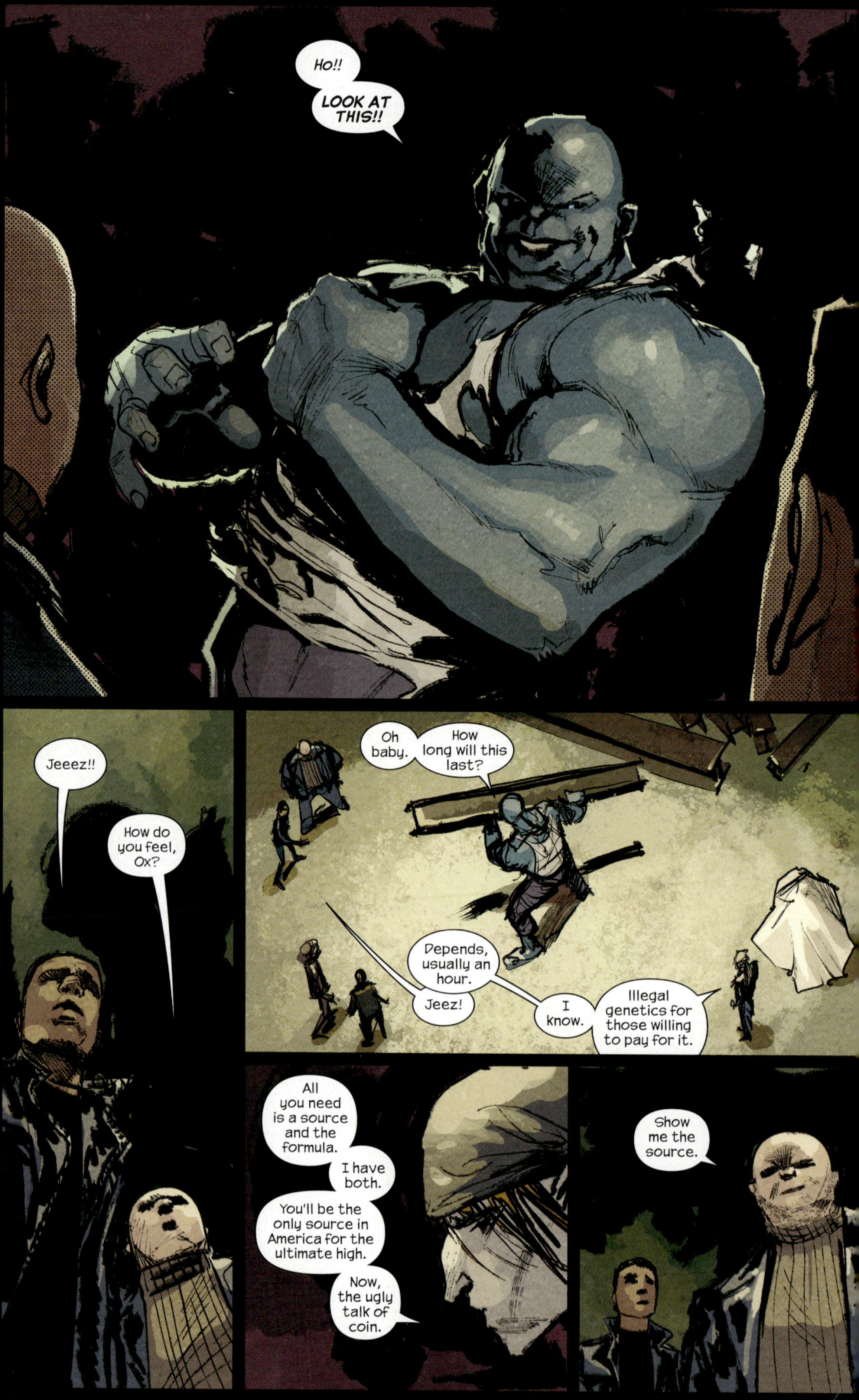
HO!!
LOOK AT THIS!!
Jeeez!!
How do you feel, Ox?
Oh baby.
How long will this last?
Depends, usually an hour.
Jeez!
I know.
Illegal genetics for those willing to pay for it.
All you need is a source and the formula.
I have both.
You'll be the only source in America for the ultimate high.
Now, the ugly talk of coin.
Show me the source.

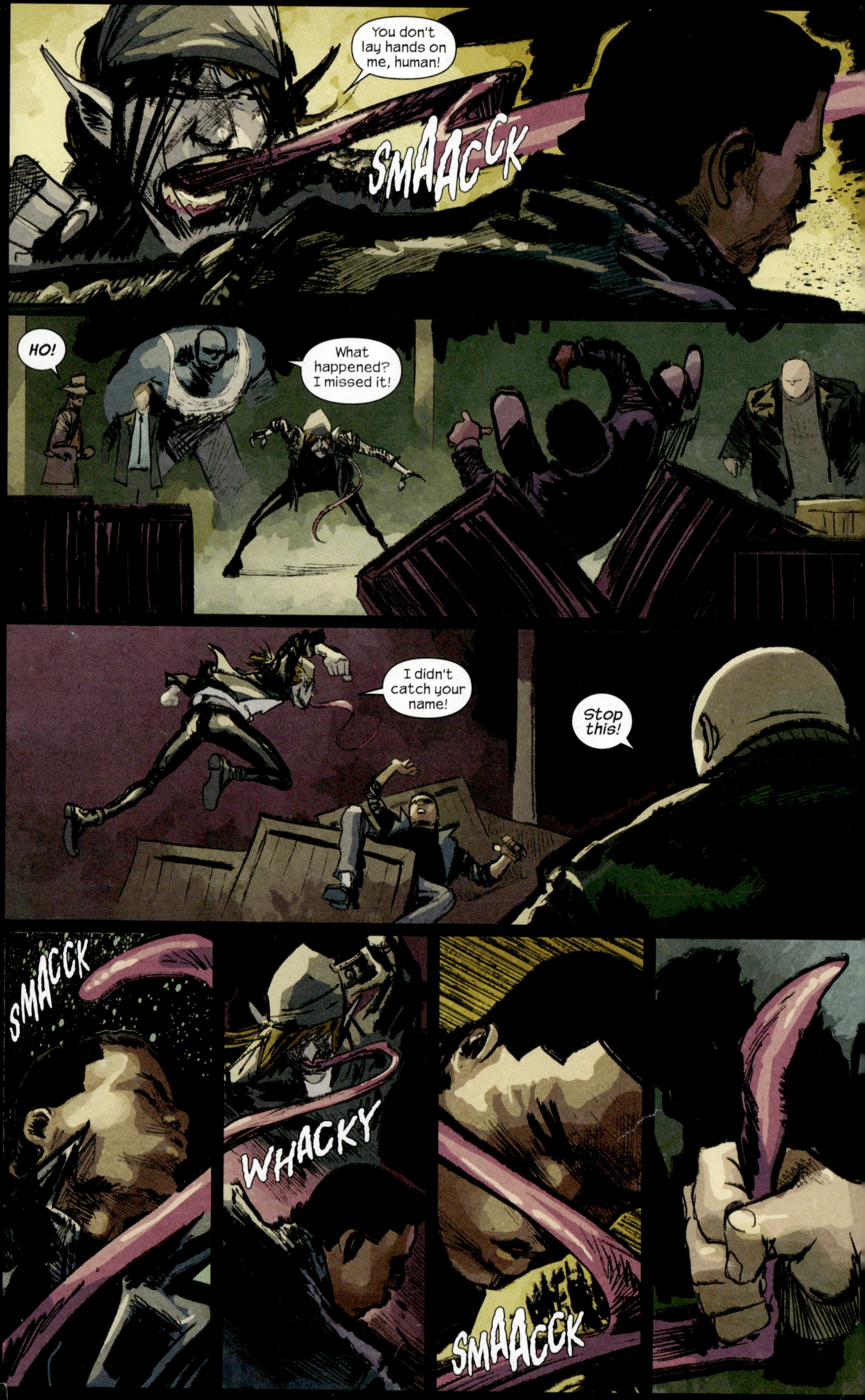
You don't lay hands on me, human!
SMAACCK
HO!
What happened? I missed it!
I didn't catch your name!
Stop this!
SMACCK
WHACKY
SMAACCK

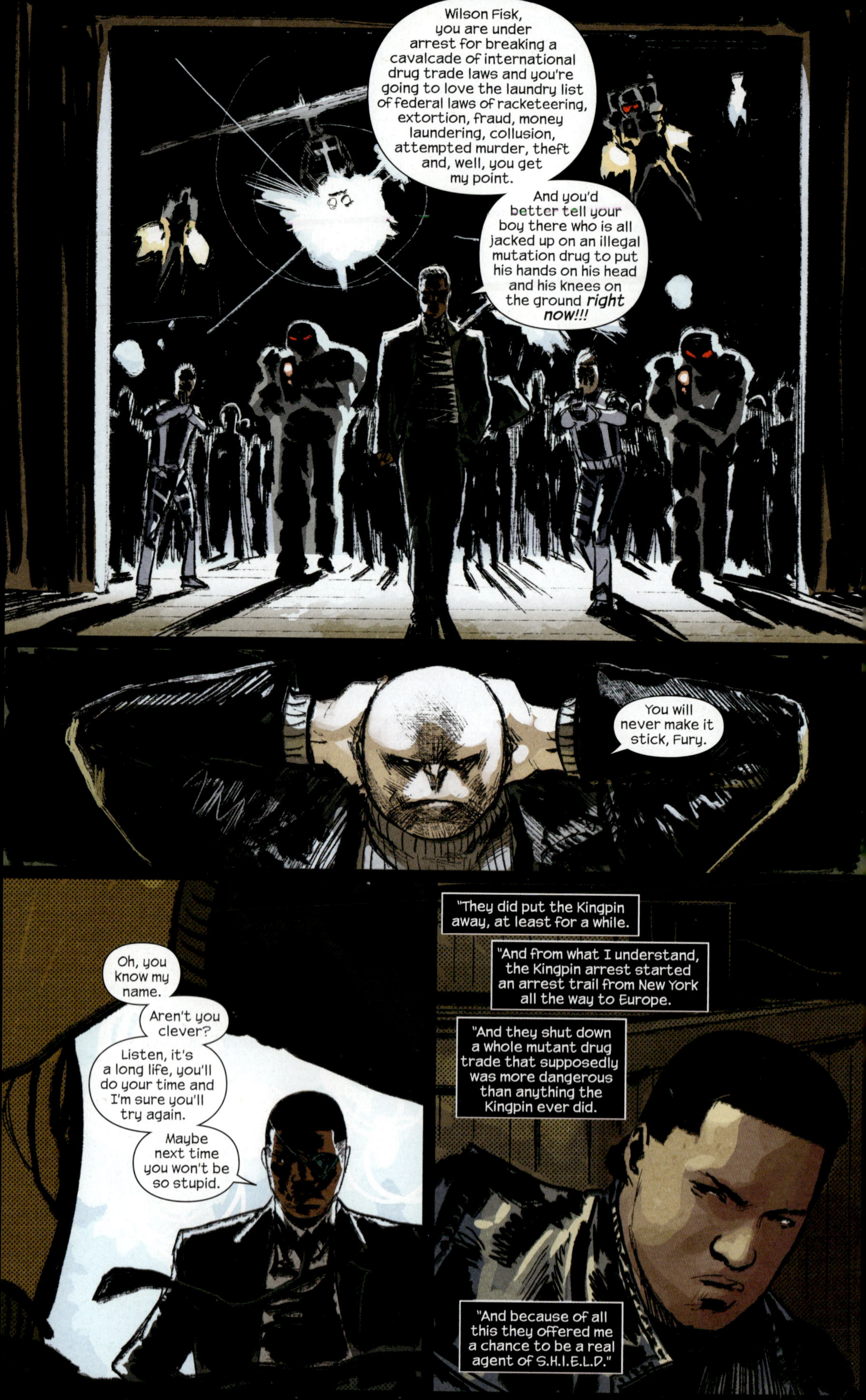

Wilson Fisk, you are under arrest for breaking a cavalcade of international drug trade laws and you're going to love the laundry list of federal laws of racketeering, extortion, fraud, money laundering, collusion, attempted murder, theft and, well, you get my point.
And you'd better tell your boy there who is all jacked up on an illegal mutation drug to put his hands on his head and his knees on the ground *right now!!!*
You will never make it stick, Fury.
Oh, you know my name.
Aren't you clever?
Listen, it's a long life, you'll do your time and I'm sure you'll try again.
Maybe next time you won't be so stupid.
"They did put the Kingpin away, at least for a while.
"And from what I understand, the Kingpin arrest started an arrest trail from New York all the way to Europe.
"And they shut down a whole mutant drug trade that supposedly was more dangerous than anything the Kingpin ever did.
"And because of all this they offered me a chance to be a real agent of S.H.I.E.L.D."

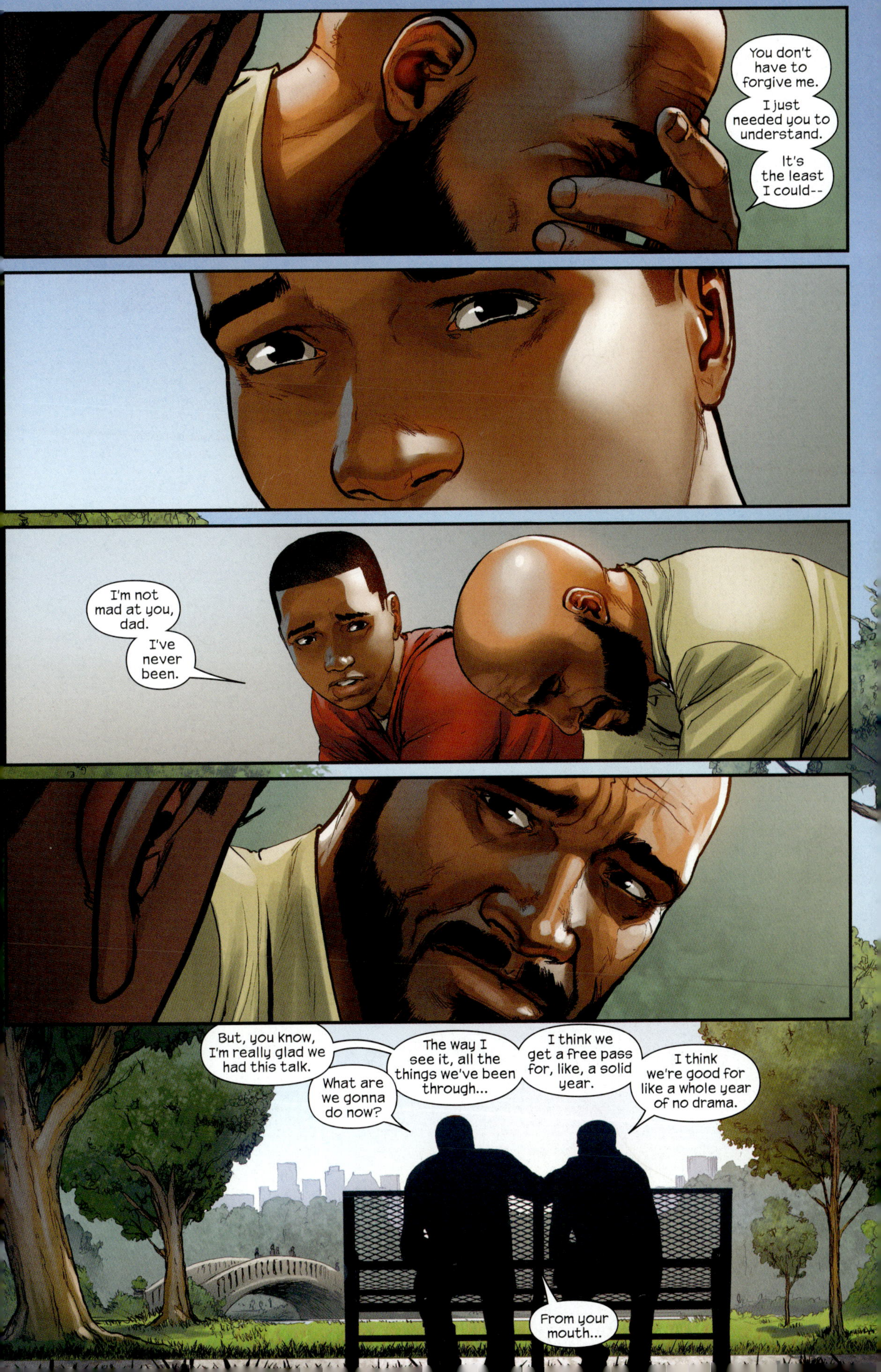

You don't have to forgive me.
I just needed you to understand.
It's the least I could--
I'm not mad at you, dad.
I've never been.
But, you know, I'm really glad we had this talk.
What are we gonna do now?
The way I see it, all the things we've been through...
I think we get a free pass for, like, a solid year.
I think we're good for like a whole year of no drama.
From your mouth...

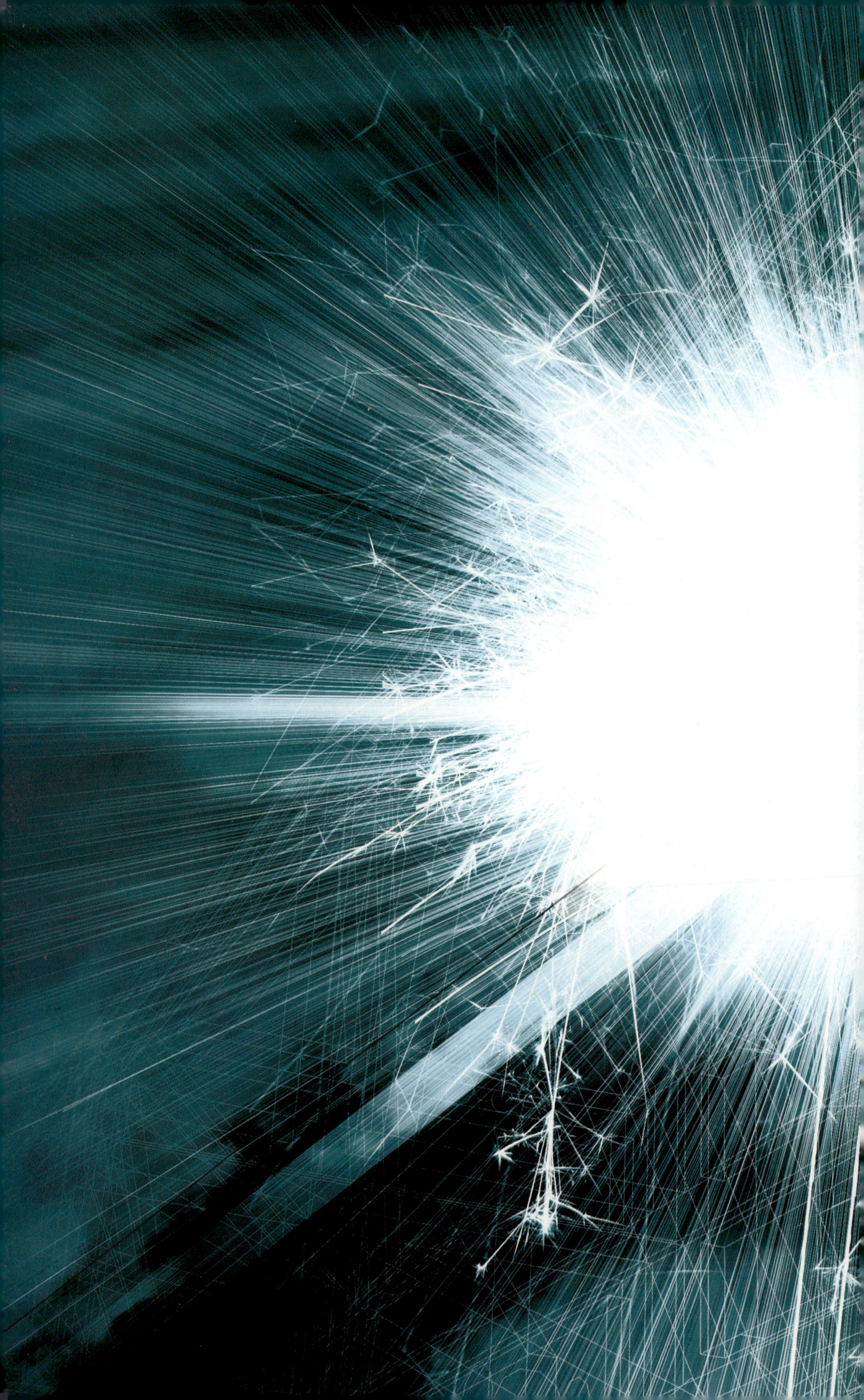

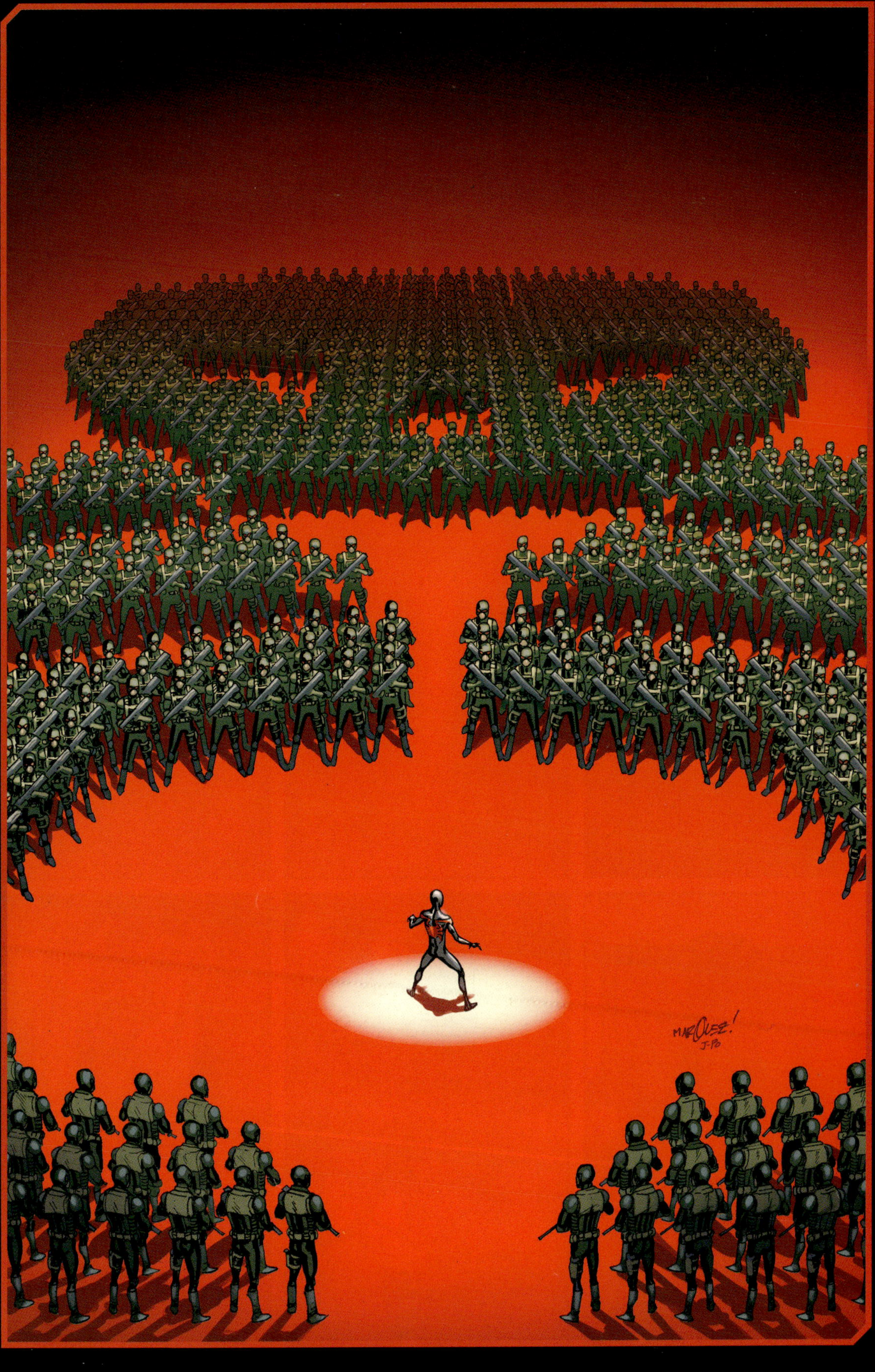
MARQUEZ!
J-Bo

MILES MORALES: ULTIMATE SPIDER-MAN #10

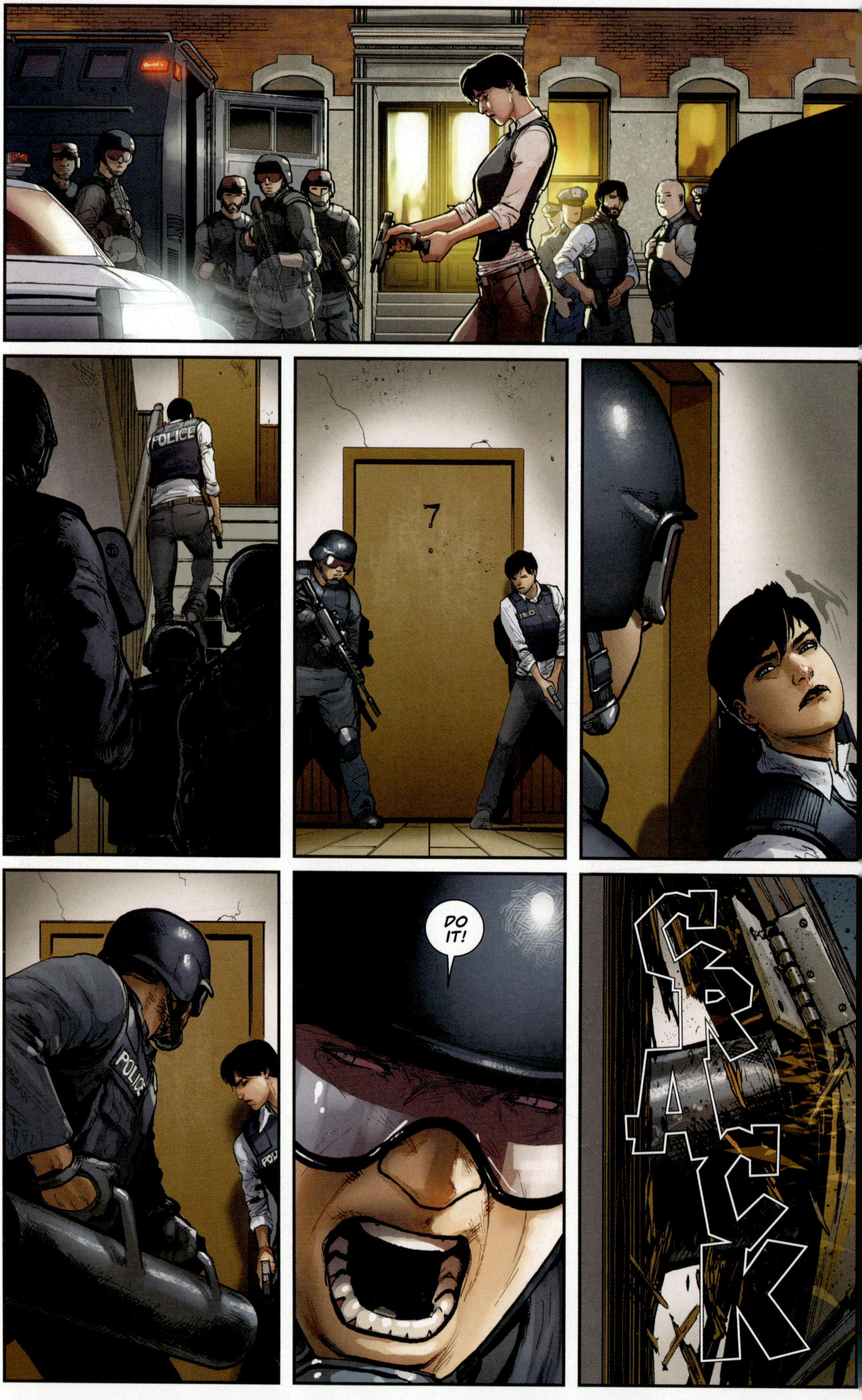
POLICE
DO IT!
POLICE
CRACK

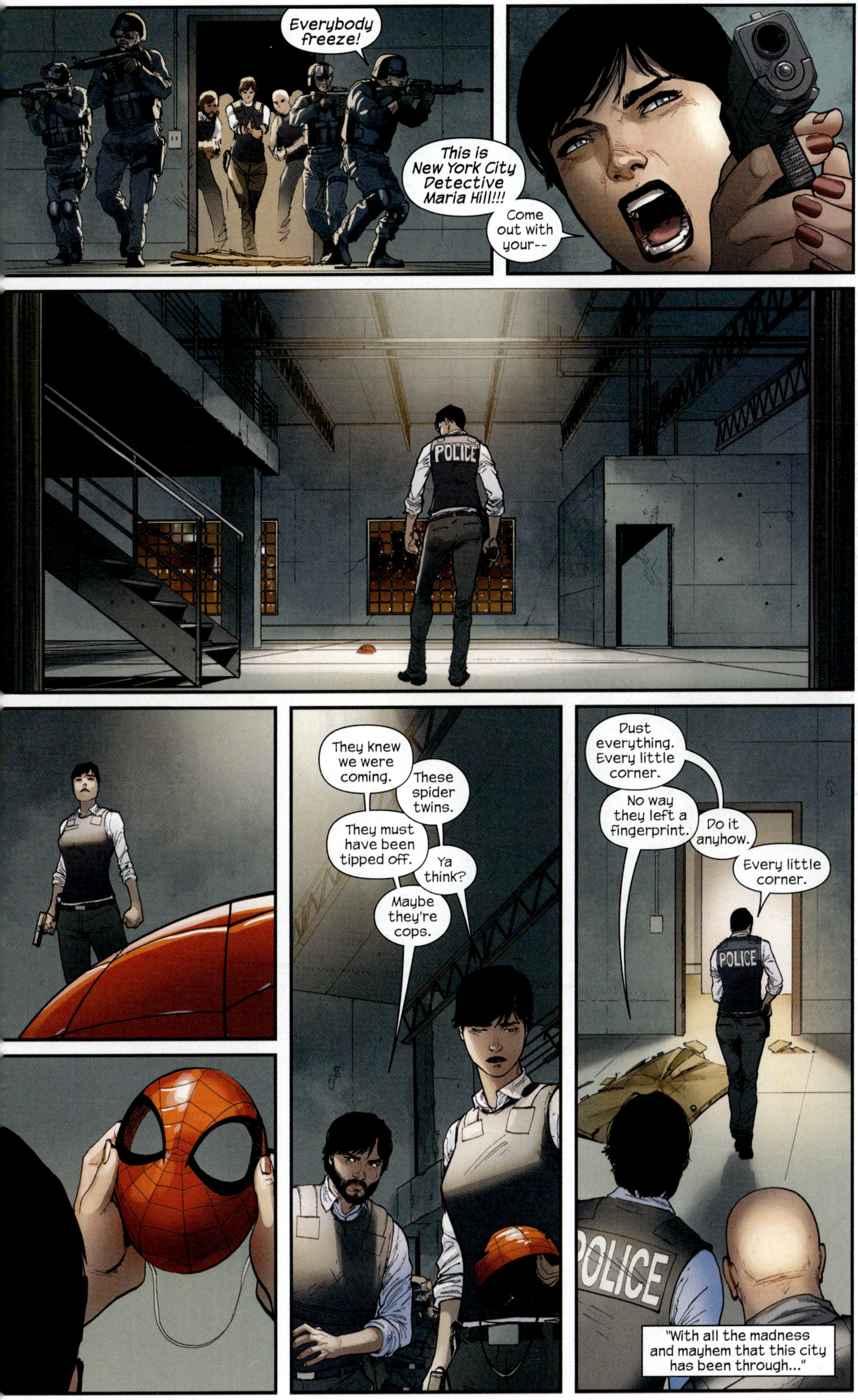
Everybody freeze!
This is New York City Detective Maria Hill!!!
Come out with your--
They knew we were coming.
These spider twins.
They must have been tipped off.
Ya think?
Maybe they're cops.
Dust everything. Every little corner.
No way they left a fingerprint.
Do it anyhow.
Every little corner.
POLICE
"With all the madness and mayhem that this city has been through..."

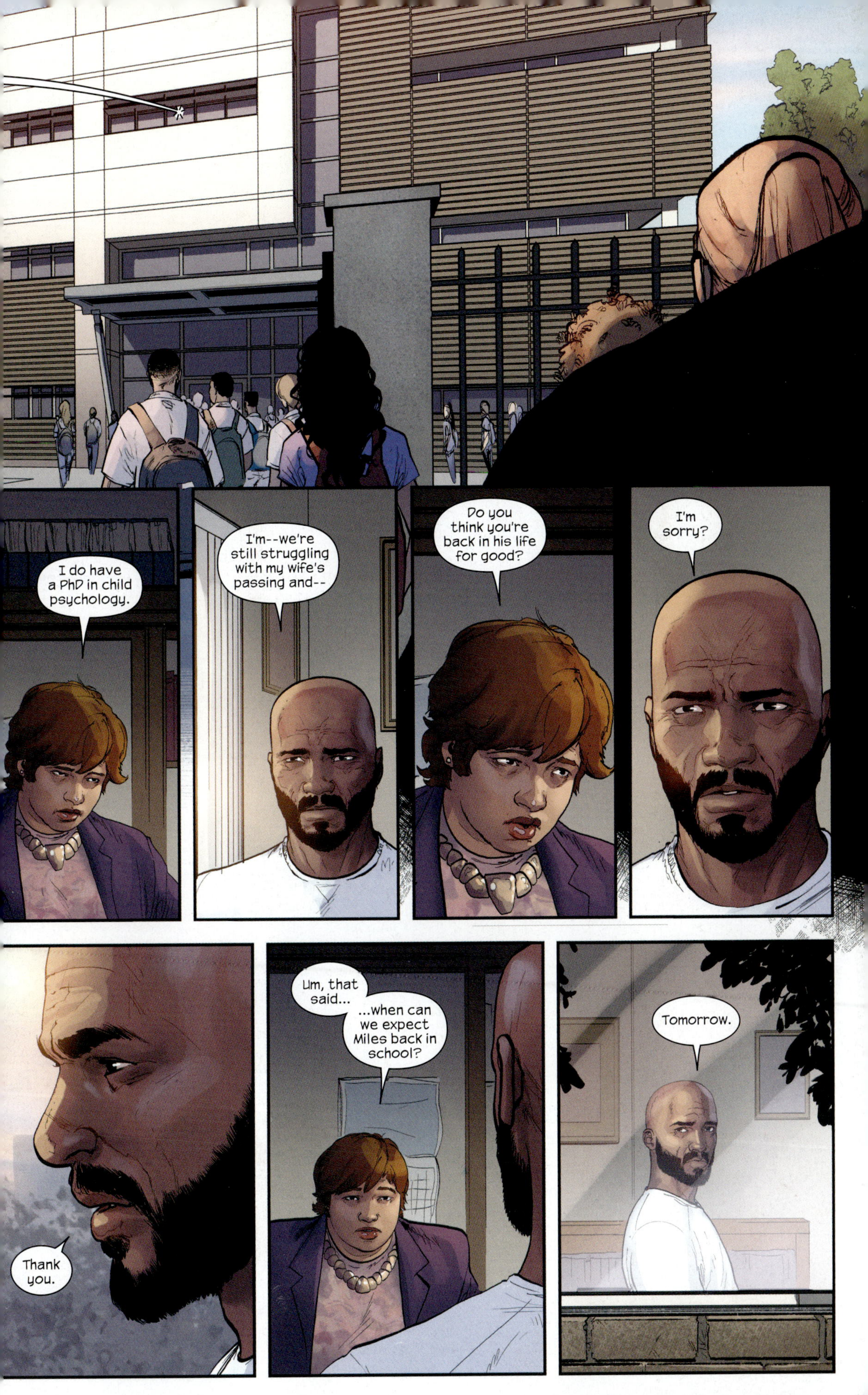
I do have a PhD in child psychology.
I'm--we're still struggling with my wife's passing and--
Do you think you're back in his life for good?
I'm sorry?
Thank you.
Um, that said...
...when can we expect Miles back in school?
Tomorrow.

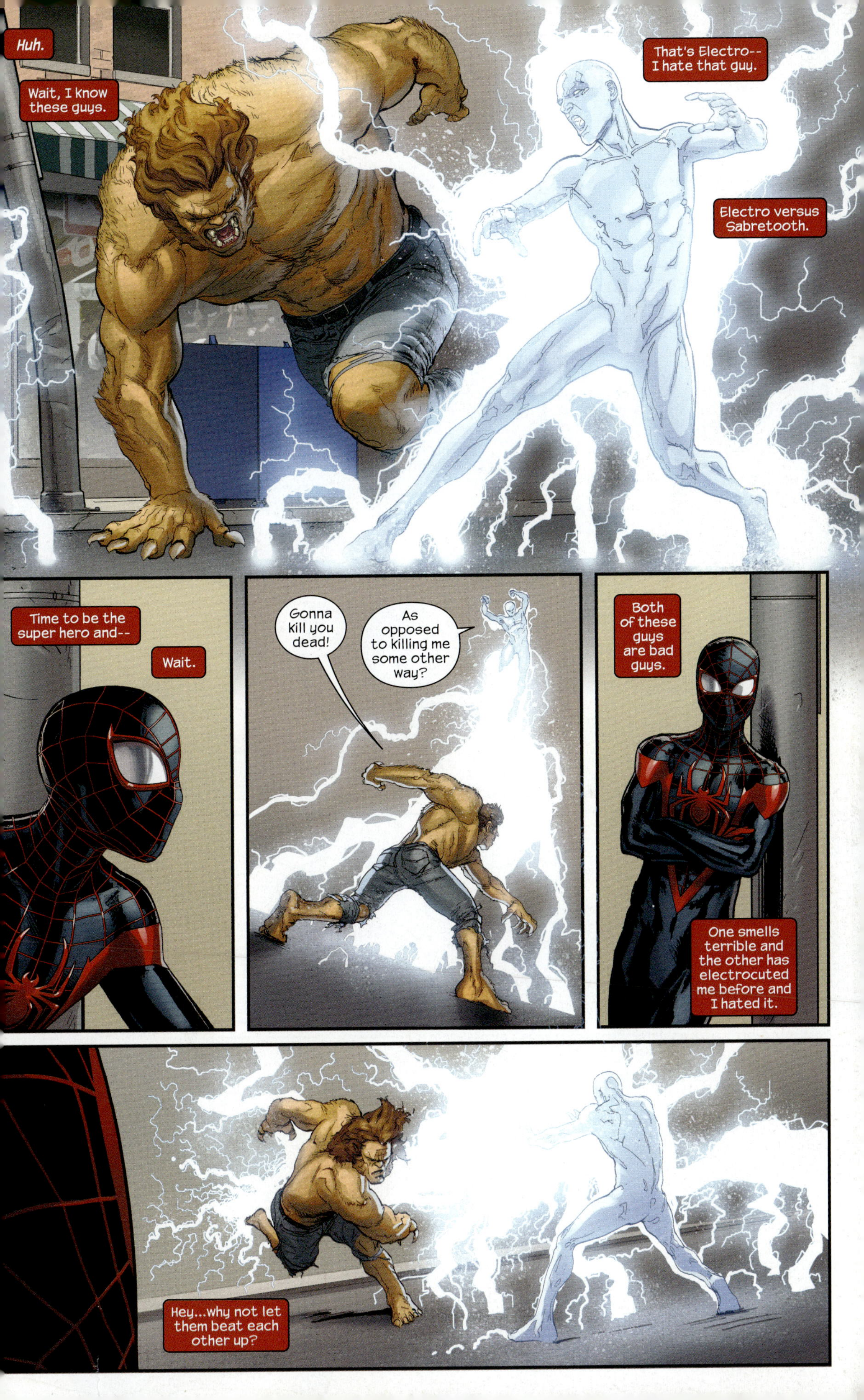

Huh.
Wait, I know these guys.
That's Electro-- I hate that guy.
Electro versus Sabretooth.
Time to be the super hero and--
Wait.
Gonna kill you dead!
As opposed to killing me some other way?
Both of these guys are bad guys.
One smells terrible and the other has electrocuted me before and I hated it.
Hey...why not let them beat each other up?

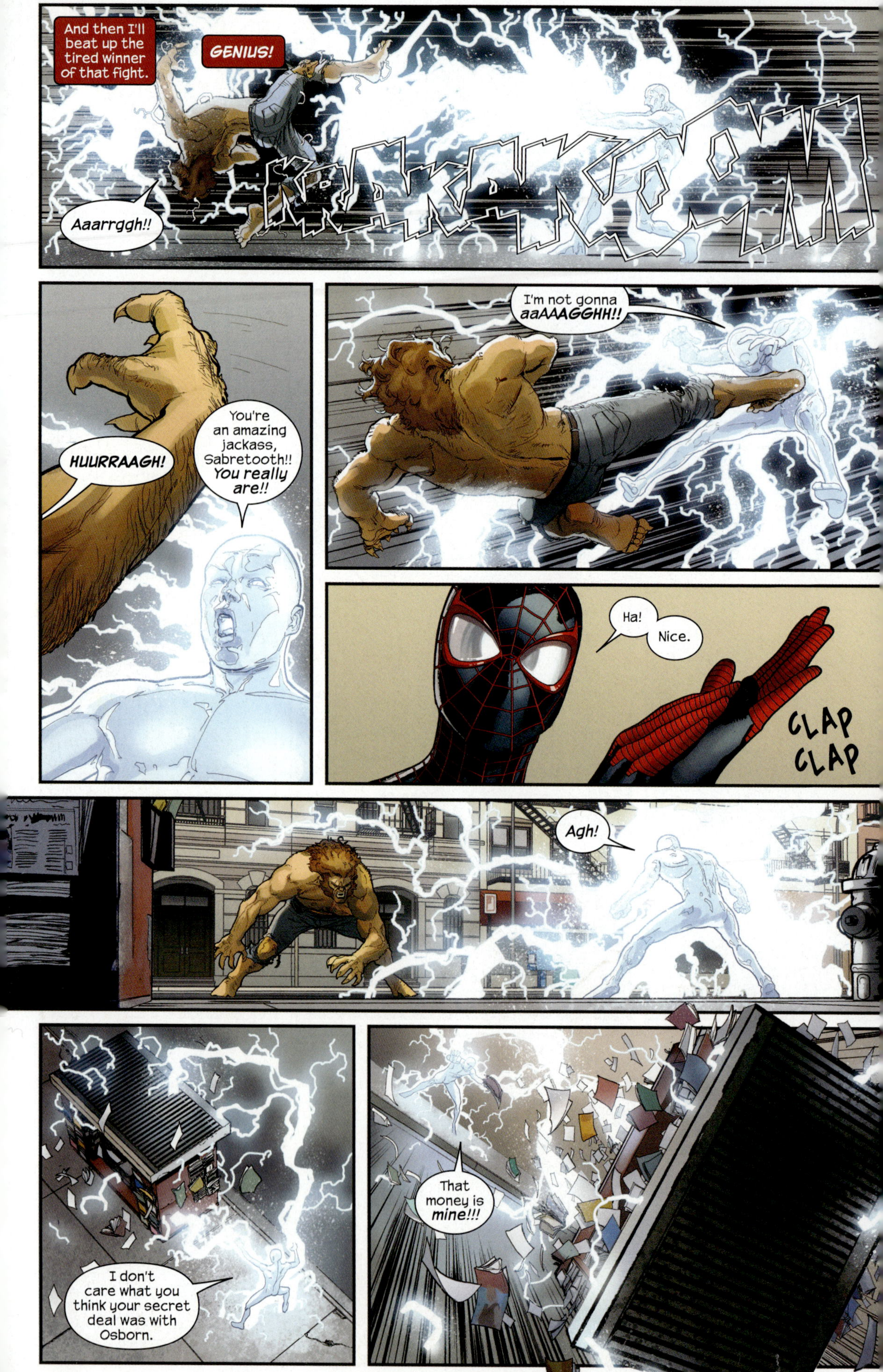
And then I'll beat up the tired winner of that fight.
GENIUS!
Aaarrggh!!
KRAKAKOOM
HUURRAAGH!
You're an amazing jackass, Sabretooth!! You really are!!
I'm not gonna aaAAAAGGHH!!
Ha!
Nice.
CLAP CLAP
Agh!
I don't care what you think your secret deal was with Osborn.
That money is mine!!!

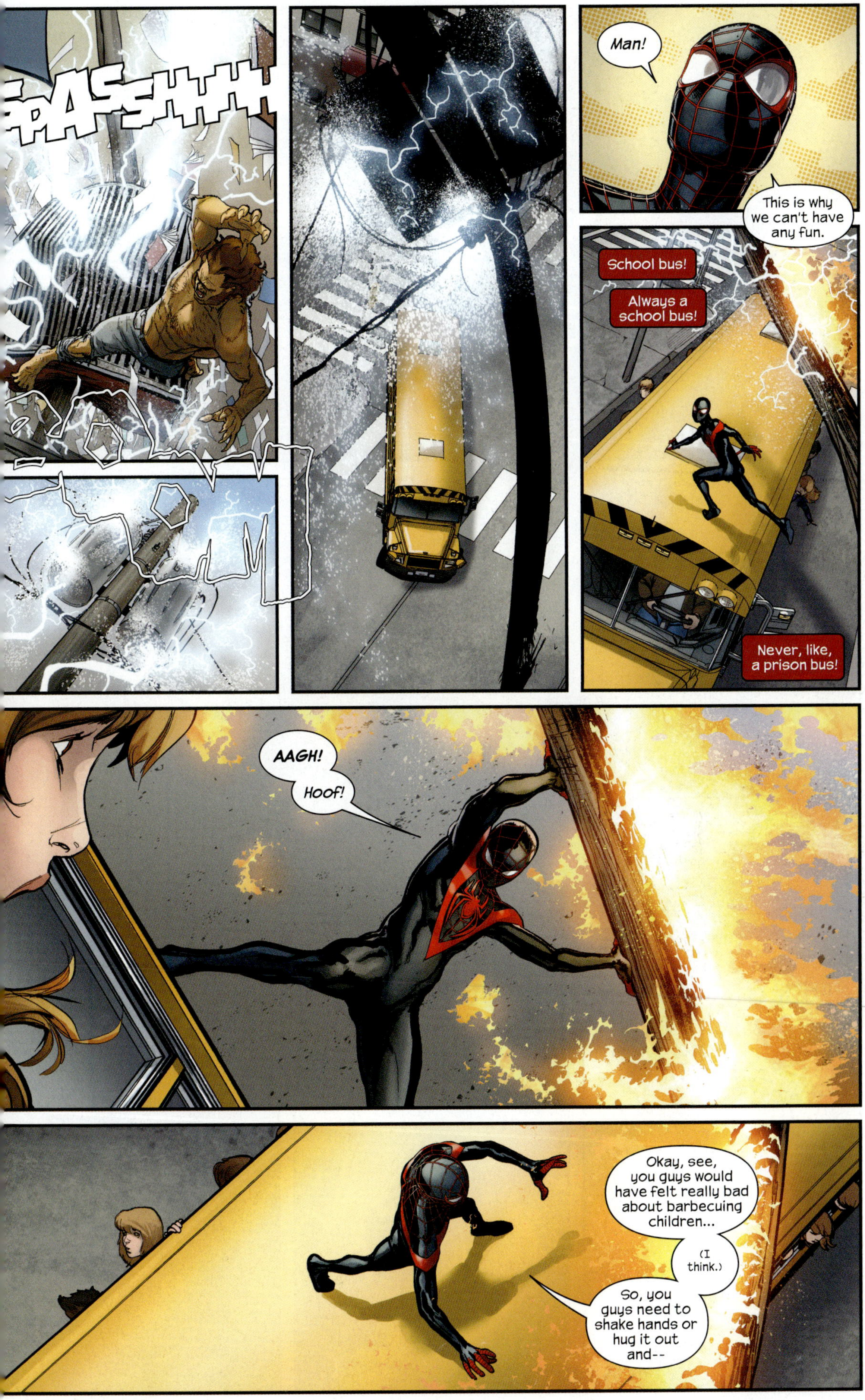
Man!
This is why we can't have any fun.
School bus!
Always a school bus!
Never, like, a prison bus!
AAGH!
HOOF!
Okay, see, you guys would have felt really bad about barbecuing children...
(I think.)
So, you guys need to shake hands or hug it out and--

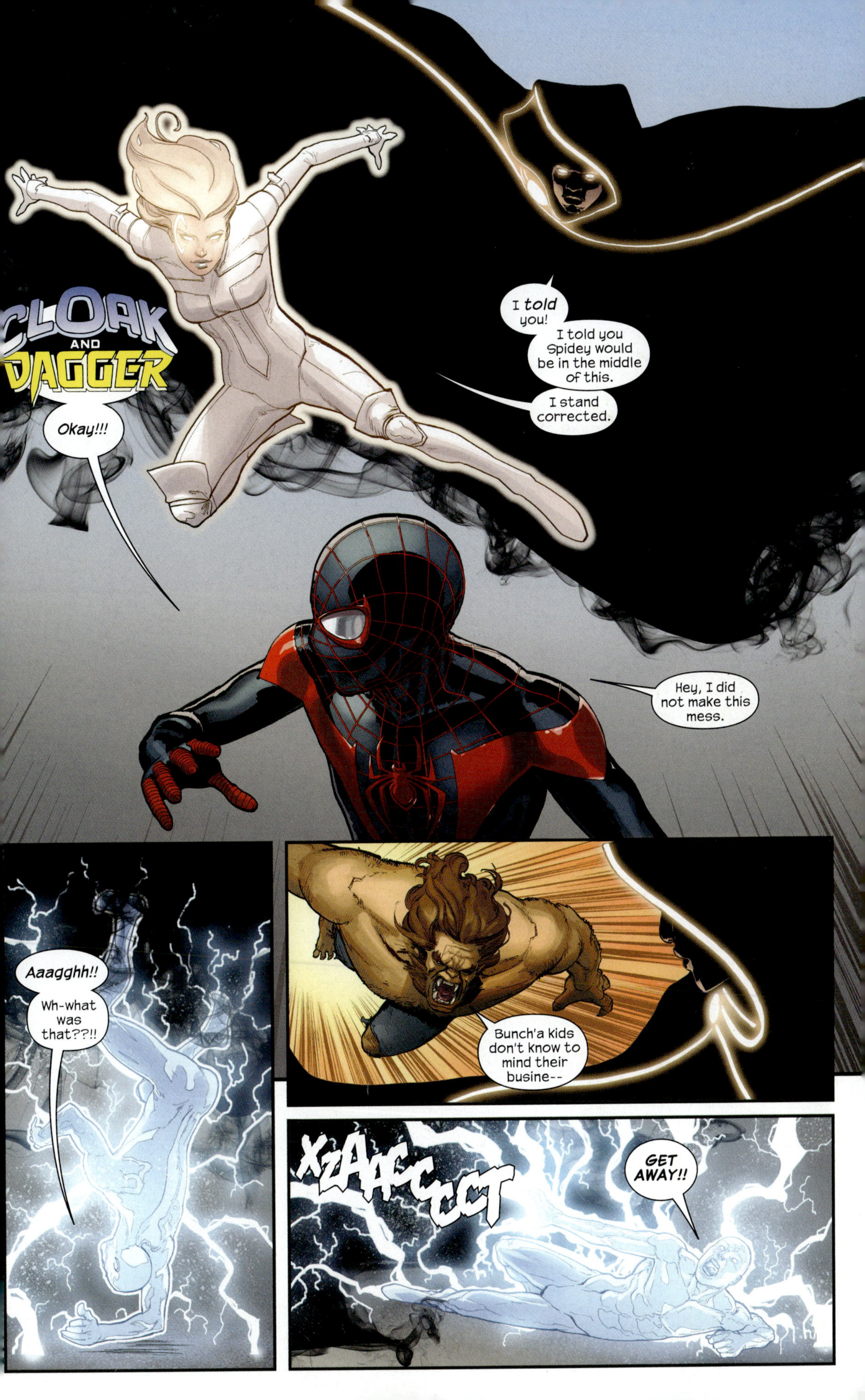
CLOAK AND DAGGER
I *told* you!
I told you Spidey would be in the middle of this.
I stand corrected.
Okay!!!
Hey, I did not make this mess.
Aaagghh!!
Wh-what was that??!!
Bunch'a kids don't know to mind their busine--
XZAACCCCT
GET AWAY!!

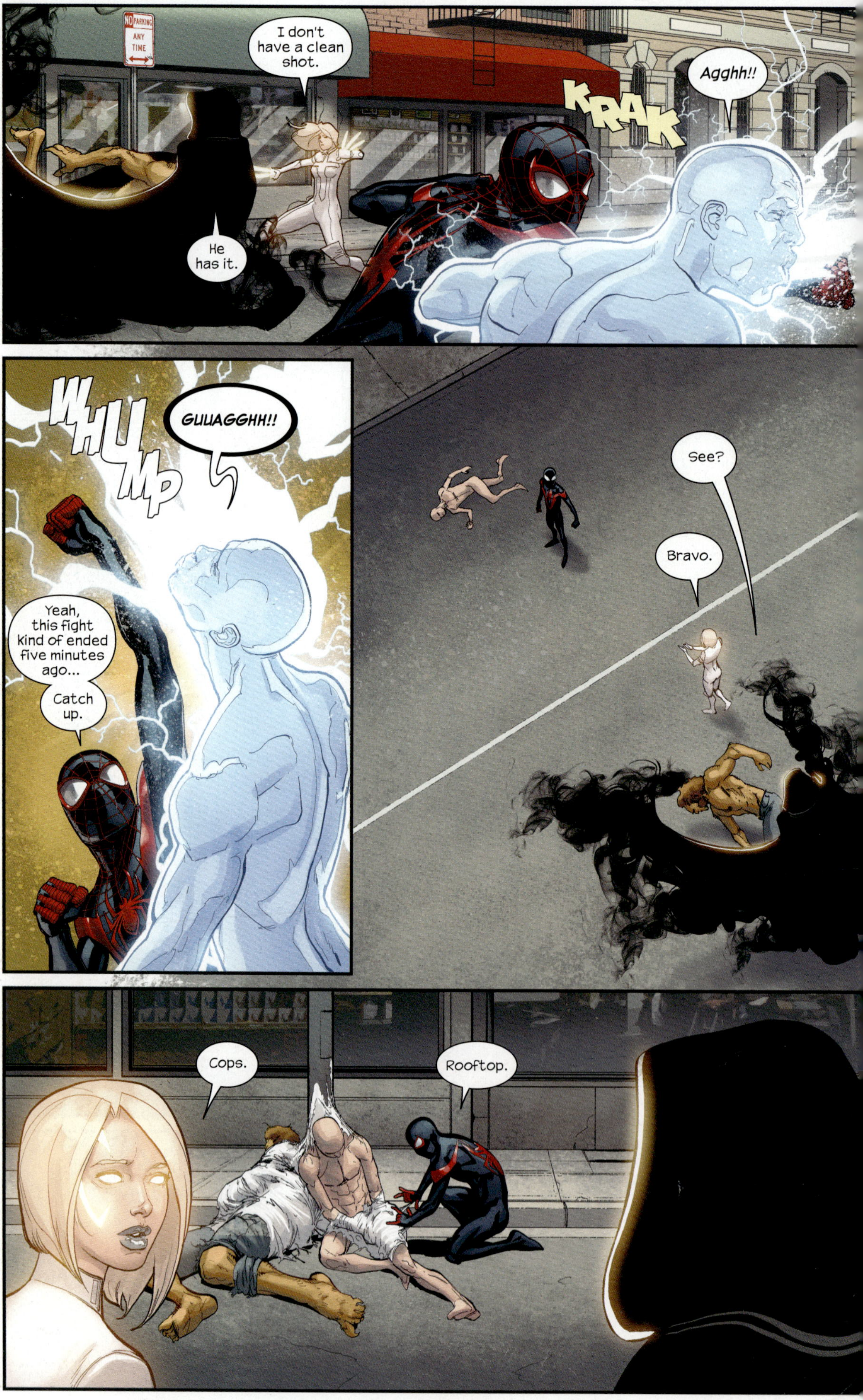
NO PARKING ANY TIME
I don't have a clean shot.
He has it.
KRAK
Agghh!!
WHUMP
GUUAGGHH!!
Yeah, this fight kind of ended five minutes ago...
Catch up.
See?
Bravo.
Cops.
Rooftop.

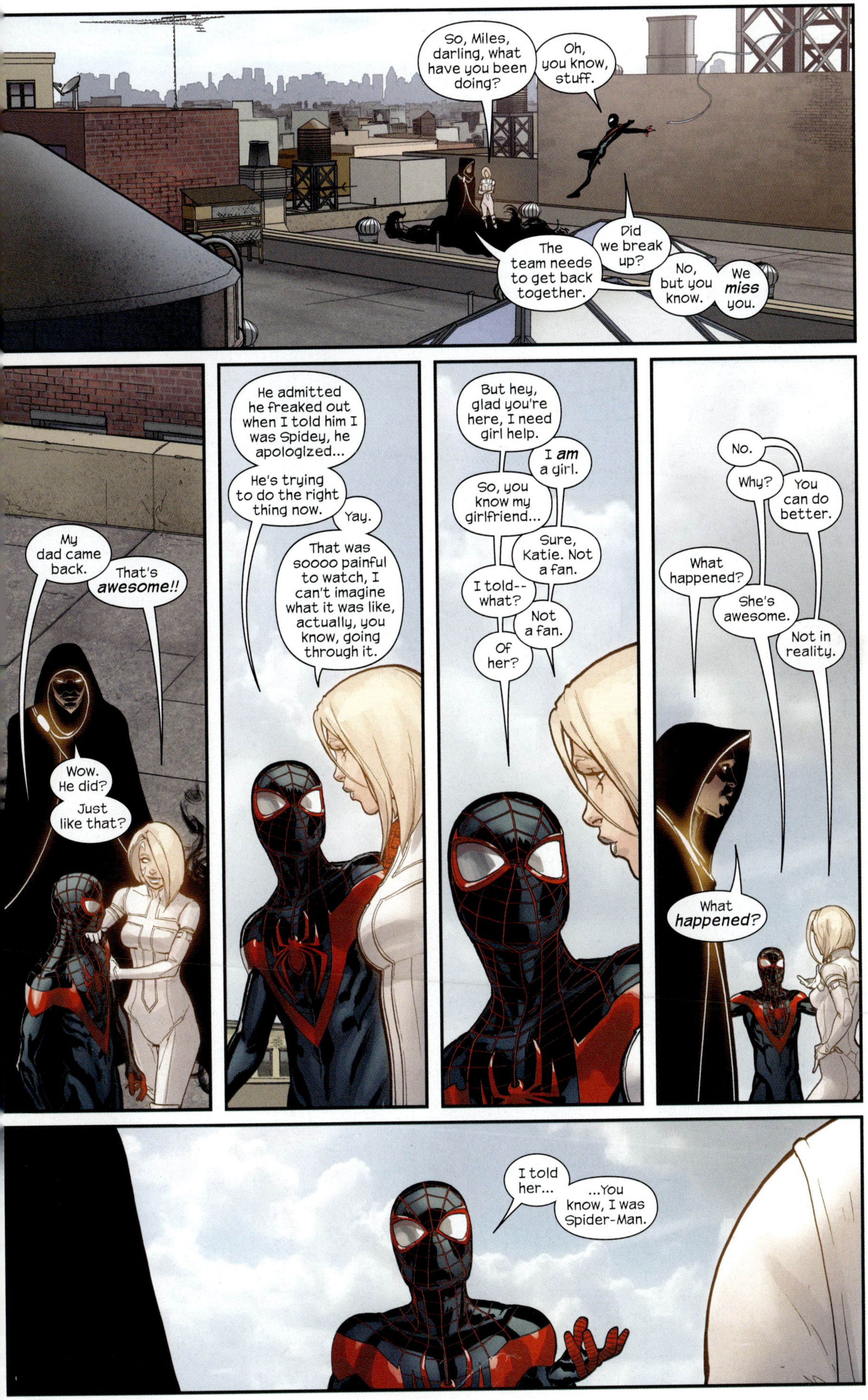

So, Miles, darling, what have you been doing?
Oh, you know, stuff.
Did we break up?
The team needs to get back together.
No, but you know.
We *miss* you.
My dad came back.
That's *awesome!!*
Wow. He did?
Just like that?
He admitted he freaked out when I told him I was Spidey, he apologized...
He's trying to do the right thing now.
Yay.
That was soooo painful to watch, I can't imagine what it was like, actually, you know, going through it.
But hey, glad you're here, I need girl help.
I *am* a girl.
So, you know my girlfriend...
Sure, Katie. Not a fan.
I told-- what?
Not a fan.
Of her?
No.
Why?
You can do better.
What happened?
She's awesome.
Not in reality.
What *happened?*
I told her...
...You know, I was Spider-Man.

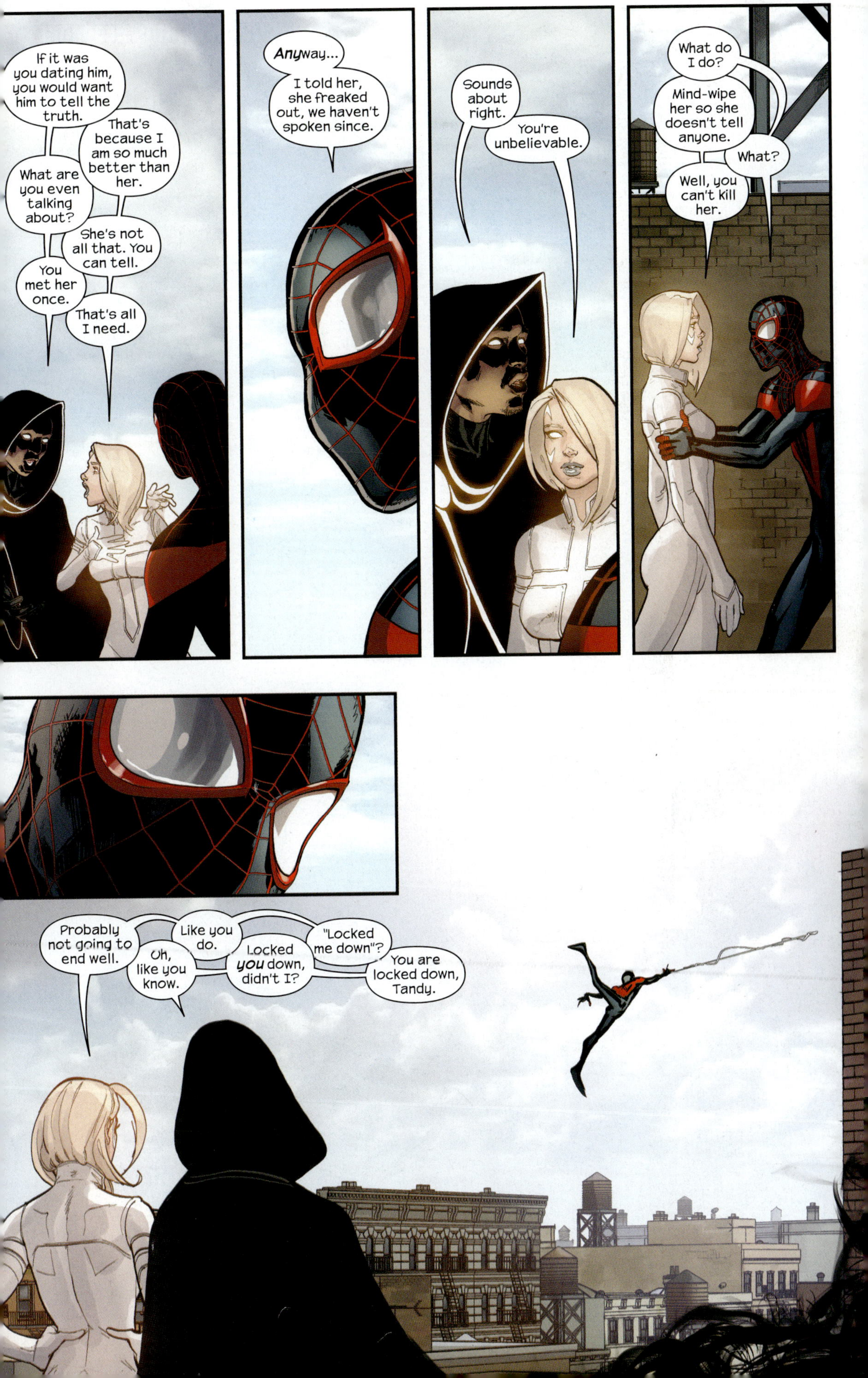

If it was you dating him, you would want him to tell the truth.
That's because I am so much better than her.
What are you even talking about?
She's not all that. You can tell.
You met her once.
That's all I need.
*Any*way...
I told her, she freaked out, we haven't spoken since.
Sounds about right.
You're unbelievable.
What do I do?
Mind-wipe her so she doesn't tell anyone.
What?
Well, you can't kill her.
Probably not going to end well.
Like you do.
Oh, like you know.
Locked *you* down, didn't I?
"Locked me down"?
You are locked down, Tandy.

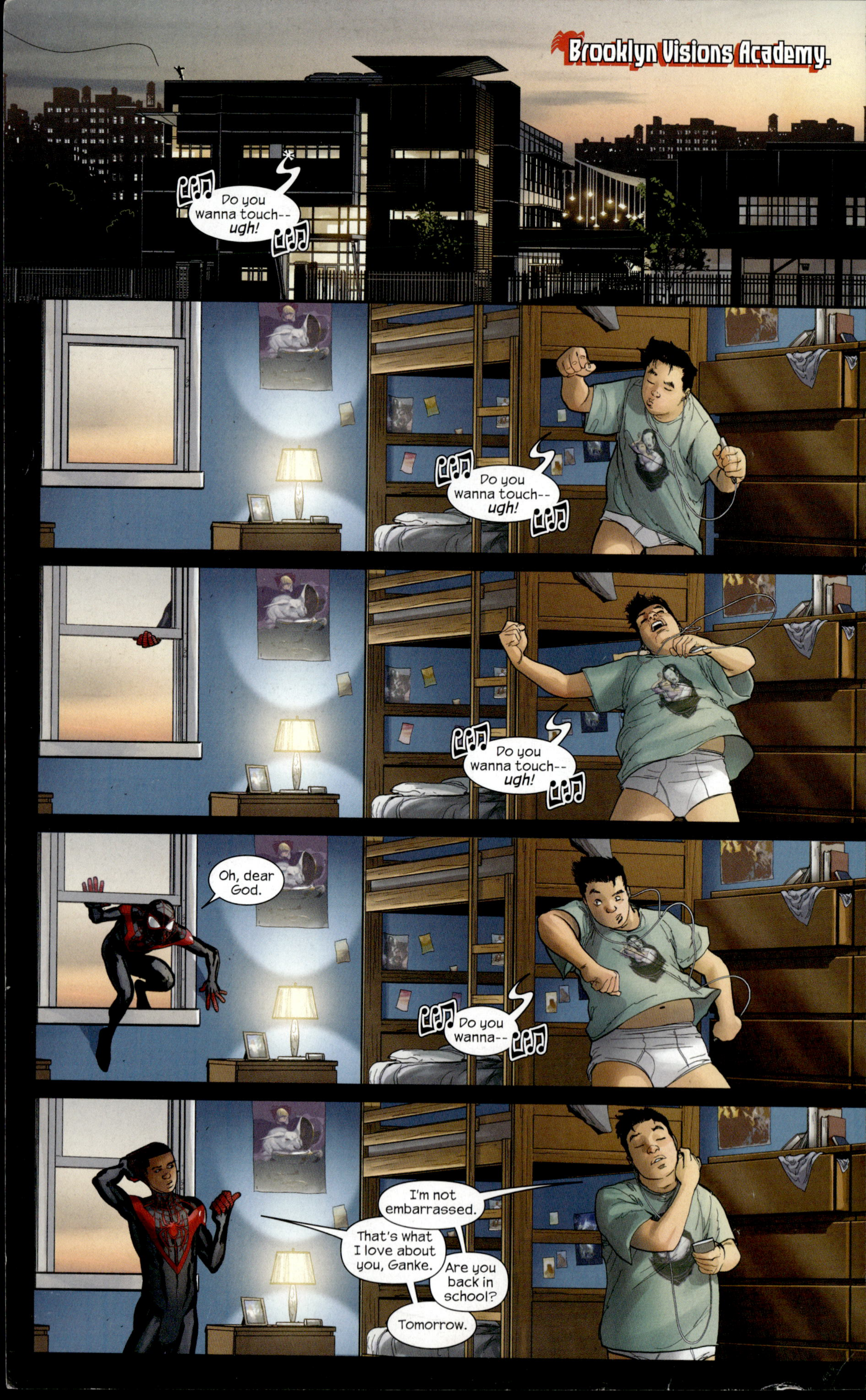
Brooklyn Visions Academy.
Do you wanna touch-- ugh!
Do you wanna touch-- ugh!
Do you wanna touch-- ugh!
Oh, dear God.
Do you wanna--
I'm not embarrassed.
That's what I love about you, Ganke.
Are you back in school?
Tomorrow.

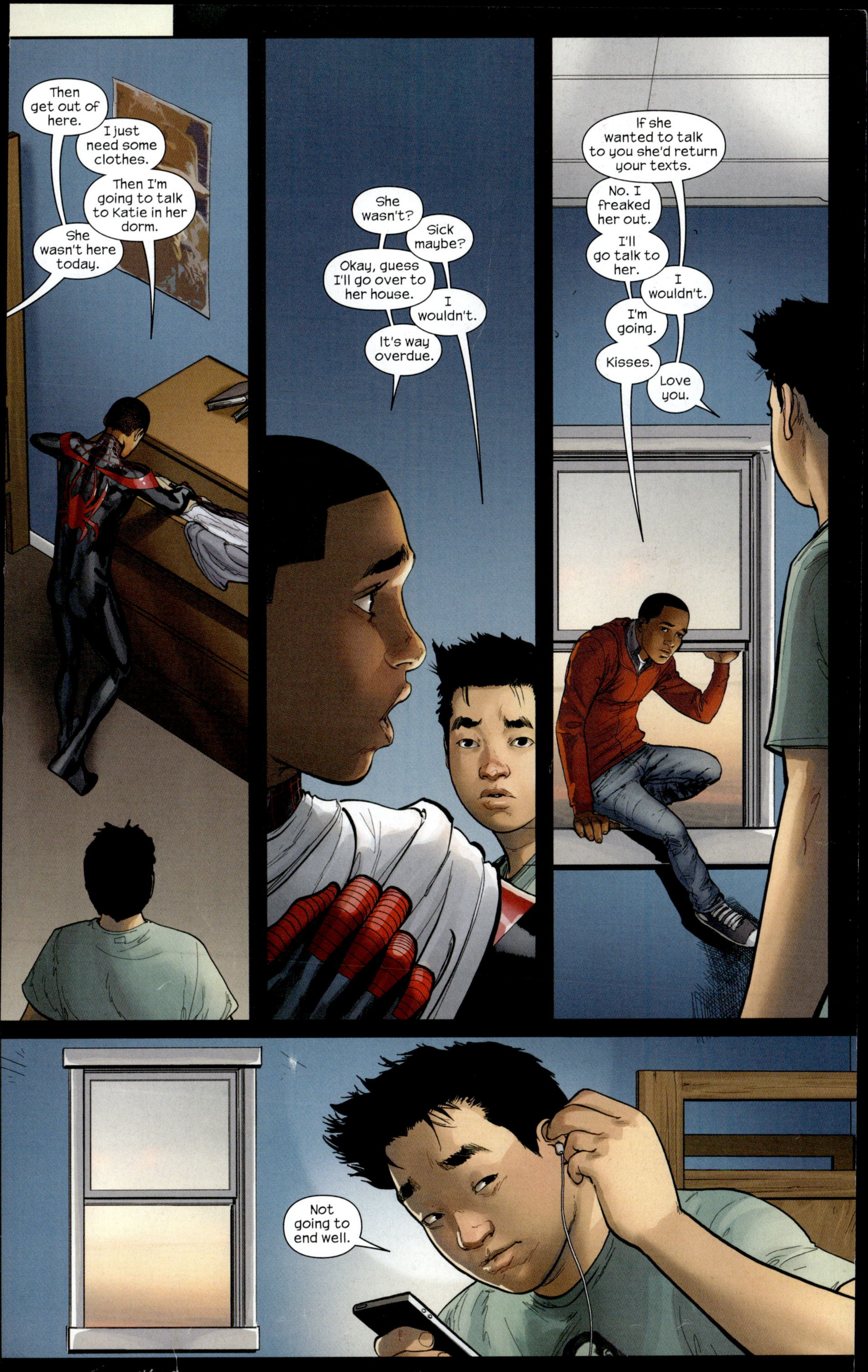

Then get out of here.
I just need some clothes.
Then I'm going to talk to Katie in her dorm.
She wasn't here today.
She wasn't?
Sick maybe?
Okay, guess I'll go over to her house.
I wouldn't.
It's way overdue.
If she wanted to talk to you she'd return your texts.
No. I freaked her out.
I'll go talk to her.
I wouldn't.
I'm going.
Kisses.
Love you.
Not going to end well.

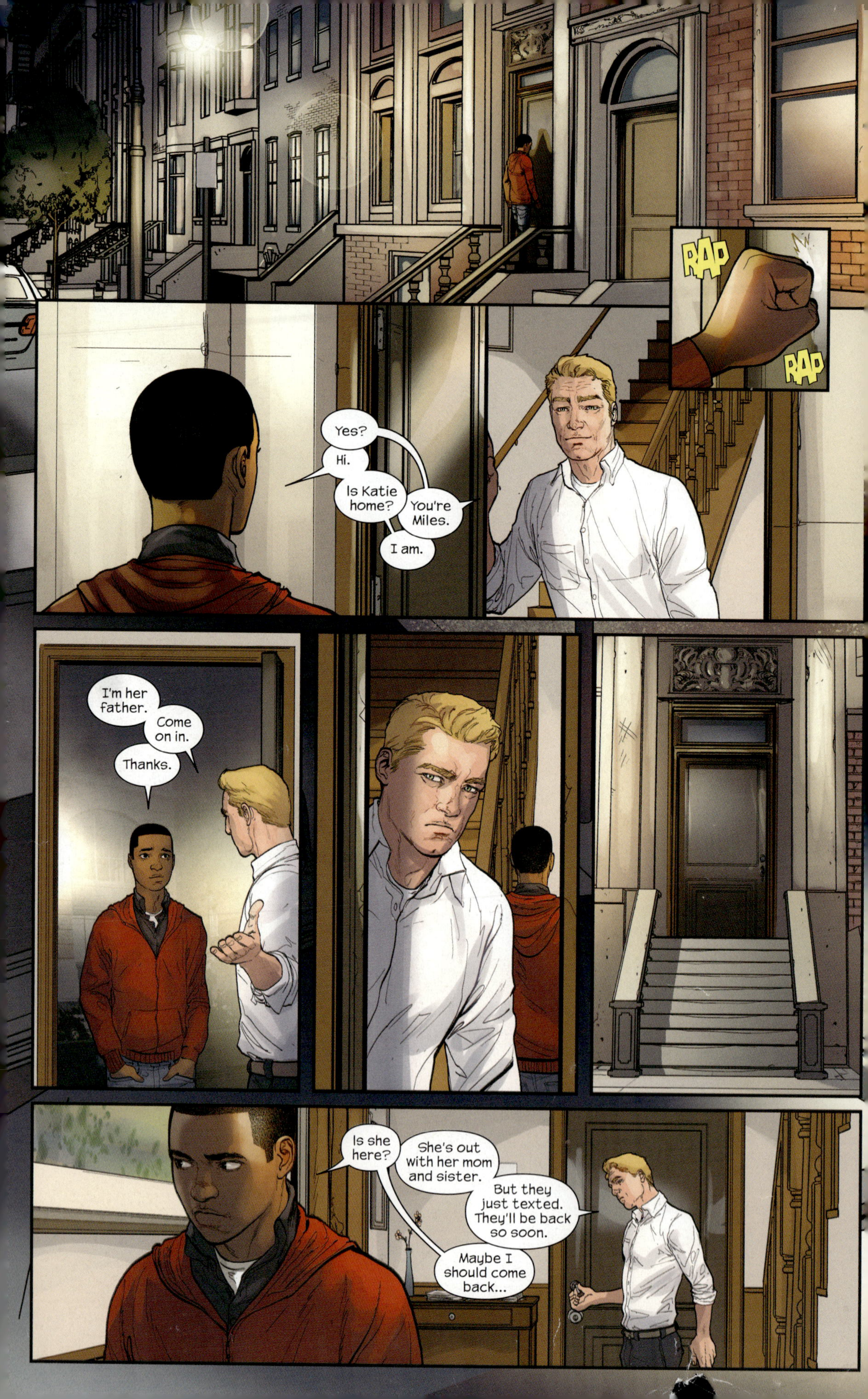
RAP
RAP
Yes?
Hi.
Is Katie home?
You're Miles.
I am.
I'm her father.
Come on in.
Thanks.
Is she here?
She's out with her mom and sister.
But they just texted. They'll be back so soon.
Maybe I should come back...

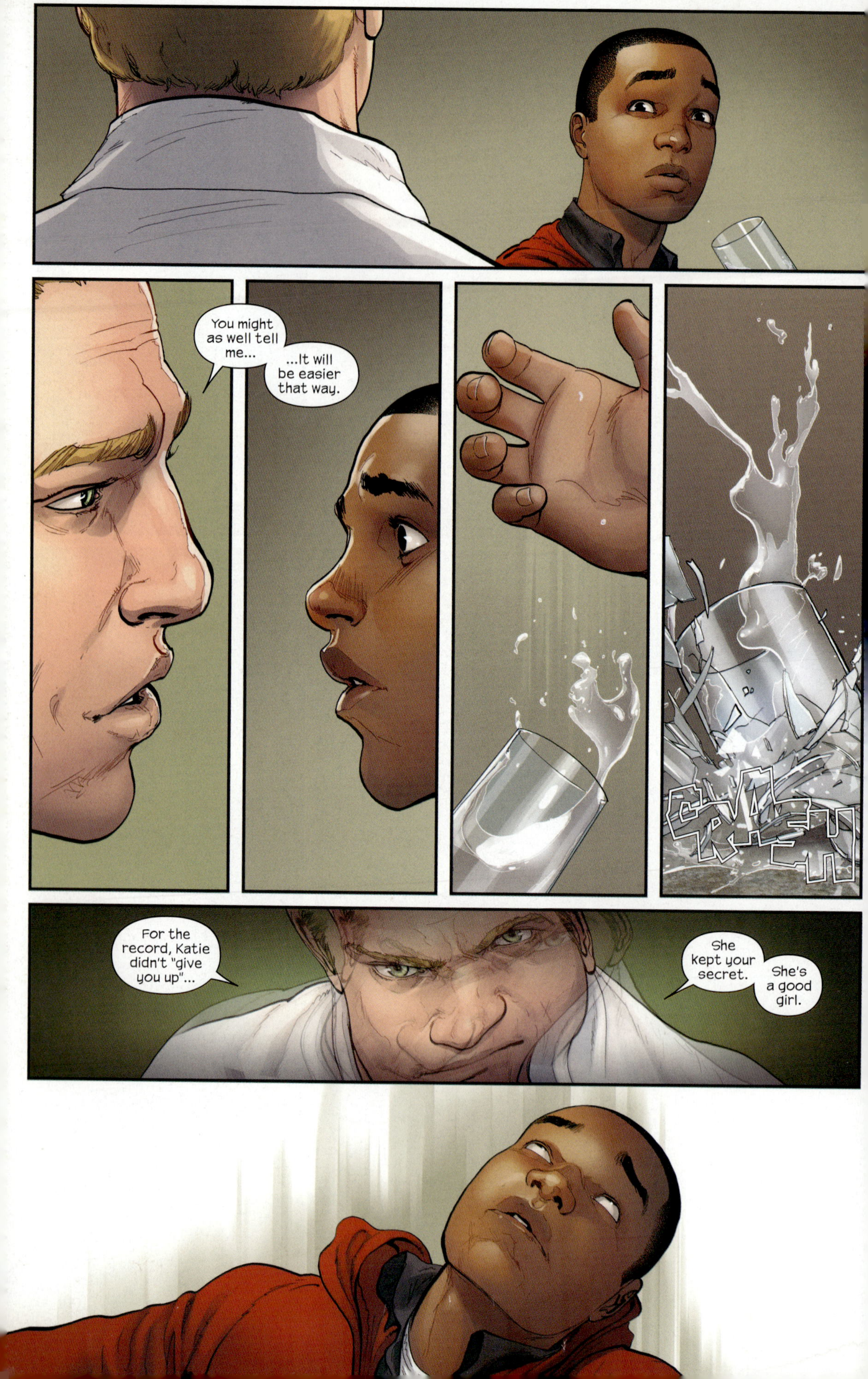
You might as well tell me...
...It will be easier that way.
For the record, Katie didn't "give you up"...
She kept your secret.
She's a good girl.

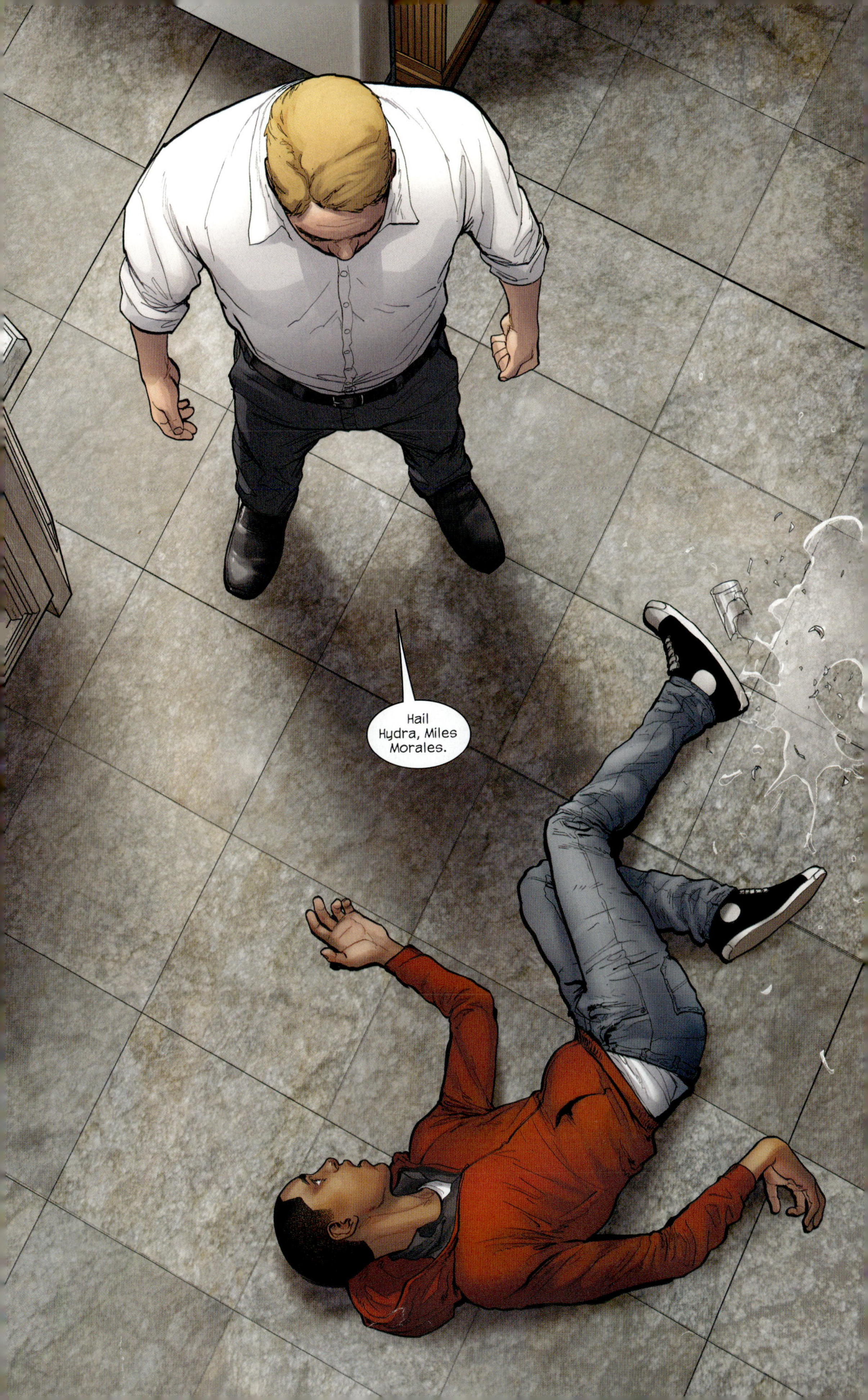
Hail Hydra, Miles Morales.

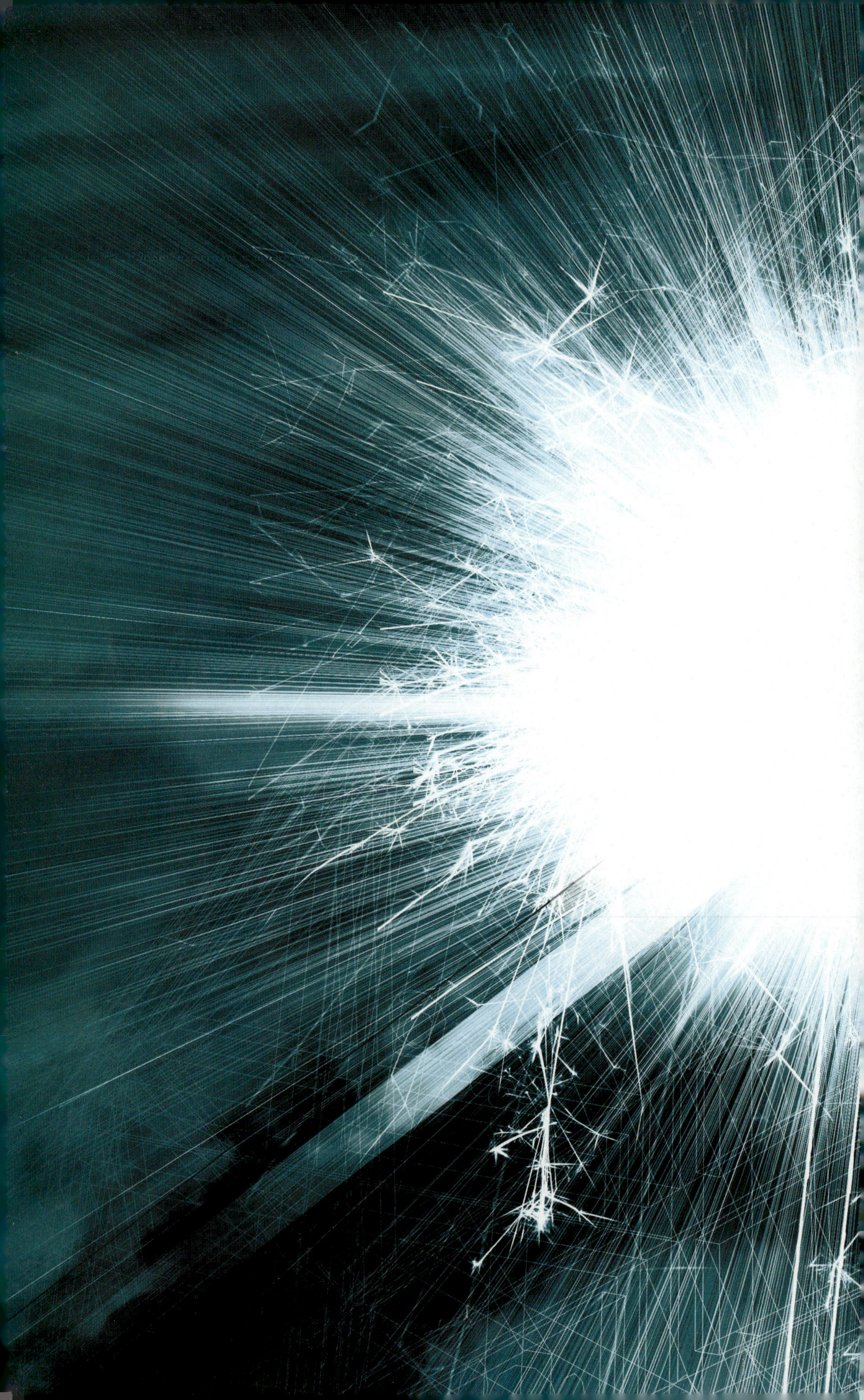

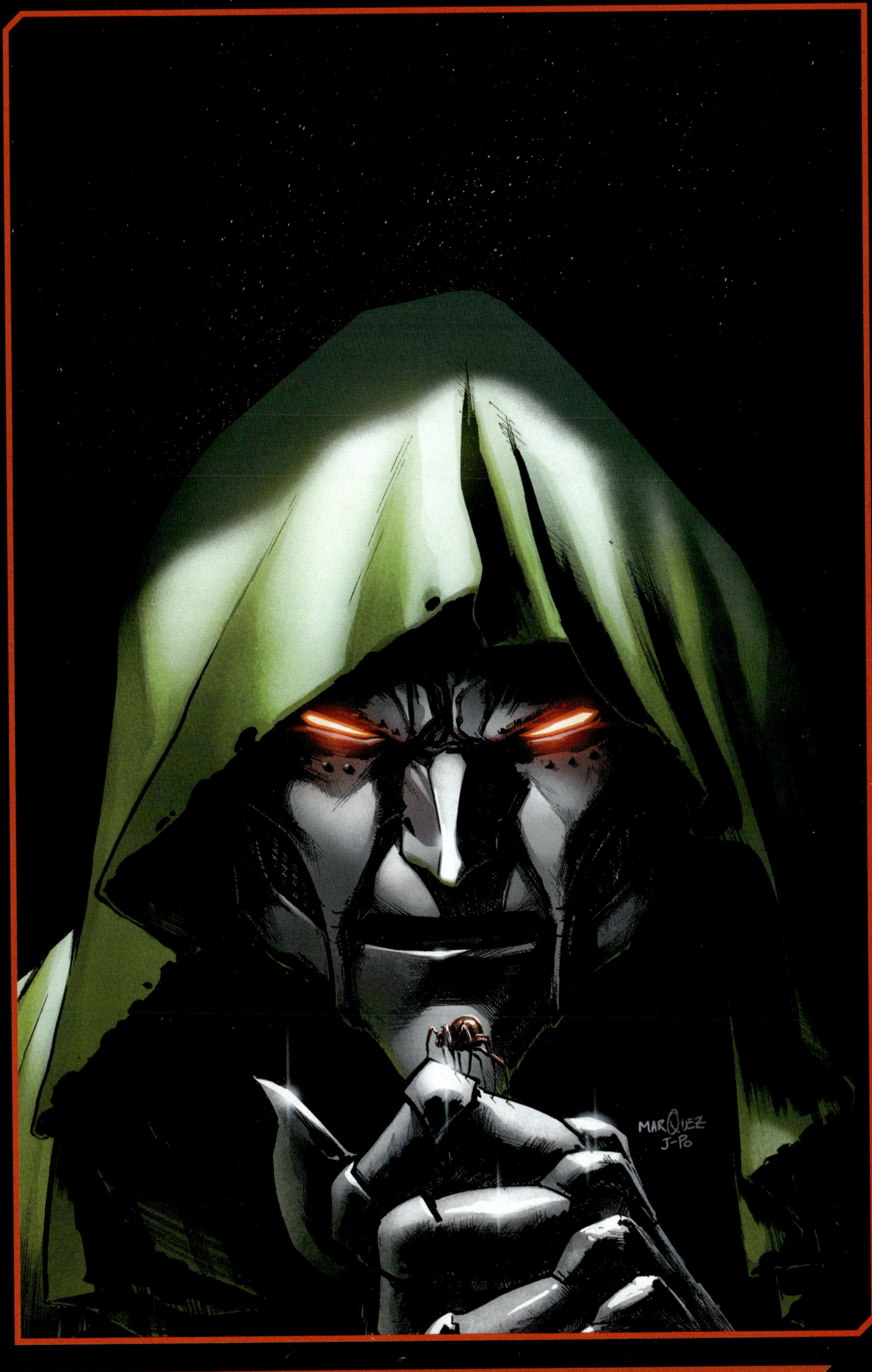

MILES MORALES: ULTIMATE SPIDER-MAN #11

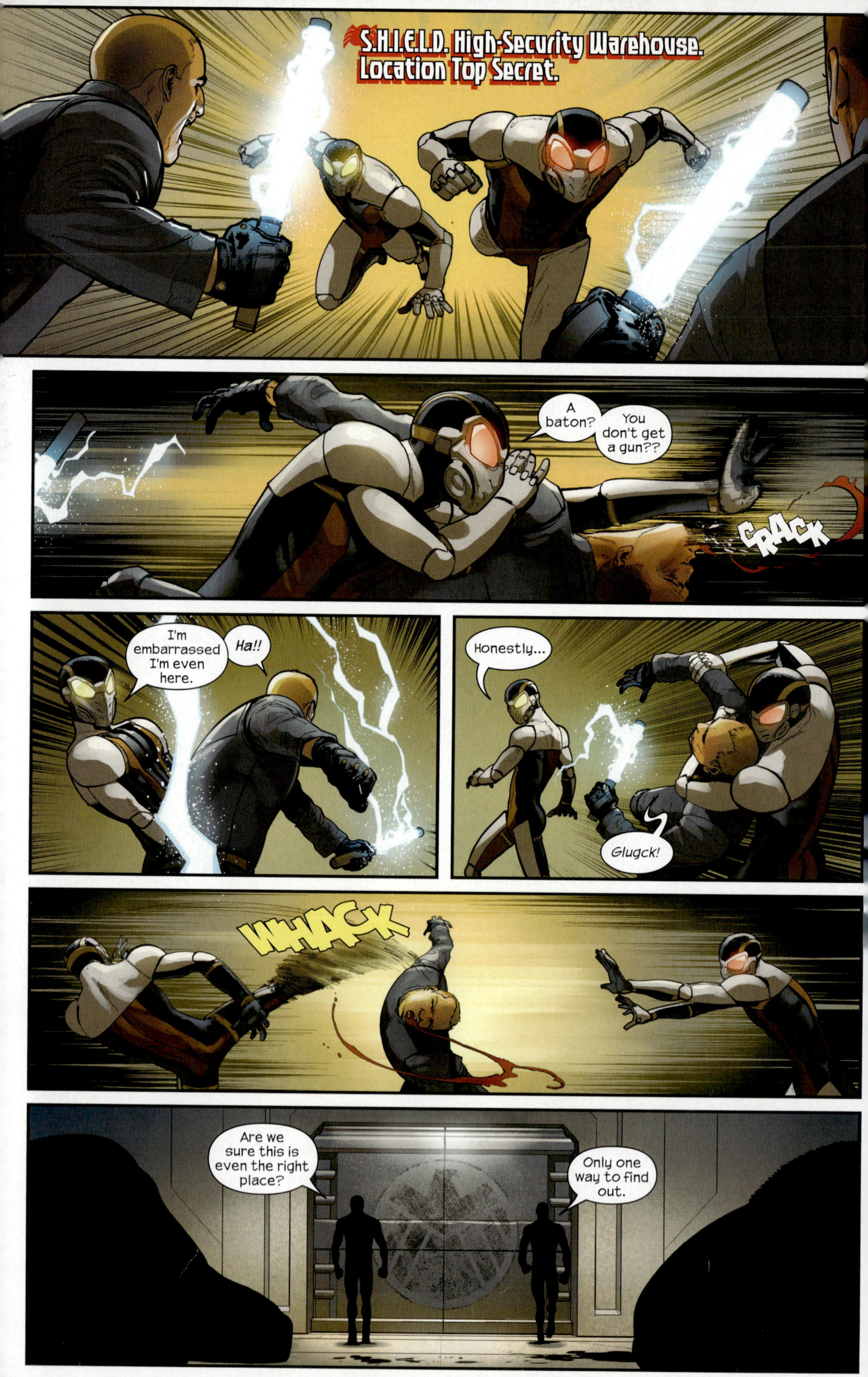

S.H.I.E.L.D. High-Security Warehouse.
Location Top Secret.
A baton?
You don't get a gun??
CRACK
I'm embarrassed I'm even here.
Ha!!
Honestly...
Glugck!
WHACK
Are we sure this is even the right place?
Only one way to find out.

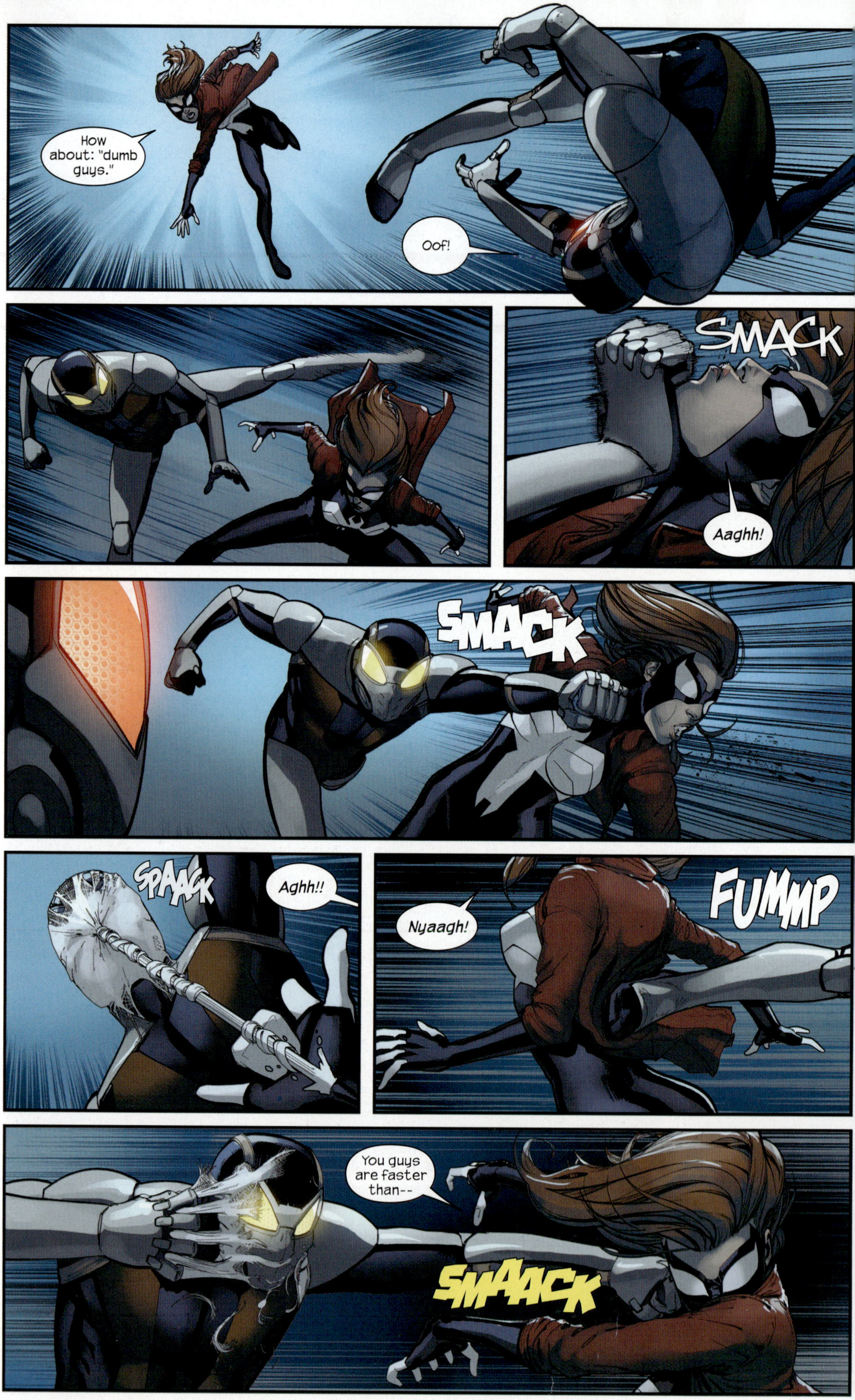
How about: "dumb guys."
Oof!
SMACK
Aaghh!
SMACK
SPAACK
Aghh!!
Nyaagh!
FUMMP
You guys are faster than--
SMAACK

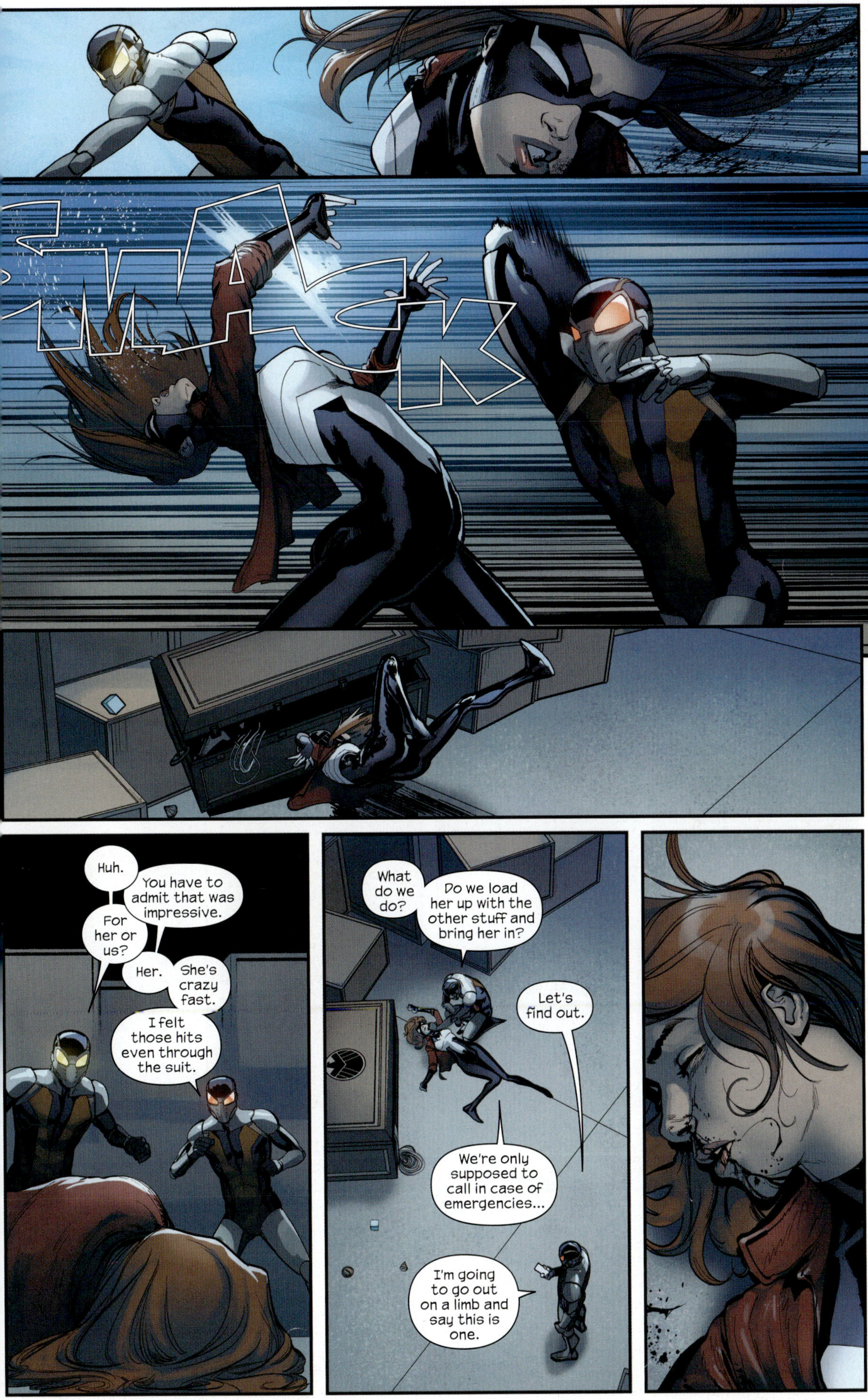

Huh.
You have to admit that was impressive.
For her or us?
Her.
She's crazy fast.
I felt those hits even through the suit.
What do we do?
Do we load her up with the other stuff and bring her in?
Let's find out.
We're only supposed to call in case of emergencies...
I'm going to go out on a limb and say this is one.

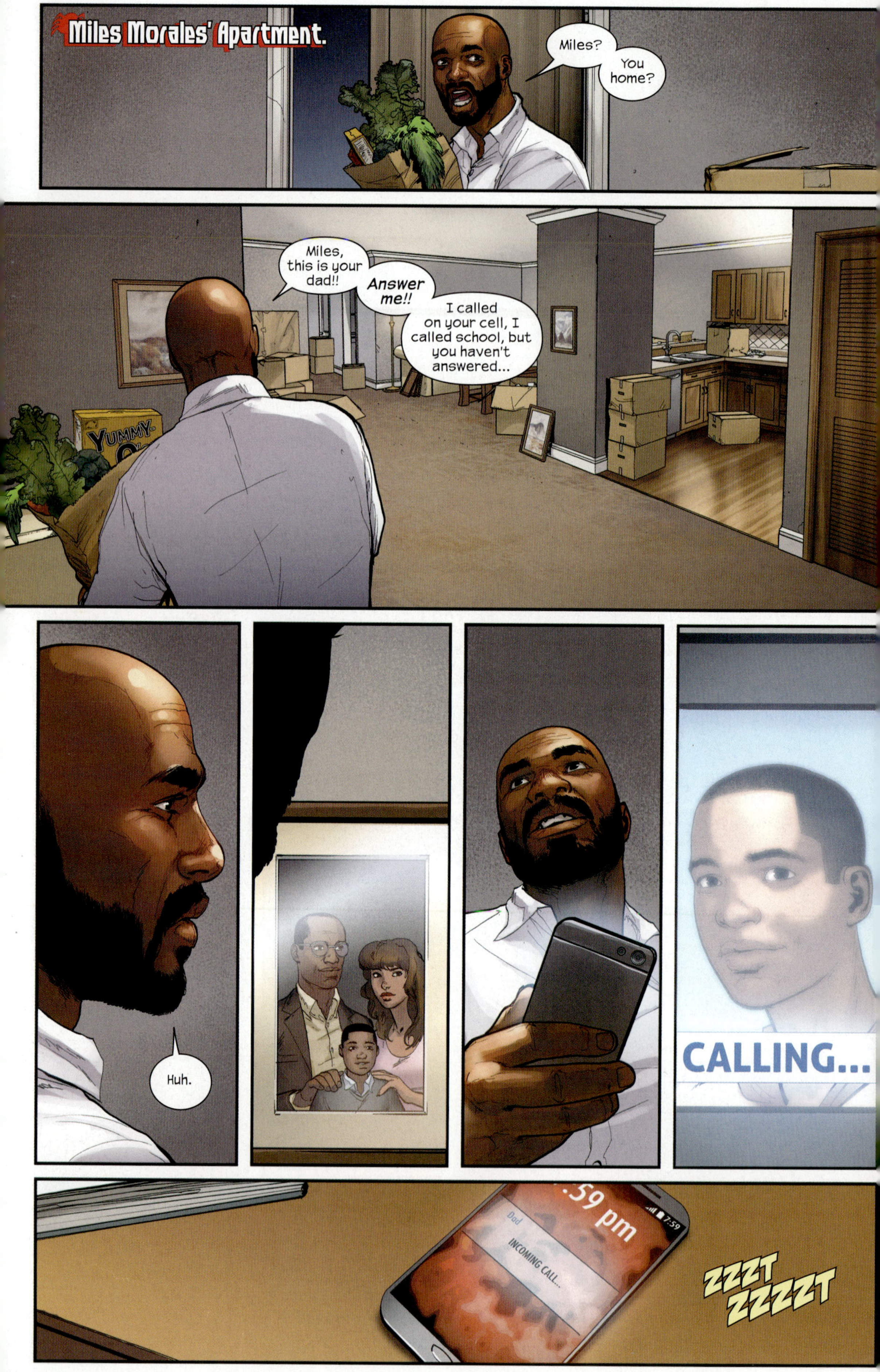
Miles Morales' Apartment.
Miles?
You home?
Miles, this is your dad!!
Answer me!!
I called on your cell, I called school, but you haven't answered...
YUMMY-
Huh.
CALLING...
Dad
INCOMING CALL...
ZZZT ZZZZT

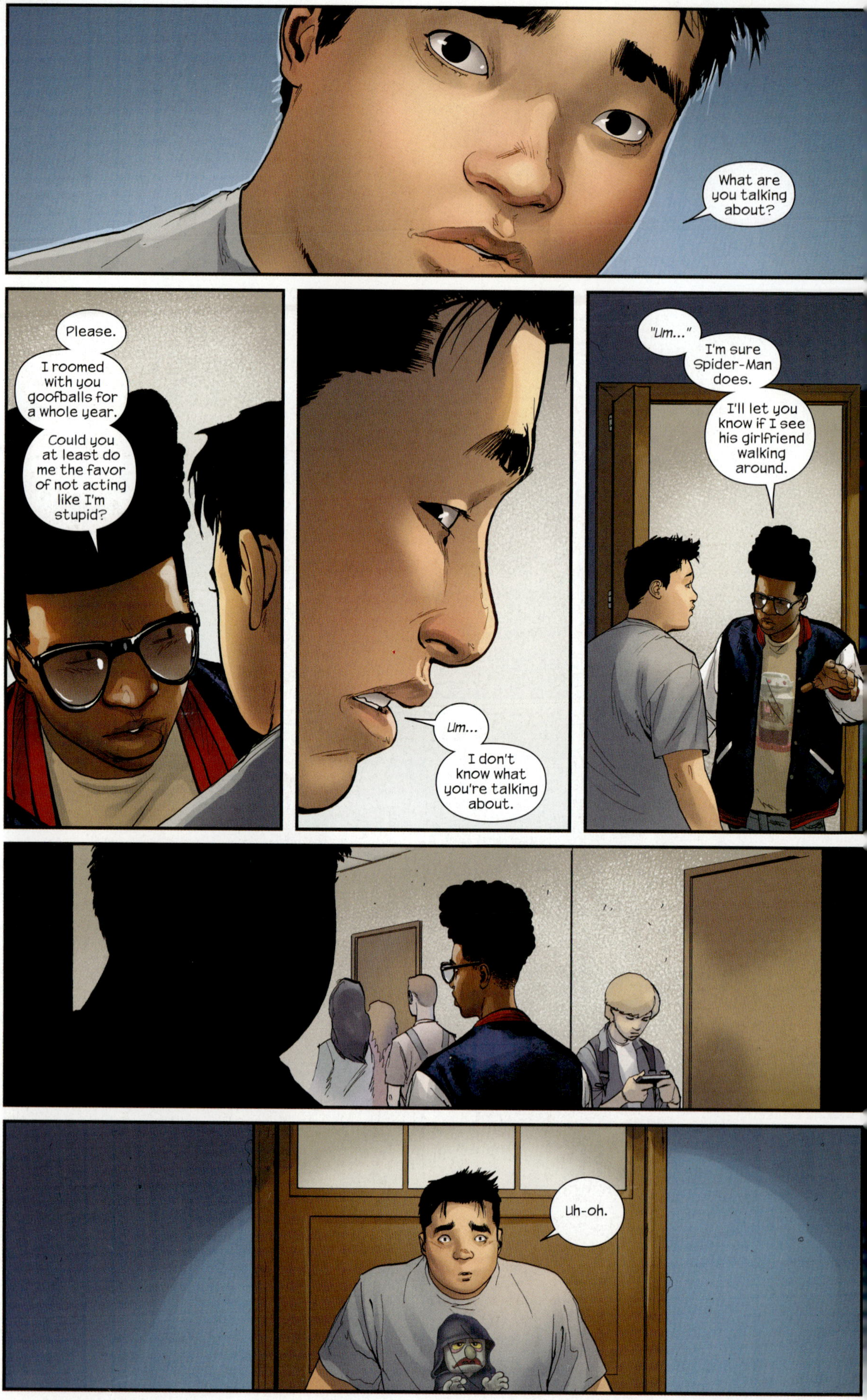
What are you talking about?
Please.
I roomed with you goofballs for a whole year.
Could you at least do me the favor of not acting like I'm stupid?
Um...
I don't know what you're talking about.
"Um..."
I'm sure Spider-Man does.
I'll let you know if I see his girlfriend walking around.
Uh-oh.

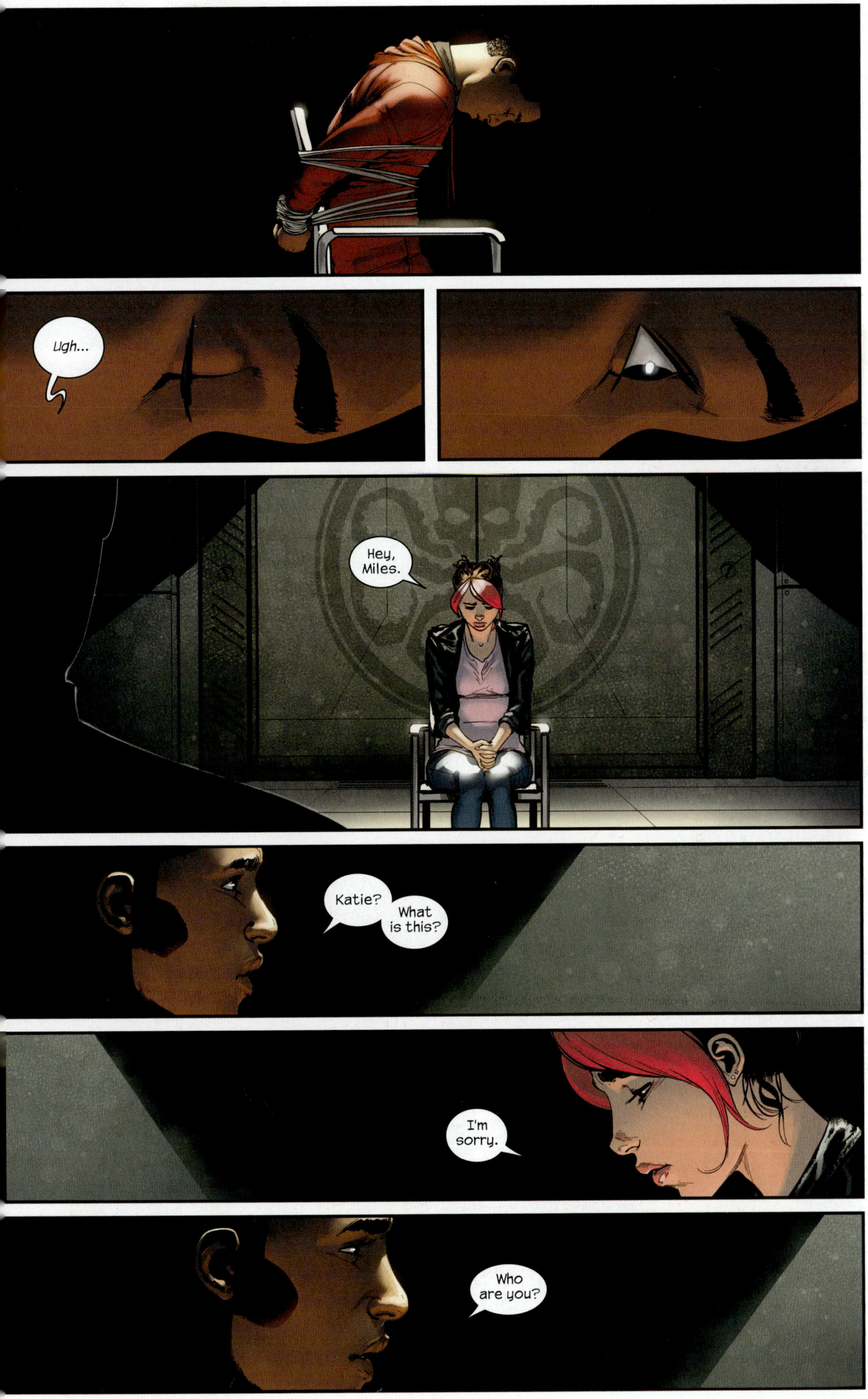
Ugh...
Hey, Miles.
Katie?
What is this?
I'm sorry.
Who are you?

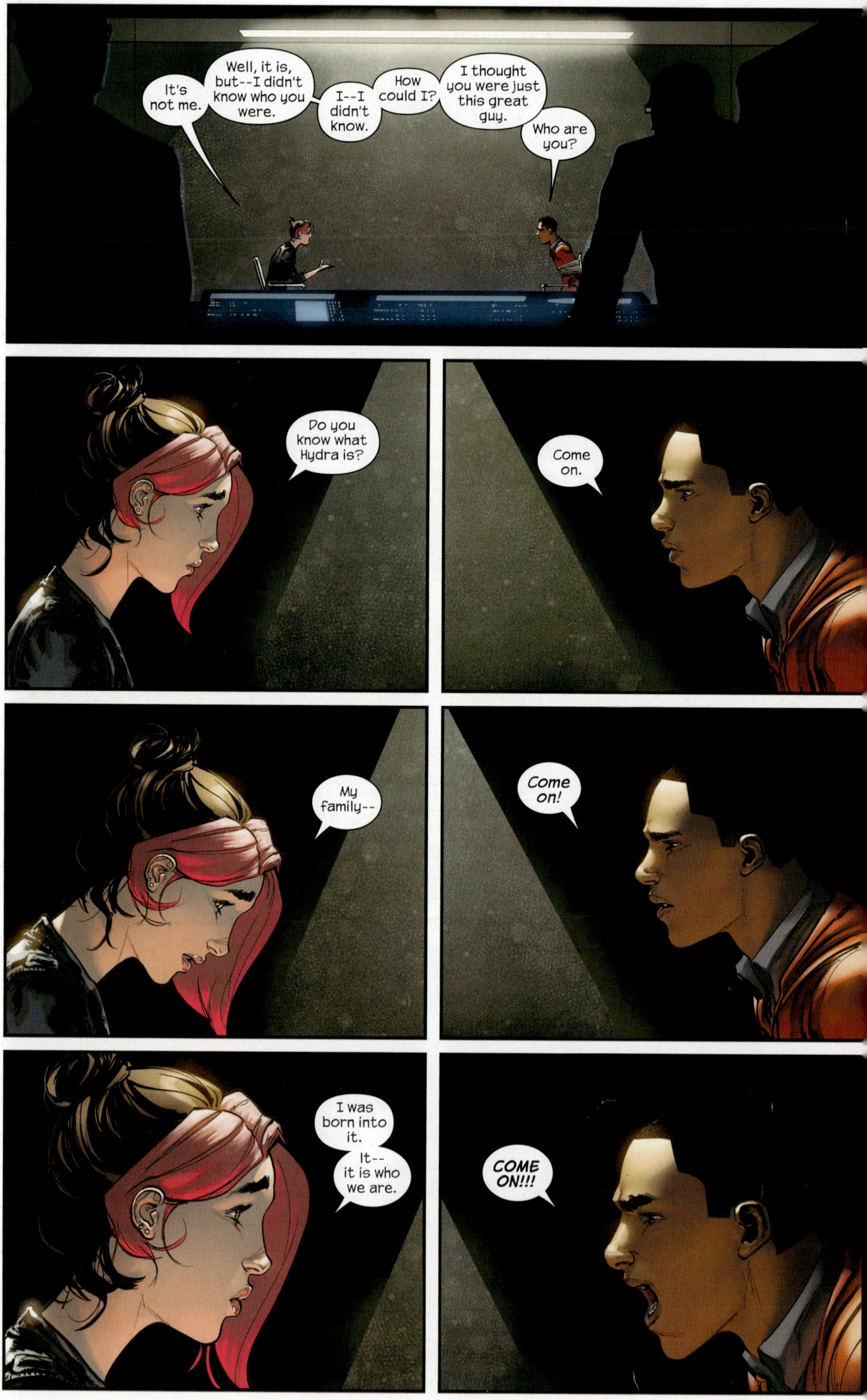
It's not me.
Well, it is, but--I didn't know who you were.
I--I didn't know.
How could I?
I thought you were just this great guy.
Who are you?
Do you know what Hydra is?
Come on.
My family--
Come on!
I was born into it.
It--it is who we are.
COME ON!!!

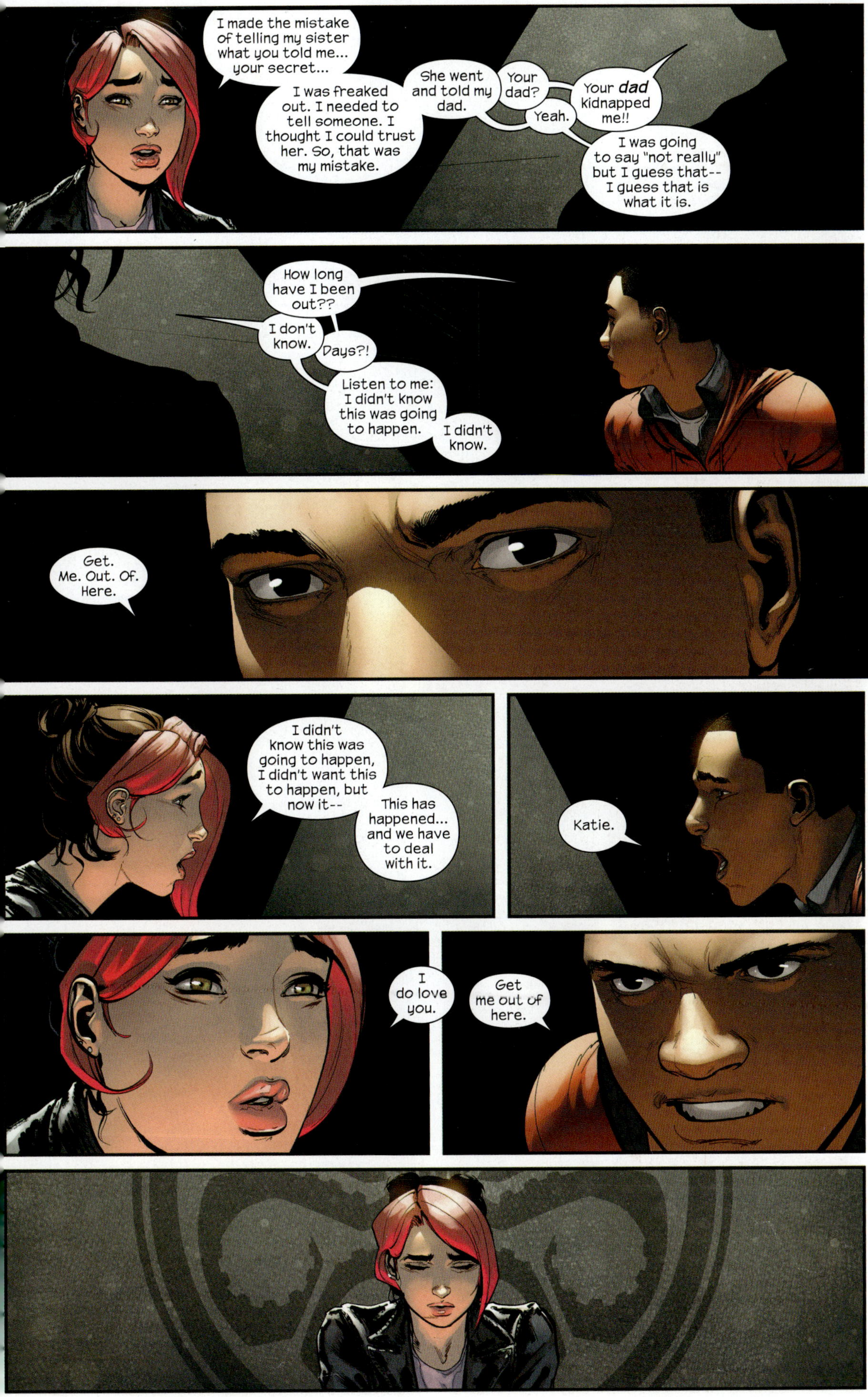
I made the mistake of telling my sister what you told me... your secret...
I was freaked out. I needed to tell someone. I thought I could trust her. So, that was my mistake.
She went and told my dad.
Your dad?
Yeah.
Your dad kidnapped me!!
I was going to say "not really" but I guess that-- I guess that is what it is.
How long have I been out??
I don't know.
Days?!
Listen to me: I didn't know this was going to happen.
I didn't know.
Get. Me. Out. Of. Here.
I didn't know this was going to happen, I didn't want this to happen, but now it--
This has happened... and we have to deal with it.
Katie.
I do love you.
Get me out of here.

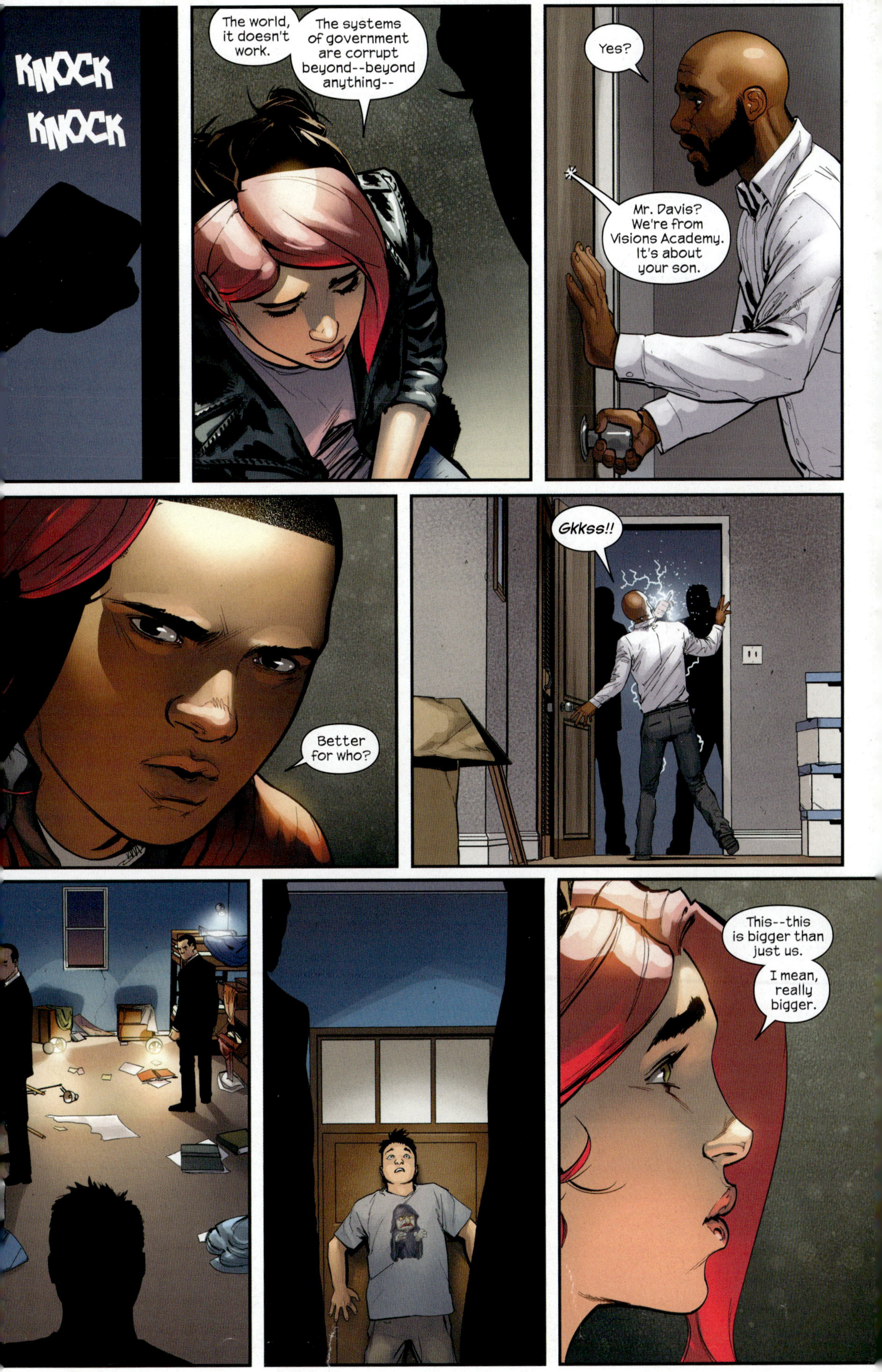
KNOCK
KNOCK
The world, it doesn't work.
The systems of government are corrupt beyond--beyond anything--
Yes?
Mr. Davis? We're from Visions Academy. It's about your son.
Better for who?
Gkkss!!
This--this is bigger than just us.
I mean, really bigger.

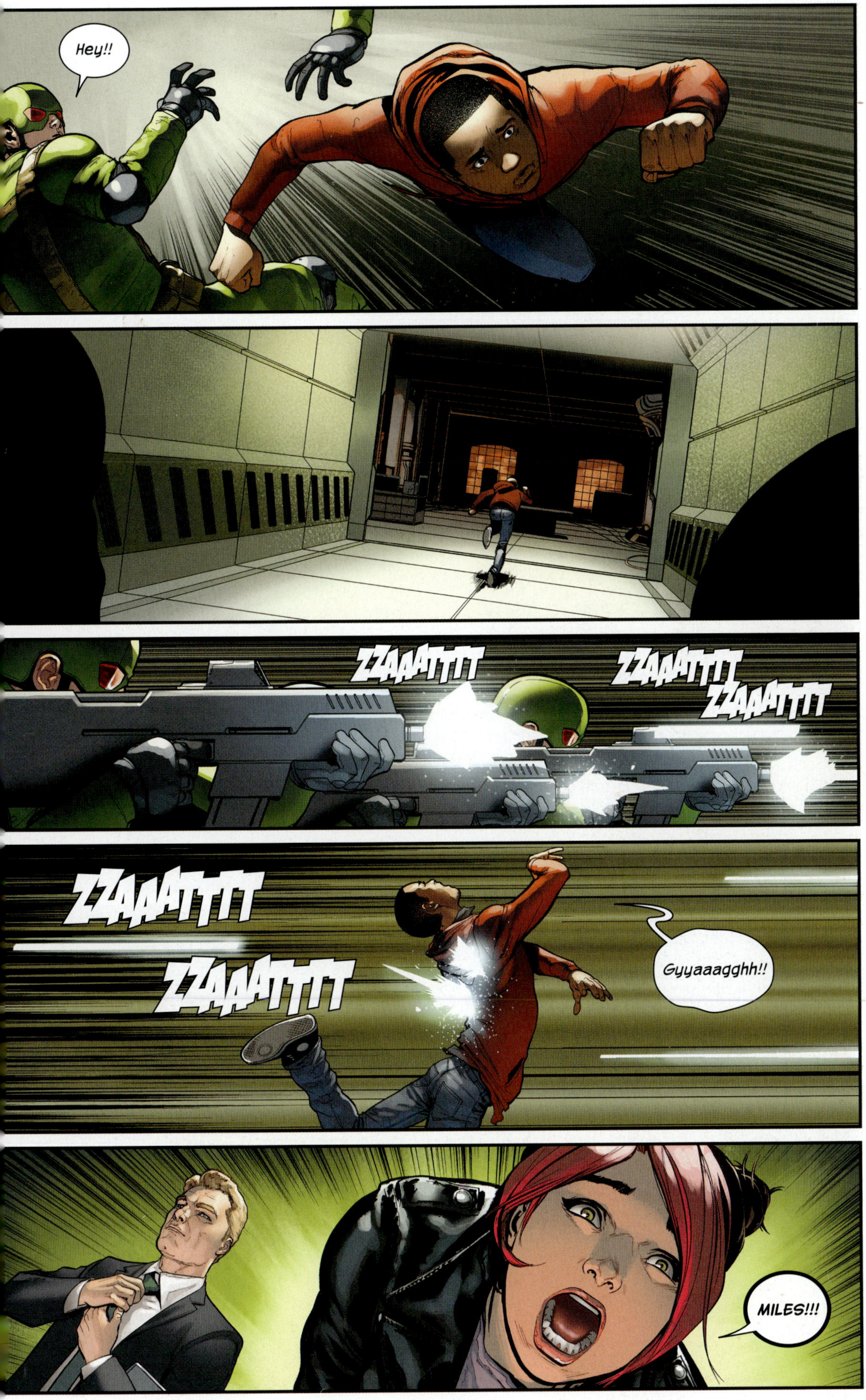
Hey!!
ZZAAATTTT
ZZAAATTTT
ZZAAATTTT
ZZAAATTTT
ZZAAATTTT
Gyyaaagghh!!
MILES!!!

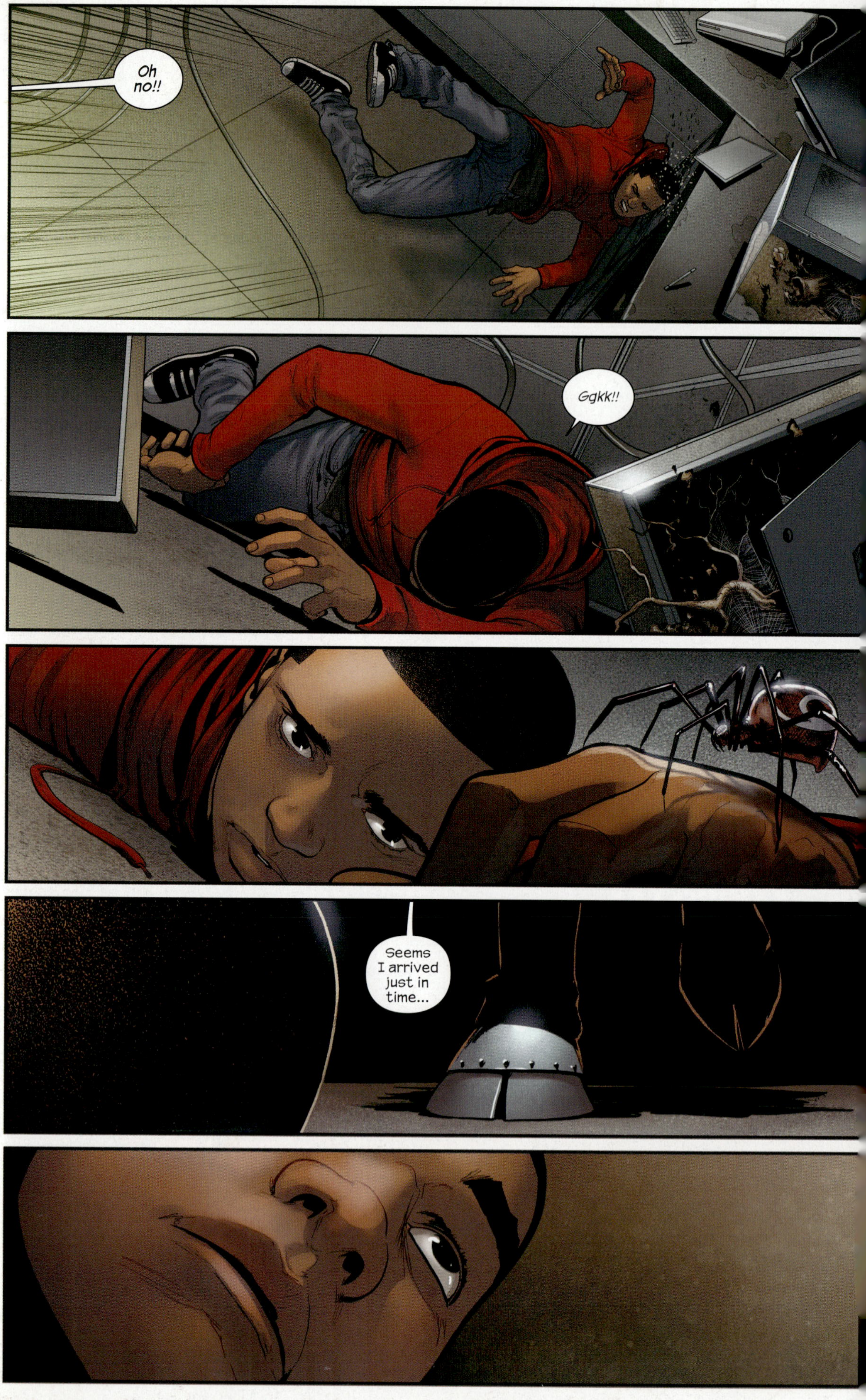
Oh no!!
Ggkk!!
Seems I arrived just in time...

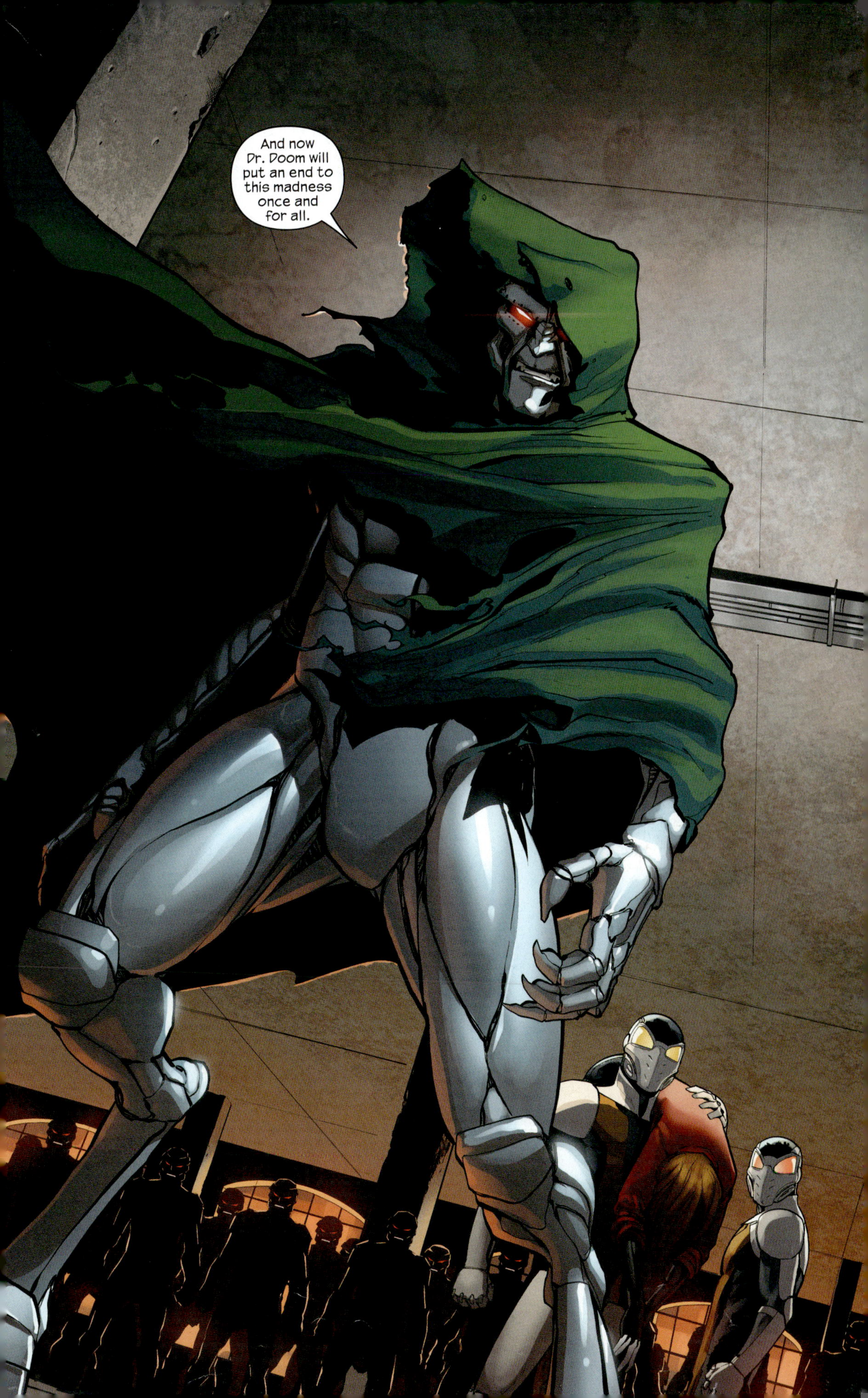
And now Dr. Doom will put an end to this madness once and for all.

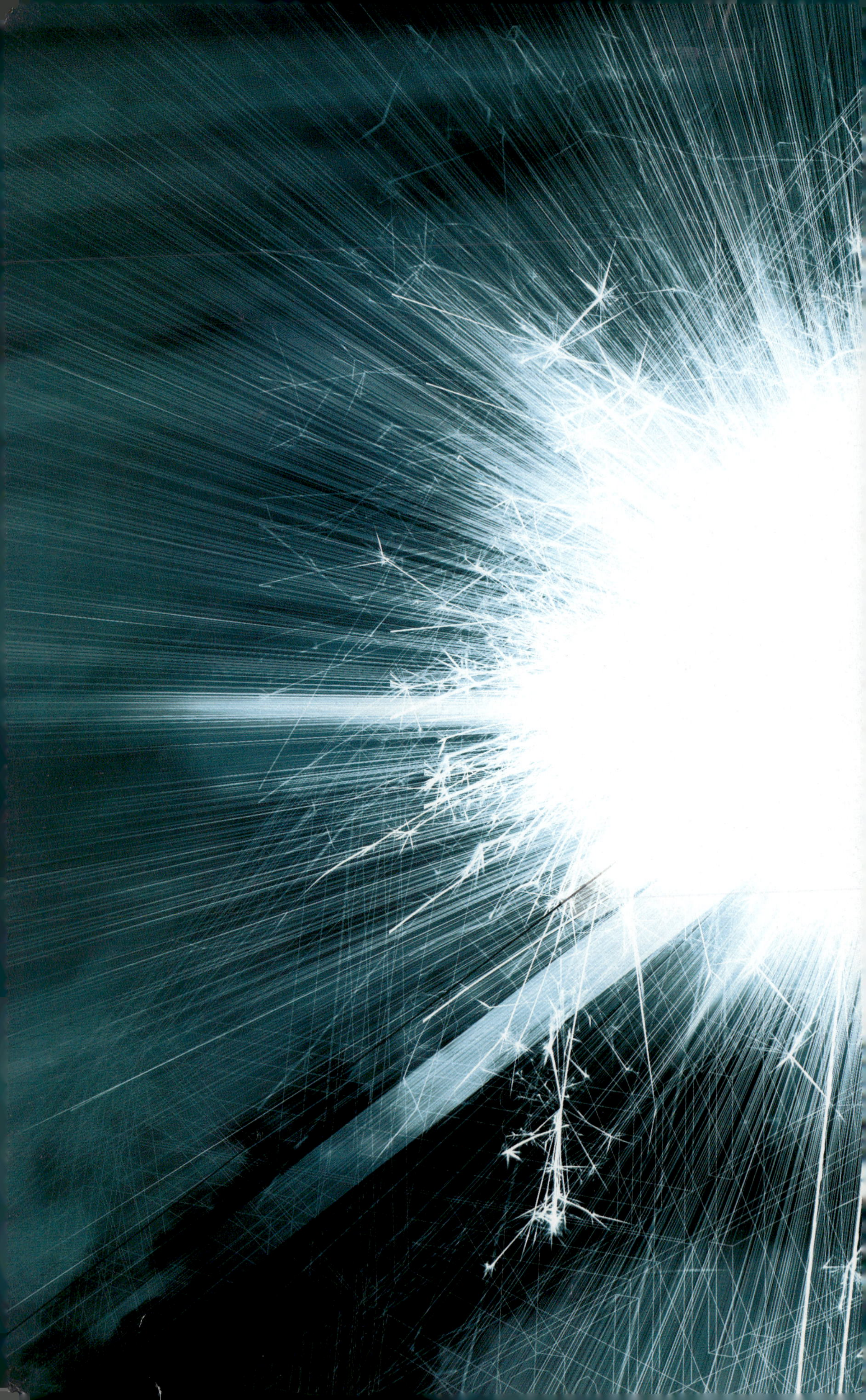

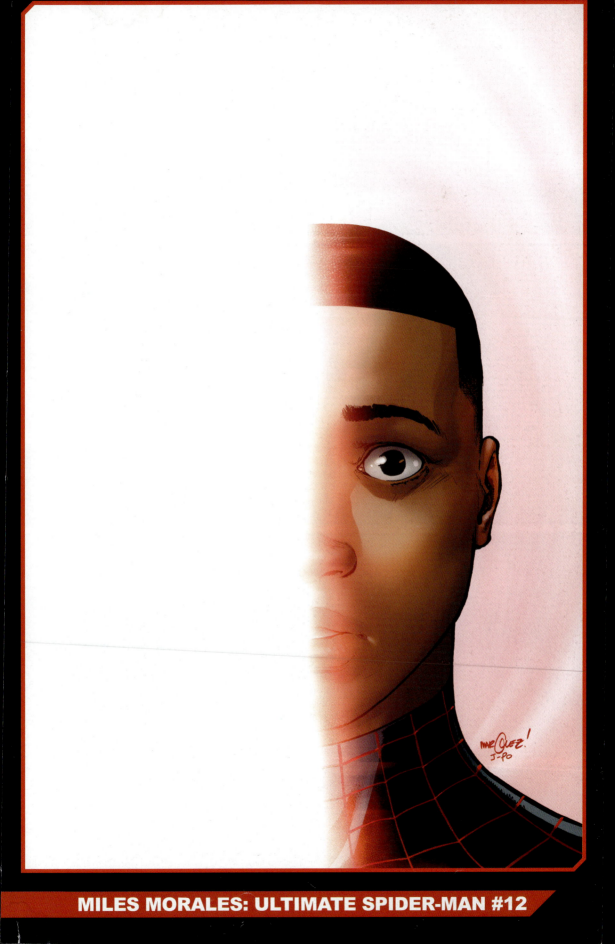

MILES MORALES: ULTIMATE SPIDER-MAN #12

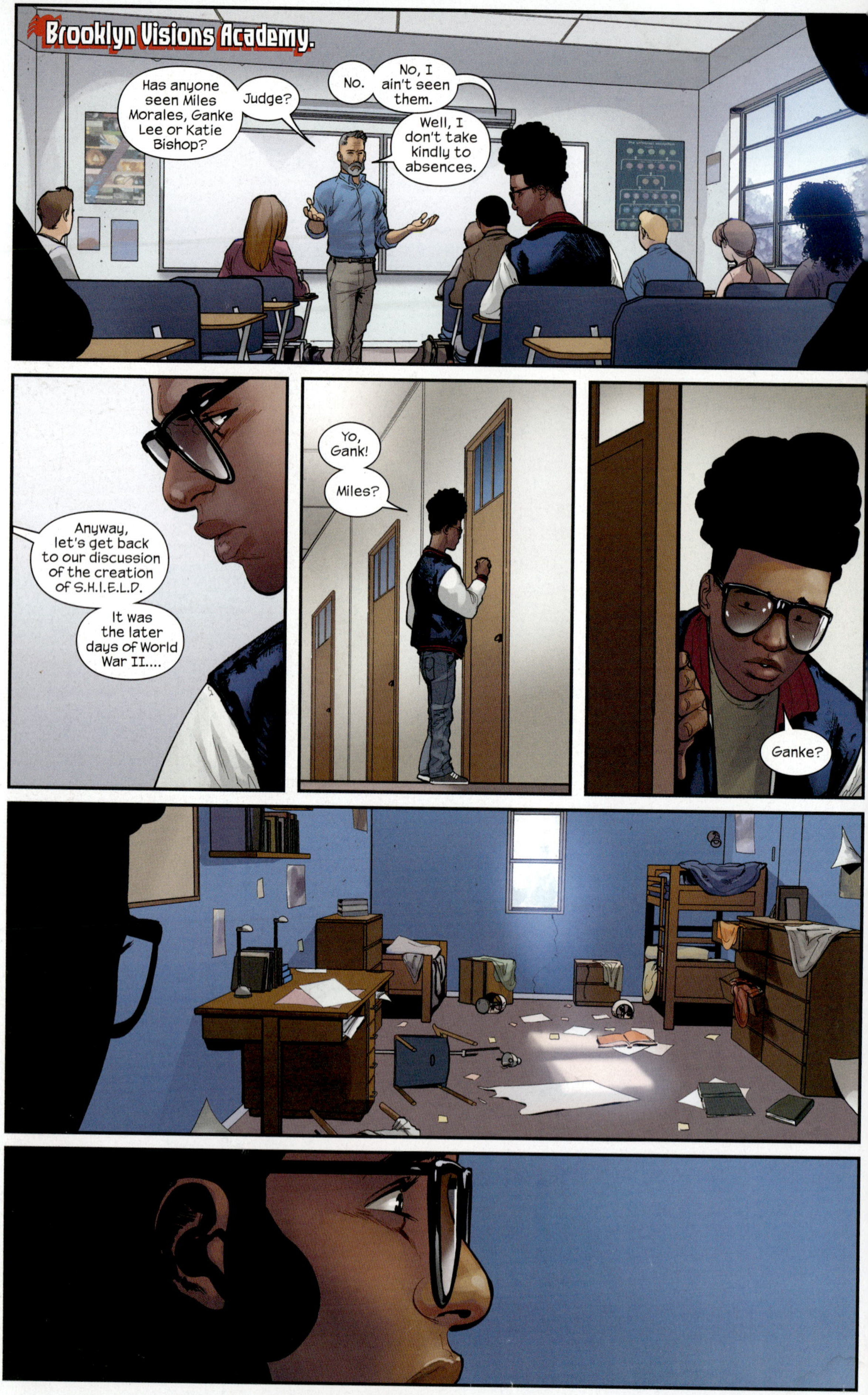
Brooklyn Visions Academy.
Has anyone seen Miles Morales, Ganke Lee or Katie Bishop?
Judge?
No.
No, I ain't seen them.
Well, I don't take kindly to absences.
Anyway, let's get back to our discussion of the creation of S.H.I.E.L.D.
It was the later days of World War II....
Yo, Gank!
Miles?
Ganke?

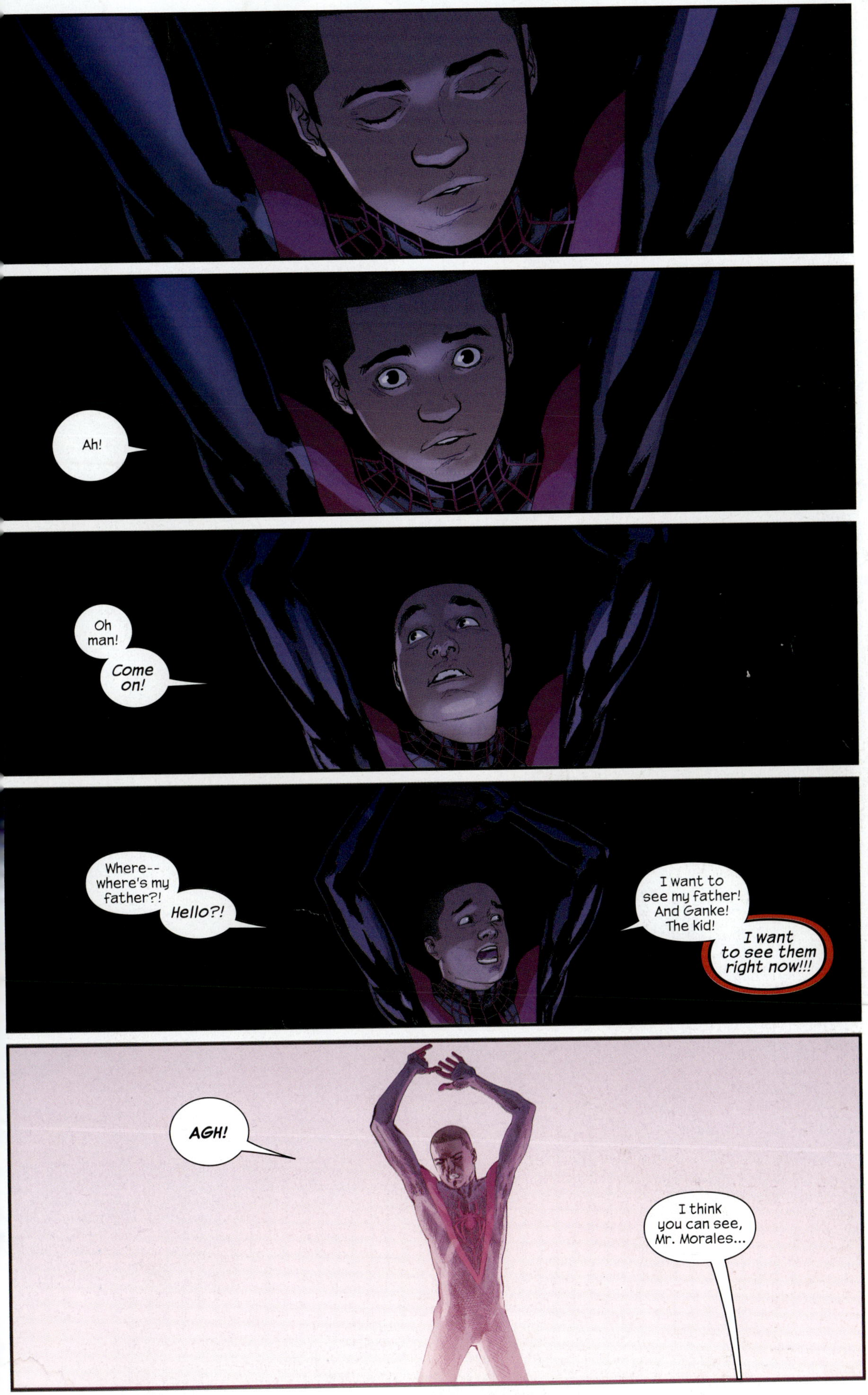
Ah!
Oh man!
Come on!
Where-- where's my father?!
Hello?!
I want to see my father! And Ganke! The kid!
I want to see them right now!!!
AGH!
I think you can see, Mr. Morales...

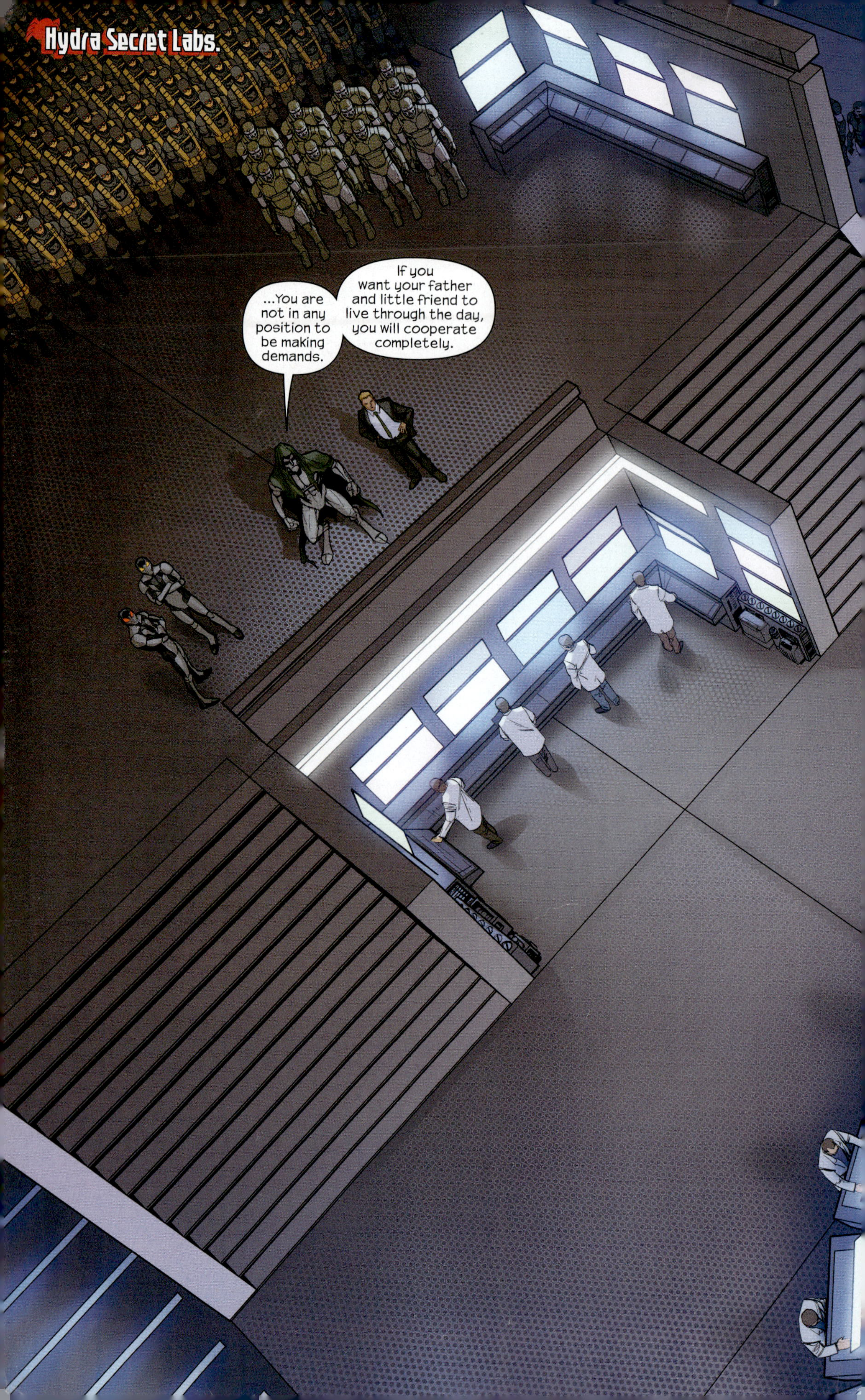
Hydra Secret Labs.
...You are not in any position to be making demands.
If you want your father and little friend to live through the day, you will cooperate completely.

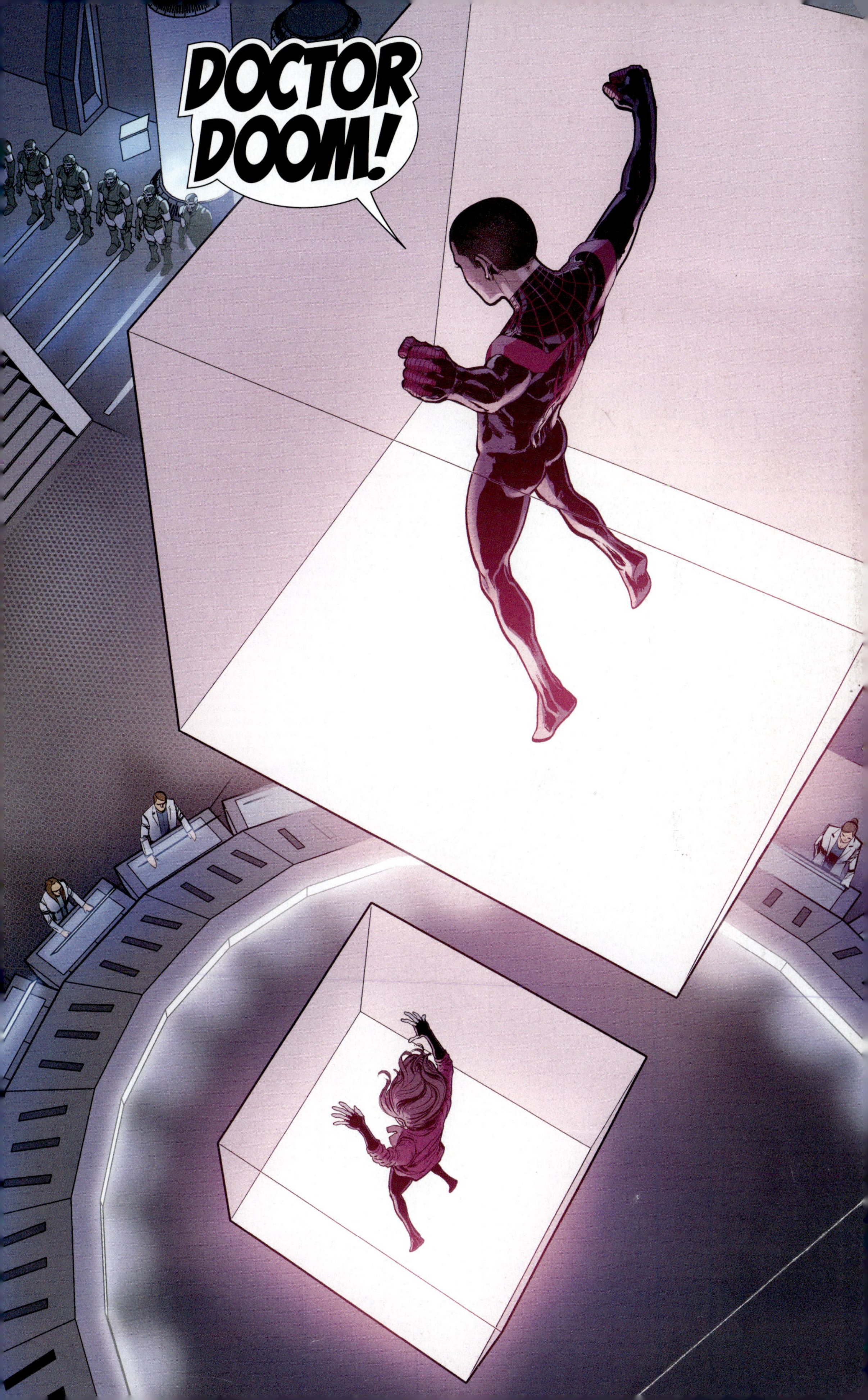
DOCTOR DOOM!

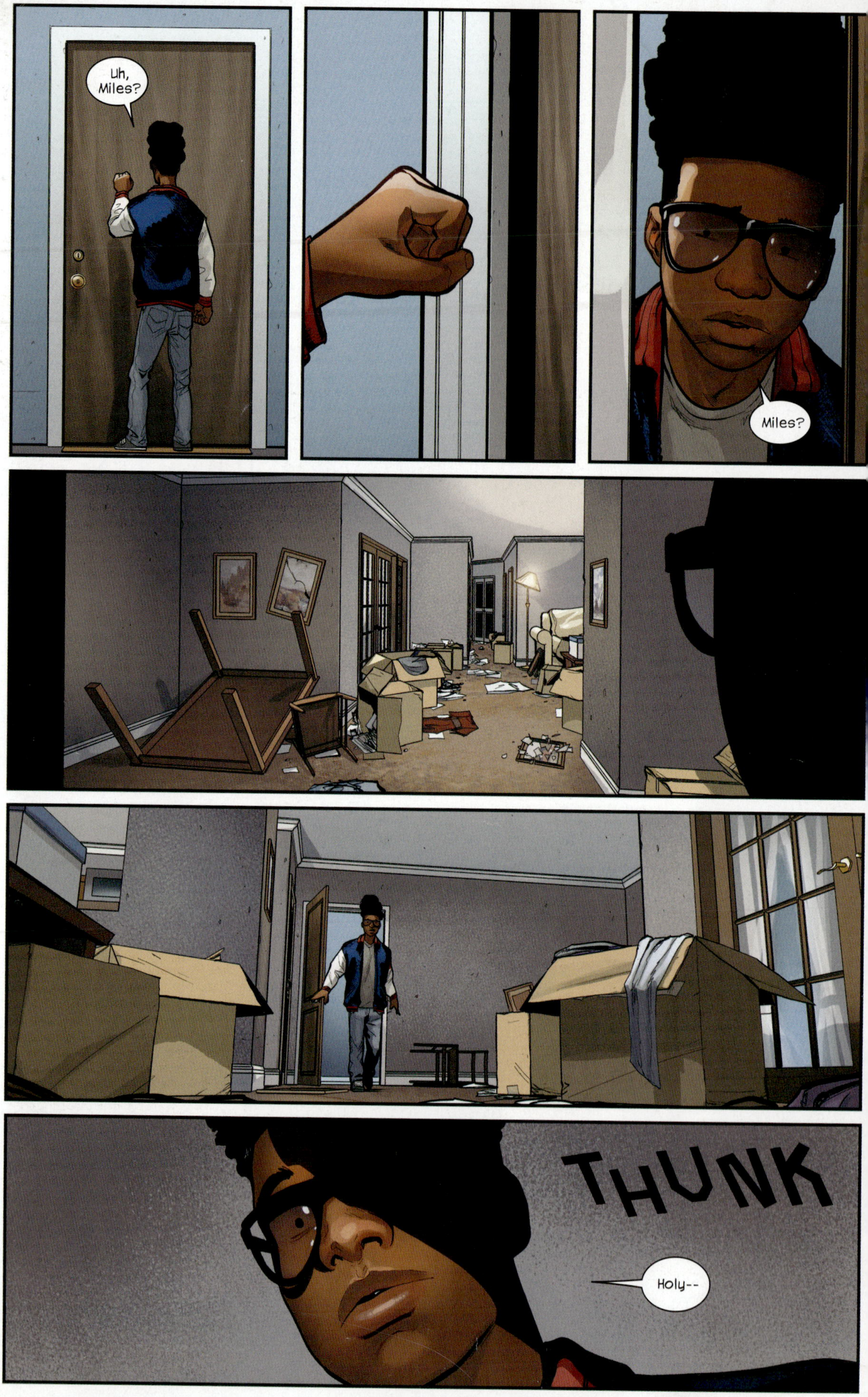

Uh, Miles?
Miles?
THUNK
Holy--

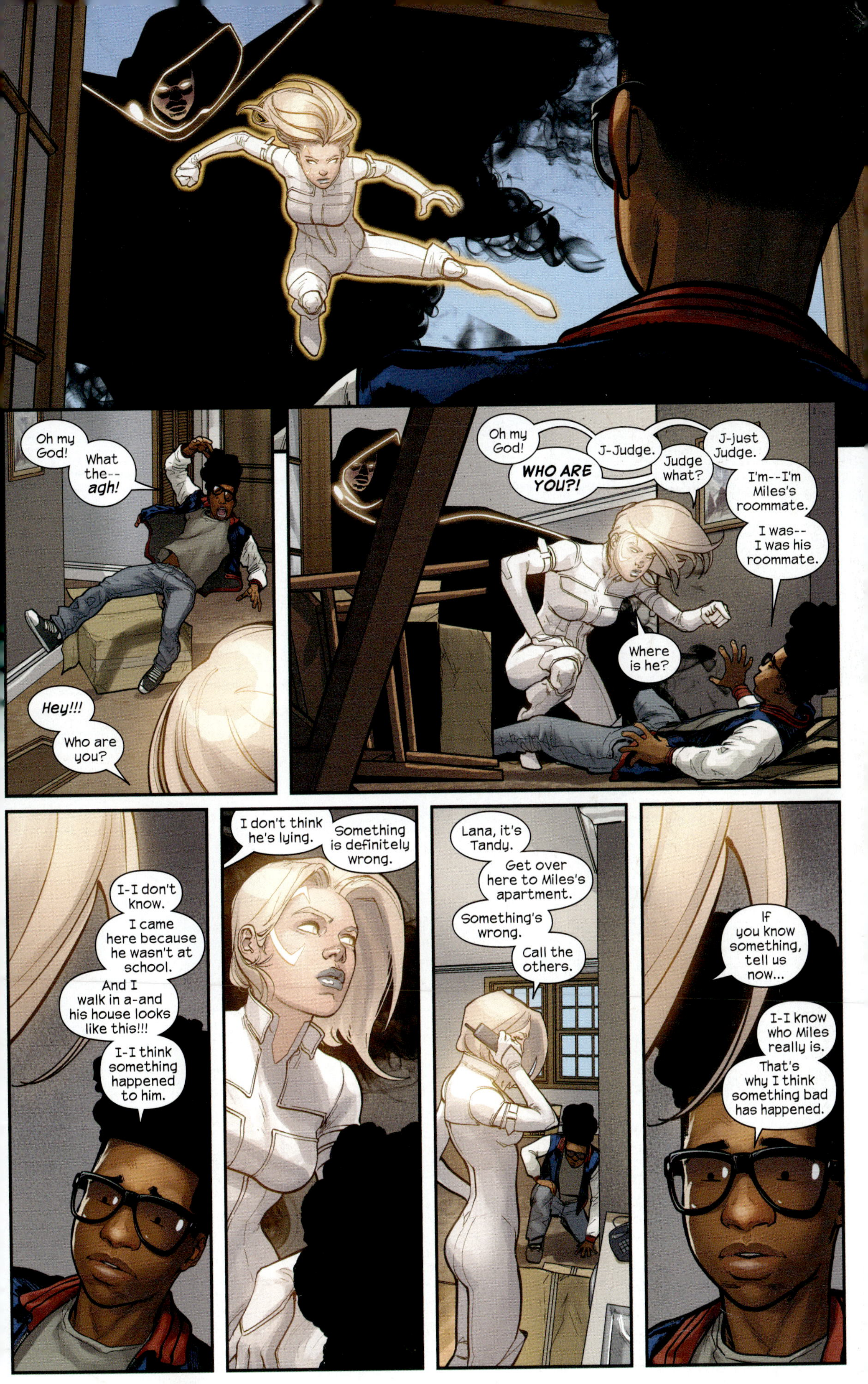

Oh my God!
What the-- agh!
Hey!!!
Who are you?
Oh my God!
WHO ARE YOU?!
J-Judge.
Judge what?
J-just Judge.
I'm--I'm Miles's roommate.
I was-- I was his roommate.
Where is he?
I-I don't know.
I came here because he wasn't at school.
And I walk in a-and his house looks like this!!!
I-I think something happened to him.
I don't think he's lying.
Something is definitely wrong.
Lana, it's Tandy.
Get over here to Miles's apartment.
Something's wrong.
Call the others.
If you know something, tell us now...
I-I know who Miles really is.
That's why I think something bad has happened.

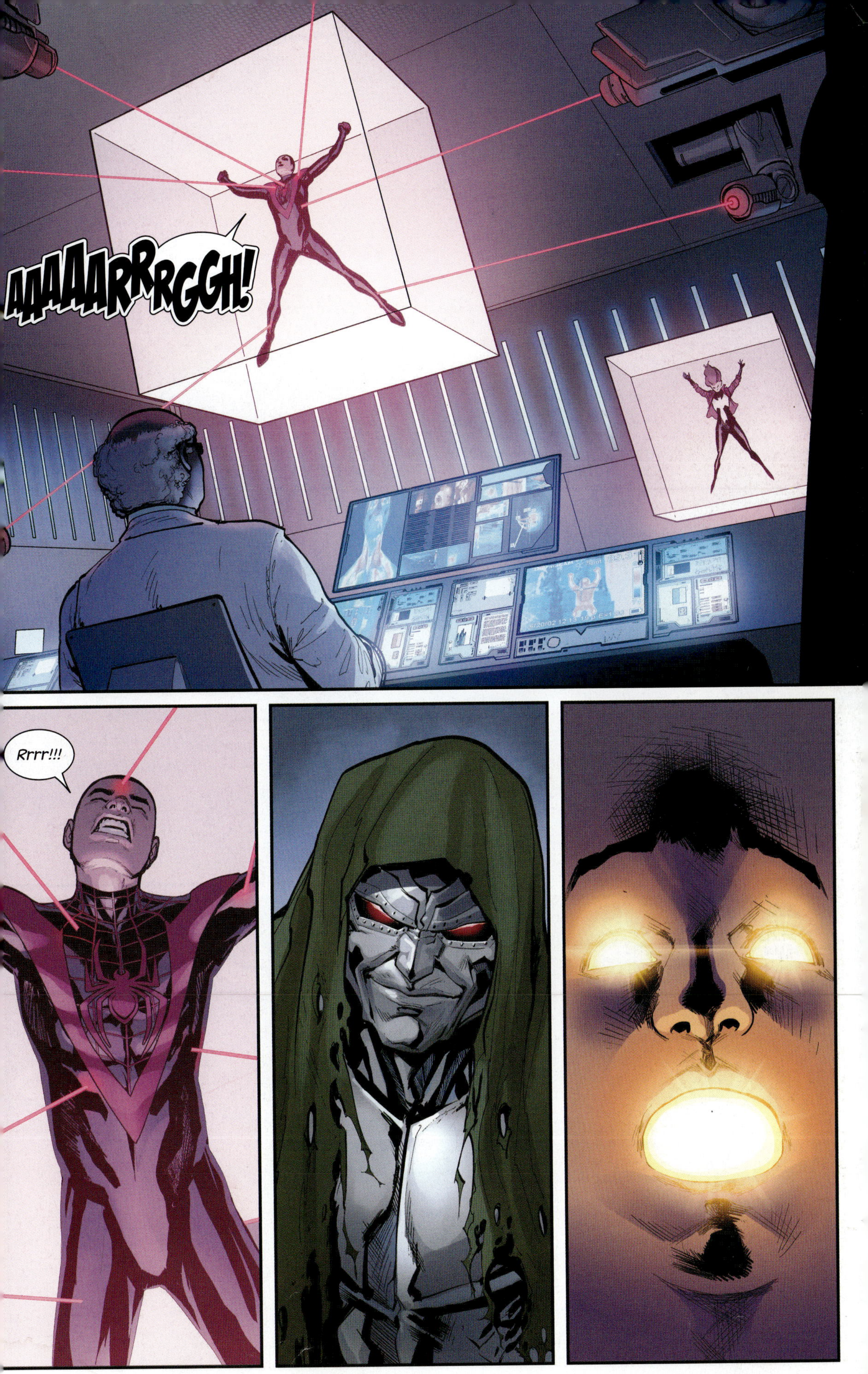
AAAAARRRGGH!
Rrrr!!!

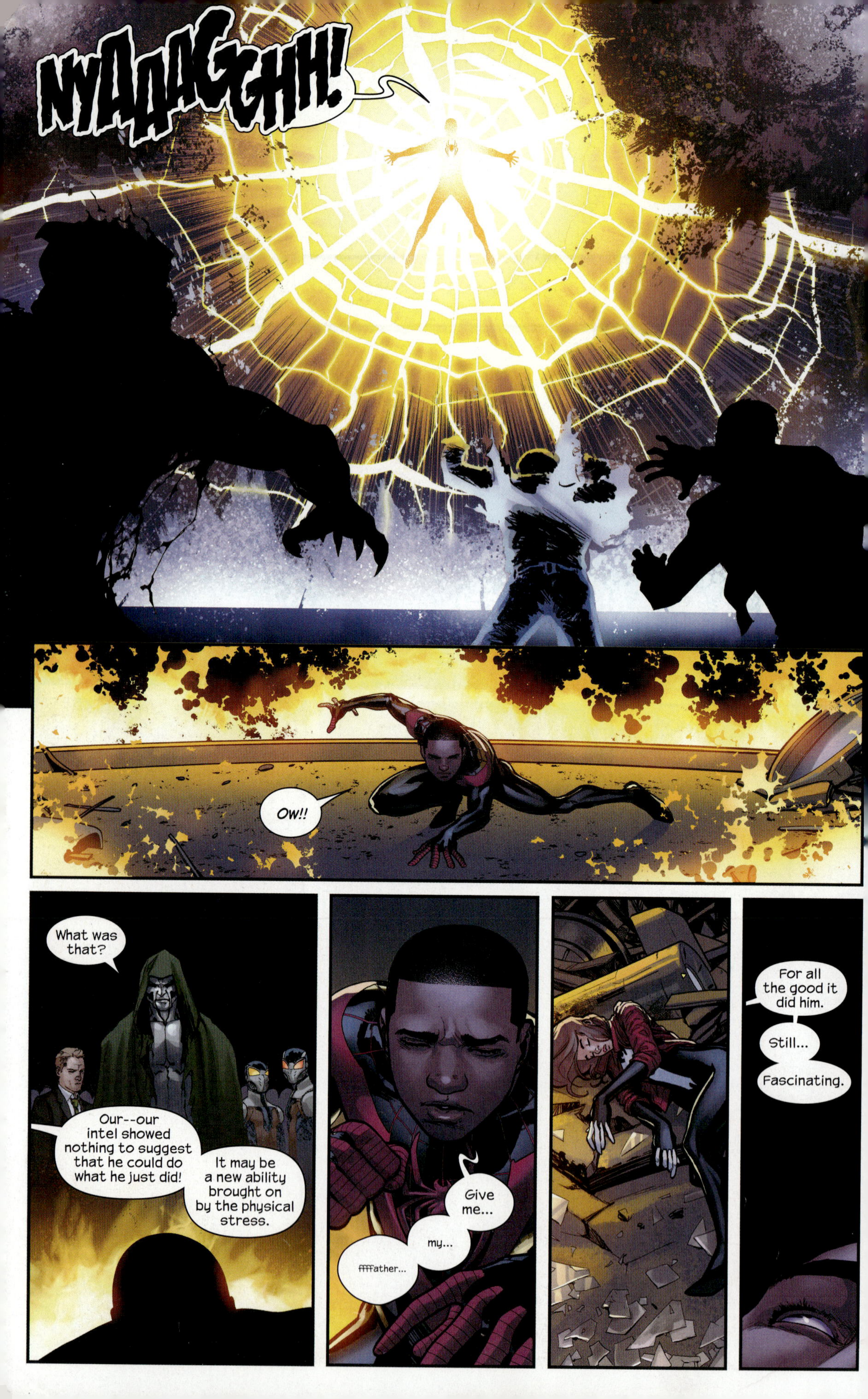
NYAAAGGHH!
OW!!
What was that?
Our--our intel showed nothing to suggest that he could do what he just did!
It may be a new ability brought on by the physical stress.
Give me...
my...
ffffather...
For all the good it did him.
Still...
Fascinating.

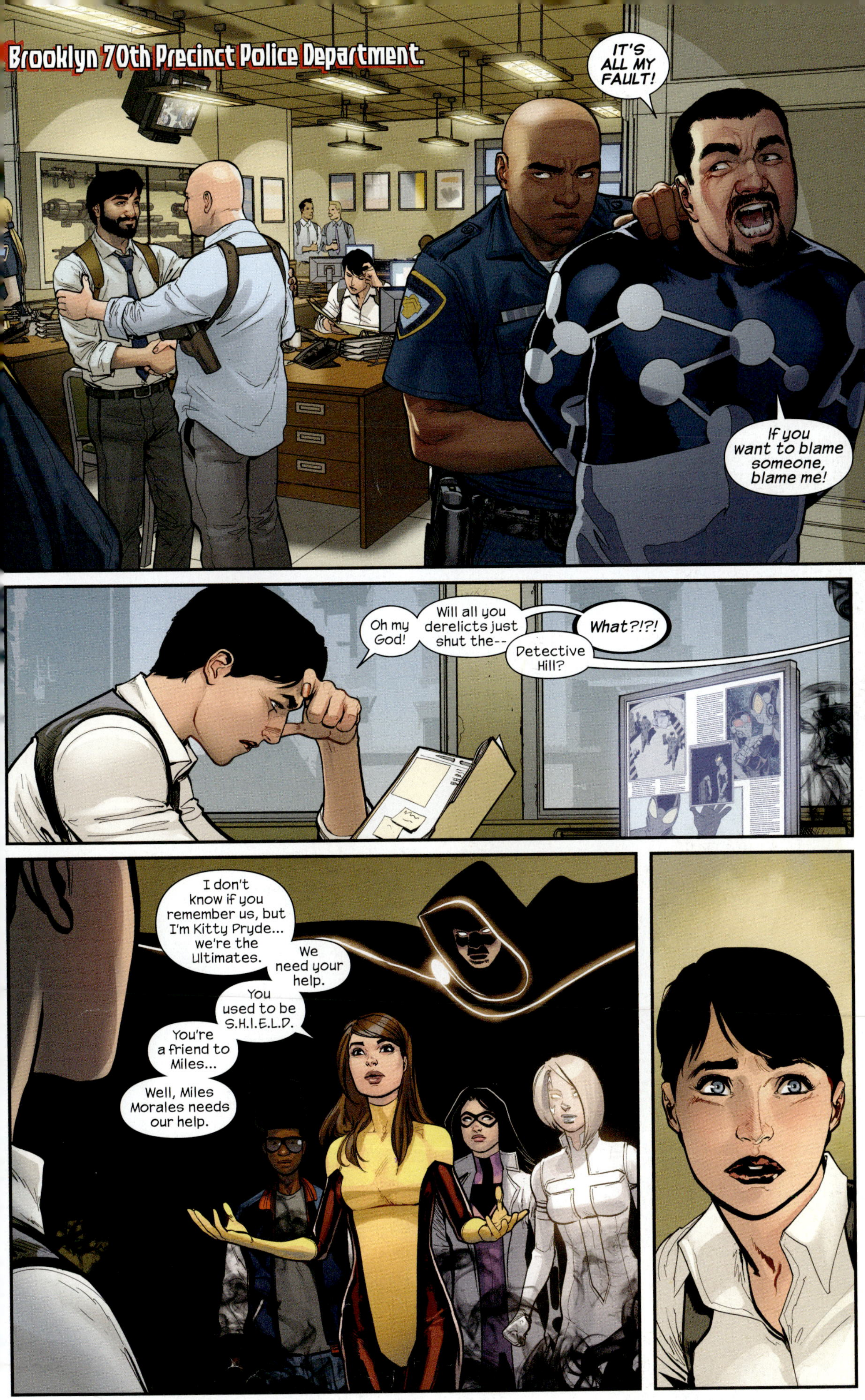
Brooklyn 70th Precinct Police Department.
IT'S ALL MY FAULT!
If you want to blame someone, blame me!
Oh my God!
Will all you derelicts just shut the--
What?!?!
Detective Hill?
I don't know if you remember us, but I'm Kitty Pryde... we're the Ultimates.
We need your help.
You used to be S.H.I.E.L.D.
You're a friend to Miles...
Well, Miles Morales needs our help.

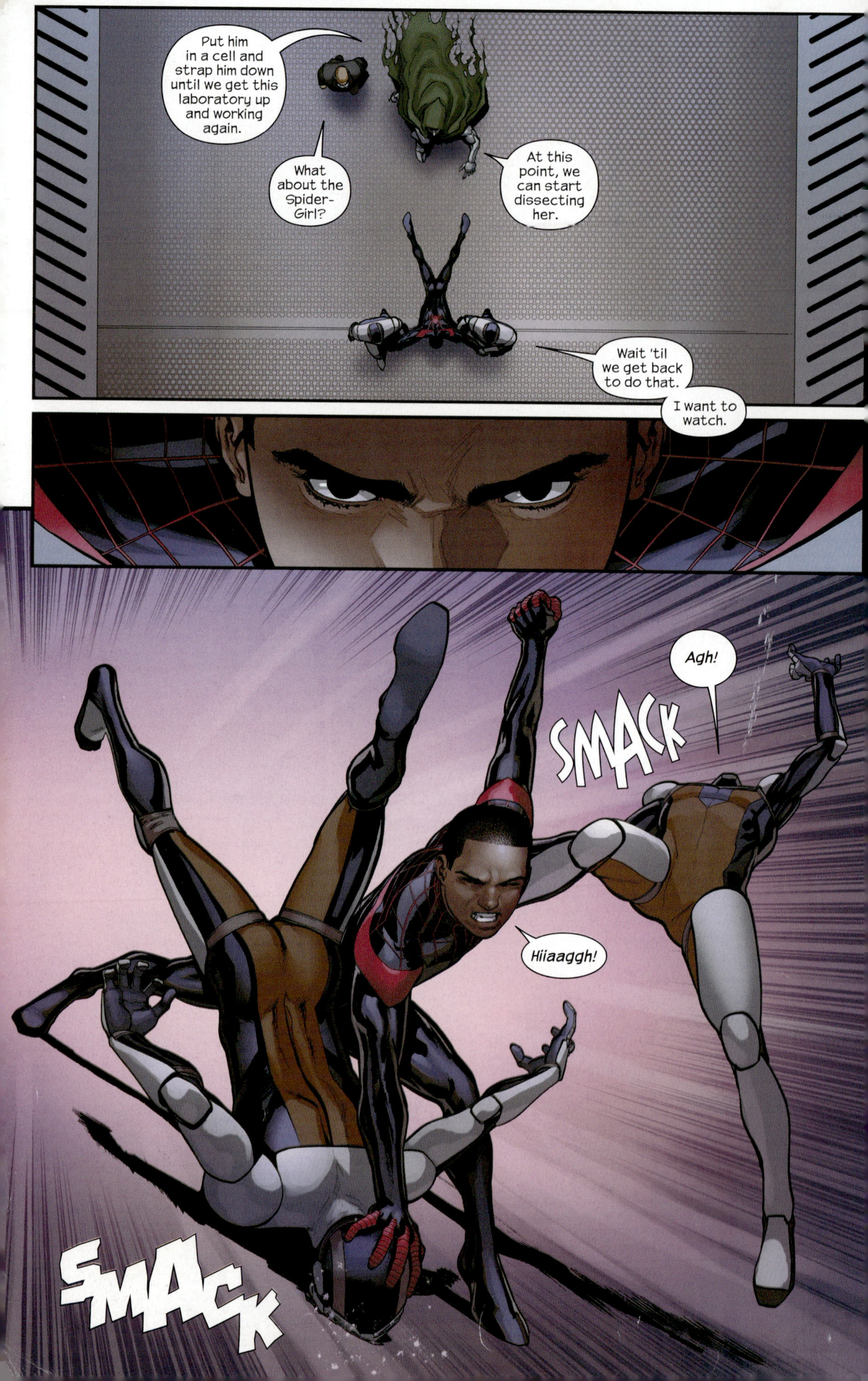
Put him in a cell and strap him down until we get this laboratory up and working again.
What about the Spider-Girl?
At this point, we can start dissecting her.
Wait 'til we get back to do that.
I want to watch.
Agh!
SMACK
Hiiaaggh!
SMACK

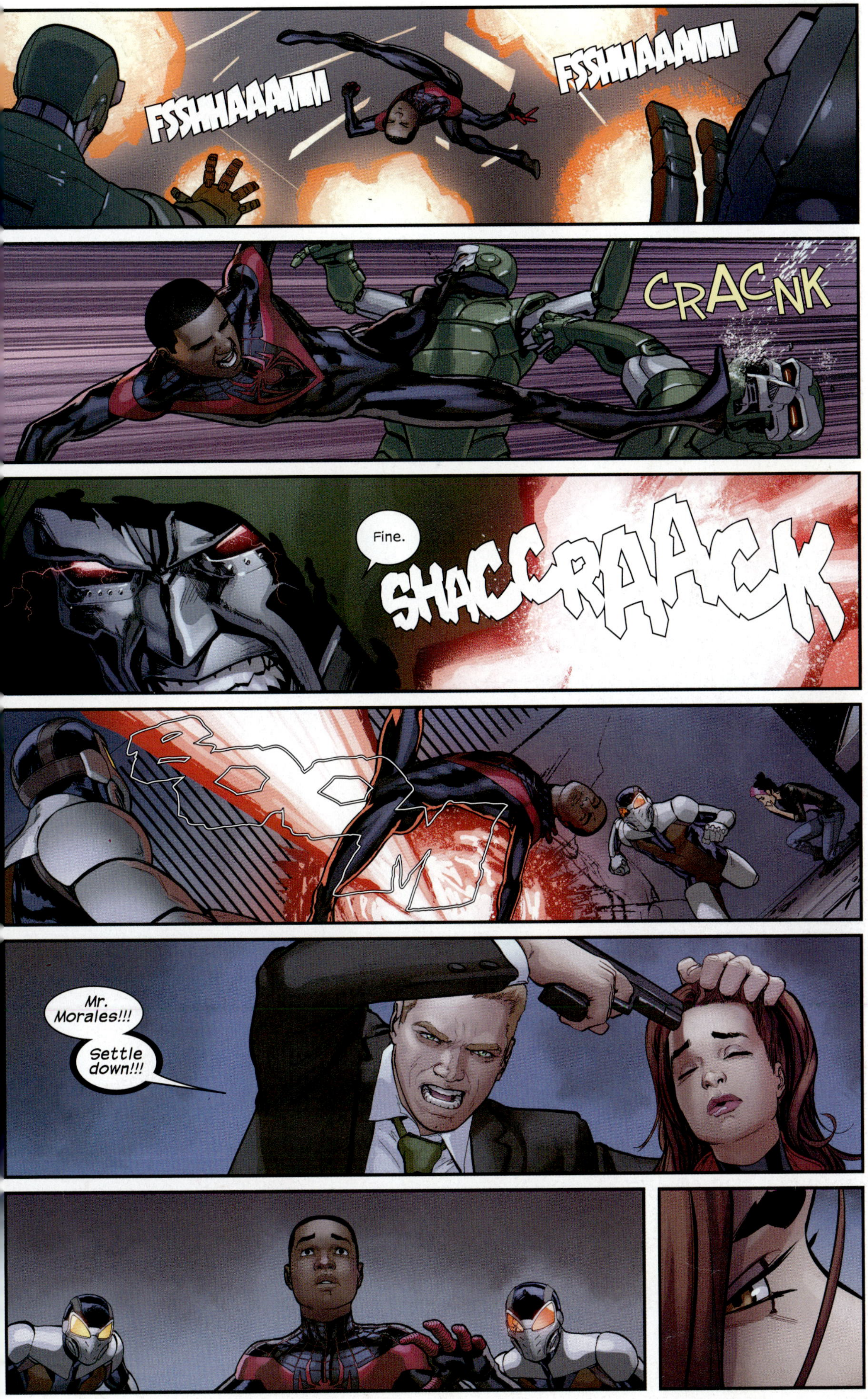
FSSHHAAAMM
FSSHHAAAMM
CRACNK
Fine.
SHACCRAACK
Mr. Morales!!!
Settle down!!!

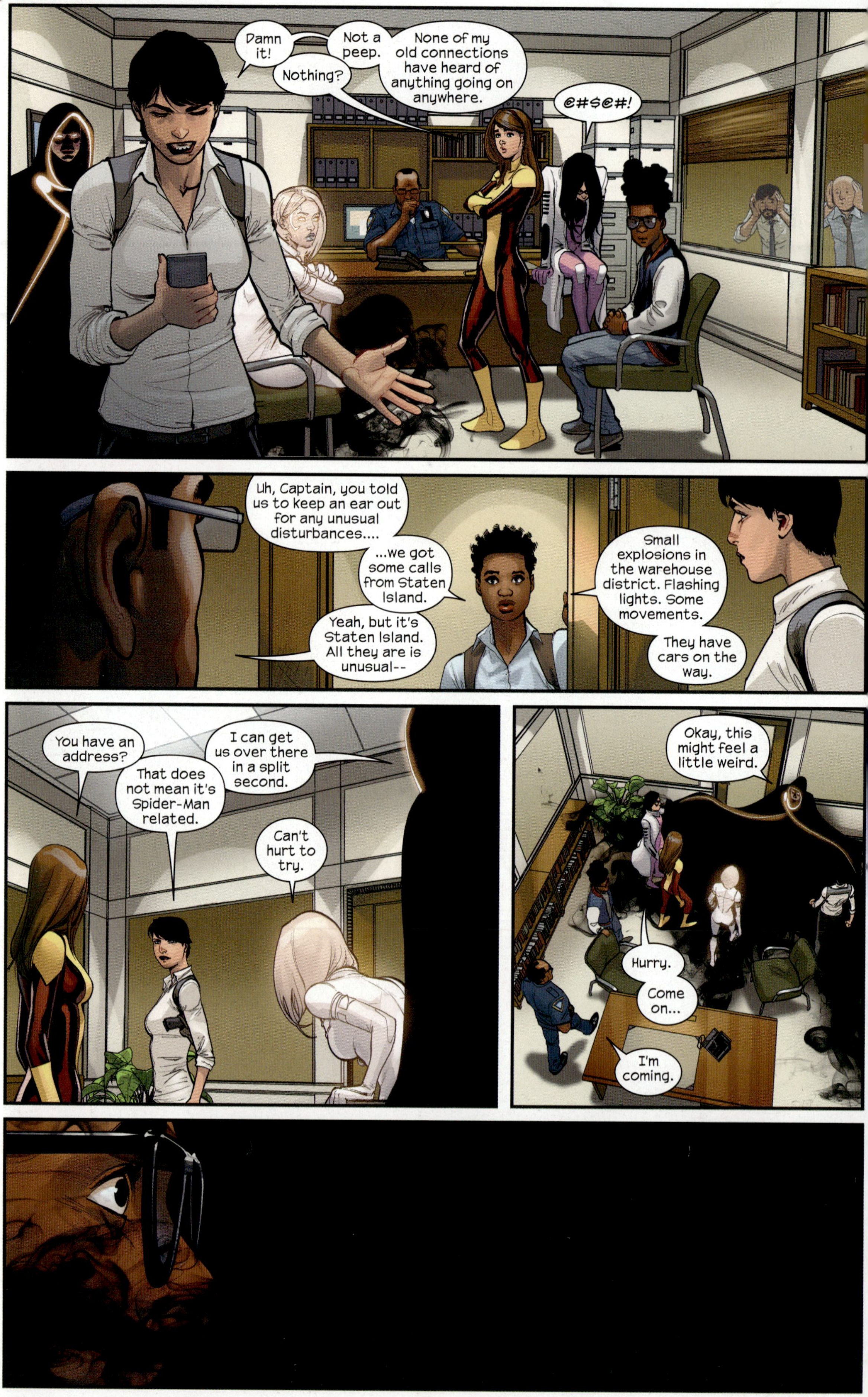
Damn it!
Not a peep.
Nothing?
None of my old connections have heard of anything going on anywhere.
@#$@#!
Uh, Captain, you told us to keep an ear out for any unusual disturbances....
...we got some calls from Staten Island.
Yeah, but it's Staten Island. All they are is unusual--
Small explosions in the warehouse district. Flashing lights. Some movements.
They have cars on the way.
You have an address?
That does not mean it's Spider-Man related.
I can get us over there in a split second.
Can't hurt to try.
Okay, this might feel a little weird.
Hurry.
Come on...
I'm coming.

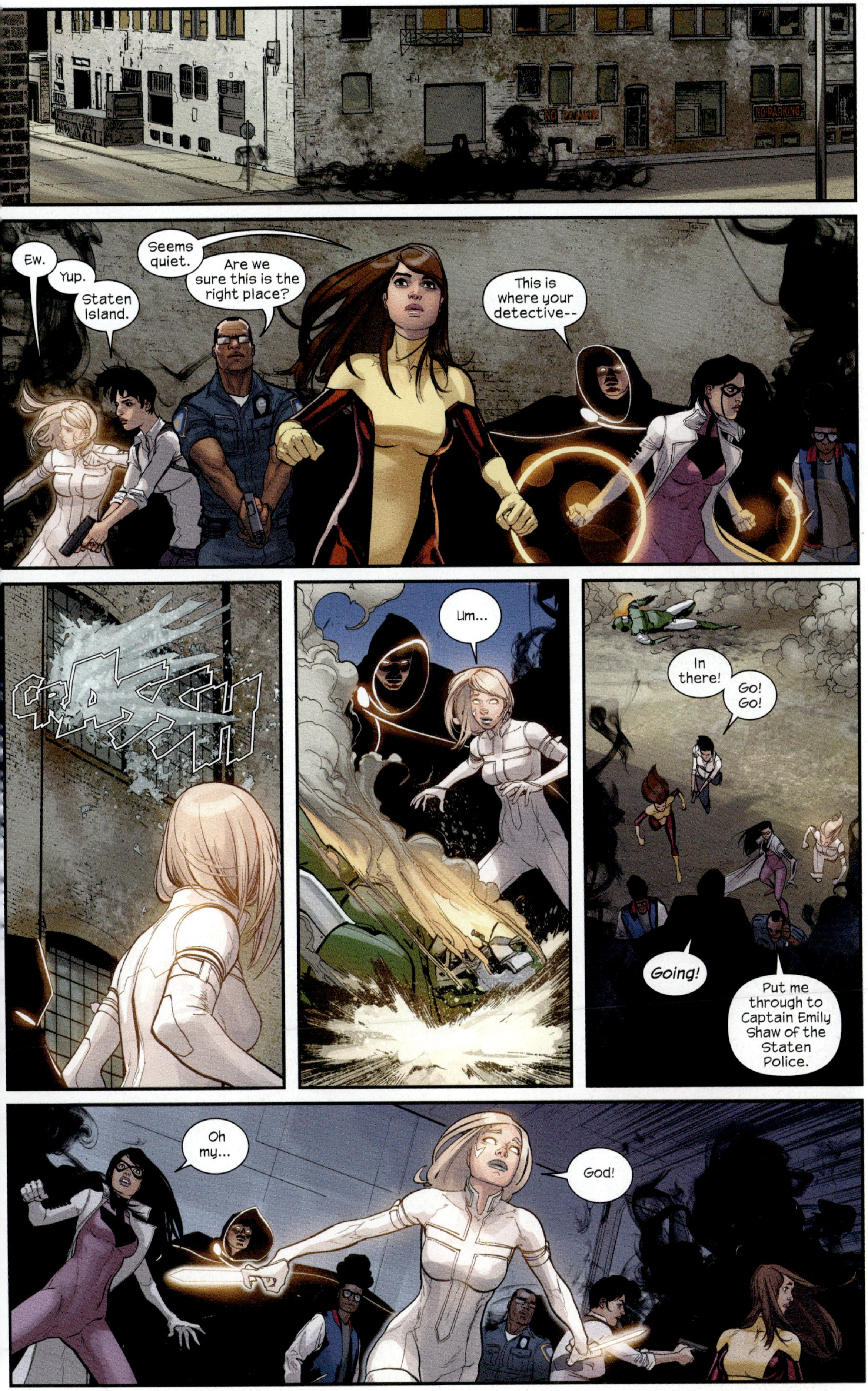
Seems quiet.
Are we sure this is the right place?
Ew.
Yup.
Staten Island.
This is where your detective--
Um...
In there!
Go! Go!
Going!
Put me through to Captain Emily Shaw of the Staten Police.
Oh my...
God!

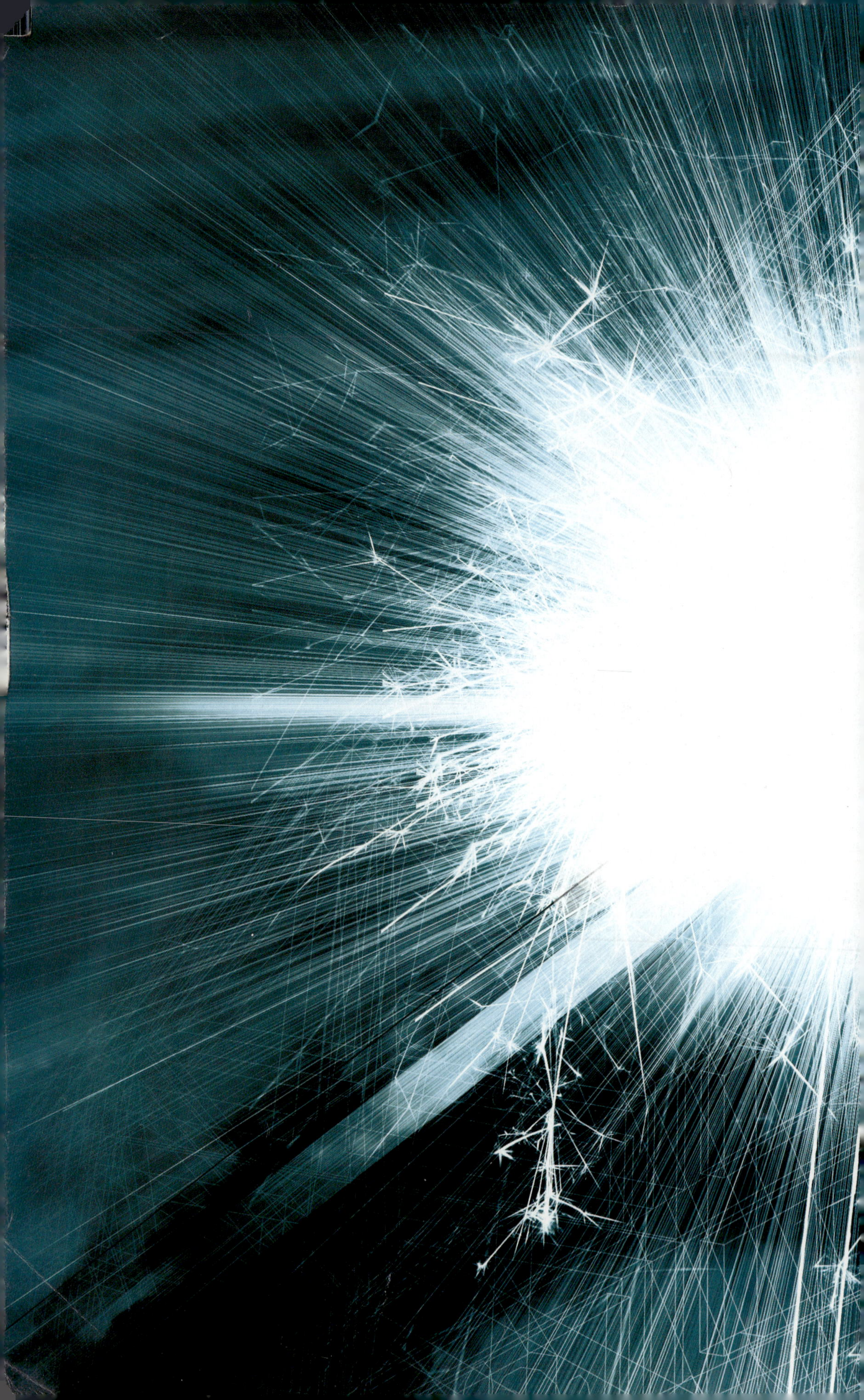

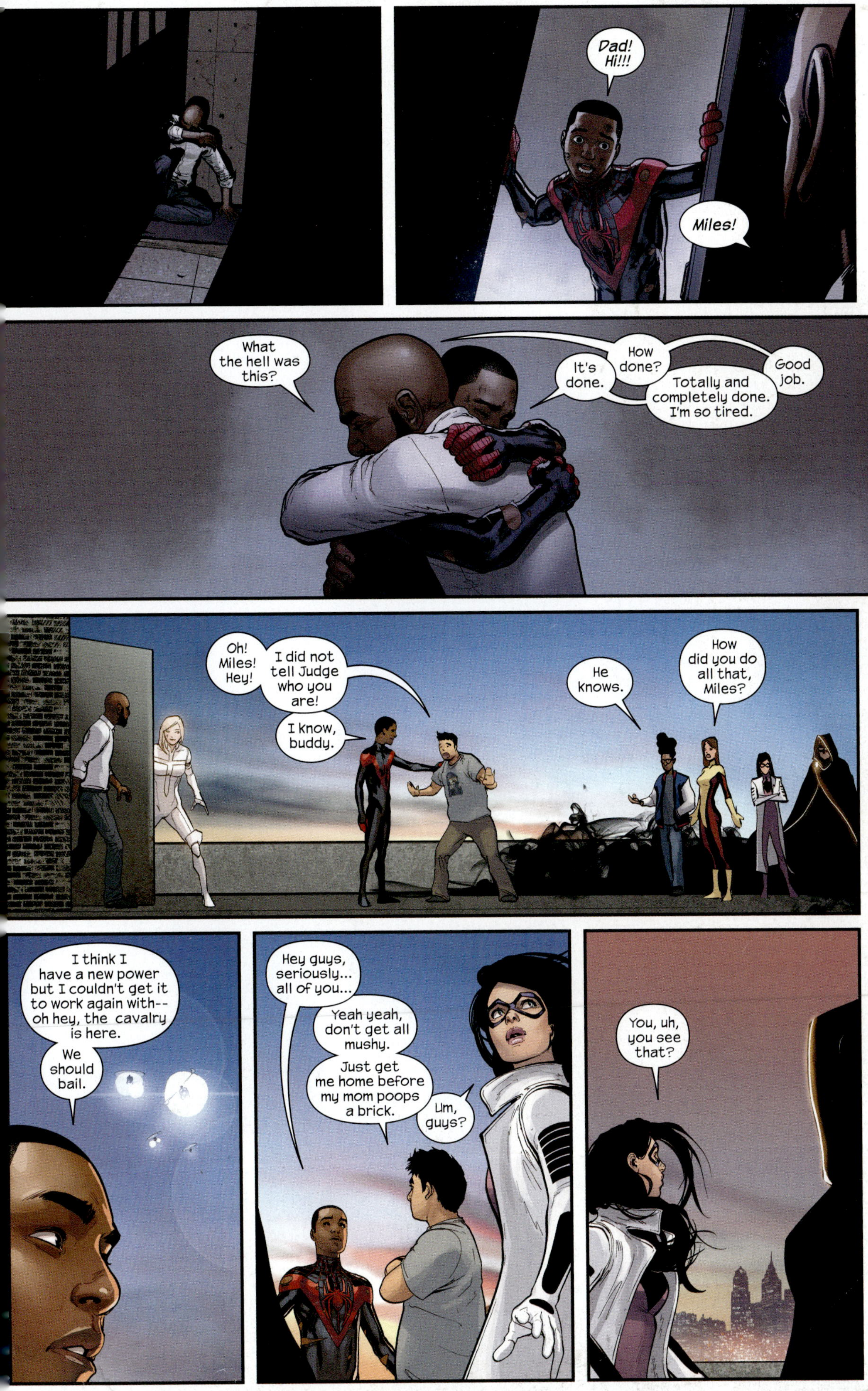
Dad! Hi!!!
Miles!
What the hell was this?
It's done.
How done?
Totally and completely done. I'm so tired.
Good job.
Oh! Miles! Hey!
I did not tell Judge who you are!
I know, buddy.
He knows.
How did you do all that, Miles?
I think I have a new power but I couldn't get it to work again with-- oh hey, the cavalry is here.
We should bail.
Hey guys, seriously... all of you...
Yeah yeah, don't get all mushy.
Just get me home before my mom poops a brick.
Um, guys?
You, uh, you see that?

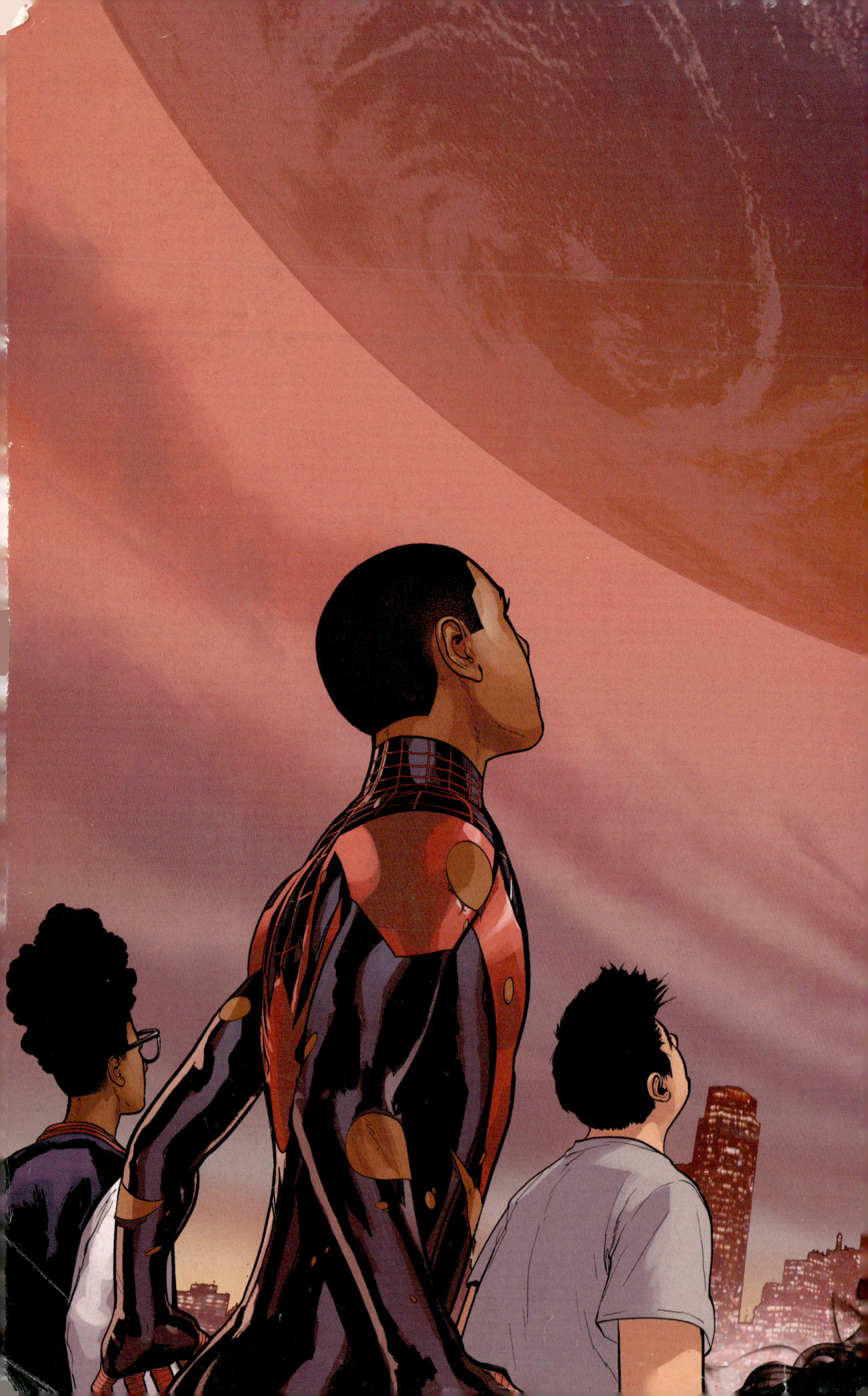

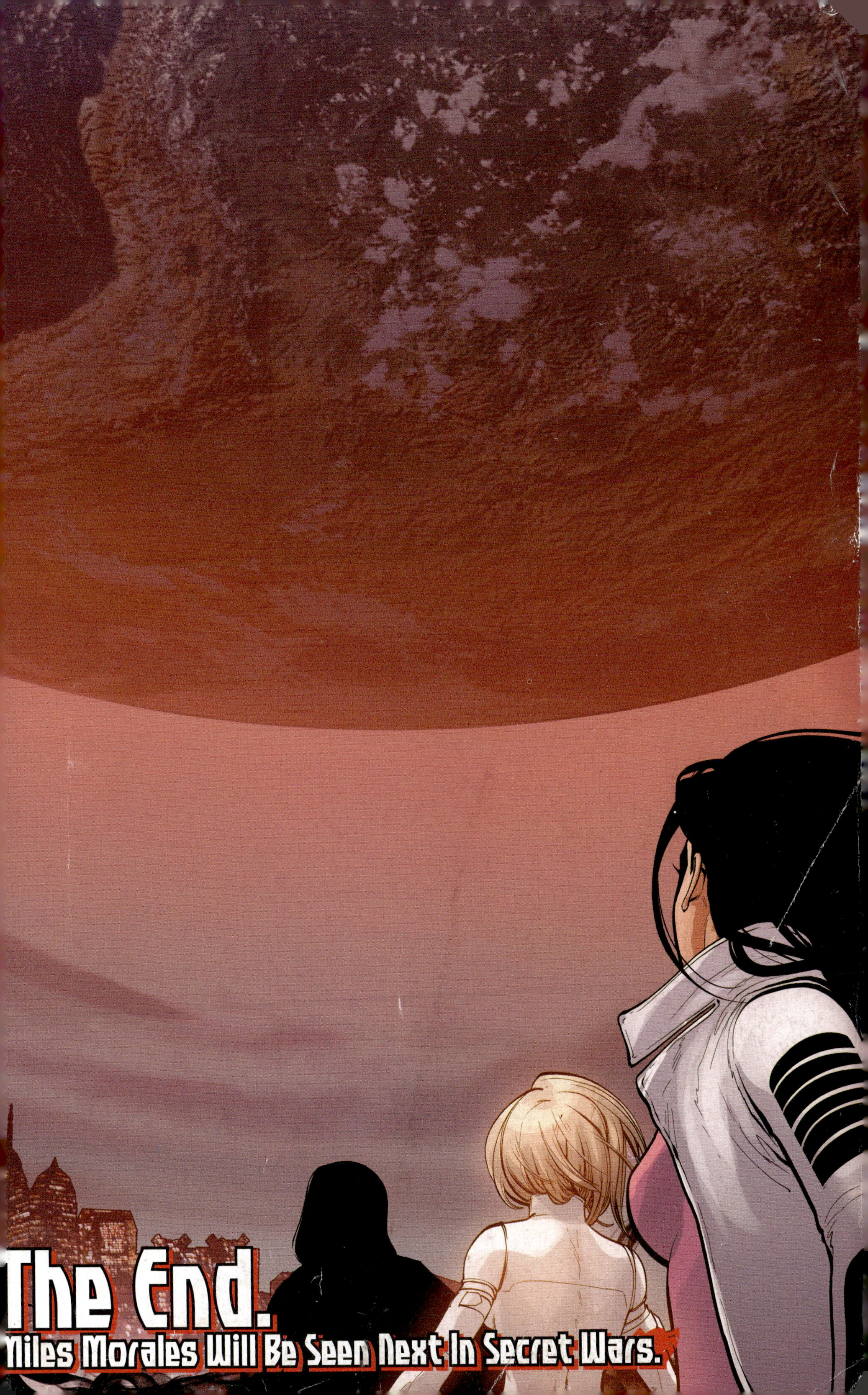
The End.
Miles Morales Will Be Seen Next In Secret Wars.

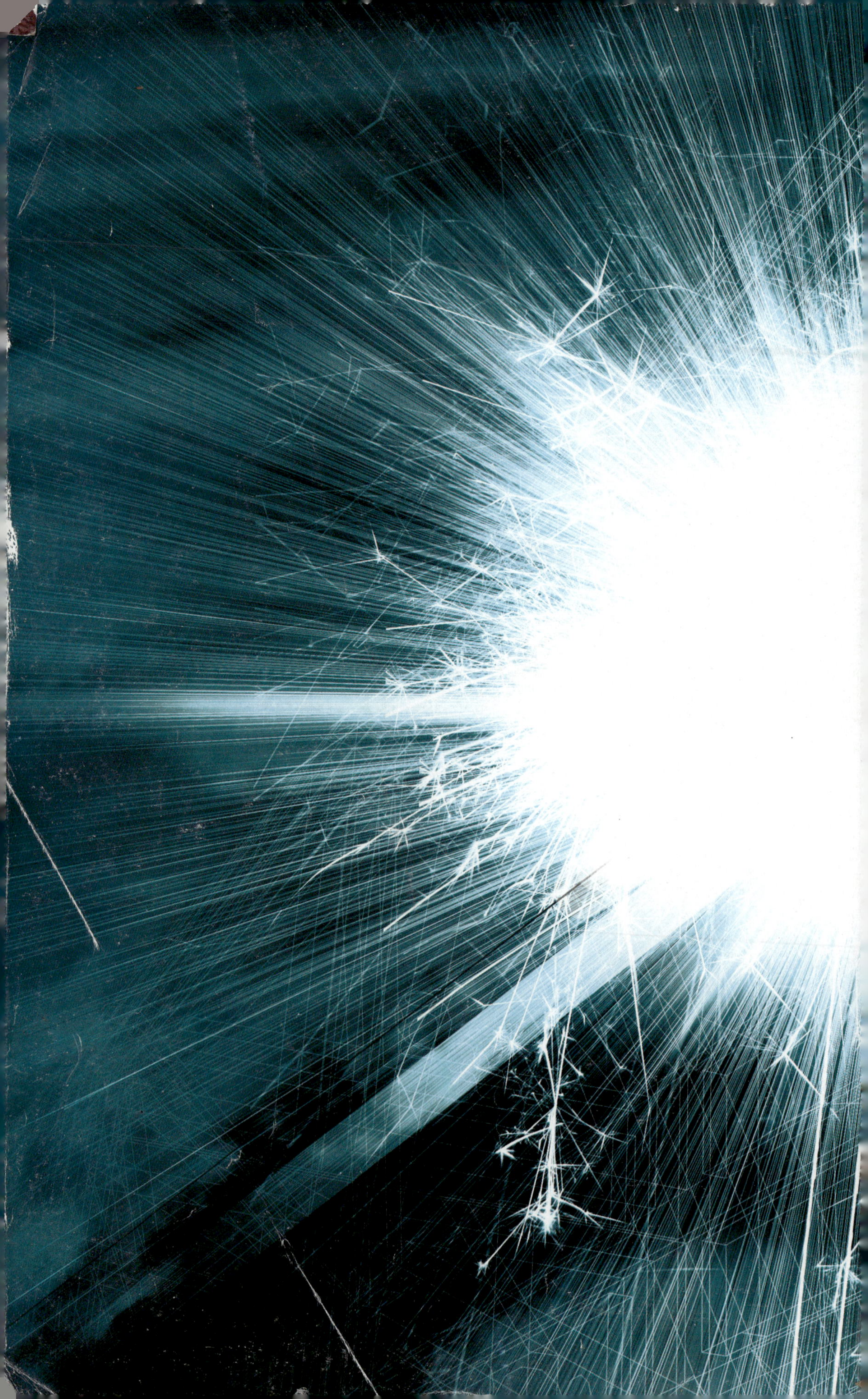